THE MAKING OF A MODERN
JAPANESE ARCHITECTURE

THE
OF
MODERN
ARCHI-

MAKING A JAPANESE ARCHITECTURE

DAVID B. STEWART

1868 TO THE PRESENT

KODANSHA INTERNATIONAL
Tokyo and New York

Publication of this book was assisted by a grant from the Japan Foundation.

Distributed in the United States by Kodansha International/USA Ltd., through Harper and Row, Publishers, Inc., 10 East 53rd Street, New York, New York 10022. Published by Kodansha International Ltd., 2-2, Otowa 1-chome, Bunkyo-ku, Tokyo 112 and Kodansha International/USA Ltd., 10 East 53rd Street, New York, New York 10022.

Copyright © 1987 by David Butler Stewart.
All rights reserved. Printed in Japan.
LCC 87-81685
ISBN 0-87011-844-7 (U.S.A.)
ISBN 4-7700-1344-2 (in Japan)
First edition, 1987

I dedicate this book to all
the Minakuchis,
and specially to those who are also Stewarts:
Toshiko, Daisuké and Tahkeru.

CONTENTS

Preface 9

Acknowledgments 11

1
The Victorian Foundations of Meiji Architecture 13
A Necessary Restoration 13 / New Towns and Foreign Building Types 15 / Enter the Surveyor 17 / With Brick and Stone under Imperial Contract 18 / Native Assimilation of Western Techniques and Styles 22 / Some Speculation about *Giyofu* Motifs 27 / Systematization and Rationalization 31

2
Tokyo and the "Problem" of Styles 33
Competing Influences and the College of Engineering 33 / Japanese Exposure to the Queen Anne Revival 37 / Proposals for a Japanese Whitehall 38 / The Rest of the City 41 / The German Neo-Renaissance Episode 43 / Kingo Tatsuno, Architect to the Nation 48 / Tokuma Katayama, Architect to the Crown 55

3
F.L.W.: Japan as a "Means to an End" 63
The Birth of Modernism 63 / "Japanism" as an Aspect of Historicism 64 / The Notion of Architectural "Truth" 65 / The Sistine Chapel and the Phoenix Hall 69 / The Japanese Print 74

4
Rebuilding the Imperial in the 1920s: Japan Gained 77
The Legend 77 / What the Building Really Was 79 / How Wright Conceived the Second Imperial 81 / The Role of Japan 83

5
Tokyo and the Beginnings of "Modernism" 90
Antithesis 90 / Tokyo in the First Quarter of the Twentieth Century 90 / Notions Bearing on Style 91 / Conflict between Structure and Expression 92 / Expressionist Trends in Public Building 96 / An Early Modern Residence 101

… / Kikuji Ishimoto's German Connection 118 / The Joint-Style
6

Rationalism and Lifestyle: The Thirties through the End of the War — 107

Nationalism and the Quest for Japanese Taste 107 / Unbuilt Manchukuo: A Lost "Opportunity" 110 / Artistic Rehabilitation of Traditional Taste 111 / A Style for the Times: P.O. Buildings and Schools 113 / Kikuji Ishimoto's German Connection 118 / The Joint-Style Modern Japanese Residence 124 / High Modern Climax: Antonin Raymond's Residential Styles 129 / The Diffusion of High Modernism in a Native Climate 142 / Group Housing and Other Social Aspects of Showa Architecture 146 / Kunio Maekawa 152 / Three German-Trained Architects in Bitter Times 159

7

Ins and Outs of Postwar Urban Rhetoric — 164

Internationalism: Sun and Shadow 164 / The Beginnings of Tange's Career 170 / Japan and CIAM: Hiroshima 172 / Otterlo, MIT, and Metabolism 177 / "The West's Favorite Japanese Architect" 182 / Fate of a "Grand" Design: Tokyo 184

8

A New Dialogue with Tradition — 186

Town and Country 186 / Le Corbusier's Parentage of the Japan Style 189 / The Next Step 190 / Home Front 192 / Third-Man Theme 197 / Abstraction with Traditional Forms 202 / Doubts about Nation and Style 205 / Le Corbusier in Tokyo 206 / "Japanese Space" 210 / Frontality or "Revolution" 213 / Shell Game and Recourse to Wit 215

9

Technology, Metaphor, and the Resurgence of Japanese Space — 219

To Build or Destroy 219 / Isozaki in Kyushu: Semiotics Replaces Semantics 223 / A New Kind of Space... 228 / ...And Its Politics 229 / Reflections and Transparencies 230 / Architecture as Metalanguage 231 / Returning to a "Space of Darkness" 233 / Implications for the City 234 / New Values in Everyday Things 235

10

The Present: Between *MAniera* and *Sachlichkeit* — 237

F.L. Wright and the Ungraspable Tao 237 / Seven Operations of Manner (*Signed* Isozaki) 239 / Chessboards and Mandalas 240 / "Hard" and "Soft" and the Formalist Literary Device 242 / Semiotics and Neo-Formalism 244 / Two Incomparables: Points in Common 244 / A Different Time and Place 246 / *Maniera* and the Cube 248 / Rhetoric of the Cylinder 256 / An Aqueous Metaphor 261 / Squaring the Circle at Kamioka 265 / Space-Time in Japan: Paris/New York 267 / Shinohara and the "Second Style" 268 / "Third Style" and Gap 269 / *Sachlichkeit* Alive and Well in Uehara 277

Notes and References — 282
Additional Sources and Further Reading — 290
List of Illustrations — 293
Photographic Credits — 297
Index — 298

Preface

The most perplexing issue in this book is that of Japanese "space," or the manner in which emptiness or void is perceived and treated in Japanese buildings. This is scarcely a matter for discussion in the first and second chapters, where examples of Western architecture are for the most part as closely imitated as possible from the points of view of facade design, massing, and ornament. In the third and fourth chapters the case of Frank Lloyd Wright, Japanese prints, and the Imperial Hotel is used, perhaps unfairly, as an opening onto the theme of divergent modes of spatial perception—but I have dealt with Wright at length because of his cardinal importance in the history of modern Western architecture. That is, most of what can be said about Wright's work can be proved axiomatically for the rest of modern architecture up until Le Corbusier's late style.

Not enough is known about Japanese architecture from the completion of the Imperial Hotel to the advent of the Pacific war, but, from the 1930s onward, *plan* becomes an essential element of consideration for architecture in the Western style. Thus the issue of space receives an increasingly detailed treatment as floor plans make their appearance for the buildings discussed. Here is published for the first time in any Western language a corpus of work examined in chapter 5—and, particularly, chapter 6—which constitutes the Japanese wing of the International Style but has never before reached the history books, written on the whole by Western authors.

The story of postwar Japanese architecture is better known, of course, although, once again, it has rarely been examined in English from a Japanese (or, at least, local) point of view. The rest of the book deals with the most important architects of the 1960s onward—Kazuo Shinohara and Arata Isozaki. Needless to say, the work of a number of good architects has been passed over, but I believe that what I have written is fairly exhaustive in taking up the notions of these two men, who are unquestionably—though in different ways—the greatest theoreticians and practitioners at work during the period covered. The final chapters are, therefore, devoted to problems of city development and architecture, climaxing in the ideas of Isozaki's "Space of Darkness" and Shinohara's "Japanese Space," with their accompanying flow of works. Some readers may find these parts of the book difficult and unnecessarily abstruse. However, my argument in favor of pursuing such topics is that they reflect a common heritage of generally held Japanese beliefs about *space*. Once more, what can be learned from Isozaki and Shinohara—what I, personally, have learned over a number of years—can usually be shown in axiomatic fashion to hold for the rest of modern Japanese architectural production.

From the Middle Ages until the advent of the Modern Movement, space in Japanese architecture was usually sequential and frequently "literary" in terms, respectively, of its composition and allusions. Even in the West, talk about buildings as spatial containers is a relatively modern phenomenon. In both East and West the discourse on "space" becomes progressively a matter of interest and concern as that on "style" falls into abeyance. In any case, this inversion of a traditional relationship is mainly what is meant by the term "modern" architecture.

Although I have tried to keep social events and context somewhat in focus, this book is neither a social history nor a sociological text. I have, therefore, accepted the term "Japanese space" at the same level as one is today easily comfortable with the idea of, say, Renaissance or baroque space—recognizing the identifiable qualities of these without feeling obliged to undertake an out-and-out examination of their origins. Moreover, Husserl and Viollet-le-Duc have both reminded us in their different ways that art is "one"—as life is—and I have tried to keep faith with this assertion.

But to return to the matter of style, there is a particular occurrence that claims our attention: the invention of the tearoom (or *chashitsu*, notably the so-called rustic *chashitsu*)—the miniscule space reserved for the preparation and drinking of ceremonial tea. In its smallest and most perfect state it dates, probably, to the Tensho era (1573–92) and involved innovations attributed mainly to the celebrated tea master Sen no Rikyu (though tea itself—even rustic tea—was a far older institution, and tea drinking had a long and distinguished history in Japan as well as China). This "style" of the *soan chashitsu* (where tea was drunk in a thatched hermitage) as eventually perfected has been referred to as the beginning of "space" in Japanese architecture. There may even have been some influence from Western post-Renaissance space, as occurred contemporaneously in Japanese painting, owing to the presence of Jesuit missionaries in Japan. Principally, however, the tearoom of this new sort represented a refusal of the *shoin* or palatial reception hall, where tea had previously been consumed, in favor of an assimilation of *minka*-inspired (i.e., vernacular "folk" dwelling) elements.

In spite of the possibility of their cross-fertilization, modern architecture in its worldwide manifestation could be assigned two reference points as a matter of speculation. One comprises the geometrically apportioned volumes of Renaissance architects, and the other is the *chashitsu*-inspired *sukiya* style of Japanese design. Here attention is accorded the bounding surfaces, and spatial content is allowed to shift for itself all in becoming the most significant element or aim of the design. Naturally, a spatial envelope is indeed produced in the latter tradition, but it is constituted by superimposed and intersecting planar surfaces in conjunction with virtual projections or extensions of these into the intervening void. Philosophically, the void is the important quality of a tea-derived building (see the first section of chapter 10), but in terms of the actual technique of production of spaces, the opposite is true! It was Wright who integrated these notions with Western space—almost certainly without a full understanding of the difference in "spatial" quality involved—to make a "modern" architecture, which thus began to exist in *spatial* terms. But, as we shall see, this happened not in Japan, but well before Wright's first arrival there in 1905.

The space of the *chashitsu*—in ways which, at least in so many words, were probably never revealed to Wright—bears within it a self-commentary. No less a scholar than Joseph Needham has pointed out that the Chinese suffered from what he calls a "lack of deductive geometry," which went hand in hand with the conception of a harmoniously patterned cosmos in which all being and phenomena composed an interactive whole. Although indeed precise and economical in its means, the rustic teahouse and, through it, the *sukiya* style of building and gardening were perhaps more inductive than deductive in their approach. Unlike Renaissance artist-architects, its masters could lay no claim to theological or proto-scientific notions, such as from time to time neoclassical building has been molded or pressured into displaying. This does not mean that the rustic teahouse—or by extension subsequent Japanese architecture in general—was denied a cosmic or world view, but its does suggest the way in which *sukiya*-style buildings may be viewed as filtering data (including *spatial* data) from their surroundings instead of offering theorems about the nature of the universe and the ordering effect of a divine presence in it. The result is a certain mode of assimilation; not the formation of an attachment to concepts. The latter produces an illusion of control and relative independence on the part of the subject or spectator, whereas the former induces a more "self"-permeating vision of "enlightenment" in the Buddhist sense. In the Japanese tradition, then, space is not approached or dealt with as a tangible aspect of a real existence but, instead, as the image of a larger world.

The story of the first 100 years of Japanese modern architecture is, through the renewal of a praxis of radical aestheticism, the story of a way back.

Acknowledgments

It is an especial pleasure to acknowledge the help of the following colleagues and friends over a long period of time in matters relating directly and indirectly to the achievement of this book: Kiyosi Hirai, Hisao Koyama, Toshio Nakamura, Koji Numasawa, Kazuo Shinohara, and Koji Taki.

As the writing of it took form, a further and particular debt was incurred to Fumihiko Maki, Kiyosi Seike, and Hiroyuki Suzuki. I am grateful to all three.

In different ways, and in friendship over varying lengths of time, Shimpachiro Ishigami, Riichi Miyake, Shigetake Nagao, Masato Nakatani, Takaharu Yamaguchi, and Hajime Yatsuka have all helped to make the book what it is.

I have received especial assistance more than once from Arata Isozaki, always graciously given over a number of years; continuing encouragement from Shozo Baba and Takeshi Ishido; and help in a very particular instance recently from Takeo Hatae and Koichi Kitazawa.

It is impossible not to mention: Junya Fujita, Hirohisa Hemmi, Nobuo Iwashita, Takeo Ozawa, and Taku Sakaushi, and, in particular, Shiro Sasano, all of whom, together with myself, are members of one of the world's most exclusive clubs, and also Takashi Uzawa, who is an honorary participant. There has been a great deal of give-and-take for which I am grateful.

Abroad, Jacques and Martine Sandjian, as well as Hiroko Kiiffner and Eberhard Kreutzer, have proved faithful friends in responding to requests for aid—last minute and otherwise.

In some ways, the actual idea for the book came from Makoto Ueda in Tokyo and from Bruce Goodwin in New Orleans, through requests for an article and a lecture respectively.

In different capacities Mack Horton and David Chesanow have read the manuscript and been of enormous help. Also, my friends Tim Clark, Grant Hildebrand, Seizou Uchida, Anne Wagner, and Nobuko Warren have all graciously accepted to read one or more of the prewar chapters and point out necessary revisions or changes, saving me from all kinds of pitfalls.

Assistance in locating photographs and drawings has been offered by Nobuo Aoki under the auspices of Terunobu Fujimori; further kindness was shown in this respect by Noriko Tsuchizaki of the Architectural Institute of Japan's Library. In addition, Tomoko Sakazume and Keiko Uchida have given all kinds of help, always unstintingly. Each of my immediate colleagues at Tokyo Institute of Technology, in addition to those already mentioned, has always been ready to provide information and support.

Finally, all the staff at Kodansha International deserve very particular thanks and most of all Messrs. Michael Brase and Nobuhiro Katakura, the ever attentive and selfless editors of this book.

We would say, of course:
"There's a buttercup!"
"There's a nice little forget-me-not...."
But Apollon Apollonovich would say simply and succinctly:
"A flower...."

Just between us: for some reason, Apollon Apollonivich considered all flowers the same, bluebells.

He would have characterized even his own house with laconic brevity, as consisting, for him, of walls (forming squares and cubes) into which windows were cut, of parquetry, of tables. Beyond that were details.

From "Chapter the First, in which an account is given of a certain worthy person, his mental games, and the ephemerality of being"

His hand resting on the marble banister, Apollon Apollonovich caught his toe in the carpeting, and—stumbled. His step slowed involuntarily. Quite naturally, his eyes lingered on an enormous portrait of the Minister.

A shiver ran down Apollon Apollonovich's spine: the place was badly heated.
He had a fear of space....

Apollon Apollonovich did not discuss his stay in Japan with anyone....

Undoubtedly the senator had been developing a fear of space.

From "Chapter the Second, in which an account is given of a certain rendezvous, fraught with consequences"

Andrei Bely, *Petersburg*

1 The Victorian Foundations of Meiji Architecture

A NECESSARY RESTORATION

Not until 1868 did Japan enter history as a modern polity, but even at so late a date Europeanization of artifacts as well as lifestyles was effected only by degrees. The brusque arrival of American warships in the guise of a trade embassy fifteen years earlier had presaged the demise of the Tokugawa. The shogunate could offer no solution to the problem posed by the encroachment of foreign powers into northern Asian waters. In self-defense, from 1854, the shogunal government tentatively set about concluding treaties with the Western powers and opening ports for trade. Debate nevertheless persisted on whether or not to retain the exclusion policy which for the previous two and a half centuries had held sway. Pressure to depose the shogun and restore the imperial mandate was originally linked to belief in the necessity of expelling all foreigners and excluding their innovations. The position of the shogunate was inherently weak and the treaties it had signed conciliatory, but the anti-Tokugawa forces, in their turn, also came to understand the inevitability of material changes. As a consequence they, too, embraced the open-country policy, albeit in a far more aggressive and decisively independent-minded fashion than the shogunate. The upshot was that the fifteenth and final shogun, late in 1867, yielded his mandate to the emperor, and in the spring of the following year the charter of the new government was proclaimed, reestablishing imperial rule and pledging an international stance in foreign affairs.

The young emperor was to administer the affairs of the nation directly, respecting the will of his subjects through institution of a parliament. External policy was founded on a friendly and impartial internationalism, itself based on the adoption of culture and technology from other nations. The immediate burden modernization and rationalization placed on the new government was enormous, so that reforms had to be instituted gradually. Earliest of all these was alteration of the geopolitical map of Japan, with reversion of feudal domains to the possession of the emperor. Reorganization of social classes, abolition of feudal stipends, and leveling of universal military conscription followed. Most difficult of all was enforcing transmutation of the yearly rice taxes based on crop yield to a uniform land-tax system payable in currency. Most decisive from the point of view of matters treated in this book was transposition of the seat of government from the ancient capital, Kyoto, to the former castle town of Edo. This city had evolved as the administrative center of the shogunate but was, henceforth, to be renamed Tokyo, the "Eastern Capital." Concomitantly, the new Meiji era was proclaimed, thereby ending the disconcerting practice of designating several era names successively within a single reign. Virtually by fiat the forty-four years (1868–1912) of the Meiji reign were synonymous with an epoch of transitional and evolutionary culture taking Tokyo as its center and standing for Japan's initiation into the contemporary world.

In the realm of change by decree which Japan became practically overnight, speed of transformation was to vary. For example, the calendar was realigned by fixing the third day of the twelfth month of the fifth year of Meiji as January 1, 1873. On the other hand, a cabinet system was not established before the end of 1885, and the so-called Meiji Constitution (the first to be proclaimed in Asia) at last provided in 1889 for the de facto establishment of that parliament (or Imperial Diet) first mentioned back in 1868. Meanwhile, as the physical evolution of the new capital was necessarily based on the swiftness with which administrative decisions were returned, its development was extremely uneven.

Here began an unevenness persisting to the present day which any student of the dynamics of the world's great cities fails to understand at his own peril. But Tokyo, as it lay dormant at the beginning of the Meiji period, was not, or was no longer, one of these. Probably within living memory—at the end of the eighteenth and beginning of the nineteenth centuries, perhaps earlier—Edo had been the most populous city on earth (with 1.3 million inhabitants). At the start of Meiji the capital, Edo-Tokyo, was sadly and massively depleted. In its heyday the city had lived off the Tokugawa bureaucracy, plus the provincial aristocracy forced to maintain dwellings there. Therefore, when the regulation enforcing secondary residence in the capital was deemphasized as early as 1862, the economy of the metropolis was at once forced into abeyance. Yet it was impossible—even in the state of uncertainty to which political events tended in the last years of the shogunate—for the ordinary townsmen, including merchants and artisans, simply to pack up and leave, and the city thus retained a population base of around 500,000. That is the estimate after the shogun's departure, at a time when the population of London was approximately three million.

We possess a final vignette of the desolation of Edo, its mansions left to ruin, together with the drying up of a vast network of service industries (not least those of prostitution, theater, and entertainment), which constituted the city's chief livelihood. Otherwise, surprisingly little is known about the

1.1. Tokyo–Yokohama Railway, 1872, showing Yokohama terminal at Sakuragi-cho by Bridgens. Woodblock print by Hiroshige III.

metabolic workings that underlay the buildup and eventual decline of an extensive chain of cities throughout Tokugawa Japan. Perhaps for this reason the fact has never attained much prominence that the new Japanese nation born out of the run-down clockwork of the Tokugawa era was larger than any European country, with the exception of neighboring Russia. Indeed, by the time the first post-Restoration civil registry and census had been carried out in 1873, Japan's approximately thirty-three millions placed her within five million of the population of post–Civil War United States. At the end of the Edo period, when such crucial figures must have already been intuited, not to say throughout the Meiji era, these data could not have been lost on the plague of foreigners seeking admission to hitherto secluded Mikadoland. Though without a real explanation of causes, such was the demographic context of the years after 1850 and up until the time Japan achieved full status as a nation in successful wars against China and Russia on either side of 1900.

Japan was initially goaded by the United States toward realization of her potential destiny, but it needs to be borne in mind that she did not take that country as exclusive model until World War I—nor in an out-and-out sense until after World War II. In fact, regarding the sudden effects and paradoxes of Westernization, Japan during the Meiji period bore a certain resemblance to Russia, or at least to that famous aspect of Russia which has never been quite Europeanized. Moreover, the full effects of the Industrial Revolution, as largely accomplished in Britain by 1850, were retarded in both the United States and in Germany until the aftermath of the Civil War and national unification respectively. Therefore, it is possible to view Japan's late but rapid industrialization as being on time according to an international timetable. Haste, in any case, not only determined the ethos but was of the absolute essence in implementing Japanese goals. For, as President Fillmore had observed in a letter to the emperor, the Japanese islands now lay only eighteen days' distance by steamship from Oregon and California. After delivering the presidential missive and conveying even more pointed observations of his own in 1853, Commodore Perry returned to Japan the following year under instructions from President Pierce to conclude a treaty. Among the gifts he bestowed on the Japanese were a miniature steam locomotive and a telegraph apparatus. At that time, of course, the tide of exclusionism had not as yet turned in favor of Westernization. It is, therefore, an especially impressive index of the about-face which followed that by the earliest years of Meiji the first telegraph line was in place (1869) and the first railway link established (1872), both joining Tokyo with the newly created port of Yokohama some miles to the south (fig. 1.1).

The precipitant mechanization that was part of the foundation of the Japanese state cannot be sketched here in any detail. By 1870, however, a Ministry of Technology was set up in order to expedite the buildup, with foreign expertise, of a number of state-supported enterprises. Thus, for example, during the 1870s mining was made a state monopoly and the help of Western technical advisers enlisted to improve the mines. Likewise, government-operated model factories were the responsibility of a new Ministry of Home Affairs, notably in the all-important textile field, which had hitherto functioned as a cottage industry. Nevertheless, from the beginning of the eighties a substantial portion of government-aided operations was sold off to the private sector.

Even before the Restoration, proto-industrialization is known to have centered on the production of iron and armaments, and this is assumed, in early cases, to have been based on textbook knowledge from Holland. The modernization of shipbuilding eventually gave cause for the importation of foreign technicians and equipment. Military applications of technology received high priority irrespective of the change of regime, and the French were among the first in this field, their prestige remaining considerable until the Prussian victory of 1870. Afterward, French military missions were resumed as early as 1872 and continued until 1890, when the Japanese government definitively turned its attention to German development with its impressive groundwork laid down by Prussia.

Another aspect of continuity between the old and new Japanese regimes, one intimately linked with armed forces and defense, was the patent inequality of the treaties concluded by the Tokugawa shogunate with various foreign powers. Inequity centered on the question of privileged legal status for foreign nationals in Japan as well as refusal to allow Japan to establish her own tariffs. The Meiji government was pledged to observe some fourteen such pacts, and the greatest objective of Meiji diplomacy was to revise, redraft, or abolish them. The bitter experience of these agreements had convinced the new Japanese leaders of the necessity to conform with outward standards and behavior of the mid-Victorian age, initiative in which devolved upon the Meiji emperor and the court. This is abundantly clear in the iconography of court functions, and proscription against Japanese traditional dress has been scrupulously maintained down to the present day in all public ceremonies. Superficial Westernization of costume and manners gained rapidly in momentum and complexity, and within a short time de-Japanization had evolved as a norm of progress and a behavioral ethic. This Westernization also achieved its original goals, for by 1899 Japan was able to enforce the abolition of consular jurisdiction and in the last year but one of the Meiji era insisted successfully on complete tariff autonomy.

NEW TOWNS AND FOREIGN BUILDING TYPES

In response to changes in politics, industrialization, and diplomacy, the realm of material culture grew increasingly at odds with the stereotype of an eternal Japan. This is not to deny that traditional lifestyles persisted to a great extent, notably outside the capital and major towns. Indeed, even in the cities all but the upper classes remained at the beginning virtually unaffected in their daily lives by the implementation of the new political order. Yet, all the same, and within a relatively short period of time, an altered environment began to take shape. Naturally, as is still the case today, architecture, as well as food, manners, and dress, played a vital and accepted role in this process.

What is nowadays known as "Meiji architecture" (and, as such, studied for its own sake) was a version of contemporary post-1850 European practices but with certain idiosyncratic differences owing to Japanese variations in climate, technology (or lack of it), and local customs. For the most part, the style of building that resulted from this combination was utilitarian, eclectic, and, possibly, to Western eyes, commonplace. To the Japanese it was nothing less than astoundingly original and inaugurated a new trend in taste wedding hitherto unknown modes of conspicuous consumption and compliance with official ideology.

We can now see how Meiji building was the earliest portent of a momentous sea change, but at the time, about the middle of Queen Victoria's reign, it might have seemed to a Western observer as if a certain Regency flavor had lately invaded Japanese architecture. Whether situated in the environs of the capital or the foreign precincts in Yokohama and Kobe, none of the buildings that arose before the 1880s even begin to resemble the up-to-date blocks illustrated by Sir John Summerson in his remarkable little monograph entitled *The London Building World of the Eighteen-Sixties*.[1] From the middle of the century Western building techniques were, in isolated instances, being introduced to factories or shipyards as part and parcel of the early industrial development we have already noted. Then—from the 1860s—consulates, churches, commercial establishments, and residences for foreigners began to make their appearance under the impact of trade and diplomacy. Such designs, as far as can be known, originated with the users, but they were realized by Japanese builders, namely traditional carpenters and house-fitters. In this way, the gradual setting-up of a simplified industrial infrastructure—together with the growth of a class of foreign advisers, traders, diplomats, and missionaries—brought into being buildings and townscapes that anticipated in visual terms the consequences of an official turnabout in politics.

All these works, whatever the level of skill they exhibited—and for the most part refinement of detail eluded them—were regarded as being simply in the "foreign style." This label was attributed, at least by one Englishman, to the fact that it designated an aesthetic "foreign to all known styles of architecture."[2] There was, certainly, a pleasing though outlandish quality about a lot of Meiji architecture, the more so as it has today become a rarity (fewer than 1,300 examples of non-native-type structures survive from the period throughout the country, including only 33 in Tokyo). At a more serious level, however, three major notions are entailed. The first, to be blunt, is that an exoticism has always attached to the persons and lifestyles of foreign residents in Japan from the earliest times to the present. The second is that, in her search for a contemporary identity, Japan was totally without traces of a colonial past such as centers of colonization in India, the old Dutch Cape Colony, or the eastern seaboard of the United States all evinced at one time or another. In each of

1.2. The Bund, or waterfront, at Yokohama before 1866. Woodblock print by Hiroshige III.

these places various vernacularized traditions of neoclassicism evolved. By contrast, for example, the vast region of Australia beyond the original boundaries of New South Wales, the more recently colonized regions of southern Africa, such as Natal, and such parts of the western area of the United States as remained unoccupied by Spain were without this inheritance. Japan resembles these latter instances but with the addition of an interesting tendency to employ the heritage of classicism—to borrow a Summersonian coinage from another era—as an exotic "artisan mannerism." A third point which bears emphasizing is that architecture and townscape in Meiji Japan reflected the vigor and optimism with which any new cultural age is undeniably infused.

As regarded influx of aliens into Japan, "concessions," later to be known more simply as settlements, were set aside for their use in a restricted number of open ports designated in several parts of the country. This model was derived from China, a recent precedent having been furnished by the Treaty of Nanking in 1842. That pact concluded the Opium War, ceded Hong Kong to Britain, and regularized the earlier European presence elsewhere in China. When pushed to the wall, the Japanese authorities therefore reopened Nagasaki in Kyushu as a trading base for foreigners. By the Ansei Treaties signed in 1858, Hakodate in Hokkaido and Kanagawa, a fishing village just south of Tokyo near the site that later became Yokohama, were also established at the same time. Ten years later Osaka was duly opened up to foreigners, and Kobe—soon to become a thriving port in its own right—was created, like Yokohama, completely from scratch. Finally, in the following year foreigners were given access to Niigata, an existing port on the Sea of Japan facing Vladivostok, itself a new town inaugurated by the Russians in 1860.

These foreign communities were begun as rough-and-ready makeshift places, with the exception of Kobe, which profited from the experience of the others. Just as in the gold-mining towns of the 1840s in California, a man could be made or broken overnight, and there was a chronic shortage of women. First would spring up a rudimentary hotel, saloons, and a church or two, to be followed by clubs and amenities.

By far the most important among the Treaty Port Settlements was Yokohama (fig. 1.2), which, established in 1859, is today the second largest city in Japan. While little is known of its earliest buildings owing to a fire in 1866, the town as rebuilt shortly afterward became "an observation post and a laboratory"—the cradle of the new Meiji civilization.[3] In other words, Yokohama took Nagasaki's place as the main dissemination point in Japan for Western learning as well as every sort of newfangled technique and goods.

From their earliest inception, two separate streams of development came to be associated with Yokohama and the other open ports, reflecting the division of these towns themselves into foreign and Japanese sectors. First were the buildings foreigners put up for their own use, but of these virtually none survives, though some are represented from a distance in sketches or photographs, where they appear to be naive and retardataire. They were simplified structures with a modicum of what was reckoned to be correct detailing, and any flourishes were culled from some built source or possibly a pattern book. Early examples of such work were invariably framed in timber, even if certain of the more important would later be faced with stone. In most instances, not only have the buildings themselves disappeared, but rarely, if ever, can the name of a builder be supplied. In the best of cases he would have been an engineer or surveyor but more commonly a plain merchant, missionary, or Catholic priest. A world apart from this display of Western architectural genius stood the Japanese town, but it should be kept in mind that here was also the source of materials and all labor.

In the early days the settlements wore an inevitably raw and temporary aspect. They are remembered as uncomfortable, if not unhealthy, with concern for rudimentary sanitation making an appearance only after prosperity stimulated growth and expansion. It was recalled, for instance, that roadmaking, street lighting, and drainage all constituted problems in the early days of Yokohama. This was partly because, after the fire of 1866, a new residential district was laid out on the bluff overlooking the town, and the area which had made up the original foreign enclave reverted to business. Thus,

1.3. Nagasaki at the beginning of the Meiji period.

1.4. British and other "factories" at Canton, eighteenth century. Chinese export ware bowl in the Idemitsu Museum of Art, Tokyo.

streets in the older part of the settlement remained unpaved and unlit long after the Japanese part of town had installed gas lighting in 1872. In all cases, the buildings that survive today from the last century are not those which originally composed the old Bund, or waterfront. Instead, they are later examples built on higher tracts beyond the confines of either the settlement or the Japanese town.

At Nagasaki, too, the old "Dutch factory" dating from more than three centuries before Meiji has long since disappeared under the pressures of native and Chinese occupation. Owing possibly to this history of prior foreign settlement, the town, shortly after it was reopened to Westerners just before the end of the shogunate (fig. 1.3), could already boast a few homes constructed as villas in the Oura district overlooking the magnificent bay. One such dwelling, situated at some distance from the settlement itself, is the Glover Residence of 1863, among the oldest of all Western-style buildings left standing in Japan today. Still other houses were constructed in this more healthful hilltop district at the beginning of Meiji, while a few have been removed to the same vicinity quite recently in a bid to establish a parklike, open-air architectural museum.

So, while Nagasaki retains a distinct atmosphere of former times, it is the panoramic setting which, as at Kobe, sways the imagination in combination with (mostly) later nineteenth-century buildings. This will be what the tourist, rightly, comes to see, in the same spirit as the Sunday visitors who throng the old Foreigners' Cemetery in Yokohama. Comparatively less well known, Hakodate, in Hokkaido, likewise evokes life in the settlements, but on my visit there in the late 1970s, it had more appealingly kept a share of its old unpaved streets and lanes. Perhaps the most enlightening suggestion put forward about the appearance of the open ports, but one that is difficult to verify, is that they may architecturally have resembled the already established ports of the China coast[4] (fig. 1.4). This notion is strengthened if one attempts, as we shall do only very schematically, to reconstruct a vision of the architect's role in the old colonial-imperialist context. At the same time, taking into account the large quantity of or-

dinary, utilitarian mid-Victorian buildings that have vanished from the scene at home, one need not overemphasize the role of these foreign settlements in terms of an architecture which, today, is merely unfamiliar.

ENTER THE SURVEYOR

In England, the 1850s and 1860s were decades (here again I have recourse to John Summerson) when the architectural profession was "tragically split between art and piety on the one hand and 'bread and butter' on the other."[5] And one may guess that the general run of non-native architecture in the trading ports of the Far East largely answered to the second description. Let us try to discover how this situation—with its implication of a decline in building quality—came about, for it is in sharp contrast with the example of India, whose Presidency towns before the reign of Victoria are referred to as citadels of neoclassicism.

Early Victorian times in Britain witnessed the phenomenal rise of the "surveyor" trained in techniques of measurement and quantification. The architect, whether or not he was still an amateur, nevertheless considered himself primarily a man of taste. Although the surveyor was eventually to become a necessary adjunct to the architect as the range and scope of building activity expanded, it cannot be denied that the promotion of the former to independent status at about this time occurred at the expense of the latter. It is true as well that visibly lowered standards of design and levels of craftsmanship—resulting from an increased rationalization of building methods and cost-estimating procedures—came to dominate certain sectors of the building trade at about this time.

The whole trend represented by the incursion of the surveyor into the realm of the architect happily occurred too late to affect the standards of Anglo-Indian building, at its height during the reign of George III. It follows, however, that building in the classical style was never afterward to achieve great distinction east of Singapore, and the fact mirrors a changed age. Although layout and design of the Presidency towns were largely the work of military engineers

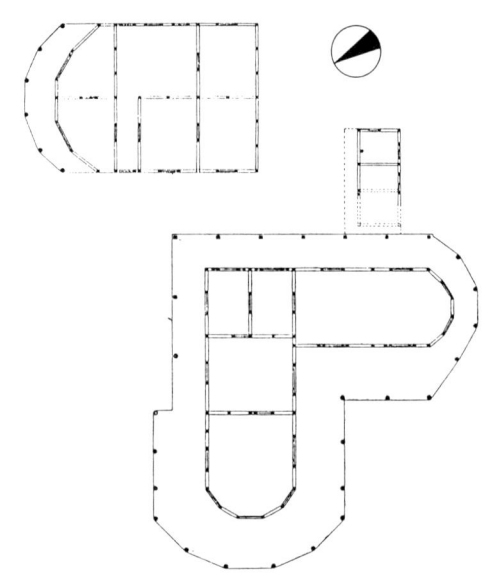

1.5. Glover Residence at Oura, Nagasaki, 1863. Painting by Soko Ochiai in the Nagasaki Prefectural Museum and early plan with dependencies.

who were East India Company men in the employ of the British army, style in places like Calcutta and Madras was determined by the aristocratic taste of their governors. These men, during their brief moment as patrons of architecture, were scarcely disposed to consider themselves mere servants of a trading company. As a consequence, they ignored the vociferous protests of the East India Company's directors to desist from lavish expenditure.[6]

Yet colonies were business enterprises, and the case of Singapore seems to illustrate the transition between the unsanctioned burst of extravagance in India and the reversion to a more characteristically mercantile standard farther east. It was here that in 1833 an Irishman named George Coleman was appointed the first Government Superintendent of Public Works. Nothing is recorded of his training, although he is known to have designed houses for merchants in the Calcutta district. In Singapore he executed a modest residency for Sir Stamford Raffles, but his first official employment under Raffles's successor was as revenue surveyor, and he was later employed on a topographical survey of Singapore before at last attaining superintendent's rank. Meanwhile, Coleman enjoyed an extensive architectural practice in the colony and, as he had already learned to do in India, made significant use of native materials in carrying out even Palladian-style projects. Coleman's questionable practice of combining public service with personal speculation plainly anticipated those careers of the following generation of architect-surveyors who worked their way eastward in the years to come. His death in 1843, however, at the age of forty-eight and after a quarter century in the East, marks the end of a colonialized architecture secure in the basic elements of the Anglo-Palladian legacy. Whatever their training, the men soon to follow in Coleman's footsteps lacked the fixed support of any established architectural tradition. They would be surveyors and no longer "architects" in the older sense of that word. And, in the case of those who went to Japan, they embarked, just as Coleman himself is known to have done—initially— without the backing of any colonial authority. As we shall see, however, more than one among them shortly managed to be employed by the new imperial Meiji government. Later, their successors would be brought out to Japan from England or the Continent, or over from the United States, once the Restoration was on course, with intention to further the express diplomatic and political aims of the young state.

WITH BRICK AND STONE
UNDER IMPERIAL CONTRACT

Fittingly for the theory that sees early Western-style Japanese architecture influenced by the style of building in the Chinese treaty ports, at least one British surveyor (now believed to have been in Japan from as early as 1863–64) had embarked in China. Thomas James Waters landed at Kagoshima in Kyushu, chief town of the powerful and pro-imperial Satsuma fief, sometime after the siege imposed by the Royal Navy, which had been of some value in helping to turn the tide toward an open-country policy. He was to supervise the construction of a new steam-powered cotton mill housed in a simple gable-fronted building of stone. This was completed in 1867 after designs which accompanied the spinning machines from Manchester.

Also in Kyushu, Waters became acquainted at Nagasaki with a young British trader from Hong Kong. He was a typical figure named Thomas Blake Glover, and he dealt in ships, armaments, and coal in addition to gold and silver, tea, seaweed, and silk thread. It used to be believed that Waters designed for Glover his villa overlooking Nagasaki port, already mentioned as one of the oldest surviving Western-style structures in Japan. The Glover Residence (fig. 1.5), a bungalow-type structure with extensive verandas on three sides, is datable to 1863 and was the work of a Japanese builder who is first encountered as an assistant on the Nagasaki Roman Catholic Cathedral (1862–64).

Both the cathedral and the Glover Residence have gained iconic status as pre-1868 artifacts of foreign-style Japanese building. The church, later expanded, was first built of wood in a pointed neo-Gothic variant, replete with a now lost baroque frontispiece, according to the design of French priests. In fact, one need look no farther than the example of St. John's Cathedral of 1849 at Hong Kong, constructed in a neo-perpendicular manner, to gauge the relative ordinariness of either church. Similarly, the Glover Residence carries more than a suggestion of Anglo-Indian precedent and probably

1.6. Waters: the Mint at Osaka, 1868–71. Riverfront alignment of foundry and outbuildings.

1.7. Waters: the Mint at Osaka, 1868–71. Portico of the foundry building.

also reflects the example of Hong Kong, where Glover himself had connections. In any case, unlike Japan, Hong Kong may be seen from photographs to have had a large stock of Italianate and other Western-style buildings, many of which were extant before 1860.[7] To reiterate, it is the grandeur of the Nagasaki site that lays hold of the historical imagination, imparting its own uniqueness to the remaining buildings. As for these, it now seems probable that Glover's house was only later enlarged to its present size, though it did provide a nucleus at Oura for a cluster of other early foreign dwellings. Among them, the Alt House, for instance, is a single-story building of neoclassical format, but it remains of greater interest from a technical point of view, including the provenance of its materials, than for its style.

Thomas Glover facilitated Thomas Waters's career by presenting him to the new Meiji government. Waters was thus enabled to procure a contract from the Public Works Bureau of the Treasury for construction of a new National Mint at Osaka. Concomitantly, Glover arranged for purchase at discount of London-made minting machinery, originally used for two years by the Hong Kong authorities in their unsuccessful attempt to supplant the Mexican silver dollar as the standard unit of currency in the East. Waters's new mint went up between 1868 and 1871 (fig. 1.6), with an interruption due to fire. It is recorded as the largest, most up-to-date Western-style factory of the early Meiji period, the machinery it housed contrasting favorably with the antiquated Dutch equipment previously used by the Japanese. Architecturally, it consisted of a long, low foundry block with an attached vestibule that bore a monumental facade. This section of the mint survives and consists of a hexastyle Tuscan portico elevated on a podium, the porch masking a round-headed doorway flanked by arched windows (fig. 1.7). Excepting the Yokohama Cathedral of 1862, now known only from an engraving, this porch may represent the earliest pedimented portico built anywhere in Japan (if the simple distyle porch of the Alt House at Nagasaki is also discounted). Nevertheless, judged by strictly purist, that is, Greek Revival, standards, it seems strangely awkward and misproportioned. One wishes to attribute this feeling of unease to a later rebuilding of the parapet behind, but more likely we are encountering firsthand a typical example of the undoing touch of the surveyor.

1.8. Waters: the Mint at Osaka, 1868–71. Sempukan, or reception pavilion, to the rear of the foundry.

Rearward of the foundry itself, and detached from it, stands a two-story reception pavilion known as the Sempukan (fig. 1.8). Built of brick rendered in stucco and covered by a roof of Japanese tiles, this purely ceremonial structure is surrounded by a veranda that displays an identical Tuscan order at both levels with coupled columns at the corners and a gabled prostyle porch. More than with the villas at Nagasaki, one senses this building to be reminiscent of a naive architectural consciousness. For the Sempukan's refinements are artisanal instead of being merely conventionalized, and it possesses, overall, quite a strong craftsmanlike flavor. For instance, instead of a parapet there is only the direct overhang of the tile roof, recalling those earlier verandaed structures, now vanished but known to have lined the waterfront at Nagasaki and elsewhere in the port settlements. A comparatively correct entablature, incidentally, is cast in shadow by the overhanging tiled eaves at second-story level.

Originally the Sempukan stood along the riverside in a single line with the director's residence and technicians' quarters, which once flanked the foundry building. These dormitories resembled the Sempukan in general layout though without the ceremonial note imparted by the latter's prostyle porch. They appear to constitute some refinement of the foreigners' quarters at the cotton spinning mill in Kagoshima with which Waters had earlier been associated. Indeed, the amply proportioned, nearly cubical structure with a hipped roof and surrounded by a continuous two-story veranda can safely be regarded as typifying the majority of Western-style building in very early Meiji Japan. Still, the Sempukan is a virtually unique and unusually stately survival.

In American architecture, the continuous veranda had a Spanish, or Spanish-American, provenance. It was diffused mainly through New Orleans as a residential form, and institutional examples, other than hospitals, are comparatively rare. A striking instance was the design for the Customs House at Galveston by Ammi B. Young, architect for the U.S. Treasury Department between 1852 and 1860. It was to have had a *three*-tiered veranda, although this was never incorporated in the work as built, which remains one of the finest classical revival buildings on the Gulf Coast. While this Texas port, settled from the 1830s, in some ways recalls the history of Far Eastern treaty settlements, may it not have been the Public Works Bureau of the Japanese Treasury itself that imitated the thriving Construction Branch of its U.S. counterpart? This bureau was at first in charge of all public building in Meiji Japan, the mint being but a single example. The fact that under Young's supervision the Corps of Engineers and Engineering was implicated in jobs initiated by the Construction Branch for the U.S. Treasury may also explain the resemblance of certain features of Meiji architecture to standard American military building of the period. In 1855 Young published a complete engraved work with the title *Plans of Public Buildings in Course of Construction, under the Direction of the Secretary of the Treasury, including the Specifications Thereof*. Though there were other books of this type, Young's is just the kind of source that would merit further checking in order to determine the real origins of surveyor's architecture of the Meiji period in Japan and elsewhere.

By 1871 Waters was in Tokyo, where he designed the Commercial Museum, said to have been the city's first brick building. He is known to have first imported brick from Hong Kong and later set up a brick kiln or two. Here he made some of the bricks for the mint, as well as those for the museum and other Tokyo buildings like the Takebashi Barracks (1870–74) and the British Legation (1872). Much British architecture, wherever found in the East, has a strong whiff of military building manuals. Thus, it is in the Takebashi Barracks (figs. 1.9–10), perhaps, that a clue to Waters's formation, about which we know nothing whatsoever, may be found.

Early in the eighteenth century, during the period following the reinstatement of the Duke of Marlborough as Master of the Ordnance in 1714, buildings designed in the Office of the Surveyor-General of the Ordnance developed a profoundly Vanbrughian feeling, an example being the Old Board of Ordnance at Woolwich (1718–20). The Takebashi Barracks echoes this curious arched-and-pedimented style of the ordnance offices of that period, except that the imperial chrysanthemum device in the pediment replaces the ocular window, or the rondel, that is such a popular feature of English baroque. In itself, this rondel-centered pediment is emblematic, from Calcutta to Hong Kong via Singapore, and even oc-

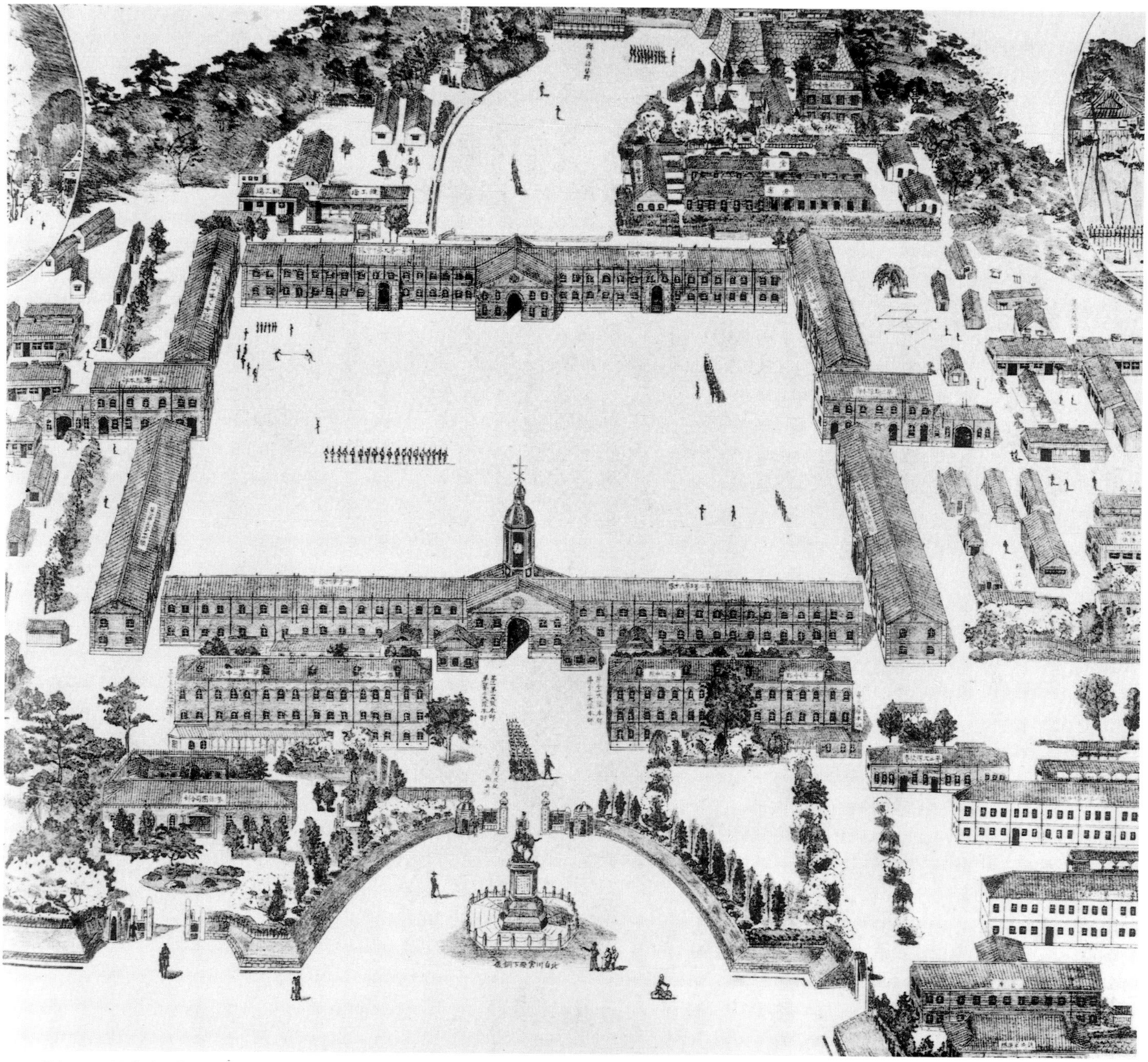

FOUNDATIONS OF MEIJI ARCHITECTURE 21

1.9. Waters: Takebashi Barracks, 1870–74. Bird's-eye view, from a popular engraving.

1.10. Waters: Takebashi Barracks, 1870–74. Main front.

1.11. Waters: redeveloped Ginza district, or so-called Bricktown, 1872 onward. Woodblock print by Kuniteru II.

curs in military buildings in the United States. Meanwhile, the arch-pediment combination reappeared during the Regency, especially in utilitarian architecture, such as Charles Fowler's Covent Garden Market in London, as well as in his conservatory for Syon House at Hounslow, from which Waters might have taken it.

Yet another habit links Waters to the heritage of the Regency (whose successes surveyor-architects recalled, somewhat as the Ordnance men appropriated late baroque devices for enlivenment of their own designs). That was his predilection for using the Tuscan order in functional buildings. This was a tradition consecrated by Palladio, who found Tuscan columns well suited to the barns of country villas. Waters, with his brick factory to hand, was called in to recreate the main thoroughfare of the Ginza district in Tokyo when, in 1872, one of the periodic great fires endemic to the capital ravaged some ninety-five hectares in the area we now think of as its center. In his design he made use of more or less continuous colonnaded facades (fig. 1.11) that screened terraces of brick-built units which Waters hoped to be able to promote as fireproof dwellings for the displaced populace. He took as his model for these colonnades, evidently without regard for the straightness of the main Ginza street as laid out, Nash's magnificent design for the Quadrant (1819–20) in Regent Street, London (removed in 1848). Every bit as much the improviser as John Nash himself had been, Waters simplified the stately cast-iron Roman Doric of the Quadrant to an unfluted Tuscan order for the Ginza.

The significance of Waters's new Ginza development was nothing less than that it was the first street improvement in modern Japan. In addition to his "fireproof" houses, some 916 of which were built (although this amounted to only a fraction of the number originally envisioned for the scheme), Waters determined to pave the roadway in brick as well. In emulation of the Quadrant, it was broadened to ninety feet but had, in addition, twin rows of trees to guard pedestrians from vehicles. The new street became a popular promenade, gas lamps making a debut in 1877 and, later on, trolleys. The new buildings, however, were not immediately favored with occupancy on account of both dampness and fear of earthquakes. Thus, from the year following the construction of the "bricktown" prototype, old-style wooden residences, which had been banned in the new area, were once again built. Eventually, Waters's buildings also came to be accepted, and a number of newspapers, newly founded on the model of the journals which appeared in the settlements, established their offices in the Ginza. At this same time, just to the south of Ginza, at Shimbashi, Tokyo's earliest railway terminus was constructed (assuring the historic link with Sakuragicho in Yokohama). Here was a fact of life that once and for all altered the predominantly residential character of this part of the city.

NATIVE ASSIMILATION OF WESTERN TECHNIQUES AND STYLES

The matter of exactly which style, or styles, were imported into Japan, as well as the issues of "when" and "from where," are questions that we can probably never resolve. Waters, the surveyor, was essentially concerned with getting things done as, of course, was the Meiji government, and neither may be reproached for ignoring archaeological exactness. Eclecticism and variety, in the context of workaday historicism, were viewed as positive architectural attainments, an attitude in no way repudiated by the surveyors. On the whole, Waters was better at architecture than the foregoing, slightly grudging account might suggest. He appears to have stuck to the generalized formulae of English neoclassicism of a generation or two before his own and went about his business without an attempt to confront or display more up-to-date Italianate, let alone Frenchified or High Victorian Gothic, notions. Now, in any case, we must produce the other side of the coin and examine the results Japanese practitioners were achieving in the styles of building exposed to their observation through the agency of the settlements.

An entirely new architectural idiom, chiefly in wood, was pioneered in this way by Japanese master carpenters, frequently situated outside of the main cities. It lasted through the middle of the second decade of Meiji, but with certain later repercussions. This development has usually been known as *giyofu* (pseudo-Western style), although recently the new word *kaikashiki* (Restoration mode) has been coined as a

1.12. Tateishi: Kaichi Primary School, Matsumoto, Nagano Prefecture, 1876. View from main gate.

descriptive term for it. The most celebrated early surviving example of such a building is the Kaichi Primary School of 1876 at Matsumoto, Nagano Prefecture, in the mountainous region of central Honshu. It is a structure of medium size, five and six window bays on either side of a balconied frontispiece (figs. 1.12, 17), and is the work of Seiju Tateishi, a carpenter previously in the service of local samurai. He based his design on sketches he drew on the site of the Kaisei Gakko (Liberal Arts College) of 1873 in Tokyo (see fig. 1.20). However, the new schoolhouse at Matsumoto surely resembles even more the Medical College of 1876, with its identically uneven distribution of bays. Unlike the majority of residential and commercial buildings photographed in the settlements, neither the Kaichi School nor either of the two educational buildings in Tokyo has verandas or any form of arcading. On the other hand, both the Kaichi School and the Medical College have lanterned towers of a characteristic type that derives from the English or Dutch baroque, where it had signaled customs houses, exchanges and markets, or variously some type of collegiate building. Square or octagonal lookout towers were frequently present in early buildings of the Meiji period, Waters's Takebashi Barracks having one of the most oddly proportioned (see fig. 1.9). Furthermore, a photograph of the Osaka Town Hall of 1874 seems to show a fully fledged Michelangelesque dome with tall drum, while the Kanagawa Prefectural Building of 1871 at Yokohama is known to have employed a four-story half-engaged clock tower as part of its more conspicuously mid-Victorian Italianate composition. So there was no shortage of models from all styles and periods.

Nevertheless, Tateishi's sources for the Kaichi School remain a mystery. His building is probably a conflation of the style of Kisuke Shimizu II, the greatest and earliest of the so-called *giyofu* architects, whose career we shall turn to now, and that of the Ministry of Technology established in 1870, which up to 1885 produced a number of buildings for which the term *kaikashiki* appears especially suitable. Taking all evidence into account, redefining the old and new labels in this way is not really as subtle as it may seem. The likeliest reason such a distinction has never been proposed is the scarcity of our knowledge about early Yokohama (due to the fire of 1866) in conjunction with the fact that none of the works of Shimizu, either there or in Tokyo, has survived.

The two most important and spectacular works by Kisuke Shimizu II, who lived from 1815 to 1881, were the Tsukiji Hotel for foreigners (1867–68), facing Tokyo Bay, and the First Mitsui Bank Headquarters (1871–72) at Kaiunbashi, in the heart of the capital. The second Shimizu was the son-in-law of the founder, and he himself later became head of Shimizu Gumi. Known since 1937 as the Shimizu Construction Company, this firm remains even today among the great "big five" Japanese architect-builders. The two most significant buildings of the founding years of the Meiji period are known to us only from drawings, prints, and dim old photographs but were, of course, internally framed in heavy timber. Yet, contrastingly, the walls of the hotel, originally

1.13. Shimizu: Tsukiji Hotel for foreigners, Tokyo, 1867–68. Woodblock print by Kuniteru II.

commissioned under the shogunate, were done up in a peculiar kind of stuccowork (fig. 1.13), while Mitsui Bank was faced with stone (fig. 1.14). Both had symmetrical front facades presided over by the kind of pagodalike cupola already discussed, which came to be admired during the Edo period. In the case of the hotel, the tower was topped by a square open belfry surmounted by a weathervane, but the second of these two works supported a closed octagonal lantern with a flagstaff at its pinnacle.

Though both buildings had Japanese-style tiled roofs, the bank was recognizably mid-Victorian in a way the hotel was not: by virtue of its two-story porticoed facade, which echoed the architecture of the foreign settlements. However, this facade was differentiated from the genuine article and also, I believe, from any recent building in Yokohama, whether foreign or Japanese, by the materials and embellishment of its porch (fig. 1.15). Although certain details relating to the first story were later modified, the original facade consisted of a two-story open gallery along its entire length, with projecting end walls that bore engaged half columns on the ground floor. These end walls were omitted on the floor above, and the upper veranda was protected on all three sides by a distinctive honeycomb-patterned balustrade of bronze. The gallery contained five bays and, therefore, had ten columns, plus the pair of demicolumns already referred to. Like the balustrade, these were also of bronze, a fact which accounts for their extreme attenuation and wide spacing. As there is barely any attempt to create an order as such, these columns behave proportionally more like rows of simple colonnettes. This is very different from the Sempukan with its astonishing Palladian rectitude, but it is possible that the galleried aspect of the Mitsui Bank owes something to the ancillary buildings constructed by Waters at the mint.

Bronze columns, or for that matter even silver fittings, are said to have been used in plantation houses near or along the Gulf Coast. Therefore, the distinctive feature of the decoration of Mitsui Bank is less to be found in its metalwork than in the naive, yet attractive, historiated designs worked into the curious bargeboard-type ornamentation underneath the entablature and between the columns of the second-floor gallery and also displayed in bracketed form on the first floor. This particular technique is of late Edo inspiration and consists of the kind of polychrome ornament carved in wood above the entrances to shrines. Motifs frequently include auspicious dragons, pine boughs, and stylized Chinese cloud forms. The latter formed the bronze brackets attached to each column, and in the upper gallery these supported longitudinal frieze elements of bronze that, in turn, bore a broader plastered frieze depicting auspicious Japanese cranes in flight. These several registers were overhung by a massive plasterwork cornice topped with copper guttering, and a wooden balustraded parapet also originally sheathed in copper. The decorative effect is reminiscent of the kind of oriental rococo motifs encountered in certain eighteenth-century European buildings or in the ornamentation of so-called Chinese Chippendale furniture or in wallpaper of the same period embellished with frets and lattices.

Carved polychrome friezework of this sort had already appeared in at least one building intended to serve the Meiji state, namely the very early Naval Reception Hall once situated in the precinct of the Hama Detached Palace. Yet such a structure had been largely vernacular and was scarcely, if at all, Westernized. Another example was the residence built in 1871 at Kumamoto for the schoolteacher, L. L. Janes, which has a five-bayed, two-story veranda as well as very simple historiated carving in the first-floor frieze, and a kind of cusped bargeboarding of trelliswork inserted between the columns at second-floor level. Needless to say, the design is executed unassumingly in wood and plaster without the aid of exotic materials.

Therefore, Shimizu's First Mitsui Bank, by making use of established *giyofu* motifs but aggrandizing the context in which they occur, created a pseudo-Westernized monument that remained qualitatively unique. A glance at its extraordinary roofline ought to allay any doubts on this score. For the customary hipped roof Shimizu substituted a complete

1.14. Shimizu: First Mitsui Bank, Kaiunbashi, Tokyo, 1871–72.

1.15. Shimizu: First Mitsui Bank, Kaiunbashi, Tokyo, 1871–72. Woodblock print by Kuniteru II.

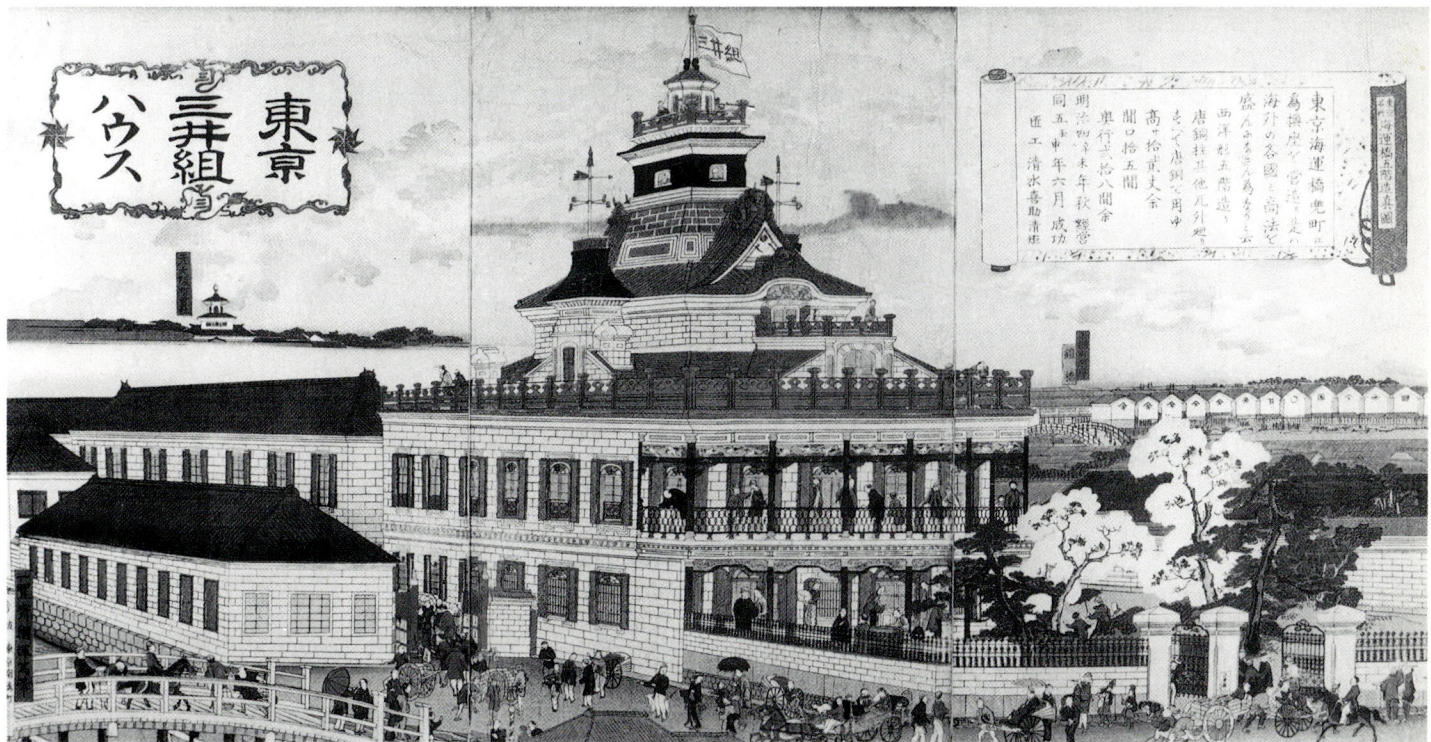

belvedere-like construction of some five different levels, including the aforementioned eight-sided lantern at its top. As if the combination of English- or Dutch-style cupola and tiled gabling that derives from Japanese feudal architecture were not enough, this already hybrid structure is flanked by a pair of French- or Italianate-looking box-turrets, each with a truncated pyramidal roof surmounted by a wrought iron parapet and a weathervane. Wondrously, the hierarchical disposition of this trio of spires succeeds in domesticating the otherwise heterologous eruption of medieval gabling, multi-tiered cornicework, and parapeted balconies.

In its way, the realization of the First Mitsui Bank at Kaiunbashi by Shimizu was as prodigious as that two centuries earlier of the flat facade of Wren's Sheldonian Theater at Oxford, with its concept taken from Palladio's reconstruction of the Basilica of Constantine. It is disappointing that the plan of Shimizu's building does not fulfill this promise of grandeur. It portrays a succession of small axially unrelated chambers while nothing at all is made of the expectation of a grand staircase. As built, the stair was a narrow affair pushed to one side of the building, a fact which seems to confirm that Shimizu was designing his work from mere elevational notions of Western monumentality, possibly engravings or even plain woodcuts. By contrast, perhaps the single most interesting feature of this plan is the inclusion of a small *tsubo* garden situated in an enclosurelike courtyard at the rear of the structure. All the same, at this point where the fabric of the building seems to go native, with a disjunction between one- and two-story wings, there was not the slightest break in the continuity of the left-hand lateral facade, whose appearance is known from contemporary woodblock prints.

Though we no longer have the least firsthand knowledge of any monumental effects of townscape in the original settlements, there can have been little there to challenge a supposition that the First Mitsui Bank was the most painstakingly elaborate of all early metropolitan *giyofu* structures.

1.16. *The "Incomparable" British Consulate at Yokohama*, completed in 1868. Woodblock print by Kunimasa IV. Smaller view shows three towers superimposed, as in perspective.

Its very complexity makes for difficulty in gaining an idea from Shimizu's design of the inherent satisfactoriness of the style. In this respect, the other important work by him, the Tsukiji Hotel for foreigners completed in 1868 (see fig. 1.13), also gives a somewhat maverick impression and is scarcely more helpful. This is because its walls were finished in a traditional technique known as *namako-kabe*.

As early as the Kamakura period (1185–1333), a particular species of fireproofing technique known as *dozo-zukuri* had appeared in Japanese construction. This consisted in the application of from ten to thirty centimeters of mud over a timber frame and was chiefly used in buildings designed for storage purposes. It later came to include an elaborate system of protective closure based on the use of several sets of doors, the outermost faced with iron. In such a building, the walls of hardened earth were plastered over with lime or, alternatively, a technique evolved in the warrior residences of the early Edo period might be applied, by means of which even the storehouses of commoners were covered in a veneer of square, flat-cut tiles. In the system known as *namako* walling used for the Tsukiji Hotel in the first year of Meiji, these tiles were applied in a diagonal pattern to achieve a distinctive bond. The ornamental effect was emphasized by means of an extruded lime plaster molding which concealed the joints between tiles and formed a characteristic crisscross design, the raised portion being semicircular in cross section. It was believed that these strips resembled the sea cucumber, i.e., *namako* in Japanese, or *bêche-de-mer*. Though originally intended to provide an extra measure of fireproofing and, possibly, an identification device in times of conflagration, the *namako* walling technique as it evolved from the common storehouse, or *kura*, of the Tokugawa period also proved a transitional step toward imitating Western-style brick and stonework by means of paint and stucco.

Except for fortification work and retaining walls, masonry construction was not practiced by the Japanese. Brick had been unknown, presumably, until Thomas Waters began to produce it at the beginning of Meiji. Therefore, the technique of mud-walling was apparently extended to the foreign settlements where it was used, from earliest times, in the construction of storehouses and mercantile buildings, mainly as an attempt at fireproofing. This was merely a continuation of the tradition of maintaining extensive "godowns" (a corruption of the Malay word for storeroom), as the warehouses in foreign posts all over the East were termed. And it would seem that, whether for practical or ideological reasons—or both—*namako*, or "trepang" (from the Malay word for sea slug), became a popular mode of construction in the earliest years of Yokohama's settlement. Incidence of the technique must have increased after 1866, the year of the fire that destroyed a third of all foreign buildings and nearly the entire native town. The Tsukiji Hotel (which itself burned, after only four years, in the great Tokyo fire of 1872) substantially resembled new structures put up in the final year of Tokugawa at Yokohama, such as the City Hall in Motomachi of 1867 and the U.S. minister's house situated on the Bluff, the new neighborhood opened to foreigners that same year.

Shimizu had been appointed as early as 1861 to a position at the Kanagawa (i.e., Yokohama) government office, which placed him in charge of construction and contract bids. Also active in Yokohama at this time (first mentioned in 1866) was an American, or possibly English, architect-surveyor, R. P. Bridgens, who built the twin railway stations in Yokohama and at Shimbashi in Tokyo. In 1867, also on the Bluff, he constructed the provisional British Legation, which was an essentially Western-type building but executed in *namako* walling. It is now known that while Shimizu obtained the construction permit and acted as builder, contractor, and later on as manager of the Tsukiji Hotel, it was R. P. Bridgens who wrote the specifications and drew up the plans for this new project in Tokyo. Yet, in terms of a style dominated by the effect of its *namako* walling, the hotel must be seen as an end rather than a beginning, the more so as the actual fireproofing proved so ineffective. Even though destined for a foreign clientele, Shimizu's hotel represents the apotheosis of a brief vernacular interregnum—derived from interests and conditions prevailing in early Yokohama—as opposed to the Westernizing tendency established among craftsmen working outside the settlements and exemplified in the First Mitsui Bank.

The ill-fated hotel opened in the first year of Meiji, the same year as Yokohama's new British Consulate (fig. 1.16). Here, except for its insistent loggie, was a building of solidly European inspiration, unlike the provisional legation. It occupied a corner site in Yokohama proper, and it possessed, in logical fashion, three towers, probably of brick with stone quoining. It was solidly in the Italianate style and, as such, a rare harbinger of John Summerson's "London building world" of the sixties. Or, if Bridgens was once more involved, as may well be supposed—and depending on his nationality—it demonstrates an equivalent idiom in the United States. It seems probable to me that the triple-tower arrangement may well have supplied the necessary inspiration for the fanciful topknot of Shimizu's subsequent First Mitsui Bank. That is because these towers regroup visually when the consulate is viewed obliquely, as it was in contemporary *nishiki-e* prints, in such manner that the end towers appear to flank the corner one. This conclusion is suggested, above all, by the squared, mansarded profile of the consular turrets as depicted in the single extant photograph of the building and repeated in the popular broadsheet topographical views of Yokohama of the early Meiji period.

SOME SPECULATION ABOUT *GIYOFU* MOTIFS

The path traced by a single architect from neovernacular pastiche in the Tsukiji Hotel to *giyofu* amplitude, however jejune, in the First Mitsui Bank has been accorded a good deal of attention here on account of its spectacular suddenness. Furthermore, both these buildings by Shimizu stand well outside the general run of pseudo-Western style work which continued to be built in the provinces until the middle of the second decade of Meiji, if only for their size and notable significance in social terms. But the First Mitsui Bank also displays a variety of characteristic motifs discoverable in a great many other pseudo-Western designs of the period. These include the cupola with weathervane (or, occasionally, a clock); the Japanese tile roof; the porch or balconied projection bearing a *kara-hafu* gable in pseudo-Chinese style; applied ornamental architectural features in the form of columns, balustrading, false quoining, and historiated brackets or friezes; casement windows of imported glass and fragile appearance, frequently tinted or colored; and a host of telltale constructional details, ingeniously and artfully camouflaged.

Tateishi's masterpiece, the Kaichi School at Matsumoto (see fig. 1.12), in its present carefully restored condition, is the best immediate source of our knowledge of many of these devices and is still early enough (1876) to suggest the directness with which *giyofu* carpentry attempted to mimic buildings constructed of masonry. But what are the real sources of such an edifice? The historiated ornamentation of the porch (fig. 1.17) with its iconic phoenix, dragon, cloud, lotus, and floral motifs is in the late-Tokugawa fashion that derives from the famous Nikko Shrine buildings with their profusion of spectacularly carved and painted decoration. Another clue is that the pair of carved *putti* exhibiting a banderol with the name of the elementary school inscribed in Chinese characters beneath the pseudo-Chinese gabled roof is tentatively identified as a borrowing from the masthead

28 FOUNDATIONS OF MEIJI ARCHITECTURE

1.17. Tateishi: Kaichi Primary School, Matsumoto, Nagano Prefecture, 1876. Porch (detail of figure 1.12).

of a woodblock broadsheet, the forerunner of today's popular *Mainichi* daily newspaper.

Yet, ultimately, the device of carved *putti* must come from the engraved frontispiece of some Renaissance, or Dutch, book or possibly the tradition of topographical engravings of architecture exemplified in Hollar's mid-seventeenth-century print of the conspicuously Flemish-style Royal Exchange, London, or the slightly later engraving by Henry Bell of his Customs House situated at King's Lynn. Therefore, there is, it seems to me, a problem of iconography in buildings of the Kaichi School type. The solution must go back to the English or Dutch baroque, as represented pictorially, and, thus, I believe, shorting out the influence of the foreign buildings of the settlements in general. A further aspect of the problem itself lies, I guess, in fully appreciating the heavy timber construction of such buildings as well as the sheer deadweight of the roof, both of which serve to endow them with a relatively archaic look. In the Kaichi School, for example, the upper and lower stories are divided by a full entablature, serving to impute visual solidity to the facade, which must appear able to support the roof.

In terms of native Japanese graphic tradition, it is their color attribute which links *giyofu* buildings to another species of architectural representation. Besides the coloration of historiated friezes, as found in the First Mitsui Bank, the architectural ornament of the buildings themselves was frequently given over to shades of blue, red, crimson, and pink. Part of the explanation of this polychromy lies in imitation of stone or brick, with its corresponding tonalities of blue and gray, red and pink. Thus, at the Kaichi School the base of the lantern is rendered as stonework and a modicum of imitation brickwork occurs in the embellishment of the porch on the surface of the projecting walls supporting the gabled roof. But the application of color goes well beyond this, since the window surrounds are of blue, and both the window shutters and the front doors are characteristically embellished with fielded (i.e., raised) panels outlined in white with a scheme of two further colors. Such is exactly the mode in which Western-style architecture, especially in Yokohama, is portrayed in contemporary *nishiki-e*. Thus, if it is true that imported paints were initially employed for *giyofu*, in a sense these also correspond to changes taking place at the time in woodblock printing technique, owing to the use of "improved" inks.

A final aspect of the puzzling relationship between *giyofu* iconography and various other species of art is related to the prominent Chinese element of decoration displayed in a number of pseudo-Western Japanese buildings. This can be seen in the Kaichi School in the painted or stenciled motifs occurring around the upper and lower doors of the main facade. In addition, though round- or segmental-arched openings with fanlights are characteristic enough of *giyofu* work, the front door at Matsumoto is fitted with a glazed surround of an unlikely Chinese type with a latticework fret displayed around its border. Finally, from the fluted colonnettes of the porch is suspended a pair of wrought-metal lanterns whose curvilinear forms are echoed in the painted design surrounding the doorway to the balcony above. There may be no connection, but this very curious motif happens to recall the design of a hanging lamp in the upper hall of Waters's Sempukan, and this is known to have been imported from Hong Kong.

A far more vexing problem than the attribution of Sinicizing motifs, present in successive variations throughout the history of Japanese art, whether in painting, cloth, ceramics, or metalwork from the earliest historical times, is the question of architectural backgrounds in the views of foreign scenes created by Japanese artists, particularly during the course of the eighteenth century in the period of seclusion. Even today the largest group of foreign residents in Japan after Koreans is the Chinese community, and this was also the case in the port concessions during the last century. Moreover, during the period of seclusion there was a continuous Chinese presence in Nagasaki, so that a certain amount of trade took place between the two countries with the Chinese themselves cast, generally, in the role of model foreigners at a time when Westerners were excluded. Cal French has pointed out the importance of the Soochow souvenir print[8] for the development of Japanese topographical art, from their reception at the beginning of the Ch'ing dynasty, in the middle seventeenth century, onward. This held true, notably, as regarded both a particular style of draftsmanship as well as a distinctive choice of locales and building types. Incidentally, the perspective-viewing machines of European derivation, which reached Nagasaki as early as 1718, came equally from Soochow.

Also at Nagasaki, of course, was the influence of the Dutch factory at Deshima. In artistic terms, this included the diffusion of Dutch scenes, including architectural townscapes, as well as views of classical, or Italian, architectural composition, at which Dutch artists excelled. Such European painted or engraved works were copied by Japanese artists, such as

1.18. Woodblock print depicting the Roman Forum, Toyoharu, before 1814.

1.19. Woodblock print ostensibly of a town in the Netherlands. Toyoharu, before 1814.

Utagawa Toyoharu (1735–1814), and French reproduces a "View of the Roman Forum" (fig. 1.18) by this artist which he calls "one of the most delightful adaptations of a European engraved prototype to the Japanese color print tradition."[9]

The color scheme of this work is described as "subtle shades of salmon and ochre" complemented by "dark green and gray," a combination not unsuggestive of the *giyofu* palette we have examined. Finally, French also proposes that in some Japanese works produced toward the end of the eighteenth century there occurred a conflation of Dutch and Chinese motifs comprising figures as well as architectural backgrounds. While certain of the direct copies of Italian scenes, for example, are flat and wooden owing mainly to difficulties in rendering single light sources and imitating perspective techniques, other views are suffused with a Gibbsian or Anglo-Dutch vitality (fig. 1.19). In reality "foreign to all known styles," it seems to make itself at home in the architecture of the Meiji period. By some mysterious transposition this atmosphere was retained in the architecture of the foreign settlements themselves by the carpenters and builders who worked there. Indeed, it was not so very different from the approach evolved by a foreign surveyor, such as Waters, seemingly equipped to provide a neoclassical design for any occasion. Later, within the Japanese tradition of foreign-style or merely "commercial" buildings, this highly

1.20. Hayashi: Liberal Arts College, Tokyo, 1873.

1.21. Hayashi: Ministry of Communications (combined with the Nihonbashi Post Office), Nihonbashi, Tokyo, 1874.

inventive and eclectic mode was fated to degenerate into what was afterward known, pejoratively, as *kamban*, or signboard, architecture. Yet such eclecticism and invention do still make themselves felt, even in today's work, as will become clear further on in the course of this book.

SYSTEMATIZATION AND RATIONALIZATION

The Liberal Arts College (Kaisei Gakko; fig. 1.20), forerunner of Tokyo University, of 1873, has already been mentioned as one influence on Tateishi's design for the Kaichi School in Matsumoto (see fig. 1.12). It was also among the last buildings designed and built under the auspices of the Treasury's Public Works Bureau, previously cited as having commissioned Waters's Osaka Mint as well as most of the important government structures of the very early years of the Meiji period. The person responsible for the Liberal Arts College was a former carpenter, Tadahiro Hayashi, having received a formation of sorts from 1865 as a builder in the new Western style in Yokohama, where he probably worked under Bridgens. He eventually joined the Treasury, and when, in 1874, the Public Works Bureau came under the umbrella of the recently founded Ministry of Technology in a merger which created a new architecture division, Hayashi moved with it. He eventually headed up this architectural section and was involved in the design of over thirty buildings, more than half of them brick.

We shall see in the following chapter that a number of foreigners were also employed by the Ministry of Technology. The majority of Western technical advisers brought to Japan by 1890, however, were hired by the Railways Bureau, and a second large group worked on civil engineering projects, including waterway improvement. These reported to the Ministry of Home Affair's Public Works Bureau, and so were not connected with architectural design as such.

Like the Kaisei School, the Ministry of Communications (fig. 1.21), a work completed in 1874 under Hayashi, provides a rather generalized example of the influence of contemporary Western sources. However, with its pedimented portico, it may reflect the specifically neo-Palladian aspect of a work by Waters like the Sempukan. In fact, though hardly "contemporary" by home standards in England, a number of arcaded ground-floors and porticos, as opposed to mere "verandas," had begun to make their appearance in the architecture of the settlements, most notably at Kobe, by (as reckoned from photographs) the mid-seventies. Both the Kaisei School and the Ministry of Communications have an overblown colonial New England flavor which, under any other circumstances, would be attributable to pattern-book copying but here probably represents a peculiar process of transmission conceivably unconnected with written or drawn documents, none of which in any case has survived. An exception is the preservation of carpenter Tateishi's famous sketch of the Kaisei School, but this leads, unfortunately, nowhere in itself. Both the Kaisei School and the Ministry of Communications were of heavy timber construction with stucco overcoating, the classical *giyofu* material, but with quoining in actual stone. The school is a long, low building whose entrances are marked by *kara-hafu*, the swelling gabled formulae for porches. However, the later Ministry of Communications possesses an urban-type elevation, which, following the street line, forms a corner. In so doing, it may obey the example of Waters's Ginza architecture or that of facade building in the settlements. In any case, major instances of new architecture from now on avoided the Chinese-style gable and other vernacular devices, such as the revival of the "flame-headed" window (*kato mado*) of Zen architecture at the end of the shogunate. That form, incidentally, still appears in the lantern of the Tsukiji Hotel by Shimizu (and, in fact, had even entered Western architecture in the previous century from Indian sources).

By the middle eighties, the Ministry of Technology itself was no longer, and the only extant example of its stucco-over-wood type of construction is the Medical College, which Tateishi would seem to have known. It was later altered and moved to an isolated spot in the Botanical Gardens of the University of Tokyo, not part of the main campus. A more up-to-date version of this same official style may be seen in the buildings for which the Ministry of Technology became responsible in Hokkaido, where immigration was encouraged at this period. The Office for Development at Sapporo (1873), for example, with its immense timber-framed mansarded dome, appears as the most sophisticated and probably also the largest non-industrial building anywhere in the Japan of its day. It was, however, entirely the work of the Commissioner of Colonization's American technical adviser, and so, to all intents and purposes, a foreign work; nor could it have been known to many mainland Japanese.

The most interesting proof of the shift toward a certain rationalization process in architectural design, owing pre-

sumably to the influence of the Ministry of Technology in matters of "public" taste, is provided by the so-called second Mitsui Bank of 1874. Japan Incorporated was not built in a day, and the original First Mitsui Bank (1871–72) was within a short time ceded to the Japanese government to be used as the First National Bank (together with the newly constructed mint, the most important of all national institutions in terms of portraying the stability of the government and keeping up its prestige abroad). A new Mitsui Bank at Surugacho was thus duly completed by Shimizu in 1874; like its predecessor, it was a large, squarish building but with three main floors instead of two. The topmost of these was set back from the lower facade or, put another way, the massively unwieldy tower of the earlier building had been expanded and simplified into a third story of usable proportions.

This second Mitsui Bank was of similar materials to the first, though apparently not faced in stone, while the material of the columns seems no longer to be known (fig. 1.22). The portico was roofed in Italianate fashion and surmounted by an open balcony. An additional pedimented porch of a single bay flanked by corbeled half-bays with half-rounded corners opened from the right-hand lateral facade. The historiated ornament of the first bank has disappeared for good, and the massive entablature was surmounted only by a tiled, hipped roof with a nominal cupola. This had no lantern but was topped instead by a huge piscine finial, traditionally of dark-fired porous earthenware tile and sometimes gilded, but here cast of bronze.

Except for this feature, the new second bank would have been at home in the likes of mid-Victorian Salem or Portsmouth, New Hampshire, though not in the newly Ruskinian Gothic or French neo-Renaissance-dominated precincts of Boston. There, from Beacon Street to the Back Bay, all the baffling modes of European historicism were being rung in something like an orderly succession. In Japan this orderliness was less than apparent, although the intention in the years to come was that it should be reflected.

1.22. Shimizu: Second Mitsui Bank, Surugacho, Tokyo, 1874. Facade viewed from the right, and lateral elevation.

2 | Tokyo and the "Problem" of Styles

COMPETING INFLUENCES AND
THE COLLEGE OF ENGINEERING

The array of historicist styles never evolved in Tokyo beyond a problematic efflorescence of manner; yet it furnished a requisite emblem of progress. For the outside observer this disparity between means and ideals has created a problem ever since, though for few Japanese. In Boston as in Europe, architectural revivalism furnished, above all, the opportunity to demonstrate an insider's knowledge of detail in a context of technical virtuosity. By contrast, the expertise of traditional Japanese builders was decisively bypassed after the *giyofu* episode on account of the sudden shift in building material from wood to reinforced brick construction by the middle of the Meiji reign. As a consequence, architects were able to control the field of public building. As they remained for the time being a class of underskilled technicians virtually dependent on foreign instruction, Japanese architecture experienced a severe loss of capacity for technical innovation that nearly brought creativity to a halt. Yet this shortfall was compensated for by a reliance on the effects of surface pattern as well as the iconic value of borrowed motifs and hierarchies, combined with a resourceful inventiveness.

A formalized provision for architectural education was nonetheless imperative, and it unfortunately happened that an eclectic approach, which esteemed decorum more than "sensibility," was instilled, mainly by a young Englishman, as we shall see. Ironically, the young architect in question, a pupil of that most innovative of revivalists, William Burges, belonged to a rather lukewarm, though highly principled, breed of eclectic designer concerned, first, with insinuating technical improvements and, second, with manipulating a particular style to fit a given commission. Mainstream Japanese architecture was, therefore, from around the end of the 1870s destined to become "improving" in this double sense.

Foundation of a technical college figured as early as 1871 among the aims of the newly created Ministry of Technology, but the Imperial College of Engineering did not materialize until after the government's historic fact-finding Iwakura Mission had paid visits to Edinburgh and Glasgow at the end of 1872. A number of the college's new staff, including Henry Dyer, its principal, were Glasgow University graduates;[1] the curriculum was drawn up by Dyer on his voyage out to Japan in the spring of 1873. It was to consist of training in the fields of mechanical and civil engineering, as well as telegraphy, shipbuilding, architecture, chemistry, metallurgy, and mining. In 1876 an art school was added, and it was also decided to hire a full-time instructor in architecture.

Much of the faculty of the new engineering college were only slightly older than the students. Thus, in 1877, a twenty-four-year-old Englishman, the 1876 Soane Medalist chosen by the Royal Institute of British Architects, arrived in the capacity of the school's first "professor" of architecture. Yet just exactly how the college determined in favor of Josiah Conder is no longer known. Not only had he no recorded Scottish connections, but also he would appear to have preempted the place of the Frenchman A. C. de Boinville (b. 1849), a surveyor, who had signed on initially with the Ministry of Technology in 1872 before the establishment of the college.

Before returning to Conder's appointment, let us here say a few words about the nearly anonymous de Boinville, about whom even less is known than is the case with Conder. As late as 1876, we find de Boinville completing the design for the Government Printing Office laid down by Waters (who, it must be assumed, was no longer in Japan). In the frontispiece of this building, known only from photographs, the tympanum was distinguished by a largish wheel window in the form of the emperor's *kiku*, or chrysanthemum, crest. At the apex of the pediment above stands a consular eagle, which is, in reality, a phoenix. In the year of Conder's arrival, 1877, de Boinville erected an auditorium building (fig. 2.1) for the new engineering college. This was a foursquare affair, Vitruvian in its detailing. Moreover, the facade is delineated in the manner of an English neo-Palladian tower house and resembles, I feel, a condensed version, significantly without the cupola, of William Kent's Horse Guards in London, as executed by Vardy (1751–58). But instead of rustication, de Boinville constructed his building of brick and made use of a triple superimposed order of pilasters. The main floor (i.e., the principal one above the ground level) is lit by three inordinately sized Serlian windows set into recesses, and each tower bears, at attic level, a similar motif, in which the arched recesses have been replaced by engaged Corinthian pilasters supporting a small, pedimented gable. In addition, the towers are punctuated by small imperial crests in such a way as almost to bring to life one of Serlio's woodcuts (see fig. 2.24). There is a certain sensitivity in the play of stringcourses and entablatures. However, the overall arrangement is mechanically repeated on the side of each tower.

Given that the middle portion of de Boinville's facade is restricted to a single recessed bay, all this is somewhat overpowering. It seems, in fact, that the auditorium was originally

2.1. De Boinville: auditorium building at the technical college, later Imperial College of Engineering, Tokyo, 1877.

2.2. Tokyo High Court, Tokyo, 1874.

intended as the centerpiece of a collegiate complex in the form of a quadrangle open on one side—in the manner of Jefferson's University of Virginia—but the extended wings this would have entailed were never actually completed. Standing in isolation, then, the auditorium was lighted by a range of high thermal windows on each side expressed as dormers, in the Roman tradition, as this was soon to become vulgarized by the Ecole des Beaux-Arts in the ensuing years of the nineteenth century. The new building for the college possessed a workmanlike integrity, if only as one man's interpretation of the relatedness of various neoclassical features. As in the work of Serlio, there is, if nothing more inventive, at least a reassuring subordination of parts to the whole. Manifestly, something of this same quality was to be felt in the work of Waters at his best and the *giyofu* idiom of architect-builders as exemplified by Kisuke Shimizu II. But all of these belonged to a preindustrial or (in the case of Waters) an early industrial past, and given the forward-looking context of the burgeoning Imperial College of Engineering, designs of a mere journeyman quality, however harmonious, were no longer acceptably up-to-date.

What was now required was a type of man more truly representative of the London building world and its newly minted professionalism, apparent in the recent royal chartering of the Institute of British Architects as the RIBA in 1866. Simultaneously, there was a good chance that in readjusting their sights toward a metropolitan style, namely that of London, the Ministry of Technology would be obliged to encounter the Gothic Revival. Mention has already been made of the appearance of Gothic in the Roman Catholic cathedral at Nagasaki, though not yet of its use for any secular building. In fact, the Tokyo High Court of 1874 (long ago destroyed, its architect forever unknown) provides an enchanting example of something akin to William Kent's "modern Gothick," which, in the eighteenth century, had set out to challenge classical supremacy. The style was seldom used for government buildings before Barry and Pugin's rebuilding of the Houses of Parliament following the fire that destroyed most of the Palace of Westminster in 1834. However, England's royal law courts were housed in undestroyed Westminster Hall until 1882. The Tokyo High Court (fig. 2.2) was a large structure two verandas in height with ten lengthwise bays

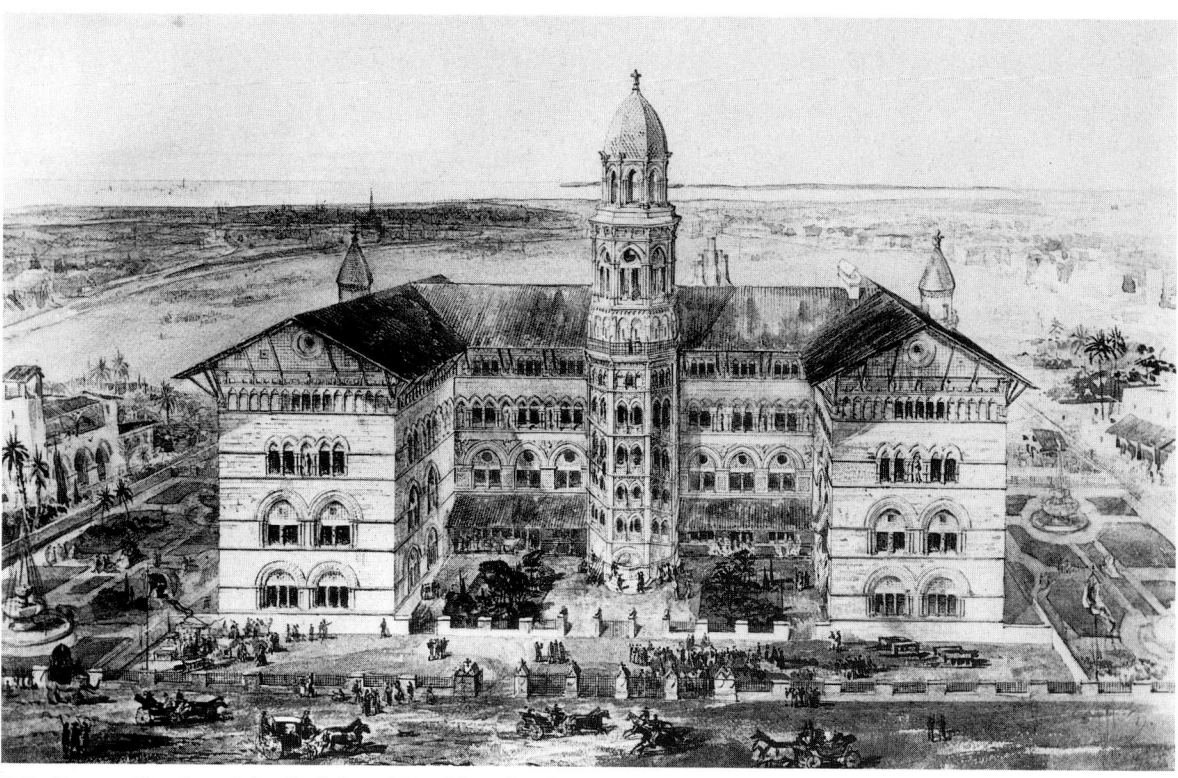

2.3. Burges: Bombay School of Art, 1865. Unrealized project.

interrupted by a possibly twelve-sided tower or, more probably, a five-sided mock centerpiece of three stories surmounted by a spiked parapet. As a stylistic exercise, the High Court, built of wood and perhaps stuccoed, is recognizable as one sort of Regency Gothic. It recalls in mood the Old State Capitol at Baton Rouge, Louisiana (constructed 1847–49 and rebuilt 1880–82), a building in its present form with twin octagonal towers but without verandas. A further reflection in Tokyo of the revival of Gothic architecture is the fact that the two earliest structures for the Technical College, before full implementation of imperial sponsorship, were created in a much simplified brick-and-stone neo-Gothic idiom by Alexander McVean and William Anderson. The names of these architects bespeak their provenance, and there can be no doubt that at least the larger building, which overlooked part of the moat of Edo Castle (that section today filled in and constituting the site of the Ministry of Education headquarters), was a modest recollection of George Gilbert Scott's towering Gothic pile for Glasgow University, finished in 1871.

Given such a beginning, it was perhaps not altogether out of place that young Josiah Conder came to Japan from the office of the celebrated Goth, William Burges. But in broaching this topic, there is a danger of the master eclipsing his apprentice, especially as Burges himself was one of the earliest Western collectors of Japanese feudal armor and woodblock prints. Characterized by his biographer as "eccentric, unstable and extravagant,"[2] Burges was also rich. He never needed to run a large office and was, moreover, too much of an individualist to have founded a school. A respected architect and the son of a successful civil engineer, his reputation today rests solidly on his colorful and exuberant neo-Gothic decoration and furniture designs. Regrettably, little of Burges's high-spiritedness is reflected in the life or works of Conder, who spent only two years under Burges before going to Japan, too short a time for influence to have taken hold.

Though he never left Europe, William Burges had earlier made a design for the Cathedral at Brisbane (1859, but modified in the building). In 1865, he submitted full drawings for a new building to house the Bombay School of Art (fig. 2.3). This project remained unbuilt and was, except for the scheme of decoration, a remarkably undigested design. The style is stated to be that of the twelfth century, but the tower and general layout, or *parti*, are, of course, nothing of the sort. It may even be noted that the jostling of facade and tower is less assured than the naive alignment of the Tokyo High Court. Yet, the relative lack of sophistication of the Bombay School of Art did not hinder an earlier Burges pupil, William Emerson, from pursuing his own career in India with something of the master's own aplomb and flair.

Burges's approach to the art of the past was eclectic and antiquarian in the best sense, as his subsequent architectural and interior works testify, especially those designs for his chief patron, Lord Bute, at Cardiff Castle and elsewhere. Conder, on the other hand, was remembered by a colleague from Burges's Buckingham Street office on account of his "capability for getting work done." Stressed also were his "characteristic thoroughness" and, not least, Conder's "dogged persistence and self-reliance."[3]

Given that the man erected more than seventy buildings in the course of a practice that extended through the Edwardian period and beyond, until his death in Tokyo in 1920, these qualities can hardly be gainsaid. Nevertheless, Conder visibly had neither the requisite muscle nor flair for High Victorian Gothic. Neither did he attempt a serious engagement with the vernacular revival which succeeded that style in domestic architecture and still less with the neobaroque classicism fashionable in England in the reign of King Edward.

As the Bombay School of Art project testifies, Burges himself was unaccustomed to manipulating complicated plans until his submission for the Law Courts—a major metropolitan competition that took place the following year. It has also been remarked rightly that "he never designed a popular work of national significance,"[4] that commodity which, above all things, the Victorian age cried out for at home and sought to export elsewhere. Possibly the Bombay

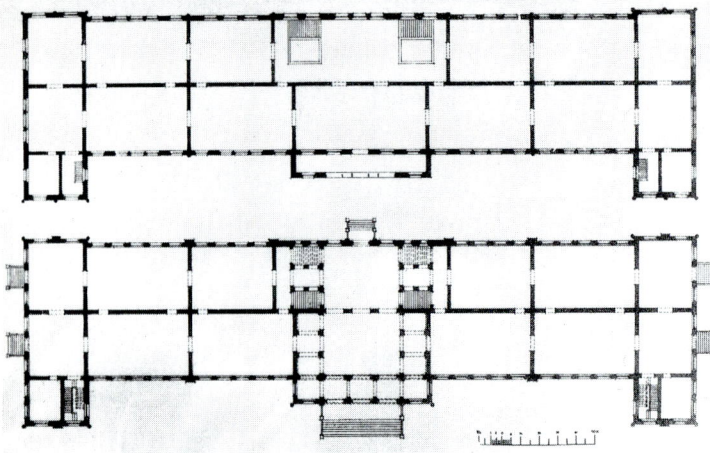

2.4. Conder: Ueno Imperial Museum, Tokyo, 1882. Woodblock print and floor plans.

project reflects the influence of the South Kensington art schools (briefly attended by Conder). Nor in England was there any better example of the type of professional college the Japanese hoped to establish. It was the German architect and erstwhile revolutionary Gottfried Semper who, during his stay in London in the early fifties, had advised Prince Albert on matters relating to the foundation of a museum and its accompanying schools at South Kensington to be based on a Continental model. Semper later left England and went to Zurich, where he taught till 1871 in the Polytechnic, an institution far closer to what the Japanese, at just this time, were contemplating.

Therefore, the position which Josiah Conder was invited to fill, and which to some extent he succeeded in creating for himself upon arrival in Japan, can be regarded as falling between two stools. In one sense, Conder's architectural production was to fail symbolically in terms of design to provide for hybrid, or colonial-type, institutions, in the same way that Burges failed in the Bombay scheme. Still, Conder, like Semper, had a genuine interest in structure and in practical institutional work which was in neither Burges's character nor manner of working. Although it is not easy to praise much of what Conder built in Japan, most of which has now disappeared, the Japanese may, indeed, have been fortunate to get Conder and keep him at the College of Engineering for almost a decade before he turned to private architectural practice. For the number of foreigners directly employed by the Japanese government had reached its peak in the three-year period 1873–76, just prior to Conder's arrival. And by the middle of the 1880s, former students of Conder were able to initiate the Architectural Institute of Japan, of which he was elected first honorary president. Like the RIBA before it, this organization sought to institutionalize functions which surveyors and architect-surveyors had previously exercised unofficially and set the most vital of these under the actual professional jurisdiction of the architect.

Though far from London, Conder assiduously kept up his professional affiliations, achieving the rank of Associate in 1878 and, in 1884, Fellow of the Royal Institute of British Architects. Therefore, by definition, the architectural design office he founded in 1888 was the first to be opened in Japan by any member of the profession as formally constituted. Yet, his earliest building had been completed by the year 1879 for the government, a model school for the blind known as the Kummo-in. In that same year the Imperial College of Engineering graduated its first architects trained under Conder's supervision, and by 1881–82 a few of his students were participating, under Conder's direction, in the construction of the Ueno Museum (fig. 2.4). This was a long, low two-story building badly damaged in the Great Kanto Earth-

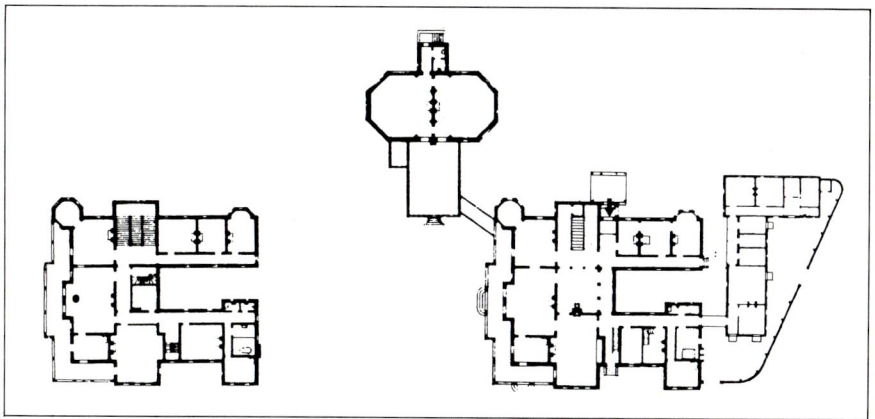

2.5. Conder: Iwasaki Villa, Fukugawa, Tokyo, 1889. Plan shows dependency with conservatory and billiards room.

quake of 1923 and now replaced. It was in the so-called Hindu-Saracenic style, in reality an orientalizing version of Venetian Gothic made popular in British India at about this time. Conder's original drawings nonetheless show the extent of Burgesian influence, both in the style of draftsmanship and the texture of the ornamentation. Even in Britain itself, museum building had not yet developed any clear-cut pattern of associationalism between contents and architectural form except for a notion that the Gothic corresponded with natural history. Therefore, it is hard to condemn Conder's design purely on grounds of its unsuitability to the Japanese imperial collections, yet it is equally difficult to find much logic in his choice.

By 1885 the Ministry of Technology had been hastily disbanded owing to the fiscal straits in which the government discovered itself. Between 1884, at which time Conder ceased to be a regular teacher at the college, and 1886, when its architectural section was made part of the Imperial University, where Conder lectured until 1888, his position and role are unclear. Strictly speaking, the opening of his own office corresponds with the end of his academic career, though it did not put paid to his work as a government servant, as he continued throughout his life to advise the Ministry of Home Affairs on topics related to building and construction. Finally, in 1892, Tokyo Imperial University made Conder a professor emeritus and, in 1915, awarded him an honorary doctorate.

JAPANESE EXPOSURE TO THE QUEEN ANNE REVIVAL

From the mid-1880s the field of architecture began to be dominated by young Japanese architects employed as civil servants. Among these were the four members of Josiah Conder's graduating class of 1879 at the College of Engineering. The best-known and the most prolific of them was certainly Kingo Tatsuno (1854–1919), who went abroad the year after claiming his diploma and bids fair as a Japanese Inigo Jones: the native apologist for a foreign style imbibed at its source. From 1880 to 1882 he attended London University, where T. Roger Smith, a great-uncle of Conder's, taught architecture at University College. Famous in his lifetime, Smith served as president of the RIBA as well as the British Institute of Certified Carpenters; his name also appeared frequently as an assessor for competitions. Conder himself had been articled to his relative before somehow managing a transfer to Burges's office, where Tatsuno, not quite a decade later, now followed. Burges, however, was to die suddenly in mid-career in April of 1881, at age fifty-three, during the course of the young Japanese architect's stay. Thus, when Tatsuno returned to Japan after a year of travel in France and Italy, the style

2.6. Shaw: Alliance Assurance Offices, London, 1881–83.

he brought with him was not Burges's; instead, it was a loose, if recognizable, version of the so-called Queen Anne revival.

The Queen Anne style flourished during the 1870s and 1880s in reaction to the High Victorian Gothic to which the previous generation in England had been committed. Had Burges lived longer, Tatsuno might not have been attracted to the new style at all, for Burges is known to have been dismayed at its lack of serious purpose, by his own standards. Nor did Conder attempt to make use of Queen Anne in any of his own works until well after the return of his pupil to Japan. At long last, the villa (fig. 2.5) for Baron Iwasaki at Fukagawa, completed in 1889, combined brick-and-stone Flemish gabling, one of the hallmarks of the developed Queen Anne fashion, with the continuous verandas that much earlier had characterized so many of the buildings of the foreign settlements. It was one of Conder's most successful works.

As for Tatsuno, we discover him already writing from England in the year of Burges's death that Queen Anne is a "cheap" style of building and one that will be "easy to learn." By this time in the early eighties, Richard Norman Shaw, Burges's slightly younger contemporary and the most notable practitioner of Queen Anne, was already receiving commissions of some prominence. It is almost certainly Shaw's Alliance Assurance Offices at 88, St. James's Street (designed 1881; built in 1882–83) which captured Tatsuno's imagination. For the building (fig. 2.6), on a highly visible corner at the junction with Pall Mall, was to attract the notice of architects throughout England. It was at this date only Shaw's second nonresidential building, after his New Zealand Chambers of 1873, and in it he elaborated a Flemish version of the Queen Anne. Therefore, the reddish brickwork of the neo-vernacular is articulated in a lively manner by means of horizontal banding and ornamental dressing of white Portland stone. If not a particularly fine building by Shavian standards, the Alliance Assurance Offices was nonetheless widely imitated at home and, in a more general way, also influenced Japanese architecture through Tatsuno's example.

PROPOSALS FOR A JAPANESE WHITEHALL

Kingo Tatsuno returned to Japan several years before the breakup of the Ministry of Technology in 1885. In 1884 he was named to a post in the College of Engineering, and in the subsequent transfer of architectural education to the Imperial University his influence succeeded Josiah Conder's, especially after Tatsuno became departmental head. Yet the disappearance of the Ministry of Technology at this time also meant the establishment of still another Department of Works, in 1886, the third in slightly less than twenty years of Meiji rule. At its head was Bancho Matsuzaki, a civil servant about whom not very much seems to be known except that he had trained independently as an architect in Germany. Under his leadership, official architecture in Tokyo was to reflect the strong Prussian bias that influenced the Meiji state in many ways during the years which followed, ending only with the Triple Intervention in 1895.

However, in the mere space of a decade, Tokyo was far from transformed into the image of Berlin, nor of Hamburg or Bremen, retaining instead the haphazard, mosaiclike quality the city still displays. Instead, priority was given at this time to a scheme for coordinating the layout of government buildings in the area west of Tokyo Bay in the neighborhood south of the former castle moats and ramparts that today constitutes Hibiya Park. At the end of the shogunate and during the first years of the Restoration, the official seat of government had been remote and ill-defined in contrast with the lively atmosphere of Yokohama or the "downtown" areas[5] of Tokyo proper. For these fairly quickly regained the bustling atmosphere they had temporarily lost in the period of the capital's decline. With the exception of Waters's Ginza redevelopment scheme, whose popular appeal was not manifested at once, the earliest Western-style architecture of the capital rose without the help of any European-style plan to bind buildings with their context. Yet it might be noted that Vienna's Ringstrasse with its sampler of architectural styles was scarcely less odd, despite its planned network of streets and institutions. In Tokyo the newly created Department of Works was determined, but on a smaller scale, to systematize the district intended as the setting for the

2.7. Ende und Böckmann: Parliament and Exhibition Grounds near the Imperial Palace, Tokyo, 1887. Existing palace moats with imaginary new construction.

emperor's gift of a new parliament. By 1887 a site had been selected, and the Berlin architectural firm of Ende und Böckmann had visited Tokyo and returned to the German capital with a contingent of about a dozen Japanese trainees.

Ende und Böckmann was well respected and could have been recommended to Matsuzaki by the German government. Hermann Ende, who had begun as a surveyor, started to work with Wilhelm Böckmann in 1859, and by 1872 their firm had been awarded second prize in the initial Reichstag competition. In 1886–87 both principals visited Japan. Submitting their proposal (fig. 2.7) for the parliament and exhibition ground, present-day Hibiya Park, they appointed as the firm's agent and representative young Hermann Muthesius, who resided in Japan from 1887 till 1891. Muthesius subsequently served as the Prussian technical and cultural attaché in London and became celebrated as the author of the book *Das englische Haus* (1904–5). A photograph of 1896[6] shows him and his wife in a discreet London sitting room surrounded by various Japanese artifacts.

It is insufficiently understood that, as well as demonstrating the far-reaching influence of Japan upon Europe and America, the art of this period became a commodity in the commercial, naval, and diplomatic struggle between Great Britain and Germany culminating in World War I. Since Muthesius was, more than anyone, instrumental in transmitting a knowledge of British architectural culture to the European Continent, it is a telling footnote that his career should have begun in Japan promoting the official Prussian style. Similarly, the French were threatened in their lucrative monopoly of decorative arts by pan-German interests, and as late as 1910–11 the young Francophone Swiss, Le Corbusier, had reported on industrial art in Germany in an attempt to redress this situation.

Except for its sharp profile and relative lack of flourish, there was nothing avant-garde about the hulking neobaroque classical scheme for the parliament building (fig. 2.8) Ende und Böckmann submitted to the Japanese in 1887. This was accompanied by a reorganizational scheme (fig. 2.9) for the area south of the palace destined to become the seat of government. It included a truly monumental dispersion of ministerial buildings along a triumphal way as well as plans for the construction of a railway spur to a new central station at a point north of the existing Shimbashi terminus. Within six months a second set of elevation drawings for the parliament was forwarded from Berlin, this time with a fantastic pagodalike centerpiece (fig 2.10), like an extremely orientalized version of Shimizu's First Mitsui Bank, now the First National Bank. The Japanese sensibly rejected this conceit and, presumably owing to expense, also the Ende und Böckmann plan for a relocated railway station with its unfunctional three-sided ceremonial approach adjoining the northeast corner of the proposed exhibition ground.

Then, in 1887, James Hobrecht, an upper-echelon Prussian civil servant who had been responsible for the Berlin extension plan of 1862, visited Japan for one and a half months and prepared a greatly simplified version of Ende und Böckmann's scheme. He retained the exhibition grounds as a park encircled with plain, unarticulated blocks of ministry buildings. The site of the parliament, which is the same as that of the present Diet building, was apparently never in question, and Hobrecht also kept the simplified southern route of approach from Shimbashi devised by Ende und Böckmann and arranged for the railway to be extended alongside the existing palace moat without the need for a further station. Afterward, Ende reappeared in Japan and modified his firm's scheme, retaining the parliament building but diminishing the exhibition grounds to the size proposed by Hobrecht, so as not to disturb the outer moat. This had altogether been eradicated in the first grand design and then restored by Hobrecht for use as a railway cutting.

A compromise solution (fig. 2.11), now finally worked out by the former surveyor Ende, took over Hobrecht's notion of what is today Hibiya Park as a public garden ringed by ministries. However, in true surveyor style the surrounding pattern of streets was to have been rationalized and the southern approach route to parliament suppressed altogether. Meanwhile, the layout of the park was made more elaborate and the palace for each ministry given a baroque articulation intended to blend the architecture with a relatively inexpensive landscaping project of radiating paths and segmented parterres.[7]

None of these German proposals was effected in its entirety. The last plan described was, however, not too different from the arrangement which resulted, except that a provisional Diet building framed in timber was hastily put in place at the southwest corner of the park in time for the opening of parliament in 1890. A Berlin- or Reichstag-type design was never built. However, the new Imperial Palace, which was also part of the Meiji grand design, was constructed in the former castle precinct between 1883 and 1888; it survived until World War II. The palace was mainly traditional but with heating and electricity. Its vast state rooms were finished in

2.8. Ende und Böckmann: Imperial Diet Building, Tokyo. First scheme, 1887 (unrealized).

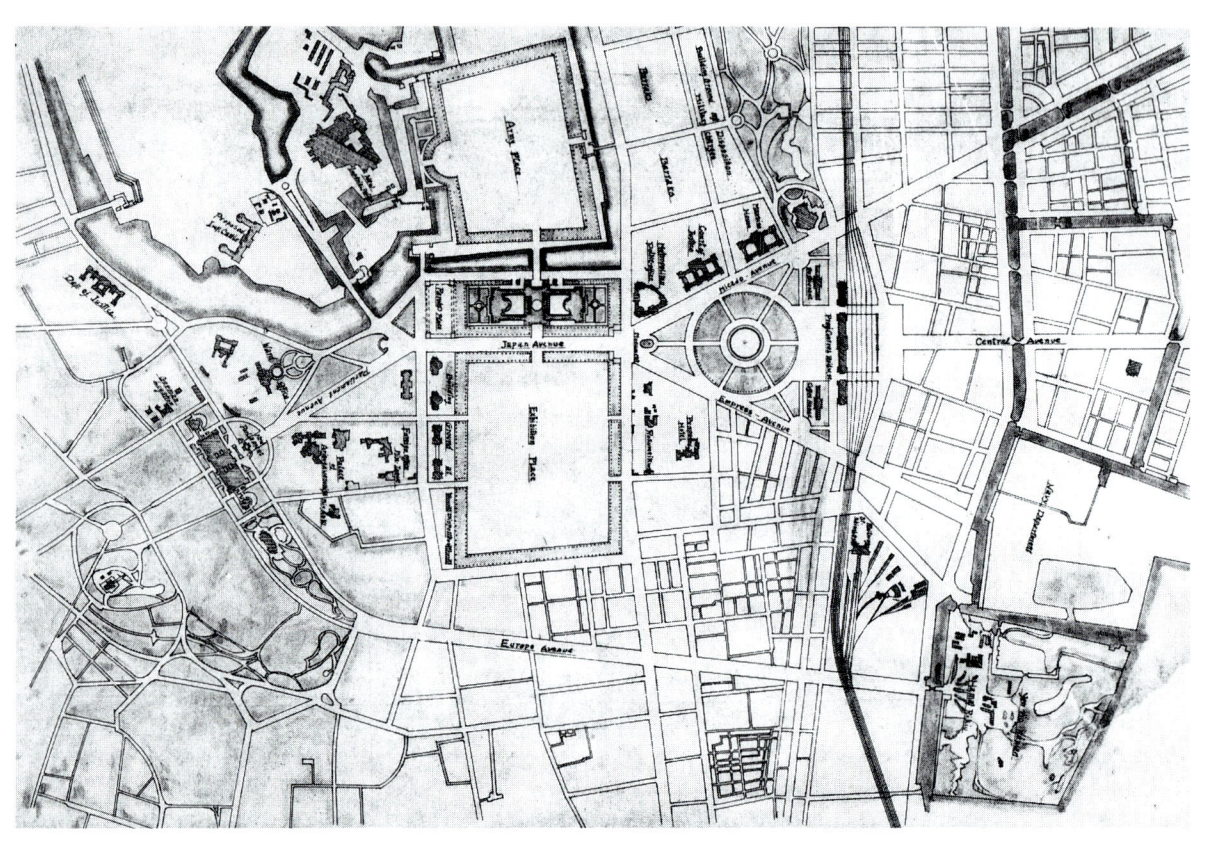

2.9. Ende und Böckmann: Parliament and Exhibition Grounds near the Imperial Palace, Tokyo, 1887. Proposal for railway extension and location of ministries.

2.10. Ende und Böckmann: Imperial Diet Building, Tokyo. Second scheme, 1887 (unrealized). From *Deutsche Bauzeitung*, 1891.

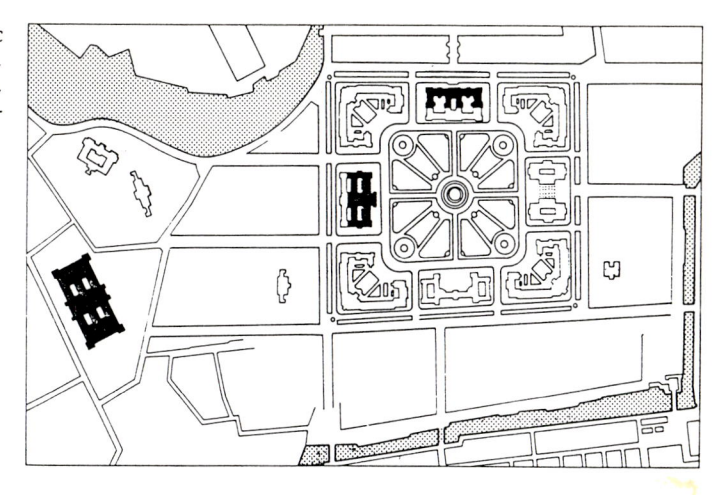

2.11. Ende: Compromise solution for a public garden (later Hibiya Park) ringed by ministries, 1887 or 1888. Site of Imperial Diet Building (at left), and proposal for Ministry of Justice (top) and National Court, are shown in black.

semi-Western style with ponderous furnishings commissioned from Germany. In terms of planning, it was secluded from public view in characteristically Japanese fashion, avoiding any decisive orientation with respect to the legislative or judicial branches of the government. Even today the emperor is still veiled in seclusion, but with the eventual building of Tokyo Station (designed by Tatsuno and begun in 1911; see fig. 2.34), a monumental axis was at last constructed leading to the outer gates of the palace grounds on the east side. This route takes the place of the bridge with which Ende und Böckmann would have spanned the inner moat on the south, in the direction of parliament and Hibiya Park, in order to accede to the palace from the grand ceremonial boulevard of their original design.

THE REST OF THE CITY

The locus of the Imperial Palace (see fig. 2.12), that of Meiji as well as the one constructed following World War II and still in use, provided the capital with a closed, "negative" focal arrangement centered on the fortifications of Edo Castle. By the standards of traditional Japanese "castle towns," Edo offered a less than adequate defensive network of bent and crooked streets, owing to the unbridled growth of the metropolis in its feudal heyday, which had oriented development toward the expanse of the bay. The castle became something of an adjunct, and it is only in the modern layout of the city that the castle, or palace, grounds again mark an empty center. In Edo-Tokyo up to, and including, the beginning of the Meiji period, ground occupation was extremely uneven. Owing to that system of enforced alternate attendance upon the shogun already referred to, between 60 percent and 70 percent of the urban area of Edo had been occupied by extensive gardens and grounds belonging to estates of the provincial aristocracy. The remaining land was shared out between highly patrolled and regulated commoners' districts of great human density and the scattered precincts of numerous religious establishments. Even when the modern state took over after a brief spell of martial law amounting to virtual civil war, never was there a plan to restructure the city as a whole. At once, new men from regions that boasted loyalty to the imperial cause took over the mansions vacated by Tokugawa administrative officials, putting them to use at first as both residences and government buildings. By 1871, in the wake of the Restoration, all were free in theory to occupy any land they could procure for themselves, as the old feudal distinction between samurai and merchant districts was overthrown. As things turned out, only a small proportion of the total land area was repossessed by the bureaucracy.

Indeed, relatively rapid amassment of urban wealth during the Meiji (1868–1912) and Taisho (1912–26) periods did stimulate in Tokyo, and to a lesser extent in other cities, a program of legislation to facilitate municipal improvement schemes. No real substitute for a planned urbanization that never happened nor was ever envisioned, this legislation is nevertheless to be seen as a vital step toward urban and economic development. These regulations, more often introduced by administrative fiat than enacted democratically, were not intended to produce a visually well-ordered utopia but merely a livable metropolis understood to be continuously expanding both in area and in population. To the extent that, today, more of the world's fastest expanding cities resemble Tokyo than do not, this response to growth that proved both crisis and asset in Japanese history merits attention. In any case, the reurbanization that occurred over the whole period from the 1880s until the 1920s and 1930s furnishes an inseparable background to the built environment of Tokyo. Moreover, in contradistinction to our lingering notion of both the European and the Chinese city as bounded by a physical shape, Tokyo seems never to have been imagined as such a place, let alone one governed by baroque axes.

It bears restatement that Tokyo, as the Meiji government's new capital, was reborn as a mental symbol projecting an ethos of progress and hope for the future.[8] More prosaically, the city was also restructured into fifteen wards, or *ku* (fig. 2.12). These, in turn, were part of Tokyo Prefecture, the remainder of which was largely composed of outlying villages as well as actual country districts. Such was the region at the eye of political power of the entire nation, a region that began once more to grow after the dramatic loss of population incurred during the brief period of civil strife and Restoration of 1868. Expansion occurred at the rate of about thirty thousand inhabitants per year, and by the mid-eighties the population had soared above a million. However, because of the large reserves of open space in the feudal city, modern Tokyo took almost twenty more years to overspill the ward area. By the end of Meiji the two-million figure had nearly been reached and suburbanization was beginning to take place in earnest. Nevertheless, as, for example, in Elizabethan or early Victorian London, these outlying areas had little about them that was attractive or desirable.

It was officials of the powerful Foreign Ministry who, in

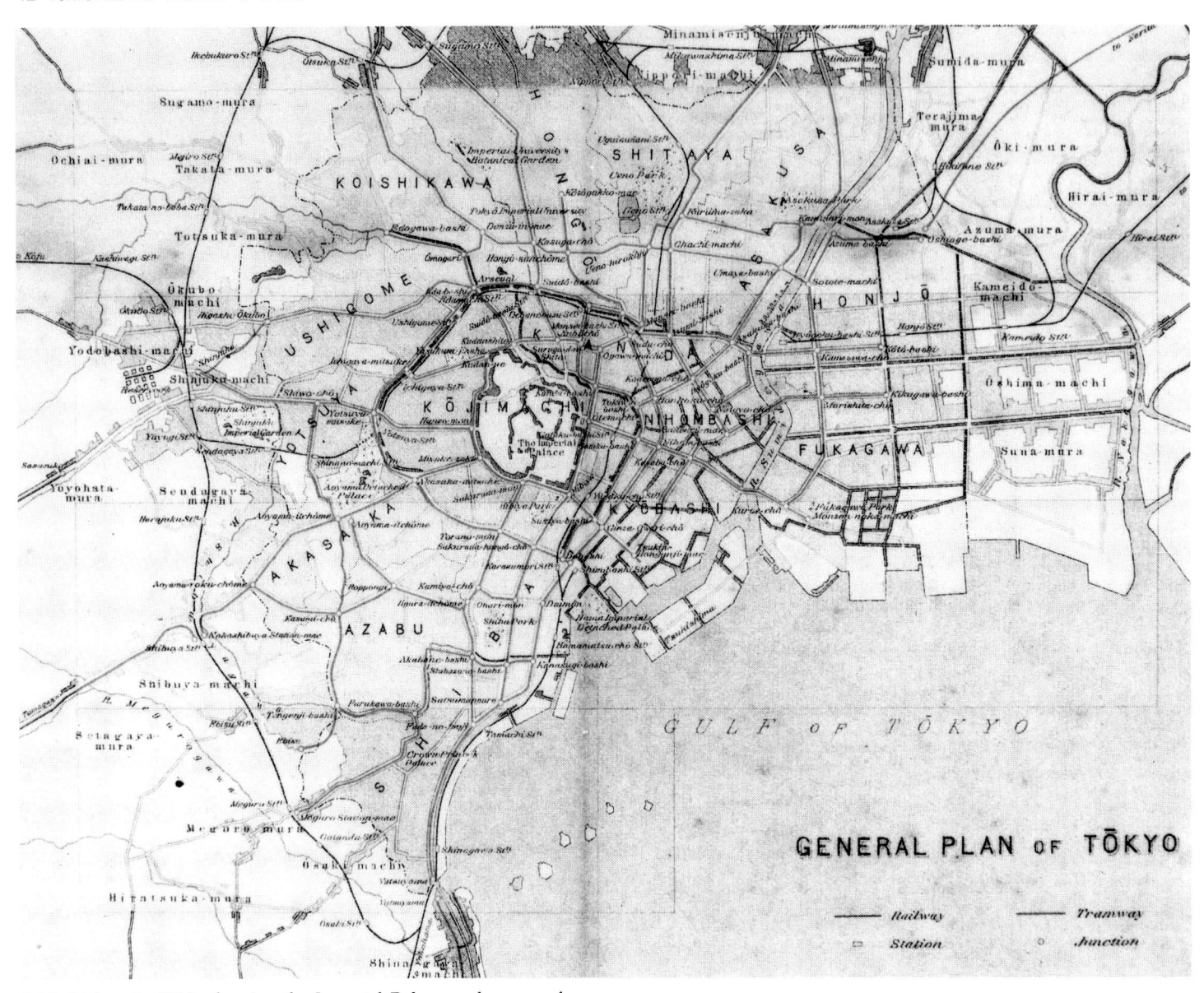

2.12. Tokyo in 1914, showing the Imperial Palace enclosure and location of the fifteen original wards.

their concern over the revision of the unequal treaties, pushed forward the plan for consolidation of a government district at Hibiya during the second half of the 1880s. The half-hearted success of this endeavor, as already chronicled, marks the demise of a *revanchard* view of Tokyo as a "showcase" of culture intended to influence foreign opinion. It was, in effect, the Ministry of Home Affairs that intervened against the essentially European-style development of a Tokyo Whitehall. The scheme had the backing of the incumbent foreign minister, and it was blocked by his fall from position in 1887. Having won this test of strength, the Ministry of Home Affairs established hegemony in the field of statutory planning.

Equally of importance, it was at about this time that the emerging Japanese business community began to nourish a sense of its own independence. Under the leadership of Eiichi Shibusawa, who was president of the government-subsidized Tokyo Chamber of Commerce, founded in 1878, a group was formed hoping to promote Tokyo as an industrial metropolis by building a new port intended to rival Yokohama. Although this scheme was never realized, a number of the proposals it contained found subsequent expression in the so-called Municipal Improvements Program, which, in turn, influenced all future legislation. The two building blocks of this policy were the national Municipality Act, which was of consequence for the whole nation, and the Tokyo City Improvement Ordinance, both enacted in 1888 (the same year as the formation of the administrative County of London). Tokyo at this time still had no elected mayor, only a governor, being administered directly by the national government, and also had very little provision for administration below the ward level. The Municipality Act formalized this situation in the case of Tokyo. The more far-reaching City Improvement Ordinance, propounded by the Ministry of Home Affairs, provided for the creation or improvement of streets, waterways, moats, bridges, public markets, a number of parks, a railway line, and cemeteries. This works program was not completed until the end of World War I. Overall, it reflects the solid Victorian tradition of public-works planning whose most significant instance was the London Metropolitan Board of Works, established in 1855 (and not superseded until London County Council jurisdiction over the newly formed metropolitan county took effect in 1889).

The Tokyo ordinance of 1888, dealing as it did primarily with infrastructures, gave no consideration to housing needs. This may have been due in part to the fact that population density could, at that time, scarcely yet have surpassed the overall rate of 600 inhabitants per hectare estimated as prevailing in the "commoners" quarters of Edo up till the Restoration. By comparison, some areas of Liverpool are known to have contained about four times this figure (i.e., 1,200 inhabitants per acre) as late as 1884. Moreover, it was not until 1875 that, in England, the Public Health Act provided for clearing away slum courts and exposing all housing on street fronts in accordance with the notion of the so-called bye-law street. Nonetheless, housing conditions in Tokyo were not bright, as is shown by books published in the 1890s of the tenor of General Booth's *In Darkest England* (1890–91), which were beginning to explore the life of Tokyo's working-class poor. These tracts revealed that up to five or six persons, sometimes comprising members of two or three different families, might conceivably be occupying a single four-to-six-mat room, or an area of less than two square meters per individual.

In the period following the Russo-Japanese War of 1904–5, small and large factories began increasingly to concentrate in the capital, but they were not able to absorb the enormous immigrant work force entering Tokyo from the countryside until near the end of the Meiji period. Thus, by the end of the 1880s there are said to have been some seventy major slums in Tokyo. These contrasted visibly not only with the new wealth of businessmen and politicians but also with the relative prosperity, from the following decade, of an emergent urban-based middle class. Bad living conditions were far from unknown in the life of Japanese cities prior to 1868: thus, it is easily forgotten how the ancient Chinese model taken for early capitals, such as those established at Nara and Kyoto, allowed for a warren of narrow, twisting alleys to be situated inside each of the neat, rectangular blocks that formed the visible planning unit. In Tokyo, as in Edo, not to mention lesser cities, frequent fires played a role in slum clearance, and so could rising land values.

THE GERMAN NEO-RENAISSANCE EPISODE

In the midst of Tokyo's formidable recrudescence in the 1880s the concept of public building was not completely abandoned in the face of the defeat inflicted on the Foreign Ministry's building program by the Ministry of Home Affairs. The notion of architecture as window dressing for the benefit of foreigners was still kept alive by the Ministry of Justice, owing to the unresolved issue of extraterritoriality. This term refers to the fact that, until 1894, the year in which Great Britain agreed to accept the authority of Japanese courts at the end of a transition period of five years, all foreign nationals (i.e., Europeans) enjoyed the privilege of remaining outside Japanese legal jurisdiction, even while living or sojourning in Japan. In exchange for the abolition of the infamous "unequal clauses," which Britain was the first foreign power to cancel, the Japanese were required to supply tangible and functioning evidence of their new legal system. It was this demand which furnished the ideological context for the new Ministry of Justice (see figs. 2.15–16) and Supreme Court (see fig. 2.17) buildings in Tokyo, both built in cooperation with the firm of Ende und Böckmann. By today's standards, neither of these was of great beauty. Yet, although only the Ministry remains at the time of writing, there can be no question of their solidity. Tradition maintains that floating foundations were introduced by Ende und Böckmann, thus anticipating the system devised by Frank Lloyd Wright for his rebuilding of the Imperial Hotel, which is the subject of chapter 4 of this book. In addition, due to cost overruns for the ministry building, including the extensive ground testing ordered by Ende, the Japanese government was forced to reconsider the entire policy of vetting official building projects abroad.

Both buildings were eventually finished in the style known as German neo-Renaissance, which possesses a complicated history but is of interest, since, together with Queen Anne, which it resembles, the style furnished a source of vocabulary for subsequent buildings all over Japan to the end of the Meiji period. Frustratingly, this so-called German Renaissance manner, much of which was, in actuality, French, is comparatively little known today on account of the ubiquitous destruction in German cities during World War II. According to Henry-Russell Hitchcock, it is a variant of the style we nowadays refer to, largely thanks to Hitchcock's own researches, as International Second Empire.[9] The Second Empire was conspicuous for high mansarded roofs that accentuated play of center, end, and corner pavilions, which were characterized, in Hitchcock's words, by "rich applied orders set far forward of the wall-plane." It was inspired by Visconti and Lefeul's Louvre extension of 1852–57 and reached an apotheosis in J.-L.-C. Garnier's Opera of 1861–74 in Paris. In early German examples, the hierarchy of orders is similar, if, indeed, closer to the wall-plane than in France, while the design is frequently transposed from stone to red brick but with Renaissance ornament added in stone. Such details consisted of scrolled pediments, corbeled arcading, roundels, fielded panelwork, and striate rustication and quoining, all drawn for the most part from German models.

2.13. North German Lloyd Lines headquarters, Bremen. Undated bird's-eye view.

2.14. Rathaus, Bremen, late nineteenth century view.

Following the Franco-Prussian War and until the end of the century, the ports of Hamburg and Bremen experienced an overwhelming growth of tonnage that greatly antagonized Britain while exciting Japanese emulation. In buildings of public or pseudopublic character, such as the gigantic headquarters (fig. 2.13) projected for the North German Lloyd shipping lines in Bremen, use of the neo-Renaissance style described above follows from the presence of Renaissance prototypes, such as the lovely old gabled and arcaded Rathaus (fig. 2.14) in the same city. Yet, a certain confusion was engendered between Flemish, or Netherlandish, and German traditions, for, as Hitchcock points out in another context,[10] the "Dutch look" of the Bremen Rathaus is stronger than in corresponding Northern Mannerist buildings in Holland of the same period. A repetition of this confusion bedevils late instances of the Queen Anne at the end of the nineteenth century, where, as it happened, English vernacular precedent was abandoned in favor of Continental motifs. Such was notably the case with Norman Shaw's variously disputed, but nonetheless trend-setting, New Scotland Yard of 1887–91. Here, incidentally, as Ende was soon to do in Tokyo, the builders had to spend the first year of construction in combating foundation problems, owing to its Embankment site. More significantly, though, New Scotland Yard was Britain's earliest adaptation of a "domestic" revival idiom to use in a public building.

The North German neo-Renaissance style, though more at home in Hamburg and Bremen, was also practiced in Berlin, where it formed part of the backdrop of that city which Le Corbusier was to find so repugnant when he went there early in the twentieth century. In a recent monograph on Italianate revival architecture in Germany during the nineteenth century, the East German architectural historian Kurt Milde[11] traces the style's origins back to Gottfried Semper's Schwerin Castle design of 1843. Eventually, this great palace was realized by other architects, who introduced typically

2.15. Ende und Böckmann: Ministry of Justice, Kasumigaseki, Tokyo, 1895. Lateral view of facade, now altered.

2.16. Ende und Böckmann: Ministry of Justice, Kasumigaseki, Tokyo, 1895. Rear facade, now destroyed.

Serlian devices garnered from Loire châteaux. However, from the point of view of Ende und Böckmann and their Japanese trainees, possibly the most characteristic Berlin occurrence of the neo-Northern German style is the deceptively plain, yet strident, facade of the Palais Reichenheim, erected from 1879 to 1881 by Kayser und Grossheim (illustrated by Milde). Here there was no order as such, except for a few demicolumns and some applied pilasters between very large plate-glass, cross-mullioned windows, combined with widely spaced stone banding. The roofline of this unimportant building comprised an indeterminate system of Renaissance ornamentation, including a domed turret and various dormers and lucarnes, with stone orbs at the corners of each of the pavilions.

Eventually, most of these features can also be discovered in the German-inspired architecture of Tokyo and the provinces built from the mid-1890s onward. The earliest and best of such works was the Ministry of Justice (figs. 2.15–16), completed in 1895, in Kasumigaseki beside Sakuradamon, the southern gate to the palace enclosure. Still occupied and now about to be restored, it occupies a site to the west of and slightly behind Hibiya Park. This location is more central than the emplacement determined by the original Ende und Böckmann plan. The Ministry of Justice was itself the work of the firm, and it displays that sophisticated and semirational approach that, in default of actual beauty, the nineteenth century sought in large-scale historicist undertakings.

In Tokyo, until an earthquake-proof means of construction was finally devised, the dilemma faced by all official buildings was how to counter lack of height while avoiding undue length; therefore, Meiji builders met with the exact opposite of today's conditions. In the Ministry of Justice the problem of an overlong facade was solved by establishing a prominent five-bay central pavilion, whose main feature is a tall loggia in the Tuscan order borne on arches. These originally formed an open arcade of double height that provided a passage through the podium into an enclosed courtyard.

2.17. Ende und Böckmann: National Supreme Court, Kasumigaseki, Tokyo, 1896, detail of frontispiece. Smaller view shows full facade.

This central element is flanked by simple, flat-roofed neoclassical porticoes indicating the twin entrances to the main building. Further loggie in antis are expressed on each of the lateral facades, a reappearance of the old veranda motif now rendered uneasy by the presence of the sliverlike roofs of mansarded corner pavilions. On the whole, I find the building improved in appearance by the new roof added in the aftermath of World War II. This involved a change to flat-arched (from fully round-headed) windows in the corner pavilions with a more uniform and less steeply inclined roofline and less fussy detail about the remaining lucarnes. In the process the various loggie became less French and more verandalike, engendering the structure with a hard-to-place but nonetheless pleasing tropical air. Recently, however, it has been proposed to restore the building to its original nineteenth-century appearance.

In 1896, one year after completion of the Ministry of Justice headquarters, a weird and ungainly pile intended to house the National Supreme Court took form (fig. 2.17). Recalling the alternative project for the parliament itself, the high court building had first been endowed by Ende und Böckmann with Japanese-style tiled roof, pagodaed centerpiece, and flanking turrets. This design, too, was ruled out as being at cross-purposes with the aim of eradicating extraterritoriality. Yet its alternative can hardly be viewed as much of an improvement, and it is not known to what extent Yorinaka Tsumaki, who supervised construction, may have been responsible for its appearance. The Supreme Court survived until the latter half of the 1970s and was all loggie and turrets, originally with matching stone-dressed brick fenceposts and gate. Both the Ministry of Justice and the Supreme Court took over the battered foundations that earlier had been a feature of the neotraditional options for parliament and the courthouse. The strength of the Nobi earthquake of 1891 had led the government to reformulate building codes based on observed structural deficiencies in existing buildings, as well as in response

2.18. Conder: Naval Ministry, Kasumigaseki, Tokyo, 1894.

2.19. Conder: Naval Ministry, Kasumigaseki, Tokyo, 1894. Atrium and grand staircase.

to the threat of fire. It is known that Ende had already been concerned with these problems, as indeed Conder was, and it may be that the oddness of the Supreme Court facade, in particular, is at least partly to be explained by considerations of structural stability where, at the same time, it was not wished to sacrifice height. Impressiveness, obtained by cleverly articulated massing and an attention-getting roof, was the main desideratum of the Second Empire style in public building, while Japanese examples were both too long and too low to profit much from anything but the style's excesses. Yet, even the strange courthouse elevation conceals a practical note, for the uppermost element was a skylight, or clerestory lantern, over the main stair.

Josiah Conder's Naval Ministry, which dates from 1894, attempts a similar exercise in dissimulation of its length (fig. 2.18), and in fact this building also possessed a centrally lit court or atrium—a glass-roofed hall with grand staircase rising to an open-arcaded second story (fig. 2.19). In the facade there is a residue of Conder's Hindu-Saracenic style of several years earlier in the alternating voussoirs of the windows. The gist of the design worked out in reinforced brick is decidedly Second Empire with its profusion of mansarded pavilions. Its chief interest is how, in this late work of a pupil of Burges, the overall aims of High Victorian Gothic and Renaissance-derived idioms can be seen to merge.

Another instance of the pervasive influence which the North German neo-Renaissance style exercised on Japanese architecture was the Tokyo Industrial Club (fig. 2.20), known also as the Chamber of Commerce, whose foundation by Eiichi Shibusawa in 1878 has already been mentioned. The building, completed in 1899, scarcely differs in its essentials from the banality of the Palais Reichenheim vocabulary of a generation earlier, and one of the curiosities of the style is its lack of interest in distinguishing between buildings of a private and public nature. The design for the Industrial Club is of surpassing coarseness and was the work of Yorinaka Tsumaki,

2.20. Tsumaki: Tokyo Industrial Club, Babasakimon, 1899.

2.21. Tatsuno: Bankers' Association Assembly Rooms, Sakamoto-cho, Tokyo, 1885.

already referred to as having supervised the two works built by Ende und Böckmann for the Ministry of Justice. Tsumaki also worked extensively for the Tokyo Prefectural Government and ended up becoming a power in the Ministry of Finance, where he is said to have groomed himself as Kingo Tatsuno's opponent and archrival. Fittingly it is to the work of Tatsuno, following his return from Europe, that we must now turn.

KINGO TATSUNO, ARCHITECT TO THE NATION

Tatsuno was Japan's first full-fledged professional architect and, like many successful Japanese of the later Meiji era, was a thoroughly eclectic personality. In this, he resembled Josiah Conder, three years older than himself; however, he exceeded the meager talents of his teacher while expanding on the Englishman's organizational abilities and professional skills. Tatsuno did not become master of his own firm until 1903 (even at this date the first to be maintained by a Japanese), but predictably he had begun to build as soon as he returned from Europe. He continued to do so from the base provided by his position at the Imperial University, until early retirement occasioned the removal of his activities from the confines of the civil service to the private sphere.

Tatsuno's initial work, the small Bankers' Association Assembly Rooms in Sakamoto-cho of 1885, was described by himself as being cinquecento-*fu*, or "of the sixteenth-century style" (fig. 2.21). The intended reference may be Serlio's treatise, and the Serlian character of the work is emphasized by the range of ocular windows just below the heavily dentilated cornice. The same device occurs in the College of Science Administration Building (fig. 2.22) designed by Hanroku Yamaguchi and built at Hongo three years later. Like Tatsuno, Yamaguchi was one of the first Japanese architects to study abroad, having returned, fresh from France, to enter the service of the Ministry of Education. Both buildings are of brick with stone trim. However, Yamaguchi's

2.22. Yamaguchi: College of Science Administration Building, Tokyo Imperial University, Hongo, 1888.

2.23. Tatsuno: Shibusawa Mansion, Kabutocho, Tokyo, 1888. Rear facade.

is larger with pavilions at the ends and center of the composition. These are framed by superimposed orders of pilasters, while, in Tatsuno's building, the central bay is made to break forward and is topped by a sculpted pediment but without the use of an order. The effect achieved by Tatsuno would be Wrenish, if not Jonesian, except for the polychrome voussoirs of the arched windows on the ground floor. Such a detail serves to complete the suggestion of one of Serlio's Venetian palaces, but via the example of Ruskin. Nearer home, of course, these arches derive from Conder's Ueno Museum, which was finished during Tatsuno's absence abroad and was itself a product of Ruskin's Venetian manner.

Other early works by Tatsuno were small and seem to exhibit traces of French medieval detailing derived from his recent travels in Europe. Then, in 1888, he erected a mansion for Eiichi Shibusawa (fig. 2.23). As Shibusawa was founder not only of the Tokyo Chamber of Commerce but also of the Japanese banking system, this must have been a spinoff of Tatsuno's first work. Shibusawa[12] was the son of a well-off indigo producer and dealer, who, in turn, was descended from humble farmers near the capital. Breaking his ties with this rural past, Eiichi departed to serve the Tokugawa and was made a samurai. But upon returning from a visit to the Paris International Exposition of 1867, he found the government deposed. Like many, he switched to the side of the Restoration, accepting a post in the Ministry of Finance but leaving it at the age of thirty-four to embark on a private career. His success in the newfound and, thus, somewhat amateurish business sector proved phenomenal, owing to both his yearlong stay in Europe and an apparently natural bent for economics. At the end of a mere decade and a half, Shibusawa was able to install himself in the palazzo which Tatsuno composed in equal parts of Serlio (fig. 2.24), Ruskin, and Conder's Venetian inspiration. The house was situated on one of Tokyo's numerous canalways, and Venice provided a decidedly appropriate metaphor. In fact the Shibusawa

2.24. Serlio: Venetian Palace from *Architettura*, Book IV (1611 English edition).

residence echoes Conder's small Venetian-style office (fig. 2.25) designed in 1878 for the Hokkaido Colonization Agency (later turned over to the Bank of Japan), in which Tatsuno is thought to have participated. But Tatsuno, typically, by not diluting his motif with elements of other more or less inappropriate styles, goes straight to the point, which is historicist, in displaying the Venetian theme locally to practical effect. By contrast, Conder seemed unable in his later works to propose, and then adhere to, a particular idea or image, let alone develop it in any meaningful way.

There survives a view of one of the parlors or drawing rooms of the Shibusawa Mansion, which, as it happens, is among the few recorded interiors of the middle Meiji period. The photograph shows a room (fig. 2.26) which is not overlarge but fully draperied and carpeted, and lit by gas. Indeed, Shibusawa himself proposed the introduction of gas street lighting, such as, in Tokyo, made its first appearance in the rebuilt Ginza and soon extended all the way to Asakusa. The furniture in the Shibusawa parlor is a neat and spare, yet not quite coherent, blend of mid-Victorian production. The only note of well-mannered exuberance is in the patterning of the draperies, as well as the swagging which conceals the feet of the simple straight-lined upholstered chairs and sofa, and the acanthus-patterned medallion from which the gas globes are suspended. There are two sorts of undraped wooden tables and a mirrored overmantel with side shelves and a festooned mantelpiece typical of English work of the period. No element of this interior is as readily identifiable, per se, as the windows of the second story, copied as these are from the Ca' Foscari, which John Ruskin had referred to as "the noblest example in Venice of the fifteenth-century Gothic." Nevertheless, Tatsuno seems possibly to have made use of Morris textiles, carpet, and wallpaper, with which, however, the French inspiration of the upholstered furniture is visibly out of keeping.

In fact, even the windows referred to, which also reappear on the land side of the building, are not precisely those of the Ca' Foscari, or of any actual Venetian palazzo. The traditional trefoil light is surmounted by an inverted semicircular-arched panel, intended to harmonize with the roundels inserted in the spandrels of the arcading, which are characteristic of the Venetian transition from Byzantine to Renaissance. Nor do the Shibusawa windows conform precisely with Ruskin's schematic "orders" of Venetian arches, as illustrated in *The Stones of Venice*. The Japanese play with circular windows and ornamental disks, seemingly derived from Serlio's Venetian-style projects if not from Anglo-baroque precedent, has already been noted, as in the building for the Bankers' Association, of which Shibusawa was president. At first, the Japanese fondness for such usage is hard to make sense of. However, the first Kabukiza, on the site of the present-day theater of the same name in East Ginza, had an identical aperture flanked by sculptured panels surmounting its three-opening arcaded entry (fig. 2.27). Viewed in a lithograph of 1902, bedecked with three rising-sun flags, the true significance of this Renaissance motif at last becomes clear as a figuration of Japan's own national device.

Just as neo-Serlian or cinquecento-*fu* activity in Japan happens to coincide, if a little uneasily, with aspects of Ruskin's Venetian Gothic, as introduced by Conder, we might cite as a comparison the importation of France's Second Empire architecture into the United States. In America this is sometimes referred to as the General Grant style, and it includes works such as the Philadelphia City Hall and the New York State Capitol at Albany, as well as Alfred B. Mullet's now recently restored State, War and Navy Department building in Washington (1871–75). In fact, the Iwakura Mission, already mentioned in connection with the establishment of the College of Engineering, was also received in Washington by President Grant, who eventually, with his wife, returned their visit in 1879. What was significant about the "General Grant" style in architecture, for a United States recovering from the Civil War, was its embodiment of the authority and assurance of the newly reunited government. Ignoring the corruption of the actual administration, not to mention the financial panic of 1873, the style provided an exercise in self-confidence and also signified the beginning of Continental training for American architects.

In Japan, the naive Franco-Italianizing gestures of Tatsuno's early work were shortly to be subsumed in the imported neo-Renaissance (i.e., Second Empire) tendencies of the 1890s already described. However, in the same year as the Shibusawa Mansion, Tatsuno completed a new building intend-

2.25. Conder: Hokkaido Colonization Agency, Tokyo, 1878.

2.26. Tatsuno: Shibusawa Mansion, Tokyo, 1888. Drawing room (exterior depicted in figure 2.23).

2.27. Kabukiza Theater, Ginza, Tokyo (1889, by Kozo Takahara), depicting the national emblem.

2.28. Tatsuno: College of Engineering, Tokyo Imperial University, Hongo, 1888.

2.29. Conder: Department of Law and Literature, Tokyo Imperial University, Hongo, 1884.

ed to house the College of Engineering (since 1886 under the auspices of the Imperial University). Despite its symmetrical disposition and axial alignment, befitting the new campus at Hongo, the Engineering College was, in feeling, Tatsuno's most Burgesian work (fig. 2.28). Its skyline was enlivened by a pair of muscular towers with the profile that was Burges's trademark. This building was a distinct improvement over the Department of Law and Literature (fig. 2.29) Conder had designed for the campus four years earlier. In his elimination of the Gothic windows and lancet-headed arcading propounded by Conder, Tatsuno moved away from the Gothic Revival while retaining the overall tautness of Burges's idiom, which Conder never understood. Both of these collegiate works clearly refer to Burges's own project for Trinity College at Hartford, Connecticut, of 1873 in the Early French Gothic style, only a small portion of which was ever built (a third and final wing was added as late as 1882).

The next milestone in Tatsuno's career was exactly that, since his Bank of Japan (1890–96) proved the largest official commission of the new decade (figs. 2.30–32). Shibusawa was prominent among its sponsors and the commission was handed to Tatsuno, who promptly went abroad for a whole year of study. The project was elaborated mainly in London, and it is believed that Tatsuno benefited from a certain amount of help from an erstwhile fellow pupil of William Burges.

The Bank of Japan is a three-story structure built of brick with iron reinforcing bands and making limited use of steel in the spans. The whole of the building was faced in stone, and steel-sash windows were made use of, almost certainly for the first time in Japan. The new bank owes its distinctive facade to a more sophisticated traditional handling than had ever been seen in Japan, one which, for the first time, is of French neoclassical inspiration. Nothing in the previous history of Japanese Western-style architecture prepares one for the appearance of the bank.

The original building (later extended) is square in plan, instead of the elongated shape we have noted in most government buildings, an appreciable innovation in itself. Within this square Tatsuno inscribed three arms of a cross, leaving space for a rectangular courtyard, which is fronted by a rusticated screen, one story in height. Displaying an order of applied pilasters and separated from the road by a narrow moat, this screen is pierced by two gates, each having one large- and one small-arched entry and recalling the triple-arched centerpiece of Tatsuno's Engineering College. This time, however, the courtyard would provide a sequential focal point; it is enclosed by a colonnade and must be traversed in order to reach the porticoed main front of the bank. The banking hall is situated in the *corps de logis* behind this portico. It is surmounted by an eight-sided domical vault,

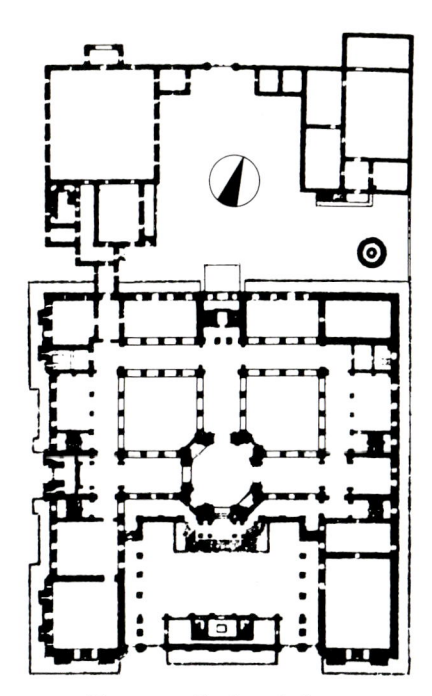

2.30. Tatsuno: Bank of Japan, Otemachi, Tokyo, 1890–96. Plan.

2.31. Tatsuno: Bank of Japan, Otemachi, Tokyo, 1890–96. Detail of courtyard.

2.32. Tatsuno: Bank of Japan, Otemachi, Tokyo, 1890–96. South front.

2.33. Beyaert, with Wynand Janssens: Banque Nationale de Belgique, Brussels, 1860–74. Facade, rue du Bois Sauvage.

2.34. Tatsuno: Tokyo Station, Marunouchi, Tokyo, 1911–14.

with a lantern and lucarnes appended externally. A baylike projection creates a balustraded porch topped by a two-storied aedicule framed by pairs of widely-spaced, nonfluted composite columns. This composition, in turn, enframes a tripartite pedimented window of a simple pilastered order. The arrangement provides a foil for the dome, and the same motif is echoed in the center and end pavilions that ornament the lateral volumes of the building. The overall scheme is a variant of the courtyard type of palace, such as the Luxembourg Palace in Paris, which was begun in the early seventeenth century. But in Tatsuno's bank, the rotunda was enlarged as a matter of function and is, therefore, pushed back from the screen front to occupy the core of the ensemble.

Among the buildings studied by Tatsuno was the Banque Nationale at Brussels, by Beyaert and Janssens, of 1860–74.[13] This consisted of a single prominent elevation (fig. 2.33) behind which a complex distribution of ceremonial and functional components made the most of an enclosed and highly irregular sloping site. The Bank of Japan site was perfectly open and regular, and Tatsuno's scheme is a more conventionally Beaux-Arts layout that seeks to build up a monumental three-dimensional composition on the basis of a complex and articulated symmetrical plan. The significance of the Bank of Japan was that it was the first building of this type by a native Japanese architect. Nor was its complexity rivaled until the construction of the Imperial Hotel by Wright a whole generation later.

Whereas the Bank of Japan veers between influences of the seventeenth, eighteenth, and its own centuries, the final work of Tatsuno's to be discussed was less diffident. Ranking in sheer confidence with Tokyo Station (fig. 2.34), about which, however, nothing need be said except that its facade *must* be preserved as both a record of Tatsuno's period style and an element of townscape, the enormous circus of the National Sumo Arena (fig. 2.35) was put up by him in 1909 to hold 13,000 spectators. Here was the most splendid stadium ring of its kind in the Far East, consisting of a vast, centrally glazed, steel-ribbed canopy roof. The facade was composed of multitiered arcades punctuated by stout domed and mansarded turrets providing stairs to the galleries. The membranelike saucer dome of the wrestling hall, which roofed this shrine to the national sport, appeared less than two decades after Conder's conventional cast-iron dome for the Russian-designed orthodox cathedral in Tokyo. Moreover, the arena was completed in the same year as Sano's Maruzen Book Company (see fig. 5.4), normally referred to as the earliest architect-designed, true steel-frame structure in Japan. The fireproofing of the Sumo Arena was, however, inadequate, and in 1917 the structure burned and had to be rebuilt. In Tatsuno's rendering of the original scheme, we see him for

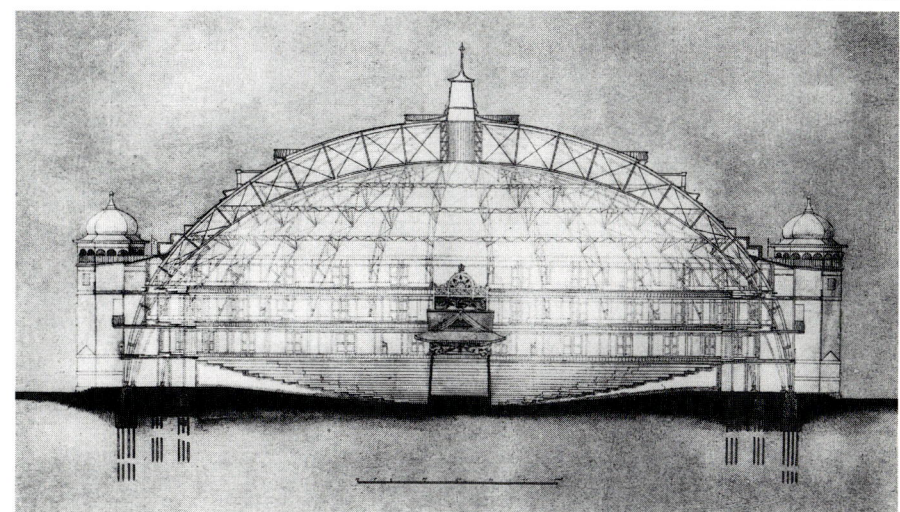

2.35. Tatsuno: National Sumo Arena, Kuramae, Tokyo, 1909. Drawing shows roof structure.

the first time intent on true Second Empire grandeur in a Hindu-Saracenic mode. The roofline was made memorable by the application of a mansarded drum as the chief exterior expression of the dome, a feature deleted from the building as reconstructed after the fire.

TOKUMA KATAYAMA, ARCHITECT TO THE CROWN

The most notable exponent of the French Second Empire style, and the other great architect of the Meiji period, was Tokuma (or, sometimes, Toyu) Katayama (1853–1917). Senior by a year, Katayama had been Tatsuno's classmate but was not among the students selected by the Japanese government for formal study abroad, despite the obvious promise of his graduation project. What this project, a school of art designed in the Burgesian manner, showed was a talent, far beyond that of Josiah Conder, for the elaboration of a facade, including the integration of sculpture and other types of ornamentation. Katayama entered the Ministry of Technology, where he spent an initial period of two years in the repairs section. After that he was detailed to work in the building department; among its tasks was the construction in the hilly southern part of the capital, at Hiroo, of a mansion for Prince Arisugawa. This was eventually completed in 1884 but is now destroyed, the grounds having been made into a park.

With the assassination of Czar Alexander II in 1881, Prince Arisugawa was chosen to represent the emperor of Japan at Alexander III's coronation ceremony held the following year. The delegation provided Katayama with a chance to go abroad, and he remained in England and in France for about two years.

Katayama's first individual official building commission was the Japanese Ministry in Peking. The ministry (fig. 2.36), which was the first foreign project undertaken for the government by a Japanese national, was completed in 1886. It appears to combine Chinese features, seen in the general proportions and tiled roof, with a type of Italianate ornament, presumably executed in terra-cotta, that probably derives in the first instance from Schinkel's Bauakademie in Berlin (1832–35) but had been popularized by Gottfried Semper, among others.

At the end of 1886, Katayama was sent to Germany for eleven months in order to oversee the selection and manufacture of furnishings for the new Imperial Palace. The imperial residence had burnt down shortly after the capital was shifted to Tokyo; a rebuilding commission was set up in 1870 but eventually, in 1883, became absorbed by the Imperial Household Ministry. When the latter decided to erect the new palace in the Japanese style, it was nonetheless resolved, for reasons of state and diplomacy, to array the interiors in the

2.36. Katayama: Japanese Ministry, Peking, 1886.

2.37. Taki: General Staff Headquarters, Tokyo, 1889.

Western manner. Formerly the commission had been independent of any ministry, but the prevailing notion of a traditional residence with Western-style amenities turned it into an on-the-spot training ground for numerous architects from the College of Engineering and the Ministry of Home Affairs under the guidance of Josiah Conder. Katayama's interiors for the palace, as completed in 1888, were executed in a massive Teutonic neobaroque idiom, and the bombastic furnishings he commissioned contrasted oddly with its opulent Japanese-style architectural trappings.

While Katayama was completing his supervision of the palace decoration scheme, he also worked as a part-time instructor at the Imperial University. He soon took his doctorate there in 1891, only the second to be conferred in architecture after Tatsuno's. He was also much occupied in designing Western-style mansions for the Meiji aristocracy, and in 1890 he erected a hospital in Shibuya for the elite Red Cross Society, modeled on the Heidelberg University Hospital, and in 1891 the Tokyo Central Post Office. But in these works there was little to suggest the boldness and grandeur of the Second Empire style, which was their chosen point of reference. The same is true of Yuzuru Watanabe's Imperial Hotel of 1890, for instance, and the point is best made by looking at Daikichi Taki's General Staff Headquarters of 1899. This building (fig. 2.37) visibly makes a gesture toward Mullet's State, War and Navy Department Building in Washington, D.C., of over a generation earlier, which I have cited as an example of the General Grant style. There are, in both buildings, the same straight-sided mansard roofs characteristic of Second Empire architecture in general, but the Tokyo version has only two stories and no orders at all to speak of. Its discreet balustraded porch attempts, I think, to extract a single bay of the fantastic, four-story centerpiece of the Washington building, but the one is only a whisper of the other.

The General Staff office replaces an earlier building, by an Italian architect, which may have been a victim of fire or earthquake. Taki's discretion could also be the result of deficits incurred by Ende und Böckmann. The greater, then, is one's surprise in confronting the next pair of works by Katayama, the imperial museums at Nara and Kyoto, executed in 1894 and 1895 respectively. They are the equivalent of Tatsuno's contemporary Bank of Japan and, moreover, they represent the only genuine, full-blown Second Empire (as opposed to the neo-Renaissance manner of the German-trained contingent of Japanese architects) buildings of the Meiji period. The grandeur Katayama achieved in these two museums is all the more astonishing as they conform to the virtually regulatory two-story-plus-attic formula of pre-steel-structure Japanese construction. These commissions were awarded by the Imperial Household Ministry in order to house what are today the national museums, the first of which, in Tokyo, had been accommodated in Conder's Hindu-Saracenic structure at Ueno some ten years earlier. The Nara Museum (fig. 2.38), the smaller of Katayama's designs, is a pyramidal composition roofed by shallow, straight-sided mansards culminating

2.38. Katayama: Nara Imperial Museum, Nara, 1894.

2.39. Katayama: Nara Imperial Museum, Nara, 1894. Detail of main entrance.

2.40. Katayama: Kyoto Imperial Museum, Kyoto, 1895.

in a substantial lantern over the principal entrance. The arched entryway is framed by a coupled columnar portico, which breaks forward slightly and supports a massive segmental pediment, a motif that derives ultimately from the Square Court of the Louvre. The facade is enveloped in smooth, banded rustication, executed in cool yellow stucco, recently restored, with an exquisite carved stone ornamentation (fig. 2.39). The wings flanking the entrance pavilion are blind with unsculpted cartouches set between pilasters articulated in the rustication.

The Kyoto Museum (fig. 2.40) has a similarly organized facade but combines stone, red brick, and stucco in a composition terminated by flanking mansarded pavilions. The central and end pavilions have decorative wrought-iron parapets but no lantern. Entry is by means of a triple-arched, triangular-pedimented Renaissance porch incorporating Japanese motifs in the tympanum. Possibly owing to its greater size, the Kyoto building is the less satisfactory of these two works by Katayama. Its overall proportions, as well as the choice of decoration and materials, are less happy. It seems to me that the model for both the Nara and Kyoto imperial museums was J. V. Dahlerup's Ny Carlsberg Glyptothek, built in 1893–95 but already designed by 1888. Even though the coloration of Dahlerup's building is more nearly imitated in the Kyoto Museum, it is the segmental pediment and scalloped arches that appear to find an echo in the Nara Museum. Another possible source is Smithmeyer and Pelz's Library of Congress in Washington, D.C. (1889–97), where Second Empire motifs were incorporated in a rich Beaux-Arts classicism. As in Katayama's smaller work at Nara, the library possesses a kind of spontaneity which eludes most of the neoclassical architecture of Washington, as much as it does Tatsuno's Bank of Japan.

Tokuma Katayama's last two buildings, the so-called Hyokeikan (1901–9) and Togu Gosho (1899–1909), brought in the new century but also marked the end of the Meiji period. The brash confidence of the Second Empire style was largely relegated to the past. Both these large works built by Katayama belie the academic tone of the Edwardian period, and both are associated with the unfortunate Crown Prince, Yoshihito. Whether ill or mad, he enjoyed a reign (1912–26, commemorated as the Taisho period) far shorter than that of his father, the Meiji emperor.

The Hyokeikan (fig. 2.41) forms part of the national museum complex at Ueno in Tokyo, standing to the left of the newer main building and facing the still more recent East Asian Arts pavilion. Originally, however, it was to serve as a municipal museum presented by the citizens of Tokyo on the occasion of Prince Yoshihito's wedding, although soon contributions flowed in from all over the country. The Togu Gosho (figs. 2.42–44), which was begun earlier though completed in the same year as the Hyokeikan, is today referred to as the Akasaka Detached Palace and serves as the official state residence for visiting foreign heads of state. Though never occupied by any member of the Japanese imperial family, the palace was intended by the future imperial couple as

2.41. Katayama: Hyokeikan, Ueno, Tokyo, 1901–9. Smaller view shows foundation structure.

their official residence, in the same manner as Kensington Palace. Following World War II and up until its recent restoration, it housed the National Library.

In this pair of works, Katayama sought to create a powerful setting for the monarchy and set the final seal on the Meiji regime's policy of uncompromising Westernization. Japan had been victorious over China in 1895, and the construction of the Akasaka Palace was paid for out of the reparations awarded Japan. In addition, both buildings were completed shortly after the stupendous triumph of the young imperial Japanese navy over the Russians in 1904–5, and also just one year before the annexation of Korea in 1910 which was its natural result. The palace, which is by far the more resplendent of the two buildings, testifies uncompromisingly to Japan's newfound position of near equality among the world's advanced nations. It is the first building in Japan incorporating something of true European grandeur and, ironically, it introduced a neobaroque idiom that, even though still fashionable, was on the point of becoming outmoded in the West. Often regarded as the "Japanese Versailles" (fig. 2.43), the Akasaka Palace bears closer comparison with the Neue Hofburg in Vienna, as brought to completion in 1894 by Karl von Hasenauer, after Gottfried Semper's death. However, the detailing of the facade is, after all, palpably French, and has been aptly compared by Hiroyuki Suzuki to the Ionic colonnaded front of Mewes and Davis's nearly contemporary Royal Automobile Club in Pall Mall.

Only a little more than half a century after the introduction of Western architecture into Japan, the erection of the Akasaka Palace was a remarkable achievement. Like the Hyokeikan, it is of reinforced brick construction (three thousand tons of iron, including a quantity of discarded locomotive rail) entirely faced with stone. Edward Shankland (formerly of Daniel H. Burnham's office), who had been chief engineer for the World's Columbian Exposition, did the structural calculation. Bruce Price, the influential New York society architect, skyscraper designer, and Japanophile, had a hand in checking the architectural work and may have done more. In particular, the pair of star-spangled orbs on either side of the front entrance, just above the point where the wings begin their outward sweep, suggest Price's influence.

For all his fame, little[14] is now known about this architect (father of the future social arbiter, Mrs. Emily Post). It appears that the cottages he erected on the Lorillard estate at Tuxedo Park in 1885–86, but not perhaps the "Japanese-style" one for Addison Canmack, were known to Frank Lloyd Wright and actually influenced him. In any case, it was in 1900 that Katayama consulted Bruce Price at his offices in New York about the design for the Togu Gosho, begun in the previous year. Price died in 1903, well before the completion of the project for the new palace in Tokyo. But in that same year, Wright was already at work on the Larkin Administration Building in Buffalo, New York. Architecturally, this was a quite different affair, but for years the Larkin Building also supported a pair of great globes, flanked by sculpted figures instead of the phoenixes that may be seen

2.42. Katayama: Akasaka Detached Palace, Akasaka, Tokyo, 1899–1909. Main front.

2.43. Katayama: Akasaka Detached Palace, Akasaka, Tokyo, 1899–1909. Aerial view of the grounds.

2.44. Katayama: Akasaka Detached Palace, Akasaka, Tokyo, 1899–1909. Grand staircase.

in Tokyo. These were untypical of Wrightian decoration and no suitable explanation was ever forthcoming, before or after their eventual removal. Bruce Price proposed orbicular ornament, especially in some of his unbuilt but published work,[15] and I think it likely that Katayama and Wright share this perhaps arcane aspect of Price's influence.

For sheer richness of ornament, the Togu Gosho interiors were unparalleled by any other Japanese building of the same or, perhaps, even of any later period (fig. 2.44). It is difficult, I believe, to assign precise influences, but Katayama had, after all, made the study of Western-style stately interiors his own, both in his work with the Imperial Household Ministry as well as the numerous commissions he executed for the nobility.[16] The interior detail of both the palace and, in simpler terms, the Hyokeikan confirm the delicacy of handling so remarkable in the carved ornament of the Nara Museum. However, in overall effect, the Hyokeikan reflects the exactly contemporary Japanese Resident-General's Palace by Katayama in Seoul, about which virtually nothing is now known. Korea was made a Japanese protectorate at the end of 1905, and Hirobumi Ito, one of the great statesmen of the Meiji period and a favorite of the emperor, was the first resident-general, although the new viceroyal headquarters was not completed until one year before final annexation of Korea in 1910. The Resident-General's Palace, in its turn, was modeled on Louis Le Vau's château, constructed for Louis XIV's Surintendant des Finances, at Vaux-le-Vicomte (1657–61). Katayama is known to have admired Le Vau, who, at the end of his life, was appointed First Architect by Louis XIV, the role that, in effect, Katayama himself filled for Emperor Meiji. The problem of styles, or the lack of any single viable idiom, had become a general condition of architecture.

By this date any fault of Katayama's in the Hyokeikan, or in the Akasaka Palace, might as credibly have been committed by a Western architect. What is, by contrast, recognizably anachronistic, owing to Katayama's own temperament and the lingering skills of Japanese craftsmen at the end of Meiji, is the astonishingly integral quality of his ornament. An instance are the reliefs that depict the liberal arts just below the line of the second-story entablature in the facade of the Hyokeikan, and rather more individual examples abound in the state rooms of the Akasaka Palace. Possibly, it was this very ingenuity and facility that aroused the hostility of the Meiji emperor toward the Togu Gosho, for the palace was condemned outright as being too luxurious for the habitation of his son, the crown prince. Resembling Vaux-le-Vicomte, which was nonetheless inhabited for three weeks by its owner before being seized by the king, Katayama's palace had a sadly circumscribed history. Katayama himself never recovered from the chagrin of having created a henceforth vacant masterpiece, although he outlasted Emperor Meiji, dying in 1917, the sixth year of Taisho.

3 | F.L.W.: Japan as a "Means to an End"

THE BIRTH OF MODERNISM

By the end of the nineteenth century, Western architecture had reached that turning point in both structure and expression which, for want of a more secure definition, has been called the Modern Movement. The name of Frank Lloyd Wright has already been cited in connection with the story of the design for the Akasaka Detached Palace. Here it is necessary to mention Wright in his capacity as the most significant figure of the Modern Movement in architecture, not to say the foremost architect America has ever produced. It would, then, in examining the roots of modern architecture anywhere be natural to refer to Wright's achievements, but in the case of Japan it becomes a virtual obligation. The reasons are two and each is of a different order of importance. The first concerns the fact that Wright's most prominent work outside the United States, the second Imperial Hotel, was built in Tokyo. The hotel as a fact of Japanese building history must be dealt with on its own merits in the following chapter. But the obverse of Wright's significance for Japanese, and world, architecture lay in what he called his "enslavement" to Japanese prints. Wright, indeed, was more than usually candid regarding the origins and nature of this attachment.

An avowed "Japanese" quality in Wright's work, declared to be self-evident, has always been taken for granted as corroborating his infatuation with Japanese art. In fact, this notion has been carried so far from the mere influence of prints, over the years, as to conclude in a quasi-reconciliation for many between the character of Japanese traditional architecture and the revolutionary proposals on which Wright's own spatial organization is based. Nothing could be more of a mistake, even though the Japanese are certainly among those most avid to acclaim the brilliance of Wright's inventiveness and imagination.

In the present chapter we shall undertake to show how Wright's sympathy with and delight in things Japanese was an overall reaction to, yet at the same time a function of, that same revival of past art forms which characterized the architecture of the middle Meiji period. In a word: "historicism." This relationship is most clearly expressed in Wright's discourse on *The Japanese Print* of 1912. In this little tract he proposes to borrow an array of means found in simple woodblock broadsheets and landscapes to right that dearth of sensibility he, like other pioneers of the Modern Movement, remarked in the art of the late nineteenth century. A related matter, which is harder to agree about, let alone account for, is the question of apparent resemblances between Wright's own buildings and those of traditional Japan. There are, of course, comparisons to be made, and Wright denied these. Most frequently, as in the case of the California architects Greene and Greene, the game is given away by the arts-and-crafts inspiration that distances American japonaiserie from its sources.

Of greater moment than the sympathetic reproduction of isolated motifs, whether on admission or denial, is the different understanding of space that is implied. This involves the overall Japanese notion of spatial feeling which tends to violate even those boundaries usually believed to separate the various representational arts, such as prints or folding screens, from the domain which we—anyway, in the West—reserve for architecture. The "no-space" architecture in which the Japanese themselves conceive their own tradition was abruptly cut off in the architecture the Meiji period gave rise to. It disappeared, except in subtle effects of flatness, abrupt juxtaposition of basic elements (where a more extended or baroque sequence might be forthcoming in Western architecture), and an occasional unexpected use of materials. All of these were indicators of an essentially non-Western point of view on the part of Japanese architects or builders, whether self-trained or not.

Of course, it is inconceivable that Wright could have remained unaware of this difference, at least following his first visit to Japan in 1905. Nevertheless, even he seems to have set the essential terms of this greatest of all contrasts back to front. In a talk at a Japanese print gathering as late as 1950 at Taliesin, he remarked of a work by Hiroshige, "Here you get a sense of tremendous, limitless space." Then, more correctly but casting a veil of paradox over the earlier statement: "On what is your attention focused? Nothing." Such is an example, then, of the type of semantic mixup, for which I do not intend to *blame* Wright, but which it is the aim of this book to point out, as more traditional notions of space reenter post-Meiji Japanese architecture. For, to conclude, the transcription of this same lecture, today in the Frank Lloyd Wright Memorial Foundation, records Wright as going on to say: "Hiroshige did, with a sense of space, very much what we have been doing with it in our own architecture."

To say as much is simply unacceptable. To be sure, there is a spatial focus in Wright's buildings, sometimes masked, but only on occasion, by antiperspective devices, perspective being notably absent from most Japanese prints, except those which sought to imitate the West. Less trivially, there is in the very conception of space a strong divergence between Japanese and Western art and architecture, even that of the nascent Modern Movement. This dichotomy inspires a hypothesis to the effect that "modernism" must have been brought kicking into our world of preestablished forms and ideas with the aid of a Japanese midwife. Neither parents nor forebears were Japanese, but the father, so to speak, ran off with the midwife. She, in turn, nourished the child, who learned to utter a few words of Japanese while the midwife, though retaining certain Japanese habits and her domestic accessories, never looked back. Eventually, modern architecture as practiced in Japan was repossessed of its heritage, but not the whole.

"JAPANISM" AS AN ASPECT OF HISTORICISM

Though not enough is known about it, Bruce Price's collaboration with Katayama on the Akasaka Detached Palace represents the most complex and sophisticated architectural dialogue undertaken on the part of a representative of the Meiji polity with an outside expert. Moreover, Price's role as consultant, whether or not it entailed an *exchange* of opinion, was part of a transaction in which the conventions and institutions established by the Meiji oligarchy appear to have been respected and even enhanced. Little more in the way of a conclusion can be drawn from the episode except that the Akasaka Palace, never subsequently used for the purpose intended, may have been an act of architectural statesmanship that succeeded all too well. Stylistically the design was a dead letter; still, the client (that is, the Japanese state) was now an equal among equals.

This example goes some way in illustrating the difference between a "society" architect like Bruce Price and a maverick such as Frank Lloyd Wright. The latter, already when visiting Japan for the first time, in 1905, and more assuredly so some years later when asked to submit plans for the Imperial Hotel, had a solid reputation as a "designer," if not much more. By contrast, the status of Price, who is today nearly forgotten, was unambiguous: his designs were understood as surehanded historicist exercises rechanneled in the direction of fashionable Beaux-Arts classicism. Furthermore, Wright had been employed, with one or two exceptions, by a conspicuously middle-class clientele and had actually rejected an expense-paid offer to study in Paris at the Ecole des Beaux-Arts to be followed by two years at the soon to be founded American Academy in Rome. He claims to have refused this proposal[1] by saying that he had been "spoiled" for Paris by his training with the Chicago architect Louis Sullivan, whose office he joined in 1888. Sullivan liked to paint his own portrait as a renegade from Paris, where he had passed just ten months in preparation for entrance to and in study at the Ecole des Beaux-Arts before abandoning his European education in 1875. In reality Price was as much a self-taught architect as either Sullivan or Wright. Like Sullivan, Price had spent about a year in Europe, while Wright went there only after visiting Japan. Had Wright accepted the chance that was offered to study in Paris and Rome, he would have opened the way to a career for himself resembling Price's but probably far more brilliant.

I have already characterized Bruce Price as a "Japanophile," which, though in no way surprising, is not very precise either; yet, by the end of the century, this want of precision no longer matters. The taste for Japanese art has been acknowledged as "almost certainly the most important single external influence on the European decorative and applied arts in the second half of the nineteenth century."[2]

Here we need not refer to the specialized discussion about the influence of Japanese woodblock prints on the subsequent development of Western painting, most notably Impressionism, and it is enough to state categorically that prints, as well as other contemporary Japanese objects, were known in both England and France from the 1850s onward. In the field of interior decoration, which includes painting and collecting but goes beyond either, it is convenient to recur to the authority of the Victoria and Albert Museum, once more in the person of the author just quoted. The following, then, is Elizabeth Aslin's schedule of the three phases into which Japanese influence was split:

In the eighteen-sixties it was a matter for individual collectors and enthusiasts, both in England and France, and in this period Whistler produced his earliest Japanese-inspired paintings, Rossetti designed a Japanese bookbinding and a few amateurs began to collect lacquer, porcelain, glass and prints. In the 'seventies, the fashion was in full swing amongst informed people and Japanism and the Aesthetic Movement were virtually synonymous, while the Philistines scoffed. Interior decoration and furniture design were based on what were believed to be Japanese principles, rather than on the superficial forms and ornament which were the hallmark of the 'eighties when what had been a movement became a mania. Every mantelpiece in every enlightened household bore at least one Japanese fan, parasols were used as summer firescreens, popular magazines and ball programmes were printed in asymmetrical semi-Japanese style and asymmetry of form and ornament spread to pottery, porcelain, silver and furniture.... By the 'nineties the fashion for anglicized Japanism had gone and Japanese art ... had become one of the contributory elements in Art Nouveau.[3]

In the United States, this timetable was somewhat retarded, especially in the Middle West, but by the end of the period the characterization of the "Aesthetic" household is accurate.

It is, therefore, in this, architecturally, rather unhelpful sense that Wright, too, as well as Price, may be called a "Japanophile." For during his Oak Park period—that is, through the 1890s and in the course of his 1905 trip to Japan and, indeed, probably right up until he left the Oak Park studio for good in autumn 1909—Wright was an active collector of oriental artistic goods. Nor, as we shall see, did his passion for Japanese and Chinese art abate during his later escapades in the Far East. This harmless diversion gradually matured into a means of livelihood and a near manic obsession. Yet the problem remains as to the connection between the Japanese vocation to which Wright readily pleaded guilty, and discussed at some length in *An Autobiography*, and the development of a "Japanese" influence in his architecture.

Going as far back as possible, the attitude toward "fashionable" Japan on the part of practicing architects raises numerous questions, although the serious-minded cases are few. Among trailblazing enthusiasts for Japanese objects were William Burges and his slightly younger fellow architect, E. W. Godwin, whose interest in Japan dates to the 1860s, falling within the earliest of the three phases described above. As early as 1862 we find Burges exhorting Gothic fanciers, of which he of course was one, to devote "an hour or even a day or two" to the Japanese Court at South Kensington.[4] The reason offered was that the workmanship of the objects which were on display rivaled those of the European Middle Ages. At this period, interest in Japan was a mere private indulgence and, in the cases of both Burges and Godwin, "Japanism" remained a submerged current between the purer shoals of medieval and, surprisingly, Greek concerns. Though a collector, Burges himself never designed a Japanese interior, as Godwin was later to do on several occasions, for which the evidence today, it must be admitted, is purely verbal—not even pictorial!

Godwin claims to have got his working knowledge of Japanese design from two of the volumes of Hokusai's *Manga*, which were certainly made use of by other Western artists working at different times. He is best known today for his simplified furniture designs (fig. 3.1), some of which were for unique pieces executed in rare woods with ornamental carved panels and painted or lacquered details restricted to well-defined areas. The majority, however, were produced in quantity and, later, pirated: "ebonised" with simplified turnings and a modest amount of incised giltwork. These have virtually nothing to do with Japan, in spite of the fact that they were publicized as "Anglo-Japanese" in inspiration. The more expensive pieces, on the other hand, resemble Chinese or, possibly, Korean furniture types, except for the areas of decoration which are patently Japanese and, in some cases, are known to be of Japanese execution.[5]

Godwin is also remembered for his subtle and intimate domestic interiors, including various rooms in at least three houses of his own executed at diverse stages of his career and the more celebrated schemes for the American painter Whistler and Oscar Wilde, the playwright, both in Tite Street, Chelsea. To the extent that, according to surviving descriptions, they seem to have approached Whistler's paintings based as those were on a restrained variation in color and tonality, Godwin's ensembles may indeed have had something of a true Japanese aesthetic quality. Whistler's occasionally almost abstract "arrangements" and "harmonies" were first familiar to me as a student, and on looking at some of them recently after a good many years in Japan, I found they do in fact succeed in their Japanizing intentions, without sacrificing their originality as works of Western art: a rare achievement.[6]

H. H. Richardson, the American architect who influenced such a number of others, was among the admirers of Burges and Godwin, and there remains a remote possibility of some kind of personal contact. Wright himself, however, was too far removed in generation to have been influenced in any way by Godwin, who died young, in 1886, shortly after his friend William Burges. Instead, the taste for Japanese art and ideas of decor soon filtered through to the wealthier suburbs of Chicago, and we know the architect who first alerted Wright to the art, as opposed to the architecture, of Japan. His name was J. L. Silsbee; Wright's family had employed him, and he, in turn, became Frank Lloyd Wright's first employer.

THE NOTION OF ARCHITECTURAL "TRUTH"
One of the established principles of twentieth-century architec-

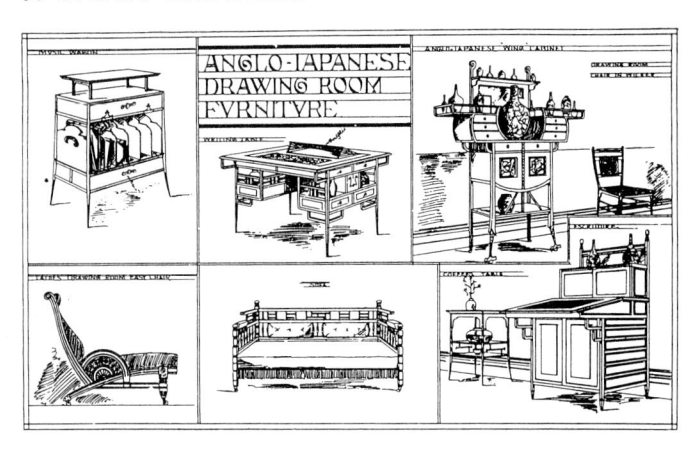

3.1. Godwin: Title-page (pl. 1) and plates 8 and 14 from *Art Furniture...*, 1877. Sales catalogue for Godwin's "Anglo-Japanese" furniture.

ture is the idea that historically derived ornament of any kind is basically untruthful. This notion stems from undeniably abusive practices on the part of nineteenth-century decorators and builders, but it also arose out of restrictive ethical convictions about the nature of art: John Ruskin's in England and Eugène Viollet-le-Duc's in France. A distinctive feature of the extensive and monumental treatises produced by these moral guardians of art is its fulsome rhetoric, yielding a kind of self-sufficiency—not a jot, or a trope, of which was lost upon the young Wright in the process of self-education. When,

late in 1893, Wright came to open his own office after quitting the firm of Adler and Sullivan, his reigning standard or motto—"I had left it off the door. But it was sitting there inside"[7]—was *Truth against the World*.

Now, nowhere in Japan will such a slogan be in evidence or even of much use, and we shall perhaps be able to discover how Wright is generally supposed to have eradicated the bogeyman of historicist motivation from Western architecture if we can discern the way in which he manipulated this motto. For get round the notion of architecture-and-truth, as well as above and below it, Wright certainly did! Secondly, we may also hope to come to grips with the conundrum of just how the stimulus afforded by Japanese pictorial and decorative art was transformed into an effective architectural incentive, but the latter must needs wait upon the former.

It has been wittily remarked, but not inaccurately, that the only architectural theorist whom Frank Lloyd Wright approved of wholeheartedly was the great Frenchman Eugène Viollet-le-Duc.[8] Viollet, who died in 1879—that is, during Wright's early youth—contended that every architectural form, whether belonging to the present or the past, must be the result of a certain ratiocination, or logic. The design of a cathedral, or of any other kind of structure, ancient or modern, was regarded by Viollet as a logical synthesis of parts. Moreover, the concise matter-of-factness of this view later contributed to the totally fresh concept of an architecture "proceeding by a process of argument from the known terms of a problem to the unknown but discoverable solution," a notion that "with all its inherent ambiguity, formed the foundation stone of modern architecture."[9]

Nowadays one can appreciate only with difficulty the newness of what, in effect, we owe to Viollet: "the theme of reason as the criterion of all good architectural performance."[10] It was indeed the "reasoned," and the "reasonable," quality of all that Wright discovered in the *Raisonné*, as he refers to Viollet's massive compendium, or *Dictionnaire*, which became the leitmotif on which he founded his own practice.[11] However, Viollet-le-Duc's public career as a teacher was short-lived. While his great medieval edifice, the *Dictionnaire raisonné de l'architecture française du XIe au XVIe siècle*,[12] stood, Viollet himself had been forced by March, 1864, to relinquish the Chair of History of Art and Aesthetics created for him in November, a few months earlier, as part of an attempted reform of the Ecole des Beaux-Arts in 1863. His replacement was not an architect at all, but the versatile and popular philosopher-historian Hippolyte Taine, who reigned in Viollet's stead until 1883.

The brief attendance of Wright's master, Louis Sullivan, at the Beaux-Arts during 1874–75 fell in the middle period of Taine's professorial tenure. It may even have been his exposure to this charismatic lecturer that constituted the most memorable part of the Ecole's legacy to Sullivan's formation, if *The Autobiography of an Idea*, written almost at the end of Sullivan's life, is to be trusted.[13] Although it is not known for sure whether Sullivan actually attended Taine's course in 1874–75, Taine's discussion of the Sistine Chapel by Michelangelo in the printed edition of his lectures was, according to *The Autobiography of an Idea*, to alter profoundly Louis Sullivan's views on the subject of artistic creation. Sullivan's account of this description and of his own experience beneath the Sistine frescoes in Rome burns with a Pauline intensity. Given Wright's worship of his master, it may be assumed that something of this fervor commuted itself to Wright's eventual notion of architectural truth based on Viollet.

Sullivan's visit to Rome took place in April 1875. But, even before setting foot in Italy, in the mere reading of Taine's lectures, he claims to have registered "three strong impressions, novel shocks":

> First, that there *existed* such thing as a Philosophy of Art; second, that according to M. Taine's philosophy the art of a people is a reflex or direct expression of the life of that people; third, that one must become well acquainted with that life in order to see into the art. All this was new and shining.[14]

This quotation expresses the kernel of Taine's collectivist determinism, which derives in spirit from Hegel's *Lectures on Aesthetics* (translated into French, 1840–52), though less in method of application. The enormous appeal of Taine's so-called idealistic positivism for the second half of the nineteenth century is difficult to reconstruct today, owing to our jaded attitude toward the accomplishments of science and to the reduced role of metaphysics in contemporary philosophy. Science remained Taine's ideal, and therefore, as both literary and art historian, his techniques were based on the minute examination of individual phenomena. Yet his most characteristic stance is to reason circularly from his own conclusions. Nevertheless, in his *Philosophy of Art* he promised to explain the arts of Europe through an investigation of the conditions that led to their creation, by means of an extension of positivist methods of investigation as used in the natural sciences. Even so, Taine was debarred from achieving his ideal of a materialistic and naturalistic aesthetics by a curious double-aspect theory of physical and psychic material. Ironically, the genius of much of his description actually depends on this ambiguity.

In our own century the appeal of Taine's flawed endeavor to account "scientifically" for cultural values has been acknowledged by as influential a commentator as Ernst Cassirer[15] as well as by Proust,[16] whose theory of literary creativity reflects Taine's predilection for conflating introspec-

3.2. Michelangelo: ceiling frescoes, 1508–12, and altar fresco of the *Last Judgment*, 1534–41, Sistine Chapel, Vatican.

tive data with history and semipublic events. As it happens, Louis Sullivan's *The Autobiography of an Idea*, which, incidentally, is narrated in the third person, does exactly this, and one might even compare its approach, though only in this one important respect, to Proust's early *Jean Santeuil*. Additionally, *An Autobiography* by Frank Lloyd Wright, being based on Sullivan's example, is cast in this same mold. Not surprisingly, both these architectural autobiographies are characterized by their candidness and Stendhalian egoism, as well as their unreliability.

But, now, to rejoin Louis Sullivan in the Sistine Chapel (fig. 3.2):

> Here was power as he [i.e., Louis] had seen it in the mountains, here was power as he had seen it in the prairies, in the open sky, in the great lake stretching like a floor toward the horizon [Lake Michigan], here was the power of the forest primeval.... There seemed to come forth from this great work a mystery; he began to *see into it*, and to discern the workings of a soul within. From beneath the surface significance there emerged that which is timeless, that which is deathless, that which in its immensity of duration, its fecundity, its everpresent urge, we call LIFE.... Imagination alone could do this; ... He saw that Imagination passes beyond reason and is a consummated act of Instinct—the primal power of Life at work.[17]

In fact, the exact passage in Taine that Sullivan purports to cite in connection with his visit to Rome, but for which he gives no chapter and verse, has never been identified and may have been noted down in the lecture room. We do, however, possess Taine's celebrated remarks on the predominance of the image over the "idea" in the Italy of the Renaissance.[18] In Michelangelo's day the impulse toward strong and powerful forms had not yet suffered unduly from an excess of culture: the soil of Europe was still hard and intact, the plowshare of civilization not yet having multiplied its furrows to infinity. The seeding ground of art, so to speak, had not yet been overpulverized, and primitive vision not yet decomposed by raw ideas. Taine goes on to complain of the nineteenth century as an era made up of abstract signs and fragmented forms; modern images, should these escape the impact of cold, scientific reasoning, remain but the product of hallucinators, no longer of seers.

These thoughts may seem to contradict the overall Hegelian tenor of Taine's *Philosophy of Art*, though, in fact, Hegel in his *Aesthetics* experienced similar waverings between loyalty to his system and genuine enthusiasm in the face of actual works of art. Moreover, in 1870, following the close of his first five-year cycle of lectures about art at the Ecole des Beaux-Arts, Taine would make his mark in the field of scientific psychology with the publication of *De l'intelligence*. His ideas were to influence Ribot and Janet, among others, and this book was made available in English the next year. In other words, Taine's idealism was significantly tempered by a novel and iconoclastic approach; in turn, his determinism was more open-ended (and, of course, agnostic) than Hegel's. Finally, his thoughts on art were a good deal more stimulating, on the strength of contemporary accounts, than the famous distillation of *race, moment,* and *milieu* that has come down to us in the history books' reiteration of nineteenth-century philosophical doctrines.

Taine had been out of favor with the Second Empire authorities at the time he was admitted to the Ecole des Beaux-Arts as a replacement for Viollet-le-Duc. Yet he personifies the aesthetic eclecticism of both the regime and the school, except for a pessimistic streak apparent in our paraphrase of his comparison of the art of the nineteenth century with that of the Italian Renaissance. Viollet, on the other hand, was a civil servant and close to imperial circles; but he was a sworn enemy of eclecticism, less a relativist and more an optimist than was Taine. The two differed in their applications of the determinist principle: Taine was, above all, a vitalist, a fact which shows through in the writing of Proust as well as in the extraordinary abstracted botanical ornament conceived in the architecture of Sullivan and perpetuated, in still more abstract forms in the "organic" architecture of Wright. But something similar was already reflected in the Gothic concerns of Viollet-le-Duc, not to mention Ruskin, whose translator, incidentally, Proust also became.

Such were among the ideological cross-threads woven into the prehistory of the so-called Modern Movement in the visual arts; and these finally amount, in a cumulative way, to a basic Western prejudice in favor of "truth" as against vulgar ornamentalism. In architecture, truth to structure, as Viollet demonstrated it in Gothic vaults and flying buttresses, was a part of this notion. Still, on the whole, architectural truth was a full-blown historicist, yet ideologically rather shaky prop for a barren and fragmented process of design. Truth in buildings, it was hoped, would stimulate the recovery of a scale of values that could be felt to be wholesome, intact, and in tune with the ideals of contemporary civilization.

THE SISTINE CHAPEL AND THE PHOENIX HALL

By simple definition, the Modern Movement cannot be said to exist, or to have existed, in Japan, other than as a reflection of Western values. There are many reasons for this, quite apart from the development gap that has already been discussed in the two previous chapters of this book. For example, one major impediment to the assumption of the burden of architectural truth, in all its weighty significance, on the part of the Japanese would have been the very notion of cause-and-effect it embodies. And that in spite of our late twentieth-century perception of such a view of truth as almost oriental in its subtlety and convolutedness.

In Taine's case, this complexity was a result of what one of his best critics has referred to as Taine's "dream of certainty and synthesis [that] persisted all his life."[19] This determined his attitude to English positivism as well as German idealism, which movements he hoped to be able to fuse. Over and above any such reconciliation of opposing philosophical tendencies, there are, according to the same authority, a mathematical analogy and a pantheism in Taine's thought, which are traceable to and reinforce Taine's Spinozism. Both are inimical to, even if perhaps they *seem* compatible with, the Japanese interpretation of Japanese art. Here the spiritual intensity of *fin de siècle* European art saw its own pantheism reflected in the Japanese scene as reconstituted out of the prints, textiles, and figurine art of Japan, despite, as we shall see, doubts about technical aspects, such as actual draftsmanship. It was further believed in some quarters that the significance of Japanese architecture was negligible. This point was well taken in its way, since, traditionally, architecture in Japan was part of the domain of technology and was never included among the fine arts, as in Europe, or at least scarcely to a similar degree. This, incidentally, is one more reason for the failure of architecture in Japan to be metamorphosed internally by the Modern Movement. In short, the Japanese responded to the positivist demands of what I have chosen, following Wright, to call architectural truth at the same time as they left the idealist component aside.

Now, there was in Wright's youth one famous Japanese-style building erected in the United States which played into the hands of aestheticism and Japanism (although in accordance with the notion just mentioned of distinguishing between Japan's architecture and her other arts, it may not have had as notable an influence as has been claimed for it). *The Autobiography of an Idea*, which Sullivan wrote in order to show that "instinct is primary and intellect is secondary in all the great works of man,"[20] closes in the thirty-seventh year of its author's life with the opening on May Day, 1893, of the World's Columbian Exposition in Jackson Park, Chicago, on the shores of Lake Michigan. The 1893 World's Fair was the ominous event whose "damage" Sullivan claimed would "last for half a century from its date, if not longer."[21] In his view the "Columbian Ecstasy" was a "virus" thanks to which "we have now the abounding freedom of Eclecticism, the winning smile of taste, but no architecture."[22] The most explicit architectural significance of the fair, or great White City, was its heralding of a giantesque, neobaroque form of Beaux-Arts classicism in American public building. While there were structures at the Chicago fair in other styles, including Sullivan's part Saracenic and part Romanesque "Transportation Building," the greatest contrast of all was unquestionably provided by the Imperial Japanese Exhibit, or Phoenix Hall (fig. 3.3). And this has been pointed to over and again as a source of influence on Wright, or at least his earliest exposure to a Japanese structure of an authentic type.

The Phoenix Hall, or Ho-o-Den,[23] was designed by Masamichi Kuru for the Imperial Japanese Commission to the exposition and executed with the assistance of Tokyo Fine Arts Academy and in consultation with experts from the Tokyo Imperial Museum. It was ostensibly a replica of that hall of almost the same name, the Hoo-do, at the Byodo-in at Uji, close to Kyoto, built in 1053 by Yorimichi Fujiwara as part of the conversion of one of his country estates into a so-called retirement temple (fig. 3.4). The complex was thus a sanctuary of Pure Land Buddhism as well as a nobleman's residence, hence the "den" affix in the name of the Chicago version. The Hoo-do's shape (fig. 3.5), suggestive of the

3.3. Kuru: Phoenix Hall, World's Columbian Exposition, Chicago, 1893.

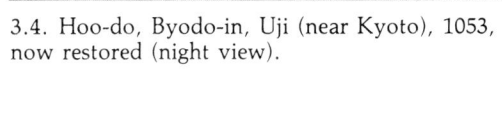

3.4. Hoo-do, Byodo-in, Uji (near Kyoto), 1053, now restored (night view).

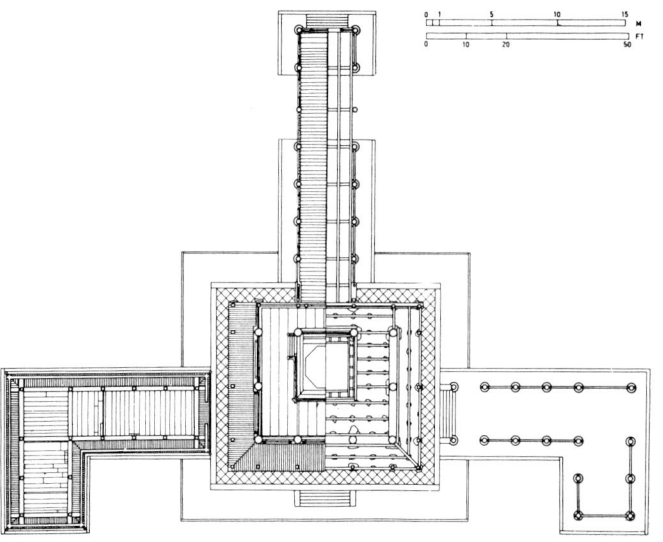

3.5. Hoo-do, Byodo-in, Uji (near Kyoto), 1053, plan.

phoenix with its wings outstretched in mythical flight, was a novelty in the canon of early Buddhist architecture in Japan. The idea of a "replica" of this ancient and sublime Amida Hall at the exposition was justified by the argument that Japan had been "from ancient times considered the birthplace of the Ho-o (or Phoenix). The United States of America, in its turn,

> has organized an Exhibition which for magnitude and magnificence exceeds anything the world has ever before seen, and which is accompanied by all those tokens of success that are believed to follow the advent of the Ho-o. Japan . . . has responded to the wishes of its promoters with the joy of the bird as it spreads its wings and carols its song in the heavens . . . [and] has come to the Exhibition laden with the treasures of that art which has been the heirloom of her people for the last thousand years.[24]

This was to prove literally true. In addition to substantial exterior alterations, the interior of the Ho-o-Den in Jackson Park was converted into a series of period rooms; it was, if viewed within the Japanese tradition, a museumlike, eclectic building. The original structure at Uji survived in 1893 in a state of near disintegration, but is today restored and may be viewed by the public.

The new Phoenix Hall was a building of its epoch, that is to say, the Meiji era. It was "somewhat smaller in size [than the original] and modified to adapt it for secular use."[25] Shipped to the fair in dismantled form, it was, after some discussion, erected according to the wish of the Japanese on the so-called Wooded Island by a crew of Japanese workmen.[26] Though visibly differing in materials, tonality, and physical scale from any other building at the exposition, this adapted version of a private aristocratic Amida Hall remained nonetheless an academic exercise in revivalism. For although its structure of unpainted wood contrasted bodily with the brilliantly plastered neoclassical facades of most of the larger buildings swathed in orders and statuary (fig. 3.6), and even if it appeared to Western eyes as a subdued unity approximating the once gorgeous hall belonging to the Byodo-in at Uji, the Japanese pavilion was a physical reconstruction of a cultural relic.

The interiors of the Ho-o-Den at Chicago, as worked out by government architect Kuru, constituted a sort of patternbook of authentically reconstructed period details selected from various eras of construction (fig. 3.7). On the left, as one faced the building, the Fujiwara epoch of the ninth to mid-twelfth centuries was represented with features from Uji itself as well as from the apartments of the Imperial Palace at Kyoto. On the right, the so-called Ashikaga style of the mid-fourteenth to mid-sixteenth centuries was depicted in a room from the Silver Pavilion at Ginkakuji in Kyoto. And, in the center, the Tokugawa age (1608–1868) was illustrated by a suite of rooms copied from Edo Castle. These reconstructions of matted rooms in various aristocratic styles ranging over a millennium were equipped in period fashion with genuine works of art selected by the Imperial Museum. The arrangement was designed logically to provide a quick notion of various spatial dispositions together with first-rate examples of traditional types of craftsmanship to anyone, such as Wright, who cared to visit the Japanese pavilion (fig. 3.8).

In 1893, however, the Ho-o-Den probably lacked readability, as has been tellingly observed by Manson:

> Beneath an ample roof—a powerful expression of shelter —and above the platform on which the temple stood, was the area of human activity, an open, ephemeral region of isolated posts and sliding screens that changed its appearance according to the activity of the hour, and that, in Occidental parlance, was not architecture at all.[27]

In other words, according to familiar Western terms of reference, the Phoenix Hall must have appeared extremely curious. Just as we do not have Sullivan's *contemporary* remarks on the architecture of the exposition, we possess no comments at all by Wright on the Ho-o-Den. We do know that the work from which the above quotation comes was written in consultation with Wright and, in some respects, represents an authorized biography of his early years. Still, it remains virtually unthinkable to assign stylistic changes in Wright's work to any imputed "lesson of the Ho-o-den," as Manson somewhat tentatively attempts to do,[28] especially as Wright's independent career had only just begun the same year, 1893, shortly after the World's Fair closed down.

In this matter of Wright's awareness of Japanese style, Tselos may be correct in emphasizing the importance, not of the Ho-o-Den, but of a smaller "Japanese Tea House."[29] This Nippon Tea House (fig. 3.9) was an entirely separate structure located on the narrow Bosporus leading from the Lagoon into the North Pond. Naturally, the tea house was built in a living idiom, a kind of loose version of the *sukiya* manner. For in the course of the Tokugawa age the "tea" style, that great invention of the grand tea connoisseurs, had not

3.6. Kuru: Phoenix Hall, World's Columbian Exposition, Chicago, 1893. Bird's-eye view of Wooded Island, with U.S. and Manufactures pavilions behind it.

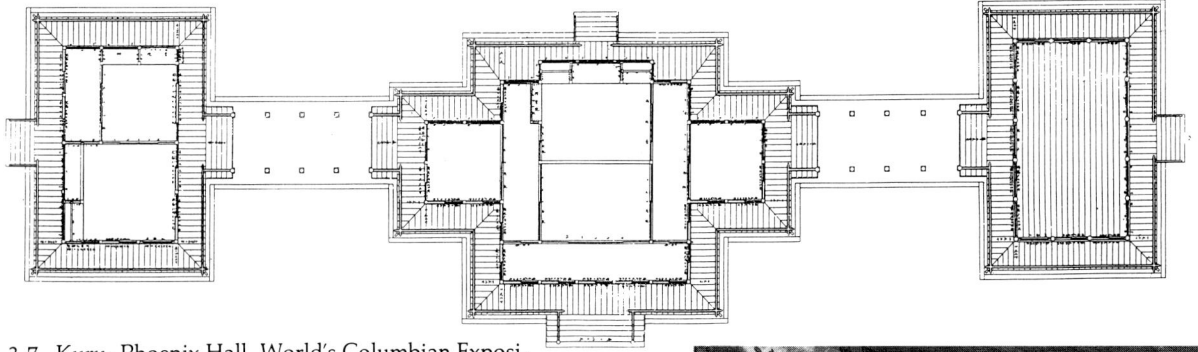

3.7. Kuru: Phoenix Hall, World's Columbian Exposition, Chicago, 1893. Plan. From *The Inland Architect and News Record*, 1892.

3.8. Kuru: Phoenix Hall, World's Columbian Exposition, Chicago, 1893. Period interior.

only come to influence the comportment, costume, and residential architecture of the merchants and townspeople but also determined the style of common entertainment spots. Tselos has pointed out, probably correctly, that the right-angled superimposition of roof ranges just visible in contemporary views of the Nippon Tea House must have discovered a vocation in the classical Prairie House prototype, such as the Ward Willits House of 1902 by Wright. In fact, there is no real example of similar crossing in the hierarchically built-up roof forms of the Heian period, as displayed in the swell-curved gable ends of the Ho-o-Den. Tselos also cites the well-known, but difficult to date, remodeling program of about 1895, which Wright undertook in regard to his house in Oak Park. Even though the details of the remodeling are ill understood today, it can still be observed that the wall treatment of the newly added dining room is markedly different from the more conventionally "Queen Anne" type of living-room wainscoting that is original to the house as it was constructed in 1889. If indeed the Ho-o-Den lacked—at various levels—either consistency or intelligibility, an interior renovation based on any one of its three Japanese-style period interiors, each of which was internally consistent, might have offered a sensible point of departure.

Possibly we shall never know more of Frank Lloyd Wright's exposure to any tangible example of Japanese architecture up until his initial visit to Japan in 1905, by which time the Prairie Style, his distinctive contribution to the Modern Movement, was already a fact of history. The Oak Park dining room was characterized by a modular, paneled decoration that seems to reflect the division of Japanese walling into rectangular segments bounded by exposed structural elements (later removed and, at present, reinstated, arguably giving a good idea of the original form). Moreover, in his new office Wright was to employ a Japanese draftsman by the name of Shimoda.[30] But he is also careful to specify, albeit at the cost of recounting a cruelly self-revealing incident, that Shimoda was not to be tolerated as an assistant for more than a very short time and soon enough became in no uncertain terms *persona non grata*.

Whatever the influences of Japanese participation in the 1893 World's Fair on Wright, we should still be on the lookout for a more "heroic" incentive comparable to Sullivan's conversion before the frescoes of Michelangelo. Such a red-letter event would account, in a more convincing way, for Wright's tenacious faith in Japanese art as a beacon of truth. Finally what for Sullivan had been a localizable experience, two days

3.9. Nippon Tea House, World's Columbian Exposition, Chicago, 1893 (right half of copyrighted photograph).

spent practically on his own and alone in the Vatican holy of holies, was seemingly for Wright a renewable one. Even so, Sullivan had been impressed by the painting, not the architecture, of the Sistine Chapel, with what Michelangelo had created "in the beneficence of power"[31] there. Afterward "he began to see the powers of nature and the powers of man coalesce in his vision into an IDEA *of power*."[32] Essential here is the all-encompassing nature of this construct which allowed for an expression of the grandeur of engineering works, such as bridges, and even of "science in general"[33] to be reflected, in Sullivan's mind, by an architectural theory and system.

3.10. Wright: title page of *The Japanese Print*, Chicago, 1912.

THE JAPANESE PRINT

For Frank Lloyd Wright the equivalent of the Sistine Chapel was not the official reconstruction of the Phoenix Hall at the Chicago fair but rather the state of grace afforded him by discovery of the Japanese print. This may have been rather apparent to anyone who knew Wright during the early phase that his career took at Oak Park and beyond, but he did not open his heart to the architectural world on this matter much before the 1930s. And by that time the vogue for Japanese art, including prints, had passed from being an esoteric, or even a popular, passion to the domain of wealthy collectors.

The story of Wright's involvement with the *ukiyo-e*, or Japanese woodblock print of the middle to late Tokugawa period, is extensively documented in *An Autobiography*, first published in 1932. So, also, are his various activities as a dealer in Japanese prints, a role that is now of historical interest but over which he had understandable misgivings. He was aware that his commercial dealing caused him to lose caste in the high circles in which he moved in Japan. As substantial amounts of money from American buyers were involved in his transactions,[34] the business side of his infatuation with the Japanese print possibly stood in the way of any earlier explanation of what, after his arrival in Japan, became an undisguised passion.

On the matter of Japanese influence in his work, the colorful remark of Wright's which follows is emphatic, and belongs as well to this later period of self-revelation: "No, my dear Mrs. Gablemore, Mrs. Plasterbuilt, and especially, now, Miss Flattop, nothing from 'Japan' has helped at all, except the marvel of Japanese color prints."[35] Clearly, a defensive note is being sounded here, but the emphasis also derives from the fact that, based on teachings of Viollet, Wright believed all forms of architectural expression to be committed to similar, if not identical, logical aims. We shall, I think, never know the extent to which Wright was able to reconcile this rationalist doctrine contained in the *Raisonné* with actual specimens of Japanese building. But, in any case, an unassimilated influence, whether from Japan or stemming from another source, would have been inconsistent with Wright's brand of truth. Indeed, a middle term *had* to be admitted into the equation linking Japan and Wright's concept of architectural truth.

That this was so is suggested by certain remarks made by one of the apostles of the Aesthetic Movement, a younger contemporary of Burges and Godwin, the book illustrator Walter Crane. During 1891–92, while Wright was still in the office of Sullivan, Crane, an Englishman, spent five weeks of a nine-month American tour in Chicago. An exhibition of his work was held at the Art Institute, where Crane lectured on "Design in Relation to Use and Materials." Writing in 1896, Crane, who was in possession of some Toyokuni prints from about 1870, reiterates the notion that Japanese art in general reflected a living medieval tradition, by this time a commonplace assumption.[36] What is interesting in Crane's case is that he is careful to specify that his remarks apply to Japan "as regards its arts and handicrafts with the exception of architecture." He then goes on to state that "in the absence of any really noble architecture or substantial constructive sense, the Japanese artists are not safe guides as designers."[37] And he notes, finally, that a distinction must be drawn between mere "decorative sense," as possessed by the Japanese, which is "finesse . . . taste, in short," and "real constructive power of design."[38] Crane is here actually referring to the contemporary revival of book design and illustration in England and, in particular, to what he calls the "satisfactory filling of spaces" in the process of page layout. Hence there can scarcely be any suspicion of self-interest, as there might in the case of Wright, in Crane's totally unanticipated and apparently dismissive remarks on Japanese architecture.

Walter Crane's was a major voice, albeit on the arts-and-crafts side, in the progressive nineteenth-century tradition from which Wright's architectural and interior ideas are descended. Even so, in his opinions, we find surprisingly little cultivation of a true understanding of Japanese art on its own terms. This lack of comprehension also affected Wright but did leave him free, at least, to pursue his own instincts with regard to Japanese prints. Twombly has called Wright and his first wife, Catherine, "virtual proselytizers for things Nipponese"[39] in the year following their return from Japan, both having local speaking engagements on the topic. In March, 1906, an exhibition was held by the Art Institute of 213 works by Hiroshige, which must have been the fruit of their Japanese trip and for which Wright prepared a catalogue. Wright's subsequent escape to Europe, with the wife of a client, from this intimate and Aesthetic suburban Oak Park scene leaves us with something of a gap in our knowledge of Wright's pursuit of Japanese art. But, in 1912, thus after his return from Berlin, and Italy, was published the short treatise entitled *The Japanese Print*[40] (fig. 3.10).

Wright begins his text by explaining that in order to understand the "unpretentious colored wood-cut of Japan" we "as a people" and, in particular, "our artists" must take up an *unfamiliar* stance, namely "the aesthetic viewpoint."[41] In a footnote, he includes a brief bibliography of works on the subject,[42] which, as he says, he intends to "neglect." Instead, the aim of Wright's work will be "to tell what these colored engravings are in themselves and more particularly of their cultural use to us," namely: "in awakening the artistic conscience, or at least in making us feel the disgrace of not realizing the fact we have none."[43]

This notion of an "artistic conscience" was a pillar of the Aesthetic doctrine, which during the latter part of the nineteenth century had inclined so toward Japan and her art. It may be understood essentially as a gesture of truce in that century's struggle waged between ideas and sensations, as exemplified in Taine's passage which has already been referred to on the art of Italy in the Renaissance. Sullivan, as we saw, had resolved this in favor of the "Idea" of "power," an analogy between *Life* as we experience it and the "life" transmitted to, and reflected by, the work of art, without worrying a great deal about the physiological or mental equipment that might account for this kind of transfer. Wright repeats his arguments but refers far more delicately to what he calls "the true vitalizing power of art," which relies on an instinctual or intuitive perception of the "subjective quality" of a work of art.

Although nothing has been lost in terms of moral fervor, this move away from the Michelangelo of the Sistine ceiling toward a more selective, intimate, and, ideally at least, ephemeral nature is part and parcel of Wrightian strategy:

> You may personally feel in these aesthetic abstractions of the Japanese mind the innocent and vivid joy which ... is yours in the flowers of field or garden.
> A flower is beautiful, we say—but why? Because in its geometry and in its sensuous qualities it is an embodiment and significant expression of that precious something in ourselves which we instinctively know to be Life ... a proof of the eternal harmony in the nature of a universe which is too vast and intimate and real for the mere intellect to seize.[44]

Although the determinist element will come flooding back at the end of the essay, and remains obvious in the passages of *An Autobiography* dealing with Japan and Japanese graphic art, the emphasis here is on a generalized but authentic Nature, which is in fact that of Wright's upper Midwestern childhood in Wisconsin.

A single but well-timed and significant shift away from conventional or received ideas on Japanese art, like the ones expounded by Walter Crane and quoted above, is revealed:

> The most important fact to realize in a study of this subject is that, with all its informal grace, Japanese art is a thoroughly structural art; fundamentally so and in every medium. It is always, whatever else it is or is not, structural.[45]

This is, however, followed by a rather retrograde discourse on the "spell power" of geometric form designed "to 'build' the Idea," which constitutes the major part of Wright's essay. Though nothing that is harmful or wrongheaded is said, the little book by Wright turns out to be fairly conventional after all.

Now, Wright, like Viollet and most of the other nineteenth-century writers on architecture, great and small, had seized on what John Summerson has termed "the irresistible analogue of a *new style*."[46] Thus, he was able to declare, just three years after his return from Japan: "From the beginning of my practice the question uppermost in my mind has been not 'what style' but 'what is style?'" And his answer is the neo-historicist one: "the forms must be born out of our changed conditions, they must be *true* forms, otherwise the best that tradition has to offer is only an inglorious masquerade."[47] In a still earlier piece of writing, the text of the famous Hull House speech entitled "The Art and Craft of the Machine," he deduces that the basis of the *new style*, and henceforth of "style" itself, must be "SIMPLICITY."[48]

But simplicity, here, no longer implies a cry of protest against mechanization as it did for William Morris, the English prophet of art reform. Instead, for Wright, the machine becomes a "marvelous simplifier," as well as "the Forerunner of Democracy." The second notion accounts for the emphasis both Sullivan and Wright placed on a national, or American, style, while the two phrases taken together bridge the gap between the free-floating idealism propounded by Sullivan and the increasingly insistent utopian ideals of the Modern Movement.

As agent of this transition, Wright assimilated much that was to prove grist to his mill, including Japan. He was also quickly moved to observe that others had done likewise, for example: The Japanese "saw nothing to admire in Western culture except that as *a means to an end*, it would serve them better than their own in the undertaking now ahead—the defense of the East against the West."[49] The meaning this may have had shortly prior to World War II was not exactly what

I have in mind, but for Wright himself the statement was probably without irony, although he may have been trying to hedge his bets, particularly in later editions of his autobiography. Yet the same phrase occurs, back in the article of 1908, in which Wright is describing his own style and architecture: "Simplicity is not in itself an end; it is a means to an end."[50]

The new art detailed by Wright, of which the first principles were Simplicity and Repose, is that of Nature,[51] "this school" which "Japanese art knows . . . more intimately than that of any people."[52] In *The Japanese Print*, four years later, its interaction with art is made more precise: "To the smallest fraction of Japanese lives what was divorced from Nature was reclaimed by Art, and so redeemed."[53]

Furthermore, Wright's understanding of the Japanese print is directly connected with his view on "style" in architecture by his notion of simplification.

> Broadly stated then, the first and supreme principle of Japanese aesthetics consists in a stringent simplification, and consequent emphasis of reality. The first prerequisite for the successful study of this strange art is to fix in mind at the beginning the fact that it is the sentiment of Nature alone which concerns the Japanese artist; of Nature as beheld by him in those vital meanings which he alone sees and alone therefore endeavors to portray. . . .[54]
>
> This process of elimination of the insignificant we find to be their first and most important consideration as artists, after the fundamental mathematics of structure.[55]

As already mentioned, the work on the Japanese print must have been postponed by Wright's European sojourn of 1909–10. But this "flight," as it has been termed, provided a viewpoint from which Hokusai and Korin could be compared with Velasquez and even Rembrandt. Thus, from Fiesole, Wright was able to adjudge:

> Then, too, we should learn the more spiritual lessons the East has power to teach the West so that we may build upon these basic principles the more highly developed forms our more highly developed life will need if the Machine is to be a safe tool in our hands.[56]

In the next chapter we must try to get a closer look at these new-age and cross-cultural theoretical pronouncements of Wright's and their application. The opportunity to make a manifesto in brick and stone came at the conclusion of lengthy negotiations for the design and commission of a large hotel to be situated in the heart of Tokyo. While technology—or Wright's version of it—was to have a well-publicized role in the overall conception of this Imperial Hotel, the Machine was not all that much in evidence, since the 270 guest rooms, plus 10 suites, were for all intents and purposes hand-built by an army of local craftsmen and laborers. The Imperial Hotel evolved as a fortunate conjunction of misfortunes and accidents which was to make a name for Wright. At the same time, the design itself led him some way from the path of "stringent simplification" which he habitually mentioned in the same breath as the Japanese print. The paradox of an architectural Truth which forever remained the "means" to some continually receding "end" was to haunt the Modern Movement. Such was the strain of rationalism inherited from Viollet which could produce the Imperial Hotel as a transitional work situated between nineteenth-century ideals and the architecture of modernism. Wright's efforts spell out the dissimilarity between Western architecture and the "rationality" of Japanese traditional construction, which is so patently antispatial in its logic. It is the recovery of this essential antispatiality of all Japanese art—which, incidentally, was better realized through the midwifery of a Manet or a Degas than Wright's—that will prove the goal of Japanese architecture in the twentieth century.

4 | Rebuilding the Imperial in the 1920s: Japan Gained

THE LEGEND

The Imperial Hotel in Tokyo, as reconstructed by Frank Lloyd Wright, was the first Japanese building erected by a Western architect of repute and talent (fig. 4.1). Although the entrepreneurial history of the present hotel goes back to 1890, the Imperial became internationally celebrated only after Wright's new building opened on September 1, 1923. The hotel's fame was, in part, architectural until closure—late in 1967—of the fantastic edifice Wright had designed and its destruction the following year. Its reputation depended, for the rest, on effective management, assured by the Inumaru family since shortly before the inauguration of Wright's famous building. Almost certainly, both components were necessary to the achievement of the Imperial Hotel's legendary status. And a third must also be added, namely, the unlooked-for occurrence of the Great Kanto Earthquake just before noon on the Imperial's opening day.

Prior to this event, Wright's direction of the project had been strongly criticized in both Japan and the United States. His failure to respect costs, or even apparently to take the notion of costing into account, was an open scandal, the budget being prodigious by standards on either side of the Pacific. In America, however, gibes against the architect of the Imperial Hotel were at least partially motivated by personal and ideological concerns. The assault seems to have been silenced by survival of the hotel in the Tokyo earthquake, once this fact had been noisily established stateside by Wright, who had already left Japan for good.

The best account of the hotel's rebuilding is by Wright

4.1. Wright: Imperial Hotel, Hibiya, Tokyo, 1913–23. Principal Facade.

4.2. Wright: Imperial Hotel, Hibiya, Tokyo, 1913–23. Ornament in dining room and on exterior parapets.

4.3. Driving piles on site of the Imperial Hotel (probably 1920), with National Supreme Court and Ministry of Justice at rear.

himself in *An Autobiography*, where—despite the idealization of his own role—he does not spare a presentation of the difficulties. However, certain details of Wright's participation, notably the manner in which the project was commissioned, for a long time eluded his biographers. Inconsistencies have now, for the greater part, been set in satisfactory order through recourse to Wright's own correspondence of the period.[1] All the same, Shinjiro Kirishiki's valiant and diplomatic attempt from the Japanese side to piece together a construction history of the building at the time of its dismantling early in 1968 remains a necessary corrective to each further retelling of this most controversial of all Wright's undertakings.[2]

Apart from the question of its vast expense, the sheer physical extent of the hotel, some 34,500 square meters, seems to me of importance. It seemed so to Wright, too, in terms of helping to promote his own reputation, although, in Japan, larger buildings, such as factories and office blocks, had already risen by the early 1920s. But, most of all, Wright was self-absorbed in an unusual, but not revolutionary, type of antiseismic construction he thought he had invented, and at the same time in a highly idiosyncratic program of ornament. These jointly defined the Imperial Hotel for him. Pairing the two features established the "truth" of the design. This, we saw in the previous chapter, Wright had come to find in the "organic" qualities of a style which in some abstruse, Carlylean sense he also believed compatible with the Machine. The building Wright realized in Tokyo was an elaborate metaphor linking a hidden antiseismic structure to an ornamental system created by chiseling tufa-like stone into crystalline, gossamer, lobed, or frondlike forms of a kaleidoscopic geometry (fig. 4.2). Here, indeed, was the enchantment, or "spell power," which Wright mentioned in *The Japanese Print* of the previous decade. It was rendered flesh in the Tokyo hotel by coupling a structural expression, heroically symbolized everywhere by open-ended cantilevers with rhythmed tracery fashioned of "living rock" and deftly interwoven from the interior to the exterior of the building's concrete-and-brick shell.

It is now generally believed, though it can scarcely be demonstrated,[3] that the Imperial's success in withstanding effects of earth movement during the Great Kanto Earthquake was largely fortuitous. Its survival was certainly not unique; while Wright, who never revisited Japan, was at some pains to imply that it was. Soil conditions were bad at best, and it seems less the actual structure of the hotel that was at issue than the problem of devising subfoundations that would be effective in what Wright described as soil that was like "soft cheese." As in the matter of the hotel's superstructure, Wright's "floating" foundations reposing on piles (fig. 4.3) were neither unique nor original; nor in a worst-scenario case would they have proved adequate.

As for its ornament, the Imperial Hotel was in some ways a building of its time, and attempts have been made to fit it into the Art Deco style. Yet the logic of Wright's ornament derives, rather, from that of Sullivan, which itself hardly resists categorization as Art Nouveau. By virtue of a similar integrity the Imperial ornament refuses assimilation to the rhythm of sub-Cubist decorative impulses from Europe, though if we take into account Wright's own earlier Midway Gardens in Chicago (see fig. 4.9) we may find the association comes more readily. The "spell power" of Wright's hotel in Tokyo has never sat well with professional historians, such as Hitchcock,[4] yet it seems in many ways an ultimate expression of Wright's end-of-the-century aestheticism. This was nothing short of Epicurean in terms of its values, a condition which the Wright legend has been far less willing to consider than was the man himself on the evidence of almost all his writings.

WHAT THE BUILDING REALLY WAS

Wright's commission originated in the decision to replace the earlier hotel designed by Yuzuru Watanabe in the Second Empire style (fig. 4.4; erected 1888–90), which had just sixty guest rooms and ten suites. Significantly, the history of the concept put forward in the Imperial goes directly back to the hotel built at Tsukiji in 1867–68 by Kisuke Shimizu II (see fig. 1.13). It had been managed by a consortium which Shimizu himself headed, perhaps the earliest example of a joint-stock venture in Japan. The theory it embodied was that foreigners were to be segregated for the sake of their own comfort and to the mutual benefit, as the government professed, of all. After the destruction of the Tsukiji Hotel, the same notion was reexpressed in the Rokumeikan, or "Deer-Cry Pavilion," a kind of assembly room where wealthy and aristocratic Japanese could mix socially with foreign residents and guests. Like the Imperial Hotel, the Rokumeikan stood near Hibiya Park; it was put up in 1883 to a design by Josiah Conder and became so celebrated as a place of resort that its name is today synonymous with an entire era of Meiji culture at the end of the last century. Each of these buildings was, so to say, a "halfway" house and responded to a par-

4.4. Watanabe: Imperial Hotel, Hibiya, Tokyo, 1888–90.

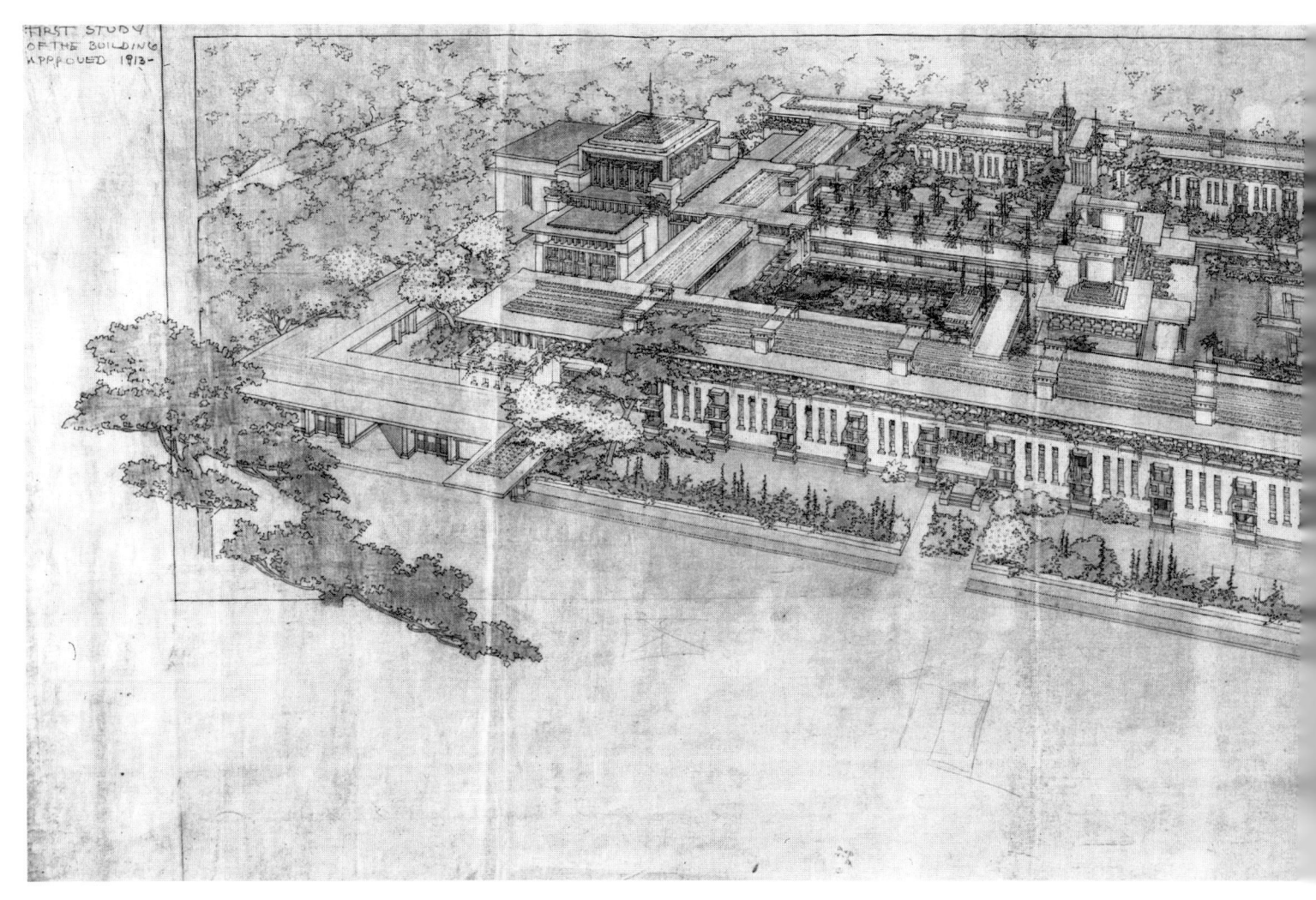

ticular phase in the socialization and development of Japan. Culminating with the Imperial Hotel by Wright, each was swept away in its turn as the nation evolved.

The persons responsible for the formation of the joint-stock Imperial Hotel corporation, following the Tsukiji episode and the Rokumeikan interval, were Eiichi Shibusawa, later raised to the rank of viscount in 1900, and Kihachiro Okura, ennobled as Baron Okura in 1915. Shibusawa's Venetian-style residence by Tatsuno was finished in the same year, 1888, which saw the beginning of the first Imperial Hotel. Okura, who was made president of the hotel partnership, was, in addition, an important collector of oriental ceramics, painting, and decorative art. The imperial household held stock in the firm from the beginning and was also the leasor of the land on which Wright's hotel eventually came to stand. Thus, while the Imperial Hotel was never the direct property of the emperor or his family, as Wright was content to imply, its association with the Japanese imperial household remained in virtual force until the American Occupation, when both land and stock were placed in other hands.

The period of its greatest élan, comparable in some ways to the brilliance of the Rokumeikan era of a previous generation, was the decade and a half between the completion of Wright's building and the outbreak of the Second World War. In those brief years, the Imperial Hotel enjoyed a role in the social life of Tokyo like that of the Hotel Adlon in Berlin.

4.5. Wright: Imperial Hotel, Hibiya, Tokyo, 1913–23. First study. Marginal notation "approved 1913."

HOW WRIGHT CONCEIVED THE SECOND IMPERIAL

The American, Wright, was recommended to design the new Imperial Hotel by Frederick W. Gookin, "a prominent Chicago banker, whose expertise in the field of Japanese prints made him one of the nation's foremost authorities."[5] This was in 1911, and Wright's involvement with the hotel did not terminate until midsummer of 1922, when his Japanese assistant, Arata Endo, was left on his own to complete the entire south wing of the structure. Of these eleven years approximately one third were spent in Japan: from shortly before the close of 1916 until the end of the spring of the following year, and at intervals from the end of World War I until Wright's ultimate dismissal some four years later.

The design of the hotel can be related conceptually to the sequence of Wright's own works that preceded it in the United States. On the other hand, the building for the Imperial Hotel was intimately connected with a certain image of Japan held by Wright as a personal vision, or dream, and, thus, with his reverence for Japanese *ukiyo-e*.

The greatest success of the Imperial Hotel was the boldly monumental spaces Wright contrived to create in spite of restraints posed by the earthbound profile of the building with its purposely lowered center of gravity (fig. 4.5). Related was the Beaux-Arts sophistication of its plan, already mentioned in connection with a certain family resemblance to Tatsuno's fairly recently constructed Bank of Japan (see fig. 2.32). This type of plan remained for the entire age up until World War I, and even after that, the ideal for virtually all public buildings. It was valued for the opportunity it presented to distinguish building types by displaying a building's character through a distinctive combination of ornament and plan. The nature of the individual solution aimed at is not always easily perceived today, and particularly so in buildings constructed toward the end of the period. Nevertheless, what remains obvious in practically any successful Beaux-Arts design is the desire to communicate a sense of the finished architectural whole, both plan and ornament uniting toward that end. Wright's skill in this was precisely the reason he had been invited to study abroad in Paris and to help initiate the American Academy in Rome. His unwillingness to accept reflects, I think, a recognition that the day of buildings like the Bank of Japan or the Akasaka Detached Palace was over and the vocabulary they employed unclear; this accounts for his horror of academies and distaste for the indiscriminate use of classicizing ornament. Otherwise, his choice to remain in the Midwest was in no way a blanket refutation of the rhetorical functions of architecture.

The design of the Imperial Hotel is proof of this state of affairs, in terms of which Wright hoped, as he always did, to rehabilitate and redefine architectural Truth. Whence came the aesthetic perfection, and perfectionism, inherent in the hotel scheme: the same precision of proportion or spatial sequence that rarely failed Wright even in his earliest works. Yet, the "grand hotel" building type itself, and probably the budget, which Wright apparently imagined unlimited, were his undoing. These factors led to a blurring of what he wished to state, as much as any overlay of neoclassicism would have done. This detracted from the whole idea and its realization.

4.6. Wright: Imperial Hotel, Hibiya, Tokyo, 1913–23. Looking north along the second-floor promenade.

4.7. Wright: Imperial Hotel, Hibiya, Tokyo, 1913–23. Crossing and north rear entrance.

By contrast, in the Prairie houses, Wright had rethought and retooled the very concept of the new-age dwelling, that is, the middle-class residence with relatively few servants or staff. In returning to a completely serviced installation, like a hotel (especially in pre–World War II Japan), the architect was in yet another sense undoing what he had so often accomplished in earlier work, just as in purely formal terms he now reverted to an image of bilateral symmetry. Nevertheless, one thing not lost was the vertical interpenetration of spaces, as well as their horizontal-and-vertical interlocking, one of the most distinctive of all features in Wright's residential architecture of previous years. For instance, in the Imperial, both front and rear lobby areas reached through more than one floor (the front lobby extending into the third level), as did the dining room and the auditorium, as well as the so-called promenade (fig. 4.6). The latter formed the crossbar of the hotel's H-shaped plan and constituted a transverse axis connecting the symmetrical north and the south wings in which guest rooms were located (fig. 4.7).

In the Imperial Hotel, hierarchy of ornament was thus matched with hierarchy of spatial arrangement, as in many other Beaux-Arts works of the period. The prior substraction of classicism in all but a few of Wright's beginning works, the absent column or missing entablature, had rarely led to any ambiguity in Wright's residential style. In the Imperial Hotel, on the other hand, the return to an earlier hierarchy, pairing plan and decoration, decreased the sense of abstract spatial freedom while shifting the onus of abstraction onto the system of ornament. Yet, at the same time, here was a decoration so highly articulated as to appear virtually scenographic. The effect was charming and unusual, as many still alive will not hesitate to attest, but divorced from any context, including Wright's own unique spatial sense.

Still, if we consider some of the great nineteenth-century spaces we have lost, there were perhaps precedents for the Imperial, not in any city hotel, but possibly in the deluxe resort hotels of the West. Each time he traveled to Japan, Wright was obliged to traverse the whole northerly portion of the American continent to take passage from Seattle or Vancouver. Was he, I wonder, familiar with Robert C. Reamer's Old Faithful Inn in Yellowstone Park of 1902 or Glacier Park Hotel in Montana, built in 1913? The lobbies of both, heavily rusticated, were multistory spaces in which whole trees created a forest of columns, always, of course, with the fireplaces Wright loved, sometimes made of piled-up boulders suggesting living rock. Was the informality, composed of a daunting and immensely picturesque naturalness, of such hotels what Wright now in Japan hoped to recreate at the Imperial?

Wright's trees were, in the event, concrete ones. To be sure, timber construction on this scale—such traditional examples as Todaiji notwithstanding—is unthinkable in a modern metropolis in an earthquake zone. As for stone, Wright tells how he had purchased a quarry's worth of the soft, porous white tufa at Oya, near Nikko. This material was employed throughout the new Imperial, everywhere wrought by hand in accordance with a semiabstract naturalism amazingly similar to the neo-Ruskinian ornament that the young Corbusier, in the Swiss Jura, had wrung from his Alpine surroundings nearly two decades before.

The same carved ornament burst out over the hotel's facade, where, it must be added, all similarity to the U.S. Far West abruptly ceased. Here, on the outside of the building, we are once more back within the Wrightian canon. It is, though, his brick style, long narrow Roman bricks laid over a stone watertable—not the white rendering over timberwork that is alleged to resemble a certain kind of Japanese construction. Overall, the buildings of which one is most reminded are Wright's own home at Taliesin, in Wisconsin (fig. 4.8), and the open-air music hall and restaurant called Midway Gardens (fig. 4.9), in Chicago, both contemporary in various degrees with the Imperial project. Not surprisingly, the greatest resemblance lay in the drawings, or bird's-eye views, rather than in the final, realized phase of any of the three. In addition, the Imperial's facade, minus most of its ornament, was related in design to some of the grandest of Wright's early residential schemes, such as the palatial Darwin D. Martin house of 1904, in Buffalo, which he built for the owner of Larkin, the soap manufacturer and mail order firm whose headquarters was alluded to in connection with the Akasaka Palace's orbicular sculptures.

THE ROLE OF JAPAN
Wright labeled the Imperial as being in various ways a transitional work:

> A world in itself—a transition world—began to take shape in that transition-building. It was created spontaneously as any ever fashioned by the will of a creator in the Middle Ages. Most of all the plans I had prepared at Taliesin were thrown away and my presence on the work enabled me to make such changes in the work itself as were required or I desired. . . . I could take off my hat to the culture I had learned to revere. Something no foreign architect had ever done before.[6]

What Wright stresses in this passage is less the shift from orthodox nineteenth-century monumentality to an ahistorical, and abstract, formalism, such as is characteristic of his work in general, than a new amalgamation between East and West. On the one hand stands Japan, as "the culture I had learned to revere," and on the other is implied the tradition of Rationalism reinvented for the West by Viollet-le-Duc out of his own medieval pursuits. It is no secret that Wright claimed Viollet as master, but he could, at the same time, doff his hat to an alien aesthetic. Here, it seems, is a fairly late manifestation of what Edward Said refers to as "the *idée reçue* 'Europe-regenerated-by-Asia' " underneath which "lurked a very insidious hubris."[7]

In Wright's case this pride was fueled in part by the presence of a cheap, yet highly skilled and also deeply committed coolie labor force. Ironically, Wright had proclaimed once and for all how "the machine was the great forerunner of democracy."[8] "Invincible" and "triumphant," it would go on "gathering force and knitting the material necessities of mankind ever closer into a universal automatic fabric."[9] In consequence, "the Art of old [which] idealized a Structural Necessity [was] now rendered obsolete and unnatural by the Machine."[10] But not only had Wright found a purportedly antiseismic structural principle to serve him as a real and also a metaphorical core device for the Imperial Hotel, he also now commanded a great band of independent-minded yet, in the end, formable oriental hand-laborers to realize the scheme (fig. 4.10). And this, incidentally, was one of the complaints urged against Wright on the part of the American construction industry until the earthquake disaster delivered him from persecution.

As for the Japanese aesthetic, whose improving influence Wright claims to have assimilated, two texts contained in *An Autobiography* are devoted exclusively to Wright's Japanese experience. These, called "A Song to Heaven" and "Yedo," following on each other,[11] constitute a subtext within the main body of autobiographical material relating to his stay in Japan.[12]

Wright visited Japan twice before actually securing the commission for the Imperial Hotel. The first of these journeys,

4.8. Wright: Taliesin, the architect's house and studio, Spring Green, Wisconsin, 1911 onward. Study of about 1916 (after fire of 1914).

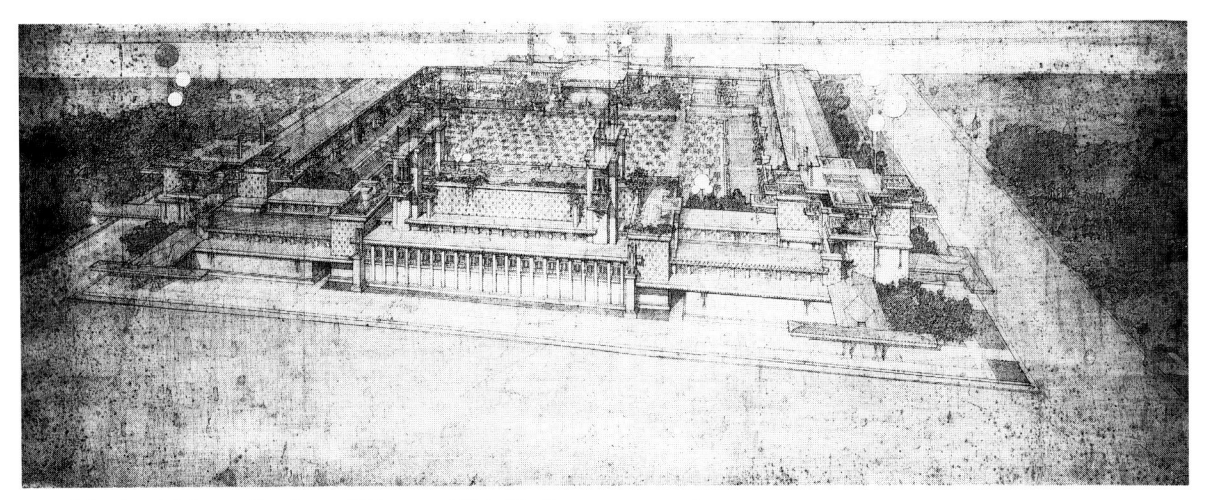

4.9. Wright: Midway Gardens, Chicago, 1914. Bird's-eye perspective.

which was also Wright's earliest trip abroad, had been from February to April, 1905, in the midst of the Russo-Japanese War. It followed the Louisiana Purchase Exposition of 1904 at St. Louis, where Wright had gone down to see a landscaped replica of the famous Temple of the Golden Pavilion, Kinkakuji, which was the official Japanese exhibit. At the beginning of 1905, then, Wright and his first wife, Catherine, traveled to Japan in the company of Mr. Ward W. Willits and his wife. Willits was an executive of a brass and bronze foundry[13] and the client for whom, in 1902, Wright built the first masterpiece among his Prairie houses, the Willits House on the edge of the Illinois prairie in the Chicago suburb of Highland Park. Sheet brass was widely used for artillery shell cases, as well as for small-arms ammunition, and Willits may have made the trip to Japan on some kind of business connected with military supply. Mr. and Mrs. Wright, however, were intent on purchasing Japanese art objects in the divestment occasioned by the war effort. Wright, however, always referred to this trip as having taken place in 1906, after the signing of the Portsmouth Treaty.

4.10. Japanese workmen erecting one of the eight stone peacocks for the Imperial Hotel's Banquet Hall.

The 1913 visit to Japan, from January to May,[14] was totally suppressed in Wright's own autobiographical account, possibly because it was too painful. For Wright was accompanied this time by Mamah Borthwick Cheney, wife of a client, with whom he had previously fled to Europe; she was assassinated in 1914 by the deranged servant who also set fire to Taliesin. Additionally, Wright wished his readers to believe the Japanese had sought him to design the second Imperial Hotel on the strength of his Berlin publications a few years earlier.

It was clearly, nonetheless, this voluntarily suppressed visit that inspired Wright to compose what he called "A Song to Heaven," which deals with Japanese religion, aesthetics, and life-style in *An Autobiography*. In fact, the reverie, which opens with a second anchor-dropping in Yokohama Bay, goes on to conflate the second visit of 1913 with the third of 1917, when Wright was accompanied by the third woman who became a part of his life, the sculptress Miriam Noel.

What Wright earlier referred to as those "spiritual lessons the East has power to teach the West"[15] turned mainly on two themes: the Japanese dwelling house and the life-style it engendered, and the print, together with the subjects it portrayed. In "A Song to Heaven" he draws attention to "clusters of straw-thatched villages nesting in the nooks of the mountainous land naturally as birds nesting in trees." This is but one metaphor drawn from three opening paragraphs of conventional Aesthetic imagery depicting Japan as viewed from the ship in Yokohama Bay. The discussion then veers toward the topic of cleanliness and the Shinto religion, for Wright stresses that the Japanese way of living depends on this religion, while the Japanese house is for him "the dwelling ancient Shinto religion built there."[16]

More precisely, Wright defined "the native home in Japan" (fig. 4.11) as "a supreme study in elimination—not only of dirt but the elimination of the insignificant."[17] The "simplicity" which this entails is understood to be the point in common between the dwelling he admires and the woodblock print which he adores. In addition, he noted: "I found this ancient Japanese dwelling to be a perfect example of the modern standardizing I had myself been working out."[18] And, in conclusion: "By heaven, here was a house used by those who made it with just that naturalness with which a turtle uses his shell."[19]

Wright's argument, however, leads back with a fatal inevitability to his notion of architectural Truth: "The truth is the Japanese dwelling is in every bone and fiber of its structure honest and our dwellings are not honest."[20] He characterizes the Japanese religion, its elevated aesthetic (including the tea ceremony of Rikyu), and, in fact, the whole Japanese way of life as a "song to heaven," a "simple everyday singing of the human spirit."[21] But his interpretation is limited, in the manner of true Epicureanism, to admiring the vision of a "practical way of beautiful life" thus evoked. At last he was forced to admit: "I have learned as much for us in our lives from this singing as I could hear or bear."[22] This is similar to the impulse of the emperor Marcus Aurelius which Walter Pater described as a desire "to perpetuate, to display, what was so fleeting, in a kind of instinctive, pathetic protest . . . against the 'perpetual flux' of all things. . . ."[23] Perhaps that, in the end, is what the curious and florid vision of the Imperial Hotel also amounted to: an attempt to rationalize and somehow localize Wright's own sensations of Japan.

The Japanese house, as Wright at the beginning of the present century would have known it, has disappeared together with much of the ritual accompanying daily life as he refers to it in "A Song to Heaven." Thanks to the Impressionists, and also to Wright himself, the aesthetic of Japanese prints is deeply and thoroughly ingrained in our twentieth-century sensibility. On the other hand, the space of the traditional dwelling as experienced by Wright firsthand (which left him "too delighted with the problem to attempt to solve it"[24]) has never received truly serious-minded consideration. Nor has

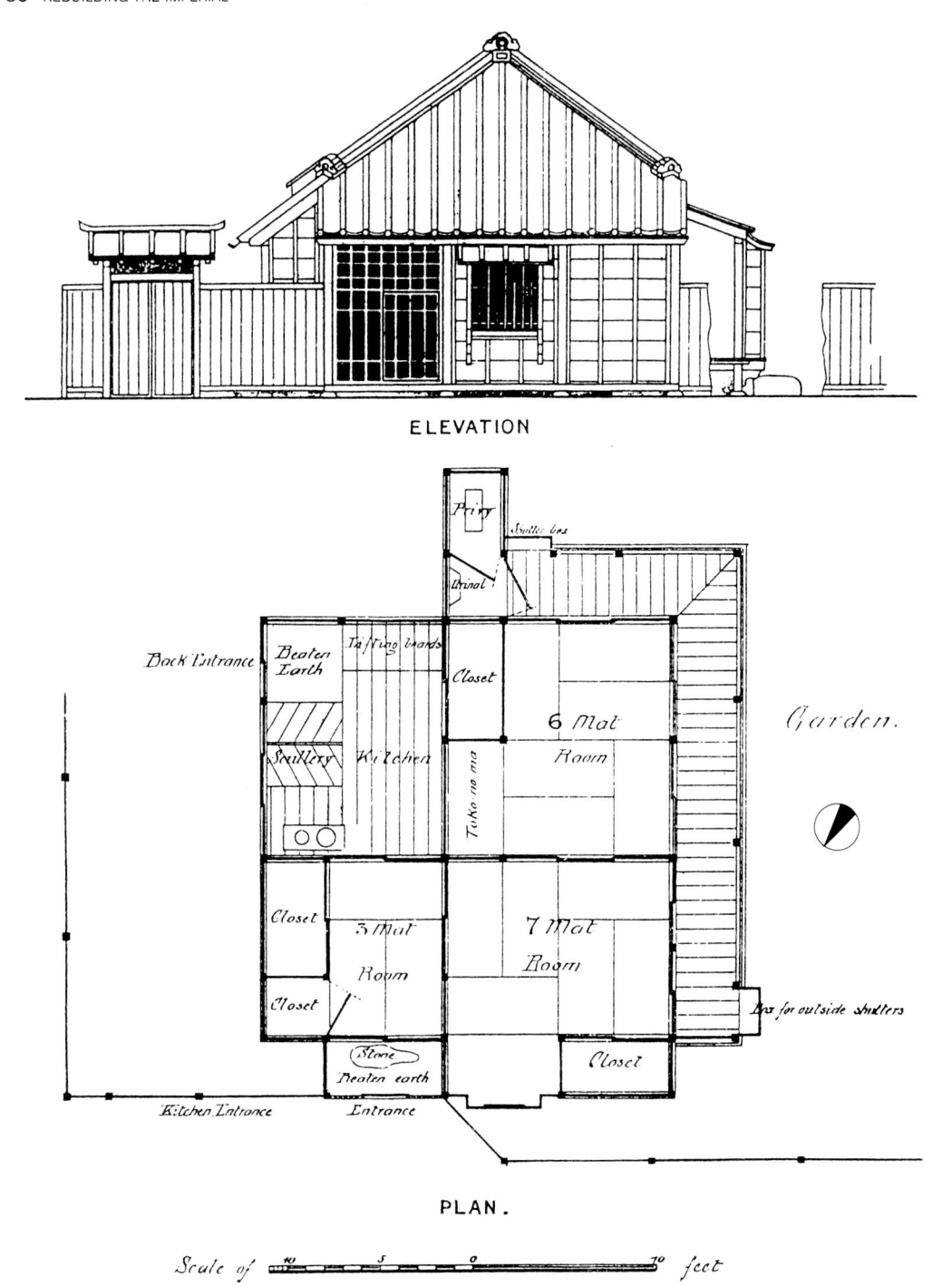

4.11. "Middle-class Japanese Dwelling," drawn for Josiah Conder by R. T. Conder. Elevation and plan. From *Transactions of the RIBA*, 1887.

it been successfully assimilated into Wright's or any other Western architecture.

Wright's American work, such as both the projects for Taliesin and Midway Gardens—the latter realized by the outbreak of World War I and the former a continuous pattern of changing ideas—displays a kind of Persian intricacy. Together with the hotel they composed a single mazelike vision (fig. 4.12), whether caravanserai or seraglio, which, however beautiful, was not one of Japanese-style "simplicity." Wright viewed Midway Gardens as "an 'Arabian Nights' in architecture"; moreover, he used this same image to sum up his various stays in Japan during work on the Imperial: "this romance of one thousand and nine days and nights in Tokio—once upon a time Yedo."[25]

Wright seems to have used "Yedo" as the title for his second Japanese reverie because, as his conception of the new work in Tokyo grew, it enhanced his historicist longing for a golden age: "Yedo was a presence always in which to search for the invaluable record of that time, in the print...."[26] "Yedo" is an evocation of the Tokugawa city *par excellence*, in which Wright allows realistic impressions to cut across and merge with scenes and figures known, even in his time, only from prints. Together with "A Song to Heaven," it adds a fresh episode, or chapter, to Taine's ethno-analysis of the relationship between diverse cultural formations and the finished work of art.

Tokyo is seen by Wright in its still ancient, yet rapidly disappearing, manifestations as a setting for his Imperial Hotel, that masterpiece and crowning ornament of a latter-day present: "Teeming, enormous area is fascinating Yedo. A vast city channeled with wide bare-earth streets swarming with humanity their interminable length...."[27] And further on: "Mystery is everywhere. Maintained—as privacy? ... notwithstanding tremendous activity, brooding quiet is over all as though some enchantment had purposely wrought unnatural scenes."[28] After a general description,

4.12. Wright: Imperial Hotel, Hibiya, Tokyo, 1913–23. Pair of views detailing circulation.

4.13. Late nineteenth-century view of women awaiting clients in a brothel, Yoshiwara, Tokyo.

Wright moves on to Yoshiwara: "Ahead of us looms a great black gate. Directly in front of the gateway a great cherry tree is in bloom . . . innumerable red and white lanterns." Here, explains Wright, "is the ceremonial glorification of something we of the West never understood. . . . Here it appears a woman [is] raised to nth power as a symbol among men. . . . Woman aggrandized, institutionalized. Demoralized? No. Only *professionalized*. . . . Here a compelling power is made artistic and deliberately cultured."[29] The view Wright derived was Aesthetic: "As the prints show it to us we see that love of life and beauty was a poetic theme running like a thread of fine silk through all that Yoshiwara life of the Edo courtesan."[30]

It is not difficult to guess, even though Wright's description is riddled with images of the *ukiyo-e*, that he must indeed have known the institution of the prostitutes' quarter (fig. 4.13) at first hand. This may have been Yoshiwara as it survived in 1905 with its main gate of wrought iron, dedicated early in 1881 (to which he appears to refer above). Possibly it was in 1913, two years after the great fire of 1911 that virtually destroyed the place. Some two hundred brothels and teahouses disappeared. Only the former were rebuilt, a fact which meant that the old high culture and the refinement, one aspect of the fame of the district, were gone forever.

Wright was aware of the vocation of the rebuilt Imperial as what he himself termed a "social clearing house"[31] (fig. 4.14) and must have conceived of the building in one sense as a microcosm of sorts. To this end he seemed virtually to endow it with a metaphorical sense of that city, Tokyo-Yedo, which made its immediate surroundings and had furnished Wright's own Japanese experiences, both in reality and art. In rhetorical terms, the hotel operated in some measure as a synecdoche, standing for the city and its mysterious, captivating street life, which it purified and rendered up as art. Especially coming as it did after Midway Gardens, a dining and entertainment mecca with cultural aspirations, the Im-

4.14. Tea on the Imperial Hotel's terrace, probably late 1930s; and dinner about to be served in the banqueting hall.

4.15. Wright: Imperial Hotel (1913–23). Lobby and *porte cochère* reconstructed at Meijimura, Inuyama, Aichi Prefecture. *Oya*-stone detail has been recarved.

perial could easily have been identified in Wright's mind with the fabled, but now defunct, pleasure quarters of Edo. That, at least, may have helped to situate an opulent and labyrinthine cast of feature that made this steamship-set oasis of diversion and repose comparable, in all but the essential, with the vanished splendor of Yoshiwara before the fire.

One person who might have had little patience with this explanation, or could have endorsed it in a negative sense, was Wright's assistant, the Czech-American Antonin Raymond. Raymond, with his wife, Noémi, a diminutive Frenchwoman—notable artist and, later, interior decorator in her own right—had several years before spent about a year working for Wright at Taliesin. In New York, after spending World War I in Europe, Raymond had just set himself up in practice when he was co-opted by Wright, construction of the hotel being about to get under way in earnest. With Wright and Miriam Noel, the Raymonds sailed for Japan, arriving at Yokohama on New Year's Eve of 1919. Admiring Wright as deeply as they did, the Raymonds nonetheless were European-born and some twenty years younger; in addition they were allowed a greater freedom to participate in day-to-day Japanese life than Wright could enjoy. At last, they grew to resent Wright's treatment of the Japanese personnel as well as of his companion.

Raymond eventually became bored with work on the Imperial, at which he remained approximately one year as Wright's chief assistant. The immediate trouble lay in the repetition of what Wright called "grammar" (fig. 4.15) but which Raymond came to regard as "mannerisms" that were "devoid of content, particularly in Japan."[32] When Raymond found himself no longer able to continue in his role, he incurred Wright's bitterness but did not sacrifice his friendship altogether. In severing his connection with the Imperial, Raymond stayed on in Japan to become one of the few foreign architects to conduct a lifetime of practice in the country.

Raymond retained his respect for Wright, but his ultimate verdict on the Imperial Hotel was decisive. It is of more than just historical interest to record that, for him, "the design had nothing in common with Japan, its climate, its traditions, its people and its culture. I do not believe that this ever occurred to Wright, whose thoughts were entirely concentrated on the expression of his own personal imaginings. The hotel finally turned out to be a monument to himself."[33] There is a sense in which such a conclusion was inevitable and just, and we must now investigate alternate possibilities.

5 | Tokyo and the Beginnings of "Modernism"

ANTITHESIS

In ancient Rome,[1] philosophy, not religion, trafficked in metaphysics and virtue, whereas from the time of the Renaissance an onward flow of ideas mired Western architecture in ethical considerations. Even though Japanese architecture is frequently governed by ritual, such prerequisites recall the old Roman religion and do not necessarily entail a behavioral ethic. Antonin Raymond detected this disparity within a year of his arrival in Tokyo; Wright, on the other hand, could never countenance it, and did not wish to. With hindsight, reflecting on the Imperial Hotel episode, Raymond half a century later wrote: "I could not help but form the definite opinion that Wright's motivation for the design [of the hotel] was minor as compared to the [everyday] motivation behind the design of Japanese artists." By way of precision, he adds, "It was a liberation to realize that motivation behind a creative effort in the form of novelty, astonishment, the assertion of one's own personality or the desire to create things which nobody has ever done, was a minor and mean motivation." Then Raymond, at the brink of a lifetime of experience in Japan, elucidates his own position: "I began to realize that there perhaps exists such a thing as an absolute, in philosophy and in life's artistic expression; that the Japanese and other Oriental people through the centuries had pursued the idea of acquiring a knowledge of the Universal in Philosophy and therefore in the arts."[2] Thus he came to feel the "existence of an agelong philosophy of life" which provided "the basis or the starting point of the design of every single component of Japanese expression...."[3] This, Raymond concluded, differed fundamentally from Western ideals.

Wright himself had been aware of a similarly far-reaching difference, as his discussion of Yoshiwara shows. He was, above all, attracted to the ritual and amoral aspects of the "floating world," as the realm of entertainment and sex—the world of prints—was referred to. The whole issue seems colored by an obsessional fervor and once more called forth a classical allusion: "The 'moral' element that could make it bestial was lacking. As it was with the Philosopher and the Hetaira in Athens itself, so probably here in Yedo...."[4] And, here, Wright returns to the point that it was all an "esthetic rite." Yet again we discover the print—"a window through which I looked upon my own work. A byroad by which I saw it"[5]—as the vehicle of, but also this time (by means of an effect of framing and, in turn, distancing), a hindrance to, Wright's understanding.

Even Raymond (though not wedded to the notion of "reform," or committed to architectural truth, with the same strength as Wright) was unable, finally, to resist the occasional temptation to arrange or improve upon the Japanese aesthetic. But no longer was Japan to be a "means to an end," either for him or for his wife. Still, Raymond—in addition to his experiences in New York and in Western Europe, and leaving aside his early art training in Prague—was influenced deeply by Wright. Raymond's attitude and intentions may be summed up by what Wright wrote, later, in 1937, concerning the Imperial Hotel: "I wanted to help the Japanese get to their feet indoors and learn to live in fireproof masonry buildings, without loss of their native aesthetic prestige where the art of architecture was a factor."[6]

TOKYO IN THE FIRST QUARTER
OF THE TWENTIETH CENTURY

Early architectural "modernism" in Japan is poorly recorded, since, at first, it was not a particularly self-conscious movement at all. In terms of production and the economy, the Japanese during this period were indeed, to use Wright's expression, "getting to their feet." The age of Taisho (1912–26) includes all the time Wright spent in Japan, except for his earliest visit. Tokyo during that period experienced a volatile and unstable phase of development, climaxed by the earthquake of 1923. In contrast with our perhaps rather too orderly concept of Western "modernism" and its now neatly documented cultural achievements before and after World War I, the Japanese reflection of these events is more fragmented.

Japan's engagement in the European war was nominal and, as such, provided culture with no particular impetus. But the overall shock produced by the introduction of Westernizing processes, attitudes, and material artifacts continued apace, while Japan, as a whole, now became involved for the first time in the birth of full-scale urban mass industrial society. Just as previous urban improvements had proved more functional than beautifying, the ensuing phase of Tokyo's growth was forced to confront mainly practicalities, and that within a few short years. Major considerations were to be the extension of infrastructures (above all, transport) to outlying districts and the provision of housing, mostly without other amenities. A city planning section was set up in 1918 within the Ministry of Home Affairs, which itself had been instrumental in overcoming the earlier "showcase" approach to planning advocated by officials of the Foreign Ministry in the mid-Meiji period. The following year a City Planning Act became law, succeeding the old ordinance of 1888. This new planning tool applied specifically to the six principal ports and industrial cities of central Japan: namely, Tokyo, Yokohama, Nagoya, Kyoto, Osaka, and Kobe. In the case of Tokyo, the population had reached a full two million inhabitants, with an additional million distributed in the five counties peripheral to the capital.

Gradually, from the mid-1880s, various pieces of a new Tokyo railway system had been placed in service, including a circular line situated at an appreciable distance from the center and elevated over most of its course. Finally, in 1911, the municipality took over a 190-kilometer streetcar network after eight years of private operation; half a million passengers were by this time being carried daily. The combined rail and tramline capacity was augmented by an additional main trunk line running due west from the city, as it still does today—the Chuo Line—which became the capital's first relatively "long-distance" commuter facility. In obvious contrast with the better residential districts centered on the old, and now increasingly subdivided, estates along the circular, or Yamanote, line, this new railway served areas in which raw agricultural land was beginning to give way to small and hastily built homes for rent to salaried workers. Although the Taisho era promised rapid capital and industrial growth, houses averaged only about forty square meters per family. In the recently developed areas, streets were unpaved, water and electricity unavailable on any organized basis, and sewage disposal primitive.

Rapid growth on this pattern, especially in the six principal centers mentioned, which today constitute Japan's three major conurbations (Tokyo-Yokohama; Nagoya; and Osaka-Kobe, with Kyoto at a short distance), set a precedent for the infamous "rabbit hutch" dwellings of the late twentieth century. Development of planning strategies could scarcely have been, and evidently never was, a main concern amid Taisho political and economic perspectives. Parliamentary democracy and internationalist orientation were achieved during the Meiji period, but now a thriving urbanizing culture immersed in *modanizumu* (modernism) failed during the twenties to achieve the economic expectations of the previous decade. Thus, while manufacturing output was good, overall growth was only moderate during this period, owing chiefly to an inappropriate fiscal policy and stagnating agriculture. In comparison with successes achieved for the same period by German administrators, or even under the weak British Town Planning Act (1909) with its numerous defects, Japanese planning policy suggests that the Ministry of Home Affairs was still obsessed with basic rural improvement. This, however, had become a losing battle, while the equally critical field of urban planning, where a fresh start might have been made, was allowed to proceed as a mere exercise in public-works administration.

In Japanese cities, planning representation at a local level was still being effectively denied. The same had been true of London throughout most of the nineteenth century, although Birmingham offers a contrasting example. London's main excuse for lack of a democratic process had lain in the extreme fragmentation of the metropolis itself. By contrast, in Tokyo, despite the inclusion of formerly separate communities, lack of administrative coordination was never a reason for autocratic methods; rather, such policy evolved by choice on the part of the central government. Nevertheless, on the favorable side, the City Planning Act of 1919 did incorporate numerous current ideas, such as zoning, building-line control, and land consolidation. The number of cities the act applied to rose in 1923 from six to thirty-one, a figure which trebled by the end of the decade. Yet, because the twenties in Japan were an era of social upheaval and widespread public protest, the authorities proceeded with considerable discretion in individual applications. Thus, the Tokyo Metropolitan Government, which set an example throughout Japan during the period preceding World War II as well as after, matched its authoritarian stance with technocratic standards of a conservative cast. Its orientation in favor of road improvement and public works was validated, during the reconstruction of Tokyo after the Great Kanto Earthquake of 1923, with this policy surviving more or less unchanged to the present day.

NOTIONS BEARING ON STYLE

Through Taisho and into the early 1930s, two aspects of national life seem to have persisted despite profound changes of direction in economic and political currents. One of these was the growth of applied technology, which Japan shared with the Western world. The other was a noticeable resurgence of popular urban culture, a field in which Japan was able to lay claim to a considerable wealth of precedent. Far more than in the West, here was the *continuation* of a historic mass phenomenon. To all intents and purposes Japan's prototypical urban mass culture had peaked, as Wright must have been aware, during the Tokugawa period, to which the

5.1. Nakamura: Tokyo-Taisho Exhibition, Ueno, Tokyo, 1914. View of the grounds, and main gate.

ukiyo-e belong. In the West, the Modern Movement seems to reecho this phenomenal cultural liveliness of the world's largest city, Edo. Its style was what Wright called "elimination of the insignificant."

Yet, after Meiji, the culture of Taisho and early Showa (the present reign, from 1926) tended toward trivialization in its material artifacts, even if less tangible components were surely deeply felt, in conjunction with the very real social changes of the modern era. Architecture, in particular, suffered greater indignities than in the Meiji period. The moment had come—after that of the alienation of carpenters by architects—when, in a kind of technological backlash, engineers now expected architects to compromise their newfound identity. As is well known, or should be, the Modern Movement in the West is also about this usurpation of architecture by technology. Yet, in spite of today's rehabilitation of the *moderne* and other banalities, early twentieth-century architecture possessed adepts who were able to stage-manage the marriage of art and technology. Japan, at that stage, did not, although skillful personnel were in the process of formation. As regards the emergence of the so-called International Style, we shall be able to discuss them in the following chapter dealing with the 1930s—a development which ranks second only to growth of the modern cinema in Japan but is less familiar.

For the moment, we must content ourselves with a cursory examination of Japanese architectural culture in the guise of a native expressionism, and one early residential design by Antonin Raymond.

CONFLICT BETWEEN STRUCTURE AND EXPRESSION

It is hard to tell with precision when modern architecture entered the Japanese field of view, but, in 1913, Japan's oldest architectural publication, which was entitled simply *Kenchiku-zasshi* (Architecture Magazine), began to publish illustrated articles dealing with contemporary Western architecture. Then, at Ueno the next year, buildings of the Tokyo-Taisho

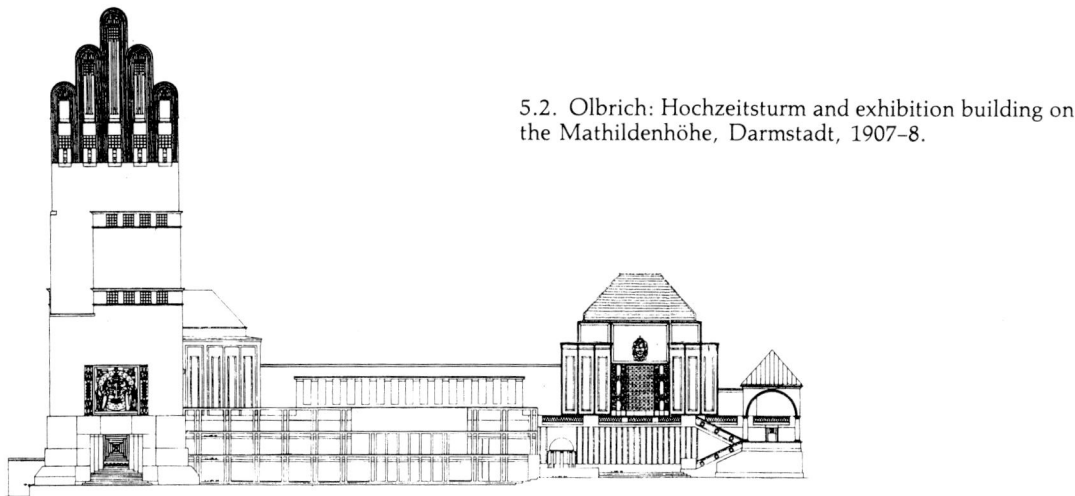

5.2. Olbrich: Hochzeitsturm and exhibition building on the Mathildenhöhe, Darmstadt, 1907–8.

5.3. Nakamura: Josui Kaikan, Kanda, Tokyo, 1918. Rear terrace.

Exhibition (fig. 5.1) erected by the recently founded Sone-Chujo partnership marked the coronation of the new emperor and can be sensed as proclaiming a new stylistic influence. The firm's architect for the exhibition, one Jumpei Nakamura, was perhaps the first to display an awareness of the so-called Secession style of about 1900, which by now had migrated from imperial Vienna throughout central Europe and Germany. In the Secessionist manner are aspects of Art Nouveau, elements of expressionism, and at the same time the breath of a revived classicism. The most relevant European comparison to the temporary Tokyo-Taisho Exhibition buildings is the Mathildenhöhe artists' colony near Darmstadt with its central Hochzeitsturm (fig. 5.2) and exhibition halls of 1907–8 by the Viennese Joseph Maria Olbrich, who died in the year of their completion. In Japan an actual imitation of Olbrich's peculiarly shaped tower was not to appear for another eight years, in the year 1922, with the centerpiece of the Commemorative Peace Exhibition (see fig. 5.7) held also at Ueno Park. Meanwhile, the echoes of Secessionism in the buildings of the 1914 coronation exhibition were sufficiently radical to influence the design of places of amusement as well as kimono patterns and the forms of other everyday goods in the Japanese capital. The new manner stood in obvious contrast with the baroque conventions of the Akasaka Detached Palace, the new emperor's intended residence, as it had in Austria.

The Tokyo-Taisho Exhibition was a mere ephemeral display in the history of Japanese public building. A more lasting example of the Secession's influence was Nakamura's Josui Kaikan (fig. 5.3), which until a few years ago stood in the Kanda district of Tokyo. It was an alumni club for one of the more prestigious universities, and although each room was decorated in a different style, the rear terrace and elevated pergola show how well, by 1918 (when the building was constructed), Continental themes could be assimilated. Even before this date, in Europe, former Secessionist architects no longer

5.4. Sano: Maruzen Book Store, Nihonbashi, Tokyo, 1909.

5.5. Sano: Seitoku Memorial Gallery, Aoyama, Tokyo, 1926.

limited the style and its mannerisms to their original aim of breaking with the style and purposes of official art. In Germany, most noticeably, the stylish mode of applied ornament was increasingly employed in a modified form for industrial and even government buildings. Peter Behrens was the clearest case of an artist and architect who had militated against the establishment briefly but, shortly afterward, reaped the benefits of its sponsorship. This early sowing of wild oats became a confirmed pattern in the Japanese educational and employment system, so that Behrens's association with the giant AEG electrical combine merited scrutiny by Japan's academic civil servants. With the advent of World War I the Secession style disappeared in the German-speaking countries. Jumpei Nakamura had perhaps no choice but to enroll at the Ecole des Beaux-Arts in 1920. In four years he emerged as an architect licensed by the French government.

In 1915 the architectural section of Tokyo Imperial University decided to separate its departments of design and structure, with Kyoto instituting the same split five years later. It has been observed that the market for architectural work had not yet developed and matured sufficiently to warrant such specialization. However that may be, a silently enforced structural bias emerged and has remained in effect ever since in Japanese architectural education.

The year 1915 also saw the publication by Toshihiko Noda (1891–1929), at only twenty-four years of age, of a paper entitled "Architecture is not Art" in *Kenchiku-zasshi*. The controversial theme Noda propounded, which reflects the structure-versus-design argument, was based on his undergraduate dissertation at the Imperial University. He called his graduation paper "Reinforced Concrete and Building Style," and the views it expressed must have been influenced by Noda's professor, Riki Sano. Sano may represent both Behrens's expanding conservatism regarding styles as well as the same architect's pioneering "neorationalism." Sano eventually succeeded Kingo Tatsuno in the chair of architecture

5.6. Bunri Ha Kenchiku Kai, active 1920–28: four projects.

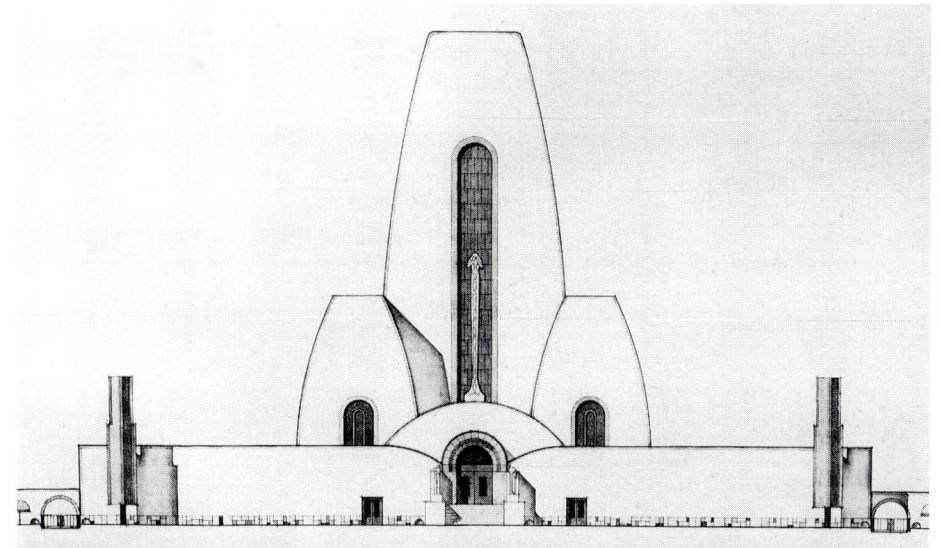

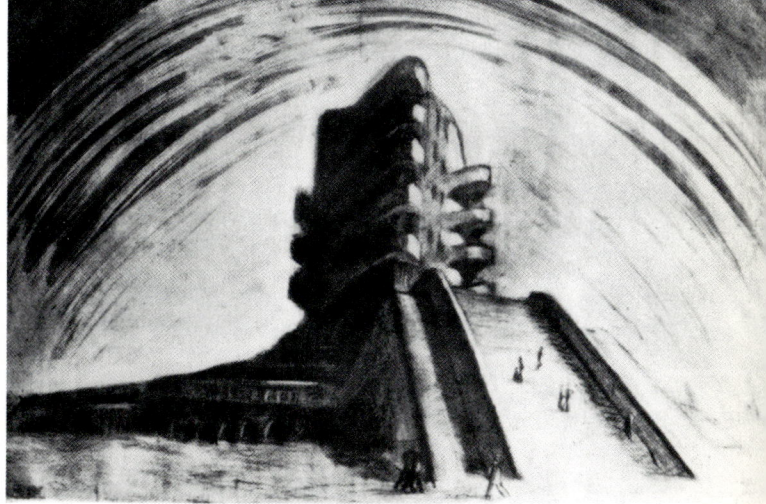

at the Imperial University. He had studied in Germany in 1911, and in 1916 published a book entitled *The Theory of Anti-Earthquake Structures*. He is best remembered today as the architect of Japan's first true steel-frame building, the three-story-and-attic Maruzen book store of 1909 at Nihonbashi in Tokyo. The Maruzen building (fig. 5.4), since destroyed, had curtain walls of brick and was in terms of style a late rendition of Queen Anne, with large expanses of window and a surface that was too taut not to be suggestive of what was behind. In spite of its "honest" construction, Sano's detailing remained elaborate even in its restraint, and there are some hints of influence by Hennebique, the early French expert on concrete.

A later work by Riki Sano (sometimes referred to as Toshikata instead of Riki) was the Seitoku Memorial Gallery of 1926, which still stands in Tokyo's parklike Meiji Shrine Garden in Aoyama. An interesting deployment of economy and decorum, the gallery (fig. 5.5) is in a sense devoid of nationality. Nevertheless, it distinguishes one particular strain of Japanese architecture, definable from that time to this. What is more, despite its stripped Romanesque or Byzantine classicism, the Seitoku Memorial Gallery internalized—inadvertently or not—some of the characteristics of the opposed Bunri Ha Kenchiku Kai (Secessionist Architectural Society), whose works we shall now examine briefly.

Five years after the publication of Noda's offending doctrine, the anti-aesthetic atmosphere it summed up brought forth a reaction. This was the romantically conceived Bunri Ha Kenchiku Kai, established in 1920. The Bunri Ha lasted until 1928 and held a total of seven exhibitions (fig. 5.6) at various Tokyo department stores (not an uncommon choice of venue). The organization came to be thought of as representing a kind of neo-Secessionism, but its real inspiration was the "expressionism" that, in the immediate post–World War I years, was for a brief time the most dynamic force in German architectural life. The Bunri Ha consisted of only six

5.7. Horiguchi: Memorial Tower, Peace Exhibition, Ueno, Tokyo, 1922.

members, one of whom was the first Japanese translator of Vitruvius. Three others were to achieve architectural notoriety and, eventually, fame.

These three expressionist activists were Kikuji Ishimoto, Sutemi Horiguchi, and Mamoru Yamada. Ishimoto studied briefly with Walter Gropius in 1922, at the end of that architect's, later on greatly downplayed, expressionistic phase. Horiguchi, among his early achievements, constructed the temporary Memorial Tower (fig. 5.7) at the Peace Exhibition in 1922, which has already been referred to in connection with Olbrich. Yamada was to have one of his later, postexpressionistic works included in the International Style exhibition[7] at the Museum of Modern Art in New York in 1932, the only Japanese candidate in this official baptism of the "modern" style.

The Asahi Newspaper Offices (figs. 5.8–10), which once stood at the busy and famous Sukiyabashi crossing near Ginza in Tokyo, was the best-known work from Ishimoto's office and the longest-surviving major building in the Japanese Secessionist style. This structure dramatically enhanced its site near the reconstructed Sukiyabashi Bridge, recalling the past of downtown Tokyo as a city on the water. Unfortunately, this waterway has now disappeared, making it hard to visualize the languidly futuristic superimposition of the double-arched stone bridge's roadway over the water traffic. Ishimoto's building, which dated from 1927, is bound to have benefited from the lessons of the 1923 earthquake, and was, therefore, as ponderous as any ten-story structure might be. It adopted the plan of its irregularly shaped site, while its mass was enlivened by exaggerated stringcourses, cantilevered balconies, and a tower bearing a radio mast. Fenestration, likewise, served expressive requirements. Since a number of the windows were of "beehive" profile, the appearance of the Asahi Offices was reminiscent of the early works of Mendelsohn in Germany as well as the still earlier Amsterdam School of protoexpressionism.

The importance of the Japanese Secession lay mainly in its iconoclastic newness and opposition to all prevailing tendencies. But in contrast with the northern European, largely German parent movement, conceived at a time when most actual building had ground to a halt, Bunri Ha's insistence on separation from structural preoccupations provided a salient theme and rallying point. Hence the claim that Japanese expressionism arose in opposition to Noda's declaration that "Architecture is not Art," for there is little suggestion within Bunri Ha of any reaction either to the recent war in Europe or to economic or social conditions. The ultimate contribution of the movement was to have prepared the terrain for arrival of the International Style as a new language, one that was neither specifically Westernizing nor dominated by technology in other than a symbolic sense. However, the designs—mainly plaster models and a few sketches—displayed by Bunri Ha in its yearly shows were largely formal exercises that reveal little about the movement's goals.

EXPRESSIONIST TRENDS IN PUBLIC BUILDING

By the 1930s Mamoru Yamada and Sutemi Horiguchi had become well-known as residential architects. Ishimoto's chief designer, Bunzo Yamaguchi, who studied under Gropius between 1930 and 1932, was another expressionist offshoot bound to become, as we shall see later, one of Japan's foremost International School practitioners, if not quite, like Horiguchi, a theorist in his own right. Meanwhile, because Japan was still engaged in building up her network of infrastructures, the number of reasonably large works by modernist architects in Tokyo and other cities was fairly remarkable even though housing, for the time being, was left to job carpenters and developed no particular style.

At the second Bunri Ha exhibition, held in 1921, Mamoru Yamada exhibited a project, unique by any standards, for a Central Telegraph Office (fig. 5.11). Although long ago demolished, this was actually built in 1925 across from Tatsuno's Tokyo Station, with which it certainly contrasted oddly. As in the Asahi Newspaper Offices, soon to be completed half a kilometer south, there was a tower with a communications mast. The rest of the building consisted of a narrow five-story frontal range surmounted by a barrel vault and secured by blade-shaped buttressing piers that alternated with double-window bays terminating in elongated parabolic cross-vaults. One entered by ascending a flight of steep steps beneath a cantilevered porch to one side of the structure. Above this entry a window soared to the full height of the roof, ending in a stepped arch inscribed within the vault, over which rose the telegraph mast. The work space of this new communications facility necessitated a rear wing perpendicular to the first. Its special features were a massive cavetto cornice and a second parabolic cross-vaulted tower next to the stack rising from the heating plant.

Obviously, a lack of conventional skills in delineation and massing bedeviled the composition of a building like the Central Telegraph Office, but it is hard to judge the real extent to which this was a problem. One complicating factor, es-

5.8. Ishimoto: Asahi Newspaper Offices, Sukiyabashi, Tokyo, 1927. Main facade.

5.9. Ishimoto: Asahi Newspaper Offices, Sukiyabashi, Tokyo, 1927. Rear facade.

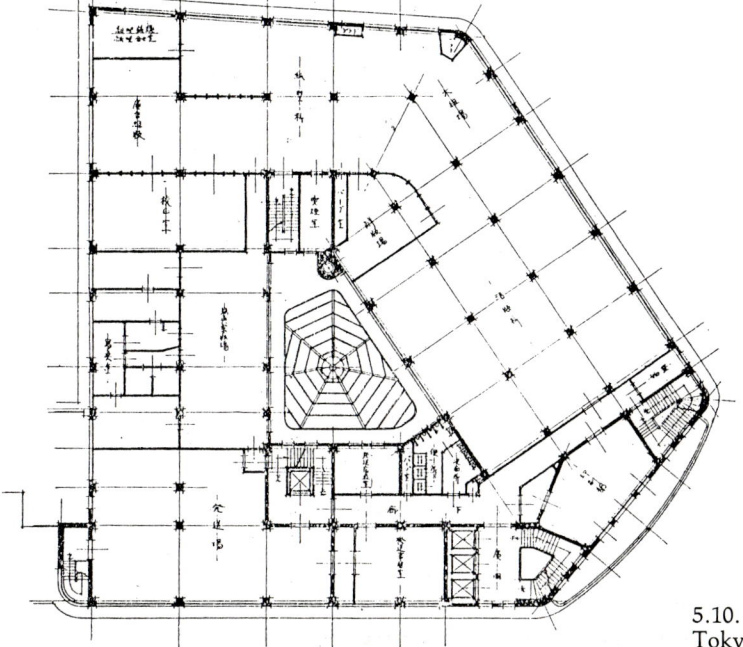

5.10. Ishimoto: Asahi Newspaper Offices, Sukiyabashi, Tokyo, 1927. Plan of the second floor.

5.11. Yamada: Central Telegraph Office, Tokyo, 1925. Inset shows roof terrace.

5.12. Kamahara: Kosuge Prison, Kosuge, Tokyo, 1929–30.

5.13. Horiguchi: Oshima Weather Station, Oshima Island, Shizuoka Prefecture, 1938. Tower.

5.14. Horiguchi: Oshima Weather Station, Oshima Island, Shizuoka Prefecture, 1938. Plan.

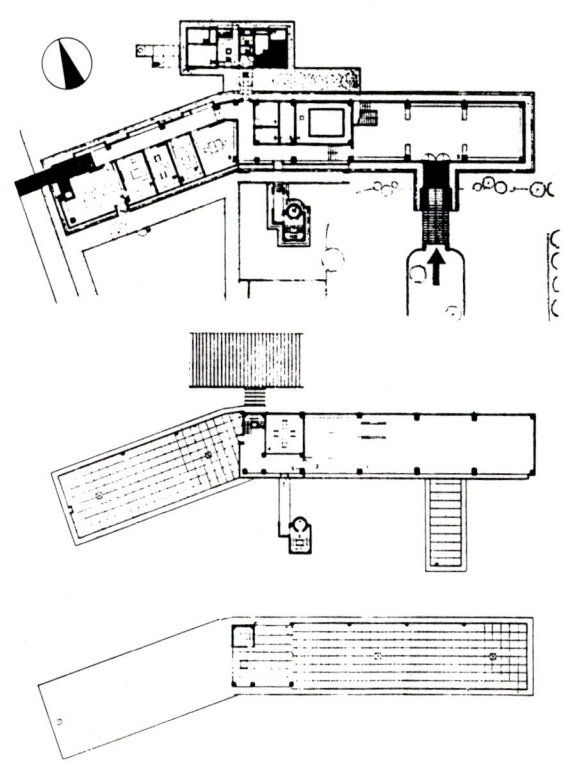

pecially in Tokyo, was that sites tended to be more awkward, and structural requirements more stringent, than in Europe. Moreover, one-time European expressionists, such as Hans Poelzig, had now turned to work in a more rational idiom. For instance, in Poelzig's radio headquarters (the Haus des Rundfunks) in Berlin-Charlottenburg (1929–31)—comparable in size and purpose to Yamada's telegraph office—only the lancet-shaped ground plan remains as a token of Poelzig's pioneering expressionist tendencies.

In Japan, a still later building than Yamada's is the redoubtable Kosuge Prison (1929–30), designed for the Ministry of Justice by Shigeo Kamahara and located in Tokyo (fig. 5.12). It retains all the excitement of the expressionism of a decade earlier in Germany (or nearly two, should we look back to Poelzig's earliest works). A more orthodox blending of expressionism with the International Style is achieved in Horiguchi's Weather Station of 1938, which has been in the news of late owing to its site, the still active volcanic island of Oshima, southwest of Tokyo (figs. 5.13–14). In these two works, both of which are signaled by useful towers, a certain functional adaptation of the Bunri Ha outlook bore fruitful results. Here, too, a working relationship between structure and expression accommodated reinforced concrete construction to a degree that would make some of the intervening work of the International Style look shoddily unsubstantial in comparison.

5.15. Uchida: Yasuda Hall, Imperial University, Hongo, Tokyo, 1925. Main front.

5.16. Uchida: Yasuda Hall, Imperial University, Hongo, Tokyo, 1925. Auditorium ceiling and plan (facing page).

But before leaving the subject of the influence exerted by the Japanese Secession, let us return for a moment to its heyday at the end of the Taisho period. One building still with us—though, unlike the prison tower and the weather station, unused at present (but earlier than either)—recalls the expressionism of North Germany and of architects working mostly in Hamburg, such as Fritz Höger. It marks the center of the former Imperial University, which a little later on was to have its entire campus unified by transformation into an expressionistically tinged collegiate Gothic. Shozo Uchida's university auditorium of 1925 (Yasuda Hall; figs. 5.15–16) can now be seen as the flagship of this metamorphosis. It is a symmetrical reinforced-concrete structure with a cladding of maroon tiles and must have been, at the end of the Taisho era, one of the Japanese capital's most up-to-date buildings designed by a Japanese architect. Apart from the North German expressionism already mentioned, it recalls aspects of work by Paul Bonatz or the ecclesiastical architect Dominikus Böhm of the same period. The concave "Egyptian" cornice echoes that of Yamada's telegraph office, but it is, above all, the dark hue of Uchida's lecture hall and the studied application of one style, not yet known as streamlined Gothic, which distinguishes Yasuda Hall and sets it apart.

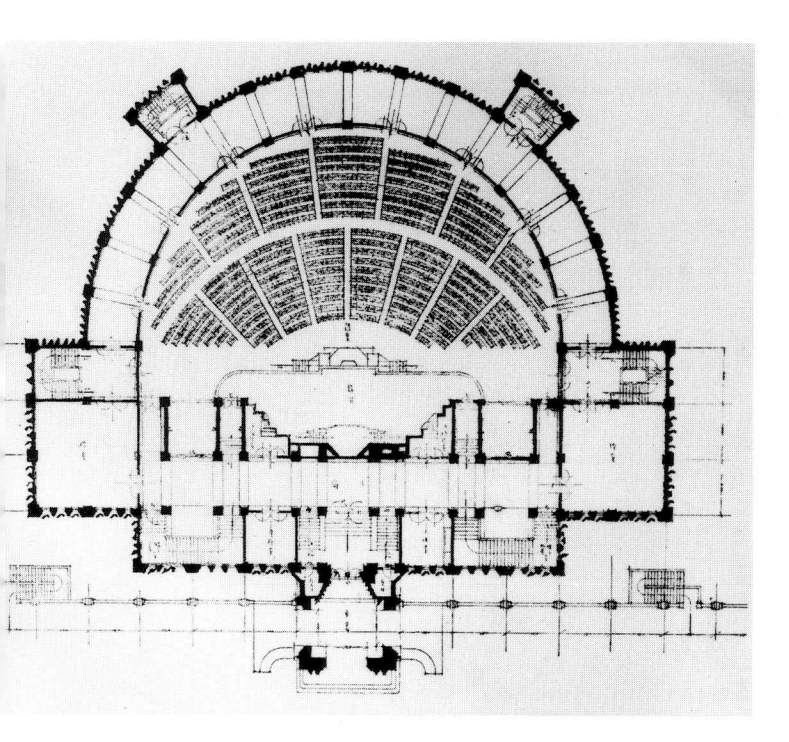

AN EARLY MODERN RESIDENCE

So far the Modern Movement, in such form as it reached Japan by the mid-1920s, had produced nothing in the way of small up-to-date town residences. On the eve of the Great Kanto Earthquake, Antonin Raymond, self-employed now for more than two years, set about to remedy this situation. Here is his account:

> At that time there was little modern architecture in Europe and hardly any in the United States. The Reinanzaka House [figs. 5.17–21] was a monolithic, earthquake-proof structure in architectural reinforced concrete, without any cement mortar or any other finish, perhaps the first in this respect anywhere. . . . It included all the adjuncts of our modern planning. The only ornament in the building was the structure itself, revealing the columns and the beams and in every way expressing the ideas which finally prevailed in contemporary design philosophy.

But Raymond explains in the following paragraph that the concrete shell of the house was not its only important feature:

> We [husband and wife] designed the furniture, the textiles, electrical fixtures, the garden, the mechanical equipment—simply everything. We succeeded in making it possible for Japanese workers and artisans to handle these modern materials. At that time very few architects and designers had any knowledge of them.[8]

The Raymond House dates from 1923–24 and was nearly complete, though not occupied, at the time of the Great Kanto Earthquake. It was located in central Tokyo, but not "downtown," so there was no particular problem about subfoundations, as there had been in constructing the Imperial Hotel. In fact, the Raymond residence was situated on a slope near the inner edge of the Yamanote district, and Raymond's reference to a "Reinanzaka House" names the place. Incidentally, the house still stands today but has been modified almost to the point of unrecognizability.

From Europe Raymond was familiar with the styles of expressionism and Cubism in painting, although he probably knew little of expressionism in architecture at first hand. However, he must certainly have been aware of the direction being given to architecture and the arts in the aftermath of the Russian and German revolutions, and, indeed, as influenced in general by World War I. These movements are

5.17. Raymond: Reinanzaka House, Azabu, Tokyo, 1923–24.
Front and rear views.

TOKYO AND "MODERNISM" 103

5.18. Raymond: Reinanzaka House, Azabu, Tokyo, 1923-24. Living room.

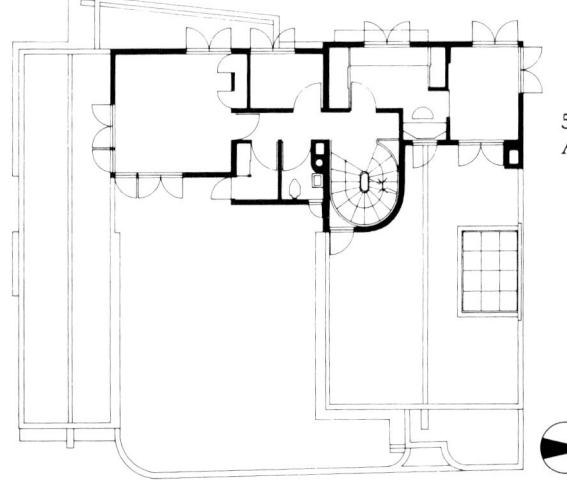

5.19. Raymond: Reinanzaka House, Azabu, Tokyo, 1923-24. Plans.

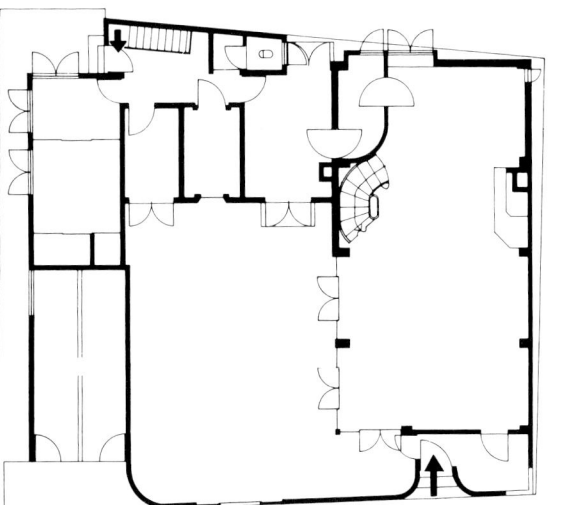

frequently lumped under terms like Constructivism or New Objectivity, although tendencies whose expression was purely painterly, such as Cubism or Surrealism, also remained important. Gropius's Bauhaus art school at Weimar furnished one point of convergence for many of these influences, and the first "Bauhaus Book" published after the institution had moved to Dessau was *Internationale Architektur* (1925) by Walter Gropius himself. It included buildings by Behrens, Poelzig, and also by Gropius, besides numerous works and projects by other German, as well as Dutch, architects. We are shown the visionary Robie House (1909) in Chicago by Frank Lloyd Wright and the so-called Villa at Vaucresson (1923) by Le Corbusier, but also the atelier for the painter Ozenfant designed by Le Corbusier at about the same time, which combines a town house with an artist's studio in Paris.

How many of these almost one hundred examples Raymond might have known either at first hand, as he certainly knew the Robie House (see fig. 10.2), or from the architectural press, is uncertain. At any rate, the new Reinanzaka House, with its stark rectilinear silhouette and rejection of all ornament, is spiritually part of this "international modern" idiom—or

5.20. Raymond: Reinanzaka House, Azabu, Tokyo, 1923–24. Early model.

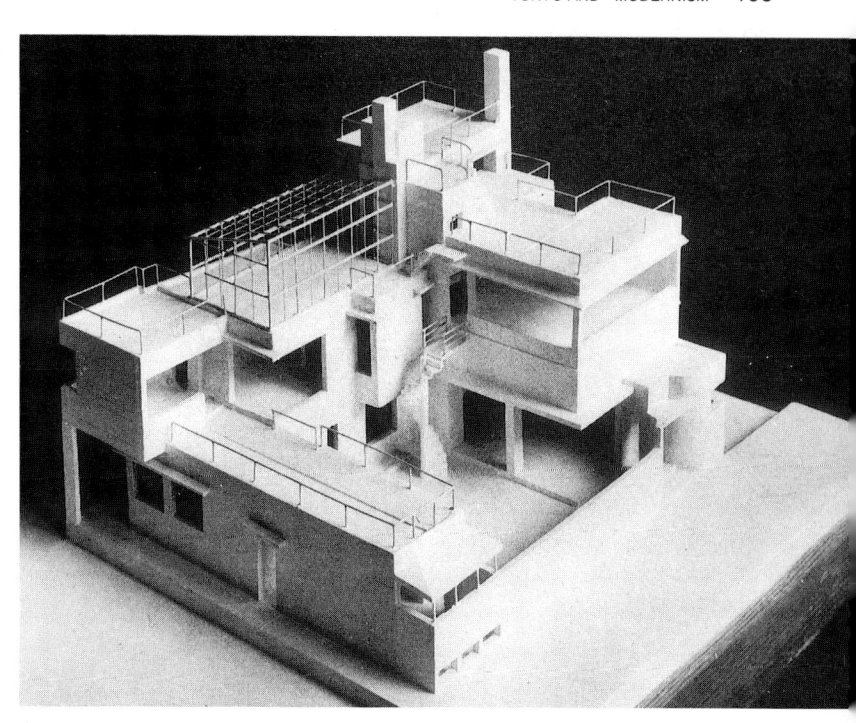

5.21. Raymond: Reinanzaka House, Azabu, Tokyo, 1923–24. Later model.

rogues' gallery of contemporary design—even though evidently not known by Gropius. Like most of the other examples, it united the visual appeal of modern "abstract" art (or *Japanese* art for Wright) with a rationalized system of construction based on industrially available materials. (The account of the Imperial Hotel which best illuminates this attitude was written by its structural engineer, Julius Floto.[9]) For Raymond, Wright's experience in Japan with concrete was certainly germane—but, on the whole, Raymond calls Reinanzaka "a real departure and liberation from Frank Lloyd Wright and his mannerisms."[10]

In combination with this pragmatic approach to style, we find Raymond exploiting the radically simplified method of internal planning inherent to most boxlike, early modern architecture. Wright's incredible facility with his own version of Beaux-Arts–type planning opposed itself to such strategy. Yet in G. T. Rietveld's iconic Schroeder House of 1924, at Utrecht, Holland, it nonetheless proved possible to finesse a compromise between an essentially cubical exterior form and the much vaunted openness of the classical Wrightian Prairie House design. This was in the same year as Reinanzaka, but the Schroeder House, admittedly, was engineered out of wood and plastered brick plus the clever external use of steel I-beams, and not the more restrictive monolithic concrete envelope Raymond essayed.

Wright had quickly perceived the inherent rationality of the Japanese dwelling as an expression of lifestyle, while all the time regarding the way of living such a house entailed to be impossibly austere. Raymond was less easily convinced that such a lifestyle was unattainable, and in fact an earlier house he had put up on the Reinanzaka site was conceived as virtually Japanese. The Raymonds lived in it, just as the German architect Bruno Taut and his wife were to occupy a traditional-style farmhouse a few years later. Afterward this temporary Reinanzaka home was moved to Hayama on the coast, where it served as a vacation dwelling.

Raymond succeeded less well in conveying the charm of the Japanese dwelling when he came to design the second, or permanent, version of his Tokyo residence. In spite of the fact that the design was changed at least twice (on the evidence of photographs of the models; figs. 5.20–21), the garden remained at the core of the scheme. But it appears that the

5.22. Raymond: Rachel Reid House, Azabu, Tokyo, 1924. Facade.

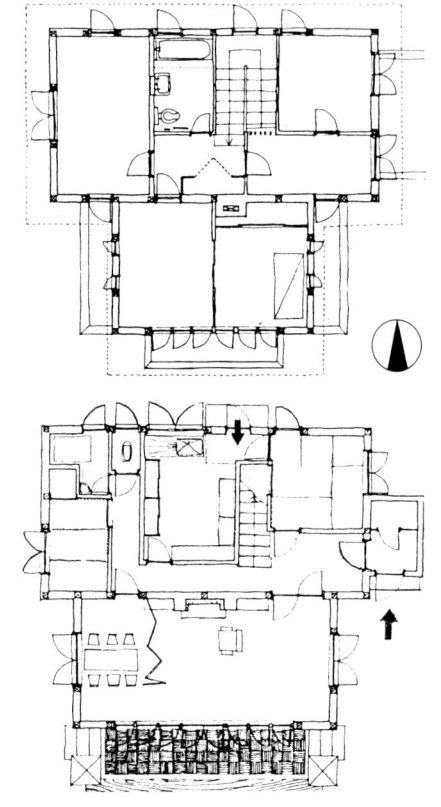

5.23. Raymond: Rachel Reid House, Azabu, Tokyo, 1924. Plans.

general openness of the house had to be reduced during the work on the plans, owing to both structural problems and considerations of cost. Raymond was by anyone's view a gifted and clever problem solver, so that the theoretical and ideological rigors of early Modern Movement experimentation sat ill with him. Thus, in spite of a number of difficulties he overcame one by one at Reinanzaka, the design was never really resolved. It represents, instead, a middle point between the competent, sub-Wrightian exercise, such as the house Raymond executed next door for Dr. Rachel Reid in 1924 (figs. 5.22–23), after the earthquake, or the temporary ambassadorial residence for Paul Claudel (1923), and his leisured exercises in the International Style executed in the following decade.

It bears emphasizing that the Reinanzaka House was not the post-and-infill type of concrete structure in frequent use today but, rather, a poured monolithic shell, such as we shall reencounter, some fifty years later, at the end of this book. Basically, there was no call for this kind of building in northern Europe, and even Le Corbusier dropped it, though never quite definitively, from about 1919 until after World War II. While there were technical reasons for abandoning it, most of all this monolithic approach did not accord with the aesthetic direction of "high modernism" during the later twenties and earlier part of the 1930s.

Raymond's temperament as a jack-of-all-styles, as well as his need to earn a living in a foreign land, led him to employ various idioms and techniques almost simultaneously in different projects for a wide range of clients. The variety of his early work is described in a lively manner in *An Autobiography*, and he was obviously fascinated by the possible geotechnical applications of concrete in Japan, about which so much less was known in the years of his first Japanese stay than today. His work of the 1920s ranged from the extensive campus he designed for Tokyo Women's Christian College at Kichijoji, with its monolithic poured-concrete missionary dwellings, to a row of concrete geisha houses he projected for Soichiro Asano, founder of the Japanese cement industry. Sadly, mainstream architectural history is fraught with discontinuities, so the post–World War II development of concrete houses in Japan is less likely to be based on Raymond's timely experiments than on the influence of Le Corbusier's style of the 1950s, especially his residential work in India.

6 | Rationalism and Lifestyle: The Thirties through the End of the War

NATIONALISM AND THE QUEST FOR JAPANESE TASTE

Since the 1890s the extraordinary nearness to Japan of Russia's eastern maritime province—as well as competition among Western powers in China—had served to stimulate Japan's fears and ambitions. After 1900 the Japanese population was no longer able to depend on its own capabilities for the production of food, while favorable trade patterns of the 1920s were brought to a more or less sudden end by the wrecking of Japan's foreign markets in the Great Depression. In northeast Asia the timeless issue of hegemony reemerged preponderant and critical: the 1930s began with the Japanese occupation of Manchuria in autumn, 1931. The puppet-state of Manchukuo was established the following spring. Annexation of Jehol Province came in 1933. By the start of the Pacific war, at the end of 1941, northeastern China had been developed as the preeminent supply base of the Japanese Empire.

Despite the restlessness of the military and its broad distrust of party government and parliamentary procedure, Japanese politics retained a veneer of constitutionalism, since the Meiji institutional structure was bypassed, not changed. During the brief Taisho interval, business interests had entered the political arena in force, and these were now enabled to contribute indirectly large amounts of capital and technology to the development of Manchukuo. National policy veered uneasily between a face-saving liberalism adapted to the pace of prevailing urbanization and industrialization, encouraged by a brief upturn in the economic situation, and the unmistakable reality of growing military control.

As early as 1932, the spectacular bombardment of Shanghai had been recorded on the spot by newsreel cameramen, shocking the world and turning opinion against Japan. By 1937, war was under way in earnest in North China, where the Japanese displayed an organizational talent allied with brutality that lends support to the term "fascist," as used by younger Japanese historians. Culturally the situation entailed a paradox, as the culture of the colonizer, Japan, was indebted to that of the colonized: to China and, incidentally, Korea. Moreover, Japan was far from being considered a racial equal by the Western powers, as indicated by the fact that the Japanese delegation to Versailles in 1919 had felt itself compelled to stipulate an equality clause. Ironically, too, the image of a self-serving pan-Asian solidarity nourished during Japan's buildup of her relatively short-lived empire contradicted the prior equation of Western culture with technology and progress. Thus, in the immediate prewar years of the early Showa era, even mild forms of Westernization risked censure. Just as in the Soviet Union or Nazi Germany, any attempt to imitate Western avant-garde movements was deemed worthy of reproof, although the precise ideological justification varied.

The so-called Imperial Crown style (*teikan yoshiki*) was, in architecture, the recognized emblem of Japanese nationalism and, later, expansionism. Still, as its name suggests, this form of ideology corresponded more closely to the reign-name styles of the nineteenth century (Victorian or Edwardian in England, Wilhelmine in Germany, and Umbertian in Italy) than to the Fascist or Nazi architecture of the 1930s in Europe. The term goes back to a competition of 1917–18 for the Imperial Diet Building, although the scheme itself miscarried and the prizewinning design announced in 1919—like the original Ende und Böckmann project for the Diet of the 1880s—was not built. Thus, the first building to make actual use of elements later acknowledged as denoting the "imperial" manner is the Hobutsu-den (1921) at Meiji Shrine in Tokyo, a repository for works of art, designed by the architects Keiji Goto and Shintaro Oe (fig. 6.1).

Meanwhile, completion of the Diet Building was put off until 1936, with the result that its streamlined Hallicarnassian bulk is inevitably associated with the consolidation of Japan's military government. In terms of scale and finish, the Diet was perhaps significant, but as a symbol of the constitution granted to the Japanese people by the Meiji emperor, it was erected far too belatedly. As architecture, it deserves no greater consideration than, say, Goodhue's Nebraska State Capitol at Lincoln, though that has a *round*headed tower, or the Los Angeles City Hall, which, however mausolean, is actually a thirty-two-floor skyscraper. Owing to the delay in construction of the Diet Building, responsibility for representing the *teikan yoshiki* devolved on two different works, one military and the other cultural. These were Soldiers' Hall (Gunjin Kaikan) at Kudan (fig. 6.2), designed by Ryoichi Kawamoto (1934), and the Imperial Museum in Ueno (figs. 6.3–4) by Jin Watanabe (1937).

The Imperial Crown style has at times been referred to as *yane no aru* (possessing a [Japanese-style] roof), and this neotraditional component is its most easily recognizable feature. Such a roof can be seen in Meiji Shrine's Treasure Hall mentioned above. Used as a sort of museum, it consists basically of a single story. Later examples with expanded functions contained more floors. To offset the excess of height this

108 RATIONALISM AND LIFESTYLE

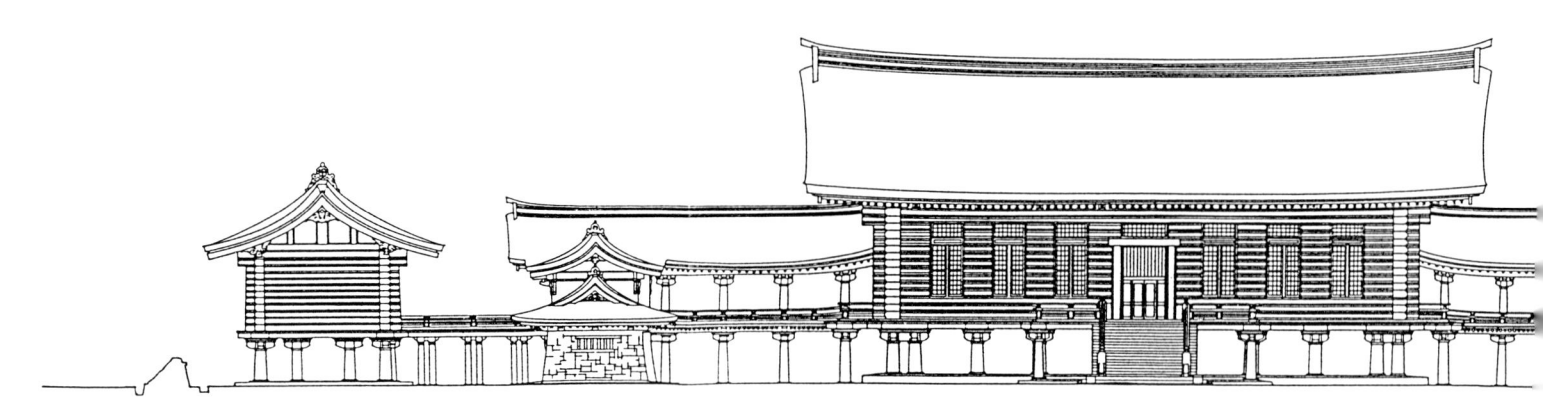

6.1. Goto and Oe: Hobutsu-den, Meiji Shrine, Tokyo, 1921. Elevation.

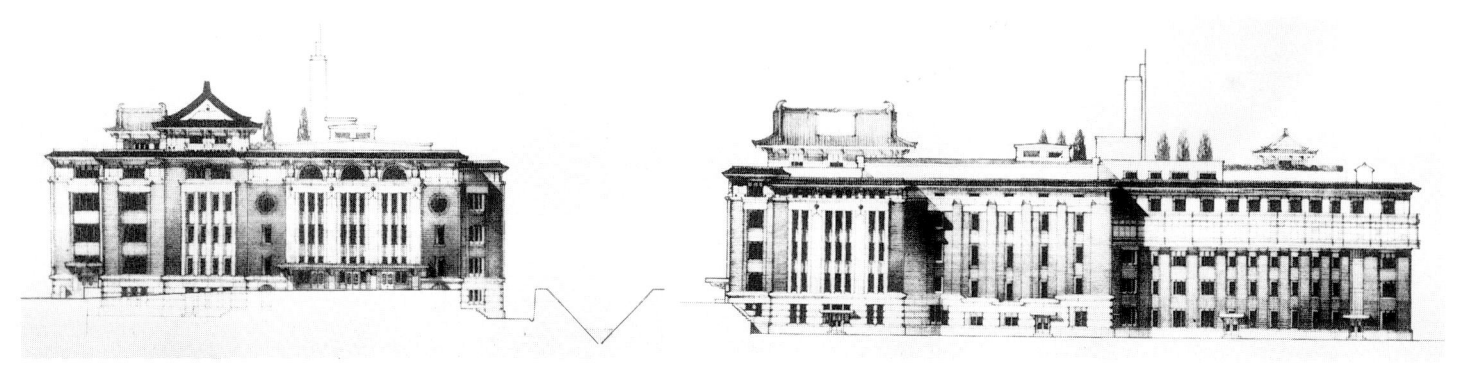

6.2. Kawamoto: Soldiers' Hall, Kudan, Tokyo, 1934. Front and side elevations.

6.3. Watanabe: Tokyo Imperial Museum, Ueno, Tokyo, 1937. Main front.

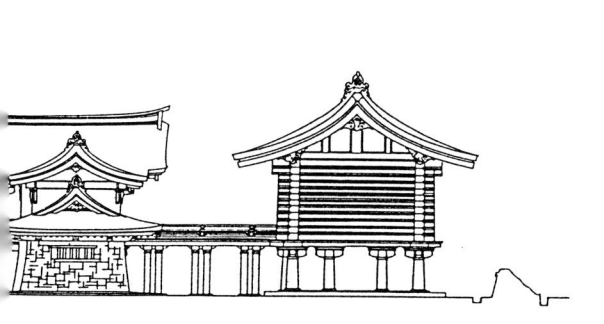

6.4. Watanabe: Tokyo Imperial Museum, Ueno, Tokyo, 1937. Composite rendering of ornament, 1931 or after, and architect's view of the proposed building.

6.5. Municipal Office Building, Nagoya, mid-1930s.

6.6. Kanagawa Prefectural Office, Yokohama, mid-1930s.

created, the final floor below the projecting eaves was often set back, or indented slightly, to produce the sensation of a roof supported in the traditional manner on cantilevered raftering.

This trick may be derived from Frank Lloyd Wright's related treatment at the Imperial Hotel ten years earlier. Its adoption in the *teikan yoshiki* was intended to deemphasize the role of the structural steel members which upheld the roof. Needless to say, such a method of treating a steel-framed or reinforced-concrete structure never attained the level of unqualified *trompe l'oeil*. And the curious high-shouldered effect obtained by the clerestorylike usage is apt to appear more continental than Japanese. Yet the ubiquitous popularity achieved by this feature of the *teikan yoshiki*, both at home as well as on the mainland during the thirties, suggests that it may have been a convenience, if not a virtue, in the pursuit of Japan's new pan-Asian stance.

Likewise, in the manner of the Imperial Hotel, which enjoyed its heyday in the years of the Empire, the *teikan yoshiki* frequently made use of an ashlar podium that served in lieu of the open system of supports associated with most traditional Japanese buildings. But, untraditionally, fenestration was bound to be grouped vertically, as in one school of skyscraper design. Soldiers' Hall, which still stands just below one of the gates of the Imperial Palace precinct, beside the moat, and was based on ideas contributed by the theoretician Chuta Ito, depends nevertheless for much of its effect on picturesque asymmetrical massing more or less reminiscent of the Prairie School. But unlike works by Wright or his disciples, any impression of modernity is dissipated in the overinsistent application of false corbels and heavy tiled gables. In sharp contrast with Soldiers' Hall, the Imperial Museum is a vast block, horizontal in appearance but square in plan, using courtyards to entrap light and air. The facade is flanked on either side by recessed endpieces of a single bay, all decidedly in the academic manner. However, the whole is roofed in a massive sweep of neotraditional tiles, and on its own terms Watanabe's building attains considerable distinction and repose for a work of such great scale. Inside the museum a sense of tranquillity is borne out in the dimly lit upper-floor galleries devoted to painting and calligraphy. The ground floor is less successful. Except for the display of monumental religious sculpture, its galleries are overlarge, while its blatant daylighting is outmoded and undesirable.

A different use of the *teikan yoshiki* is illustrated by the treatment of the Municipal Office Building at Nagoya (fig. 6.5), which is virtually identical to that of the Kanagawa Prefectural Office at Yokohama (fig. 6.6). Both buildings resulted from 1930s competitions. In order to achieve monumentality, such blocks were outfitted over a standard industrialized frame in the style that has already been described. A massive square tower topped by a pagodalike roof was then added, yielding an appearance very similar to the bizarre, tile-roofed University Library (1931-34) built by Sir Giles Gilbert Scott at Cambridge.

A final element suggesting the influence of Wright's Imperial Hotel on the Imperial Crown style is the nearly inevitable presence of a *porte-cochère*. In Wright's building, however, the covered entryway designates a true focal point. It also reposes visually within the context of repeating horizontals that compose the front elevation, and provides a backdrop for the reflecting pool at the center of the design. In the *teikan yoshiki* buildings, on the contrary, the *porte-cochère* is usually endowed with a diminutive Japanese-style roof, possibly in imitation of the covered exterior stair of many Shinto shrines. Such canopies as these had, centuries before, found their way into the residential *shinden* style of the mid-Heian period. Reflecting this development, though built much later, the old Imperial Palace at Kyoto also furnished a prototype for the prewar nationalist style.[1]

UNBUILT MANCHUKUO: A LOST "OPPORTUNITY"

The final elaboration of the *teikan yoshiki* recalls—though only distantly—the grandeur of the British capital for India at New Delhi as envisioned by Edwin Lutyens. Mainland Asia possesses numerous monumental buildings of both stone and brick, while the Japanese islands were without a masonry tradition, until the nineteenth century, of the type required to conceal the structural props of the twentieth, namely concrete and steel. Japan's architects sought nevertheless to establish their vocation in the Japanese colonial undertaking in Manchuria and northern China. A good deal was actually built, but the mastery exhibited in Lutyens's breathtaking scheme with its baroque layout was inevitably lacking, and so were the nineteen years (1912-31) given Lutyens, Herbert Baker, and other architects to realize their task.

Today few details of the architectural and planning side of the Japanese drive into northeast Asia remain in focus, but one can surmise that it encompassed the best energies of a generation. Unlike the Italians, for example, who attempted to start new communities in the "Agro Romano" near

6.7. Hsinking (Changchun). Capital of Manchukuo, late 1930s.

Rome and develop agricultural bases in Libya from scratch, the Japanese set out to "improve" a far-flung existing urban network. The Manchurian Railways Corporation and its associated companies was an experienced organization exploiting a route which Americans were once eager to finance. Moreover, as an extension of the home economy, Manchukuo had the makings of a profitable undertaking, in contrast with, say, Mussolini's Ethiopian expenditures which did little but attract a caste of administrators. Given time, a thoroughgoing development of Manchuria would have wrought a new chapter in Japanese physical planning, however repellent and unacceptable in geopolitical terms (fig. 6.7).

We have seen that the habitual Japanese approach to planning was to concentrate on improvement schemes at the expense of more comprehensive goals. Though numerous undertakings were certainly realized and are still in use in northeast China today, the Manchurian dream was short-lived. Yet the scale of ideas was relatively grandiose, à la Lutyens, since projects were formulated by an autonomous authority with sweeping powers of control. The more ambitious enterprises would have been unrealizable either in metropolitan China or in the Japanese home islands, where for the most part unplanned, high-density settlement prevailed. In the event— and less than a decade and a half after the Japanese expansionist adventure had begun—Tokyo and other principal cities, with the exception of ancient Kyoto, were reduced to ruins. Except for the gridiron scheme put into effect by the Nagoya authorities, postwar planning reduplicated the piecemeal, if largely humane, tradition that had predominated during the era of Japan's modernization with its benign neglect of utopian strategies.

The mainland story is less utopian than merely tragic, for there can be no doubt of Japan's determination in China, and by the end of the thirties the Japanese architectural press was strewn with projects for "monuments to the loyal dead." It may be supposed that these demonstrate the influence of designs produced for the Imperial War Graves Commission in Britain, at the end of World War I, by Lutyens and others. Such arches and cenotaphs make up the final balance sheet, for the demise of the Japanese military regime, when it came, was absolute and entailed the annihilation of all previous support; with it, the Imperial Crown style was discredited and abandoned.

One question, withal, could not be avoided and continued to be asked: "What is the essential nature of Japanese taste?" It was of sufficient immediacy to sustain a perennial awareness of the notion of style, even though the *teikan yoshiki* in itself had neither achieved a general transformation nor provoked a full-scale reaction. This question in different forms had been postponed over and again, during the near half-century of Meiji rule and the brief Taisho interlude, while the modernization of the country was rendered complete.

ARTISTIC REHABILITATION
OF TRADITIONAL TASTE

A further paradoxical aspect of the ethos surrounding the *teikan yoshiki* was that the style, despite strong encouragement, was not altogether enforced in officially sponsored competitions until the second half of the 1930s. By this time industrial materials were not only being diverted to the military for use on the mainland but also stockpiled in preparation for the likely possibility of general war. Finally, at the end of the decade, then, reactionary aesthetics converged with a utilization of Japan's traditional material: wood. For the first time since the Restoration, the government both advocated the use of a neo-vernacular style and was forced to override the rigorously entrenched notion that architecture must reflect sociotechnological advance to the exclusion of aesthetic principles.

Official policy had been variously defined over the years with regard to other branches of the arts. An attitude similar to the brusquely utilitarian view taken of architecture was responsible for the establishment of a school of Western painting at the technical college in 1876. In addition, a sharp decline in local patronage had nearly succeeded in eradicating the market for traditional art and artisanry, in spite of the fact that the Japanese exhibit at the Vienna World's Fair of 1873 suggested excellent prospects for export. However, in a matter of years the newfangled art school had closed its doors for want of finances, while at the end of the 1870s a private association was founded to encourage revival of the moribund traditional arts. In 1888 the American scholar Ernest Fenellosa became director of both the Imperial Museum and the newly founded Tokyo Fine Arts Academy, following a bitter debate over the direction which art education should take in the elementary schools. Thus Fenellosa toured the United States and Europe to evaluate art education methods, as well as techniques of art conservation, in the company of one Baron Hamao and a second young Ministry of Education official named Kakuzo Okakura, who was to become Japan's foremost art historian. As Fenellosa was to prove an undyingly enthusiastic pioneer supporter of the

6.8. Yoshida: Tokyo Central Post Office, Tokyo, 1927–31.

Japanese national artistic patrimony, the early years of the Tokyo Fine Arts Academy witnessed the total exclusion of courses in Western painting from its curriculum.

Thanks mainly to Fenellosa's efforts, the edifice of Japanese art was never completely dismantled, and a program of teaching and conservation was ultimately instituted in its favor. By 1891, the historian Okakura was delivering the first lectures on Japanese art at the Fine Arts Academy in support of his "natural development theory." These views were remarkably devoid of eclecticism yet took into account the development of art in both East and West. Okakura elaborated a line specifying that future development in the arts would have to be based on what he called the "unfolding of life"; but above all he believed that "for the Orient significance lay in the Orient." In 1893, it was Okakura who wrote the booklet that accompanied the Japanese government's adapted replica of the Phoenix Pavilion, or Ho-o-den, shown at the World's Columbian Exposition in Chicago that year. In 1906, his most celebrated publication, *The Book of Tea*, was issued in New York. Originally written in English, this was the volume Frank Lloyd Wright later recalled having perused at about the time of his preparation of the designs for Unity Temple at Oak Park.

Meanwhile, Fenellosa had already returned to the United States for good and Okakura was to die, at fifty-two, in the second year of Taisho (i.e., 1913). It was not until some years later that the question of an "orientalizing" taste penetrated Japanese discussions of architecture. One of the earliest recorded instances is the much cited reaction of the younger architect Sutemi Horiguchi on returning from Europe in 1924. Horiguchi graduated from the Imperial University in 1920 and became a member of Bunri Ha the same year. In Europe he was a visitor at the Bauhaus school, but mainly he was impressed by expressionism and De Stijl in Holland, publishing his *Modern Dutch Architecture* in 1924. It was, however, he later reminisced, his encounter with Greece that revolutionized his sensibilities and convinced him that Japanese architects must think in earnest about the problem of Japanese taste. After this, he said, he recognized that Japanese architects could never really succeed by imitating European buildings. Apparently he believed, as Okakura had, that the obvious divisions between Eastern and Western art were based on real differences in thinking, if not perception. Eventually, it was this notion that furnished a kind of *rapelle à l'ordre* for the generation of Japanese architects who, like Horiguchi, were born a few years after Raymond. It may well be that Horiguchi's belief in the importance of national expression in architecture was not a little influenced by the closely knit philosophy of the De Stijl movement and the coherence of the distinctive Amsterdam School that had preceded it. However, Horiguchi's generation was still young and green by Japanese standards, and concerns such as these did not put in a significant appearance until the 1930s.

A STYLE FOR THE TIMES: P.O. BUILDINGS AND SCHOOLS

Although note has been taken of a resuscitant orientalism as well as an important realization of Bunri Ha's tardy dreams of expressionism, pursuit and domestication of rationalism constitute the major theme of Japanese building during the thirties. Such was the case throughout an industrializing world, which in those years still included the great isolated centers of the East, such as Tokyo and Shanghai. The modernism it produced could be unnervingly superficial, but at a distance of fifty years even this impervious lightheartedness appears as merely another aspect of the times.

A key building, not in the least frivolous, and one which may well be regarded as the very image of rationalism, is Tetsuro Yoshida's Tokyo Central Post Office[2] (fig. 6.8). It still occupies a site in front of Tatsuno's Tokyo Station, there being no purer contrast than the charming, awkward idiom of the station, whose period of construction (1911–14) spans from Meiji to Taisho, and the gleaming rectilinear facade of the Post Office, begun in 1927 and completed in 1931. The Communications Ministry took pride in the image of speed and efficiency created throughout the nation—and, indeed, the Empire—by its Architectural Department. Post offices were the most numerous and representative building category, though other work turned out by the department included telephone and telegraph facilities, electrical and marine experimental stations, aerodromes, and lighthouses. It was here that the dream of a modern Japanese architecture was, in one sense, most completely realized by combining functionalism and rationalized post-and-beam construction. The earlier Central Telegraph Office of 1922–25 by Yamada (see fig. 5.11; influenced, perhaps, by the Dutch proclivities of his fellow Secessionist Horiguchi) displayed a pioneering version of the new style, but by the mid-thirties was already understood as romantic and untypical.

Yamada's Electrical Laboratory of 1930, published three years later in Hitchcock and Johnson's catalogue of orthodox International Style examples,[3] denotes the switchover from

6.9. Yoshida: Osaka Higashi Post Office, Osaka, 1931. Entrance.

Bunri Ha expressionism to a rational idiom (though these arbiters of taste regretted that rounded edges blurred its "effect of volume"). For, in 1929, Yamada, after Horiguchi, betook himself to Europe. There he attended the second of the *Congrès Internationaux d'Architecture Moderne* (CIAM) meetings. This was held in Frankfurt at the instigation of the city architect, Ernst May, at a time when CIAM still retained its orientation toward functionalism and *Sachlichkeit* ("objectivity"). The influence was decisive, and two other clean-lined Communications Ministry buildings of the early 1930s were the Osaka Higashi Post Office of 1931 by Yoshida (figs. 6.9–10) and the Ogikubo Telephone Office of 1933 (fig. 6.11; located in a suburb of Tokyo) by Yamada.

Martin Punitzer's's electricity-gauge factory (Steglitz, 1928) and Max Taut's Dorotheen-Schule (Köpenick, 1929) are late, little-remembered European examples of the new style in Berlin, which, like Yoshida's Tokyo and Osaka post offices, happen to be faced with tile. A far earlier building of the same general type was completed in Tokyo in 1923, though it lacked the aesthetic cachet of subsequent European designs. This was the famous Marunouchi Building, facing Tokyo Station, realized by the Fuller Company of Chicago (with its own patented system of reinforced concrete) to plans drawn up by the Real Estate Section of the Mitsubishi Corporation (fig. 6.12). Here was Japan's first modern office building, certainly the first which included a ground-floor shopping arcade. Upon completion, it was the largest structure in Japan, with a total floor area of nearly 60,000 square meters distributed over eight stories. Not surprisingly, perhaps, the Marunouchi Building (known affectionately as the Marubiru) proved of greater interest to Japanese architects than Wright's Imperial Hotel of the same year. A few years back the building was restored, using fiberglass panels to replicate the original ceramic facing, although by the time Yoshida's building had come to be constructed next door, the Marubiru was seemingly already relegated to the history of the previous Taisho reign. Today she stands a resplendent reminder of the age of *modanizumu*, but Mamoru Yamada, writing in *Shinkenchiku* in 1932, dismissed her as mere "matchbox" architecture in comparison with Yoshida's Central Post Office. In Yoshida's work, Yamada declared, column, wall, window, and door supply the bare elements of a new, unenhanced type of beauty.

Such restraint was itself about to give way to a fully classicizing treatment, exemplified in the giant order of composite columns rising through five floors upon a fully rusticated basement story in Shinichiro Okada's nearby Meiji Insurance Building of 1934. Similarly, the Mitsukoshi Department Store of that same year brought to Nihonbashi, farther north, a new breadth of academicism worthy of Marshall Field's or Selfridge's. In contrast with this spread of affluence in Tokyo's central business district during the years of the early Showa period prior to the war, Yoshida's Central Post Office was a masterpiece of functional planning simply expressed. Concealed at rear was a 126-meter vehicular dispatching platform while the three lowermost stories of the post office were serviced by a 1,200-meter conveyor system.

To these floors, all of greater than average height, was appended a fourth topped by a plain linear cornice (which, however, Yamada regretted as an anachronism). Over this rises an attic ending in a simple coping, making for a vertical rhythm of a-b-b-c-d. The two facades that, respectively, front the square and face the station form a continuous range masterfully expressing the underlying reinforced-concrete structure. They are joined at an angle that follows the line of the road out of the square between post office and station.

The infill of Yoshida's concrete frame consists of gigantic steel-framed windows having about them, nevertheless, the lightness and perfection of traditional *shoji*. In addition to its rational appearance, Yoshida's work incorporated up-to-date heating, ventilation, and fire-prevention apparatus. It was also linked with the railway station by means of an underground electric tram car. The sole decorative element, in itself functional, is the magnificent clock, four and one half meters in diameter, which fills an entire bay over the principal entrance at fourth-story height. Such was the building, which the German emigré architect Bruno Taut, arriving via the Soviet Union in 1933, praised as "the most modern in the world." As regards post offices, Taut's appraisal antedates the founding of the WPA in America by two years but does scant justice to Libera and De Renzi's new structure in Rome's via Mamorata, opened the same year as Taut's arrival in Japan. Above all, of course, Taut's comment refers to the untimely curtailment of the Modern Movement in Germany following the still recent Nazi takeover.

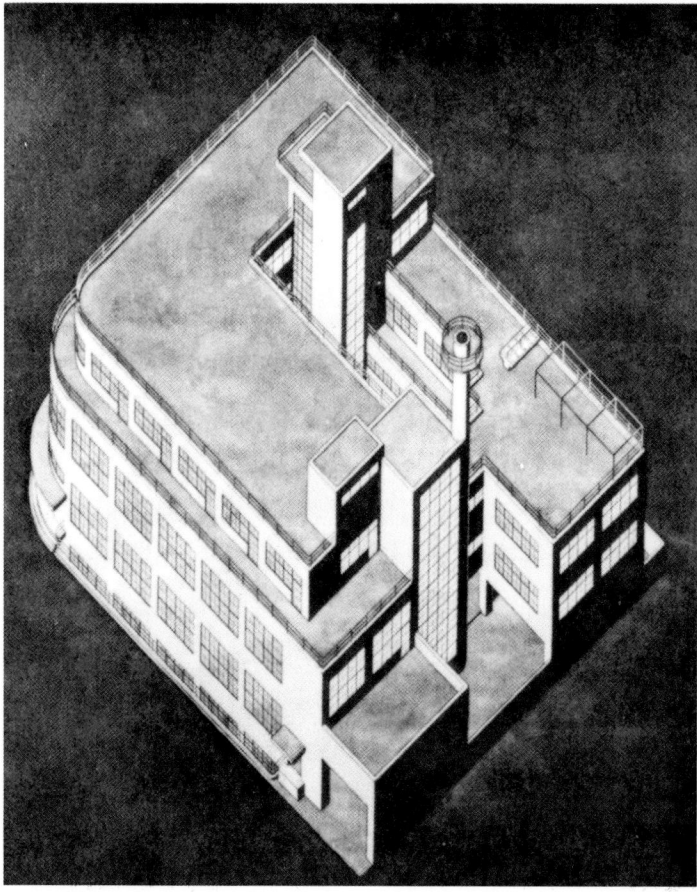

6.10. Yoshida: Osaka Higashi Post Office, Osaka, 1931. Rear and axonometric rear views.

6.11. Yamada: Ogikubo Telephone Office, Tokyo, 1933.

6.12. Mitsubishi Corporation: Marunouchi Building, Tokyo, 1923.

Entirely consistent with the support afforded by the Communications Ministry, Japanese architecture received another boost when a program of rational school construction was adopted by the architectural department of the Tokyo municipality after the Great Kanto Earthquake. Their designs (figs. 6.13–15) had matured by the mid-thirties, at which time there were over 10 million primary-school students in Japan, constituting 99.5 percent of all school-age children in the country. Of course, the majority attended class in the simple yet dignified wooden schoolhouses still seen today in some parts of rural Japan. However, the disastrous experience of 1923 dictated a new standard for central Tokyo. Among the best works were the Yotsuya Fifth Primary School (1934) and the Takanawadai Primary School (1935), followed by the sixteen-room Nagata-cho Primary School (1937) practically in the shadow of the recently completed Diet Building. Takanawadai had a broadcasting studio while Yotsuya was the very first public school in Japan to have floor heating throughout. Taken as a group, these were among the most interesting examples anywhere in the world of late International Style institutional work.

Owing to the relative scarcity of city land, schools had in most cases to be architecturally integrated with sports facilities, while all classrooms, and other indoor spaces, were disposed to obtain maximum sunlight. Though few frills were admitted, the occasional glazed stair block of curved profile or continuous row of windows smartly cantilevered beyond the structure, amid white-rendered walls, lent an air of ab-

6.13. Tokyo Municipality: Yotsuya Fifth Primary School, 1934. Glazed stairway (above), plan, and general view (below). On plan, corridors are tiled and spaces other than classrooms are as follows: (1) auditorium and gym, (2) sports ground with fifty-meter track at left, (3) swimming pool, (4) children's play area, (5) workshop, (6) teachers' room, and (7) music room.

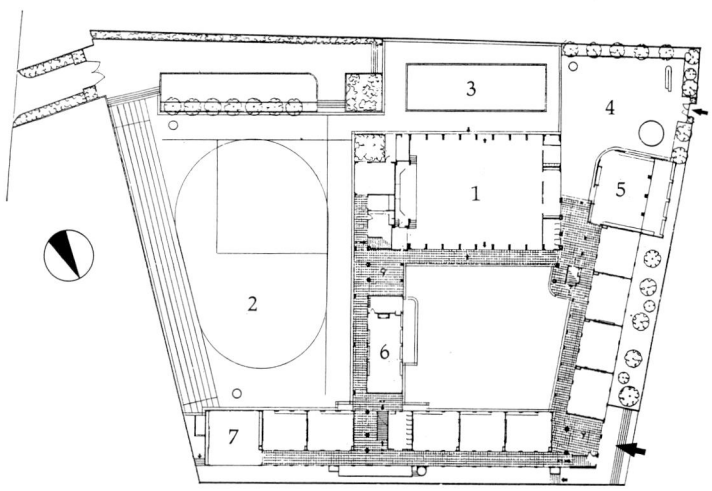

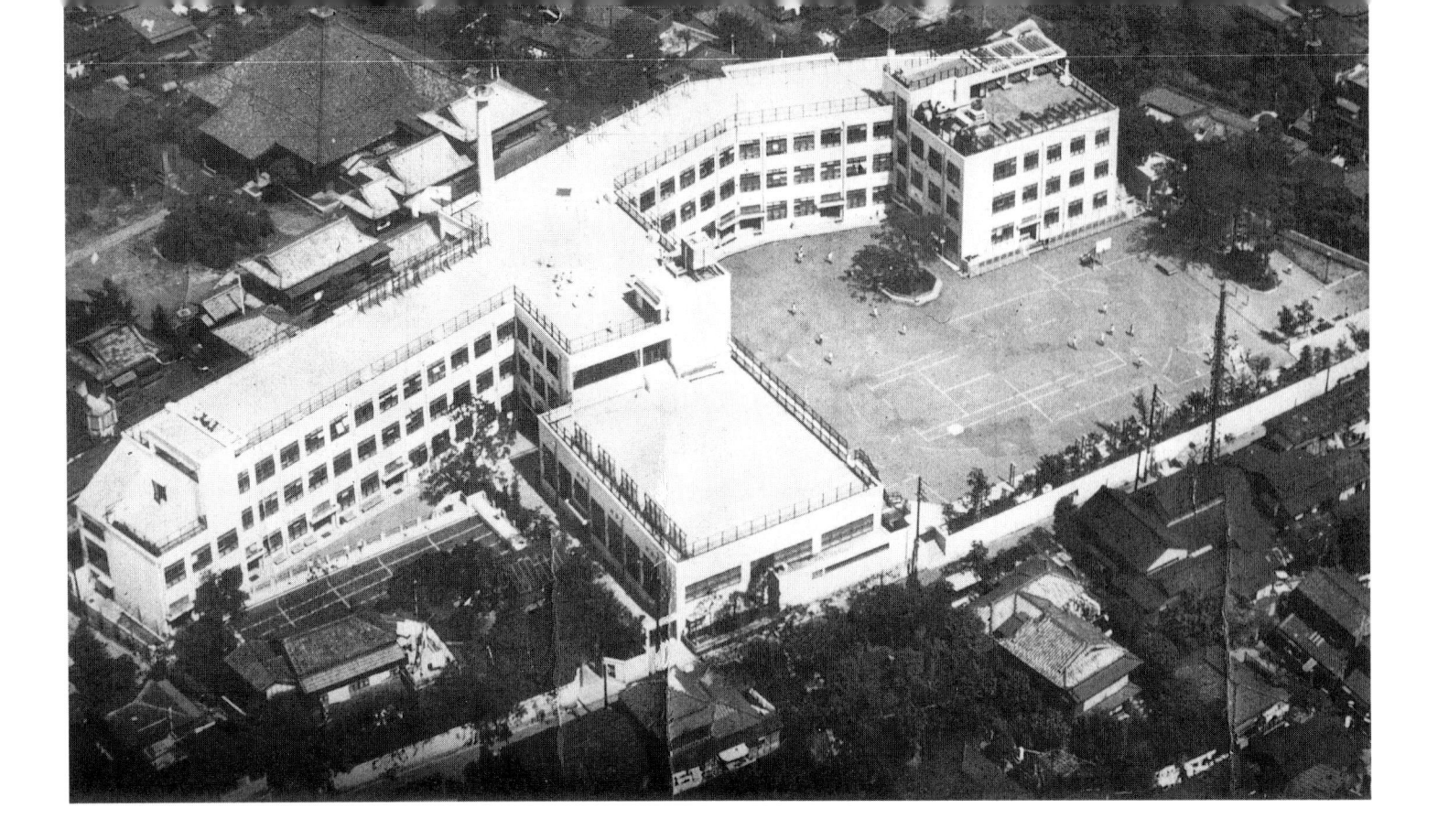

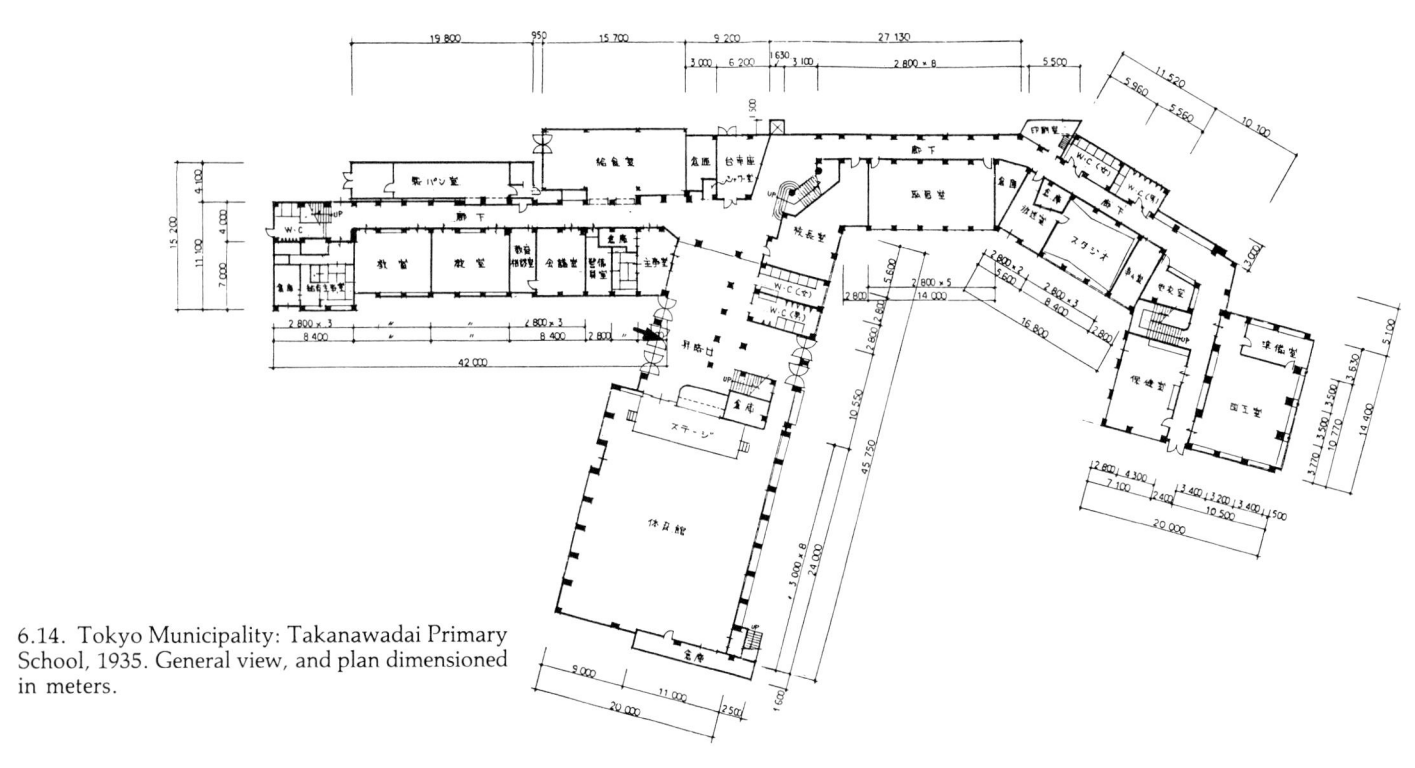

6.14. Tokyo Municipality: Takanawadai Primary School, 1935. General view, and plan dimensioned in meters.

stract modernity to the face of starkly traditional neighborhoods. Even if totally different in aspect, these schools merit comparison with the London Board Schools of the 1870s through the nineties, mainly executed in Queen Anne or its allied styles, which Sherlock Holmes is made to refer to as rising above the horizon of the city like "lighthouses" or "beacons of the future."[4]

KIKUJI ISHIMOTO'S GERMAN CONNECTION

Born like Yamada and Yoshida in 1894 (one year before Horiguchi), Kikuji Ishimoto became the first Japanese architect ever to study with Walter Gropius. That was in 1922, and Ishimoto remained one of the best internationally connected younger Japanese architects at work in the early thirties, partly owing to the fact that Bunzo Yamaguchi, a former assistant of Ishimoto's, worked with Gropius from 1930 until 1932. Consequently, Ishimoto's Shirokiya Department Store (figs. 6.16–18), finished in 1931, appears more "modern" than his Asahi Newspaper Offices (see figs. 5.8–10) of four years before. The newer work makes use of horizontal bands of almost continuous glazing yet produces a quite different effect from Mendelsohn's contemporary German department stores. Moreover, the use of real transparent curtain walling, such as Mendelsohn increasingly tended to favor, would have set Ishimoto outside his budget as well as beyond prevailing structural norms in Japan.

6.15. Tokyo Municipality: Nagata-cho Primary School, 1937. Plan with indications in meters, and general view.

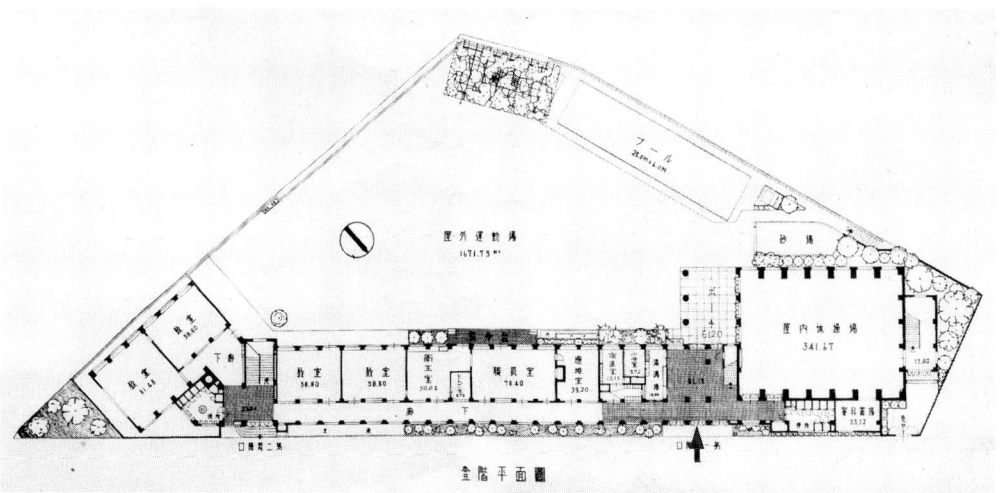

What Ishimoto did was to articulate his facade by means of balconies, vertical elements, nonstructural window surrounds, and a recessed entry in such a way that structural members are virtually concealed. The net effect plays on the formal language of Russian Constructivism, first introduced to the West almost a decade earlier, and the rendering of the store (fig. 6.19) made by Yamaguchi as early as 1927 suggests the influence of Russian-inspired perspective drawings of the mid-twenties. Today the Shirokiya has been totally remodeled, but as built, the building it most resembled was Dudok's Bijenkorf store (1929-30) in Rotterdam, now lost.

The Tokyo Airport Office of 1932 was conceived by Ishimoto more in the idiom of other Communications Ministry works with rationalist, late Bauhaus-style facade detailing (figs. 6.20-21). As in the Shirokiya, certain interior features seem more reminiscent of early Bauhaus-style expressionism or the type of decoration Taut had encouraged during the early twenties, such as the Barasch store facade, painted by Oskar Fischer, which Ishimoto could have known in Germany. Moreover, the airport waiting room suggests that same lack of acceptable modern furniture which persuaded the Raymonds to design their own (see fig. 5.18), such as steel-tubing chairs (claimed to be even earlier than Breuer's).

In fact, in the Shirokiya, Ishimoto had produced elegant and elaborate interiors, but he could also design in a traditional Japanese fashion, as in the Daikokuya restaurant in Tokyo. It had a Western-style reception lounge but also Japanese-style private dining rooms with updated traditional fittings.

The Togo House (figs. 6.22-23), in a suburb of Tokyo served by the then newly opened Odakyu Railway, was commissioned by the well-known painter Seiji Togo and offers precise evidence of Ishimoto's close contact with Europe at this time. Dating from 1931, it makes use of a semicircular partition which frames the dining room in exactly the same way as in Mies van der Rohe's Tugendhat House (fig. 6.24) at Brno, Czechoslovakia, of the previous year! It is well known that Mies's house is set on a hillside, so one must enter at bedroom level and descend to the living room below, with its full 100 feet of glazing commanding a view of the garden. But the Togo residence occupies a perfectly level and much smaller site, although it does manage to make provision for an atelier in the otherwise single-floor plan. The results bore small relation to Mies's masterpiece, yet Ishimoto, for good measure, also included a token motif derived from Le Corbusier's 1923 house at Vaucresson.

6.16. Ishimoto: Shirokiya Department Store, Tokyo, 1931. Facade.

6.17. Ishimoto: Shirokiya Department Store, Tokyo, 1931. Lounge.

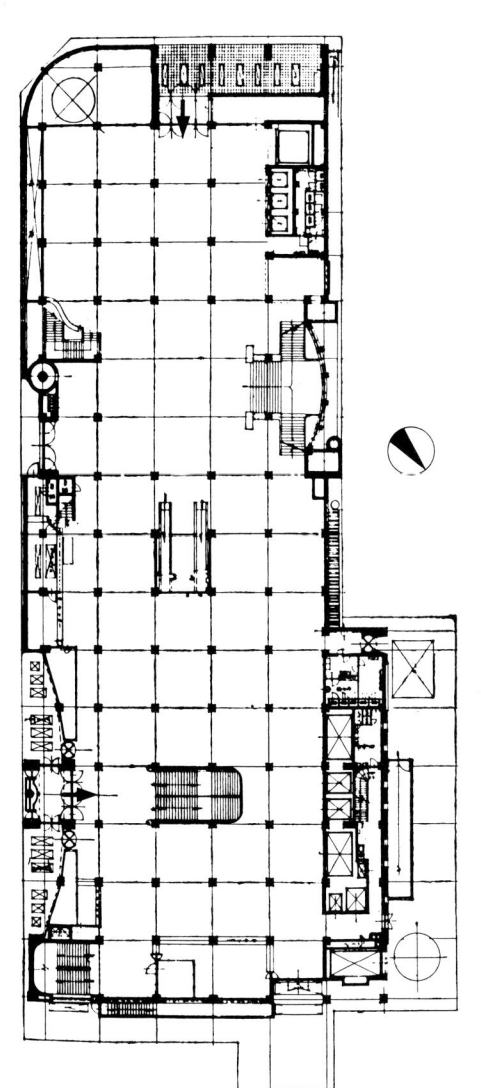

6.18. Ishimoto: Shirokiya Department Store, Tokyo, 1931. First floor plan and grand staircase.

6.19. Yamaguchi: rendering of Shirokiya, exhibited 1927.

122 RATIONALISM AND LIFESTYLE

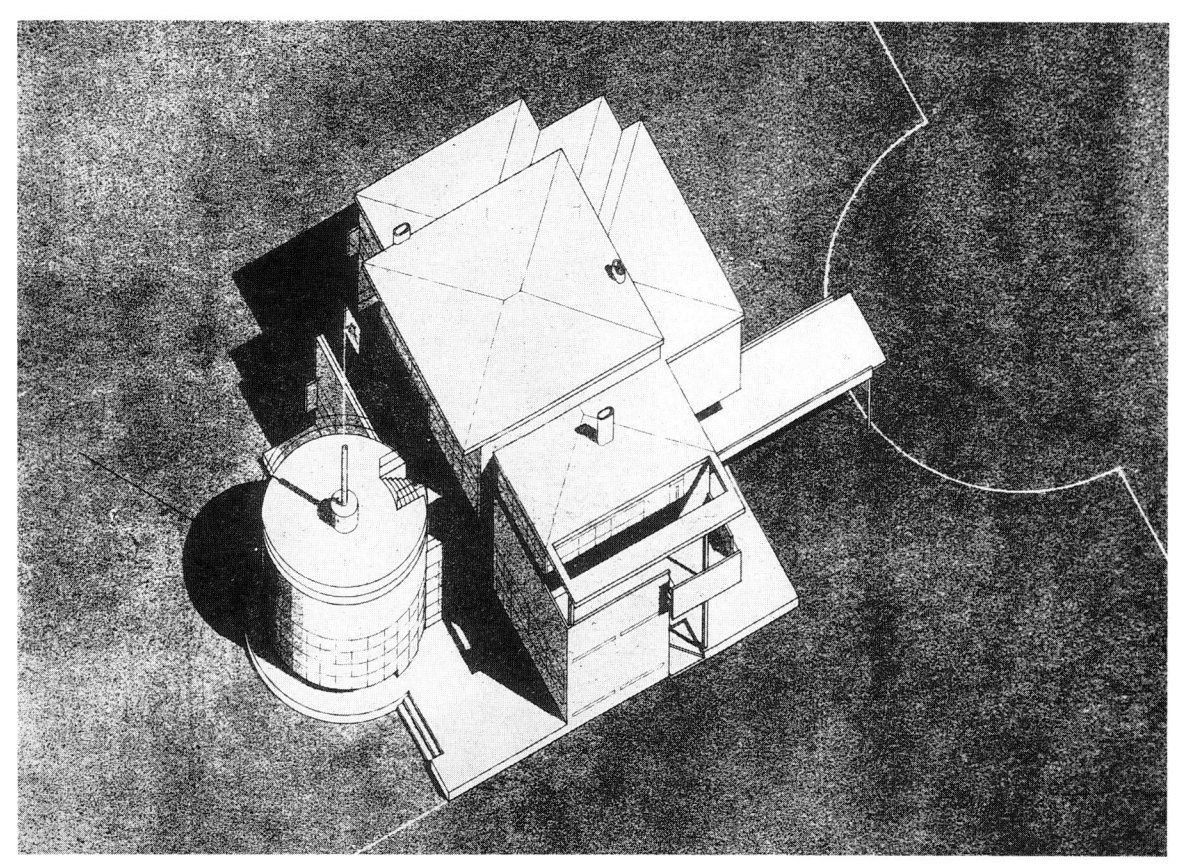

6.20. Ishimoto: Haneda Airport Office, Haneda, Tokyo, 1932. Axonometric proposal.

6.21. Ishimoto: Haneda Airport Office, Haneda, Tokyo, 1932. Terminal building.

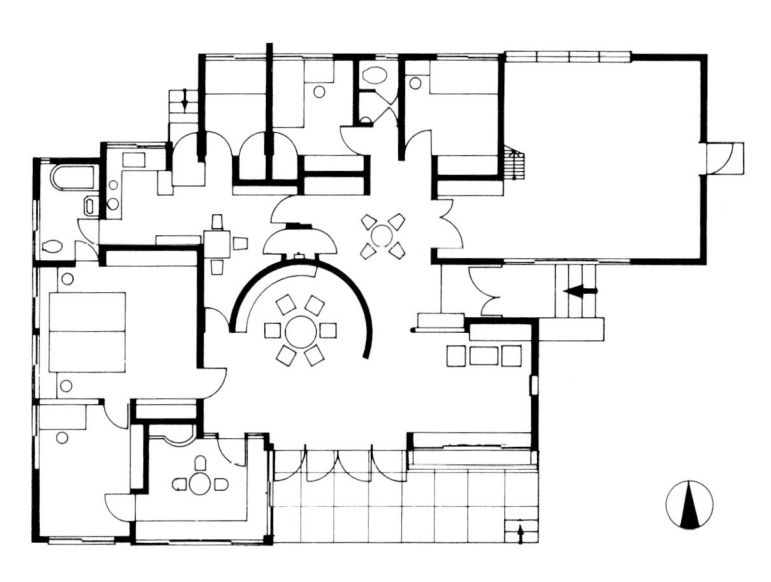

6.22. Ishimoto: Togo House, Seijo, Tokyo, 1931. Entrance and plan.

6.23. Ishimoto: Togo House, Seijo, Tokyo, 1931. Atelier.

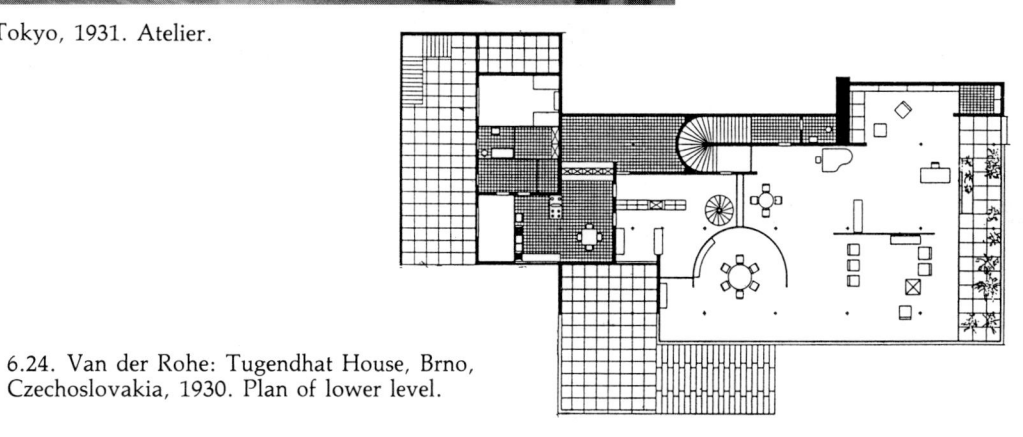

6.24. Van der Rohe: Tugendhat House, Brno, Czechoslovakia, 1930. Plan of lower level.

6.25. Ishimoto: Aoki House, Seijo, Tokyo, 1931. Garden facade.

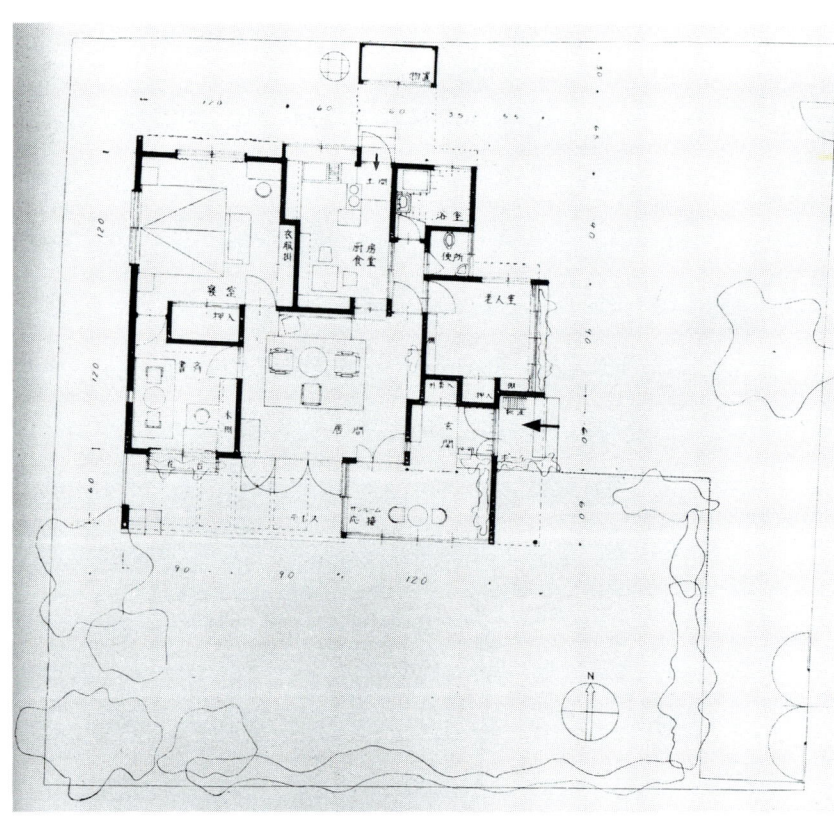

6.26. Ishimoto: Aoki House, Seijo, Tokyo, 1931. Plan

THE JOINT-STYLE MODERN JAPANESE RESIDENCE

The discrepancies which accrue in Japanese residential schemes of the early thirties—even those on a modest scale, such as Ishimoto's Togo House or his centrally planned, yet ambiguous, Aoki House next door (figs. 6.25–26)—stemmed from several sources. Possibly the most obvious was the distinction observed until World War II between three house types, namely, *wafu-jutaku* (the Japanese-style house), *yofu-jutaku* (the Western-style residence), and the so-called *wayo-kongo jutaku* (combined Western- and Japanese-style dwelling.) Among the well-to-do this stylistic division was more or less rigorously adhered to, and the choice between models was based on the observance of social proprieties as well as a concern for convenience and, not infrequently, simple preference. According to Raymond, who during these years was catering to the requirements mostly of an up-market clientele, these well-defined typologies satisfied only a part of "the elaborate arrangements necessary in the double life of the Japanese."[5] Among the more easily specifiable issues, he cites "separate entrances for guests, for the family, for the servants; several reception rooms of various types for those not admitted into the intimacy of the house; quarters and offices for the intendant; Japanese and western facilities in the kitchen; and Occidental as well as traditional rooms with mats on the floors."[6]

Yet another aspect of changing social conditions was the separation, by choice or necessity, of a number of middle-

6.27. Raymond: Hamao House, Tokyo, 1927–28. South facade.

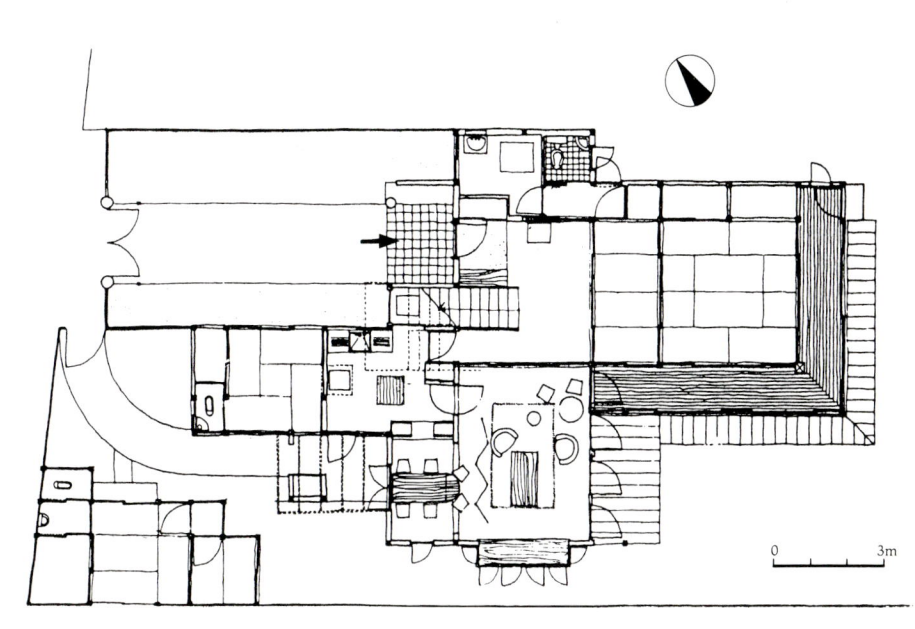

6.28. Raymond: Hamao House, Tokyo, 1927–28. Plan with caretaker's house at lower left.

class families into nuclear groupings, and a consequent demand for smaller, individually equipped houses. The design of these was no longer based on the well-established needs and resources of the extended family constellation. A further point to be kept in mind is the surprising number of dwellings constructed for artists, having the requirements of an atelier or studio. These form a small, but significant, subcategory of all residential work built during the prewar decade.

Raymond claims to have first come to terms successfully with the problem of combining Japanese and Western lifestyles in a modest house (figs. 6.27–28) he built in 1927–28 for Viscount Hamao in Tokyo. It was characteristic of the simplicity of Raymond's best post- earthquake designs and was also prophetic of the small, typical middle-class dwelling of the postwar years right up to the present. During the early 1930s a number of Japanese architects also stepped forward to propose a solution to the puzzling *wayo-kongo jutaku* typology, in aesthetic as well as functional terms.

The attempt to harmonize oriental and occidental aspects of contemporary lifestyle fell first to the two former Secessionists Yamada and Horiguchi. Yamada's House of T (published in the spring of 1932 by *Shinkenchiku* as *Ein Wohnhaus*) was not an entirely successful design, but it may have furnished an idea for Horiguchi's treatment of the Okada House of 1934 (see below). In the autumn of 1932 another house appeared in project form, in *Shinkenchiku*, which strikingly epitomized the difficulties faced by an architect

6.29. Fujiyama Mansion, Shiba, Tokyo, ca. 1932–33. Rendering of the garden facade.

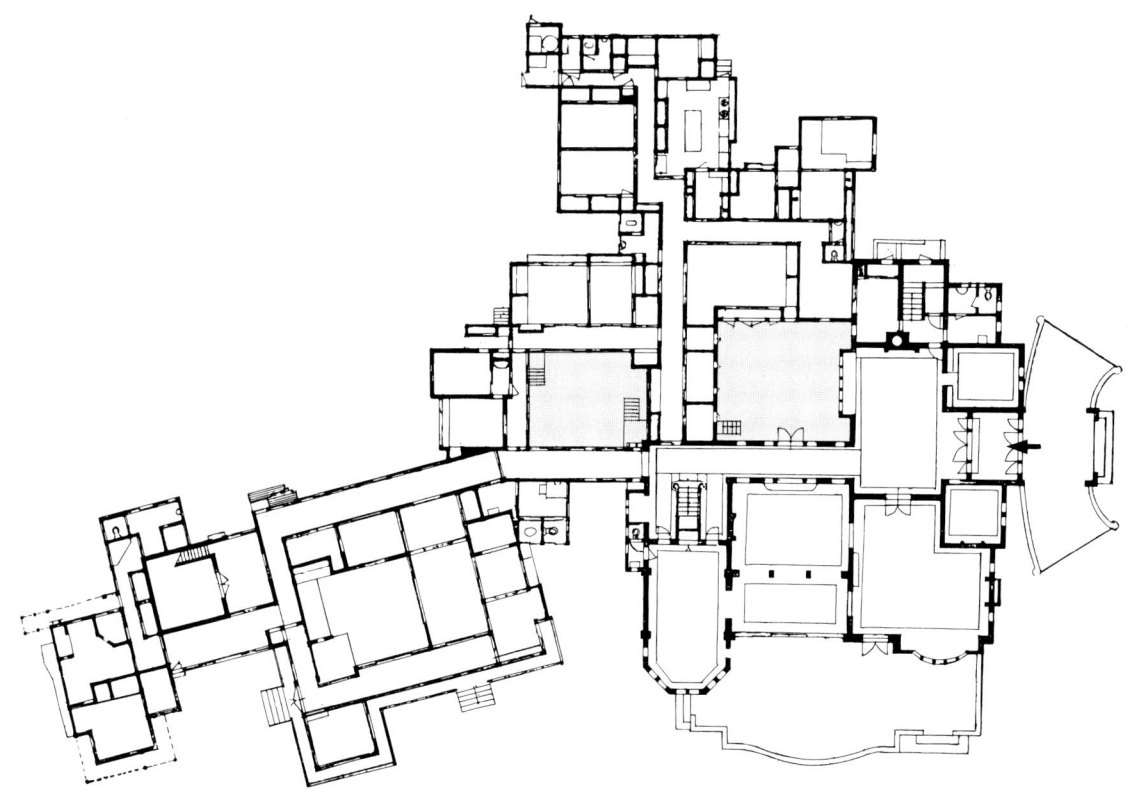

6.30. Fujiyama Mansion, Shiba, Tokyo, ca. 1932–33. Plan. Shading indicates enclosed gardens.

obliged to combine two radically different ways of life in a single work. The Fujiyama Mansion in Shiba, Tokyo, may be the ultimate example of a *wayo-kongo* residence ever designed (figs. 6.29–30). The main block was a three-story neo-Tudor edifice with half-timbered gables and carved stone ornament. The Japanese portion, on the other hand, represented a nobleman's dwelling conceived, like one wing of the Phoenix Pavilion at Chicago, in the style of late Muromachi (Ashikaga; 1336–1573). The one is crowned by a pagodalike lantern whose summit would have stood level with the filigree stone cornice of the other. Viewed from the gardens, the two facades have the appearance of separate entities. The plan nevertheless reveals the Japanese-style wing, with rooms disposed in traditional "random" sequence, to have been joined to the brick, Tudor-style structure by means of a courtyard space. Notwithstanding the extravagance and anachronism of the palatial Fujiyama Mansion, its use of a traditional central court, or *tsubo*, to weave together contrasting halves of the plan is significant. For the same device was employed by Horiguchi, and somewhat incidentally also by Yamada, to accomplish the bonding function in their more up-to-date versions of the *wayo-kongo* house.

By the time he built the House of T (figs. 6.31–32) in Aoyama, Tokyo, Yamada had already surrendered his earlier expressionism after returning from the second CIAM meeting in Frankfurt. He thus attempts to unite a reinforced-concrete house of severely plain, boxlike *Sachlichkeit* with an apparently preexisting Japanese-style dwelling, the latter containing most of the residential functions. The modern Western-style block, which Yamada added on, makes provision for a reception room, dining room, and enclosed sun-porch on the ground floor. Above are a bedroom, a study, and an open terrace, the whole topped by a roof-garden in Corbusian fashion. The sun-getting areas are expressed in a stairstep rear facade (fig. 6.33), with the Japanese-style rooms of the original main house slightly recessed to one side. The purpose of the rather desultory courtyard was to provide lighting and ventilation to the kitchen as well as to separate the traditional

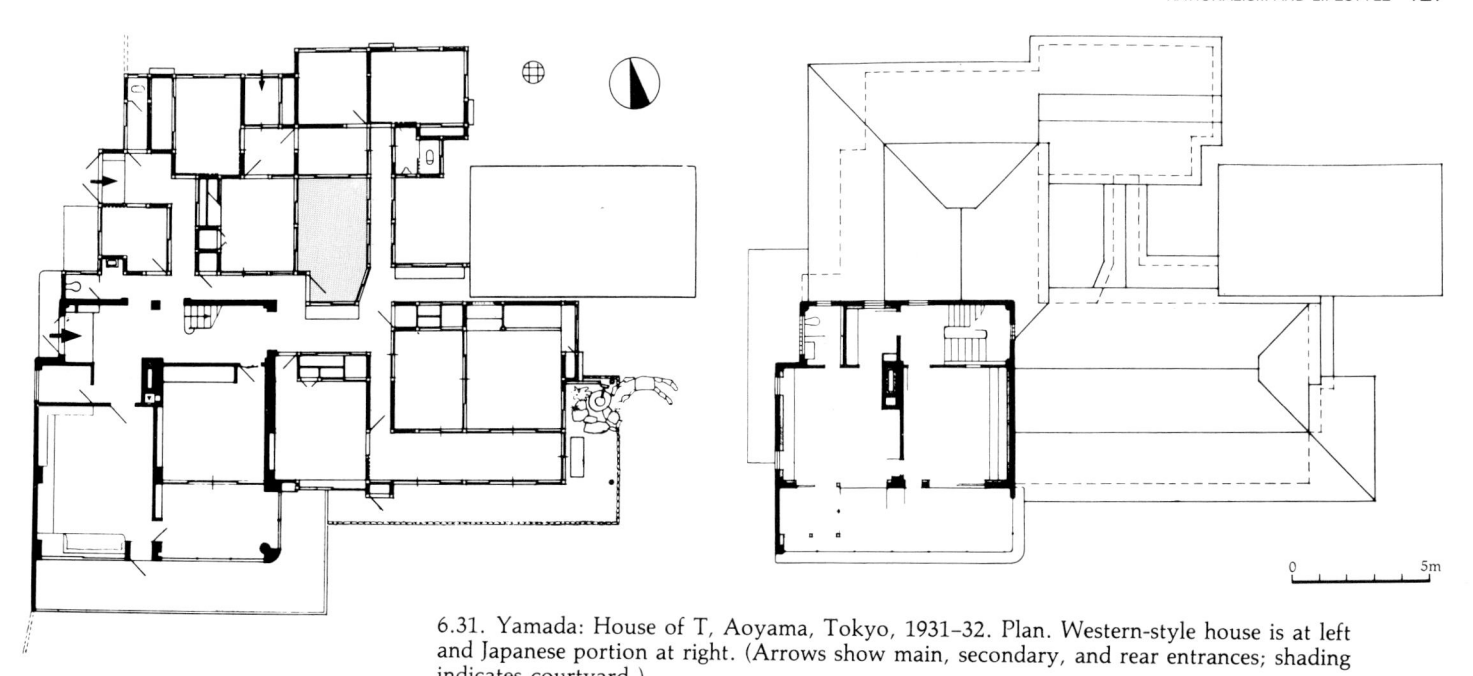

6.31. Yamada: House of T, Aoyama, Tokyo, 1931–32. Plan. Western-style house is at left and Japanese portion at right. (Arrows show main, secondary, and rear entrances; shading indicates courtyard.)

6.32. Yamada: House of T, Aoyama, Tokyo, 1931–32. South-facing interior.

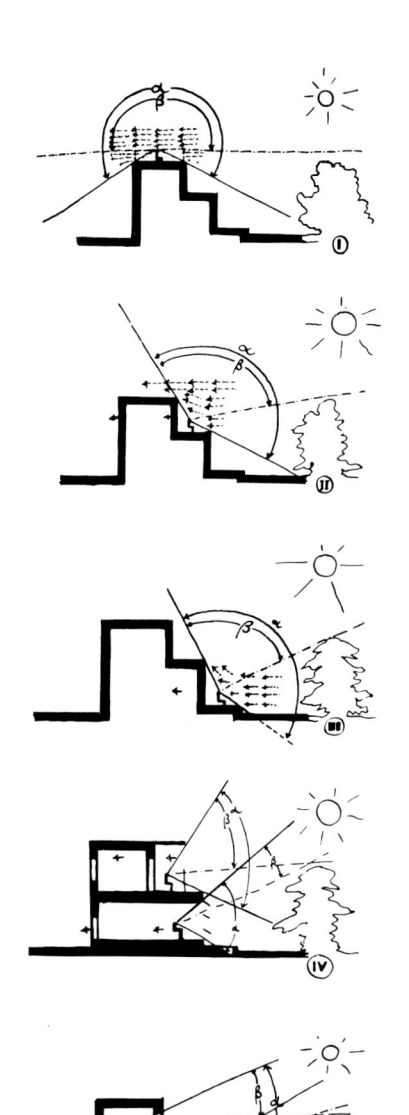

6.33. Yamada: House of T, Aoyama, Tokyo, 1931–32. Sunlight diagram.

128 RATIONALISM AND LIFESTYLE

6.34. Horiguchi: Okada Residence, Omori, Tokyo, 1934. Rear (south) facade showing juncture between Japanese- and Western-style portions.

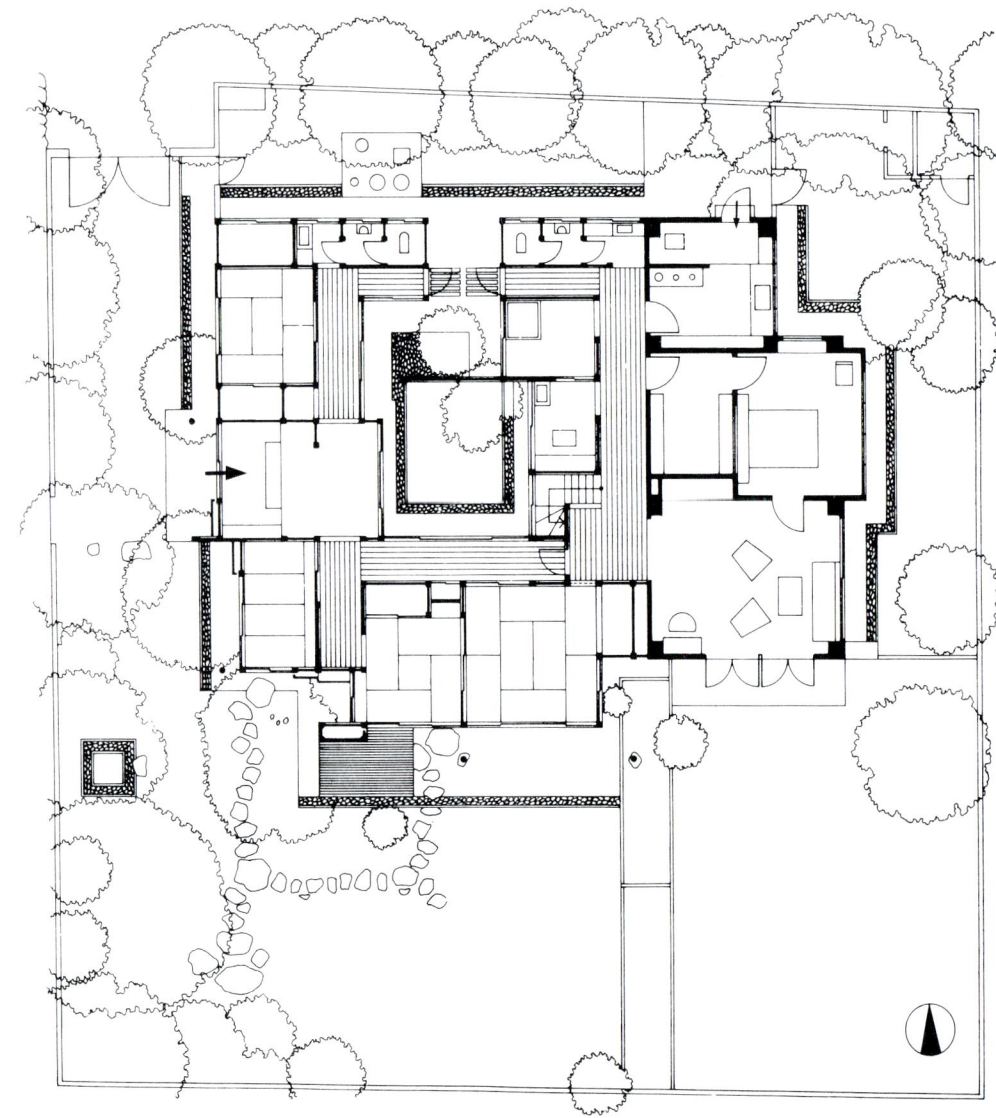

6.35. Horiguchi: Okada Residence, Omori, Tokyo, 1934. Plan.

storeroom and the bathing facilities from the rest of the house.

Only two years later, in one of the most famous houses of the period, Sutemi Horiguchi reversed Yamada's arrangement. In his Okada Residence (figs. 6.34–35) at Omori, just south of Tokyo, it is the pair of Japanese-style rooms whose expression is given priority on the garden facade, while the glazed wall of the Western-style living room is recessed slightly. The Japanese range of glazing plus *shoji* is articulated as in the *sukiya shoin* style and sheltered by an overhanging eave. Where it juts out beyond the wall of the Western wing, the conjuncture of cultures is marked by a narrow, rectangular pool which meets the foundation perpendicularly. The projecting eave is carried on a slender wooden post, which rests on the support of a natural stone set in the pool's midst. This arrangement recalls a similar composition at the Shogetsu-an teahouse of the abbot's residence of the Sampo-in at Kyoto, while opposite we have a bamboo platform reminiscent of the "moon-viewing platform" of the New Shoin at Katsura Villa. On the interior of the Okada House, an ample courtyard surrounded by verandas becomes the key planning device which separates, while joining, the two components of the structure. Horiguchi thus attempted in various ways to make use of the tea style, or *sukiya*, and its corresponding manner of garden layout to emphasize—but, at the same time, divert attention from—the interface between Japanese and Western halves of the building. The subtle dramatization this entailed had the effect of conferring classical status on the Okada Residence. Thus, today, although the house stands virtually in ruins, it is felt to supersede all other examples.

HIGH MODERN CLIMAX: ANTONIN RAYMOND'S RESIDENTIAL STYLES

By his fortieth year, the Czech-American architect Antonin Raymond (honorary Czech consul under President Masaryk from 1926) and his French interior-designer wife were well launched in the milieu of business, society, and diplomacy. That year, 1928, Raymond completed the American Embassy; in 1929 the Soviet Embassy was built more or less according to his designs; and in 1930 he finished remodeling the French Embassy. Clearly, in the world in which he now moved, large residences, embassies, clubs, and second houses were all requisite forms of expression. In 1928, also, design was undertaken for seventeen units of earthquake- and fire-proof housing destined for employees of the Rising Sun Petroleum Company in Yokohama. These were designed to be built in reinforced concrete on two types of standard plan, and each would have resembled a more or less compact version of the Reinanzaka House of 1923. The model displays rather severe, functional, boxlike dwellings having vertically integrated plans of two and a half stories, a usable roof, and a small garden.

An executive residence for Rising Sun—Raymond's first large, modern private residential work—was a more gracious design (fig. 6.36). The scheme is an elongated one and in scale it approaches his designs for the three embassies of 1928–30. This residence is somewhat vague in date but was published in the April 1931 issue of *Shinkenchiku*, volume 7, which was, incidentally, the first to appear in a modern format on good paper with clear photographs. The manager's house was followed by the better-known Rising Sun Petroleum General Office Building, possibly the first air-conditioned building in Japan. It need not detain us, however, as the style mainly reflects Raymond's enthusiasm for the work of the great French architect Auguste Perret as transmitted by a Czech assistant of Perret's named Feurstein, who worked for a time with Raymond in Tokyo. Finally, Raymond also designed two service stations as prototypes for Rising Sun, one in steel and the other in reinforced concrete (fig. 6.37). Though not entirely original, they rank among the most striking designs of Raymond's career and were duplicated for many years, as models, by the firm.

The Rising Sun Manager's Residence may have been completed as early as 1929; it is more appealing, yet more monumental, than anything else Raymond had attempted in a strictly modern idiom. The plan seems formal and French, and there are intentional classicizing touches, in the manner of Le Corbusier's final works in Switzerland and the earliest in Paris, like the *initial* project for the La Roche/Albert Jeanneret House at Auteuil of 1922 (fig. 6.38). Possibly owing to this gap in transmission, we find in Raymond's works of this period a somewhat brittle quality. Until a few years ago, they would have been condemned as "just missing" the rather strict qualifications of the International Style, as those were set forth by Hitchcock and Johnson for the Museum of Modern Art.

During the later twenties in Europe the so-called International Modern was moving toward sophisticated exploitation of visually spectacular Constructivist-inspired motifs of the same kind Raymond himself made use of in his service station designs for Rising Sun. This development gave meaning to the famous dictum about building plans being reduced

6.36. Raymond: Rising Sun Petroleum Executive Residence, Yokohama, 1931.

6.37. Raymond: Rising Sun Petroleum, steel and concrete service station prototypes, 1930.

6.38. Le Corbusier: La Roche/Albert Jeanneret House at Auteuil, Paris, 1922. Initial project.

6.39. Le Corbusier: House for Mr. Errazuris, unrealized project in Chile, 1930.

6.40. Raymond: Raymond House, Karuizawa, Nagano Prefecture, 1933. Rear facade.

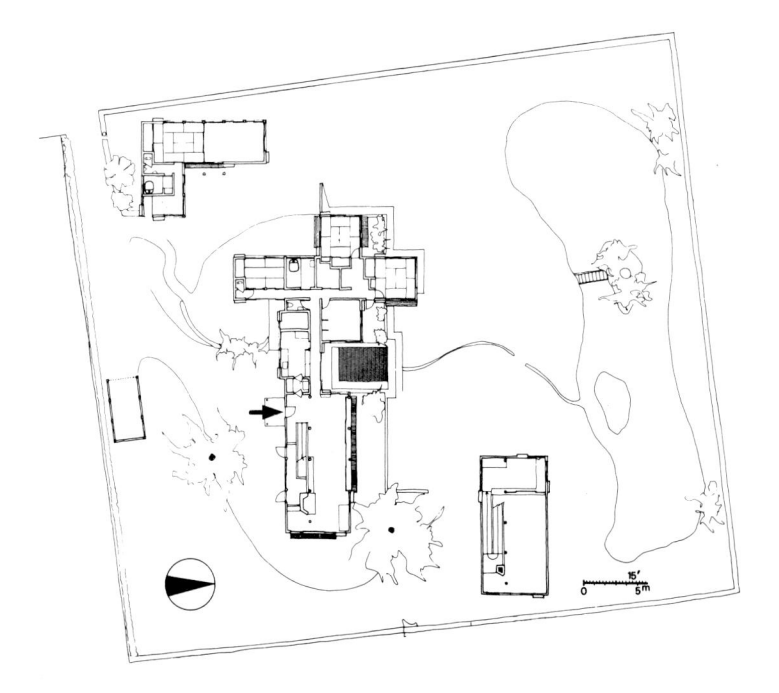

6.41. Raymond: Raymond House, Karuizawa, Nagano Prefecture, 1933. Site plan showing caretaker's cottage (upper left) and ramp leading to second-floor study (displaced, right). Shading indicates swimming pool.

6.42. Raymond: Raymond House, Karuizawa, Nagano Prefecture, 1933. Living-dining room, view toward rear garden.

to "points representing support and lines representing separation and protection from the weather."[7] Naturally, requirements for service stations and those for residential buildings are different; nevertheless, in the next few years Raymond succeeded in reconciling poured monolithic concrete with the ideals of high modernism. But, as so often is the case in Japanese architecture, events telescoped in a way that calls for a digression. For, by 1933, Raymond was actually pursuing the next, and up-to-date, phase of Le Corbusier's style but, in doing so, he turned to Japanese vernacular materials—and produced one of the most surprising buildings in the whole history of modern architecture.

This remarkable work originated in an unbuilt residential project on the coast of Chile—designed by Le Corbusier in 1930 for a Mr. Errazuris (fig. 6.39)—a scheme the Raymonds duly transformed, in 1933, into their own summer house (figs. 6.40–42). It was located at the resort colony of Karuizawa, among the mountains of Nagano Prefecture several hours to the northwest of Tokyo. For the rough masonry and tiled roof which Le Corbusier derived from the Andean vernacular, Raymond—ever resourceful—substituted log construction with cedar siding and a larch thatch. Le Corbusier was too astonished to be angry!

6.43. Raymond: Shiro Akaboshi Cottage, Fujisawa, Kanagawa Prefecture, 1931. Elevation.

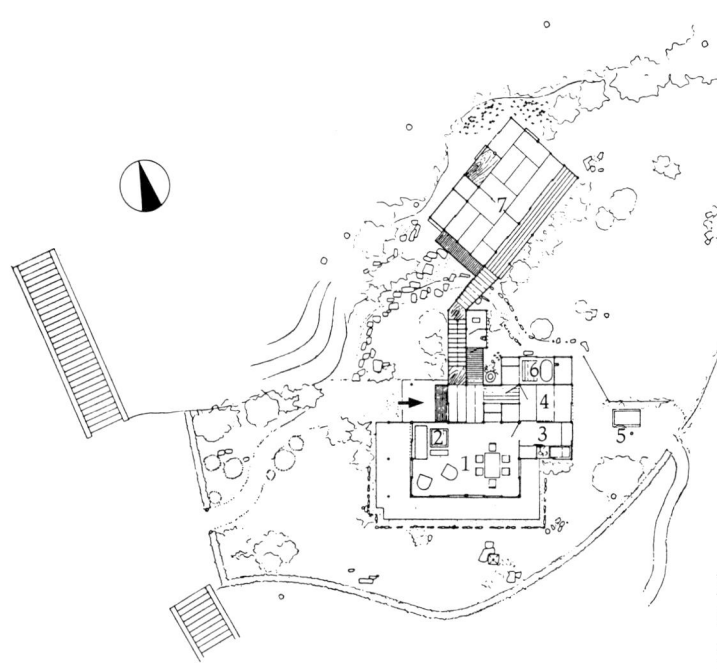

1. living rm.
2. open hearth
3. kitchen
4. servant's rm.
5. well
6. bathroom
7. bedrooms

6.44. Raymond: Shiro Akaboshi Cottage, Fujisawa, Kanagawa Prefecture, 1931. Plan.

6.45. Raymond: Shiro Akaboshi Cottage, Fujisawa, Kanagawa Prefecture, 1931. Interior.

Raymond had enlarged the sleeping quarters, giving the house a more picturesque and complex silhouette than shown in Le Corbusier's original study with its distinctively inverted style of pitched roof. The large, double-story living room fairly resembles that sketched by Le Corbusier for Mr. Errazuris, the main feature being a ramp similar to those of the Villa Savoye. But the predominance of wood in Raymond's version also lends it the air of a Japanese farmhouse, or *minka*, interior, a notion of architectural ambiance to which Raymond was to return. Befitting conditions at Karuizawa in that far-off time, furnishings were of the simplest. Tables and chairs, for example, were knocked up out of leftover lumber. Yet, having been obliged to sink a well for washing and drinking water, Raymond—with characteristic flair—inserted a swimming pool between the living and sleeping wings of the house. Finally, the Karuizawa House exuded a rough and shaggy look, owing to its thatched roof and the *sudare*, or reed blinds, that hung before the windows in summer, inspiring Raymond to quip that it resembled an African chieftain's quarters.

This one-shot vacation villa (one up on Le Corbusier) was not Raymond's first vernacular exercise. That had come with the weekend cottage at Fujisawa he built in 1931 for the famous Japanese golfer Shiro Akaboshi (figs. 6.43–45). In 1922, in fact, the prestigious Tokyo Golf Club admitted Raymond to its membership—a decisive moment in his career as a Japanese architect. Adjoining the links of the Fujisawa Golf Club, whose clubhouse Raymond designed (in modified Spanish colonial style), the Akaboshi Cottage was quintessentially Japanese in overall treatment and handling. This makes it notable as one of the earliest works associated with Junzo Yoshimura, Raymond's young manager in charge of the Akaboshi project. For Yoshimura after World War II was to become the most famous of all contemporary masters of Japanese classical architecture in a modern vein.

And, speaking of golf, when the Tokyo Golf Club elected to move from Komazawa to Asaka, in Saitama Prefecture, Raymond was of course asked to design its new clubhouse (figs. 6.46–47). This was an eminently photographable work of 1932, now virtually destroyed, and one of the most extensive private, nonresidential buildings ever put up in the International Style, certainly in Japan at any rate. The club's appearance—only the rear facade seems known—was unexpected, to be sure, but the design possesses an unassimilated textbook quality, and I am hesitant to endorse the masterpiece status sometimes claimed for it.

The Akaboshi family proved a source for Raymond of several residential commissions in the early thirties. A house for Kisuke Akaboshi, also supervised by Yoshimura, was designed in 1932 (figs. 6.48–50). It stood on a narrow, raised site overlooking a valley toward the sea. Thus the south facade consists principally of windows and was conceived by Raymond, oddly enough, in the manner of Le Corbusier's Cook House (1926), preeminently a town dwelling near the Bois de Boulogne. The plan of the Kisuke Akaboshi residence derives from Le Corbusier's Citrohan prototype, which by that time had been realized at Stuttgart, and makes use of a double-height living room overlooked by a dining room at mezzanine level. Offsetting the informality of this arrangement, the east facade is attained by a circular drive—in Raymond's consular style, so to speak—where the main entry leads to a formal vestibule, hall, and stairs sequence. On the left is a small reception parlor, of the sort noted by Raymond in his discussion of Japanese house organization, as quoted at the beginning of this section. This is balanced by a service wing on the right with stairs to the kitchen above. The ingenuity of the plan itself is not greatly inferior to Le Corbusier's own, even if the quality of the resulting spatial sequences is hard to envision. Noémi Raymond may have had a hand in these, as she did with the furnishings. Overall, of

6.46. Raymond: Tokyo Golf Club, Asaka, Saitama Prefecture, 1932. View over roof, and the model.

6.47. Raymond: Tokyo Golf Club, Asaka, Saitama Prefecture, 1932. Rear facade and view of bare concrete work.

course, the exterior massing is largely without the compelling, idiosyncratic logic of Le Corbusier's tenser and more punctual facades. Here, as elsewhere in Raymond's work, a prominent feature derived from Wright's practice are the fireplaces. But, in fact, they are also a commonplace of Le Corbusier's work during the twenties and thirties, although the hearth seems rarely, if ever, to have been regarded an essential part of the International Style.

The phase of Raymond's activity under discussion culminated in two large and luxurious houses completed by his office in the course of 1934. These show how well by this time he was able to respond to the requirements of the upper middle-class Japanese dwelling in a contemporary setting. Together with a seaside villa for Kikusaburo Fukui erected at Atami the following year, the Tetsuma Akaboshi and Morinosuke Kawasaki houses (see figs. 6.52–57) fall midway between Raymond's visit of 1931 to Italy, France, and the United States and his abrupt departure from Japan precipitated by the events of 1937. Each of these three major houses was entirely of reinforced concrete. All were designed by Antonin and Noémi Raymond in every detail, including the gardens, furniture, rugs, textiles, and electrical fixtures. In short, the Tetsuma Akaboshi House and the Kawasaki House, and to a lesser extent the Fukui Villa, record a high point in Raymond's prewar career in Japan.

The two Tokyo houses of 1934 also represent the major contribution by the Raymonds to the International Style, resolving in addition—and on a grand scale—the requirements of joint-style, or *wayo-kongo*, planning. The Tetsuma Akaboshi and Kawasaki residences produce variant resolutions

6.48. Raymond: Kisuke Akaboshi House, Tokyo, 1932. South facade.

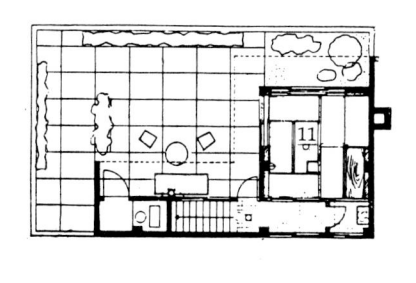

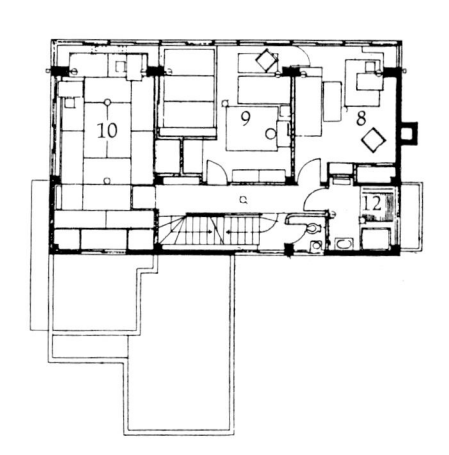

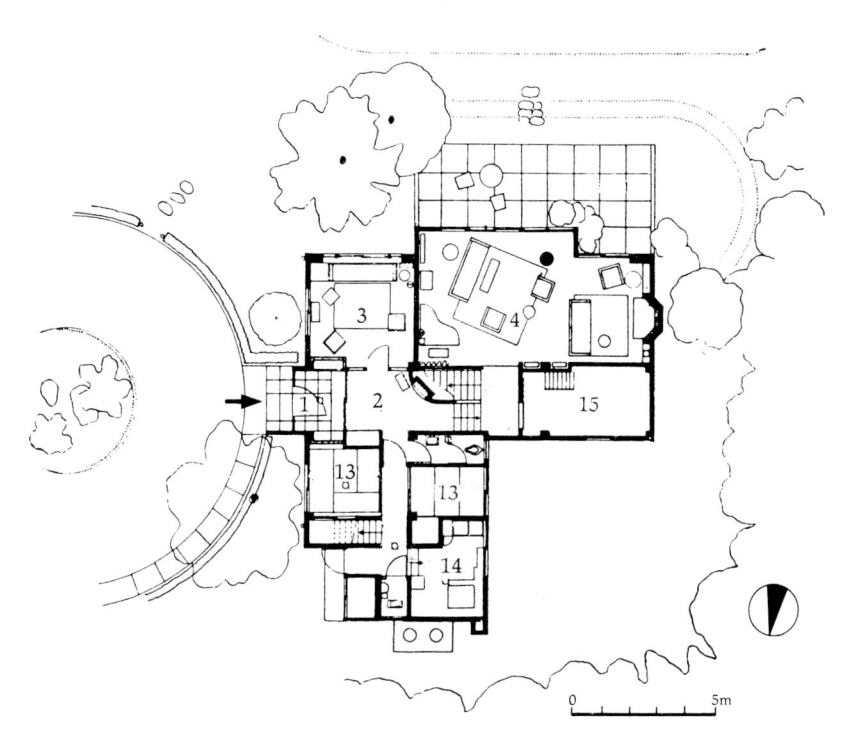

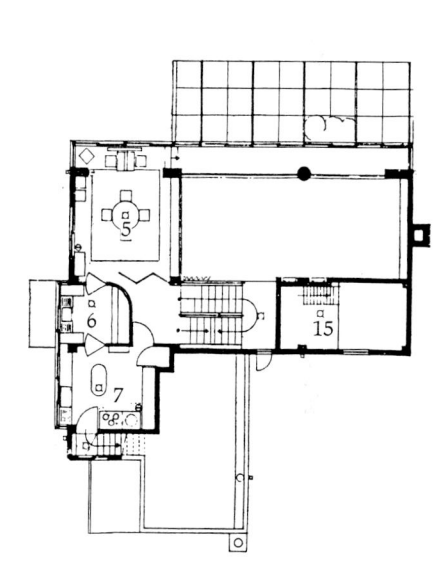

1. vestibule
2. hall
3. reception rm.
4. living rm.
5. dining rm.
6. pantry
7. kitchen
8. master's rm.
9. madam's rm.
10. children's rm.
11. Japanese rm.
12. bathroom
13. maid's rm.
14. boiler/laundry
15. storage

6.49. Raymond: Kisuke Akaboshi House, Tokyo, 1932. Plans.

6.50. Raymond: Kisuke Akaboshi House, Tokyo, 1932. East elevation.

6.51. Le Corbusier: sketch (1927) for the Pavillon des Amis at Ville-d'Avray, near Paris, 1928–29.

6.52. Raymond: Kawasaki House, Azabu, Tokyo, 1934. East facade.

of near-identical themes worked out in similar garden-enclosed surroundings. Precedents might be Le Corbusier's restoration (fig. 6.51) of the Ville-d'Avray property of Mr. Church, in 1928–29, and Mies van der Roche's celebrated Tugendhat House in Raymond's native Czechoslovakia, already mentioned in connection with Kikuji Ishimoto's Togo House. Similarly, Raymond's own remodeling of the French Embassy, and its grounds, in Tokyo affords an example of the type of project he returned to four years later in 1934. Less obvious, perhaps, though Raymond was an American citizen, is an International Style work of the same year in the United States by Edward Durell Stone, the Kowalski House at Mt. Kisco, New York.

Working for enlightened Japanese clients freed Raymond, to a degree, from his habit of subdividing plans axially into sequences of formal rooms, such as he had encountered ready-made, for instance, in the French Embassy, whose banquet hall was one of the last works executed by the team of the Parisian decorator Ruhlmann. In turn, unfamiliar demands were imposed: whether the need for a *kura* (Japanese-style storehouse) or the expectation of three separate entrances for guests, members of the immediate family, and tradespeople respectively. Furthermore, in the Kawasaki House, another project supervised by Junzo Yoshimura, Raymond adopted a feature that immediately brings to mind Horiguchi's Okada House of the same year.

Thus the main block of the Kawasaki House (figs. 6.52–54) was disposed around a courtyard. However, in a way unlike Horiguchi's composition (where two dissimilar halves, Japanese and Western, are in a sense separated), Raymond's enclosure is more of a glazed "patio" set in the midst of a columnar grid imitated from Le Corbusier. One enters a narrow vestibule leading to a small reception parlor, on the left, or else chooses the Western-style entry, on the right, with its broad hall and sweeping horseshoe stair. Facing south beyond the patio is the living room. It is flanked by a dining area and study, the latter terminating in a semicircular bay meant for a grand piano. The spaces of these three rooms flow informally between columns and over the low half-walls on either side of the free-standing chimney between living room and study. The "living-dining" continuum overlooks a terrace, with an expanse of lawn beyond it to the south. Between dining room and kitchen a passageway leads out of doors, makes a double perpendicular turn, and becomes a corridor to the Japanese-style wing of the house. This is separated from the Western wing in the manner of the Fuji-yama Mansion and looks out over a Japanese stroll garden. This native extension of the main house is balanced on the opposite side by a formal pool that is fed by a fountain in the courtyard garden of the patio opposite the main entry. The water channel forms part of a simple design composed of a path, some gravel, and a few Japanese plants.

The Kawasaki House, with its extensive gardens to the rear, was built in Azabu, not far from Raymond's own Reinanzaka property and the French Embassy compound. The house Raymond designed for the Tetsuma Akaboshi family, though located in suburban Kichijoji, is even more strictly linear in plan (figs. 6.55–57). It stretches along a central corridor with only a slight double perpendicular turning to separate the living and sleeping halves, which form a broad angle opening toward the south. The house is entered at the east end, its horseshoe stair expressed on the facade as a short of apse. Proceeding from the vestibule, rooms exposed to the south are a living room and a dining room, a twelve-mat Japanese-style room, and, past the corridor turning, "madam's bedroom," with no fewer than four small children's rooms in sequence farther along. The kitchen is situated behind a secondary stair on the north side of the break in the hall and is prolonged by a servants' wing set at right angles to the main structure. To either side of this sizable projection, the north facade is enlivened by a series of three small semienclosed courtyards, landscaped as *tsubo* gardens, and herein lies the single most original feature of the Tetsuma Akaboshi House.

The largest of these outdoor spaces is intended to separate the kitchen from the Japanese-style bathroom located at the rear of the house. A second slightly smaller one protects the family's private entrance from a view of the kitchen. The third garden is parallel to the circulation flow determined by the spinal corridor. Accordingly the hallway is glazed on the north side to afford a view across the intervening corridor from the living-dining area. The miniscule reception parlor next to the family entrance also profits from a glimpse onto this well-ordered, verdant space.

At the far end of the house there is a large foursquare *kura*, while the second story contains the master's bedroom aligned with an ample study and a ten-mat Japanese-style room all at the front of the house and opening onto a south-facing balcony. Located at the same level are a small family shrine, a further pair of children's rooms, and a second bathroom situated over that of the first floor. On the third floor there is a roof terrace with a diminutive outdoor bathing pool. A more complex network of open terraces punctuated the sec-

RATIONALISM AND LIFESTYLE   139

6.53. Raymond: Kawasaki House, Azabu, Tokyo, 1934. Living room with view toward inner garden.

1. vestibule	10. service entrance	19. patio
2. hall	11. maid's rm.	20. master bedroom
3. reception rm.	12. laundry	21. dressing rm.
4. study	13. Japanese wing	22. children's rms.
5. living rm.	14. *kura* (storeroom)	23. guest rm.
6. dining rm.	15. garage	24. bathroom
7. kitchen	16. servants' quarters	25. pantry/storage
8. family entrance	17. kennel	
9. intendant's rm.	18. pool	

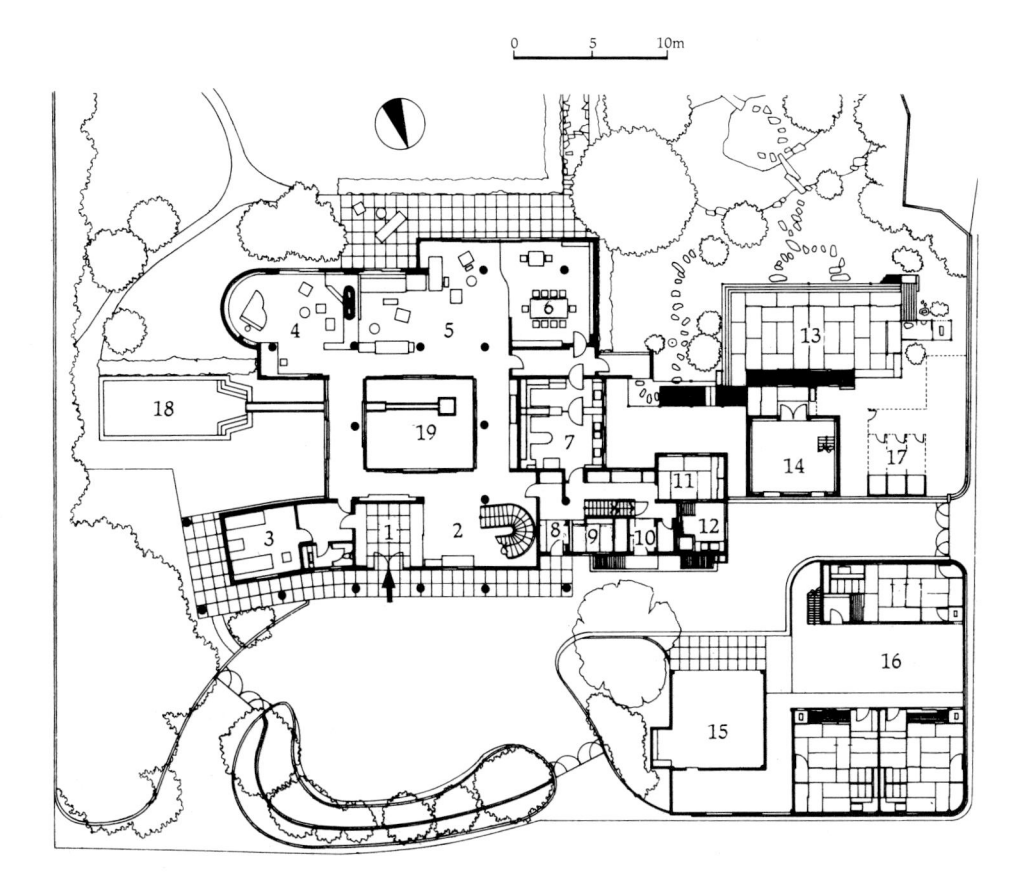

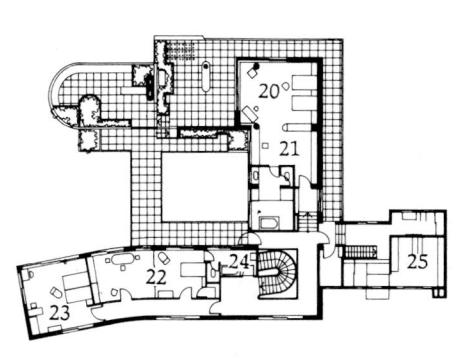

6.54. Raymond: Kawasaki House, Azabu, Tokyo, 1934. Plans.

6.55. Raymond: Tetsuma Akaboshi House, Kichijoji, Tokyo, 1934. North and south facades.

6.56. Raymond: Tetsuma Akaboshi House, Kichijoji, Tokyo, 1934. View from "madam's bedroom" toward dining room.

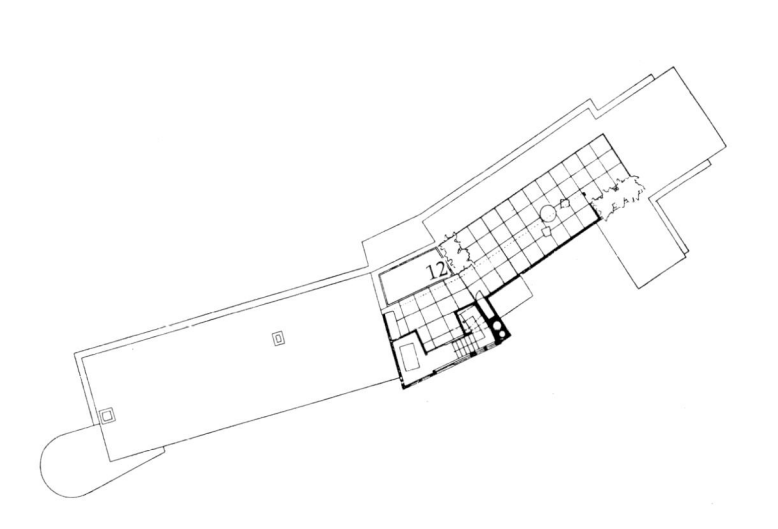

1. Japanese rm.
2. study
3. master bedroom
4. dressing rm.
5. hall
6. pantry
7. children's rm.
8. pantry/storage
9. shrine
10. bathroom
11. *kura* (storeroom)
12. pool

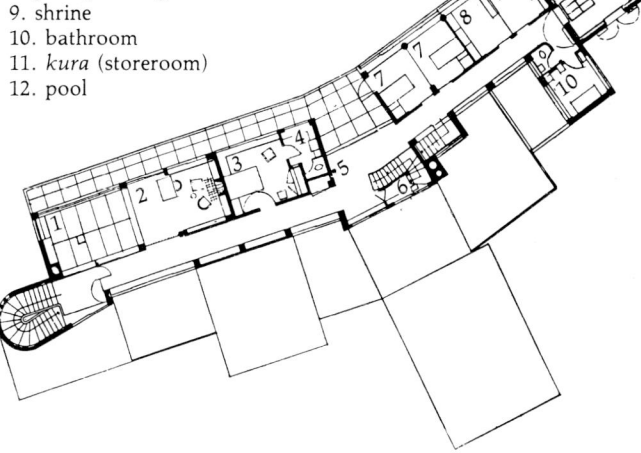

1. vestibule	11. bathroom
2. hall	12. family entrance
3. living rm.	13. reception rm.
4. dining rm.	14. intendant's rm.
5. Japanese rm.	15. pantry
6. madam's bedroom	16. kitchen
7. children's rm.	17. servants' rms.
8. *kura* (storeroom)	18. laundry
9. pantry/storage	19. service entrance
10. dressing rm.	20. patio

6.57. Raymond: Tetsuma Akaboshi House, Kichijoji, Tokyo, 1934. Plans.

6.58. Murano: Morigo Shoten office building, Tokyo, 1931.

ond floor of the Kawasaki House, all overlooking the gardens in Corbusian fashion. These two up-to-date and relatively informal houses are extremely grand by most present-day Japanese standards. With their gardens, they afford a yardstick of gracious prewar living by which it is convenient to measure examples designed by native architects.

THE DIFFUSION OF HIGH MODERNISM IN A NATIVE CLIMATE

Inclination and ability to manipulate more than a single idiom, such as Raymond demonstrated in his Japanese works up to 1937, was anathema to proponents of the International Style. Although Japanese would not have been bothered by this heterodoxy, it does seem likely, nonetheless, that Raymond's influence on Japanese architects was not much greater than we saw in the case of Frank Lloyd Wright, outside the immediate circle of office staff. One reason is that Japanese society tends to function in airtight compartments, in expression of allegiances; another is that on account of the plurality of styles it encompassed, Raymond's output lacked an easily assimilable imagery; but, most important of all, I believe, is that merely by being in Japan, his works were denied the usual cachet of exoticism possessed by foreign-built architecture—as long as it is situated abroad. Paradoxically, the closest allegiance Raymond inspired may be the devotion that Junzo Yoshimura, an exponent of the Japanese neoclassical tradition, professed for his master.

In the mid-thirties there was only one Japanese architect working in comparable modern idiom who, at the same time, enjoyed patronage on a scale similar to Raymond's. This was Togo Murano. He had graduated from Waseda University, then joined the Kansai office of Setsu Watanabe, a respected and orthodox representative of early architectural rationalism, who had spent time in America. Murano happened thus to be based in Osaka and opened his own practice there in 1929. He was three years younger than Raymond, and four older than Horiguchi. The appeal of his early writing is difficult to render in English, but suffice it to say that his youth was marked by architectural pronouncements on the order of the famous "*Yoshiki no ue ni are*" ("Be above style!") manifesto of 1919. His initial work, the plain and neat yet distinctive Morigo Shoten (fig. 6.58), was a small seven-story brick-faced office building in Tokyo of 1931, the product of ideas expressed in a 1926 article entitled "The Economic Environment of Architecture." It was an up-to-date work without surplus ornament that does not traffic in the romantic allusions which were the stock in trade of the International Modern. Indeed, Murano was convinced that, under capitalism, the only suitable and saleable architectural commodity was the restrained, ennobled kind of detailing exemplified by Ostberg's City Hall in Stockholm (1909–23). In the very year of the Morigo Shoten, Murano published another article, this time under the attractive title "*Ugokitsutsu Miru*" ("Looking While Moving,") in which he repudiated the entire Modern Movement. His dissatisfaction encompassed Le Corbusier as well as Gropius and extended to British as well as Italian modernism. In place of the International Style he announced that the panorama of Manhattan, all its skyscrapers motivated by money and technology, conveyed his new ideal of architecture—in recognition of New York as the epitome of an architecture "based on progress."

Togo Murano experienced a long and full architectural life and was by any standard an architect's architect. However, the deceptive simplicity of his work appealed especially to a clientele who had been brought up to appreciate works in the Japanese tradition of high culture embodied in the refin-

6.60. Murano: Nakayama House, Ashiya, near Kobe, 1934. Vestibule.

6.59. Murano: Nakayama House, Ashiya, near Kobe, 1934. Garden facade and plans.

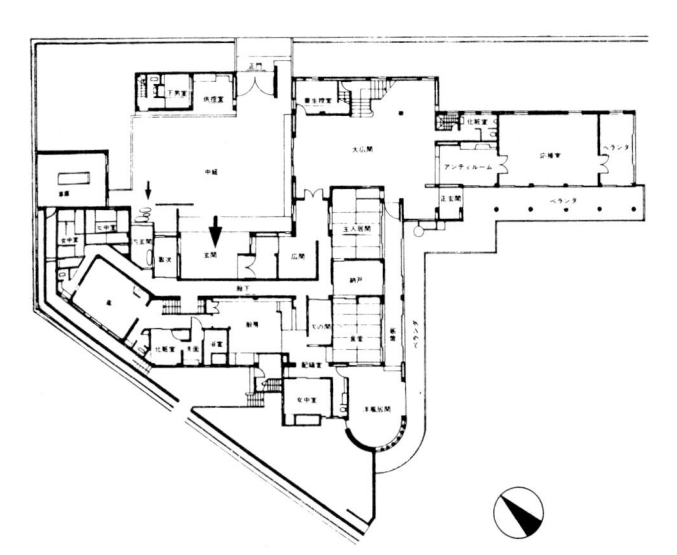

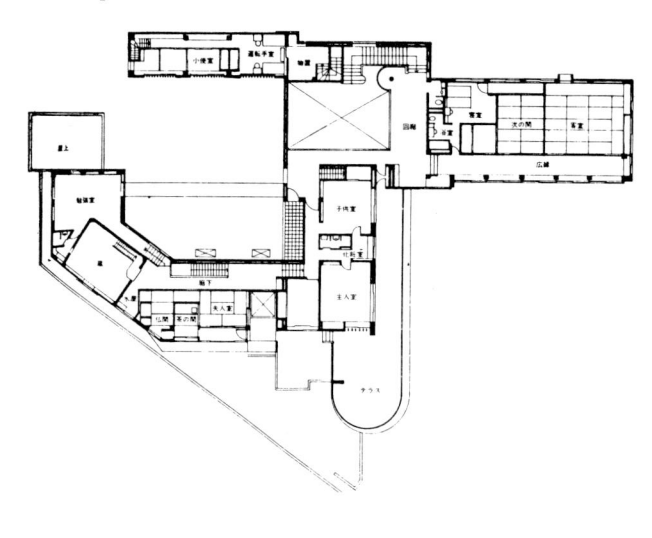

ed ethos of tea and its contributory arts. We can suppose this a very different attitude to Raymond's. For, though Raymond was largely uncommitted to the International Style *qua* style (and, in this, he resembled Murano), his interest in Japanese tradition lay with the popular arts, such as *minka*—though, of course, tea *may* provide for this as well. For a Westerner, no doubt, Murano's work seems dry, or at least aridly elegant, and, in fact, the notion of up-to-date progress apart, it embodies a very Japanese conceptual elegance whose expression is practically alien to rustic tea and its stylistic canons. Nor is it in any way "popular" or related to folk art.

The ineffability of Murano's style grew in his later oeuvre and was of course increased by reputation. There are possible parallels to be drawn with Adolf Loos in the degree and kind of Murano's aestheticism, while one problematic feature of his work is an inclusion of items of vocabulary that in the West were espoused by the official architects of fascist governments in Italy and Germany. In fact, had Japan succeeded in winning recognition for her fledgling empire, Togo Murano might have acceded to international reputation, over and above the fame he commanded in Japan throughout his lifetime. In the new democratic context that emerged after the war, the younger Kenzo Tange stepped into this role instead, and made it his own.

In 1934 Murano built the Nakayama House near Kobe in the affluent residential enclave of Ashiya (figs. 6.59–60), where Frank Lloyd Wright's Yamamura Villa (completed by his disciple Arata Endo) stood since 1924. Murano's work

144 RATIONALISM AND LIFESTYLE

6.61. Horiguchi: Kikkawa Residence, Meguro, Tokyo, 1930. Garden front.

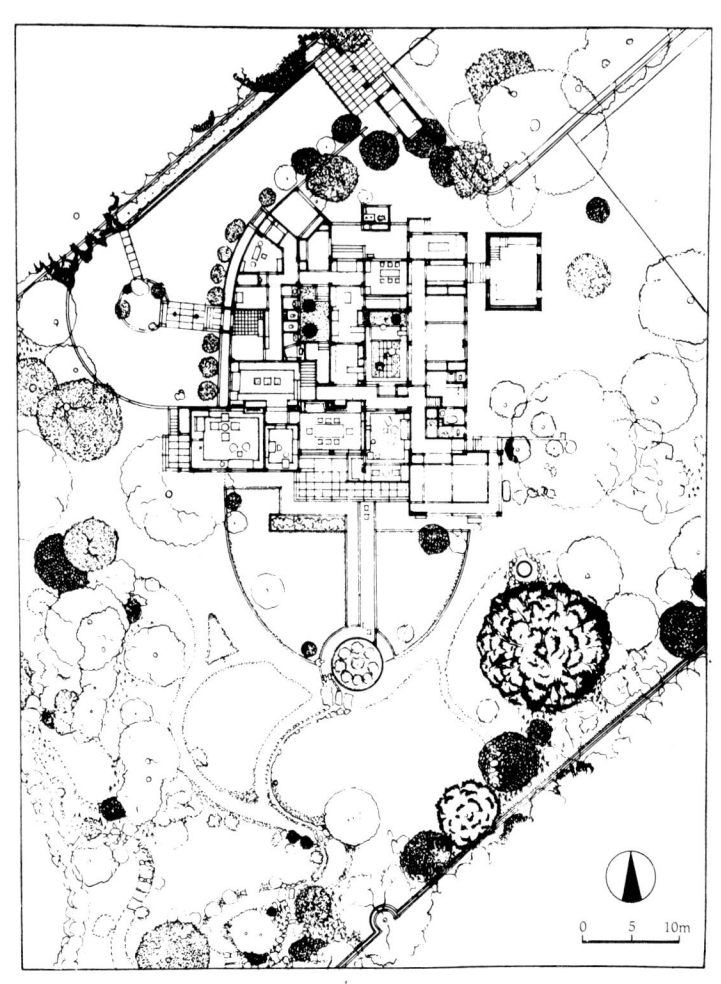

6.62. Horiguchi: Kikkawa Residence, Meguro, Tokyo, 1930. Plan.

is one more instance of the attempt to combine the virtues of upper-class lifestyle in the older, traditional Japanese and new, up-to-date Western vein, as we have seen in the work of other architects, especially Horiguchi and Raymond. Yet the Nakayama House does not afford the overall economy of previous examples, though it possesses most actual features of the two houses designed by Raymond the same year. Still, like Raymond, Murano treats the entire spatial organization traditionally, as a function of deploying the maximal southern exposure. Otherwise, their works could not be more different.

The Nakayama House is entered on the north, owing to topographical constraints of its irregularly shaped site. Here the formal guest entrance and more intimate family entrance are merely screened from each other by a partition. This is suitably decorous but disqualifies further cross-fertilization, such as we saw in the two Raymond houses. Nor is wit anywhere much in evidence, as it was in Horiguchi's famous Okada House (see figs. 6.34–35). Thus the Japanese part of the Nakayama House appears, from the plan, at least, as a murky backwater, while the Western wing features a dramatic, cinemalike stairhall not in tune with most people's idea of home. Materials such as teak veneer, Circassian walnut, and applied silver leaf produce the more or less breathtaking elegance that later became the hallmark of Murano's mature style. The rooms are too many to be enumerated. Upstairs, they occur mainly in single depth and are interspersed with terraces. Most have a view to the gardens, much as in Raymond's two houses. Still, the whole is complex and knowingly virtuosic, an ambiance furthered by sheathing the reinforced-concrete structure in mosaic tile and travertine. The appeal to Japanese aesthetics is the exquisite appropriateness of each detail, viewed in succession, enhanced by the architect's ability to wrest effects of beauty within the strict rules enforced by decorum and convention. The two sides of the house sustain, in this way, an air of cold equality.

In terms of style and scale the work most clearly comparable to the Nakayama House is Horiguchi's palatial Kikkawa Residence of 1930 (figs. 6.61–62). But it is altogether more conventionally Constructivist-minded in its welding together of mutually opposed planes and would scarcely have been out of place, say, in the outskirts of Brussels. In spite of Japanese touches here and there, and the *de rigueur* provision of several small *tsubo*-type gardens, it lacked the value of a manifesto or icon achieved by Horiguchi's Okada Residence of 1934. There, as we have seen, traditional Japa-

6.63. Horiguchi: Villa at Warabi, Saitama Prefecture, 1926. Lateral elevation and view of garden.

nese aesthetic potential was artfully merged with a schematic modernism in a way engineered to afford a collision of viewpoints. A gentle shock of recognition or confrontation is, in itself, a favorite *sukiya* device. As such, it contrasts with the somewhat anachronistic strain of elegance referred to earlier (reigning from after Buddhism's introduction until *sukiya* modified it) which Murano's work attempts to embody.

Murano's strategy in opposing "modernism" was to pursue the goal of simplicity as it accrues in technically and economically rationalized structures, like some American skyscrapers, but then, through a kind of laconic self-indulgence, to permit himself a range of spatial and material embellishments. His approach to the Japanese notion of elegance may be set beside Loos's recourse—some decades earlier, in the midst of Secession-crazed Vienna—to eye-catching slabs of plain marble and carriage-trade English furnishings, to enliven his own harshly reductive straight lines and cubes. Yet Murano was less concerned than Loos with spatial manipulation. Moreover, the variety of Japanese elegance he unleashed was deeply rooted in absolute simplicity, while an imported Englishness in the capital of baroque and Catholic Austria was relative.

Horiguchi, for his part, was on the verge of becoming an authority on Japanese-style building and garden design, for in 1932 his "Japanese Taste as Expressed in Modern Architecture" was published in the prestigious cultural journal *Shiso*. He followed this up by elaborating the notion "*yoshiki naki yoshiki*" ("style which is no style") three years later, in 1935. The phraseology brings to mind Murano's earlier notion of "surpassing" style in his "*yoshiki no ue ni are*" statement, but was also intended as a reference to the weighty interference

of the *teikan yoshiki*, or Imperial Crown style, in the affairs of the architectural profession. Yet Horiguchi, as early as the beginning of Showa, had exhibited an independent return to vernacular preoccupations. This is seen in his celebrated thatched villa at Warabi, in Saitama Prefecture, of 1926 (fig. 6.63; though on the whole the precipitating inspiration, it may be assumed, was the Dutch farm vernacular style).

While neither Murano nor Horiguchi would have anything to do with the Imperial Crown style, Murano's Institute of German Civilization of 1935 in Kyoto looks mighty like a reactionary statement, for it combines a Japanese-style roof with pergolas derived from the homely pseudoclassical style in favor with some Nazi architects. An anagrammatic statement of the work's contextual significance was the result. Yet this kind of Biedermeier jollification of modernism had originated with Speer's teacher, Heinrich Tessenow, himself a fervent anti-Nazi. A decidedly less ambiguous indication of the way things were going was the foundation, in 1936, of the Nihon Kosaku Bunka Remmei, in part as an organization for promoting the Tokyo Olympics planned for 1940. It was patterned on the model of the deservedly famous Deutscher Werkbund, whose historic role in the Modern Movement had, however, ceased by the time of that organization's Nazification in 1933. And by 1936 the Werkbund no longer even existed, except on paper. It is, therefore, certain that against such a background Horiguchi's slogan, a "style which is no style," must be interpreted as an emblem of resistance to the enforced return of a nationalistic style. Or his words may also have been an evasive tactic based on the earlier Bunri Ha ethic that to create architecture must entail an act of pure expression, asserting personality over style. At any rate, Horiguchi appears genuinely torn between personal failure to comprehend Western aesthetic notions, namely ideal categories, and his own naturalistic interpretation of Beauty. More involvedly theoretical approaches, such as Murano's strain of cultural pessimism based on his personal and avowedly materialistic interpretation of art, must have been condemned by Horiguchi from the start.

In time, Horiguchi's growing interest in tea architecture and Japanese-style gardening led him back to the minimalistic notion that art was to *make something beautiful*. Here was the prime idea which younger architects of Horiguchi's ilk—outside the academic tradition of institutionalized architecture-as-engineering—returned to in the debate concerning function (i.e., *use*) and beauty. To all obvious intents and purposes, the interest shown in Bunri Ha times in art as a form of personal expression receded, just as it had in the West nearly a decade before. But more pointedly than in the West, practice was realigned to take into account revival of a traditional concern for how materials themselves were to be "used." Such thinking contributed in early Showa to an impersonal "third-person" construct regarding architectural expression. At the same time it nurtured a heightened sensibility with respect to native idiom, which, until now, had been virtually banished to craft or minor art status. In reality, of course—all questions of nationalism apart—the new trend implied, without stating as much, a radically up-ended view of architecture itself.

GROUP HOUSING AND OTHER SOCIAL ASPECTS OF SHOWA ARCHITECTURE

Except as filling the need for a palpable "architects' vernacular," we know today the International Style was myth. Nevertheless, its ultimately Constructivist point of view, in alliance with the contemporary evolution of photography and the cinema, did much to establish the notion of *Sachlichkeit* securely in modern architecture. This way of seeing the world reaches as far back as the nineteenth century or, possibly, even to the Industrial Revolution itself. Still, the 1920s and 1930s glorified and enhanced the anonymously "impersonal" quality of national-and-industrial civilizations in a way that was new and untoward. Yet for latecomers to Western culture, such as the Russians and Japanese, the notion of architecture and urban design as a yardstick of progress was part of the history of their acquisition of Western values, preempting in an important way the claims of any particular "style."

That having been said, Constructivism—as tried by the Soviet Union for a brief period after the Revolution in the role of a quasiofficial propagandist medium—provoked greater discontinuity and, afterward, reaction than ever occurred in Japan on behalf of *modanizumu*. Such a difference might be attributable to the gradual nature of the way in which Japanese society was being continuously transformed. On the other hand, the individual—let alone the "revolutionary" individual—accounted for little in Japan. This fact may even have adaptively prepared him for the new alienation of metropolitan life and the qualitative leap imposed by industrial urbanization. For the impersonality of *Sachlichkeit* as an aesthetic ideal finds an echo in the normative "transiency of the cognitive subject" which permeates classical Japanese aesthetics—notably, but not exclusively, in the art of tea.[8]

We shall return in later chapters to this resemblance when, much later on, it begins to be sought out and pieced together by a few young architects, themselves born in the twenties and thirties. Thus, by the 1960s, there will develop a strong perception of linkage between the roots of modernism, including a sense of radical alienation, and the principal tenets of native aesthetics. For the time being it is enough to remark that Murano and Horiguchi may well have grasped this similarity in an intuitive fashion by their different ways of reapproaching the national style, however dissimilar their works may be.

So far, in our descriptive account of architecture in the early Showa period, we have dealt with the theme of the individual residence and the attempt to reconcile within it native Japanese and acquired Western ways of life. While much of the International Style's chic repute in all countries derived from villa-like private housing, the politically serious wing of the movement concentrated its efforts in the production of collective schemes. Indeed, World War I had emphasized the need to provide cheap, decent housing for an increasingly urbanized population, and not merely in those countries where existing housing stocks were destroyed. Still, in Japan—where the overall population was growing at the rate of roughly a million per year—any useful comparison with Europe is difficult.

Tenement dwellings in Japan had been a commonplace from feudal times onward, but such buildings were horizontal in layout and included even fewer amenities than their counterparts in European towns and cities. Such "long houses" (*nagaya*) survive even at present, but the principal meaning of cheap, basic urban housing is nowadays ascribed to the English, or French, "apartment." The term *apato* thus refers

6.64. Murano: Osaka Pantheon, Osaka, 1933. Entrance, and wall of main block.

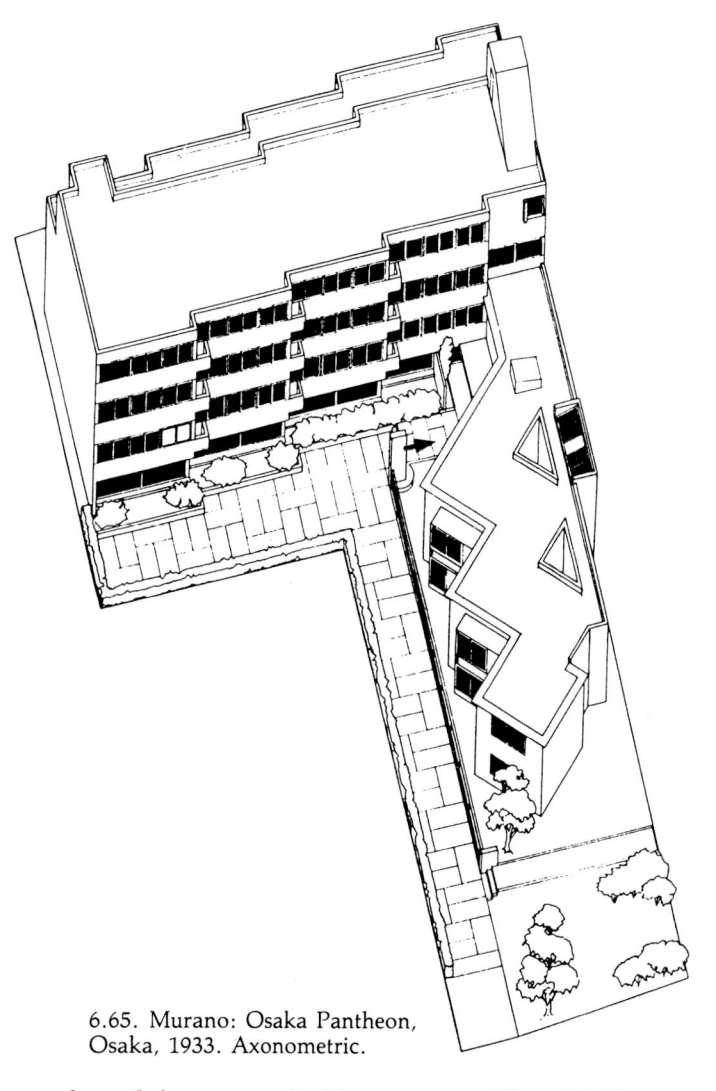

6.65. Murano: Osaka Pantheon, Osaka, 1933. Axonometric.

to small, multiple dwelling units of approximately forty square meters or less constructed in rows of one or two stories, using wood-frame or other nondurable construction. By contrast the mid-Victorian usage of "mansion" to designate flats of a better quality currently refers to collective housing constructed of reinforced concrete, except social housing blocks, which are known as *danchi*. But this latter type of flat, originally financed semiprivately, has no history whatsoever in Japan until after the earthquake of 1923.

About the time of World War I, special provisions regarding loans, sale and transport of building materials, building taxes, and right of eminent domain were enacted when an urban housing shortage was first perceived. These measures correspond in date with Japan's first employment and social security legislation passed during the early twenties, and creation of new housing was regarded mainly as a form of social relief work. However, the Great Kanto Earthquake provided the impetus for enactment of a housing association law, and the government itself established the so-called Dojunkai as model for this type of organization. So by the mid-thirties housing was to some extent identified in the mind of the public as a need not merely related to alleviation of hardship. Yet it was only one item among many in a scarcely comprehensive social agenda which was the responsibility of a government branch known as the Department of Local Affairs, a dependency of the Ministry of Home Affairs. This catchall agency supervised the operation of public markets, hostels, pawnshops, bathhouses, clinics, sanatoria, and child-care centers, probably an impossible range of tasks for any bureaucracy at that period, yet one which affords an interesting picture of the priorities of public life at the beginning of the Showa reign.

At the narrower end of the social scale, however, stood a few small, private, high-class residential developments that, architecturally, shared some of the pretensions of individual residences. Among the earliest of these, two were situated in western Japan. Their aim was to cater to life outside the bosom of the extended family, an institution which in Tokyo had already been significantly eroded by the fact that the capital of the country was also its prime labor market. One such early example was a student hostel at Kyoto University, while the other was a private complex, designed by Togo Murano, known as the Osaka Pantheon. It must have been used by young salaried employees, or possibly artists and musicians. Both are of 1933 and provide, incidentally, a suggestion of economic recovery by that date.

The Osaka Pantheon (figs. 6.64–65) is perhaps the most likeable and accessible of all Murano's youthful works. It was

6.66. May: Bruchfeldstrasse Siedlung, Frankfurt/Main-Niederrad, 1925.

6.67. Tsuchiura: Rakuto Apartment, Kyoto, 1933. Perspectives of facade and a representative room interior.

termed an "apartment house" by *Shinkenchiku* but appears more like a residential hotel in its arrangement and provision of services. Compact, individual sleeping rooms were spread over four floors, which also included several larger units with their own kitchenettes. All accommodation had a view onto either a narrow landscaped terrace or a tiny bit of garden. Here, any *tsubo*-like effect is residual, yet it is the nature of the *tsubo* form, if not of Japanese "space" in general, to emphasize the surfaces of bounding planes and not the voids they contain. Japanese space is exactly, so to say, a residue, and Murano's idiosyncratic use of staggered planning, a common enough feature in itself of the International Style, points up this nonspatiality of space.

Apart from its function to vary and increase the footage of southwest exposure on the sun-getting facade of the Osaka Pantheon's inner courtyard, the stagger device is in itself a quotation. Still, it will be remarked that the totality of visual (i.e., spatial) effect is very different from the baroque symmetry of a work such as Ernst May's iconic Bruchfeldstrasse Siedlung of 1925 at Frankfurt/Main-Niederrad in Germany (fig. 6.66). But whereas the latter was intended to form a good-size community, Murano's work of eight years later remains at a scale familiar from some of the small apartment buildings of pioneering West Coast modernism, as represented by the work of Gill or Schindler in southern California. Nevertheless, the Osaka Pantheon contains public rooms, such as a double "salon" combined with a dining room and bar, not to mention a billiards room. Bathing provisions seem virtually nonexistent, and it was probably assumed that residents would resort to a local bathhouse.

The other 1933 example of an up-to-date residential facility was the Rakuto Apartment (fig. 6.67) located in the vicinity of Kyoto Imperial University. It is the work of Kameki Tsuchiura, whose reputation as a modernist, based on a period of apprenticeship with Frank Lloyd Wright at Taliesin, is greater within Japan than we shall have the opportunity of suggesting. Strange to say, most of his work presents variants of the International Style, to which Wright was more

6.68. Yamaguchi: Bancho Siedlung, Bancho, Tokyo, 1933. View from street.

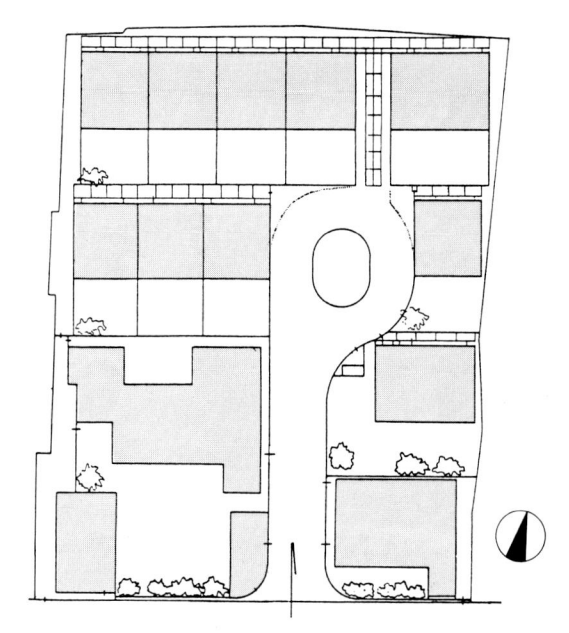

6.69. Yamaguchi: Bancho Siedlung, Bancho, Tokyo. 1933. Site plan.

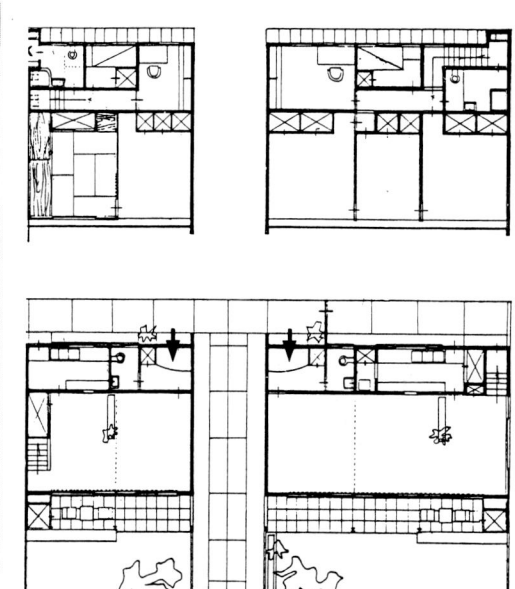

6.70. Yamaguchi: Bancho Siedlung, Bancho, Tokyo, 1933. Unit facade and plan of rear block.

or less consistently opposed throughout his lifetime, while very little of Wright's own influence may be seen in Tsuchiura's works. The Kyoto student hostel contained 100 rooms distributed over five floors on a T-shape plan. The design was not staggered, as in the Osaka Pantheon, but a setback was used for the last two floors. This device, together with porthole windows and prominent continuous railings for balconies and staircases, gives a clear idea of what was sometimes known as the *paquebot* style, to which Tsuchiura added a mast with a flying pennant for good measure. Students' rooms were small (the equivalent of six *tatami*) but not minimal, and there were a dining room, a tea room, and an in-house hairdresser's shop. It should be remarked that during the prewar years most students still lived in innlike lodging houses beside the campus, so that the Rakuto Apartment is both a continuation as well as an interesting departure from this tradition.

Tsuchiura's building at Kyoto can be described as "modernistic," somewhat in the manner of Sauvage or Lurçat. In terms of the International Style, the best example of a collective housing project ever to be realized in Japan is a contemporary work by Bunzo Yamaguchi, the erstwhile assistant of Ishimoto. Yamaguchi had returned from Germany in 1932 and his Bancho Siedlung in Tokyo (designed the following year it would seem), recalls the Deutscher Werkbund's Weissenhof Siedlung of 1927 at Stuttgart, which succeeded in bringing together architects from all over Europe. The new Bancho Siedlung (figs. 6.68–70) in Tokyo was a private housing compound and consisted of a cul-de-sac road with terrace houses based on two models differing only as to number of bedrooms, two or three according to type. Each unit affords a combined living-dining area confronting its own small garden. The stair ascends without ceremony from this living area to the bedroom floor, still with its diminutive maid's room. The kitchens were "equipped" in the new German manner, which, as we shall note later, was a revolution in itself. Detailing of the ensemble of units is already recognizably Yamaguchi's own, daintier perhaps than that

6.71. Dojunkai: Harajuku Apartments, Aoyama, Tokyo, 1926.

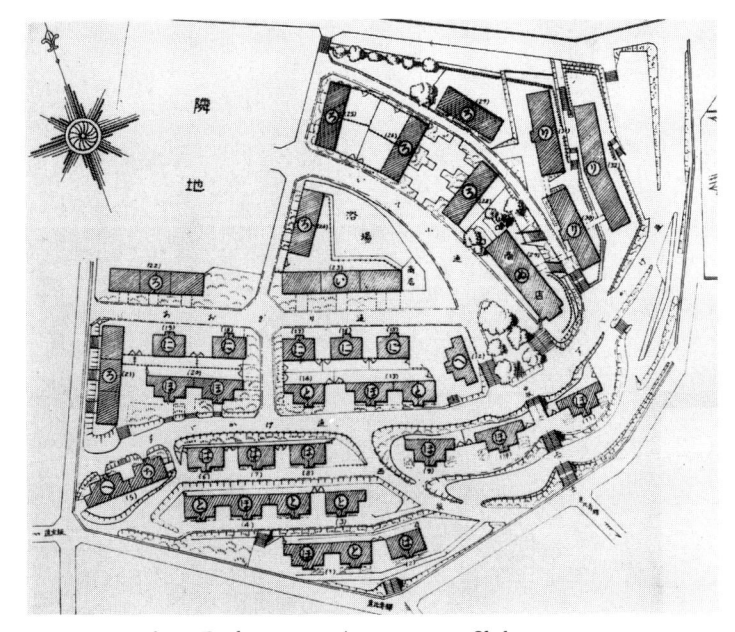

usually associated with his master, Gropius. The exterior of Bancho Siedlung was finished in white mosaic tile, with the trim, a little surprisingly, painted a shade of deep purple, while concern for integration of style extended even to the design of street lighting.

By the mid-thirties the Dojunkai, or government-sponsored private association—already noted as the principal purveyor of social housing during this period—had completed numerous realizations before it, too, fell victim to military priority, as did most nascent social services. Some of its subsidies were spent on reinforced-concrete group housing of several stories, while the rest were extended to help finance traditional-style Japanese housing units. On the whole, the former seem to have appealed to the upper middle classes, whether by intention or not. At the time of writing, such early Japanese examples of collective housing are an endangered species, notwithstanding a vogue some acquired in the seventies. The most prominent instance is the so-called Harajuku Apartments in Omotesando, Aoyama (fig. 6.71), which was allowed to go downhill until inexplicably, in recent years, numerous units have been taken over by boutiques. At any rate, the entire complex is now scheduled for comprehensive redevelopment by a private land corporation. Another group about to be razed was built in 1927 in Daikanyama, Shibuya (figs. 6.72–74), and was well documented photographically in its heyday. Both installations are of post–1923-earthquake reinforced-concrete construction, having cement stucco detailing applied over battens. In keeping with their status as social housing, individual units were smaller than those Yamaguchi designed in Bancho, a more aristocratic neighborhood to the north. The Daikanyama Apartments also included some communal facilities, such as a meeting room as well as a residents' restaurant, the latter possibly to compensate for the inadequacy of individual unit kitchens.

6.72. Dojunkai: Daikanyama Apartments, Shibuya, Tokyo, 1927. Site plan.

The most celebrated of all Dojunkai enterprises is the now half-century-old Edogawa Apartments in north-central Tokyo, built in 1934 (figs. 6.75–76). This was also the final and culminating statement made by the housing association before its demise. Not, therefore, a typical instance of Dojunkai work, this from the beginning fashionable—because big and massively built—block of flats was delineated in two ranges, one of four and the other of six stories. Edogawa was also exceptional in enjoying central heating, whose apparatus was later removed on behalf of the war effort. Necessarily, its flats were equipped with flush toilets, an unusual rarity in the Tokyo of that day. The basic unit contained one

RATIONALISM AND LIFESTYLE 151

6.74. Dojunkai: Daikanyama Apartments, Shibuya, Tokyo, 1927. Room interior.

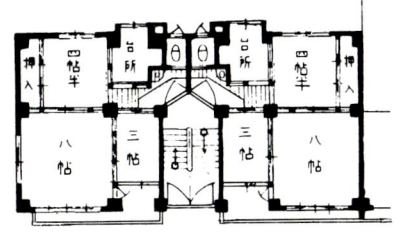

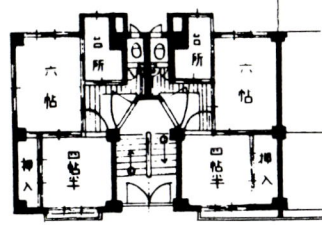

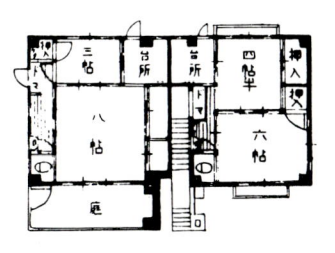

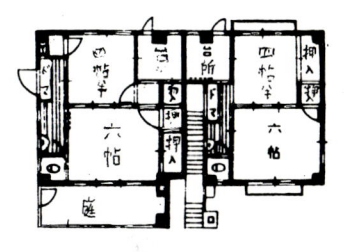

6.73. Dojunkai: Daikanyama Apartments, Shibuya, Tokyo, 1927. Representative facade and diverse floor plans.

6.75. Dojunkai: Edogawa Apartments, Edogawabashi, Tokyo, 1934. View from the central court.

6.76. Dojunkai: Edogawa Apartments, Edogawabashi, Tokyo, 1934. Model.

6.77. Tsuchiura: Ninomiya Apartments, Tokyo, 1937. Rear view.

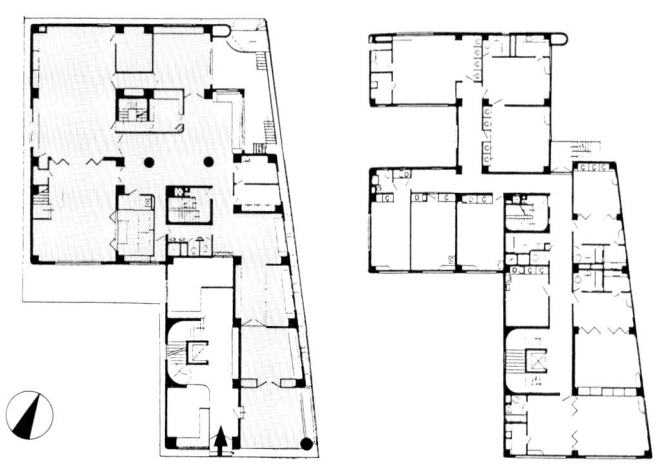

6.78. Tsuchiura: Ninomiya Apartments, Kudan, Tokyo, 1937. Plans. Shading indicates photographer's ground-floor studio.

generous-size room as well as two smaller ones, plus a good-sized entry hall, but two- and four-room flats could also be leased. The upper two floors of the rear block were reserved as bachelor accommodations and, therefore, are without the balconies considered essential for daytime occupation by children and housewives (a reminder of the traditional-style dwelling with its *engawa*, or continuous verandalike porch). The court formed between the two sections of the building provided a landscaped garden wrested from the city, as exemplified in the European theory of community residential blocks.

The Dojunkai was largely successful in promoting flats as respectable urban accommodation, at least among the upper middle-class bohemian fringe (many of the original Edogawa Apartments' tenants were involved with literature or the arts). In the private sector it was the Ninomiya Apartments (figs. 6.77–78), located at Kudan and constructed in 1937 to designs by Tsuchiura, that confirmed this tendency. Standing as it did near Soldiers' Hall in the Imperial Crown style, this block was visibly a manifesto of modernism—one of the last, in fact. It rose seven stories, with alternating bands of blue and white tile concealing a concrete frame set with flush, horizontally aligned windows. The ground floor contained a photographer's studio complete with imitation zebra rug in the waiting room. For the flats above, there was a fully glazed ground-floor lobby furnished with chrome-plated, tubular steel seating. Both one- and two-room living units were available, all with heating and hot water provided in common. Rooms were ample and airy and had beds and wardrobes built in. Finally, in contrast with Dojunkai accommodation, floors were of hardwood and there was not a *tatami* mat in sight.

KUNIO MAEKAWA

From 1938 Kunio Maekawa, a young architect without immediate family in Tokyo, occupied a flat in the Ninomiya Apartments. He had decided his vocation at the age of fifteen after seeing Horiguchi's Memorial Tower at the Ueno Peace Exhibition in 1922 (see fig. 5.7). He was admitted to Tokyo Imperial University, where he studied Keats, Browning, Yeats, and Hardy, without being able to discover any trace of the latter's early ambition to be an architect. He was advised by a professor to attend to Ruskin's *Seven Lamps* instead of bothering his head with the works of Karl Marx, and he made copies of the Greek orders. Having once discovered Le Corbusier's Villa at Vaucresson in the sepia reproductions of *L'Architecture Vivante*, Maekawa grew convinced of his own disposition toward latinity in contradistinction to the practical-minded German tradition reflected by the university's curriculum. It also happened that Professor Kishida, returning from Europe, made Maekawa a present of several books written by Le Corbusier, including *L'Art décoratif d'aujourd'hui* (which Maekawa was to translate in 1930). He was quite naturally struck by the lyrical "Confession" appended to that work, with its description of the French architect's journey across Europe as an impecunious student in 1908–9, including the revelation to him of Greek architecture while camping amid the stones of the Acropolis in Athens. In 1928, Maekawa finished his course and, having an uncle living in Paris, set out immediately to find employment with Le Corbusier. He was granted admission to the atelier in April after a seventeen-day trip from Japan across Siberia. This was the year in which Le Corbusier reelaborated his League of Nations project for the second stage of the competition (fig. 6.79) and of the first CIAM meeting at La Sarraz. The original scheme for the Villa at Carthage was on the drawing board, and Maekawa himself was engaged in working up the design for the Wanner flats later built at Geneva.

After a two-year stay with Le Corbusier, Maekawa returned to Japan in 1930. He then spent five years in Antonin Raymond's office in Tokyo, which spanned the period of the French Embassy remodeling as well as the important Kawasaki and Akaboshi houses. Following cancellation by the Japanese government of the Ford Motor Company's project for a factory which Raymond was to have designed at Tsurumi, Raymond was placed in the awkward situation of having to ask his staff members to solicit work. Maekawa had obtained the offer to do a candy store for the Morinaga Company and, after a dispute erupted between the two architects in September 1935, he was in a position to undertake this job on his own. Although the shop was duly built and published the next year, Maekawa preferred to consider the competition for the new Imperial Museum as the beginning of his career as an architect.

Maekawa, in fact, had already refused an increase in pay at Raymond's office and asked instead to be granted a portion of each afternoon to work on competition entries. Apart from several important private houses, the bulk of Maekawa's published work for the remainder of the thirties consisted of competition drawings. The schemes that he produced in this manner were frequently premiated but seldom, if ever, ac-

6.79. Le Corbusier: League of Nations, Geneva, 1928. Unrealized competition entry.

6.80. Maekawa: Tokyo Imperial Museum, Ueno, Tokyo, 1931. Unrealized competition entry.

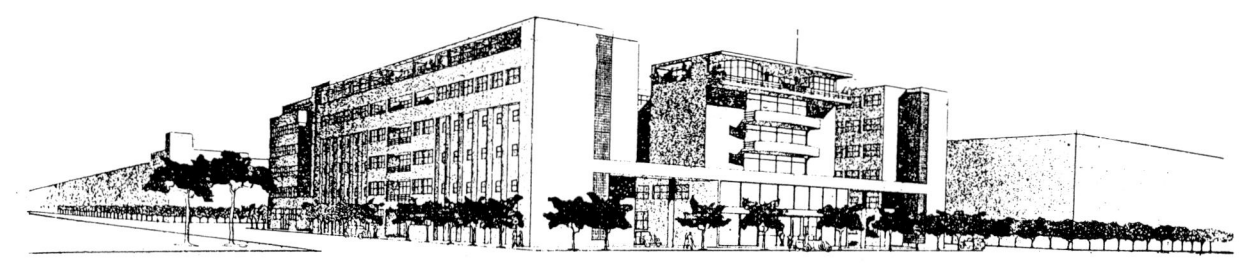

6.81. Maekawa: First Mutual Life Insurance Company, Tokyo, 1933. Unrealized competition entry.

6.82. Watanabe: Dai-ichi Seimei Building, Hibiya, Tokyo, 1934–38.

tually built. The winning entry in the Imperial Museum Competition by Jin Watanabe in the Imperial Crown style has already been discussed (see figs. 6.3–4). Maekawa's entry (fig. 6.80), dating from 1931, had no hopes for winning as it did not follow the competition's predetermined plan. Instead, Maekawa seems to have taken the opportunity to express his idea of modern design for the education and enlightenment of the jury. This contentiousness can only have been imitated from Le Corbusier, and Maekawa's scheme for the museum is, indeed, strongly related to the League of Nations project already referred to.

Maekawa submitted a similar scheme for the headquarters of the First Mutual Life Insurance Company in a competition held in 1933, one year after the Imperial Museum results were decided (fig. 6.81). The Dai-ichi Seimei Building, as the project is referred to in Japanese, was also won by Watanabe. As completed in 1938, Dai-ichi Seimei (fig. 6.82) became the fourth largest structure in Japan in terms of floor space, after the Marubiru (1923), the National Diet Building (1936), and Mitsukoshi Department Store (1934). It possesses a reinforced-concrete frame faced with granite and there are seven stories above ground and four below, the latter reflecting preoccupation on an international scale with bombproofing and defense against poison gas. Watanabe's design was Japan's prime contribution to the vogue for stripped classicism during the prewar years, sometimes still referred to as the "international fascist" style. Dai-ichi Seimei is admired today in some quarters—perhaps not altogether unjustly, if account is taken

6.83. Le Corbusier: Centrosoyus, Moscow. Submission drawing of 1929.

6.84. Maekawa: Tokyo Municipal Hall, Tokyo, 1934. Unrealized competition entry.

of its magnificent site looking out over the Imperial Palace moat. In any case, the building achieved lasting fame after World War II as the GHQ of the American command headed by General MacArthur.

While Watanabe's winning design reflected a trend of the times in favor of a certain monumental ahistoricism, Maekawa's submission must have been inspired at least partly by Le Corbusier's Centrosoyus project for Moscow (fig. 6.83), whose working drawings were remitted in 1929 during Maekawa's stay in Le Corbusier's office. Moreover, in the Dai-ichi Seimei Building as executed, there can be detected more than a hint of Maekawa's side elevation in the main facade of Watanabe's design. This is ascribed to 1934 and was probably the result of a runoff stage. The same year Maekawa himself was to win third prize in the competition that was vetted for a new Tokyo Municipal Hall (fig. 6.84) to be situated on one of the islands adjacent to newly reclaimed land in Tokyo Bay. Maekawa's scheme is still close in conception to the museum and insurance company entries but this time includes a central tower, which the description somewhat guiltily notes may be left off if desired. Bruno Taut, writing about the whole assortment of entries in *Shinkenchiku*, cannot generate much enthusiasm anymore. In 1937, Maekawa secured first place in a competition for the Showa Steel Factory Administration Building; however, his winning entry distinctly resembles Watanabe's Dai-ichi Seimei, then nearing completion (but Maekawa gives it a central tower).

Maekawa's first-prize entry in the Dairen Civic Hall competition of the following year is a more considered design (fig. 6.85), localizable somewhere between Italian *razionalismo* and American WPA. The dilemma of whether or not to insert a tower is cunningly solved by "borrowing" (as the Japanese landscape gardening tradition has it) the Monument to the Loyal Dead which stands on a hill behind the building. This had become a familiar feature of most Manchurian towns and settlements and can be clearly seen in the submission rendering over the esplanade dividing the two halves of Maekawa's civic hall. Though not part of the architecture, it manages to afford the crowning element of the design. Its presence allows Maekawa the luxury of an essentially unadorned modern building at a time when "modern" architecture was no longer permissible. Incidentally, in the same year (1938) as the Dairen Competition, a young architect, Kenzo Tange, entered the Maekawa office fresh out of university, attracted by Maekawa's entry for the Tokyo Hinomoto Kaikan Competition of 1935.

Tange stayed with Maekawa until returning to graduate school in 1942. During 1939 the office was engaged to design new employee housing for the Shanghai Commercial Bank— and a Shanghai Branch of the Maekawa firm remained open until the end of 1943. The following year Maekawa designed a house for himself in Meguro (see figs. 8.6–7), to which the remnant of his office transferred after the bombing raids of 1945 had destroyed the Ginza studio he had opened a decade before. At all events, the office did not want for work during the years of the Sino-Japanese conflict and the Pacific war against the Allies. Maekawa designed two power stations and the Kishi Memorial Gymnasium, all in 1940, and in 1941 he built an office for Toho Films and designed several exhibitions, including the so-called Pacific News Exhibition. In 1942 Maekawa opened a Manchurian branch at Mukden and in 1944 a local branch at Tottori in western Japan. It is perhaps not surprising that Maekawa has written of these first ten years of practice—with the exception of his residential designs, which we shall discuss later—as a period of growing ambivalence toward the principles of modern design and their significance for Japanese architecture.

In 1936 Maekawa's participation in the limited competition sponsored by the Japanese Foreign Ministry for the design of the Japan Pavilion at the 1937 Paris Exposition already provided an interesting case in point. The style of Maekawa's premiated entry (figs. 6.86–87) appears less influenced by Le Corbusier than by Gunnar Asplund's marvelous buildings for the Stockholm Exhibition, despite the fact that Maekawa's plans and interior perspectives are drawn in characteristic Corbusian fashion. The Foreign Ministry was looking for a work in the Imperial Crown style, more or less in the same vein as the Japanese Pavilion at the Cité Universitaire in Paris, and it is not known how Maekawa managed to prevail against these expectations. Writing in *Kokusaikenchiku*, and with one eye on the censor, the architect spoke of the difficulty of achieving a "real" Japanese style of modern architecture. Such

RATIONALISM AND LIFESTYLE 155

6.85. Maekawa: Dairen Civic Hall, Dairen, 1938. Unrealized winning competition entry, rendering and plan.

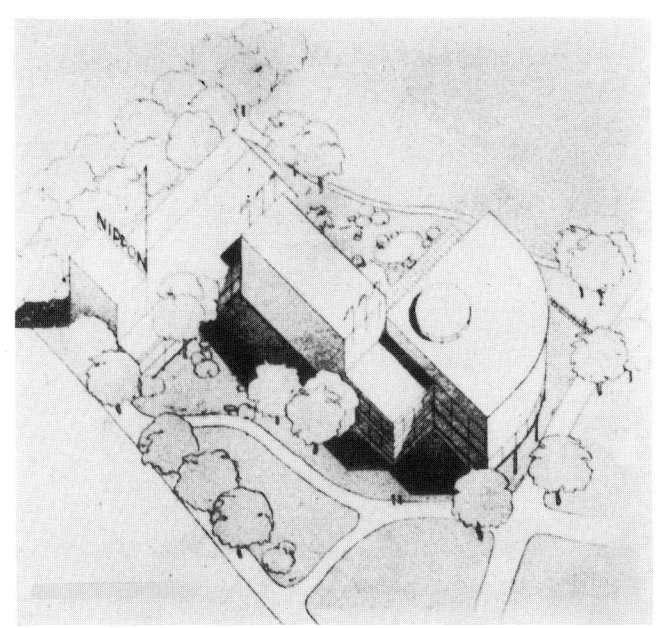

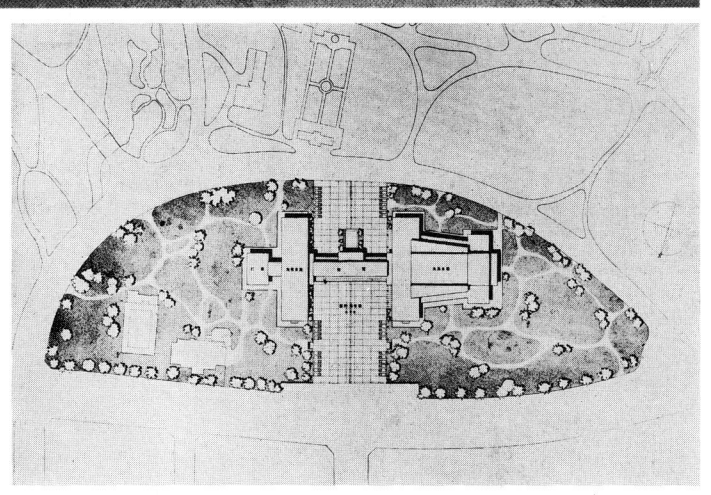

6.86. Maekawa: Japan Pavilion, Paris Exposition, 1937. Unrealized project. Axonometric and site drawing.

6.87. Maekawa: Japan Pavilion, Paris Exposition, 1937. Unrealized project. Night perspective rendering.

6.88. Sakakura: Japan Pavilion, Paris Exposition, 1937. Facade.

a style must, he maintained, be characterized by the mildness and ordinariness which distinguish Buddhist thinking and cultivate an awareness of beauty such as can only be produced by the experience of true enlightenment. Maekawa's winning project, however, was superseded by an entirely new scheme by Junzo Sakakura, who was not even one of the five participants invited to the original competition.

Sakakura had graduated one year before Maekawa from the Imperial University with a major in art history. In 1929 he went to France, where from 1931 he took over Maekawa's position in the office of Le Corbusier, remaining there until 1936. It seems clear that, through his presence in Paris, Sakakura was able to go over the heads of the Japanese authorities, parrying their objections with persistent references to the difficulties of the sloping site. He also had the support of José-Luis Sert, a fellow disciple of Le Corbusier and architect of the Spanish Pavilion. In all this, Maekawa remained without grudge. The French side were anxious to make use of local materials in the construction of all the exposition buildings, and it is probable that Sakakura was eventually able to suggest a way of doing this.

Sakakura's design, as actually built, is extremely hard to put a label on (figs. 6.88–89), except to call it a more individualized work than Maekawa's well-conceived yet somehow bloodless proposal. The Japan Pavilion was constructed on the type of exposed rubble foundations favored by Le Corbusier since their early appearance in several informal works of the late twenties. It took advantage of the

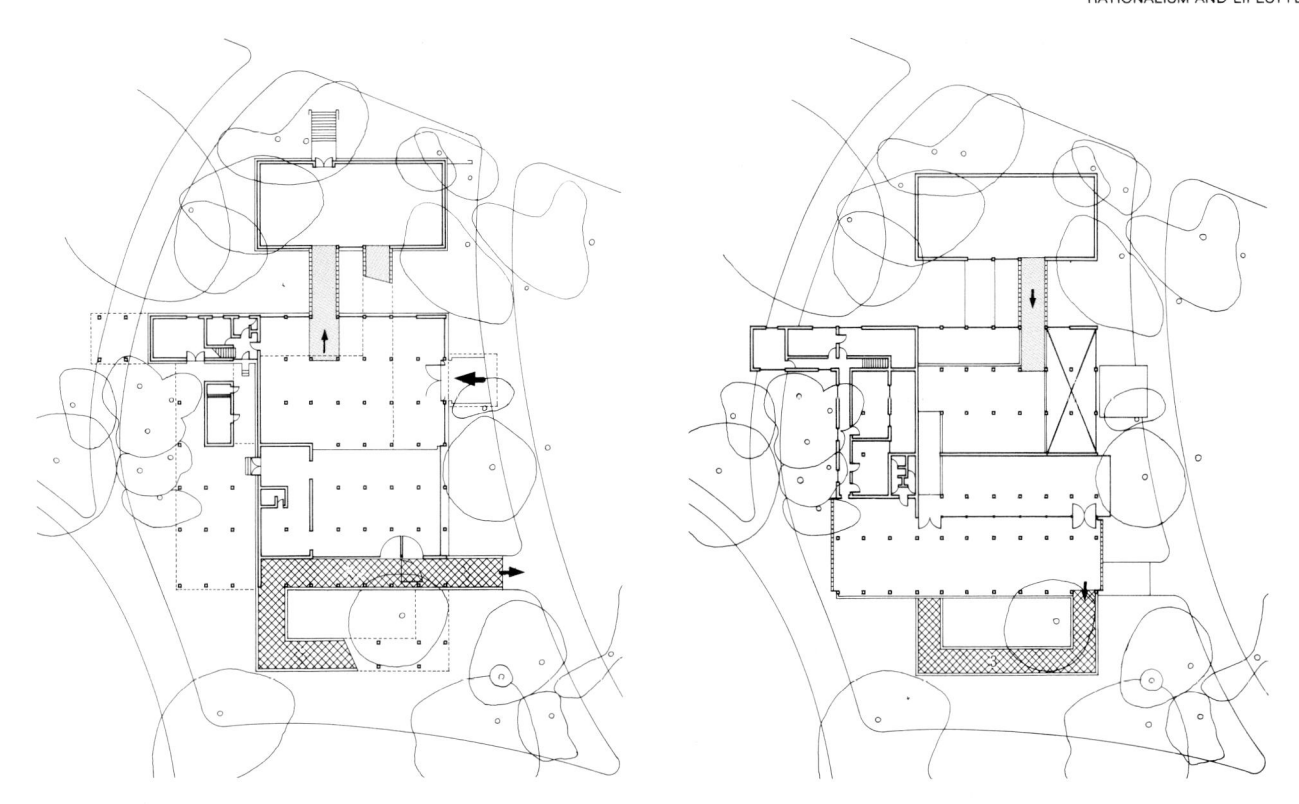

6.89. Sakakura: Japan Pavilion, Paris Exposition, 1937. Plans. Shading indicates ramps used to link ground floor (left) with upper level (right).

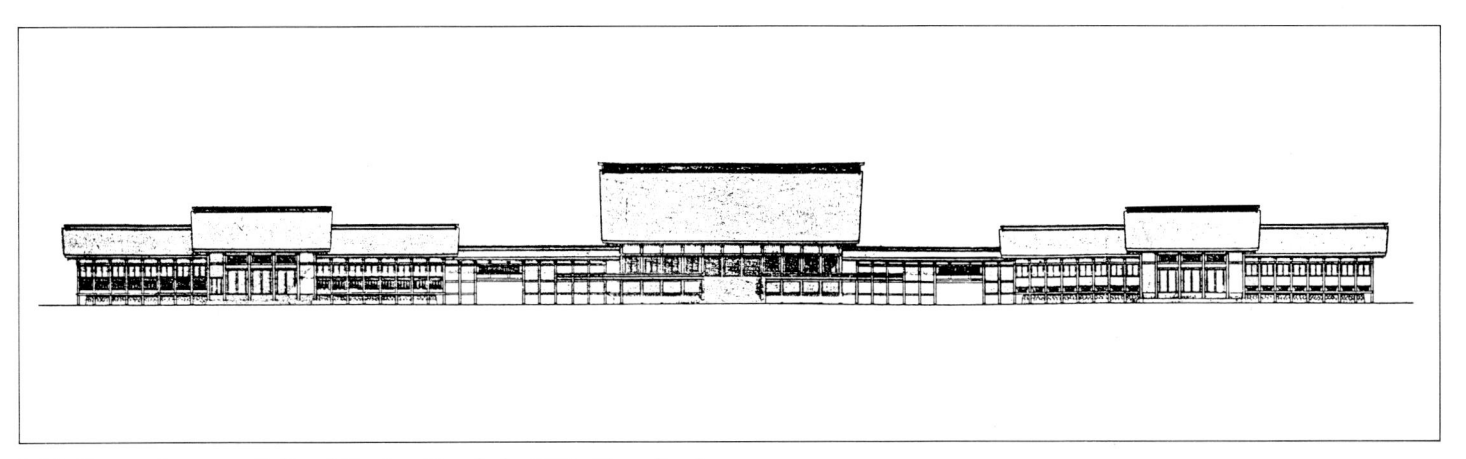

6.90. Tange: Japanese Cultural Center, Bangkok, 1943. Unrealized winning competition entry. Main elevation.

natural slope of the gardens at Chaillot by a generous use of ramps, which, as has been noted, were also a Corbusian device. In fact, as an exhibition hall, the Japan Pavilion constituted an architectural promenade, such as Le Corbusier had for some time advocated but was rarely able to achieve on a large scale. Sakakura may have been using his neo-Corbusian material in a tenuous allusion to the traditional *shinden-zukuri* style of architecture—for long known only from pictures or literary accounts—but the idea, though sometimes proposed, seems farfetched.

Maekawa later on claimed to derive a certain satisfaction from the fact that his design for the Paris pavilion, like that for the Imperial Museum at Ueno (see fig. 6.80), had not been realized. He had by then begun, he says, to sense too great a gap between modern Western architectural production and earlier Japanese practices. Indeed, by 1945, there was little left of the Japanese capital, Tokyo being reduced to a virtual ruin by recent American bombing raids. Maekawa's reaction was that the "limits of modern architecture" had been attained. Indeed, shortly before, in 1943, Maekawa for the first time had prepared a competition entry in the ancient *shinden-zukuri* style—for the Japanese Cultural Center at Bangkok, Thailand having earlier become an "ally" of Japan. In this, however, Maekawa was preempted by Kenzo Tange; in 1942 Tange won the competition for the design of the so-called Holy Precinct at Mt. Fuji, and then took first prize for Bangkok. Maekawa's Bangkok entry placed second (figs. 6.90–91).

158 RATIONALISM AND LIFESTYLE

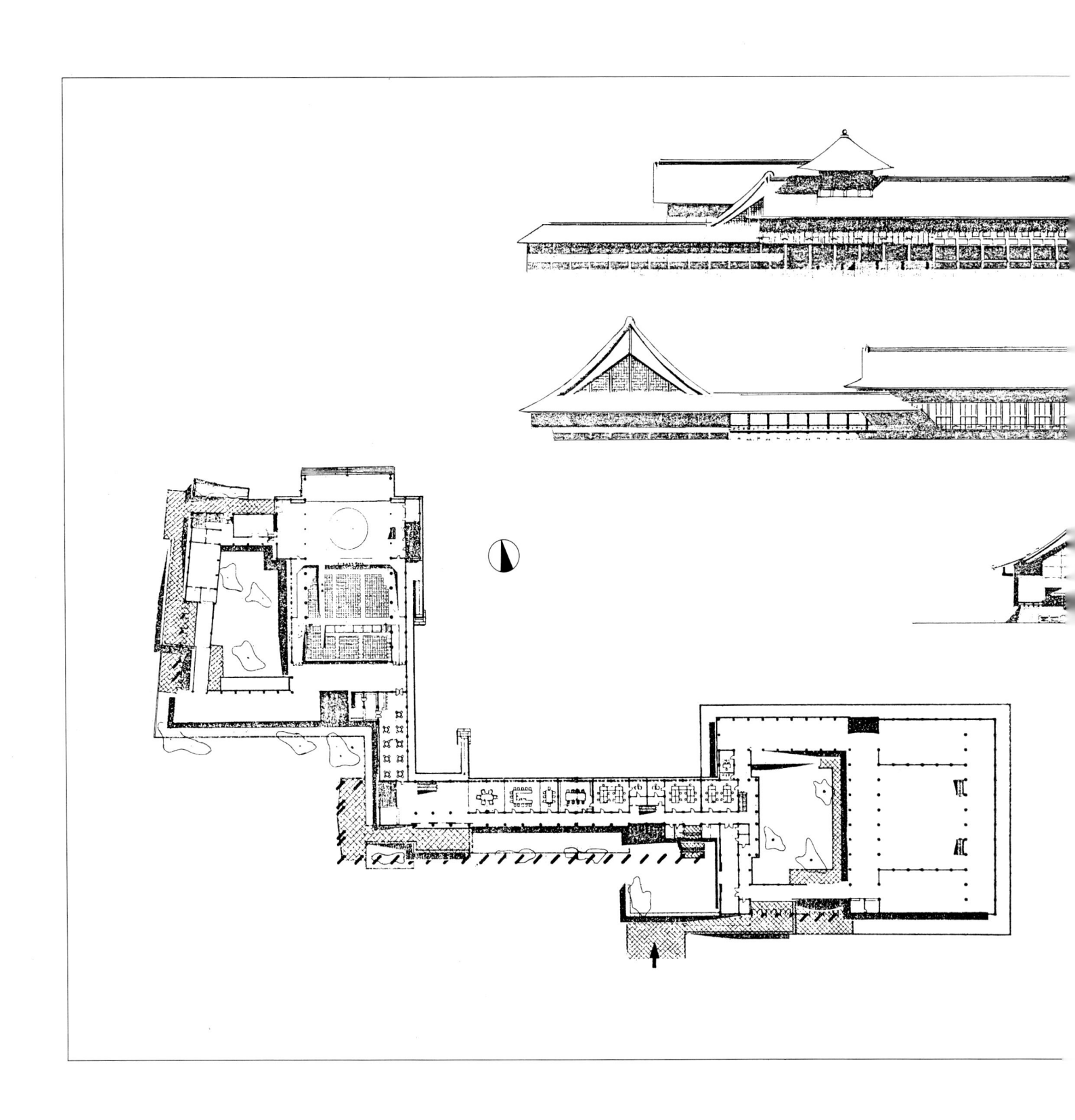

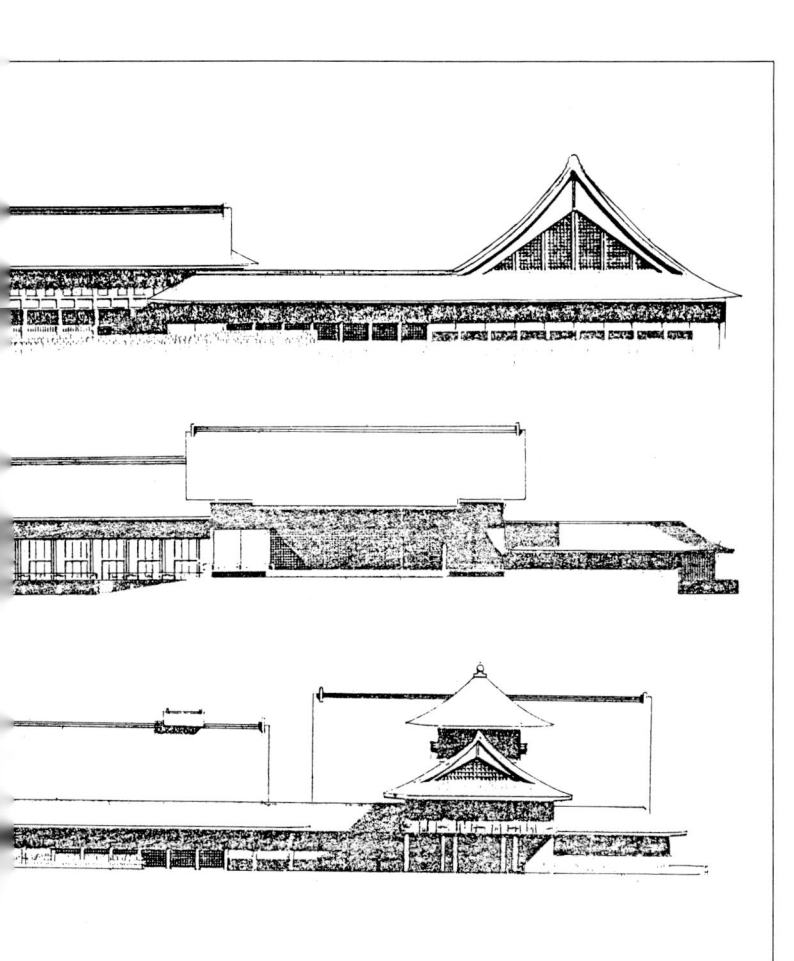

6.91. Maekawa: Japanese Cultural Center, Bangkok, 1943. Unrealized competition entry. Elevations and plan.

THREE GERMAN-TRAINED ARCHITECTS IN BITTER TIMES

The International Style survived for a few more years until the mid-thirties in the residential work of architects like Tsuchiura, but most strikingly of all in the designs of those returnees from Germany, who had either studied with Walter Gropius personally or been members of the Bauhaus. One of these was Iwao Yamawaki, who had been a student of architecture at the Bauhaus from 1930 until its final move from Dessau in 1932. Yamawaki designed a joint atelier (figs. 6.92–94) for the Migishis, a couple who painted in a neosurrealist style; it provides an attractive instance of *Sachlichkeit*, here adapted to suburban Tokyo. The atelier itself forms the main facade, which is glazed, as is the rear wall of the cubical *genkan*, or entry, projecting from it. The colored detail that characterized much International Style work, but could not be recorded in black-and-white photographs, found especial favor with the Japanese. In the Migishi House, the (wooden) window sash must be imagined dark blue; the front door was lacquer red with a handle of white bronze. In front the garden is largely paved, with only a small rectangular patch of lawn retained in one corner and a pool of distinctly architectural character opposite. The rear garden is screened from view in the Japanese fashion by a section of wall set at right angles to the east wall of the studio. This is provided with a flat overhang and appears to form part of the house, transforming a traditional motif into a Constructivist-like design.

One of the best-known works of the 1930s is the Yamada House (figs. 6.95–96) designed by Bunzo Yamaguchi at Kita Kamakura, near Tokyo, in 1934. Although Yamaguchi spent two years with Gropius following the latter's ultimate departure from the Bauhaus, the house at Kita Kamakura was inspired, obviously and directly, by the Lovell House of 1927–29 built in Los Angeles by the Austrian Richard Neutra (fig. 6.97). Neutra had visited Japan in 1930, and Maekawa, as well as Yamaguchi—just before leaving for Berlin—had the opportunity of meeting him. The Yamada House was built largely of wood, a sign of the times already referred to and to be discussed at greater length in the following chapter. So it is remarkable that Yamaguchi was able to simulate a bit of the drama of Neutra's cantilevered concrete design. However, the pillars supporting the characteristic overhangs were of steel, and this combination of materials provoked some eyebrow-raising. The plan of the house is extremely ingenious, though it required three sets of stairs

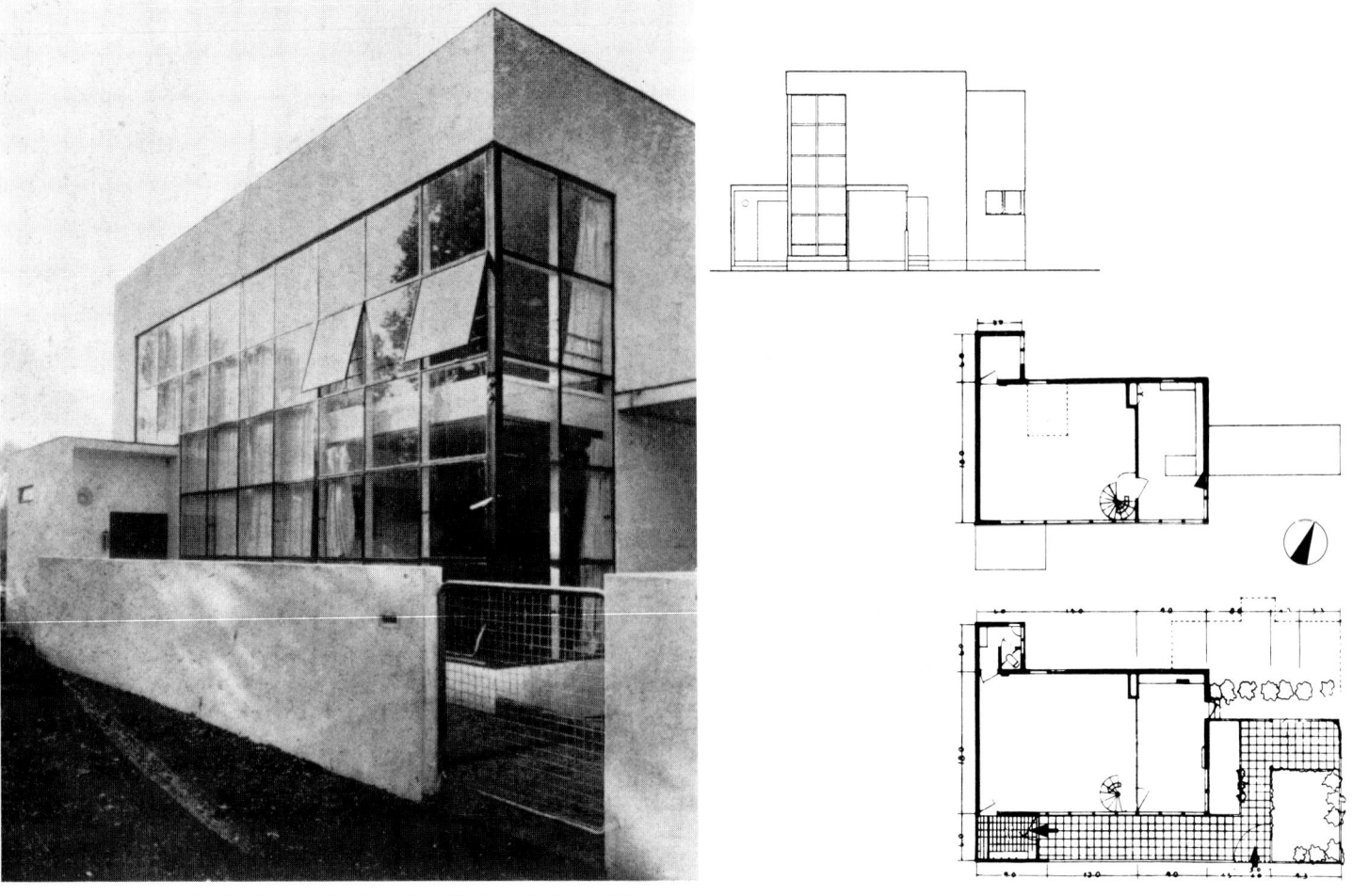

6.92. Yamawaki: Migishi House, Saginomiya, Tokyo, before 1935. Main (south) facade and east elevation (above, right).

6.93. Yamawaki: Migishi House, Saginomiya, Tokyo, before 1935. Plans.

6.94. Yamawaki: Migishi House, Saginomiya, Tokyo, before 1935. View from atelier into conversation area.

6.95. Yamaguchi: Yamada House, Kita Kamakura, Kanagawa Prefecture, 1934. Facade.

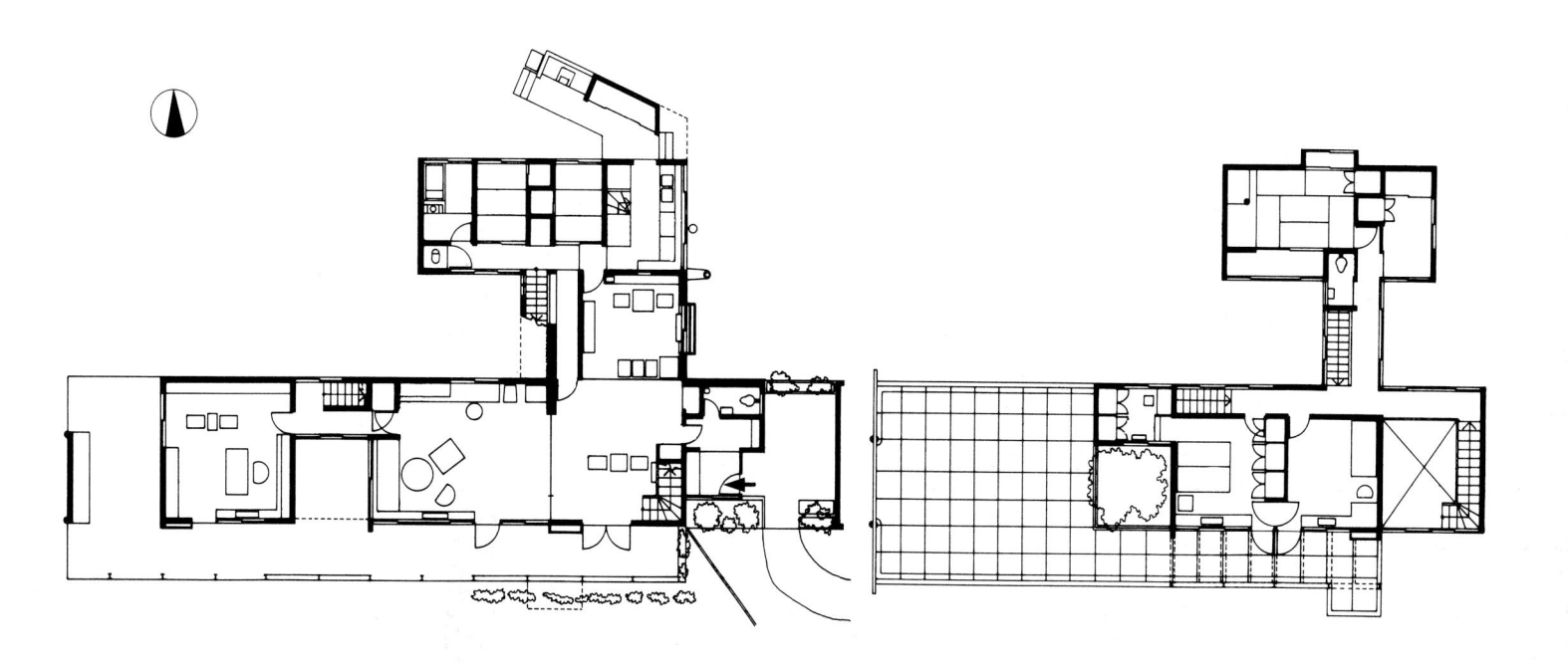

6.96. Yamaguchi: Yamada House, Kita Kamakura, Kanagawa Prefecture, 1934. Plans.

6.97. Neutra: Lovell House, Los Angeles, 1927–29.

6.98. Kurata: White Pillar House, Hakone-Sengoku, Kanagawa Prefecture, before 1937. Facade.

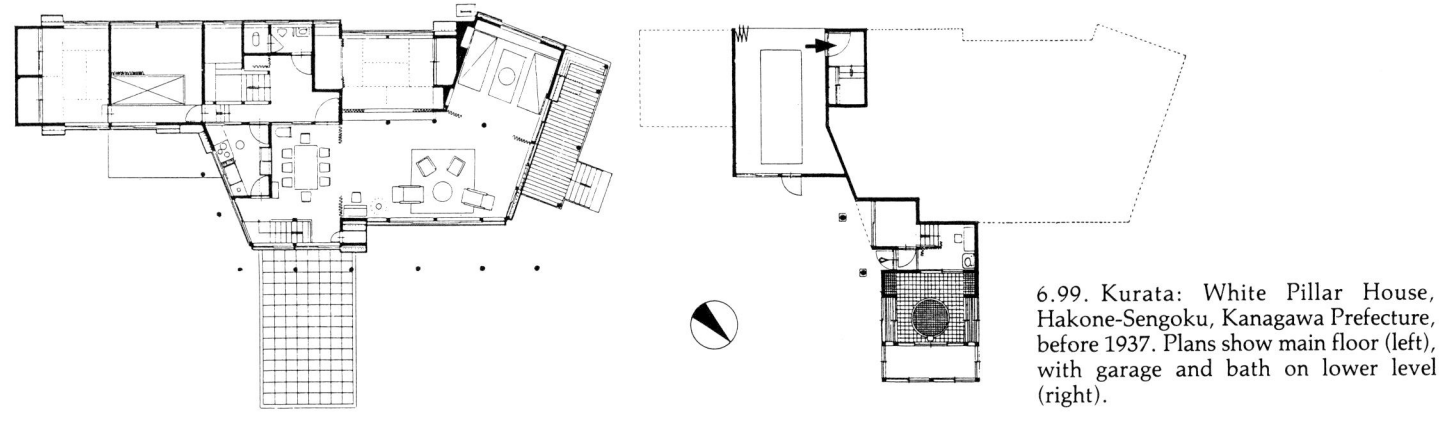

6.99. Kurata: White Pillar House, Hakone-Sengoku, Kanagawa Prefecture, before 1937. Plans show main floor (left), with garage and bath on lower level (right).

for a simple two-story residence far smaller than Raymond's 1934 dwellings (see figs. 6.52–57). The principal rooms are ranged along the south facade, just as they would be in a traditionally Japanese-style layout; all other elevations remain essentially closed. The double height of the stairhall is used as a pivot for an L-shaped arrangement of living and dining areas, which may be joined together or closed off. The rear section of the house forms a utility wing, while all south-facing rooms, upstairs and down, have access to outside terraces. The vertical stairhall is balanced out-of-doors by a square court separating the living room from the study. This recalls Raymond's use of the *tsubo* motif in the Akaboshi House. But at Kita Kamakura verticality was emphasized by planting a large evergreen in the space, thus also recalling the tree in the midst of Le Corbusier's model housing unit at the 1925 Paris Exposition. On the whole, the house at Kita Kamakura is one of the wittiest and most successful double-takes in the history of modern Japanese design. It is also one of the final notes of determined optimism in Japanese architecture of the period.

An interesting parallel to the Yamada House is offered by a villa called the White Pillar House in the mountains at Hakone, near Mt. Fuji (figs. 6.98–99). This was the work of Chikatada Kurata, who had spent 1930–31 with Gropius in Germany. The first flat-roofed house built in this attractive resort area west of Tokyo, it makes use of an exterior of white and pearl-gray siding as a foil to the surrounding green, while strong, bright colors come into play only in the furnishings. As a residence for summer use only, Kurata's work provides an example rare in Japanese architecture: functional reversal of the north-south orientation. The house is situated on a slope with a fine north view, and this accounts for placement of the living-dining area on that side, with sleeping rooms and maid's quarters relegated to the south. The

6.100. Yamaguchi: extension to Nihon Dental College, Tokyo, 1934.

6.101. Yamaguchi: Kurobe Power Station, Kurobe, Toyama Prefecture, 1938.

white pillars which give the house its name occur, then, on the back, where they support an overhang that is little more than the product of a desired aesthetic image. Both garage and Japanese-style bath are situated underneath the first story, with the bathroom jutting out to profit from the view. Thus, the White Pillar House by Kurata attains topographical interest in a way almost unknown to Japanese architecture, since building into a slope is in general scrupulously avoided on account of problems of dampness and rainwater runoff.

Thus—at approximately the same time as the Yamada House, set amid ricefields though surrounded by hills—the White Pillar House recalls *the* essential element of Neutra's masterpiece which Yamaguchi had been forced to omit from his charming *jeu d'esprit* at Kita Kamakura. Even Frank Lloyd Wright, at Fallingwater, took up the play of different levels exhibited in Neutra's work. In prewar Japan, by contrast, a building of more than just structural *trompe l'oeil*, such as Kurata produced, would certainly have been courting seismic risk.

Now, in any case, the game was up for the International Style in Japan, except for the field of utilitarian structures or civil engineering works. Such were not expected to have ideological implications but only to express efficiency and strength. In both these areas Bunzo Yamaguchi remained daringly in the forefront. As an example of the first type, we illustrate his extension to the Nihon Dental College Hospital (fig. 6.100), a work of 1934. Of the second, we recall only the Kurobe Power Station for Nippon Denryoku at Kurobe (fig. 6.101), finished in 1938. Yet the impression of well-being in the first of these works and that of solidity and stability in the second was illusory. As in the West, so in Japan: the vigor and variety of culture during this period belied the state of the world; *modanizumu* concealed fatal flaws and even seems to have left out of account the human condition.

7 | Ins and Outs of Postwar Urban Rhetoric

INTERNATIONALISM: SUN AND SHADOW

The hitherto most extensively chronicled period in the history of Japanese architecture is the 1950s and early 1960s, when Kenzo Tange—a staff member of the Maekawa office from 1938 to 1942—came to occupy a place in the vanguard of renascent international modernism. The same flamboyant decade and a half witnessed the avatar of Le Corbusier in his capacity of sculptural formgiver and the unforeseen leap into prominence of Brazilian, Italian, Mexican, and Scandinavian architects. There also appeared a serious-minded Japanese school presided over by Maekawa and Sakakura. In Japan, as elsewhere, rationalism, with its functional-symbolic (i.e., neo-Constructivist) point of view, was strikingly rechanneled in favor of an intensely sculpturesque and tactile approach, opening up, incidentally, a bonanza for architectural journalism. Some formal tendencies were direct expressions of structural technique, yet a great deal of imagery was also abstracted, knowingly or otherwise, from the repertoire of prewar Surrealist art. An additional factor was a gnawing presentiment of worldwide urban growth. In 1950 only New York, London, and Shanghai had populations of greater than eight million, while at the time of writing there are already fifteen such agglomerations. By the end of the century there will be twenty-five of these, 80 percent located in the Third World. Though few non-Japanese are acquainted with the details of Tokyo's metamorphosis, the resurgent capital of the country—so recently in ruins—nonetheless offered a foretaste of momentous events occurring today on a global scale. Tange, for his part, determined to give voice and expression to Japan's expanding metropolitan network, which, though immersed in frenzied development, failed to impress outwardly because the inchoate format of its cities lacked conspicuous drama.

From the start of his career Tange dreamed of reforming the rampant urban growth which had already become a pressing issue in Japan before the war accelerated natural trends. He sought an evocative language based on Western classical precedent as a framework for his own double-edged vision of past and present, East and West. There is no question but that Kenzo Tange's architectural notions were stigmatized by wartime attitudes and conditions; however, his eventual success was closely bound up with Japan's rescue from the so-called dark valley of the prewar years. For, having watched from a safe distance the masterful unfolding of Le Corbusier's highly contentious and largely unachieved urban and architectural projects of the 1930s, Tange remained until early maturity almost as serenely wedded to an architecture of beneficent and magnanimous aims, as, until old age, did Wright. Yet he was neither a lyricist, like both Wright and Le Corbusier, nor a man to be caught out—after the vagaries of 1930s and 1940s propaganda—hymning anything less epical than the return of a peaceful and free society. In the event, this proved overwhelmingly utopic for a mere architect—or even a self-made urban planner, like Tange—if only because *ideological concerns* were increasingly overshadowed, possibly outshone, by *the immediacy of change*. A further difficulty was that Tange had no concrete experience of the West. Memories of Shanghai apart, he shared the same airy and detached fascination with ancient and baroque planning devices—hence, pictorial-style cityscapes—that had characterized Japanese knowledge of Western urban life from late Tokugawa through the early Meiji period. Had the onset of the war not precluded it, he might have discovered a more nuanced stance, such as numbers of other Japanese architects before him had built up in the intervening three quarters of a century. Thus prepared and armed, however, Tange would perhaps never have dared to set forth. For his self-appointed task consisted in nothing less than to restore—within an evanescent and, indeed, vanishing Japanese tradition—a semblance of urban form.

The young architect's fond intention, as we shall see, had originally been to explain the principles of Le Corbusier through a study of Michelangelo. A broad view of Kenzo Tange's overall achievement cannot, of course, be measured using this proposal as a direct yardstick. Rather, it would be fairer to say that ambiguity in Tange's oeuvre reflects the success/failure of his early idol, and Maekawa's, that is, Le Corbusier himself. In questioning the internationalist assumptions of the period—symbolized to some extent by the Tokyo Olympic games in 1964 and a resplendent stadium complex (see fig. 8.57) Tange designed for them at Yoyogi in Tokyo—it is only right to remark how easily, in turn, Le Corbusier brushed aside his own radical inexperience of non-Western cultures. He made this attitude strikingly clear at Chandigarh, in India (1951–65), where pretensions to an "international" style evaporated in the amazing unworkability of the new Punjabi capital's circulation network and the awesomely self-referential character of its monuments. Nevertheless, my aim here is not to point out how Chandigarh perpetuated what might be labeled the "Imperial Hotel syndrome," or try to decide whether, within a particular historical context, this ought to be considered a good thing or not. Instead, there was one person, close at hand, who perceived Le Corbusier's postwar style, as elaborated at Chandigarh and elsewhere, as a danger for Japanese architecture. He was, predictably, Antonin Raymond.

The postwar rebuilding of Japan began masterfully with a work of Raymond's, and like the gestation of Chandigarh, its short life (1951–64) exactly spans the era under discussion. This work was the Reader's Digest Building at Takebashi (figs. 7.1–3), the first "permanent" new building in Tokyo after the end of World War II. Raymond had petitioned General MacArthur for permission to reenter occupied Japan in order to participate in the work of reconstructing the country. Arriving in Tokyo in 1947, he discovered former staff members had painstakingly preserved all documents and drawings left behind ten years earlier and only awaited his instructions to reopen the office. Raymond's business sense, together with his capacity for putting practical and humane solutions into action, were aroused by all that he saw and felt in the aftermath of the war. In addition, his prewar idealism was rekindled by the crude way in which some of his own earlier works, such as the Akaboshi and Kawasaki houses, had been vandalized by the Occupation authorities in an attempt to transform them into billeting for high-ranking American military personnel. In short, Raymond became more than ever committed to principles of contemporary design as he envisaged them.

The Reader's Digest Building was a particular concern of Mrs. DeWitt Wallace, who had first tried to interest Frank Lloyd Wright in the job. She expected a design that would serve Japan as a model of the best America had to offer, and she commissioned it from Raymond when he returned to his New York office from Tokyo in 1949. The site he acquired for the magazine was opposite the Hirakawa Gate of the Imperial Palace, about a kilometer to the north of Wright's Imperial Hotel, and Raymond's conscious intention in choosing it was to establish "a pattern for future city-planning by setting the building into a garden"[1] (fig. 7.4). By his own account, Raymond was the first architect in Japan to pursue the inspiration afforded by the early works of Le Corbusier—an influence reaching its peak, according to Raymond, in the planning of the Tokyo Golf Club of 1930–32. Then, a little later, along with architects all over the world, Raymond must also have felt the impact of the perfected vision of the *ville radieuse* published by Le Corbusier in 1935, hence during that same decade which saw so few actual commissions accrue. The Reader's Digest Building—with its gardens by the Japanese-American sculptor Isamu Noguchi—was, in fact, contemporary with Le Corbusier's own belated and partial realization of the *ville radieuse* schema in the so-called Unité d'Habitation at Marseilles of 1947–53.

The building for Mrs. Wallace was a two-story longitudinal structure recalling the Tokyo Golf Club in scale and layout (see figs. 6.46–47), though not in its construction or details. The clubhouse had been commandeered by the Japanese military before the war and was later modified out of all recognition by the Occupation forces. Meanwhile, on account of the war, the Reader's Digest Building was to benefit from a decade of prior activity in America on Raymond's part. In addition, the latest technical innovations and materials available in the United States were now copied in Japan under his supervision. These included such things as both asphalt and acoustical tiling, under-floor ducts for electricity and telephones, fluorescent lighting, a heat-pump system, and floor-to-ceiling glazing. The backbone of the Reader's Digest Building was a double cantilevered frame supported on a single row of concrete columns and buttressed for rigidity at the outer edge by steel props of circular cross-section. By tilting these slightly out of the vertical, Raymond may have hoped to echo the graceful contour of the adjacent palace ramparts. His modified cantilever system allowed for an earthquake-proof frame eliminating all load-bearing walls save on either end. Unlike the Imperial Hotel down the street, the building's oblique profile was "international" rather than continental. And in contrast with most later Japanese work influenced by Le Corbusier, Raymond's used a concrete structure to guarantee stability in a way that did not call undue attention to itself as sheer material mass.

All in all, it seems natural to consider the Reader's Digest Building as the masterpiece of the architect's long and varied Japanese career. It was the first large building in which Raymond had succeeded in applying the Japanese-style principles he had made use of so freely in much of his residential work. Conceived in terms of simplicity, economy of material, lightness, and elegance, the entire structure is based on a module of three by six Japanese feet. As for Western influence, there is as much of Mies as Le Corbusier in the Reader's Digest Building: for practical reasons it was a Miesian building—designed in a concrete cantilever form instead of steel—yet recalling Marseilles and conforming to antiseismic norms. Office space was deployed around a central core comprising stairways and toilets with movable partitions situated

7.1. Raymond: Reader's Digest Building, Takebashi, Tokyo, 1951. Facade.

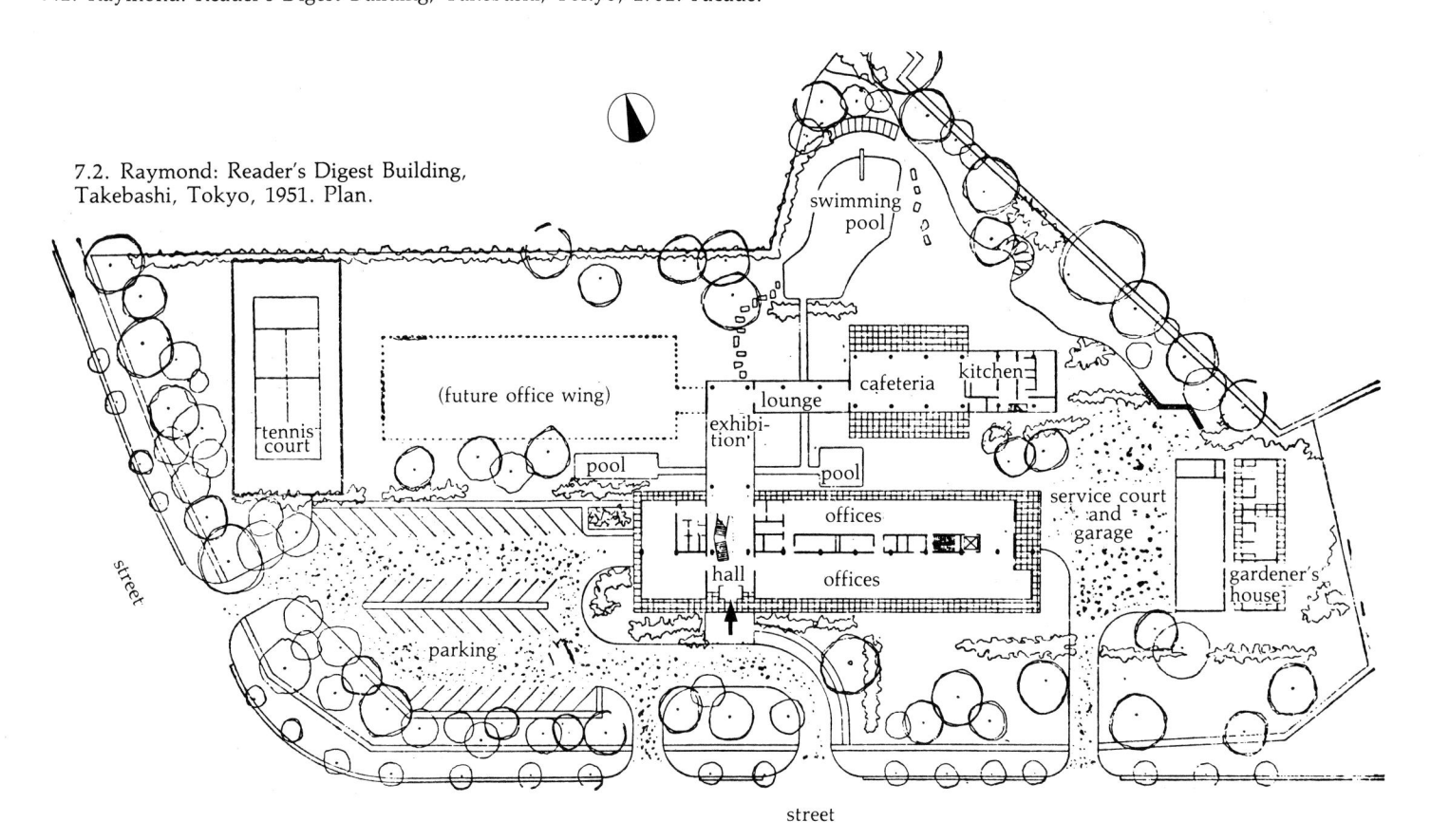

7.2. Raymond: Reader's Digest Building, Takebashi, Tokyo, 1951. Plan.

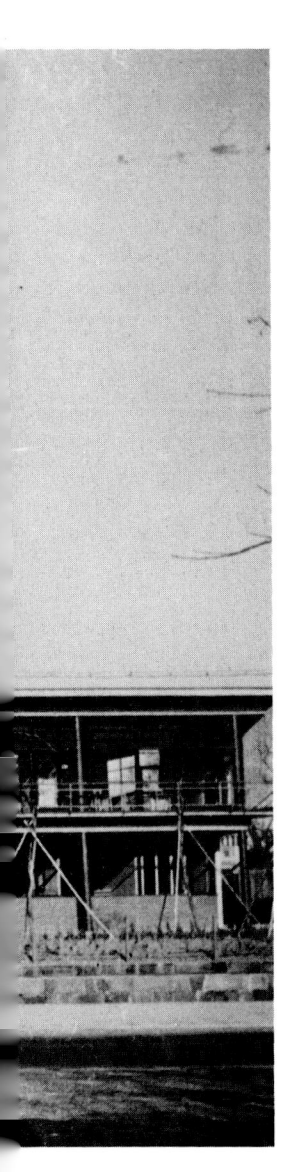

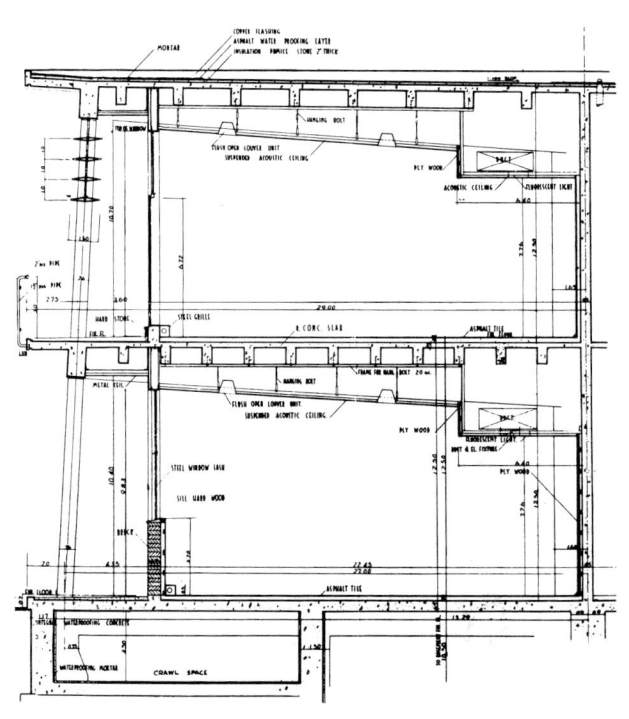

7.3. Raymond: Reader's Digest Building, Takebashi, Tokyo, 1951. Half-section.

7.4. Raymond: Reader's Digest Building, Takebashi, Tokyo, 1951. View from Imperial Palace moat.

7.5. Sakakura: Museum of Modern Art, Kamakura, Kanagawa Prefecture, 1951. View of Japanese-style supports, and axonometric showing plan of upper floor.

everywhere else. A lounge and cafeteria were placed in a separate pavilion to the rear, reached by an open exhibition hall prolonging the entrance foyer of the main building.

Before the war Raymond had never been unduly concerned with his influence on Japanese architects. But as the Reader's Digest Building reflected his position fresh from the United States—and on account of the virtual cessation of Japanese architecture for a period of ten years—this situation changed. Thus Raymond cites the design of the Hiroshima Peace Center (see fig. 7.12), Tange's first major work, presented in competition in 1950 and realized in 1955, as foremost among the imitations of the Reader's Digest by Japanese who were apparently "attracted by the exterior only."[2]

A full twenty-five years separated the two men, and Raymond later felt called upon to recognize Tange. But the older man reacted understandably with skepticism and disbelief when, on being interviewed for radio by Tange, he first heard Tange's proposal that Japanese architects ought to foster the development of a "new tradition."[3] The very notion of a distinctive neo-vernacular Japanese style seemed to Raymond to fly in the face of everything he had worked for since as long ago as Tange's entry into elementary school. With vehement decisiveness Raymond also deplored the influence of Le Corbusier's later works, such as the pilgrimage church (see

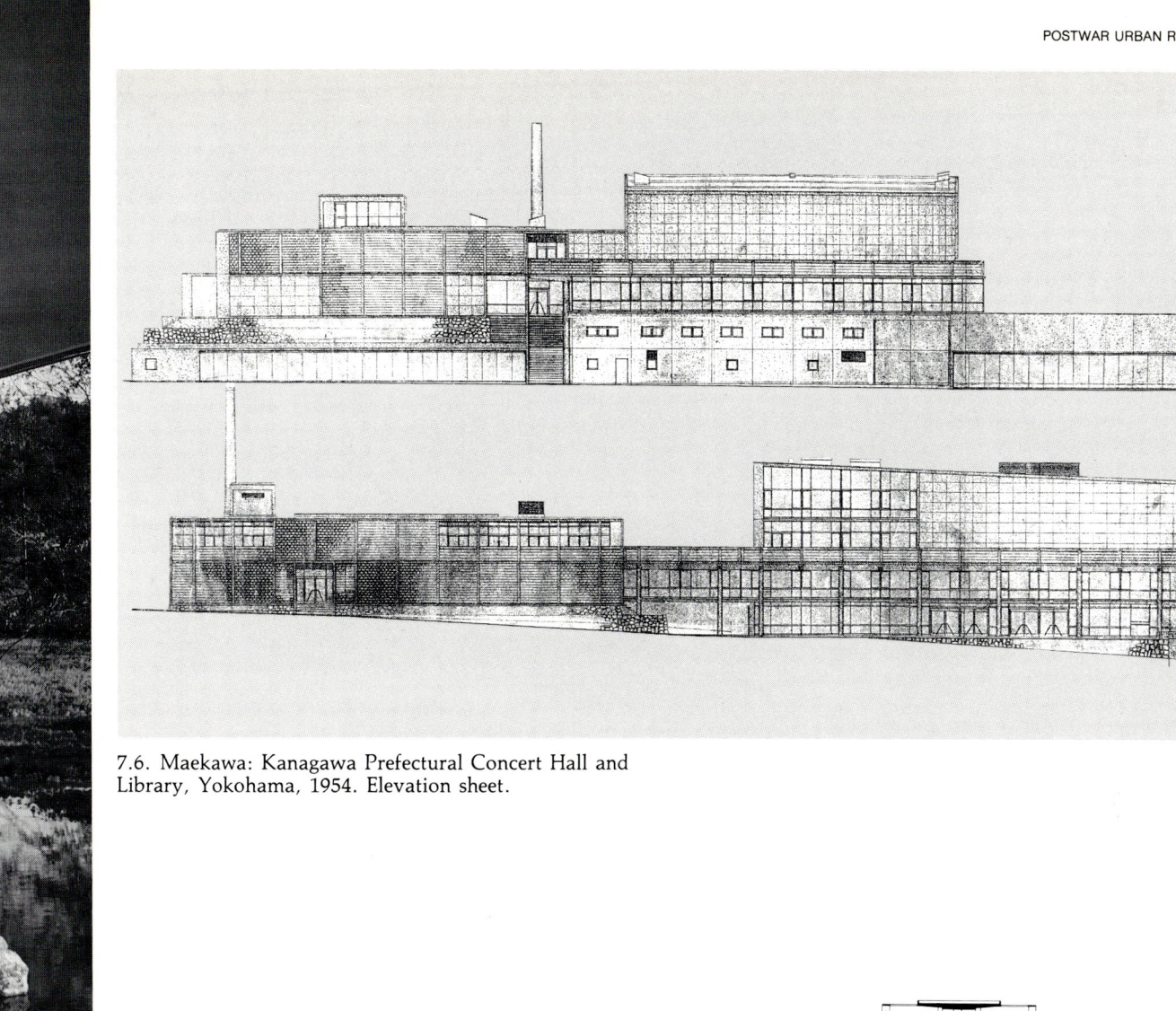

7.6. Maekawa: Kanagawa Prefectural Concert Hall and Library, Yokohama, 1954. Elevation sheet.

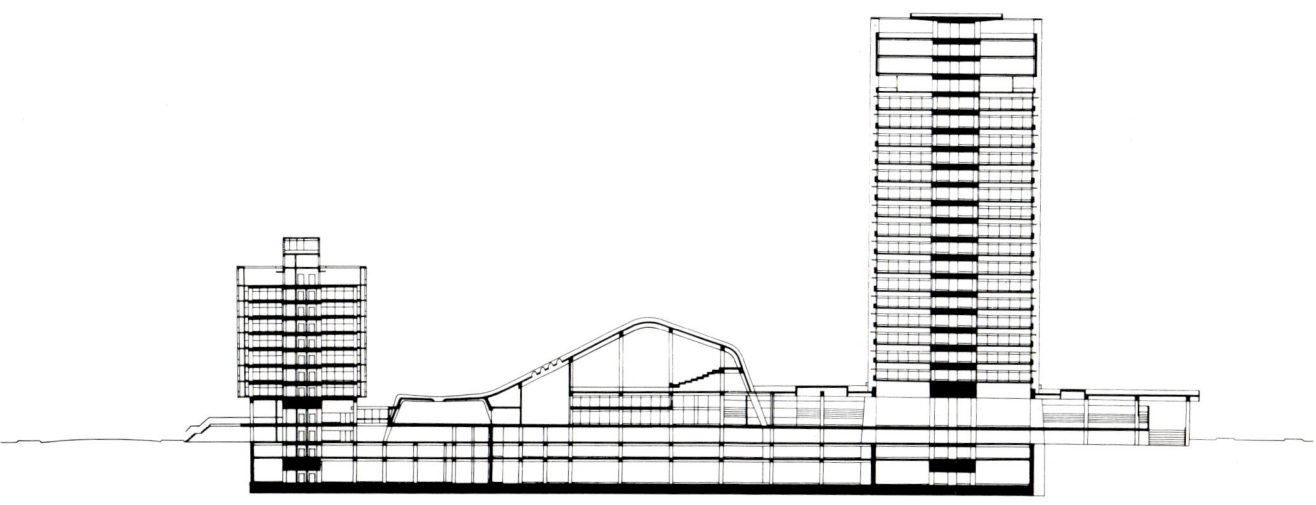

7.7. Tange: Tokyo City Hall, Tokyo, 1957 (right-hand portion unrealized).

fig. 8.50) at Ronchamp (1950–54) and the various government buildings at Chandigarh designed from 1951 onward.[4] He viewed these as having paved the way for the production of "brutalities" in postwar Japanese architecture, an opinion which, although in the minority a generation ago, deserves a rehearing.

But to return to strictly chronological considerations, the four major buildings which J. M. Richards cites as "the classics of the early years of modern architecture in Japan" need not have been influenced at all by Le Corbusier's postwar style, despite the fact that Tange in 1951 had visited Europe for the first time. They were Tange's Peace Center at Hiroshima (see fig. 7.12), Sakakura's Museum of Modern Art at Kamakura of 1951 (fig. 7.5), Maekawa's Kanagawa Prefectural Concert Hall and Library at Yokohama of 1954 (fig. 7.6), and Tange's Tokyo City Hall (fig. 7.7), left two-thirds complete in 1957.[5] In the late fifties, then, the buildings which Raymond was to characterize as "brutalities" were still in the future. None of the four works selected by Richards presents any problem of influence, as all of the prewar work of the Le Corbusier office was well known to both Maekawa and Sakakura, and through them to Tange. All the same, Tange has, in fact, acquainted us with the precise building by Le Corbusier—it was, rather, a project—to which he was attracted.

THE BEGINNINGS OF TANGE'S CAREER

The first encounter with Le Corbusier's work occurred for Tange when he was still at Hiroshima High School, where he had gone in 1930 after completing middle school in his native Imabari on the island of Shikoku. The family had been in Hankow and Shanghai but returned to Japan upon the death of an uncle, resettling in the Tange family's hometown in the prefecture of Ehime. Both Tange's elder half-brothers were at school in Tokyo, and it was natural that he should also be sent away to be educated in a larger town. At Hiroshima, Tange had enrolled in the science department but was soon longing to change to literature, when one day he came upon Le Corbusier's competition entry for the Palace of the Soviets (fig. 7.8) in a foreign art journal,[6] an incident that set the young Tange on the road to becoming an architect. Nevertheless, having neglected courses in mathematics and physics, he was obliged to spend two years as a *ronin*, a high-school graduate seeking entrance to university, before achieving admission to the architecture department of the Imperial University in Tokyo in 1935. In the meantime he recalls having read Valéry, Gide, Proust, and Dostoyevsky, as well as Hegel and Heidegger, in addition to lounging about in the classical-music coffee shops of the capital. In order to obtain a draft deferment, he prudently enrolled as a student in the film division of the art department, Nihon University, but rarely attended classes there.

The Palace of the Soviets dates from 1931 and, although it was never realized, is one of the most flamboyant and scenographic of all Le Corbusier's early schemes. It is symmetrical on one axis and dominated by two vast unequal halls, one for 15,000 spectators and the other for 6,500, not to mention provision for four smaller auditoria. The two halves of the project are connected by an esplanade designed to accommodate outdoor spectacles, and there was to have been an immense "forum" located underneath the larger of the two main halls and containing numerous restaurants as well as facilities for Soviet and foreign journalists. Le Corbusier envisaged the whole as outshining the glories of the neighboring Kremlin. More than the Centrosoyus of 1929, which was actually built in 1935, the Palace of the Soviets design was intentionally Constructivist-oriented. The volumes of the two main assembly halls at either end of Le Corbusier's model were sculpturally articulated and their roofs suspended by means of enormous cantilevered steel trusses converging like the ribs of a Japanese paper fan toward the podium end of each room. In the case of the larger assembly hall, the ends of these girders were upheld by means of vertical cables strung provocatively from a gigantic parabola, similar to the 630-foot arch eventually constructed by Saarinen at St. Louis in 1966. But for the Soviet Union in the thirties, Le Corbusier's project was anachronistic, since, as the architect later recalled, Stalin had already decided that the architecture of the proletariat was to be achieved in a "Greco-Latin spirit."

We can assume that Tange was not world-wise enough at this time to be dismayed by the poignant irrelevance of Le Corbusier's exercise in neo-Constructivist pyrotechnics. His earliest memories were the green lawns and brick terraces of a childhood spent in the former British settlement at Shanghai. From the urbane life there he was precipitated into the still-intact vernacular ambience of one of the most remote, though cultured, of Japan's provincial districts, where Tange's family occupied a large thatched-roof farmhouse set amidst a spacious Japanese-style garden. By comparison, Hiroshima was a large city, though it could, of course, hardly compete with the cosmopolitanism of Shanghai. At any rate, the radically discontinuous environment of Tange's childhood was already a principal ingredient of social and material culture at the beginning of Showa. So it is not surprising that the utopian vision of urban continuity and homogeneous architectural development which permeated the ensemble of Le Corbusier's work attracted an intelligent and romantic young man from the provinces. Or, perhaps, the context of discovery may have made a certain difference. Taken at face value, and on its own, the point to be made about the Palace of the Soviets project is certainly that Tange found it "awe-inspiringly beautiful." At this date there was, in Japan, no building in which architecture was as closely allied to art or so much resembled a piece of modern abstract sculpture. In any case, Tange's mind was now suddenly made up: "Into architecture, I felt I would be able to pour all my dreams, sensitivity and passionate enthusiasm."[7]

We have little knowledge of Tange's university career, which began in 1935 and ended four years later amid those darkening horizons already alluded to in regard to the work of Raymond and other architects at this time. Tange's major professor was Hideto Kishida, while the most important figure in the department was Shozo Uchida. These two had cooperated ten years earlier in designing the Imperial University auditorium, Yasuda Hall (see figs, 5.15–16), whose proto-streamlined Gothic idiom has already been discussed. Kishida, young even at the time of Tange's matriculation, was a historian as well as a designer. More than once, Tange has

7.8. Le Corbusier: Palace of the Soviets, Moscow, 1931. Unrealized competition entry.

commented on the strong impression which photographs taken by his teacher of Katsura Villa and the Imperial Palace in Kyoto made on him as a student. These were published in *Kako no Kosei* (Compositions of the Past) and enlarged versions were also displayed behind Professor Kishida's desk. Nevertheless, Tange's own graduation project was so thoroughly Corbusian in its execution that Professor Uchida was moved to comment, "It looks exactly like Corbusier's work."[8] This was a seventeen-hectare development hypothetically situated in the midst of Tokyo's Hibiya Park and entitled Château d'Art. So Tange—even as a young man—was already preoccupied with the notion of setting up a monument to architecture as "art" in the heart of the government district—where, indeed, so many similarly intentioned projects had been deferred or cast aside. In fact, he was never to build for the nation, except in realizing the national gymnasiums for the Tokyo Olympics (1964) and, ten years afterward, the Japanese Embassy in Mexico City.

Upon graduating, Tange contrived to avoid employment in one of the five major construction firms, as this would certainly have entailed rustication for an unspecified number of years in some far-flung outpost of empire, probably Manchukuo. Instead, he entered the office of Kunio Maekawa, where by proxy, at least, he could remain in contact with the work of Le Corbusier. But instead of being content, like Maekawa, to emulate the master in silence, Tange records that "one of my most important undertakings was the effort to try to uncover the secret of his appeal."[9] Logically, perhaps—given his sheltered background—he connected the innate appeal of Le Corbusier's way of designing with Michelangelo's, whose works Tange was equally drawn to, although he had never actually seen the work of either architect. Incidentally, Le Corbusier himself edged toward a rapprochement with Mediterranean tradition—both vernacular and classical—and had placed himself with the Greeks, as early as the famous analogy between the Parthenon and the motor car in *Vers une Architecture*. Such a comparison would, of course, have been rejected out of hand by Wright, who had abandoned Western classicism in favor of a new direction founded on the example of Japanese design. Tange, at any rate—inclined to flights of high feeling and expression—seems to have been led to the influence of the romantic-nationalist (i.e., leftist-turned-conservative) aesthetician and literary critic Yojuro Yasuda (1910–81).

Tange eventually set his views on style before the public in a ten-page article in *Gendai Kenchiku*, entitled "Eulogy for Michelangelo as an Introduction to a Study of Le Corbusier,"[10] which "stirred up considerable comment."[11] That in his youth Tange was given to romantic views there can be no question, although in Japan his name is ordinarily not associated with right-wing ideology. Yet even Le Corbusier's own prewar career disguised apparently ambiguous sympathies—these, however, being offset by a subsequent radical leftward swing. The young Tange continued to work in Maekawa's office, traveling at least once to Manchuria in connection with the National Bank competition there and stopping off afterward to tour the Japanese-occupied Jehol Province of China. He remained with Maekawa until 1942, when, owing to the war, "there were no buildings to design."[12] Hurriedly, no doubt, he reentered the Imperial University as a postgraduate student, having paternal permission to remain in school until the age of thirty. Understandably, his enrollment was extended until the surrender, shortly before Tange turned thirty-two.

These additional years of enforced study at university may have changed the direction of Tange's career. For he recalls: "This was the time when I began considering the importance of urban design, not in the sense of mere city planning involving land-use and street-network composition, but three-dimensional urban design."[13] Still, he found very little material along these lines in the university library, except for certain folio volumes containing engravings of Greek and Roman marketplaces, which he began to study with enthusiasm. By a process of analogy similar to the one which led him from Le Corbusier to Michelangelo, Tange began to transpose the concepts of *agora* and *forum* in terms of a spatial order derived from Buddhist temples, Shinto shrines, and the Heian-period *shinden* residences. Absorption in these potential techniques of physical planning was to produce useful results. For with the initiation of intensive American bombing, Tange was asked by Tokyo officials to make a study of areas of the capital most likely to survive destruction. At no time in modern Japanese history had a designer been so cut off from the realities of the Western tradition while being at the same time engulfed in events which would necessitate a total reconstruction and, to some extent, a rethinking of planning goals. The perverse network of available resources and enforced taboos (e.g., the Imperial Crown style and the ban on the use of industrialized building materials) occurred for Japan—or rather for Tange—at a critical juncture in Modern Movement development.

Meanwhile, Tange's new preoccupation with native sources

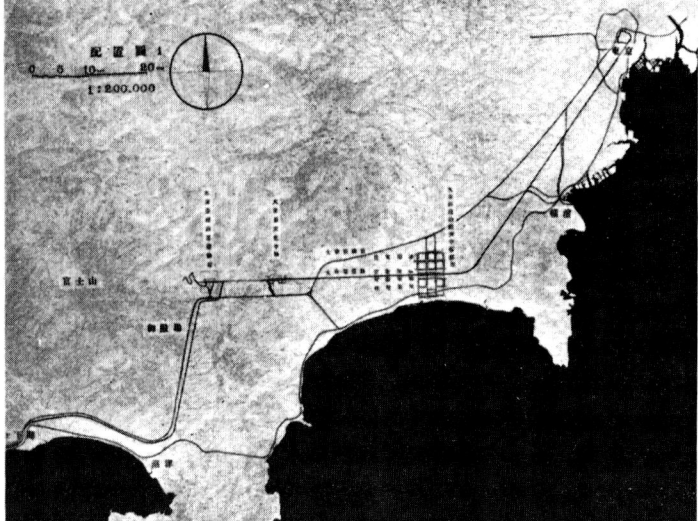

7.9. Tange: Greater East Asia Coprosperity Sphere Memorial Building, near Mt. Fuji, 1943. Rendering, and approach map from Tokyo.

7.10. Michelangelo: Capitoline Hill reconstruction, Rome, 1538 onward.

was stimulated by three competitions, among which that for the Japanese Cultural Center in Bangkok has already been touched upon. Even more significant was the ultrafascist project for a memorial building dedicated to the cause of the Greater East Asia Coprosperity Sphere, to be located at the base of Mt. Fuji (fig. 7.9). In his entry, which took first prize, Tange combined what he refers to as "the pure image of [Japan's] Ise Shrine" with Michelangelo's scheme for the reconstruction of the Capitoline Hill and the piazza at its summit (fig. 7.10).[14] No comparable transmutation of cultural icons had ever taken place on this scale in Japanese architecture, unless it was the wholesale importation of Chinese ideas and means during the period of formation and consolidation of the Japanese monarchy. In the Meiji period, no such permutation could have survived the stringent test of ideology as "a means to an end," and in the history of Western culture only the Hellenistic age could, possibly, have conceived of such a scheme.

The Mt. Fuji design of 1942-43 was, of course, never realized, nor ought it to have been. Moreover, Tange postponed the idea of propagating Michelangelo's Capitoline reconstruction until his project for the Hiroshima Peace Center (see fig. 7.12)—submitted under very different circumstances and conditions. It is not clear to what extent Tange's interest in physical urban layout was influenced by Le Corbusier's *La Ville Radieuse*, published in 1935, shortly after Le Corbusier and the French had assumed the leadership of CIAM from the exiled German faction. What is certain is that Tange's own chosen vocation of urban planner came about as a result of the war. Indeed, this might have been the case whatever the war's outcome. However, there was also the totally independent factor of the destruction of Hiroshima and the manner in which it occurred. Immediately after the war ended, Tange became a member of the Government Agency for Reconstruction and asked to be put in charge of the Hiroshima survey team, an act which for numerous reasons required considerable courage and even greater vision. During 1946-47 he also performed land-use surveys at Maebashi, Isezaki, Fukushima, and Wakkanai, among other localities. It was through such work, as he later reminisced, that Tange gradually learned the uncompromising truth that "cities did not redevelop as a result of urban plans."[15] Instead, he continues, the redevelopment process was "a product of the power relationships" reflected in "layer upon layer of political, economic and social realities behind these burned cities."[16] The cynicism and *Realpolitik* implicit in this statement acquire an extra historical dimension if it is remembered that, even before the advent of the new situation created by World War II, most attempts to implement conventional planning strategies in Japan had failed.

JAPAN AND CIAM: HIROSHIMA

Tange's disillusioning postwar experiences as a neophyte planner and policy determiner preface a failure of nerve which would eventually overtake the Modern Movement as a whole, but was somehow more admissible at the level of planning at an earlier date than in architectural design. The crisis this betokened was entwined with Le Corbusier's increasingly personalized views on urban planning and is reflected in the postwar history of the CIAM, to which reference has already been made. Founded in 1928, this organization had at first pursued a "realistic," or pragmatic, approach to situating architecture in its economic and social context. However, by the time of its fourth meeting in 1933 and under the influence of steadily worsening political events in Europe, its policies came to be largely determined by the positivistic yet idealizing mode of rhetoric peculiar to Le Corbusier. The historic fourth gathering of planners and architects under the CIAM banner assumed as a general topic of debate the theme of "The Functional City." It resulted in the elaboration of a commanding series of proposals on town planning known as the Athens Charter.[17] This document seems to have had the effect of paralyzing creative research into most aspects of the subject by directing the efforts of architects toward a rigid alignment of functional zones in town layouts and the projection of high-rise blocks of flats, in such a way that other notions were virtually excluded. By the time of CIAM VIII, held in England after the war, in 1951, the high-flown generalities which the Athens Charter had sanctioned were recognized by younger members for what they were. This meeting took as its topic of discussion "The Urban Core." Here was a theme extending into the domain of symbol, one that promised more in terms of scope than Le Corbusier's rhetorization of an elementary grammar of function. The very selection of a conference theme which broke through the bounds of the charter and called into question the model of the *ville radieuse* laid the implicit claims of both of these open to serious doubts. All the same, it was not until the tenth meeting, held at Dubrovnik in 1956, that the impossibility of going on in this same way became evident to a majority of the participants. Nor, indeed, in looking back, is it quite clear from whence the CIAM, this informal gathering of architects under the influence of Le Corbusier and a few other bright stars of the prewar firmament, had derived its portentous notion of authority and self-importance.

Kenzo Tange, then in his late thirties, had been invited to attend the 1951 meeting on the strength of his prizewinning scheme for the Hiroshima Peace Center, which in a unique and unprecedented way qualified for inclusion in the so-called urban core discussion. The manner by which the formerly thriving city had met with destruction and the enormity of its continuing predicament precluded all possibility of any ordinary solution based on a merely functional rehabilitation of the city as it had existed prior to the dropping of the bomb. At the same time, it is arguable that the event of atomic annihilation had, in one quantum leap, pushed the entire concept of architecture, let alone that of city planning, beyond the reach of all possible symbolization.

Tange's position in the face of this new "dimension" created by the reconstruction of Hiroshima appears at first to be inexplicably vague. That, however, is more than misleading. In the seventh article of the Athens Charter, Le Corbusier had expounded the notion of a continual change which determines the "spirit of the city" over the years, with mention of the "moral value" this phenomenon entailed—a preeminently Tainean mode of acceding to an experience of the urban past. In this text, made public for the first time under the German occupation, Le Corbusier was nonetheless writing prior to the destruction of either Dresden or Hiroshima, to cite only the most spectacular examples of later wartime desecration. However, by the time CIAM first met again at Bridgewater in England (1947) to "reaffirm its aims" and, again, at Bergamo (1949) to "put the Charter into practice," an innocent sample of Corbusian rhetoric could undergo a change of emphasis or even a shift in meaning. Thus, "Death overtakes buildings and cities as well as human beings. Who will make the choice between what should remain and what must disappear?"[18] The catechismal response was as follows:

> The spirit which prevails in the oldest part of the city is built up over the years; ordinary buildings acquire an everlasting significance insomuch as they come to symbolize collective consciousness; they provide the skeleton of a tradition, which, without attempting to limit future progress, nevertheless conditions and forms individuals in much the same way as do climate, country, race or custom. Since cities, and especially historic town centers, are nations unto themselves, there is a sense of moral value that holds a meaning and to which they are indivisibly linked.[19]

It can, therefore, be said that the Athens Charter, in spite of its functional bias, contains the kernel of the notion that was discussed as "The Urban Core" in the 1951 meeting of CIAM at Hoddesdon, England, attended by Tange.

Whether or not Le Corbusier's statement applies to Japanese cities in the same way as their Western counterparts is open to argument. Especially in castle towns, such as Tokyo or Hiroshima, the notion of the empty center—or "unattainable" core—is usually applied as a theoretical definition or description. The castle and its fortifications constitute a simple land-

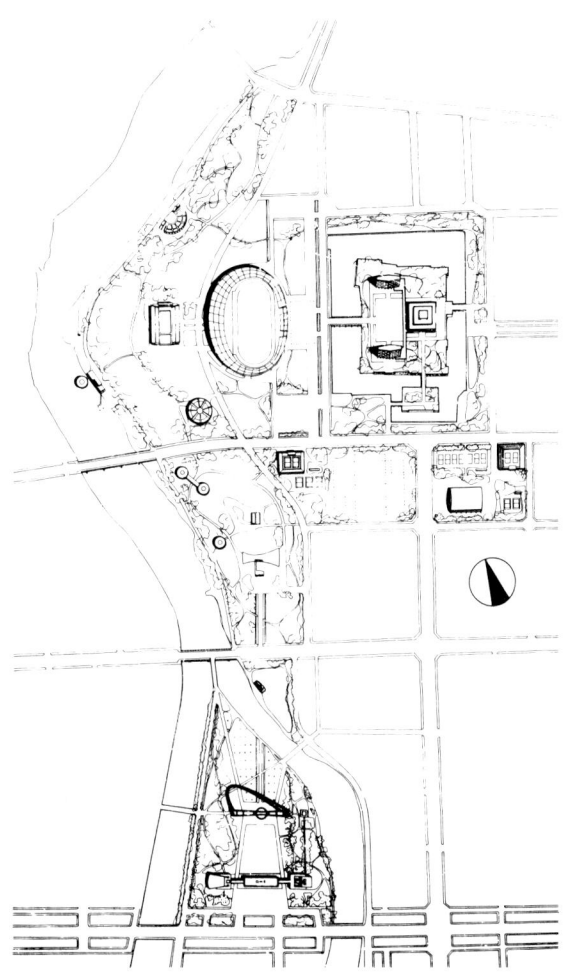

174 POSTWAR URBAN RHETORIC

7.11. Tange: Peace Park with sports and cultural facilities, Hiroshima, 1949–55.

7.12. Tange: Atomic Memorial Museum, Hiroshima, 1949–55.

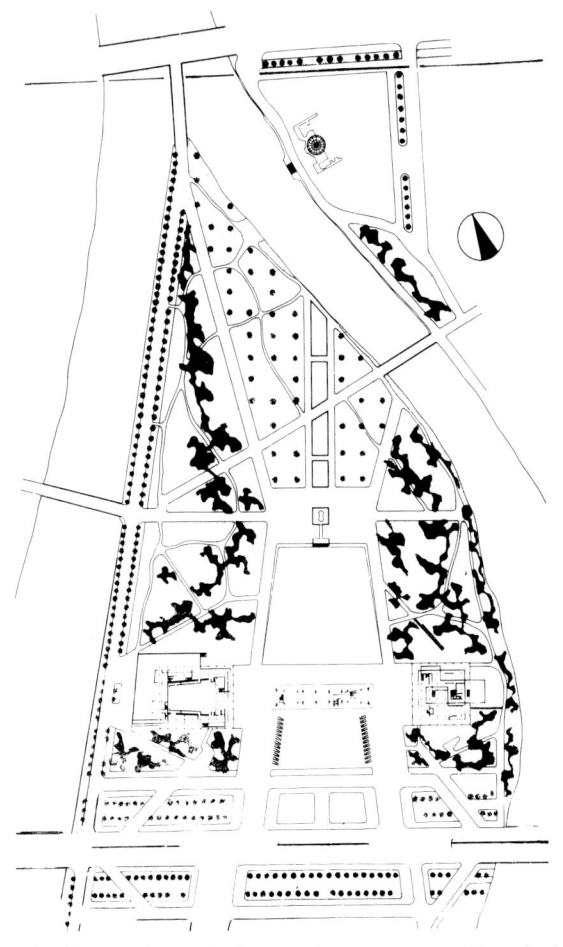

7.13. Tange: Peace Park, Hiroshima, 1949–55. Detail of figure 7.11, as realized.

mark but one that is without any participation on the part of the general populace of such a town, as entry into it would normally have been forbidden. Rather it is the commoners' districts, the great houses (particularly the sumptuary gates), and religious establishments, all of which are scattered randomly throughout the plan, that give a sense of Le Corbusier's "collective consciousness" to such towns without centers. Be that as it may, the compulsive attraction which Hiroshima suddenly came to exercise, and which it holds for us today, is that all such considerations were obliterated at a single stroke. As a result, a new "soul" or collective focus was created as a function of national and, eventually, of world attention. This imposed meaning, having nothing to do with the "spiritual" life of monumental features in the town itself, creates its own unique situational ethos as a kind of antithesis.

We know from other sources[20] that this upsurge of outside interest in the fate of the stricken town was far from being unanimously welcomed by its inhabitants. In any case, immediate needs after the disaster were of a basic and practical nature not admitting of much reflection. When Tange's land-use survey team arrived, plans for a new road network and the establishment of a green zone were already in force, conflicting, incidentally, with such sociological data as Tange's group was able eventually to put together. It was not until 1949 that the Hiroshima Peace Memorial City Construction Statute was passed by the Diet and the Peace Memorial competition set up. Tange won this in the same year and his scheme was executed by 1955, though the layout (fig. 7.11) apparently originated in 1946, the year of the Tange team's master plan. The Atomic Memorial Museum (fig. 7.12) resting on 6.5-meter *piloti* forms the centerpiece of the main architectural grouping (only one of the two flanking structures is the actual work of Tange). As the scheme for the Peace Park (fig. 7.13) was built on what is virtually an island in the center of the city, it in some ways resembles Schinkel's Altes Museum in Berlin, but that is perhaps an accident of topography. Much more to the point is the resemblance to the Capitoline layout embodied in the Greater East Asia Coprosperity Sphere memorial at the base of Mt. Fuji, Tange's unrealized wartime competition entry. Otherwise, the most famous feature of the Hiroshima composition is the axial arrangement of Tange's new buildings with the fragmented shell of a neoclassical dome—the only structure now surviving, even in part, in this area of the city—known laconically as the Atomic Dome.

Like members of the medical profession, the team Tange brought in to Hiroshima in 1946–47 was forced to make a pragmatic response to the reality of the situation created by the untoward effects of the new bomb. This killed 100,000 people on the spot and resulted in chaos, homelessness, and an ever-increasing number of fatalities which, it was soon realized, were traceable to radioactive poisoning. Although Tange, too, was later to criticize the Athens Charter, the basic and practical alternatives confronted in the Hiroshima Master Plan can only be characterized as a reversion to function in the wake of the near-total destruction of one of the largest cities in the country. If he has since described his architectural philosophy at that time as "a certain criticism of functionalism,"[21] Tange has also characterized his methodology in the fifties as deriving from "typification of function." By that, he meant that the functions singled out as relevant and influential in a given design project should, out of need, be limited to the "most human, most essential and most future-oriented."[22]

This simple and dignified concept of function was well suited to the exigencies of the moment during the early years of Japan's reconstruction. Within a short time, however, some hazier notions made their appearance, in which Tange was much given to employing the terms "structure" and "symbol." As already mentioned, Tange attended the eighth CIAM meeting in 1951, held in England the same year as the Festival of Britain. The invitation was issued to Maekawa by his erstwhile colleague José-Luis Sert, who encouraged the older man to bring his former assistant and protégé to Europe, where the latter spent "a very meaningful two months."[23] This was, of course, Tange's first encounter with CIAM's two founding spirits—Le Corbusier and his compatriot, the historian Siegfried Giedion—as well as with Walter Gropius. After the conference he spent time touring Europe's classical monuments and visiting works of Le Corbusier, notably his Unité d'Habitation, then nearing completion at Marseilles. In ad-

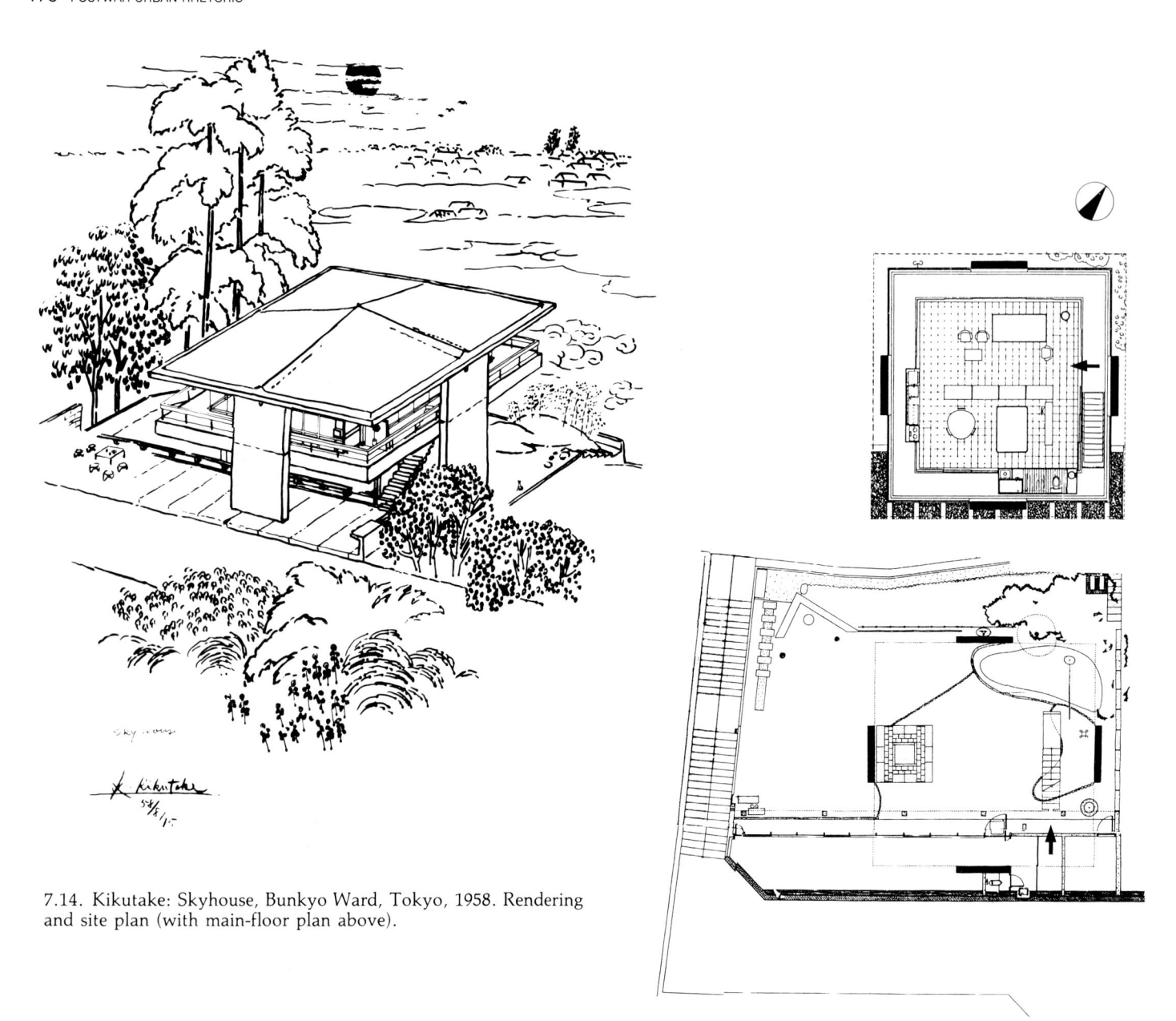

7.14. Kikutake: Skyhouse, Bunkyo Ward, Tokyo, 1958. Rendering and site plan (with main-floor plan above).

dition, Le Corbusier had with him in England photographs of his model for the new capital of Punjab at Chandigarh as well as drawings and sketches of this important and influential project. Yet the general results of the Hoddesdon conference cannot be considered much of a success, and Banham has termed the group's report on the "Urban Core" theme "little more than a compendium of fashionable clichés."[24] There was another meeting at Aix-en-Provence in 1953, but it was at the tenth conference, held at Dubrovnik in 1956, that the organization collapsed. This was owing to the determination of a group of younger members, the same age as Tange, to oppose the vagueness of the Athens Charter with respect to just those issues which were most at stake in the expansion and reconstruction of already existing cities. It is, perhaps, significant that neither Le Corbusier nor Kenzo Tange attended this Dubrovnik meeting, though for the one this was a gesture of relinquishment, while for the other sheer distance was probably the obstacle. Despite the fact that Tange became a member of the organization considered as the "new" CIAM under the leadership of those Team X contemporaries who had supervised the Dubrovnik program, his own ideas never progressed beyond those of the "old" CIAM he had first known in 1951. Banham observed that the aims of Team X were to comprise "the personal, the particular and the precise."[25] However, the conference that took place in Otterlo, Holland, in 1959, revealed these aims to be difficult of attainment. Or, once more, as put by Banham: "Close discussion of the particular could often be as trivial as broad discussion of generalities. . . ."[26] As for Tange, he has never gone further than to opine that "typified function, structure and symbol" were "what is lacking"[27] in the Athens Charter. This is not much to go on, even if one allows for the rhetorical boost inherent in the choice of an ideogram, or written character—incapable, perhaps, of being adequately rendered in translation. Nor do Tange's more pointedly architectural statements help much to clarify his rhetorical image of the city.

Presently the forty-five-year-old architect began to moot his idea of a new "charter" for the second half of the twentieth century, an effort in aid of which he enlisted support from a younger generation in Japan. At Otterlo, Tange had presented his Tokyo City Hall (see fig. 7.7) and Kagawa Prefectural Office (see fig. 8.38), works said to combine a Japanese traditional feeling with concepts derived from the Modern Movement in a way that, as was pointed out in the discussions following the meeting, was virtually inimitable.[28] However, he also brought with him to Holland seeds of a

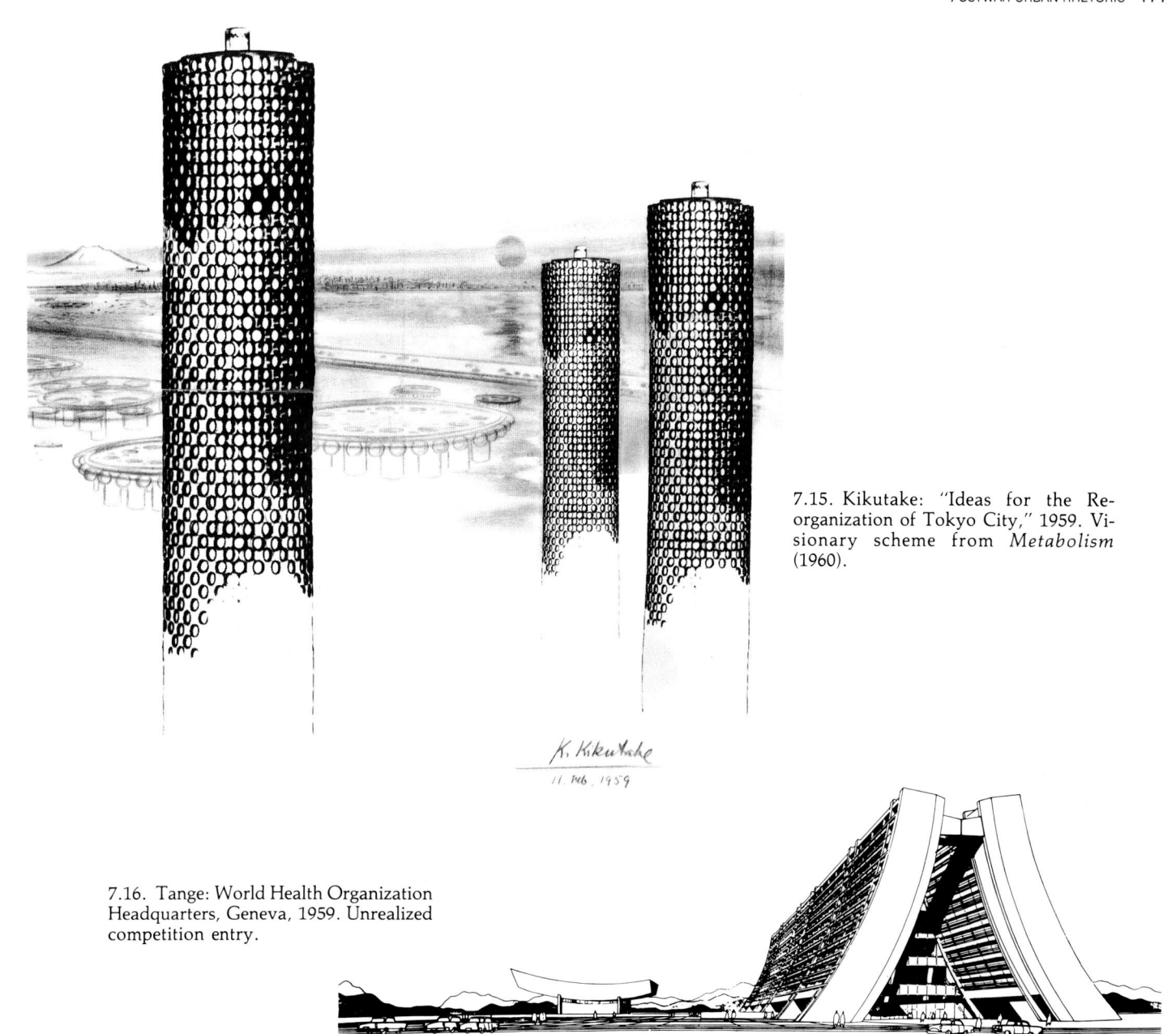

7.15. Kikutake: "Ideas for the Reorganization of Tokyo City," 1959. Visionary scheme from *Metabolism* (1960).

7.16. Tange: World Health Organization Headquarters, Geneva, 1959. Unrealized competition entry.

movement later to be known as "Metabolism" and from which his personal design program eventually borrowed some needed vitality and enhanced imagery. These seminal items consisted of one work and an unrealized project by Kiyonori Kikutake, a Waseda University man who had commenced practice in 1953 after a period spent in Togo Murano's office. The realized building was Kikutake's own house, later "Skyhouse" (fig. 7.14), erected in 1958 not far from downtown Tokyo. The project (fig. 7.15) was entitled "Ideas for the Reorganization of Tokyo City," or "Land for man to live, sea for machine to function [sic]," and is dated 1959. It proposes that, owing to the scarcity of land, coastal areas be reserved for human habitation in the form of cylindrical tower blocks, with heavy industry relegated to floating circular platforms in the sea. Both Kikutake's residence and his bay-area reorganization scheme were presented by Tange to the general session at the Otterlo meeting as an addendum following Tange's discussion of his own works.[29]

OTTERLO, MIT, AND METABOLISM

Kenzo Tange left Otterlo one day early that September for America, where he was to be visiting professor at Massachusetts Institute of Technology. Thus, he missed the controversial vote by which it was formally decided to end association with the CIAM acronym. In any case, the Kikutake land-use project, together with that for the young architect's house, was conceived much more in the problem-solving spirit of the later CIAM-Team X resolutions than were either Tange's Tokyo City Hall or the Kagawa Prefectural Office, which might have been built anywhere in Japan. Kikutake's project was keyed to the notion of land scarcity in the greater Tokyo region, while his house illustrated this plight by being raised on four slablike *piloti* at the edge of a slope. Although the idea stems from a California hillside tradition—beginning with Neutra's Lovell House (see fig. 6.97)—Kikutake's version predates, for example, Pierre Koenig's celebrated Case Study House 22 (1959), to have been situated in the Hollywood Hills.

Meanwhile, Tange's tenure at MIT was to extend for four months. On the day of his arrival in Cambridge, armed with a telegram, he abruptly broke the news of the demise of CIAM to Walter Gropius and Siegfried Giedion.[30] It may have been the reception of Kikutake's project at Otterlo which determined Tange to set a fifth-year design problem for MIT students consisting in a 25,000-person residential community to be erected in Boston over the bay. However, Tange's

7.17. Maekawa: housing at Harumi, Tokyo, 1957–58. Facade of main block.

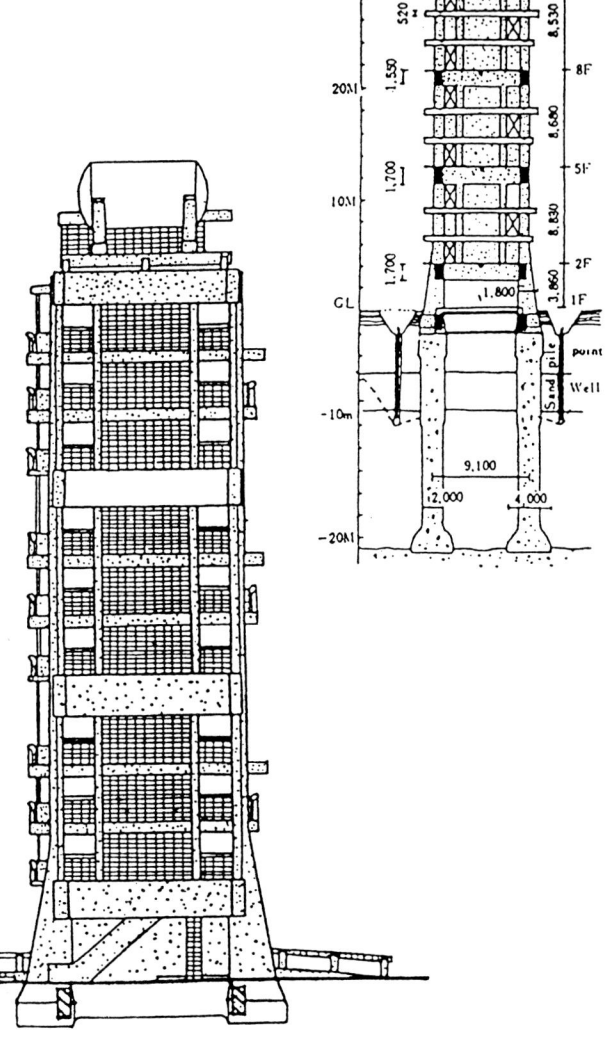

7.18. Maekawa: housing at Harumi, Tokyo, 1957–58. Side elevation and structural section.

specifications reversed the sense of Kikutake's formula by placing the residential function over the water—a much more dramatic idea—only one that was, incidentally, fraught with problems. Indeed, such housing has never been realized, although, at great cost, offshore drilling rigs à la Kikutake have since been set in place. As worked out, the MIT scheme comprised two giant linear A-frame constructions. Their design would appear to be based on Tange's own 1959 submission to an invited competition for the design of the World Health Organization headquarters at Geneva (fig. 7.16). That project, cited by the jury as unbuildable, derives in turn from Maekawa's massive public housing scheme in Harumi, Tokyo (figs. 7.17–19; near but not *in* Tokyo Bay, it is situated on an island), realized between 1957 and 1958. The vertical members projected for each block are massive and slightly splayed at the base of the prototypical ten-story unit. In Tange's WHO project the splay is exaggerated to form an intermediate space inside the building. Such a space is finally realized on a lesser, though still monumental, scale in the hotel at Disney World erected on drained swampland near Orlando, Florida, about a decade and a half later. In the MIT version, the building's profile is oblique, while each of the two linear units is curved in plan like a boomerang.

Both the MIT student project under Tange's direction and incipient Metabolism, as represented by the two Kikutake designs shown in Otterlo, came to full flower in 1960 at the Tokyo World Design Conference.[31] This five-day meeting of designers and architects was held under the auspices of the Japanese construction industry and met in the former Soge-

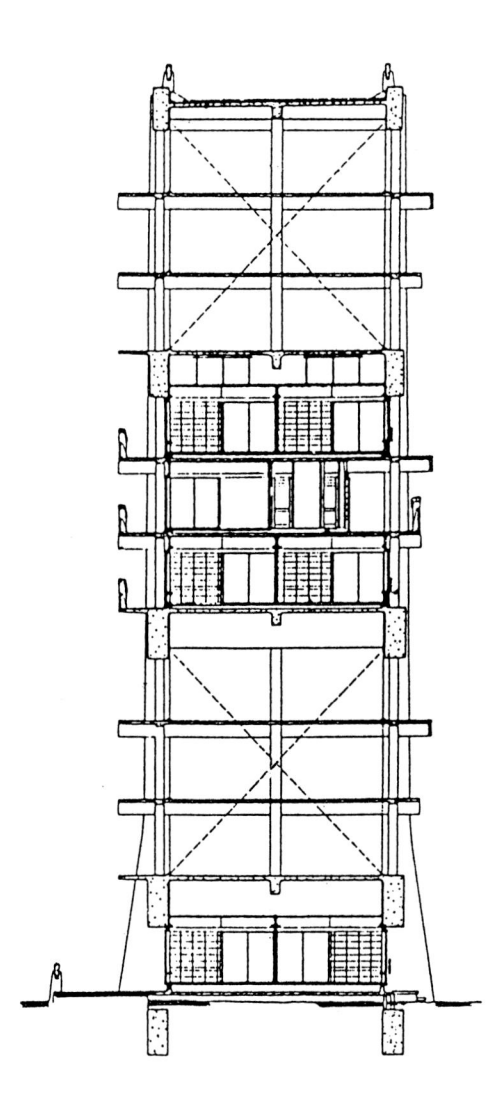

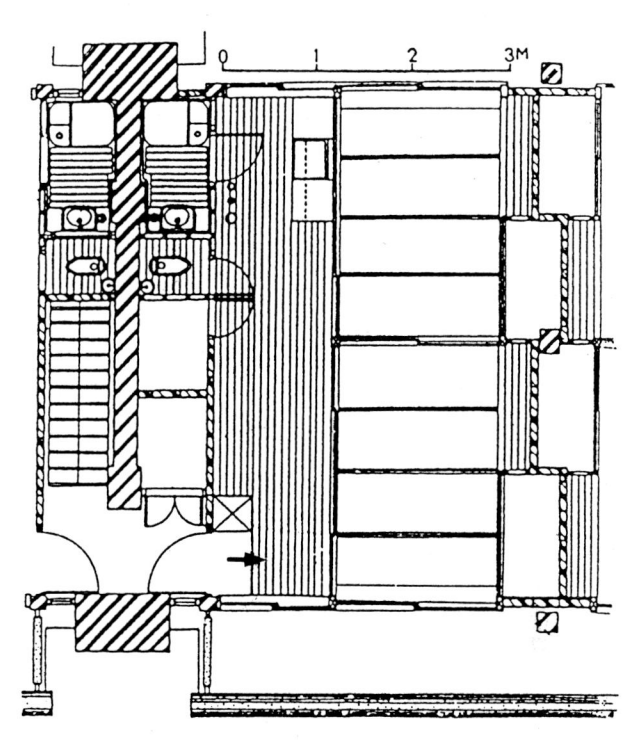

7.19. Maekawa: housing at Harumi, Tokyo, 1957–58. Unit layout plan and sectional locator for three-story grouping.

tsu Kaikan designed by Tange in 1958. Tange's address to the gathering, entitled "Technology and Man," is suggestive of the increasing, yet always hazy, importance he attributed to this domain. In fact, a forthright concern for technology is scarcely expressed by Tange, except in his Ehime Sports Center of 1953 and Tosho Printing Works, at Haramachi, of two years later. Both works were premiated by the Japanese architects' association but in after years appear to have been dropped from the Tange canon, presumably as incorporating too little symbolism. Both are shell structures of different sorts and, therefore, lead directly to the National Olympic Stadiums of a decade later.

In his speech at the World Design Conference, Tange employed such words as "cell" and "metabolism," betokening his familiarity with a group of young architects that included Kikutake (who once hoped to become a medical doctor). In the year of the conference this group—the youngest of whom, Noriaki (later Kisho) Kurokawa, was then only twenty-six—published its manifesto, *Metabolism 1960: Proposals for a New Urbanism*. Several artists, designers, and architects had been meeting informally as a "Design Committee" since 1955–56 in preparation for this international meeting. Eventually, Junzo Sakakura became conference chairman, with Tange as program chairman. Meanwhile the Metabolist initiative seemed to have originated, as such, early in 1960 with a "Theme Committee" more or less under Tange's guidance. Besides Kikutake and Kurokawa, its members included Masato Otaka, a graduate of Tange's studio then working for Maekawa; Kenji Ekuan, the industrial designer; and a graphic designer, Kiyoshi Awazu. There was also Noboru Kawazoe, a critic and former editor of *Shinkenchiku*, although his association with the group did not extend to the Metabolist manifesto itself. Importantly for later developments, there was in addition Fumihiko Maki of Tange's studio at Tokyo University. After graduation he had left Japan to study and, eventually, to teach in the United States, where he evolved an elegant and humane architectural language with which the 1980s have at long last caught up. Maki continued, despite his absence from Japan, to work with Otaka on a project for the development of the Shinjuku district based on the theme of "group form." Though not officially a member of the Theme Committee, he returned from America in time to participate in both the World Design Conference and the Metabolist manifesto. The manifesto took Kikutake's project for a marine city, renamed Unabara, as its initial chapter, and the same scheme was also aired publicly at one of the sessions of the World Design Conference. Among Western architects attending the conference were: the two Smithsons and Jacob Bakema (all of Team X), Paul Rudolph, whom Tange had met in the United States, Ralph Erskine, Louis Kahn, Jean Prouvé, Minoru Yamazaki, B. V. Doshi, and Raphael Soriano.

Tange conceived his conference program in terms of problems of industrialized growth, so casting proceedings somewhat as a continuation of the CIAM–Team X direction of thinking. Significantly, Team X had designated the notions of "mobility," "cluster," and "growth/change" along with "urbanism and habitat" as discussion topics at the Dubrovnik

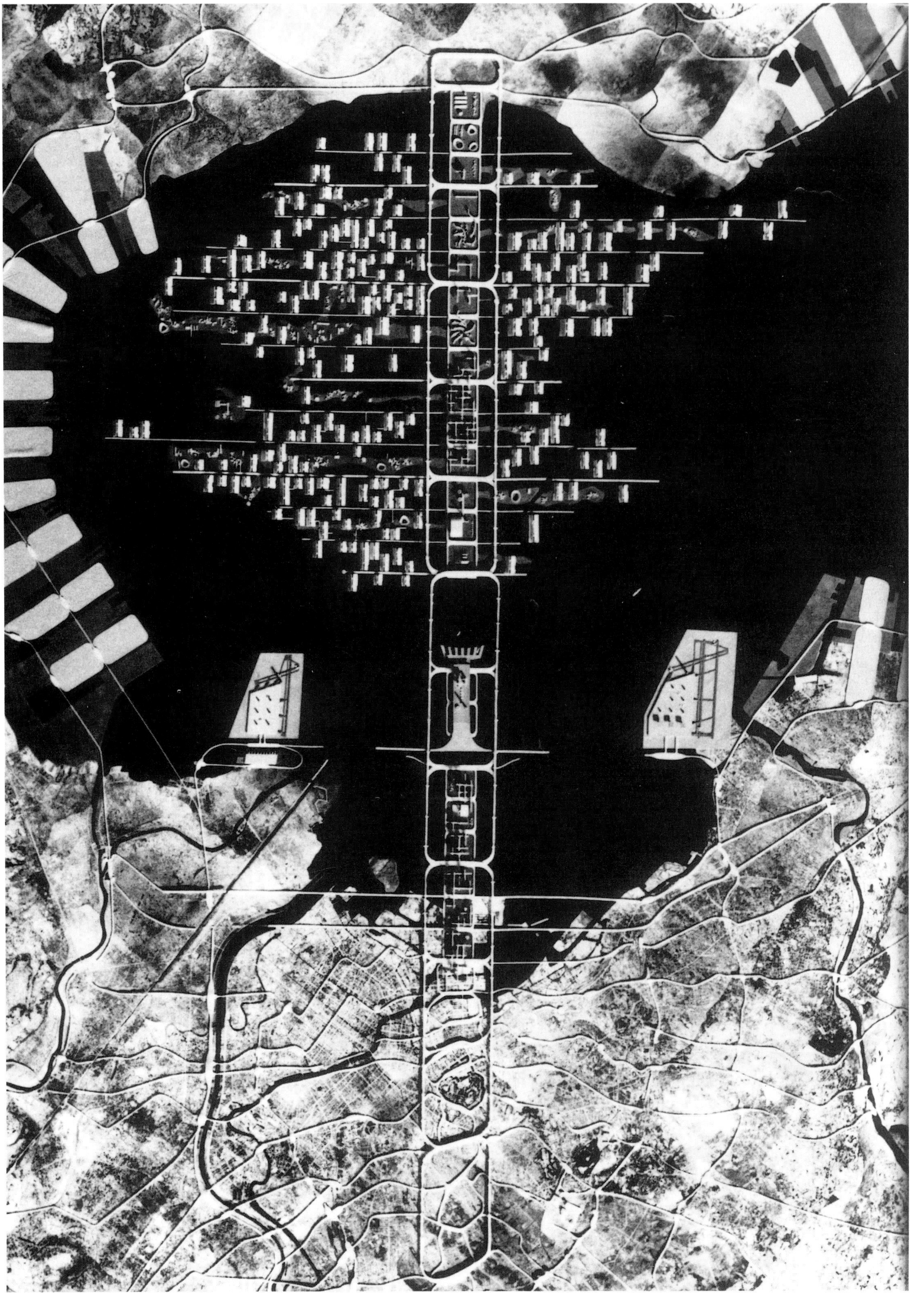

7.20. Tange: "Tokyo Plan: 1960."
View of model.

7.21. Tange: "Tokyo Plan: 1960."
Detail of figure 7.20.

meeting in 1956, and these all became key words for the Metabolists and their mentor, Tange, in Tokyo, four years later. A major difference between Tokyo and Dubrovnik, however, was that once these terms entered the Japanese ideological context, there no longer appeared to exist a metaphorical gap. In the event, the choice of Latin-derived topics for May 12, 13, and 14 (the three working days of the meeting) was unfortunate. These were all terms like "individuality," "regionality," "universality," "environment," "communication," "society," and "technology." Therefore it was the presence of the Metabolist group with their literal interpretations of Team X–type slogans in the spirit of Kikutake, as well as Tange's own intervention on the morning of May 14 under the rubric of "possibility," that proved showstoppers. Tange's talk ended with the presentation of his 1959–60 Boston Harbor project to the conference, thus paving the way for his "Tokyo Plan—1960" (figs. 7.20–21). This plan appeared in the daily press before the end of the year against a background of new economic programs announced by the Japanese government.

The Tokyo Plan was a proposal for the structural reorganization of a city of 10,000,000 inhabitants that was to have entailed a transformation of the existing radial structure into a new linear form. The scheme extending right over Tokyo Bay developed the Boston format with its convergence of notions borrowed from Kikutake and Maekawa. The linear element probably derives from the "Paris Parallèle" scheme proposed by André Bloc (director of the review *L'Architecture d'Aujourd'hui* and an acquaintance of Tange's) for the French capital earlier the same year. Tange claims that the Tokyo Plan, an outgrowth of his delayed Ph.D. thesis, marks a turning point in the evolution of his thought away from functionalism in urban planning and toward a new "structural" approach. Although functionalism is a reference to the Athens Charter, exactly what Tange meant by "structural" is somewhat uncertain. It may, however, be connected with the "megastructural" architectural notation that figured so prominently even in the reduced scale at which the vast project is represented. In Metabolism as well, megastructural imagery dominates most schemes and sketches, overshadowing elaborate theoretical points based on notions of growth and change. The entire Tange-cum-Metabolism ideology flows from the decline of CIAM, and it may be that the reorganization of the city in terms of giant, multifunctional architectural units (which is what so-called megastructures are about) offered the only possible theoretical response to this crisis. Team X, for all its good intentions, did not succeed in showing a way out of the paradoxical situation brought about by the Athens Charter. In fact, this was prolonged—rather than alleviated—by the debate on the urban core notion. The linear, megastructural approach of the Tokyo Plan accords the city a certain "readability," one major Team X objective, but at far too great a cost in actual as well as human terms. Moreover, even this ease of readability was probably illusory, as it was based—scarcely less than Le Corbusier's *ville radieuse*—on a baroque axiality incorporated *conceptually* into the plan rather than at ant's-eye level.

The illusion and metaphor incorporated in the Tokyo Plan succeeded, if at all, owing to the fantastic scale of Tange's proposed urbanistic intervention, and to the dramatic contrast between old and new (i.e., vernacular and contemporary) elements of the city. Metabolism was prepared to go even further by extending the biological life-force metaphor, for which it is named, into the realm of real-life allegory (suggestive of the entire planning process). Tange's repeated plea for "order out of chaos" appears but a thinly veiled old-fashioned modernist strategy for the rationalization of existing Japanese cities—from the disturbing viewpoint of mid-twentieth-century densities. Paradoxically, perhaps, it also makes an attempt to perpetuate the ancient concept of order exemplified in the classical Japanese city, which is to say Kyoto over against Edo or Tokyo. For the road network of the Tokyo Plan is a linearized grid superimposed over the bay, down the center of which megastructures are picturesquely disposed. To right and left the famous shrinelike habitat units, derived via the WHO scheme (see fig. 7.16), float at right angles to perpendicular service roads. The layout, shrines apart, then mimics the plan of the series of ancient Japanese capitals based upon the model of Ch'ang-an (Sian) in China. In fact, if one ignores physical appearances (which later tended to follow natural landscape contours), all Japanese settlements, from Tokyo to the smallest hamlet, are laid out in accordance with the classical administrative pattern. Land is divided parcelwise and then broken up into progressively smaller subdivisions. Thus the coordinates of any location whatsoever are given in a series of up to three numbers appended to the name of the particular district, itself usually part of a larger administrative ward. That this was less a specifically visual order than the product of a social system would probably not have disturbed Team X theorists. They themselves were out to found a "hierarchy of human associations," and thus supersede the functional planning hierarchy of the Athens Charter. In fact, already during the fifties, French planners connected with CIAM had rediscovered in Morocco their own naturally existing "structured shantytowns." Yet Tange realized how Japan, even in defeat, was not about to return to the level of a developing country. He was intent, therefore, on promoting a spatial order derived from European baroque planning via Le Corbusier, with apologies to Michelangelo and even ancient Rome. However, he invested his architectural energies in megastructures—than which nothing could have been more permanent in terms of cost-size ratio. At the same time he encouraged the young bloods of the Metabolist movement to evoke lyrical themes of mobility and change, and in so doing produced a majestic, if empty, contrapuntal harmony.

"THE WEST'S FAVORITE JAPANESE ARCHITECT"

The World Design Conference did one thing, which was to confirm the position of Kenzo Tange as the man the late Robin Boyd called "the West's favorite Japanese architect." Yet, by contrast with architects such as Maekawa or Bunzo Yamaguchi, who had spent significant periods of apprenticeship working in Europe, Tange's particular synthesis of Japanese and Western elements was something of a throwback to the mixture of native and imported themes that characterized Japanese architectural thought prior to the thirties. It will be remembered that Raymond's criticism of Tange turned on this notion of the contradictoriness of a "new tradition." Moreover, the futuristic thread of the Metabolist grand design—with its emphasis on concepts of changeability and renewal—actually goes back to very ancient Taoist conceptions of the universe, incorporated latterly in received Japanese religious doctrines. It was far from being the least important aspect of Metabolism and of Tange's personal philosophizing that such ideas, however naively, helped turn architectural thinking toward its own home ground. All the same, it needs to be realized that this expansion of theoretical horizons to include oriental religion and its ramifications had little as yet to do with precise forms of traditional architecture. The possible exception is, of course, the example of the great shrine at Ise, whose construction and reconstruction are based on the Shinto doctrine of periodical renewal. For in premodern Japan little place existed for architecture in the canon of the fine arts, which consisted essentially of painting and certain forms of Buddhist sculpture. Nor, more than in any other premodern society, was the architect accorded the role of an intellectual. Yet, in all fairness, Tange's role of high priest was never fraught with much intellectual pretension.

The World Design Conference was concerned as much with craft as architecture, and in the eyes of the ancient philosopher-sages the role of the craftsman was more amenable than that of the engineer (or builder) with his unwelcome labor-saving devices, which risked upsetting the balance of universal forces. The métier of craftsman was understood to consist in the simple transformation of natural materials, well within the laws of reciprocal harmony, and the esteem in which he was held was proverbial. Tange's self-appointed responsibility as a "mediator" between a passive humanity and a potentially disruptive technology may in part unconsciously have cast him in this role. It is true that Le Corbusier also conceived of himself as a painter, first and foremost, yet he also favored the nineteenth-century ideal image of the engineer, represented by the up-to-date figure of Auguste Perret. Above all, whether as painter or architect, Le Corbusier championed the apotheosis of the artist as intellectual. If, by contrast, Tange's views on building are seen as corresponding to an unpretentious, craftsmanly ideal, it at least becomes easier to understand how theories of Metabolism were birthed in the context of an international "design" conference. Such a notion is upheld by the rapprochement a few years earlier between Tange and the exiled German architect Walter Gropius, founder of the Bauhaus. In fact, this association resulted in the publication of a joint book, *Katsura: Tradition and Creation in Japanese Architecture*, in 1960,[32] the year of the World Design Conference. As already stated, Tange had first met Gropius at the 1951 CIAM meeting, together with Le Corbusier. The following year Gropius was to retire from Harvard, where he had taught for a decade, and the next year, 1953, saw the beginning of an association with MIT. In 1954 Gropius visited Japan on a Rockefeller Foundation grant. He made a pilgrimage to the Katsura Villa (see fig. 8.37), of course, and soon afterward Tange and the photographer Yasuhiro Ishimoto made up their minds to prepare a book on the subject of the imperial villa, to which Gropius would contribute an introductory essay entitled "Architecture in Japan." Publication followed Tange's return, early in 1960, from Cambridge, where Gropius had certainly been instrumental in arranging the four-month professorship of the young Japanese at MIT.

In the first paragraph of his introduction, Gropius postulates that "the Western mind, in its restless desire to seek new horizons in the physical world, would do well to learn a lesson in spiritual intensification from the Oriental mind."[33] His essay goes on to summarize the importance of aesthetic values in Japanese culture, citing the influence of Zen Buddhism and the tea ceremony in particular. He discusses matters both of technique and theory, grasping well the significance of incomplete and unfinished things in the Japanese aesthetic. He also speaks of a strategy which employs juxtaposition and contrasts to achieve occasional surprises within a context characterized by overall logic as well as freshness of aesthetic perception. But he acknowledges, too, "the overemphasis on playful details [which] sometimes impairs the continuity and coherence of the spatial conception as a whole."[34] Then Gropius identifies and countenances a margin of contradiction between the modern development of scientific technology as opposed to the traditional lifestyle of dignity and restraint inspired by older forms of religious philosophy. Japan, he admits, finds herself now the center of "a whirlpool of problems that defy the imagination,"[35] beginning with the pressures of overpopulation and modernization. Moreover, that traditional economy of means—whose pinnacle is represented by Katsura—had, the Japanese themselves will argue, been after all "not voluntary but imposed by circumstances."[36]

In Tange's case, Gropius's plaint seems to situate a certain "gap" or "rift" referred to by the Japanese architect in his World Design Conference speech. The notion is a measure of Tange's traditionalism as well as his distance from the philosophy of Le Corbusier. The latter preferred to trace all misapplications of technology to flaws in social organization, while Gropius had always tended, more technocratically, to localize these at the level of the industrial process itself. Moreover, both these Westerners laid a portion of the blame at the door of the consumer and client. The war had offered positive proof that both government and industry could be held accountable for technological applications but that the individual citizen was relatively powerless to influence that use or misuse of the forces that had been unleashed by science. In fact, the theme of Hiroshima, or rather—more discreetly—the peacetime applications of atomic energy, was frequently touched upon at the Tokyo conference. So was the subject of electronics, and *both* are mentioned by Tange. As neither of these topics can be associated clearly with a definite vocabulary of visual forms, it is perhaps natural that Metabolist thematics were based mainly on abstract notions.

7.22. Tange: Shizuoka Press and Broadcasting Center, Shimbashi, Tokyo, 1966–67.

7.23. Kurokawa: Nakagin Capsule Building, Shimbashi, Tokyo, 1972.

One of these was biological rhythm, implying a degree of order and control, on a new invisible scale or level. Another was spatial division, which constitutes the traditional Japanese approach to compositional technique. A third was the articulation of spatial connectors, a vaguely molecular analogy serving as alternative to the technique of spatial division.

FATE OF A "GRAND" DESIGN: TOKYO

Returning, however, to the domain of city planning, it was the Japanese city in its raw postwar aspect—with resurrected, and expanding, transport networks and frequently makeshift constructions at extraordinarily high densities—which afforded the best example of a practical application of Metabolist theory. Kikutake's marine city fantasies, as a starting point, had a special relevance to the traditional Japanese creation myth as well as to the association of the movement of the tides with the vitalist life-force enshrined in the Shinto religion. The interconnection with shapes and forces revered by Shinto is evidenced even more strikingly by Kurokawa's helical version of the Metabolist utopia of 1961. In addition, this recalls the double-helix structure of recently discovered DNA molecules (also the diagonally framed "Tomorrow's City Hall" project for Philadelphia by Louis Kahn). However, none of these schemes ever held a candle to Tokyo itself, which, however, it must be admitted, has grown toward the Metabolic image as a plant inclines toward the sun.

As for individual buildings reflecting details of the Metabolist grand design, there are really only two, and these stand within about a kilometer of one another in downtown Tokyo among the network of railways and high-speed motorways that make up its warp and woof. The earlier is Kenzo Tange's small Shizuoka Press and Broadcasting Center of 1966–67 (fig. 7.22), which far outshines the same architect's Yamanashi Press and Radio Center of 1964–66, in the provincial center of Kofu. The Tokyo building is better in every way, and an elegant statement of ad hoc-ism which accepts the metropolis both as background and context. The other Metabolist monument worthy of the name is Kisho Kurokawa's Nakagin Capsule Building of 1972 in Shimbashi (fig. 7.23). It reflects the throwaway quality of Tokyo architecture and consists of a cluster of prefabricated capsule dwelling units. Whether or not these might have functioned as part of a larger megastructure, they have here been arranged as a self-contained and neatly scaled statement of utopian preferences. Kurokawa's structure is a sculpture dedicated to the interreplaceability of it own parts.

Neither the Tokyo Plan nor the relatively youthful Metabolist movement, both of 1960, had much concrete influence in the domain of physical planning. Tokyo was caught up in a new wave of metropolitan expansion in which practice had already outstripped theory. In any case, as was earlier pointed out, impulses toward physical planning in Japanese cities have generally been weak, looked at from a historical perspective. Metropolitan growth was a continuation of prewar population trends, while the rise in building activity accompanying these years of Tokyo's expansion, naturally, received its initial impulse from economic conditions. More precisely, the cause lay in the amazing development of the Japanese postwar economy deriving from the American use of Japan as a staging and supply base for operations during the Korean War between 1950 and 1953. Shortly afterward, the National Capital Region Development Law of 1956 aimed at applying to Tokyo the sort of planning restrictions set forth in the Greater London Plan—and was promptly disregarded from the beginning. Within ten years, failure to establish a green belt on the London model was admitted formally, and the demolition of British-style planning principles was rendered complete by new transport infrastructures. An example was the construction in Tokyo of the Metropolitan Expressway system (fig. 7.24), begun in 1959 in preparation for Japan's hosting of the Olympics. The system, therefore, dates exactly twenty years after the California state law of 1939 that permitted construction of the first urban freeway, or parkway, in Los Angeles. However, the Metropolitan Expressway routes are emphatically not a *parkway* system and stand instead firmly in the Japanese tradition of metropolitan "works" or improvements. Nor are they in any way suburban, since the network, as first constructed, stopped at the limits of the downtown area and has only recently become linked with more than one line of an intercity system of high-speed roads now crossing much of the entire country. In spite of the noise and dirt generated, as well as the spoilation of housing and shopping districts in their paths, the core of original downtown "lines" form one of the real monuments of a city that possesses few. It is the density of these roads, and of the neighborhoods they traverse, which lends a "megastructural," hence Metabolist, aspect to these purely infrastructural devices of daily use and has led to an accidental romanticizing of everyday qualities of the city.

7.24. Tokyo Municipality: Metropolitan Expressway, from 1959 onward.

8 | A New Dialogue with Tradition

TOWN AND COUNTRY

Whereas for Tange sheer increase in the number and size of metropolitan areas outweighed all other considerations, such as the effects of depopulation of the countryside, another way of looking at the far-reaching experience of demographic shifts since before World War II would involve noting interaction between urban and rural lifestyles (fig. 8.1). From a purely demographic point of view, the statistics themselves were more dramatic than any kind of self-consciously futuristic imagery they could have inspired in urban architecture or cityscape. In fact, during the past sixty years of the present Showa reign, the relative proportion of city to country dwellers in Japan has been exactly reversed. Thus, some ninety million people, or 77 percent of the nation's total population, now live in the cities—a reversal similar to that which took place in Britain during the nineteenth century.

The number of urban inhabitants in Japan is at present greater than the entire population of the eastern seaboard of the United States. More than a third of these ninety million people are concentrated in the Tokyo region, including areas of neighboring prefectures. The metropolitan area as a whole is about the size of Northern Ireland or the state of Connecticut. Elsewhere in the country, the Osaka region in central Japan contains about a fifth of the total urban population. The Shizuoka Prefecture area, between Tokyo and Nagoya, and the island of Kyushu in southern Japan each account for a further tenth, with the remainder divided between smaller urbanized areas in other regions. This overall urban population represents a somewhat higher than average percentage for the industrialized nations and double that for the world as a whole.

Nevertheless, in 1950, roughly two-thirds of the Japanese population was still engaged in agriculture and fishing, a proportion comparable to that of the rural population of the United States in 1890. Tokyo itself at that time still contained only six million inhabitants. By 1970 this figure had doubled, and the Tokyo region, or commuting area, contained twenty-one million inhabitants. Tokyo, like other urbanized districts in Japan, is a relatively compact city with strong central area(s) and generally high densities. However, in certain *downtown* areas the absence, until recently, of high-rise structures preserved exceptionally low densities in comparison with cities in the rest of the developed world. The three central wards of Tokyo, therefore, still contain far fewer persons per square kilometer than either central Paris or Manhattan. On the other hand, millions in nearby areas are housed at densities easily matching either of those great cities. Most significantly of all, *average* densities far higher than those of either greater Paris or New York extend over an area covering thousands of square kilometers of the Tokyo region.

In the domain of architecture, those very same municipalities up and down the country that rejected any notion of comprehensive planning (the major exception was Nagoya) competed during the 1950s and 1960s to commission and build concert halls and auditoriums, sports facilities, libraries, and municipal offices. Initially, these works responded to the "urban core" formulae advanced by CIAM, as carried over into the theory of Kenzo Tange and others. Communities of all sizes came to acquire "monuments" on a scale which even the country's major cities had barely possessed before the war. But, unlike the builders of Japan's medieval defenses, for example, the originators of the new, mainly sub-Corbusian "Japan Style" had few sizable precincts of unbuilt land at their disposal by which to isolate and enframe their works. All the same, agricultural plots in the surroundings of towns and cities, the numerous bombed and burned-out sites left by the war, and the overall vernacular character of even urbanized districts invested the new reinforced-concrete architecture with impressive vistas and contrasts. The general architectural quality of these works was high, as was their level of craftsmanship, and they provided excellent fodder for architectural journals at home as well as abroad.

Soon, however, infill of empty sites, disappearance of old-style gardens, and building-over of agricultural lands on the outskirts of towns began to occur as expanding urban growth reflected newfound prosperity. With amazing rapidity, existing towns, which till the war had consisted of one- or two-story wooden buildings, presently displayed structures having three or more stories, which, of necessity, were built of reinforced concrete. Therefore, today, buildings of the redoubtable Japan Style live on in the pages of all the old architectural journals of the period while becoming increasingly blurred in their real context.

Another factor diminishing the real impact of the architecture of the immediate postwar period was sociologically derived. Namely, by the late 1950s, cultural optimism associated with the war's end and a renewal of democratic institutions had reverted to an identifiable pattern of political and economic interests. Since 1955 Japan has been continuously ruled by a conservative Liberal Democratic Party, strongly

8.1. View of Shinohara's Umbrella House under construction in
Nerima Ward, Tokyo, 1961. See also figures 8.23–24.

representative of both rural and big-business interests. For the most part its elected officials were content to delegate responsibility for physical planning to a technically oriented bureaucracy anxious not to disturb the status quo. But notably—as in the field of transportation planning—newly created ad hoc authorities were also given a good deal of power. In fact, the jurisdiction of such planning bodies was habitually ill-defined; frequently conflicts of interest arose at the local level, and due process was more often than not ignored. Yet, too little was understood about the relation of planning matters to architecture for the formation of much organized opposition. Moreover, the public-works bias inherited from the previous century was combined with notions of American postwar urban-renewal strategies. Even if one does not believe the latter to have been misguided, it remains difficult to imagine such an approach being made to work successfully under Japanese conditions.

Still, it appears that the Japanese were saved from certain fatal errors by their relative lack of choice in accepting densities imposed by the urban explosion with which they were faced. Thus, as long as basic services are maintained at a high level in urban communities, as at present, much of the population is insulated from such disruptions as major traffic arteries by virtue of sheer density of low-rise settlement, while residing in comparative—if cramped—comfort. On the other hand, the economic and physical balance of the larger cities has been upset by the perfection, approximately twenty years after the end of the war, of a flexible, aseismic building technology first applied in the Kasumigaseki Building at the edge of Tokyo's government office district. A thirty-six-story "minor" skyscraper resulted, effectively removing the prior building-height restriction of thirty-one meters. Since the Kasumigaseki Building's completion in 1968, pressure from Japan's new corporate wealth has succeeded in making formerly public land available for a park of new skyscrapers in West Shinjuku, and by a similar process ground space for additional tall buildings has been expropriated in Ikebukuro and elsewhere. While this may not necessarily prove to be a bad thing in itself, it is one of the many factors which has helped to drive up land prices beyond the value of almost any type of occupant structure.

A check against total building-over of every area adjacent to Tokyo is the informal survival of preindustrial patterns of land tenure which can still be remarked easily in most suburban areas. This consists of the same extreme parceling that historically has resisted most efforts in favor of comprehensive planning, such as the attempt made after the Great Kanto Earthquake to rationalize circulation. Population concentration and plain traditionalism are the accountable factors, as well as a cautious husbanding of spatial resources originally induced by scarcity of suitable farming terrain. On the other hand, it has been estimated that in spite of a more than fourfold population increase since the end of the Tokugawa period, the expansion of cultivated land during the last hundred years has not on average exceeded one-half of 1 percent a year. It is, therefore, not a little irrational that the old attitudes continue to influence perception of land use in newly urbanizing areas augmented by a tax structure which privileges the agricultural use of all land, wheresoever located. Yet one happy result—however anomalous to Western views—has been that, even as the metropolis swallows up outlying districts, these have kept a common homogeneous pattern of familiarity and ease. The Japanese metropolis retains, then, an analogy with nineteenth-century European towns as being a collection of continuous yet distinct villages. This medieval conception of the city remained a unifying feature in force all over Europe until baroque planning principles replaced and finally destroyed it—an eventual triumph by Haussmannization.

Neither complete Haussmannization, nor even a thorough Manhattanizing, such as has occurred in postwar Greater Paris or still more recently in the San Francisco Bay Area, has obtained in Japan. At a national level, centralization of bureaucratic functions is so much a fact of life—just as in the private sphere—that no further elaboration of the principle by "art" has ever been deemed necessary. In Tokyo, survival of the old "garden-mosaic" pattern, itself a result of political centralization, permitted gradual yet insatiable development of southern and western districts which today constitute the diplomatic enclave. Now that central neighborhoods are themselves being filled with new skyscrapers, it is most of all the advent of middle-rise construction in the more densely inhabited suburban areas that poses the greatest threat to amenities. In addition, peak-hour transport capacity to the city center over acceptable commuting distances remains inadequate by Western standards, though in all other respects level of service is remarkable. Inevitably, however, the single worst aspect of the entire picture is nowadays the amount required for permanent new housing investment per family as a percentage of total income, owing to persistent densification of existing urbanized areas. Theoretically, it was these two inadequacies,

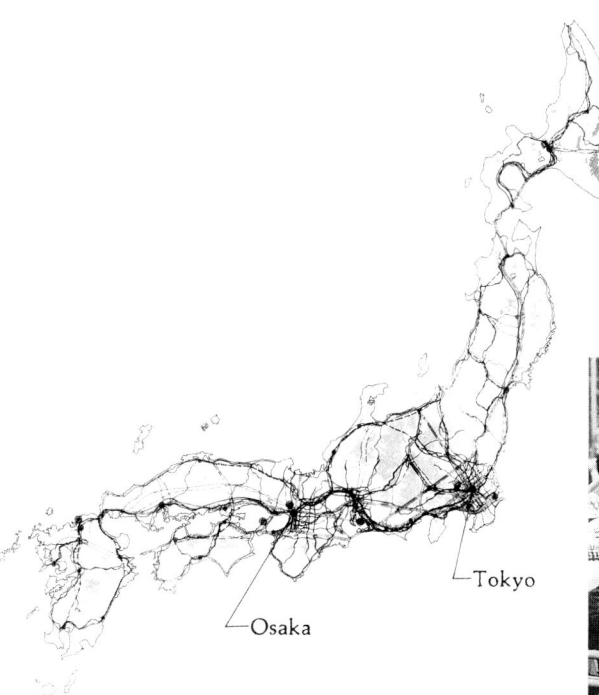

8.2. Tange: seaboard megalopolis, Tokyo to Osaka, 1965.

8.3. Demonstration against United States–Japan Security Treaty, 1960.

transportation and housing, that might have been alleviated—if not completely overcome—in a second grand proposal made by Tange, this time for a seaboard megalopolis (fig. 8.2) extending from Tokyo in the east to Osaka in the west. The scheme first received overseas publicity at an International Symposium on Regional Development organized in Hakone, near Mt. Fuji, in 1967, although Tange's ideas had been previously published in the national press.[1]

However, just as in Tange's earlier Tokyo Plan of 1960 (see fig. 7.20), initial costs would have been astronomic and the requisite technology of doubtful feasibility. All such radically utopian schemes end up providing an orchestration of images, motifs, and themes around which the aims of the establishment they seem to oppose crystallize with characteristic efficiency of purpose. The net result, as happened with Metabolism, too, is a limited progress in terms of "style" or vocabulary accompanied by a substantial growth of vested interests.

LE CORBUSIER'S PARENTAGE OF THE JAPAN STYLE

A quarter of a century later, it seems mandatory to recall that the celebration of artistic companionability at the World Design Conference held in Tokyo in 1960 contrasted sharply with protest against renewal of the United States–Japan Security Pact the same year (fig. 8.3). Eventually, more than five million demonstrators turned out to contest the ratification of this treaty, marking the outburst as the largest popular movement since the war. The psychological breach became more firmly established as Japan's power in the economic sphere evolved and the conservatism of her political establishment was openly accepted as a fact of life; disenchantment and frustration among intellectuals reached a high point in the futile revolt of the universities later in the decade. Out of all this emerged a more skeptical generation of architects for whom the vernacularized late-modern idiom of the Japan Style still exerted a formal attraction, but in a context largely deprived of meaning. Thus, as social goals of the protest movement aborted, the expected pursuit by younger men of the "architect's modern" practiced by Maekawa, Tange, and others was subtly undermined. In brief, events of the sixties imposed a tacit recognition that a specifically Japanese "new tradition" was as empty as Antonin Raymond had warned.

It is remarkable, all the same, how the richly personalized style of Le Corbusier came close to putting down roots, perhaps for the very reason that—as exemplified at Chandigarh—his vision never corresponded with a particularized view of place or culture. On the contrary, his concept of the Radiant City as a "rational and poetic monument set up in the midst of contingencies"[2]—though it might contradict Japanese sensibilities—would never prove thoroughly alien in the milieu of an industrialized, or industrializing, cultural setting. Yet the solutions self-styled by Le Corbusier as "Cartesian," from his early *ville contemporaine* onward, stem from a principle of radical doubt which Asian philosophies, in their unscathed preindustrial existence, do not share. Such systems, in other words, disregard the contradiction between metaphysics and science embodied in Descartes' conviction that the world can only be known through the mind. For Le Corbusier—builder, planner, and, hence, demiurge—regarded the "environment: places, peoples, cultures, topographies, climates" as unspecifiedly and ambiguously "contingent"—both a realm of chance prior to necessity and a wealth of resources subject to liberation by modern technology. This technology he saw to be universal, eagerly assuming that an absolute belief and a uniform material culture would flow from its application. And over all would reign Art.

From a similar Cartesian base, Jean-Paul Sartre had also constructed his conception of the work of art as a flight from contingency, like Keats's Grecian urn. But, in the event, Le Corbusier stopped short of the celebrated Sartrian formula of existence itself as radical contingency. At the same time he offered the Radiant City not, in Sartre's manner, as an agonized existential choice but as an inevitable one. For Le Corbusier "contingency" indicates either whatever is accidental or superfluous (and, therefore, dependent on something else) or, instead, a contribution or resource (from which something else may be created). The Radiant City is poised dazzlingly, therefore, as a mediating term between these worlds, a product of the three human characteristics: reason, destiny, and passion.[3] Moreover, and above all, it is "a manifestation of the human spirit itself: geometry."[4] Geometry, and the ideal city, must afford a "bearable" and "acceptable" alternative to the "chaos" of a not always perceptible "mathematics of the universe."[5]

The Athens Charter tends to play down these ideologically aggrandizing aspects of city-building, and it is curious that Le Corbusier seems ever to have believed that such notions could find sufficient, as well as necessary, expression in mere "plans." Not until the elaboration of the acropolis at Chandigarh, more than twenty years later, did a geometrically fashioned town schema yield its final lyrical convergence of passion and destiny with reason in an array of urban monuments. So it is of exceptional interest that the building, or rather project, of Le Corbusier's which Kenzo Tange seized on when still a student—the so-called Palace of the Soviets (see fig. 7.8)—is exactly the kind of building that would have afforded a similar focus. On the other hand, the Moscow scheme played on a combination of technical virtuosity, imposed by its vastness, and a specified (i.e., Marxist) ideological bias and impact. Neither of these elements could satisfy the passion for a kind of universal poetry to which Le Corbusier acceded in the passages from *La Ville Radieuse* I refer to above. Nor does the projected Palace of the Soviets presage those forms subsequently mediated by Surrealism via Le Corbusier's own painting. In keeping with this experience—and except for certain elements of pure pastiche—Tange's architecture, like that of his teacher, Maekawa, for the most part stops short at the prewar phase of Le Corbusier's development. In terms of urban planning, a similar lack of development ensnares the very work of Le Corbusier himself, who shows little progress in this field after the great functionalist, utopian setpieces of the 1920s and their reelaboration in his work of the 1930s.

There is, however, a particular quality which unifies and distinguishes the works of Tange and other Japan Style practitioners in purely formal terms. Partially ignoring Le Corbusier's pursuit of ever more dynamically sculptured three-dimensional forms, his Japanese followers exhibit a specific concern for *matière* which originates in, but goes beyond, the work of the French architect except for his chapel at Ronchamp. Much of the best building in Japan during the postwar period has a kind of calligraphic aptness that an overconcern for three-dimensional form would have vitiated. In the best cases, such works read as giant glyphs in a way that ties them more to contemporary painting than to architecture. It was just this quality that made such buildings as the Tange town hall for Kurashiki (1960) and his stadia for the Olympic games in 1964 photograph so beautifully (see fig. 8.57), even if this appeal has by now worn somewhat thin. In visual terms Tange's famous model of the plan for Tokyo displays a similar liveliness. Yet, if the works of the Japan Style could be painterly and even picturesque—terms which Le Corbusier's own works do not evoke—it was nevertheless through Le Corbusier that the Japanese discovered a working manner that allowed for augmentation in value under artisan standards at a time when labor was still cheaper than industrialized materials.

THE NEXT STEP

Le Corbusier's example, unquestionably then, provided the basis for the tradition out of which the next step evolved. The relevant general questions asked by the upcoming generation were:

(1) What is concrete?
(2) How may we best understand the great Le Corbusier?
(3) How can Le Corbusier be reconciled with Japanese methods?[6]

Nothing in this triad of rhetorical demands posed by younger architects born in the thirties relates explicitly to Le Corbusier's concern with urban planning, which, gradually, after Marseilles and Chandigarh, became part and parcel of his architecture. Several loopholes—like the epithet "great," the notion of reconciliation, and the vagueness implied in the term "Japanese methods"—might have permitted inclusion of an urban thematics. On the other hand, urban considerations could just as easily be ignored in the best Japanese tradition of straightforward avoidance of all the conventional planning strategies.[7] Most significantly of all, however, it is the spatial implications of Le Corbusier's work, be these "urban" or purely architectural, that were missing from Japanese emulation of his work. Possibly no one was more aware of their inability to deal with such spatial issues than Japanese architects themselves. Their lack of experience in these matters was mercifully bypassed on account of the simplified nature of the International Style, with its emphasis on volumes plotted on a system of points and bounded by plain two-dimensional surfaces. The relative and uncomplicated superficiality of such modern "spatial" containers invariably calls to mind the traditional Japanese post-and-beam system of construction with its lath-and-clay infill and papered apertures. This coincidental resemblance was intuitively recognized on the Japanese side a half century back and took on the appearance and value of a research datum. And it is clearly, too, a research-oriented approach that inspired those three questions typifying the reception of Le Corbusier's postwar turnabout in style among Japanese architects. In the final analysis, moreover, the revolution in Le Corbusier's concept and manner provoked a definite crisis within modernism, one for which the Japanese were no better prepared than, say, the Americans.

On the one hand, Japanese architects, on account of earthquake risk, were in a position to produce the heavy concrete work elicited—mainly for aesthetic reasons—by this Corbusian revolution. In America, a similarly labor-intensive structural apparatus could not have been rendered cost-effective in most cases. But, quite apart from that, in Japan new access to long-untapped reserves of national tradition had paradoxically been opened up by the war. This circumstance radically influenced the way in which Japanese were able to respond to the new architectural challenge that was bound up, just as throughout Europe, with a process of national reconstruction. It could be that eradication of military government in the aftermath of the Japanese defeat produced a wave of nostalgia for a past society and its lifestyle. In addition the war effort had long before made manufactured materials unavailable for ordinary building purposes, and by the end of the war even wood was temporarily unobtainable. However, official promotion of wooden-construction techniques in place of steel during the years of Sino-Japanese conflict in the late thirties stood architects in good stead in the immediate postwar years. At this time, established architects such as Maekawa first worked in wood, but turned to concrete as soon as it became once more available, together with reinforcing in sufficient quality and quantity.

To a certain extent, and notably in the early postwar style of Kenzo Tange, these two building methods came to be conflated. This certainly provided one source of the fascination that the Japan Style exercised on foreigners, and well into the 1970s examples (increasingly bordering on a tongue-in-check parody of the national past in a mixed style) could be pointed out. There is a sense, too, in which the postwar mixed style may have been a natural outgrowth of the *sukiya* style itself, since the tea aesthetic had always encouraged traditional use of unfamiliar elements, as well as unfamiliar employment of old and tried devices. In later feudal times, moreover, *sukiya* evolved from the cloistered, hothouse environment of the tea ceremony, where it had originated, to the mercantile culture of the burgeoning towns. The merchant quarters were less severely affected by sumptuary laws such as those governing architectural expression among hereditary nobility and samurai until the start of the Meiji period. Thus, in commercial and entertainment districts there existed, well before the modern age, a repository of innovative uses—in restaurants, teahouses, and private dwellings—where tradition had either pushed the conventions of serious representation to their limits or shortcircuited these altogether.

In terms of building aesthetics, the reforming attitude of the Modern Movement should have put paid to such delightful practices. In fact the phase of expressionism had contributed to further dalliance. It is such byplay—as the German visitors Bruno Taut and later Walter Gropius were particularly quick to notice—that seems most deep-rooted and typical in the Japanese approach. Or so it was at least when ceremonial purposes, governed as these have always been by sumptuary considerations, are not at stake. Nor, of course, is one concerned here with religious architecture. It is, therefore, first of all the *sukiya* style and its derivatives which must figure in any discussion of the new access to tradition, whether mediated by a forced return to wooden construction at the start of the war or more complex psychological causes.

In my belief, substantial (as opposed to mere superficial and trifling) gains accrued out of this investigation of traditional means in residential architecture, and not in public building—even if such a judgment excludes many of the acknowledged masterpieces of the so-called Japan Style. The default of the pre-Olympics style has already been discussed

8.4. Maekawa: Kasama House, Komaba, Tokyo, 1938. Facade.

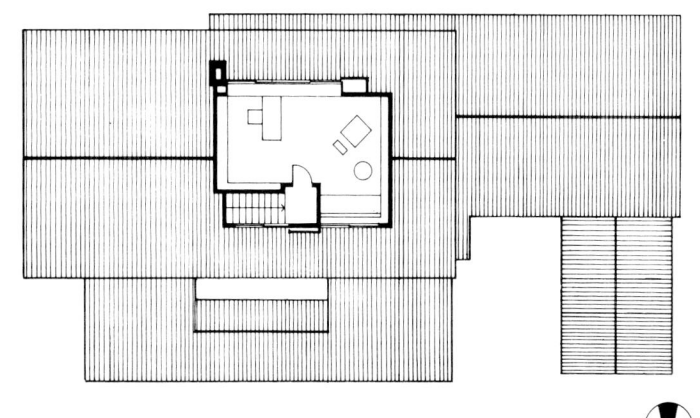

8.5. Maekawa: Kasama House, Komaba, Tokyo, 1938. Plans.

briefly with regard to external, that is, urban, considerations; the matter of housing is the reverse of this coin. Postwar building in Japan discriminates between public and private spheres in a way that has increased with the advance of the modern era. No one inside the country can remain unaware of this conclusively alienating phenomenon, if only in terms of the shrinking size of individual dwellings and splendid isolation of most public facilities. Moreover, there is some attempt to camouflage the disturbing qualitative rupture between public and private domains as a traditional virtue, beginning possibly with a misunderstanding of the philosopher Tetsuro Watsuji's[8] comments on cities and housing in the early Showa period.

HOME FRONT

After the war the Japan Style proceeded for the most part to ignore the lack of any specific and localizable urban dimension in Japanese cities—already singled out as an issue by Watsuji in 1935. If we admit the importance of the traditional distinction Watsuji cites between the "house" and the "outside," one way out of this double bind seemed to lie in upgrading the resources of the home by making it more traditional. Antonin Raymond was clearly thinking along these lines in his large joint-style residences before the war, but also in his vacation house at Karuizawa (see figs. 6.40–42). So, it seems, was Tange's teacher, Hideto Kishida, at the Imperial University, and at the same institution another historian-architect-professor, Chuta Ito, from an even earlier date. Finally, in Kyoto, Taut's great friend Koji Fujii's Japanese-style houses go back to the early 1920s.

Just before the war, neotraditional themes were embodied in works by Kunio Maekawa. Both his Kasama House of 1938 (figs. 8.4–5) in the Komaba district of Tokyo, supervised by the young Tange, and his own residence (figs. 8.6–7) of 1940–41 in Meguro are representative of a simplified and

8.6. Maekawa: the architect's house, Meguro, Tokyo, 1940–41. Facade.

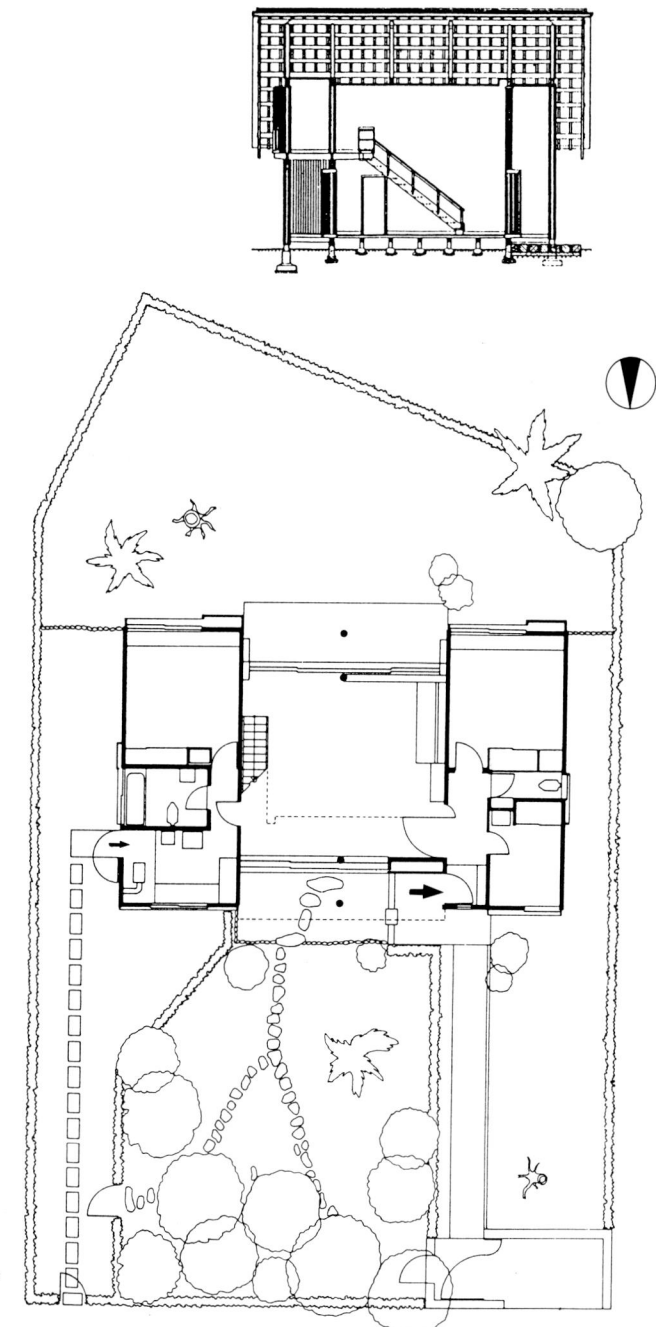

8.7. Maekawa: the architect's house, Meguro, Tokyo, 1940–41. Plan and section.

generalized, yet unorthodox, traditional Japanese aesthetic. Maekawa's robust version of this idiom was made possible by his five-year association with the Raymond office and with Junzo Yoshimura, who had joined Raymond as early as 1926, when still an undergraduate. At the time the Kasama House was erected, Yoshimura was with his employer in the United States, where he remained almost until the outbreak of the war. Raymond acknowledges his help with an unidentified house at Montauk Point, Long Island, referred to as "one of the earliest houses with definite Japanese influence but properly adapted to American conditions."[9] The interior of Raymond's big vernacular farmhouse at New Hope in Bucks County, Pennsylvania, was also partially remodeled in Japanese style during 1939, and Maekawa could not have been ignorant of such developments. Raymond reimported a similar idiom with him when he returned to Japan. The Saloman House in Shibuya of 1952, Raymond's own new home and office in Shibuya of the following year (figs. 8.8–10), and the nearby St. Alban's Church of 1955 were all executed in a related style. A hallmark of this Japanese manner Raymond derived with Yoshimura's help is its unsquared beams—a usage now touched with a more urbane flair than in the rustic prewar Karuizawa context. Notably at variance with orthodox traditional ideas are the round columns between sliding paper-covered *shoji* screens as well as the exposed diagonal exterior bracing, both of which can already be observed in Maekawa's own house of 1941.

The 1950s was also the decade of a series of so-called case-study houses built in answer to the postwar demand for low-cost housing and linked to research being done throughout the developed world, particularly in the United States. As early as 1948 the magazine *Shinkenchiku*, which had reappeared on the scene in 1946, sponsored a competition for minimal-type wooden housing. Among the most celebrated of Japanese works in this category was the series initiated in 1951 by Kiyosi Seike with his ninety-square-meter Mori

8.8. Raymond: the architect's house, Shibuya, Tokyo, 1953. Facade.

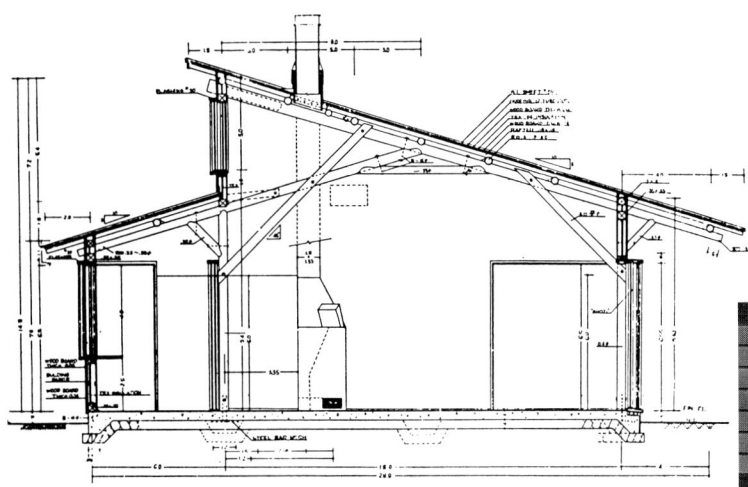

8.9. Raymond: the architect's house, Shibuya, Tokyo, 1953. Section.

8.10. Raymond: the architect's house, Shibuya, Tokyo, 1953. Interior.

8.11. Seike: Mori House, Bunkyo Ward, Tokyo, 1951. Facade.

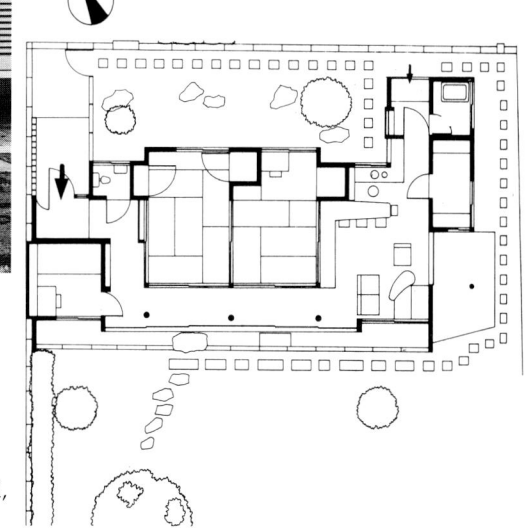

8.12. Seike: Mori House, Bunkyo Ward, Tokyo, 1951. Plan.

House (figs. 8.11–12). Its design amounted to a single room with spaces marked off by *shoji*—surmounted by a fixed *ramma*, or openwork transom—which could be opened or closed at will. Similar ideas were pursued by the same architect with increasing sophistication in the Saito House of 1952 (figs. 8.13–14), where raised islands of *tatami* afforded traditional-style seating in the midst of contemporary "Scandinavian-modern" furnishings. The adjacent Miyagi House of the following year (figs. 8.15–16) was not of wood, but of concrete block—with a roof, supported on light steel trussing, which could be pushed back to reveal the sky. As a group, these houses, including Seike's home, completed one year later, recall the design of Marcel Breuer's own residence (figs. 8.17–18) at New Canaan, Connecticut, of 1947; Charles Eames's Case Study House at Santa Monica, California, of 1949; and even Mies van der Rohe's steel-and-glass house for Dr. Edith Farnsworth of 1950. Yet, of all these, only the Breuer House shares the extreme informality of Seike's variations on a theme. The latter combine an abstract and intellectualized approach to the problem of low-cost housing, creating new, economical solutions with knowledge culled from the vernacular. The chill, costly elegance of exposed steel framing as employed in the United States was impractical in Japan, and the absolutely flat roof—which in Japan necessitates nonwooden construction—appears rarely in work of the period. In 1954 Seike met Walter Gropius and was invited by him to undertake further modular-housing research in America.

Another Japanese architect who had encountered Gropius was Kenzo Tange. At the time of Gropius's visit to Japan, Tange had recently completed a new home for himself. This was set in one of the southern suburbs of Tokyo. Like Seike's works, it consisted of a largely open plan, but the living quarters were raised a whole story into the air. The house, at Seijo, was to prove the only residential design of Tange's entire career, and its interiors afford a *locus classicus* of modified *sukiya* detailing, updated with modern materials, such as the uninterrupted plate-glass glazing at second-floor level. Except for a service core, the floors are all of *tatami* matting. The only Western-style furniture in view are a few low, lightweight sling-back chairs with frames of bent iron.

In both the Tange residence and the houses designed by Seike—all widely considered to be models of the period—the question of tradition was easily resolved. A transition was achieved in much the same way as one slipped into traditional dress upon arriving home, although that custom is virtually in abeyance thirty years later. Many of the more desirable outer suburbs of Tokyo still merged with the countryside in that far-off time, and land was neither as scarce nor as expensive as today. The urge to update tradition, or backdate the International Style, could be accomplished in more or less semirural surroundings. Indeed, Tokyo may at the time have appeared to be enjoying a neat balance between urban growth and suburban development. In retrospect, conditions—though primitive with respect to amenities—were almost as idyllic as those under which Wright's early style had flourished, at the beginning of the century, in Oak Park.

As we shall see, several of the key residential works of thirty years ago were raised, like Le Corbusier's Villa Savoye, a full story by means of *piloti*. One wonders, indeed, whether this fact may be read as somehow anticipating the subsequent

196 NEW DIALOGUE WITH TRADITION

8.13. Seike: Saito House, Ota Ward, Tokyo, 1952. Facade.

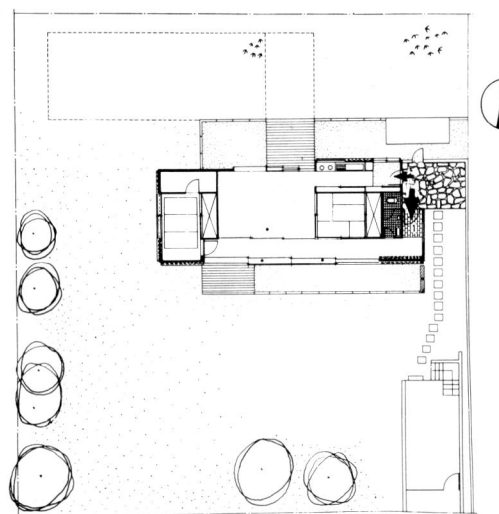

8.14. Seike: Saito House, Ota Ward, Tokyo, 1952. Plan.

8.15. Seike: Miyagi House, Ota Ward, Tokyo, 1953. Facade.

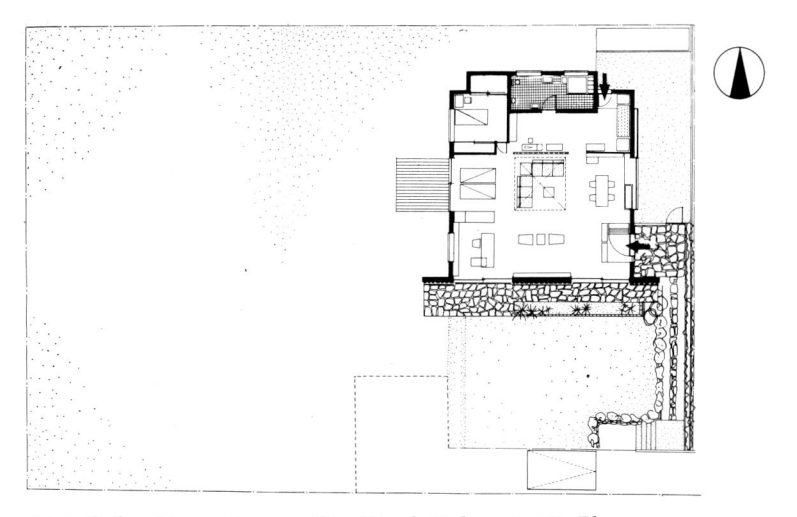

8.16. Seike: Miyagi House, Ota Ward, Tokyo, 1953. Plan.

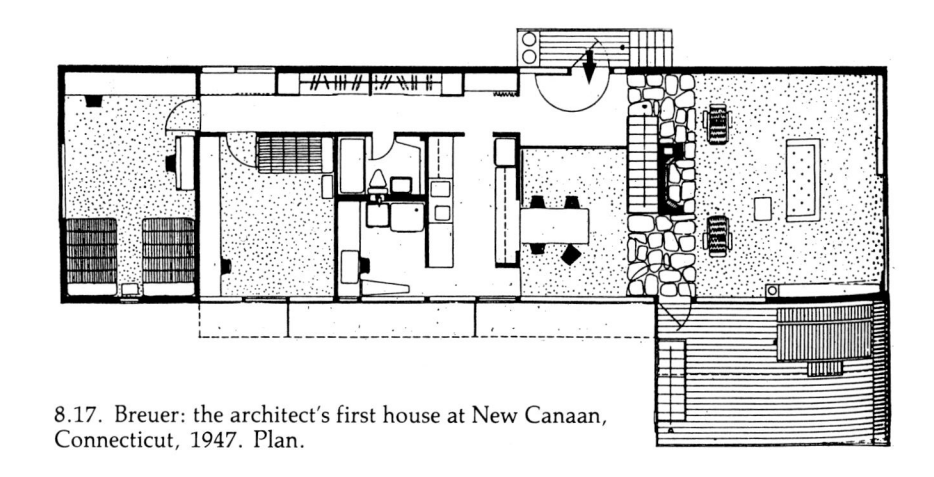

8.17. Breuer: the architect's first house at New Canaan, Connecticut, 1947. Plan.

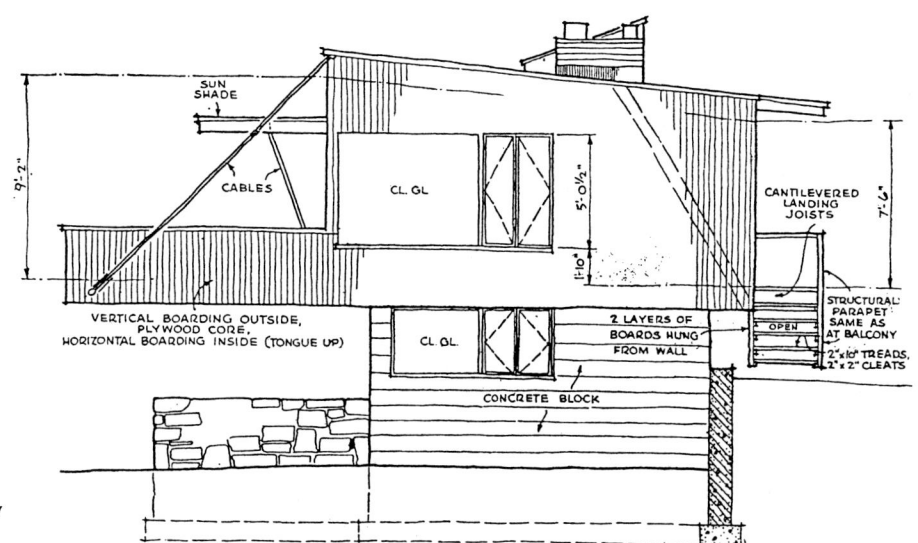

8.18. Breuer: the architect's first house at New Canaan, Connecticut, 1947. Right elevation.

decay of the environment, which was to become apparent within a single generation in Japan. The palace-style dwelling of relatively modest scale which Tange built for himself at Seijo—now swept away—offers a case in point. Although its formal vocabulary depends on the Imperial Villa at Katsura (see fig. 8.37), or even on the main palace at Kyoto studied by Professor Kishida, the framing system also recalls Tange's detailing of the Hiroshima Peace Center, including its *piloti*. Kikutake's Skyhouse (see fig. 7.14)—to be presented by Tange at Otterlo—is also raised above ground, but the structure is entirely of concrete. Here, technically, the supports are not *piloti* but slablike pylons aligned in parallel with each facade at its midpoint. From them, Skyhouse is suspended over a void at the edge of a narrow hillside almost in the center of Tokyo. Beneath the subtly modulated effect of its ceiling a single square room occupies the space created by the shell roof. The usable floor space is just ninety-eight square meters, but Skyhouse rapidly became one of the best-known of all Japanese modern buildings. This celebrity was partly owing to attention received from the Smithsons in England, though the couple disapproved of the "formalism" they saw in Kikutake's "decision-making" process.[10]

THIRD-MAN THEME

A third house (figs. 8.19–20) raised off the ground and marked—like Tange's—by the image of Katsura Villa came out of a quick, informal studio competition won by a young final-year student of Kiyosi Seike's at Tokyo Institute of Technology. The designer was Kazuo Shinohara, who in the same year, 1953, became an instructor in the university under Seike. The house was built at Kugayama the following year; it bore a remarkable coincidental resemblance to the nearly contemporary Kenzo Tange Residence (not illustrated). However, in Shinohara's house the essential framework was of steel, so that no details of carpentry were represented. There was, all the same, a low-pitched overhanging roof but with its rafter ends concealed. In contrast, the two-tiered roofing system of the far larger house by Tange plays a more conspicuous part in the overall aesthetic. His Seijo facade incorporated subsidiary bays in an a-b-a-a-b-a rhythm, while the four double bays of Shinohara's House at Kugayama were disposed in Miesian simplicity without recourse to further accent. Nor does the raised portion of the design by Shinohara include the kitchen and dining room as in Tange's house. Although the resulting separation of functions at Kugayama

8.19. Shinohara: House at Kugayama, Suginami Ward, Tokyo, 1954. Facade.

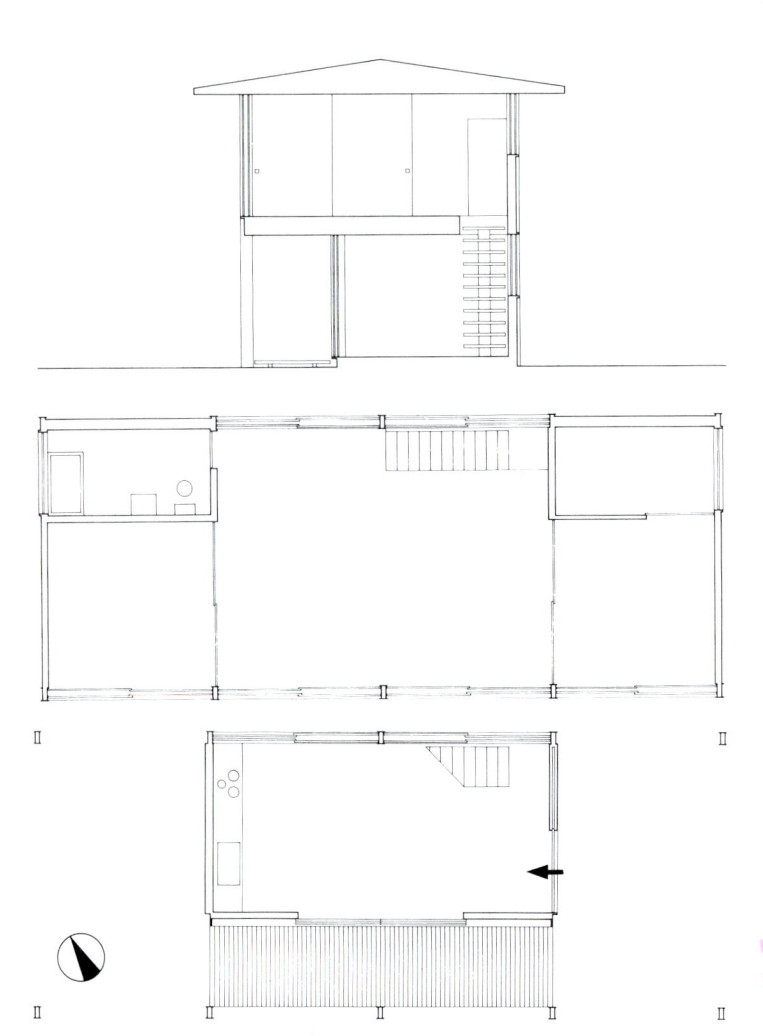

8.20. Shinohara: House at Kugayama, Suginami Ward, Tokyo, 1954. Plans and section.

was unusual, the arrangement imparted a vernacular flavor through the importance acquired by the kitchen as the informal point of entry—and, indeed, the only one.

A subsequent house designed by Shinohara—in 1958, for the poet Shuntaro Tanikawa—returned to the single-level mode initiated by Seike several years before. However, the otherwise modestly composed Tanikawa House (figs. 8.21–22) includes an oddly insistent element of mirror symmetry about its floor plan. The work would be described later as "an uninhibited attempt to create a characterless space" that could "sustain itself when an artist lived in it."[11]

Before the end of the sixties Shinohara had produced thirteen houses, all in an insistent adaptation of traditional styles and techniques, a manner in which elegance and rusticity became mixed in a curious and unnerving way. Even so, the conventions he employed were as yet rarely bent to such a degree that interiors, in particular, might not at times be confused with the work of Seike or, indeed, numerous other architects in the habit of exploiting vernacular forms and materials. Yet, fittings and furnishings apart, little about Shinohara's work was facile or commodious. It is not so much that these houses were doggedly uncompromising—a charge familiarly leveled against Shinohara by other architects; rather, each of his designs was built up in a nearly abstract manner out of the simplest of elements. Recipient of a mathematical training, the architect never hesitated to make use of structural solutions that distance his work from the domain of strict tradition. Gradually, an idiosyncratic sense of discipline evolved in these early works that sought to link tectonic requirements with decorative intentions, such as in the so-called Umbrella House of 1961 (figs. 8.23–24). Here—as in the traditional space reserved for the tea ceremony—the objective was to portray the structure of space itself. And to this day the Umbrella House of fifty-five square meters remains the smallest of Shinohara's works. Now the theme was, indeed, space, yet the spatial content of such a work is necessarily diagrammatic, immobile, and highly

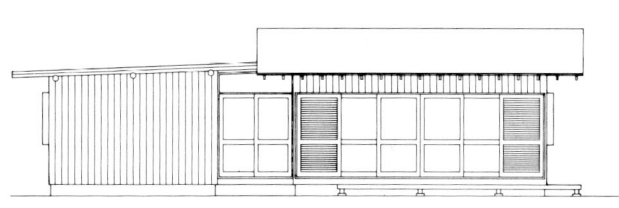

8.21. Shinohara: Tanikawa House, Suginami Ward, Tokyo, 1958. Elevation.

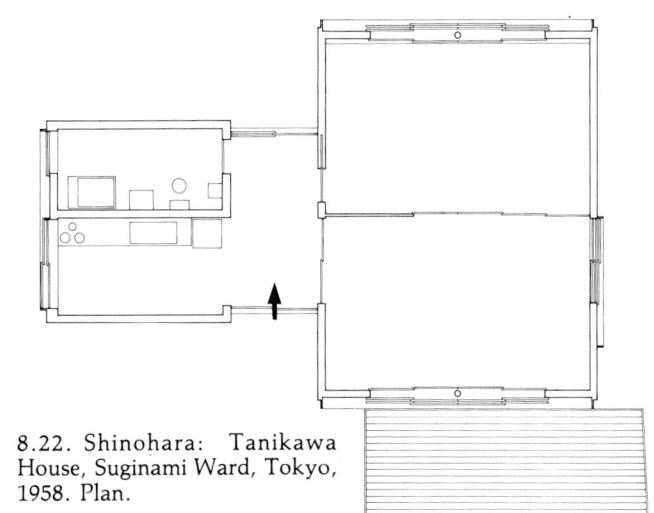

8.22. Shinohara: Tanikawa House, Suginami Ward, Tokyo, 1958. Plan.

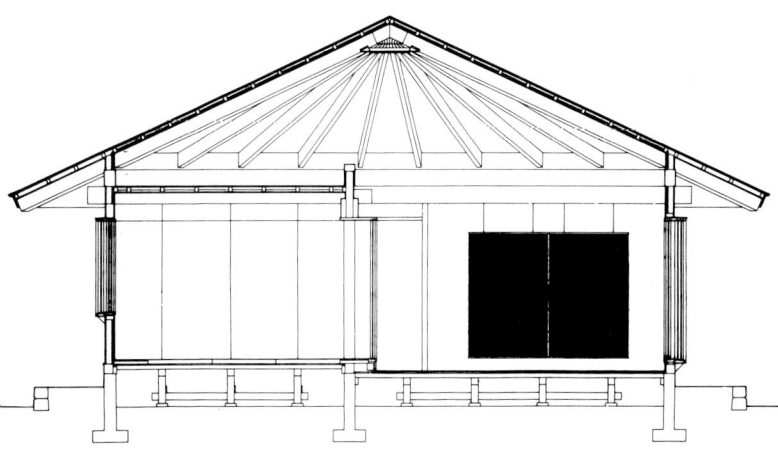

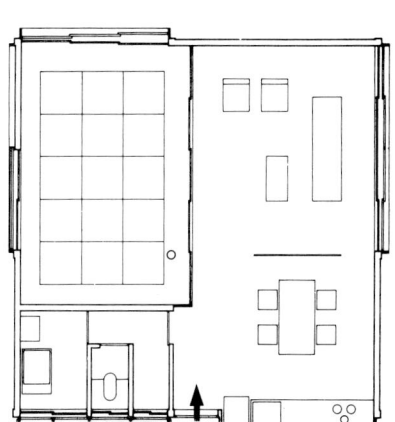

8.23. Shinohara: Umbrella House, Nerima Ward, Tokyo, 1961. Plan and mid-section.

8.24. Shinohara: Umbrella House, Nerima Ward, Tokyo, 1961. Interior.

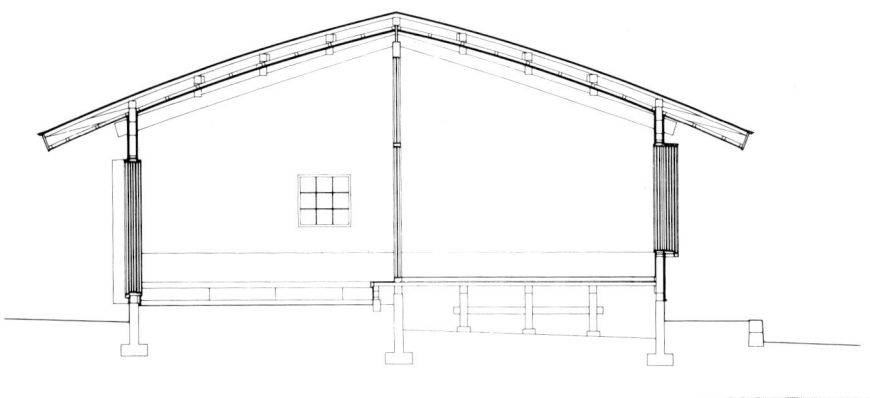

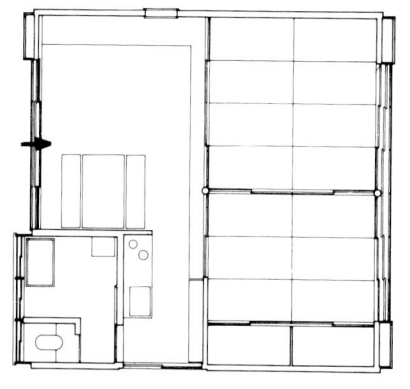

8.25. Shinohara: House with an Earthen Floor, Kita Saku, Nagano Prefecture, 1963. Section and plan.

8.26. Shinohara: House with an Earthen Floor, Kita Saku, Nagano Prefecture, 1963. Interior.

charged with a peculiar symbolism. A separate aim was to echo the spatial force of the *doma*, or earth-paved domestic working space of the traditional farmhouse, by means of a change in level between the *tatami* matting of the sleeping room and the wooden flooring of the living area in the Umbrella House. This was achieved in a more direct and obvious way, in 1963, in the House with an Earthen Floor (figs. 8.25–26)—designed as a lodgelike cottage and built with local materials in the Japanese Alps. Ordinary clay was mixed with lime and salt in the traditional manner and tamped down underfoot to form an entry plus kitchen-and-eating area.

Although there was nothing inherently out of place about provision of a *doma* in a house located in a mountain area, one is nevertheless brought face-to-face with a humble device long since abandoned by the Japanese. The symbolism invoked is of a slightly literary sort, as if conjuring up primitive origins beneath the veneer of consumer society. One is suddenly far from the optimism of the fifties as portrayed in glossy magazines, while the same symbolic rhetoric is explored further in a suburban house completed in 1966. In the House of Earth (figs. 8.27–28)—without a doubt the most un toward of all these years—the main living area is given over to a floor of earth pounded in the traditional manner described above. Down a red-carpeted stair is a belowground sleeping chamber, the sole other room in the house. In plan both upper and lower areas are slightly out of square: a fact stressed aboveground by a most unusual triangulated ceiling construction inclined at one end. Another oddity is intense use of red and black, as if portraying opposition. Shinohara's self-avowed theme of a primitive irrationalism is out of sympathy with the positive and forward-looking confidence of the Japan Style, but accords well with the decade which saw production of films like Shohei Imamura's *Insect Woman* of 1963 and Teshigahara's stylish, yet harrowing, version of Abe's *Woman of the Dunes* the following year. Just as the filmic dimension of these works (figs. 8.29–30) was impeccable, there is nothing in what Kazuo Shinohara refers to as a "black"—or "psychopathological"—space in the House of Earth to detract from its precision and geometry. It was known, however, that Shinohara objected to contemporary worship of technology in Japan. He thus intended his work of this period to be read as a rejection of the posturings of Metabolism.

NEW DIALOGUE WITH TRADITION 201

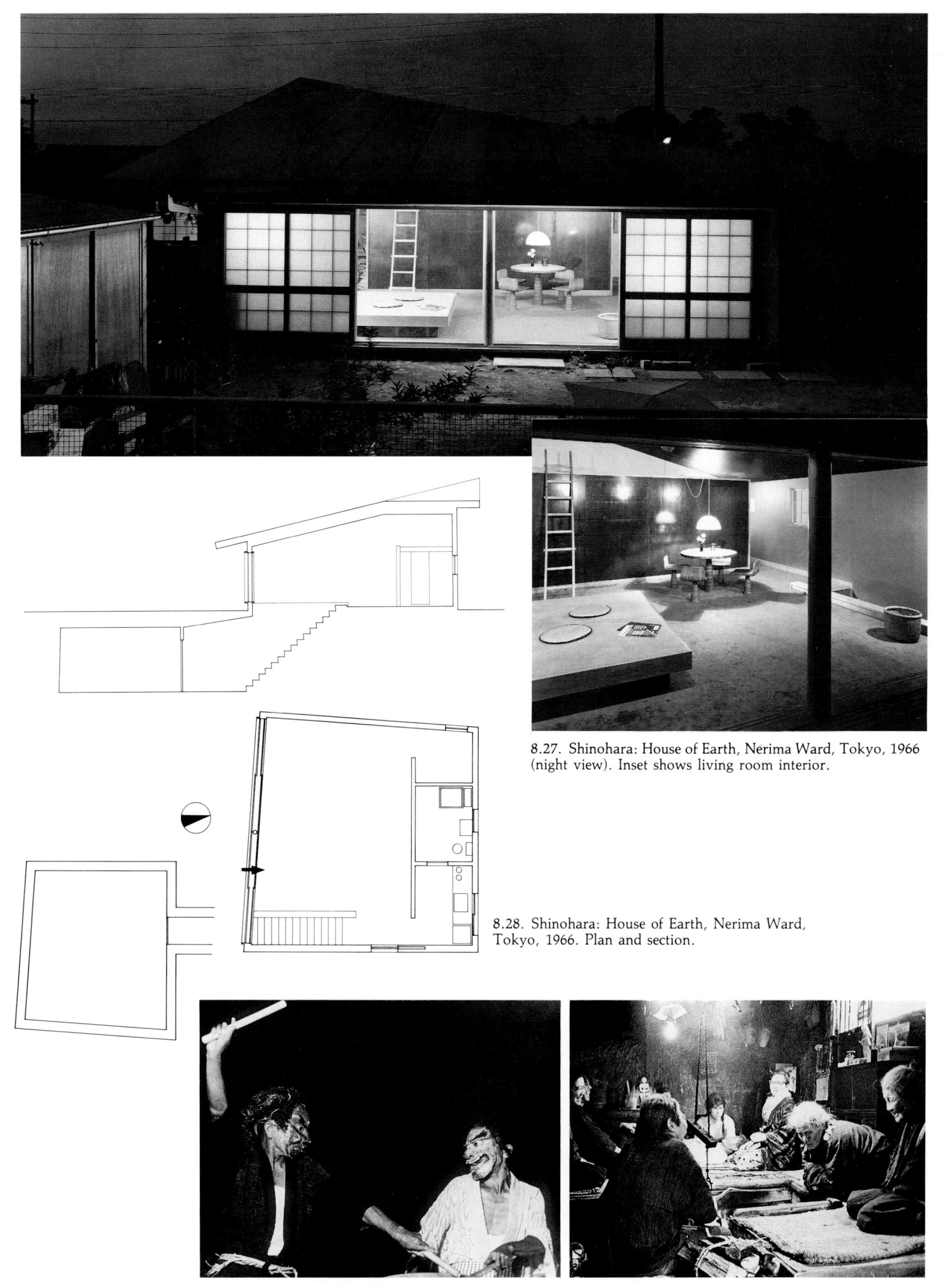

8.27. Shinohara: House of Earth, Nerima Ward, Tokyo, 1966 (night view). Inset shows living room interior.

8.28. Shinohara: House of Earth, Nerima Ward, Tokyo, 1966. Plan and section.

8.29. Teshigahara: still from *Woman of the Dunes*.

8.30. Imamura: still from *Insect Woman*.

ABSTRACTION WITH TRADITIONAL FORMS

The occult perfection of the House of Earth was matched in the same year by a counterpart named the House in White (figs. 8.31–33) in a different area of Tokyo. In this work Shinohara was at last able to give full expression to an "abstract" space by using only traditional forms. It was also in the design of his House in White that traditional syntax was first displaced by what the architect refers to as a newly "independent" spatial quality. Till then, the expressive means which Shinohara had taken over from traditional architecture were rooted in intuitive preferences, and this latitude of choice was justified by a conviction that residential architecture need not reflect those up-to-the-minute concerns posed by society at large. Gradually, however, like the cineasts mentioned above, who were his contemporaries, Shinohara realized just how social and environmental transformations penetrate the inner realm of the individual, the family, and the dwelling itself. It was at about the same time, then, that Shinohara started to consider ways in which the resources of modern architecture might be used to stake out the "space" of the individual. He would attempt to combat—at least by deployment of certain metaphors—the leveling effects exerted by industrialization and mass society.

The abstract purity of the House in White, as opposed to the more obviously metaphorical—even surreal—face of the House of Earth, may not be apparent at once. Nor is its perfection readily understood from photographs. The house comprises a square ten meters on each side surmounted by a pyramidal roof with extensive projecting eaves. It must be noted that—in Japan—this structure has not the remotest association with residential architecture. In fact, the external shape of Shinohara's House in White recalls far more readily one particular category of Buddha hall. A surviving example is the Jodoji Pure Land Hall (fig. 8.34) in Ono, Hyogo Prefecture, best known for its exceptional boldness of design. In his early work, Frank Lloyd Wright more than once drew on a similar roof form to anchor a large composition, such as the Martin House in Buffalo. This merely suggests how—in

8.31. Shinohara: House in White, Suginami Ward, Tokyo, 1966. Facade.

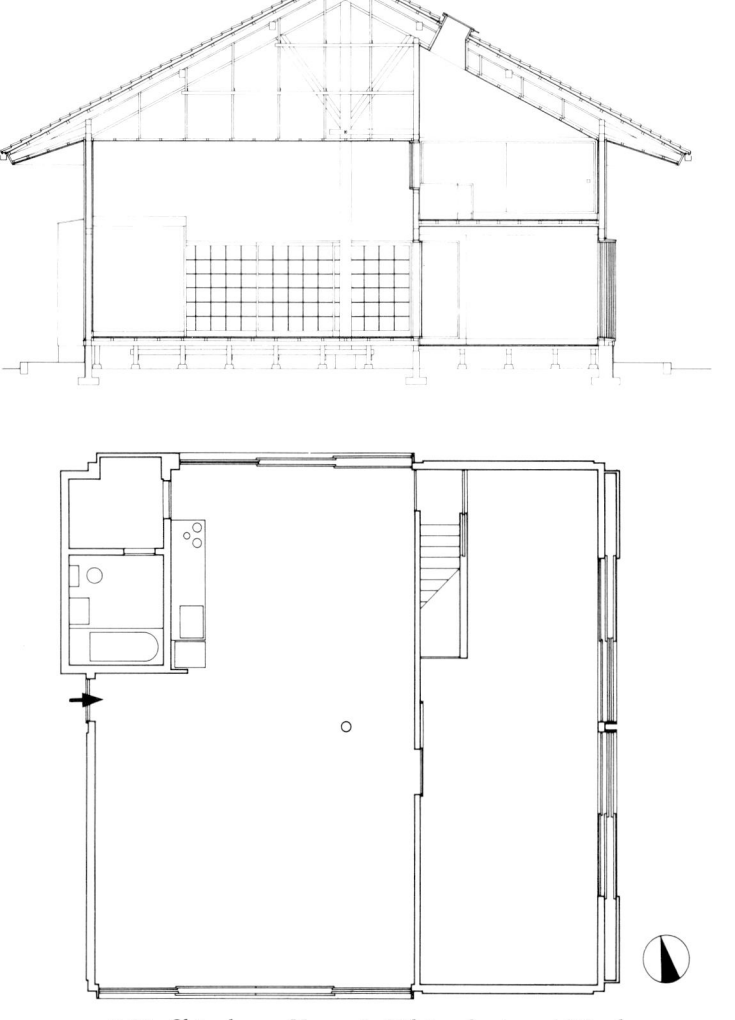

8.32. Shinohara: House in White, Suginami Ward, Tokyo, 1966. Plan and section.

8.33. Shinohara: House in White, Suginami Ward, Tokyo, 1966. Living room.

8.34. Pure Land Hall, Jodoji, Ono, Hyogo Prefecture, 1192.

8.35. Shinohara: North House in Hanayama, Kobe, 1965. View through bedroom from living-dining area.

8.36. Shinohara: North House in Hanayama, Kobe, 1965. Plan and section.

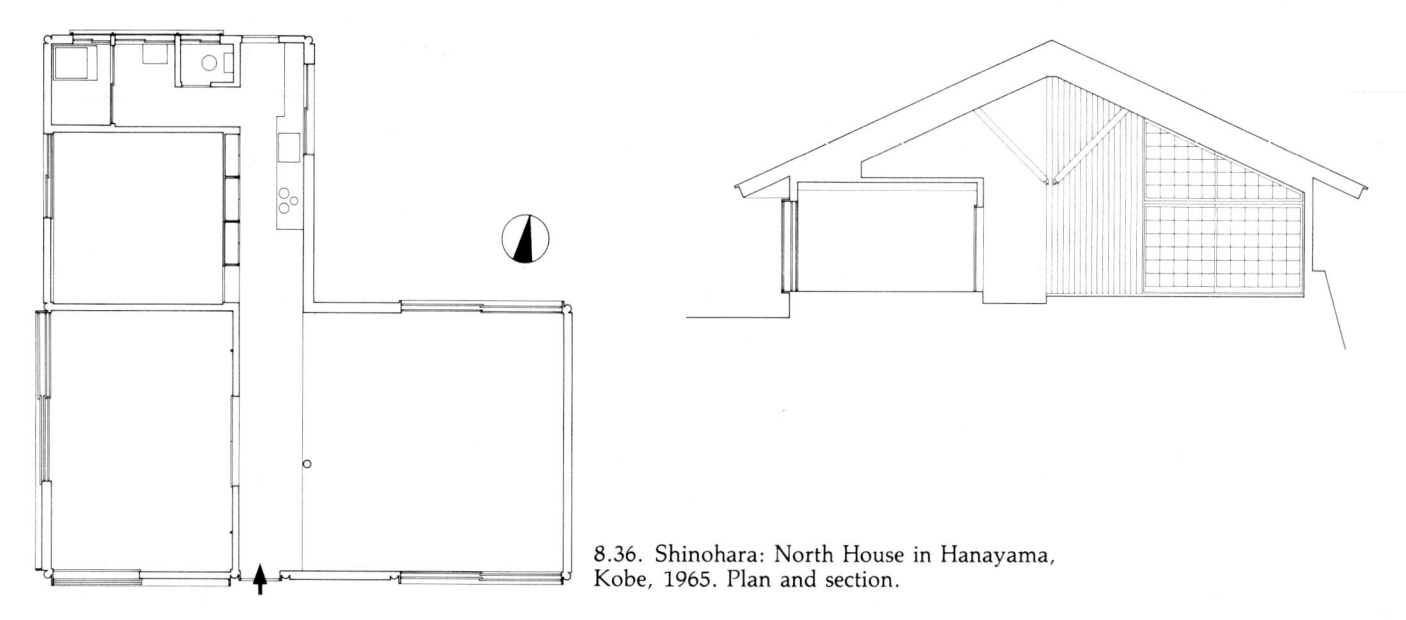

their extreme precision of forms combined with a wide-ranging selection of traditional motifs—it is possible to find a parallel between the Prairie work of Wright and what Shinohara calls his First Style, brought to a close in 1966 with the House in White.

In Shinohara's North House in Hanayama, Hyogo Prefecture, constructed the previous year, the plan was also square (figs. 8.35–36). This marginally earlier work was given a pyramidal roof but had one quadrant of its entire structure excised. This allowed for the central support system to be embedded in a corner wall, although an additional freestanding post of polished cedar—helping support the roof—is visible in the main living area. There the spatial volume rises dramatically to the full height of the roof, while nonsquared diagonal wooden struts abut against the re-entrant corner at the center of the plan. A similar arrangement of struts holds up the roof of the House in White but is concealed under the pyramid of the roof in an attic, since the ceiling of the main room intervenes at a height of 3.6 meters. The square plan is unequally bisected into two rectangular spaces, just as it was in the Umbrella House (see figs. 8.23–24). But in that work the exposed umbrellalike frame was self-supporting, as its overall dimensions were less.

In the House in White, however, the central post occupies the middle of the living room, while the sleeping area comprises two levels set into the smaller half of the plan. The upper bedroom, lit by a skylight, occupies part of the space under the roof, while the attic over the living room is merely a crawl space. The living room itself consists of a rectangular volume around the strategically placed cedar pillar; no aspect, excepting *shoji*, is related to the conventional vocabulary of Japanese interior spaces. Even these *shoji* are rendered untraditional by the extreme height of the space, exactly double that of the windows. The presence of the wooden post is enhanced by the strangeness of these proportions; or, put another way, the pillar creates a resonance within a volume that, without it, would appear unformed. Naturally, the pillar also affords a necessary diversion from the service core, but its principal function is to pin down the space, which appears to revolve about it—as if turning on axis.

According to its architect, the significance of the House in White lies in achievement for the first time of an abstract, "non-Japanese" space in spite of persisting traditional features, such as the wooden post. Shinohara's Second Style—the one elaborated in the 1970s—will build upon this event by allowing him to break altogether with Japanese compositional methods. Yet there is a significant element of paradox in that, viewed retrospectively, the Second Style may appear, in a radical sense, more "Japanese" than the First, even though bare of vernacular accouterments.

DOUBTS ABOUT NATION AND STYLE

Any attempt, moreover, to explore the terms of such a paradox is bound to bring to mind the *Kulturkritik* proposed by Kenzo Tange at about the time he was preparing his book on Katsura of 1960. Tange was interested in setting in motion a sweeping self-criticism of the entire Japanese tradition, for he claimed it was being overrated by foreign architects without due regard for inherent weaknesses. Tange put forward his argument in terms derived from Nietzsche's "Birth of Tragedy." Japanese tradition, veiled in Dionysian mystery and shadow—symbolized by the Ise Shrine—contrasts unfavorably with the Apollonian Parthenon on the Acropolis of Athens. Japanese architecture, according to Tange, reflected an essentially passive appreciation of natural phenomena viewed always as something "to be contemplated." Tange berates the "self-emptying" attitude of Zen Buddhist art that draws Japanese away from reality and causes them to lose themselves in an all-encompassing vastness of thought.[12] The "yielding disposition" peculiar to the Japanese was, he says, already part of the ancient animistic religion of prehistoric Japan. Tange argues that the same spirit persisted, yielding an emotional interpretation of reality. Thus, in spite of technical achievements imported from the Asian mainland and embodied in the construction of early Buddhist temples, such as Horyuji and Todaiji at Nara, native Japanese architecture made scant headway. In later times, notwithstanding certain practical adaptations, expression of taste overrode concern for construction and materials.

For Tange, the sense of openness in Japanese architecture and "the transient, inconstant and feeble expression accompanying it" failed significantly to "comprehend reality as something dynamic." Not even the development of an ingenious system of modular construction succeeded in fixing the conditions of "typification" necessary to express the "flux and diversity" of real life. Japanese buildings give no impres-

8.37. Katsura Villa, Kyoto, mid-seventeenth century. Bird's-eye view with gardens.

sion of unity because they are unable to combine "the functional and the expressive, the material and the artistic" as the Western tradition has consistently worked to do. Tange's criticism—offered from a designer's point of view—is valid enough, especially as regards the *sukiya* style. He remarks of Katsura Villa (fig. 8.37): "Lyricism is the prevailing impression, and the tension elevating all features to a completely satisfying whole, is absent." This is a perfectly true observation but not one that proved easy to translate into the reality of the Japan Style as a counter-praxis—unless what Tange intended was the undeniable effect of ton upon ton of concrete.

There is no question of any explicit debate between Kenzo Tange and Kazuo Shinohara, a beginning architect and university instructor twelve years his junior. Tange's line of argument as sketched here in the briefest possible terms seems to have been advanced mainly as a means of consolidating his own power among the restricted circle of architects who might eventually gain the privilege, or receive the nod, to build for the nation. His approach to the theme of a national style elicited a modicum of oblique criticism or—what is worse in the Japanese ideological arena—was met with silence. The whole issue now seems forgotten, even by Tange himself, who henceforth turned to the ever more vaguely defined goal of constructing a "communications space." Contrastingly, Shinohara's thematics dealt increasingly with that rarest of commodities: "space" in Japanese architecture. On the one hand, this notion of spatiality *qua* architectural content reveals the influence of Modern Movement architectural discussion on Shinohara's thought. On the other, the "Japanese" space that, henceforward, constitutes the aim of Shinohara's Second Style might be understood as a dialectic reply to the challenge Tange was trying to construct in his theses on the history of Japanese building and taste.

Finally, just as in Japan one is never far from the Meiji notion of a national style in architecture as handed down from the earliest generation of trained architects, so the equally important idea of modernism cannot be meaningfully separated from the presence of Le Corbusier. The construction of Tange's well-known Kagawa Prefectural Office (fig. 8.38) at Takamatsu, in his native island of Shikoku, simulates in concrete that boldness of the so-called Daibutsu style (fig. 8.39) derived from the original Todaiji at Nara, which for Tange embodied the reality of Japanese "nationhood" as no subsequent idiom had succeeded in doing. Kagawa is thus the culmination of Tange's early "trabeated" style and also, perhaps, of Maekawa's influence. For good measure, the design included a European "plaza" as centerpiece, which for Tange afforded a symbol of Western self-assertiveness. And the whole composition was played off against distant mountains, as Le Corbusier had recently done at Marseilles and would do again at Chandigarh.

LE CORBUSIER IN TOKYO

The Kagawa building by Tange was prepared from 1955 onward and completed in 1958. Almost contemporary is the National Museum of Western Art, designed by Le Corbusier —under construction at Ueno in Tokyo between 1957 and 1959 (figs. 8.40–41). Although it is scarcely one of Le Corbusier's masterpieces, the very fact of its authorship—a condition for the return of the collection it houses, seized during the war by the French government from a Japanese resident in Paris—was of great importance for Japan. The dramatic Nineteenth Century Hall (fig. 8.42), a centrally enclosed, double-story space lit from above and containing sculpture by Rodin and Bourdelle, is by far the museum's most impressive feature. Although large, the room is of a fairly intimate scale for a public building. The plan of the museum

8.38. Tange: Kagawa Prefectural Office, Takamatsu, 1955–58.

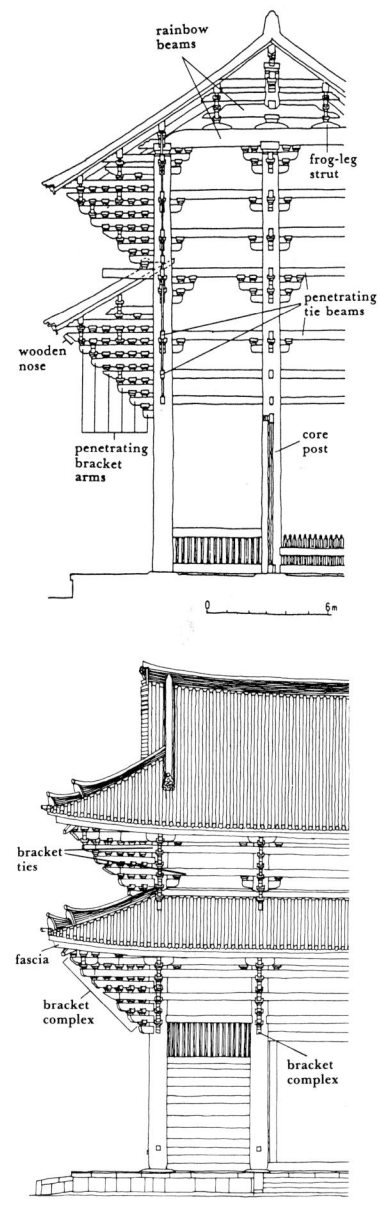

8.39. Great South Gate (Nandaimon) at Todaiji, Nara, 1199. Half-elevation and partial section.

is determined by the standard columnar grid Le Corbusier used as an expression of structural logic from the mid-twenties onward. It is of incidental interest that his method was similar in idea to the time-honored *kiwari* system of structural proportions, which was traditionally employed in *shoin*-style work before the advent of *sukiya* caused builders to rely on more arbitrary aesthetic-based notions.

In an earlier design of Le Corbusier's—for the Museum at Ahmedabad in India—the central space was simply left open to the sky. In Tokyo this was clearly out of the question: the climate dictated an enclosed structure, and a large skylight in the form of a triangular prism was intended from the beginning. Therefore, I know of no specific precedent for the Nineteenth Century Hall at Ueno. In an early drawing for the project the large skylight is expressed on the interior as a series of smaller lights.[13] Later on (fig. 8.43) it was decided to expose the crossing of the central beams supporting the roof, leaving these visible within the space occupied by the skylight itself. A similar arrangement occurs in the roof of the Council Chamber in the Assembly Hall at Chandigarh, but there the central pillar—which would have interrupted the seating—was suppressed altogether. At Tokyo the bare walls of Le Corbusier's hall were to have been relieved by a photographic mural depicting the glories of the nineteenth century. The idea must have been based on the precedent of a mural installed in the Swiss Students' Hostel in Paris in 1931 but destroyed by the Germans in 1943. The Tokyo mural was never executed, and the intended effect[14] would have been very different from the appearance of the hall today. Even in its "unfinished" state, or possibly because of it, the Nineteenth Century Hall (its name now forgotten) ranks with the significant interiors of Le Corbusier's late style. Moreover, no real description for this type of space is possible except to say that it is distinctively Corbusian.

8.40. Le Corbusier: National Museum of Western Art, Ueno, Tokyo, 1957–59. Facade.

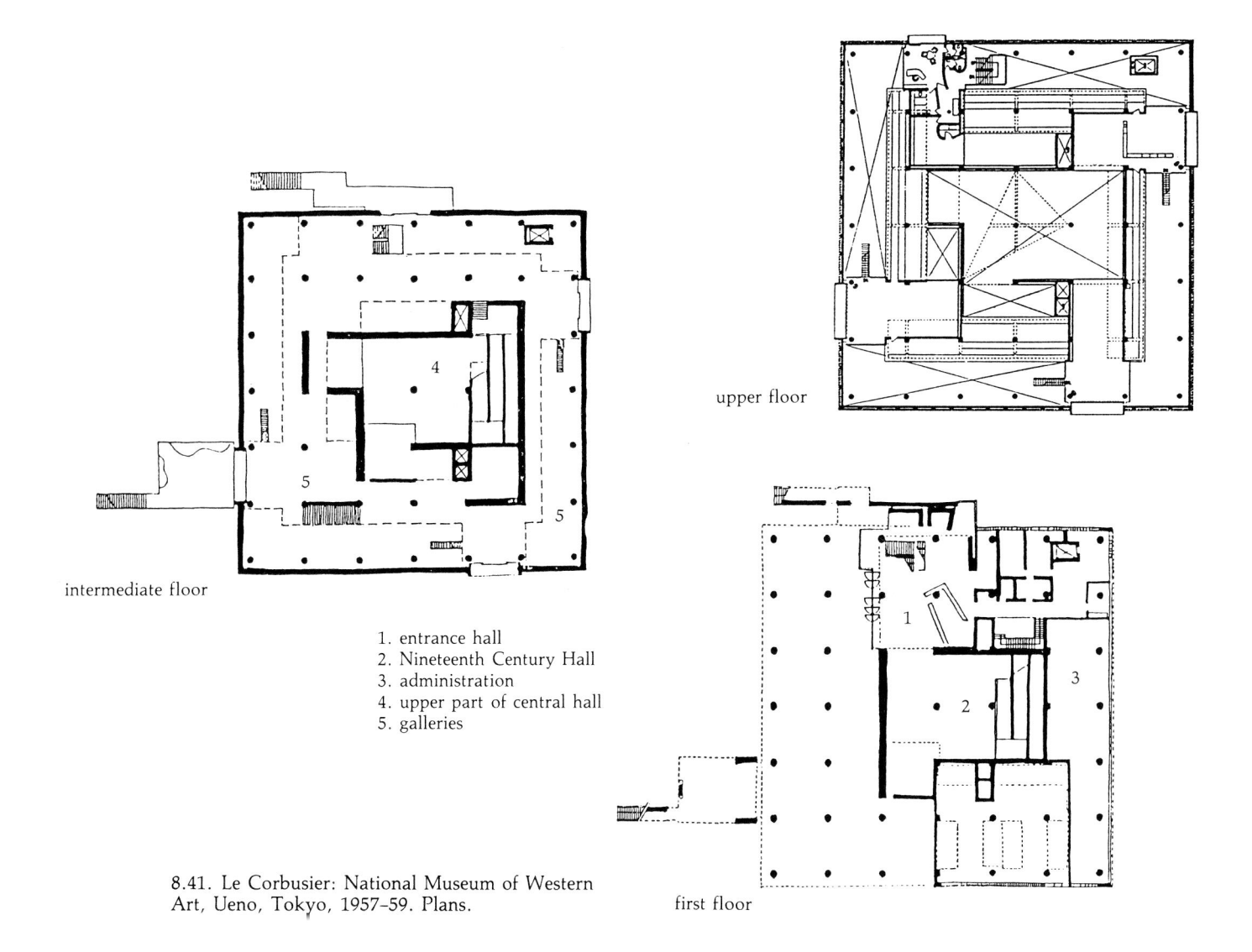

1. entrance hall
2. Nineteenth Century Hall
3. administration
4. upper part of central hall
5. galleries

8.41. Le Corbusier: National Museum of Western Art, Ueno, Tokyo, 1957–59. Plans.

NEW DIALOGUE WITH TRADITION 209

8.42. Le Corbusier: National Museum of Western Art, Ueno, Tokyo, 1957–59. Nineteenth Century Hall interior.

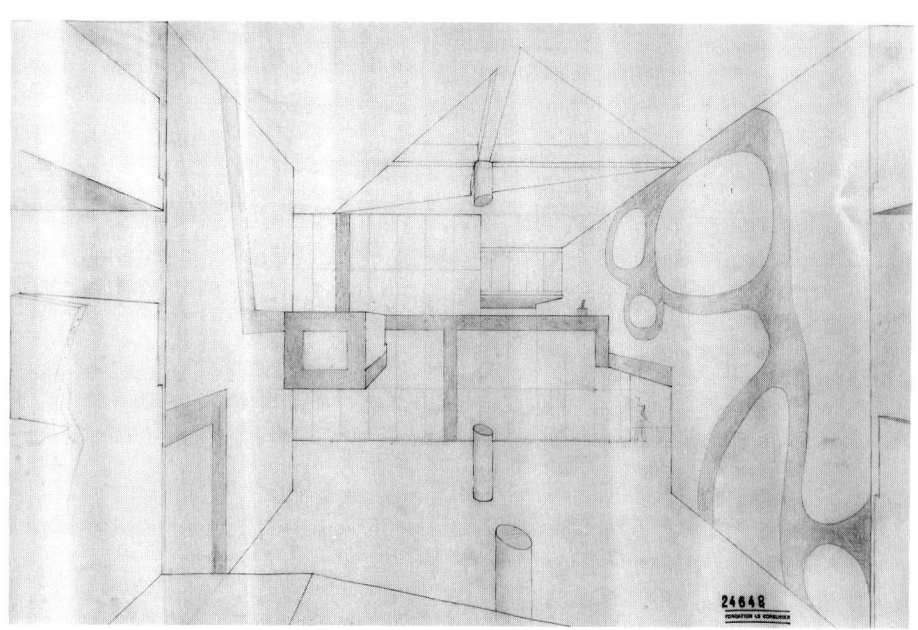

8.43. Le Corbusier: National Museum of Western Art, Ueno, Tokyo, 1957–59. Sketch for Nineteenth Century Hall.

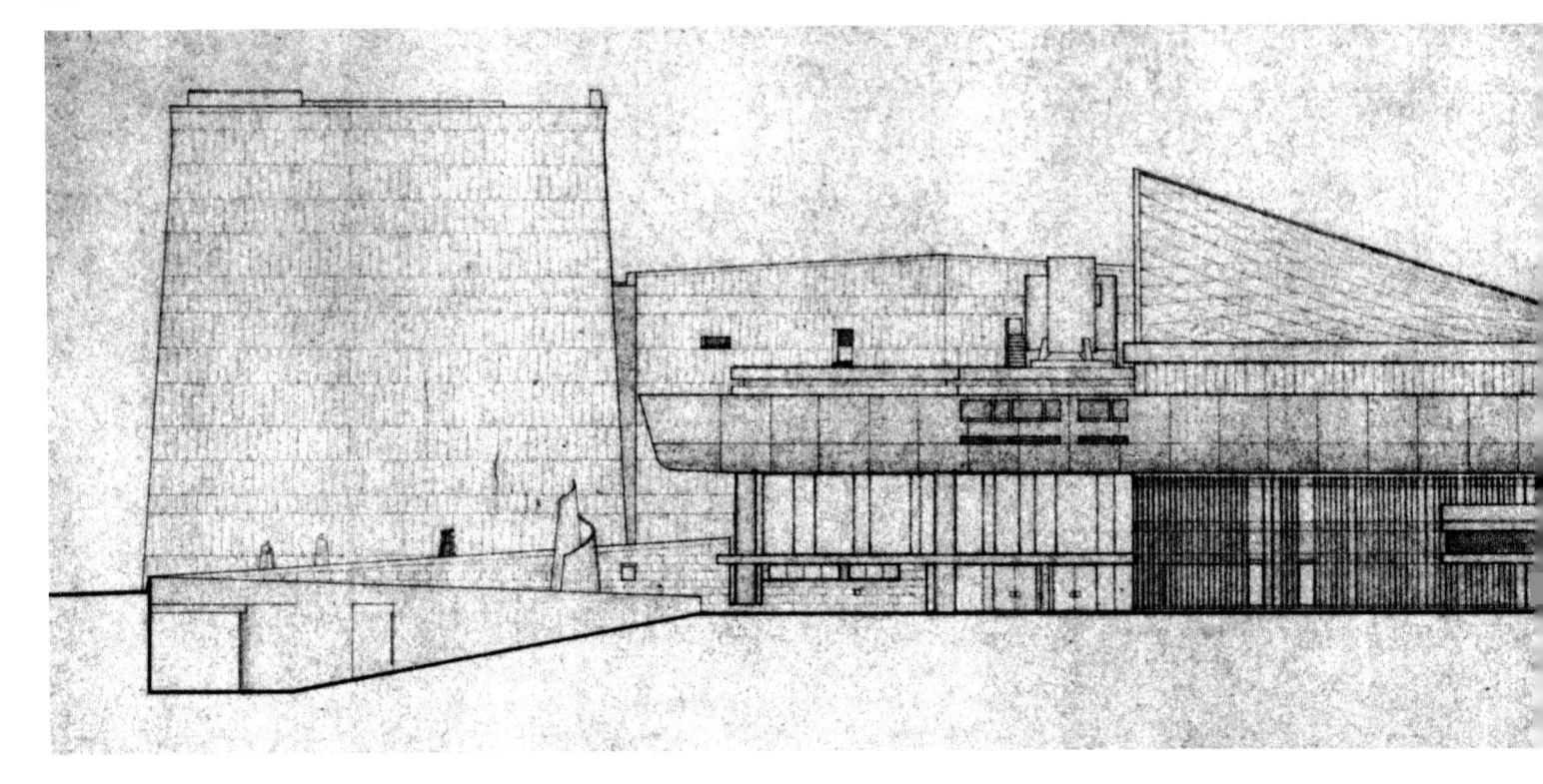

At the level of public architecture, the late style of Le Corbusier was to be diffused throughout Japan. Immediately opposite the National Museum of Western Art at Ueno, for example, may be seen Maekawa's Tokyo Metropolitan Festival Hall of 1961 (fig. 8.44), one of the best-known and indeed most distinguished among this progeny. Yet such buildings invariably attempted to present—in one and the same design—a vernacular statement that had nothing to do with Le Corbusier's late manner. For the subtle quality of the spaces Le Corbusier deemed appropriate for monks at La Tourette, art students at Harvard, or Indian capitalists and legislators was curiously irrelevant, I believe, to a country on the move, such as Japan in the 1950s had become. Thus, the ambiguity of the Janiform stance Tange had earlier taken up without regard to nation and style—an inherited dilemma—persisted in the Japan Style. Tange and Maekawa were satisfied to be confirmed in their role as elder statesmen in the eye of the public, while Metabolism—newly born—gradually faded away at the tip of a long wave of publicity in the course of the following decade.

In the end it was Le Corbusier, even in his role as a "neocolonialist" at Ahmedabad and Chandigarh, who prevailed. There, as elsewhere, his late style amounted to a broadside attack on, as well as a continuation of, mainstream modern principles (without descent into *specific* vernacularisms)—necessitating a slow and piecemeal operation of reassembly and assimilation. In Japan both the reflection and archaeological sense of disinterest this required were luxuries, neither being an attribute of the Japan Style. By way of a counter-example, the Museum of Modern Art at Kamakura (see fig. 7.5) might conceivably be understood as fulfilling these conditions. Though small, the building realized by Junzo Sakakura—architect of the Japanese pavilion at the Paris Exposition of 1936 (see figs. 6.88–89)—was one of the earliest public buildings constructed in Japan after World War II. It dates from 1951, the same year as Seike's experimental Mori House and only two years after Raymond's Reader's Digest Building. Charming and well scaled as the museum at Kamakura still appears to the visitor today, it is really a continuation of Le Corbusier's style of the late thirties.

Similarly, Le Corbusier's National Museum of Western Art, built in 1959, is related to a much earlier concept, and both the Ueno and Kamakura museums are separate versions of this. Therefore, it is only the central sculpture hall at Ueno which, despite its roots in prewar studio-*cum*-residence design, represents an adventure into Le Corbusier's postwar idiom.

"JAPANESE SPACE"

If there was a lesson to be learnt from the example of the central hall (see fig. 8.42) at Ueno, unique for its time in Japan, I find it applied in the series of residences by Shinohara already described, culminating in the House in White of 1966. After Wright, and with the exception of Raymond, Le Corbusier was only the second main figure in modern Western architecture to design a work subsequently built in Japan. The Ueno museum was locally supervised by Kunio Maekawa and Junzo Sakakura, together with Takamasa Yoshizaka. Yoshizaka translated *Le Modulor*, having spent three years in Le Corbusier's Paris office from 1950, and was, therefore, the youngest of the French architect's Japanese disciples. Kazuo Shinohara, on the other hand, had no direct connection with Le Corbusier of any kind, and he shared none of the obvious tropes of Corbusian style, delightfully abundant in the later work of Yoshizaka up until his death a few years ago. Never in Shinohara's First Style is there a conscious striving after effect, except possibly in terms of furnishings, which from time to time were selected from the "craft," or design, side of the Japan Style. Rather, it is the exotic shell roof of wood in the House of Earth (see fig. 8.27) and the positioning of the single column in the House of White (see fig. 8.33)—having no precedent in Japanese architecture—that seem to call for an explanation, if that is the right word. It does not diminish the importance of Shinohara's own compositions, which in Japanese architecture represented veritable discoveries, that these specific instances appear to match up with the quality of spatial intentions in Le Corbusier's hall as built.

With the advent of Shinohara's Second Style, in 1970 a noticeable change of orientation took place. The vocabulary of Japanese forms and materials which had marked his earlier work now disappeared. His houses, the unique building type

8.44. Maekawa: Tokyo Metropolitan Festival Hall, Ueno, Tokyo, 1961. Elevation drawing of the east facade.

subscribed by Shinohara in exact contradistinction to Tange, no longer "look" Japanese. In no case were polished wooden beams and *shoji, fusuma, sudare,* or other traditional Japanese house fittings applied, except for the one now *tatami*-floored room still *de rigueur* in nearly all Japanese residences even today. Nevertheless, the main space of the House in White, with its pillar and its *shoji* isolated—so to say, abstracted from the conventional representation of structure imposed upon the traditional Japanese interior—relates to the architecture of the tea ceremony room. In its compelling and disorienting bareness, such a space does not necessarily become less "Japanese" or more "Western." These aspects, and their meaning for Shinohara himself, were analyzed in a book he published in 1964, two years earlier than the House in White, under the disarming title *Residential Architecture*. Once again, in contradistinction to Tange's arguments, Shinohara's text attempted to set forth the main distinguishing features of the Japanese approach to planning and to space itself, in a manner free of socio-ideological criticism. The first third of Shinohara's text is devoted to the topic of "Japanese space" and is noticeable for its disregard of the structural and decorative vocabulary of the various historical styles. Issues dealt with include spatial division and connection, spatial logic in Japanese architecture, the notion of viewpoint and time, and the interpretation of vernacular dwelling houses, or *minka*.[15]

The second chapter of *Residential Architecture* by Shinohara consists of a discussion of conditions and restrictions affecting contemporary architectural production. It deals with the notion of the house as art, the idea of nonfunctional or "wasted" spatial elements, the concept of *yoshiki* (style) as personal creation, technical and prefabrication procedures, and, lastly, design as an experimental activity. The third chapter is given over to examples, namely, the seven houses constructed by Shinohara up until 1963. Only at the end of his short treatise does the author mention the possible existence of a "fourth space." That dimension might be susceptible of social interpretation, though far from such ideas as Tange or his Metabolist protégés tended to favor.

The most vital notions, however, to be culled from this brief historic text—remarkable as coming from a working architect—were those related to spatial composition itself. Among them are the distinction between spatial division and connection as well as observations on viewpoint and time, already referred to. Finally, a conclusive argument for the "nonexistence of space" in Japanese architecture led for the first time to a reliable working distinction between the respective manners in which Western and Japanese architectural traditions were established and subsequently grew. According to Shinohara, European architectural composition links successive spaces. By contrast, Japanese architecture exhibits a process of "spatial division" that involves subdividing an embracing void into smaller, relatively unstable units. This resulted in what Shinohara terms a "static" quality about Japanese space, emphasized by the lack of any indication as to possible paths of human movement, especially in the earlier epochs of Japanese building. Similarly, in later ages, gardens—like the one in which Katsura Villa is set (see fig. 8.37)—were composed of a series of viewpoints, with little attempt to coordinate or integrate these by means of an overall view of the surroundings. A similar typology of movement emerges from the act of viewing a piece of sculpture or a work of architecture. Angles of view dictated by the work itself produce a discontinuous series of separate viewing points, enforcing a notion of frontality.[16]

The fact that these discrete viewpoints were not dictated by the viewer but may be thought of instead as attached to the statue or building in question suggests that "space as we conceive of it today was unknown in Japan." The "space" encompassed by the elegant and beautiful structures of former ages was akin to "cosmic emptiness."[17] Yet, for Shinohara, nonexistence of space is primarily nonideological, though he notes that Western, post-Renaissance space must be built up from the standpoint of the "ego."[18] The same post-Renaissance space also found "room for science"—a development which, in turn, permitted the "step-by-step" evolution of architecture. In Japan, where science was little in evidence during the feudal period, such an architecture never made its appearance. However, at just that moment when contact with the West was still possible before the Tokugawa era shut out

8.45. *Chashitsu*, Ryokakutei, Ninna-ji, Kyoto, ca. 1688.

Western culture altogether: "The *chashitsu* [fig. 8.45] represented the discovery of interior space.... The concept of an 'interior' as an object of design was first conceived here." Hence, the privileged role of the tea ceremony in developing spatial tension which—in the case of previous Japanese architecture—was traditionally concentrated in the phenomena of frontality and discontinuity of viewpoint.[19]

Shinohara's definitions and propositions discussed above amount to a breviary of Japanese space, which according to him possesses a pronounced "topological" quality.[20] There is, however, an important motif in the architecture of Le Corbusier relating to this matter, namely, the famous notion of "the architectural promenade" that establishes itself from the period of the Parisian villas onward. Moreover, the majority of Le Corbusier's works of that period—and often later ones, too—are simple cubes or rectangular solids. By virtue of this, they are necessarily organized using a technique of spatial division, even when, as in Japanese stroll gardens, a path of movement through the work is clearly indicated. Such division, unlike the technique of arrangement in traditional Japanese buildings, affected not only the horizontal but also, from the beginning, the vertical plane of Le Corbusier's houses. From an even earlier moment, interlocking vertical and horizontal spaces were a salient feature of Frank Lloyd Wright's work, although in traditional Japanese buildings such sequences are restricted to certain kinds of vernacular dwellings and a particular type of townhouse invented by merchants in western Japan during the feudal age. Then, in Le Corbusier's post–World War II style, space becomes truly "topological," with bendings and stretchings occurring as a matter of course. In spatial terms, this represents the crux of the "postmodern" dilemma, especially to the extent that such spaces—in a way recalling Shinohara's House of Earth— may be interpreted as psychopathological.

For the ordinary observer as well as numerous architects

the nature of the Modern Movement's spatial revolution is best expressed through so-called Miesian simplicity. However, "space" in the modern Western sense evolved—if not pictorially, viz the case of Wright and Japanese prints—then in analogy with an imaginative blend of the great halls of the Heian period in Japan (known only through reconstructions) with their more intimate *shoin* counterparts—the latter having come in during the medieval age and reached a high point of development in the Muromachi and Momoyama periods. Both the Heian and *shoin* modes (fig. 8.46) depended on spatial division, but neither as yet possessed the high degree of tension peculiar to the miniscule *chashitsu*, or ceremonial space of rustic tea. The latter was a catalyst, so to speak, and heralded the evolution of the more widely applied—and, spatially, far more diversified—*sukiya* manner. If Western modernism has been characterized from its inception by a strong Japanese flavor—as indeed seems the case—it remained until recent times relatively free of the stylish and perverse complexities which Japanese artistic development achieved during its long seclusion until the 1850s.

8.46. Audience hall at Nishi Honganji, Kyoto, 1618, in the *shoin* style.

8.47. Le Corbusier: four views of La Tourette monastery, near Lyons, 1957–60 (north wall: top left and bottom right), plus axonometric.

FRONTALITY OR "REVOLUTION"

Notoriously, and for all the clarity of his Mediterranean vision, Le Corbusier's late style exploded in exactly this direction, both in the great apartment building at Marseilles and the pilgrimage chapel at Ronchamp. The new manner was an embodiment of a certain postmodernism before the letter, having matured in the enforced inactivity of the war. It baffled and astonished numerous established architects, especially those from English-speaking countries visiting France for the first time since the peace. One of the finest tuned and most eloquent testimonies was provoked, however, by another building: Le Corbusier's convent for the Dominican monks at Sainte-Marie-de-la-Tourette (fig. 8.47). Colin Rowe's powerful and emotive critique of this work was

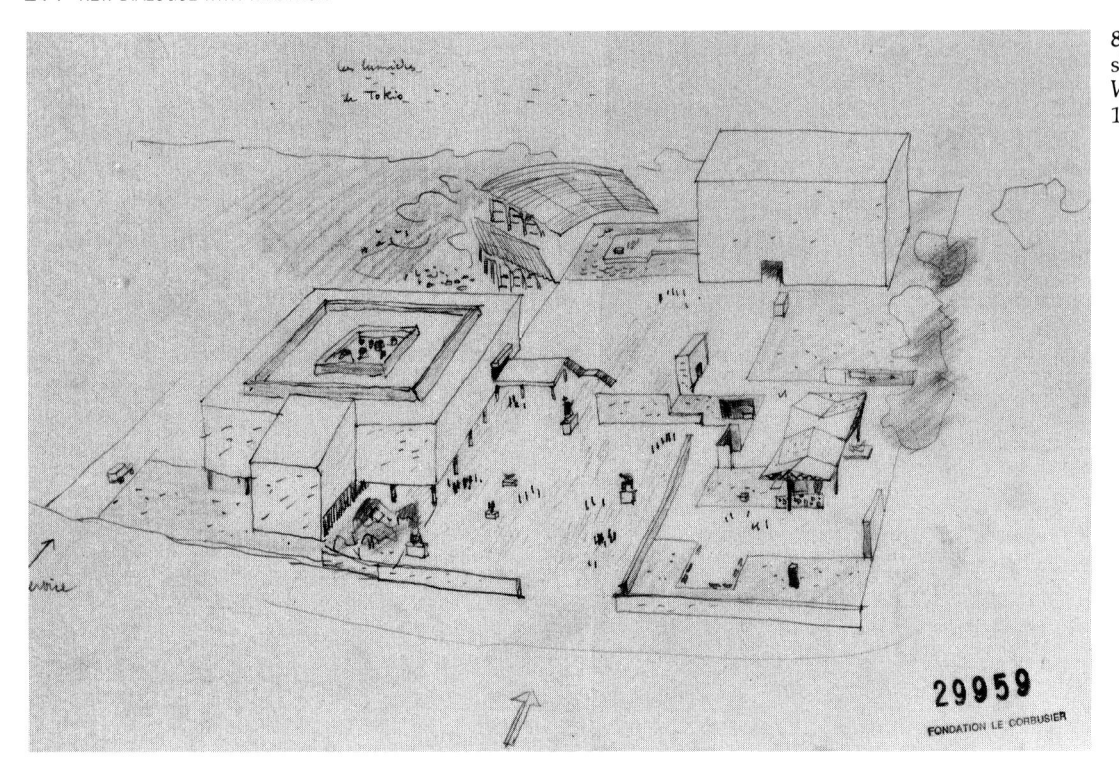

8.48. Le Corbusier: preliminary sketch for National Museum of Western Art, Ueno, Tokyo (March 1956), showing Boîte à Miracles.

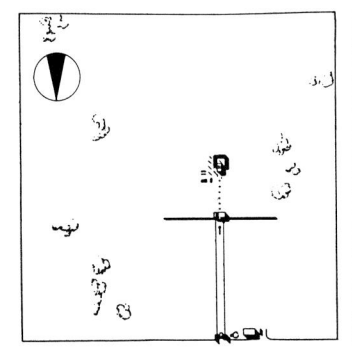

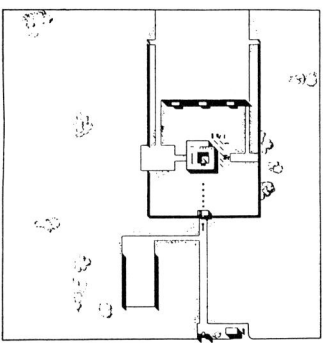

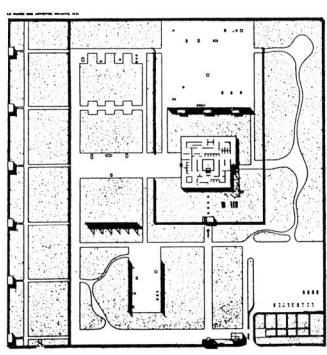

8.49. Le Corbusier: Musée du XXe Siècle, or Musée d'Art Contemporain, 1930 onward. Unrealized project.

published in *The Architectural Review* in 1961[21] and is of particular interest, as the monastery near Lyons was contemporary with the Tokyo Museum of Western Art.

Rowe boldly suggests that the layout of the precinct at La Tourette included "some very private commentary upon Acropolitan material," and thus referred to Le Corbusier's decisive early sojourn upon the Acropolis of Athens. The Ueno scheme, too, if completed as designed, would have borrowed from the ancient iconic Athenian arrangement—volumes in tension with each other and with the site. Le Corbusier's unbuilt structures included an amphitheater, a further Acropolitan feature, whose stage was dramatized by being set amid a reflecting pool. There was also to have been a proscenium, so that actors might equally well declaim while facing the opposite direction, toward an all-weather seating enclosure. Le Corbusier named the arrangement his *Boîte à Miracles* (fig. 8.48), and Rowe cites it as a possible source for the design of the chapel at La Tourette. In the end no theater was built at Ueno in connection with the museum; nor was the Temporary Exhibitions Pavilion that should have faced the museum entrance. This pavilion, however, was appropriated by Kikutake as a residential prototype that later became Skyhouse (see fig. 7.14). But instead of using the tapered *piloti* of the original design, Kikutake proceeded to apply the straight, slablike version with broad-sided face and narrow silhouette which Le Corbusier made use of at La Tourette. When later on the Ueno pavilion was redesigned in steel for erection at Zurich shortly before Le Corbusier's death, these same slab-type *piloti* were utilized

The evolution of the main building at Ueno is also of interest. Its immediate prototype was the so-called Musée d'Art Contemporain project (to house work by living artists) of 1930.[22] Later referred to as a "square spiral," this self-encircling structure was to have been begun by constructing a single exhibition room reached by a tunnel. As funds permitted, further rooms would be added, resulting in a state of perpetual construction masked by a wall extending on either side of the belowground entrance. This Musée du XXe Siècle—or "Musée à Croissance Illimitée"[23] (fig. 8.49), as it was baptized in 1939—was nonetheless designed from the beginning with walls conceived as movable partitions, so that the additive process by which the space evolved cannot be directly sensed inside the structure. Therefore, the principle of spatial division cited by Shinohara and others in connection with the history of Japanese building (and evident in Le Corbusier's own early work) is not excluded. As for the issue of "frontality" raised by Shinohara in his remarks on traditional Japanese architecture, a frontal view is imposed *a priori* by the fact that the museum was to have been hidden behind a wall of masonry—a residue of which does, in fact, remain in Le Corbusier's sketch for the whole project at Ueno.

The tensions generated by frontality—which, as Shinohara remarks, ease as the viewer changes his angle of view—remain an important element of Le Corbusier's late style. It is a weakness of Tokyo's Museum of Western Art, as built, that so little of the quality of spatial experience induced by the viewer's movement—for instance, on the Acropolis—remains. It is one of the merits of the La Tourette essay by Rowe that

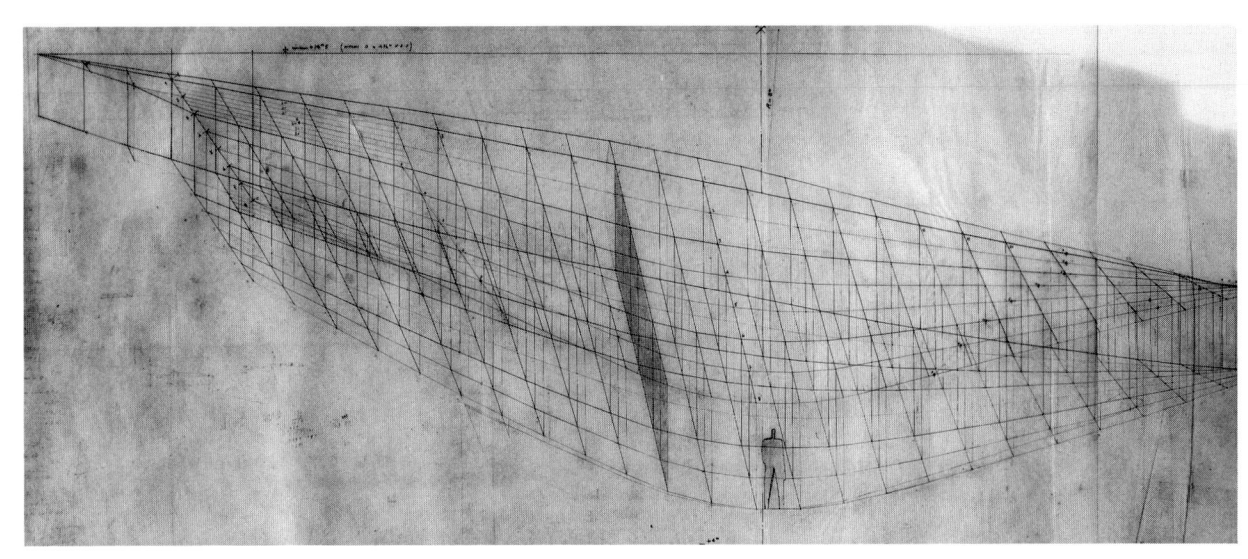

8.50. Le Corbusier: Notre-Dame-du-Haut, Ronchamp, 1950–55. Diagram showing double-shell roof construction.

8.51. Maekawa: Tokyo Metropolitan Festival Hall, Ueno, Tokyo, 1961. Overhead view (see also figure 8.44).

the author attempts an analysis of the monastery in just such terms. But, whereas Japanese buildings on the whole demand a frontal inspection, Rowe points out that at La Tourette "the anticipated frontal views never do, in fact, materialize."[24] It is only the north wall—entirely blank—that permits a frontal viewing, while all the other walls must be seen either in rapid foreshortening or from more or less oblique viewpoints. Rowe ascribes this play with, and eventual denial of, frontality to voluntary inconsistencies imposed with respect to a reading of depth by Le Corbusier. We now know that from his early maturity the architect was afflicted with monocular vision.[25] Might it be the very skills needed to compensate for this handicap that account for the fantastic game of tensions Le Corbusier was able to produce?

According to Rowe, the net result of all this complexity is that the monastery tends to "revolve, to pivot around an imaginary central spike" while resorting as well to "a supremely static behavior."[26] To a more modest yet still marked degree, the same could be said of the Nineteenth Century Hall at Ueno (see fig. 8.42). There the pinwheel construction of its central support, set beneath the aperture of the skylight, resembles nothing so much as the outline of a windmill sail poised to rotate. I have already mentioned the rotational sensation inside Shinohara's living room, with its central pillar (see fig. 8.33), in the House in White. Nevertheless, by contrast with Shinohara's remark that the angle of vision from which a work of Japanese architecture is viewed should be thought of as "attached" to the building itself, Rowe observes that a number of features of Le Corbusier's work "are obedient to the exigencies of the eye rather than those of the work, to the needs of the conceiving subject rather than the perceived object."[27] In either case, a norm of heightened spatial tension is at stake: whether exhibited in Le Corbusier's late style—for instance, at Ueno—or as it may be found in the Japanese *chashitsu*, and was revived in a work such as the House in White. Though these two approaches are the fruits of opposed traditions, the results appear comparable, though not identical, in effect.

SHELL GAME AND RECOURSE TO WIT

It is what Rowe refers to as "dichotomy"[28] that counts here, not necessarily the mathematical sign of it. But, in Japan, Le Corbusier's postwar style received, by and large, a tectonic interpretation—one unconcerned with, if not quite opposed to, appreciation of spatial values in his work. This attitude resulted in, or perhaps merely coincided with, a vogue for shell construction, where the "tension" is perceived as part of the structure rather more than of the resulting space. Notre-Dame-du-Haut at Ronchamp (fig. 8.50) was the first pure product of the Corbusian late manner in 1955, and the upper face of its great sweeping double roof seems a flat, tilted hyperbolic-paraboloid spanning diagonally its roughly square area. By 1957 Tange had already applied this solution, although without the "Mediterranean" (if that is what Ronchamp is) disguise, in his now rarely published Meeting Hall at Shizuoka. Maekawa followed suit—but the shell is merely covering for a truss structure—in the roof of the small upstairs hall of his Festival Hall at Ueno (fig. 8.51) in 1961.

8.52. Tange: Totsuka Country Clubhouse, Totsuka, Kanagawa Prefecture, 1960–61.

Likewise, Shinohara's House of Earth makes use of a simple folded "shell" built of wood without curvature (see fig. 8.27). It, too, spans on a diagonal—and is characteristically tilted by having one end raised—in order to enhance rigidity in a frame structure which, though of modest proportions, is weakened by being open on one side.

Next, varying his approach by aiming at the *appearance* of Ronchamp—although the structural aspect accords more with what Le Corbusier was currently doing in India—Tange introduced the Ronchamp theme into a profane setting at the Totsuka Country Club (fig. 8.52). With somewhat greater economy, in the same year, 1961, Maekawa recalled the billowing upturned profile of the Ronchamp roof by applying a sort of decorative cornice in his Festival Hall at Ueno. And, indeed, this is no less effective than in Le Corbusier's own work, for instance, at Ahmedabad, where in the museum a concrete cornice of similar type is used to set off brick walls.

At Nichinan, in Miyazaki Prefecture, the Nichinan Cultural Center of 1960–62 designed by Tange (figs. 8.53–54) uses decorative elements, such as apertures copied from the portico of the Chandigarh Assembly Building. The composition was developed by the architect as a series of prismatic solids, which become overlapping oblique triangles in profile and appear to radiate fanlike from a single center. Later, in 1966, Kikutake's Miyakonojo City Hall (fig. 8.55; also in Miyazaki Prefecture) afforded a Metabolist counterpart of this work. Instead of monolithic concrete as at Nichinan, the side walls of Kikutake's auditorium space are formed of radial concrete beams translated in the upper part of the building into steel ribs. Over these the roof of steel sheeting fits like the canopy of a baby carriage, one of the wittiest of all Metabolist attempts to analyze structure into its alleged respective permanent and changeable elements. The image at Nichinan was, by contrast, static and sculptural, but Tange's inspiration may

8.53. Tange: Nichinan Cultural Center, Nichinan, Miyazaki Prefecture, 1960–62. Lateral facade.

8.54. Tange: Nichinan Cultural Center, Nichinan, Miyazaki Prefecture, 1960–62. Plan (paving of courtyard, right, extends into foyer, left) and section.

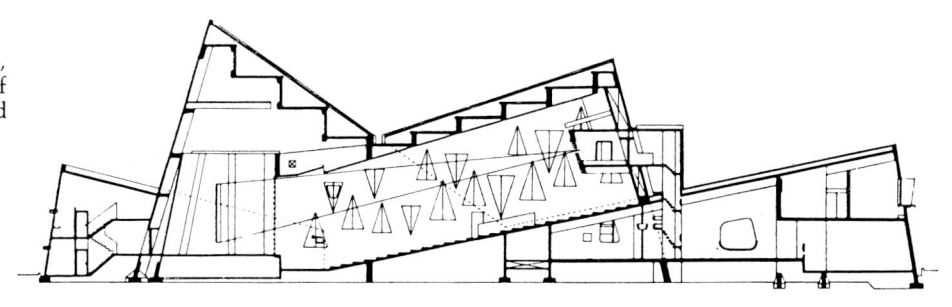

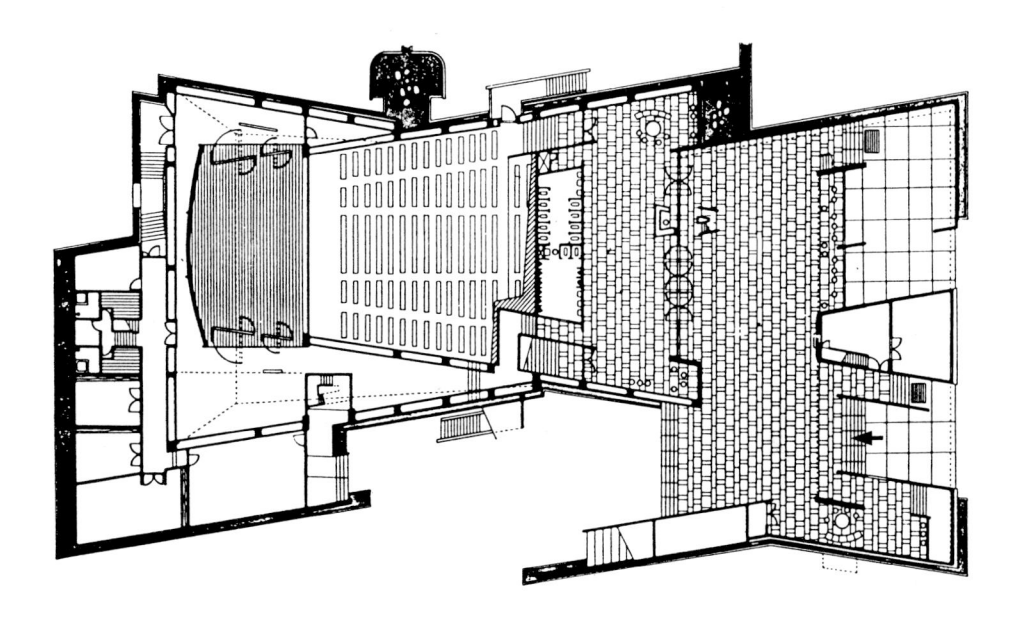

8.55. Kikutake: Miyakonojo City Hall, Miyakonojo, Miyazaki Prefecture, 1966.

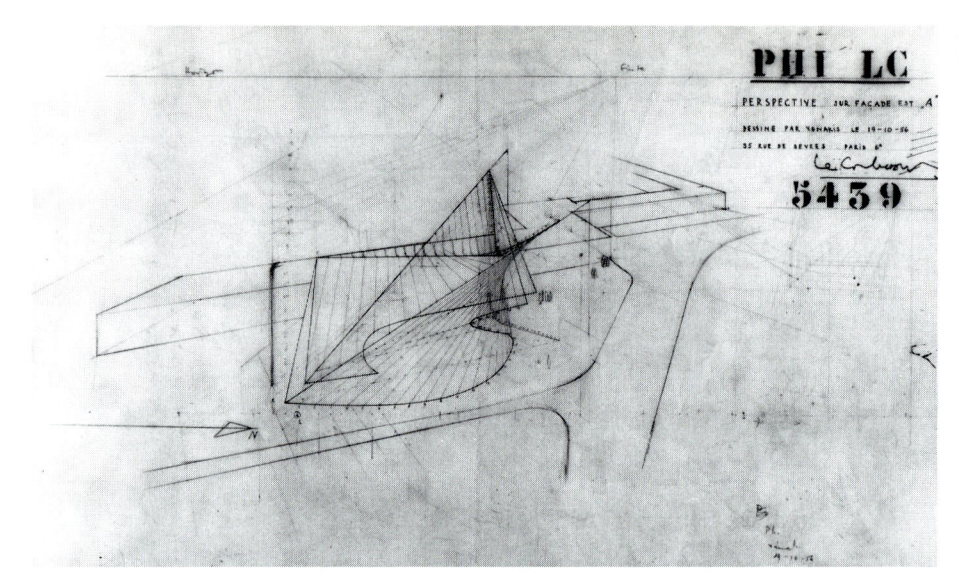

8.56. Le Corbusier, with Iannis Xenakis: Philips Pavilion, Brussels World's Fair, 1958. Schematic drawing.

8.57. Tange: National Olympic Stadiums, Yoyogi, Tokyo 1961–64.

have been the small but dynamic Philips Pavilion (fig. 8.56) designed by Le Corbusier for the Brussels World's Fair in 1958. It was a complex tentlike manifestation of saddle-shaped hyperbolic-paraboloid surfaces created by stretching cables between pinnaclelike supports in a system elaborated by Iannis Xenakis.

Wherever the Philips Pavilion's influence began in work by Tange in the early sixties, its importance is clear for the designs of both St. Mary's Cathedral and the National Olympic Stadiums of 1961–64 (fig. 8.57). The Brussels World's Fair had boasted several tensile structures of greater magnitude than the Philips Pavilion, but none was closer to being an exercise in pure geometry. A still earlier building which made use of related techniques was the Ingalls Hockey Rink of 1956–58, at Yale University, designed by Tange's great friend Eero Saarinen and the engineer Fred Severud. In both the Yale building and the Tokyo twin stadia, it was necessary to employ hybrid structural methods, though it may be supposed that Tange's engineer, Yoshikatsu Tsuboi, profited from knowledge of Severud's design. As pure sculpture—inspired, Tange says, by the broken silhouette of the Colosseum in Rome—the pair of stadia overlooking Tokyo's Yoyogi Park remains the preeminent work of the Japan Style. By contrast, the less said the better about Tange's design for the rebuilt Tokyo Cathedral, with its splayed cruciform fabric composed of eight mathematically derived hyperbolic-paraboloid shells spliced together (and lightly fudged) at the joints.

Kenzo Tange has been obsessed throughout his life with notions of monumentality and with achieving the feel (without of course, the look) of Western classical tradition. In a few works, like his small Kagawa Prefectural Gymnasium of 1965 at Takamatsu and better-known Kurashiki City Hall of 1960, he achieves this balance by uncompromisingly and unselfconsciously plumping for Japanese tradition. Kazuo Shinohara's quest lay in an opposite direction, obvious by 1966 in the climax of his First Style. Henceforth, his preoccupant goal would be to obtain a feeling of Japanese space that did not depend on mere details. But there was to be a middle figure in this equation—a student of Tange's, younger than Shinohara by only half the dozen years that separate the ages of Shinohara and Tange. The man in question was Arata Isozaki, and he shared with his mentor concern for both Western architectural tradition and urban design. Yet, he was, unlike Tange, critically aware of Japan's link with her ancient past having been severed by her own history. It was this gap, I think, that he endeavored to fill from the outset of his career by recourse to metaphor and wit.

9 | Technology, Metaphor, and the Resurgence of Japanese Space

TO BUILD OR DESTROY

Arata Isozaki, while not achieving the customary doctorate in architecture until 1961, was designated a collaborating member of the Tange team upon first entering Tange's studio at Tokyo University as a fourth-year undergraduate in 1953. After publication of the Tokyo Plan in 1960 (see figs. 7.20–21), Tange and his office committed themselves to the development of a scheme for the existing Tsukiji area of downtown Tokyo, which was to have constituted one part of the "civic axis" as sketched out in the larger plan. Whereas in Tange's original plan the tentlike auxiliary residential zones had claimed the attention of architects and public alike, the Tsukiji Plan (fig. 9.1) was an assemblage of vertical elements joined horizontally by trusslike arms approximating the scale of whole buildings. For Isozaki himself, as well as the Metabolists, it was these articulated megastructures with their erector-set possibilities that established—along with Kikutake's seaborne ideas (see fig. 7.15)—the new wave of mechanical-biological imagery.

A strict chronology no longer appears feasible, but sometime in 1961, or possibly the year after, Isozaki finished a series of Metabolist-related sketches and models entitled "City in the Air" (fig. 9.2). Meanwhile, the scheme for a "Joint Core System" (fig. 9.3), which he conceived of as an infrastructural aid to large-scale urban development, may date from as early as 1960. It seems to have had a decisive influence on certain works and projects by the Tange office. Such were, if not the buildings set for Tsukiji itself, then certainly the Yamanashi Press and Radio Center at Kofu of 1964–66 (famous for being photographed against its mountain backdrop on clear days) or subsequent related designs, like the Shizuoka Press and Broadcasting Center in Tokyo of 1966–67 (see fig. 7.22). In "City in the Air" and "Joint Core System" Isozaki proceeded by fusing the circular shafts represented in Kikutake's sketches of 1958–59 with the trabeated megastructural fantasies of Tange's civic axis portion of the Tokyo Plan, whose elements were square in cross-section. By means of this gesture he was able to fix the definitive image that the Metabolist-generated megastructure was to achieve in Tange's built oeuvre. It is likely that Isozaki's solution echoes the classical manner of joining (round) column with (square) beam perpetuated by Le Corbusier in such works as the recently completed Museum of Western Art in Tokyo of 1959.

Eventually, having founded the firm of Arata Isozaki Atelier, with its ironic initials AIA—usually read as American Institute of Architects—in 1963, the young architect would persist for nearly a decade in returning at intervals to the utopian systems architecture propounded by Metabolism. But of his initial proposals, dating from 1960–62 and including "City in the Air" and "Joint Core System," the most distinctively prophetic was also the least characteristically Metabolist in its presentation and feeling: a third scheme, the photomontage he entitled "Future City" (fig. 9.4). Here the vertical shafts derive from a gigantic and metamorphosed version of some ruined proto-Doric structure long ago abandoned to the ravages of an urban freeway. However, these ruined column shafts have been spliced and recycled as joint-core analogues with the help of modern materials. In other words, they are connected up at various angles with segments of truss borrowed from Isozaki's own "joint-core" drawing. The mood of this scenario piece is Piranesian, one portion of the recently added trussing having already crashed to the ground, while a few spectators gather to assess damage. Populated with antlike human figures as well as cars, the city promises nevertheless to function in spite of isolated disasters. Through its flirtation with classical ruins, this composition posits a theme altogether without precedent in Japanese architecture. That is the *possibility* for Isozaki—based on an analogy with the demise of the Western classical tradition—of the imminent destruction of architecture.

This metaphor of classical ruins may well owe something to Louis Kahn, who could have transmitted his enthusiasm for the subject during his short Japanese sojourn while attending the World Design Conference. Yet, it has previously been pointed out that the sporadic destruction of whole districts—if not entire cities—was a familiar occurrence in Japanese life, due to the vagaries of fire, typhoon, earthquake, and war. As a result, attitudes toward the natural and man-made environment have long been characterized by an acceptance of the precariousness of human life. Thus, a generation of architects, including Maekawa and Tange, had witnessed unflinchingly—almost without commentary—the destruction of Tokyo and other urbanized areas by the close of World War II. By contrast, we saw Frank Lloyd Wright arrive—and having spent the better part of a decade devising a structure he believed could refute the inevitable—proceed to inscribe musings on the fortuitous survival of the Imperial Hotel at the heart of his autobiography.

The conceit transforming ruins into a city of the future in Isozaki's imagination lies midway between such behavioral

220 TECHNOLOGY, METAPHOR, AND JAPANESE SPACE

9.1. Tange: Tsukiji Plan, Tokyo, 1960–64. Model of unrealized project.

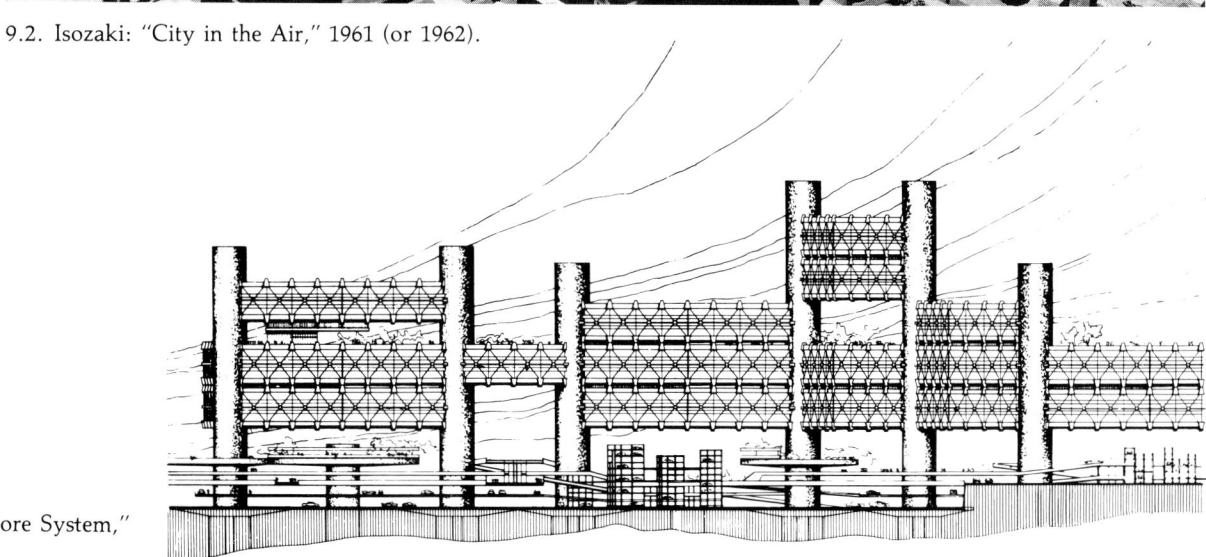

9.2. Isozaki: "City in the Air," 1961 (or 1962).

9.3. Isozaki: "Joint Core System," possibly 1960.

9.4. Isozaki: "Future City," photomontage, 1962.

extremes, and the "Future City" illustration itself is concerned, above all, with establishing transience as a monumental datum. This vision of a contemporary city rising amid classical ruins of a markedly primitive type and bespeaking an already known capacity for future growth—but also decline—is supremely an image of its time. It is tinged with the vitalistic sensibility of Metabolistic origins but, with hindsight, can also be explained as a precursor of a certain "postmodern" thinking, defined in the narrowest sense as a preoccupation with neoclassical resurgence. Interestingly, in diverging from the biorythmical imagery of the main Metabolist personalities, "Future City" raises the ante for the Metabolistic stakes. By admitting a free-floating metaphor of classicity it also permits us to glimpse a crack in Metabolism's spotless utopia.

Heretofore, the Metabolist game had involved literal-minded manipulation of straightfacedly utopian strategies; only its techniques of symbolization diverged from orthodox Modern Movement notions of a better world for tomorrow. With the new device of ruins, a flavor of vague ambivalence and subtle artificiality has been introduced, adding a formal and historical dimension to the societal and demographic references that until now furnished Metabolism's main focus. In a single stroke, the neoclassical tone of Isozaki's sketch-montage linked Metabolist ideas with the full panorama of Western classical tradition in a distinctive mode of irony, even as the Metabolist inspiration of the "Future City" was at the same time reinforced by a caption evoking the life-cycle: "The incubation process. Ruins are the future state of our city, and the future city itself will be ruins."[1]

Isozaki developed this pessimistic yet open-ended notion

9.5. Isozaki: "Destruction of the Future City," 1968.

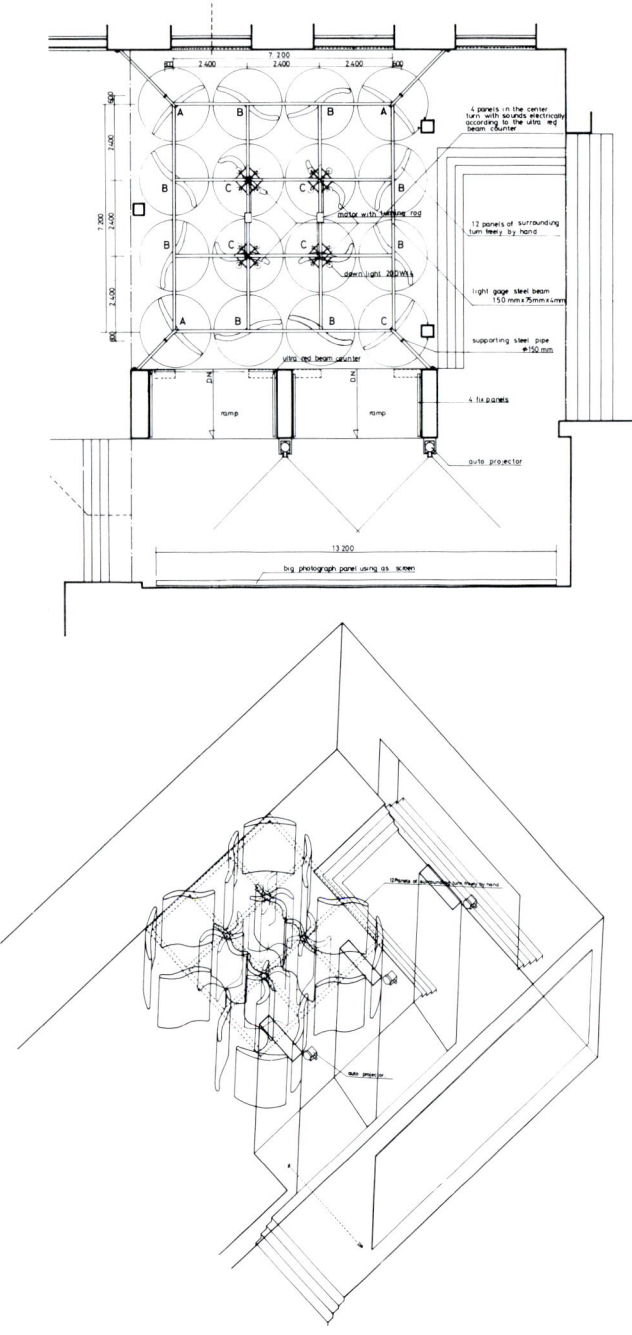

9.6. Isozaki: "Electric Labyrinth," 1968. Exhibit for the Milan Triennale, included figure 9.5 as mural background. Axonometric and plan.

in the frequently reproduced photographic panel entitled "Destruction of the Future City" (fig. 9.5). His extremely large work (also made into a poster) submits the motif of ruins to further transformation. Huddles of anguished space-frame geometries are depicted, recalling Guntis Plesums' arresting Theme Pavilion for the Montreal Expo a year before. These forms are montaged against a panoramic view of Hiroshima after the atomic blast. The panel was exhibited, in the aftermath of the university crisis of 1968, as a background for Isozaki's "Electric Labyrinth" (fig. 9.6) at the Milan Triennale, itself occupied by demonstrators that year. Isozaki's exhibit was a labyrinthine space comprising sixteen bladelike revolving panels of floor-to-ceiling height. These were made of a plexiglass material and covered with representations of hellfire from Japanese medieval painting and grotesque supernatural figures from eighteenth-century Japanese prints. The ensemble was bathed in synchronized effects of light and sound controlled by an infrared beam counter. Like many such displays, the "Electric Labyrinth" exhibits the influence of the total light-and-sound experience that was Le Corbusier's *Electronic Poem*, performed inside the Philips Pavilion (see fig. 8.56) at Brussels in 1958—now, perhaps, chiefly remembered for its orchestration by Edgar Varese.

The Hiroshima panel Isozaki designed for Milan served, ten years after Brussels, as a screen onto which transparent images of various future cities were projected. Here, the sign of the "future-urban-ruin" metaphor is reversed with respect to the architect's earlier "Future City" conception. It has been turned against itself—and us—the locus of the ultimate man-made destruction treated now as a mere vignette over which to impose the decay of a futuristic utopia. Or is it, alternatively, a prophecy of the willed self-destruction of all such utopian visions? We cannot know for sure, but clearly Isozaki used the Triennale as an occasion to present a statement regarding the still relatively recent atomic bombing of Hiroshima. Within Japan such sentiment had rarely found authentic expression—that is, beyond the eloquence of the preserved documentary remains and the chilling autobiographical accounts of survivors. Even though we lack any permanent record of Isozaki's display, the "Electric Labyrinth" must, I believe, be counted an artistic achievement of considerable originality. At a different level, the theme of Hiroshima offers a key to the "destructive" posture assumed henceforward by Isozaki in his work and writings. Like the "Future City," the "Electric Labyrinth" has never been absent from any compilation of works exhibited or published by the architect.

ISOZAKI IN KYUSHU: SEMIOTICS REPLACES SEMANTICS

Like Frank Lloyd Wright, Le Corbusier, and Kenzo Tange, Isozaki emerged from a provincial context. His earliest buildings are in Oita—Isozaki's birthplace in northeastern Kyushu—and his Medical Hall there, of 1959-60 (fig. 9.7), dates from before the establishment of his "atelier." Between 1960 and 1964, he was at work on an expanded regional plan for this prefectural capital of some one and a quarter million people. Isozaki thus appeared to follow in Tange's footsteps, and, similarly, he also lectured during the mid-sixties at the Department of Urban Engineering in Tokyo University, where Tange remained an active professor till 1974. Recognition of this field as a separate discipline in 1964 had owed a good deal to Tange, and in the years up until 1968—when the university was temporarily closed—Isozaki, too, was more often than not referred to as an urban designer. Somewhat before Shinohara had come to be known abroad, Isozaki's reputation was confirmed by his display at the Triennale. The design for the Oita Prefectural Library (fig. 9.8), which Isozaki has always considered his diploma vis-à-vis the Modern Movement, was published in both French and English magazines in 1964; the work itself, however, built in 1966, is contemporary with Shinohara's mature House in White.

The library at Oita has been compared with the work of Paul Rudolph in the United States, and precisely in Rudolph's theorizing of the 1950s one heard the idea that contemporary architecture must emerge from a world historical tradition or repository of universal forms. In certain details, Isozaki's library recalls the unbuilt scheme by Alison and Peter Smithson for the Sheffield University extensions also published during the fifties. Built on a corner site near the earlier Oita Medical Hall, the library possesses a degree of urban consciousness rare even today in Japanese architecture. This is partly owing to a willed incompleteness one senses in both these early works, by virtue of which they seem to reach out into their surroundings. In brief, it is the same awareness of the processes of growth and extension that resided in orthodox Metabolism. Yet, unlike Metabolist projects, Isozaki's expression is for the most part, at this date, remarkably balanced and sculpturesque. Moreover, as the comparison with Rudolph suggests, his work is distinguished by a determination to be part of a monolithic world tradition with emphasis on Europe, instead of simply the Japanese branch of the contemporary school. In Isozaki's case this notion had its beginnings with Tange, but if one compares Isozaki's "Future City" (see fig. 9.4) montage and its Doric columns with Tange's Nichinan Cultural Center (see figs. 8.53-54) completed the next year—which I have qualified as calligraphic—something of the difference in spirit between master and pupil can be felt.

Isozaki's early Kyushu works also include the House for Dr. N. of 1964-65 and the Iwata Girls' School, completed in the course of 1964. Like his Medical Hall and library, these are uniformly of concrete with strongly geometricizing forms. Together with the visionary schemes discussed above, all these works appeared in *Domus*[2] following Isozaki's "revelation" at the Triennale that year. Also pictured was the new Oita Branch of Fukuoka Mutual Bank (1966-67; fig. 9.9), with its open reference to James Stirling's and James Gowan's epoch-making Leicester University Engineering Building of 1959-63 (fig. 9.10). Indeed, Stirling's name will continue to be invoked with regard to Isozaki's work from this early period onward. Yet, many aspects of these early buildings are also strongly tied to the Japan Style, though not necessarily to its Corbusian aspects. Principally, it was in the bank interiors at Oita that one became aware of something new and different beginning to happen. At about this same time it was under the sign of English architecture in general—and the

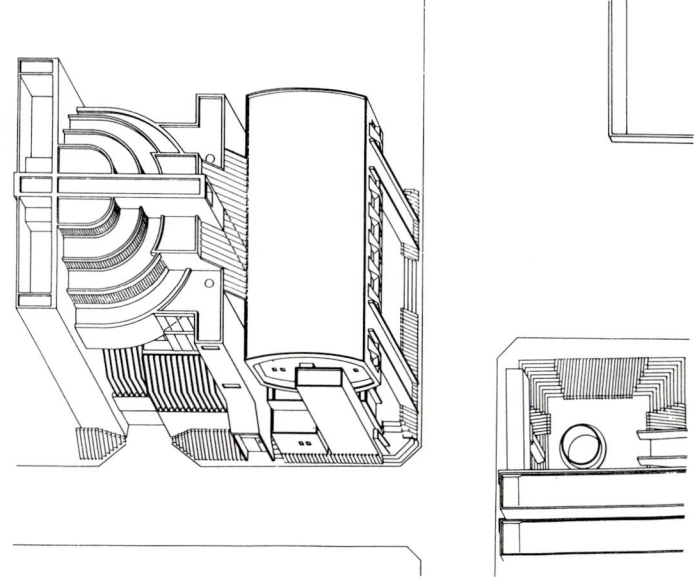

9.7. Isozaki: Oita Medical Hall, Oita, Oita Prefecture, 1959-60. Axonometric, original portion at right. (Oita Prefectural Library depicted at far right; see figure 9.8.)

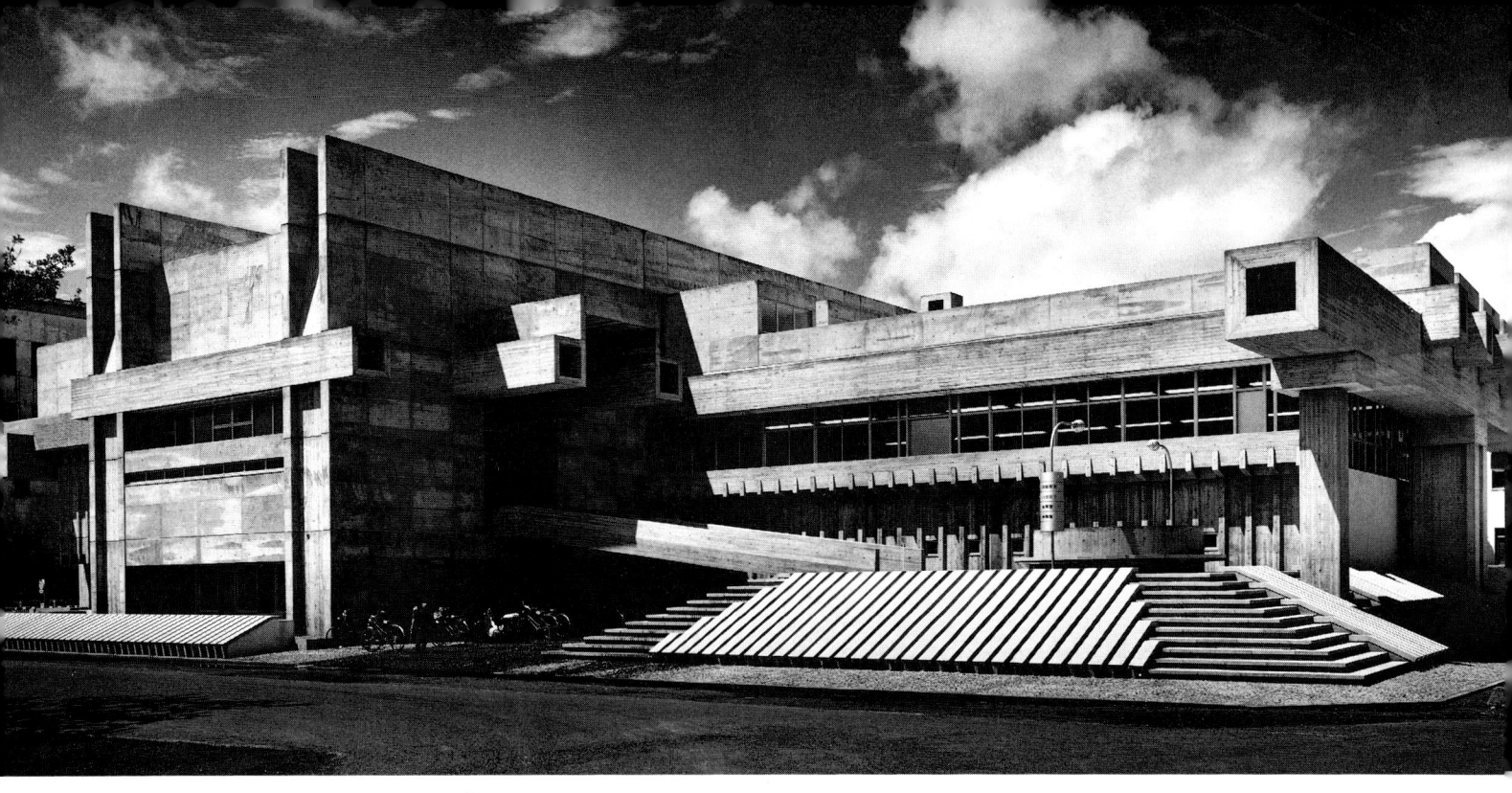

9.8. Isozaki: Oita Prefectural Library, Oita, 1966.

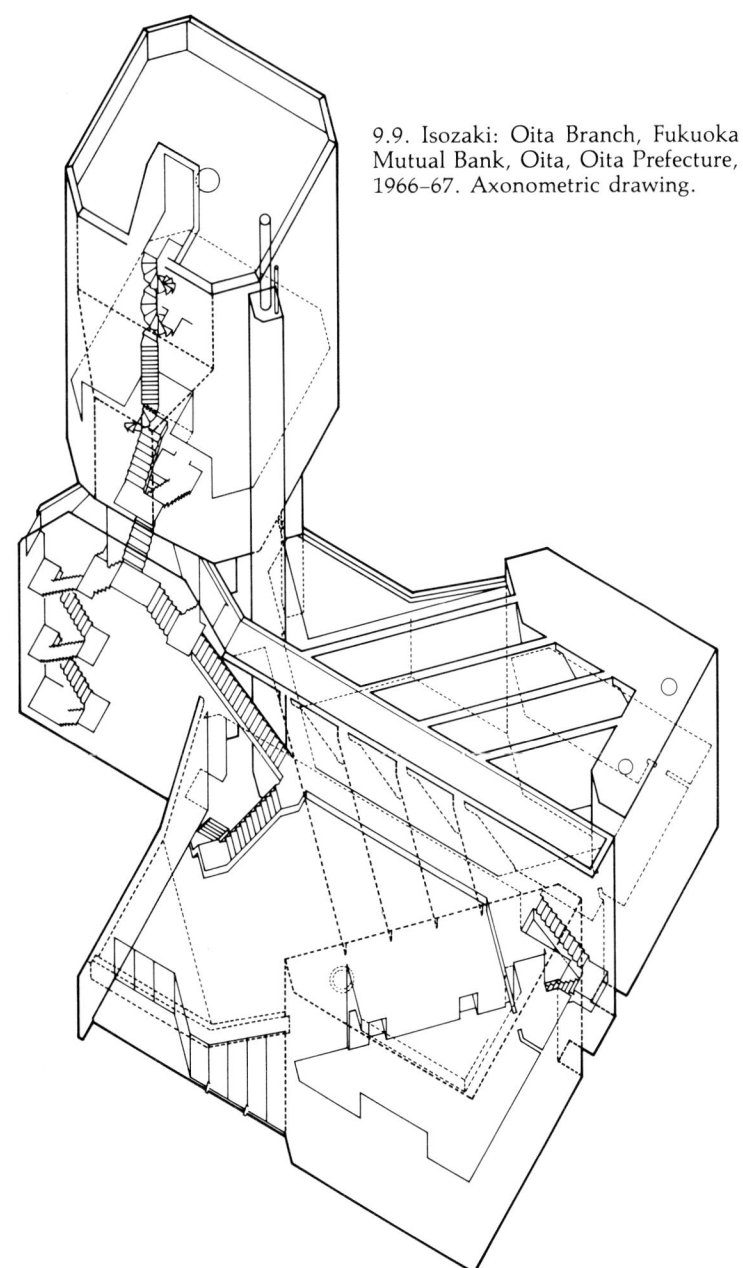

9.9. Isozaki: Oita Branch, Fukuoka Mutual Bank, Oita, Oita Prefecture, 1966–67. Axonometric drawing.

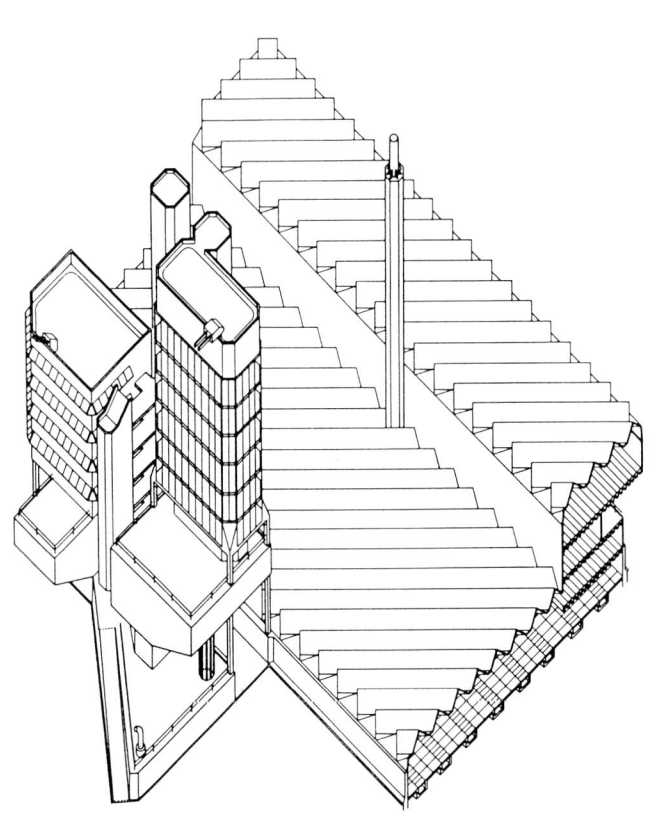

9.10. Stirling and Gowan: Leicester University Engineering Building, 1959–63. Axonometric drawing.

young Archigram group in particular—that the metaphorical aspect of high-tech began to be exploited, as opposed to Tange's straight-faced references to technology and Le Corbusier's covert ones. Isozaki belongs to the same emergent stream of development.

The Fukuoka Mutual Head Office (fig. 9.11), facing Hakata Station in Fukuoka, was designed by Isozaki between 1968 and 1971. A red Indian sandstone facade sets it apart from the customarily "poorer" materials of the Japan Style, and

9.11. Isozaki: Head Office, Fukuoka Mutual Bank, Hakata, Fukuoka, Fukuoka Prefecture, 1968-71.

it remains one of the most determinedly monumental structures anywhere in Japan. However, the branch banks by Isozaki—which, during the seventies, begin to multiply—are no longer really a part of the immediate postwar idiom. Like Stirling and Gowan's work referred to above, the branch banks depend on the Corbusian antitradition as elaborated at Chandigarh and La Tourette. Yet, what in Le Corbusier's late style might be called the rehabilitation of a semantic approach to architecture inclines toward semiotics in the work of some younger architects, while Stirling has on the whole attempted to bridge this gap between the full-blown "what" and the analytical "how" of meaning. Isozaki's significance during this recuperative phase of postmodern activity was that, working in an alien tradition, he was willing to take very little for granted. The same was, coincidentally, true of Shinohara—not only in his reevaluation of Japanese tradition, but increasingly, too, in his investigative approach to contemporary, Western-type spaces.

9.12. Stirling: Cambridge University History Faculty, 1964–67. Partial axonometric of interior.

9.13. Isozaki: Oita Branch, Fukuoka Mutual Bank, Oita, Oita Prefecture, 1966–67. "Image drawing." (See also figure 9.9.)▸

9.14. Isozaki: Oita Branch, Fukuoka Mutual Bank, Oita, Oita Prefecture, 1966–67. Main banking hall.

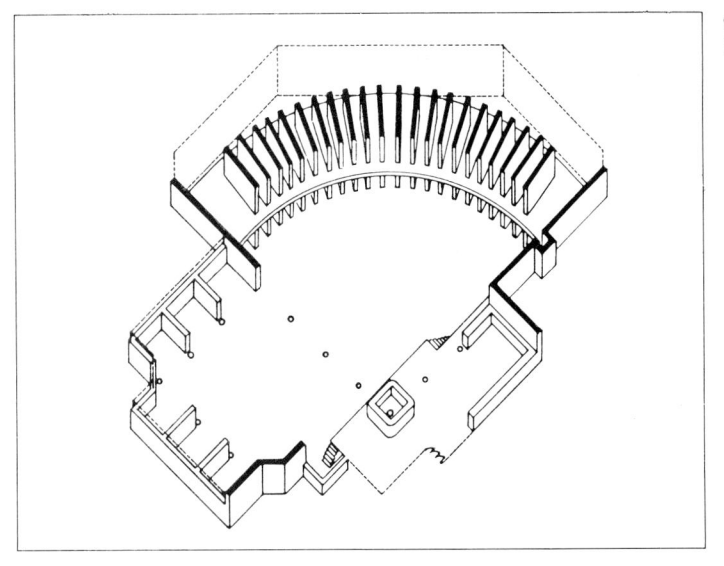

The Oita Branch for Fukuoka Mutual, completed in 1967, and the Daimyo Branch (1969), with its labyrinthine expression in plan and section, are of interest as occurring on either side of 1968, a year highlighted, for Isozaki, by the "Electric Labyrinth" at the Triennale but also marked by the university crisis in Europe and Japan. Both branches are works in search of an appropriate figural expression, denoting a gradual stylistic change from the lithic concrete work of his youthful production at Oita to representation of various "soft" systems. These included cladding of various sorts, baffling, exposed ductwork, spatial partitioning devices, and mathematical grids within an overall context of concrete construction. The main volume of the Oita bank (see fig. 9.9)—with champfered corners and raised on *piloti*—is taken over from Stirling and Gowan's Engineering Building (see fig. 9.10), which was itself a reworking of Russian Constructivist motifs. The Oita building seems to combine the influence of this work, completed in 1963, with that of Stirling's later Cambridge University History Faculty building, built in 1967 (fig. 9.12; based on a project of three years earlier). But, whereas the Engineering Building and the History Faculty were lit by means of transparent expanses of glass skylighting (notably in the workshops at Leicester and the reading room of the library at Cambridge), Isozaki's banking hall at Oita (figs. 9.13–14) is illuminated indirectly. The resultant space is subtle and individualistic.

A similar indirect overhead natural lighting had been a feature of the main reading room in the Prefectural Library at Oita—a building Isozaki later described as being about the "absence of theme." The Oita Branch bank was completed on the heels of the library, but the note of emptiness in the earlier realization has, at the bank, yielded to a new absorption in the manipulation of seemingly weightless forms. However, in keeping with his mainly semiological concerns, the architect is careful to avoid any thematic consensus. Here the interior spaces are virtual and membranelike, intended to be experienced as pulsations of light and darkness. Through such means and pursuits the unified perspective of classical Western space is dissolved in favor of an ostensible metaphor of electronic process. Consequently space itself—though, of course, still physically present—is no longer endowed with the old sense of visibility; Isozaki tries to reproduce the hallucinatory perspective of some non-Euclidean geometry. He attempts to induce in the spectator a sensation that actual, successive viewpoints are, in fact, nonsequential. The result is a kind of pantomime representation of spatiality, or

TECHNOLOGY, METAPHOR, AND JAPANESE SPACE 227

9.15. Distorting mirror: "Perhaps it is all truly 'funny'."

of such spatial knowledge as, in real terms, would defy all possibility of representation. Naturally, there is no call to label a largely semiological tour-de-force such as this with a flag of nationality; nonetheless, Isozaki's display at Oita retains more in common with Shinohara's painstakingly defined "Japanese" space than does either with the legacy of Renaissance or baroque spatiality.

A NEW KIND OF SPACE...

Experimentation in the Oita Branch bank interiors—while partly pure spatial fireworks or, to use a high-falutin expression, spatial semiotics—was at the same time a discourse on the theme of "metaphoricality." It insinuated a particular Japanese motif, as we shall see, and in spite of appearances Isozaki was by this date already deeply committed to realizing Japanese ideas about space. This fact may not have been recognized sufficiently, or at all, in Japan at the time. For, while Shinohara's important theoretical breakthrough, seen in the House in White, *seemed* barely to proceed beyond traditional accouterments—*shoji* and the rest—Isozaki began his career in modern Western architecture at roughly that juncture where Kenzo Tange—henceforward active mainly abroad—had left off. The point is that both these architects, Isozaki in the public realm as well as Shinohara in private houses, were trying to provide significant answers to the difficult question of the identity of Japanese modern architecture. And that, to be sure, is the chief issue I have wished to raise in this book.

Among the most revealing of Arata Isozaki's early writings is that entitled "Yami no Kukan," or "Space of Darkness," dating from 1964.[3] In it he enjoins the reader to visit the Magic House (fig. 9.15), or fun house, at the Korakuen Amusement Park in Tokyo. That is, one day, on being asked to submit a list of the twelve most outstanding works of architecture built in Japan since the end of World War II, Isozaki himself went to the Magic House "as a way out of this unrewarding task." He then proceeds to comment on the bizarre phenomena inside the mirror maze and trick room as if they might be interpreted as inevitable features of normal spatial experience: "Perhaps it is all truly 'funny.'"

The sense of spatial dislocation built into the architecture of the fun house with its "traps, illusions and happenings," constitutes for Isozaki "a new kind of space." At the same time, however, he feels such features may possibly "define the nature of space itself." The germ of this belief—along with these various tricks and devices—now begins to suffuse his compositional exercises and will provide tropical material for future turns of theory. Nevertheless, it comes with a certain astonishment in rereading this early essay on the "Space of Darkness" to find ourselves transported out of the Magic House at Korakuen into the Children's Home at Amsterdam, built in 1957–60 by the Dutch architect Aldo van Eyck. We realize, with surprise, that the 1959 meeting of CIAM, where van Eyck had first presented his building, was still fresh in memory. For a Japanese architect, then—or at least one like Isozaki—van Eyck's neohumanist paper, "Is Architecture Going to Reconcile Basic Values?"[4] (read at Otterlo), begged to be interpreted radically and at face value. Van Eyck, for his part, had been concerned with approximating the amazing literalness of a child's realm in built form. By this turnabout he hoped to free orphans in care of the municipality from any obligation to conform with all the perceptual distortions he suspected the syndics of wickedly favoring. Van Eyck's Children's Home is thus replete with diverse and unaccustomed spatial, formal, and scalar devices. They are not conceived, as in the amusement-park fun house, with the aim of dislocating and confusing children or adults, but for quite the opposite purpose of orienting and sheltering the Dutch orphans within their own intimate perceptual world.

Van Eyck refers to his work more or less as a recuperation of principles discovered earlier by the historical avant-garde of the Modern Movement. Those modernist achievements of Klee, Picasso, Le Corbusier, Joyce, Schoenberg, and others—"the whole wonderful gang"—deserved better, he thought, than mere mechanical or decorative repetition. Van Eyck hoped further to be able "to gather the old into the new; to rediscover the archaic principles of human nature." "In each culture," he continues, "there are things universally valid which . . . are emphasized while others are subdued." Finally, he concludes: "We can meet 'ourselves' everywhere—in all places and ages—doing the same things in a different way, feeling the same differently, reacting differently to the same."[5]

Not surprisingly, the spirit of the design of van Eyck's Children's Home moved Isozaki to refer to its spatial image as a "phenomenological" one; he characterizes the aim of the Dutch architect as making human beings "the major subject—not the object—of architecture." The remainder of Isozaki's discussion of van Eyck consists of an admiring paraphrase of the Dutchman's personalized usage of the terms "occasion" and "place" as more humane substitutes for the notions of *time* and *space*.[6] That is, as van Eyck put it: "Whatever space and time mean, place and occasion mean more. For space in the image of man is place, and time in the image of man is occasion. . . ."[7] For Isozaki, these two terms translate as "the instant at which a human being enters and perceives a space in relation to himself." Meanwhile, van Eyck was anxious to establish what he calls an "in between" in order "to reconcile conflicting polarities," and he cites the philosopher Martin Buber's phrase "das Gestalt gewordene Zwischen."[8] At the same time van Eyck plumps for a cybernetic interpretation of this—which was probably significant for Tange, who, of course, was present at the Otterlo meeting. As Tange's disciple, Isozaki would also take up the cybernetic theme in his own theoretical writing, shortly to be discussed. Yet, the most exciting implication of Isozaki's treatment of van Eyck's "timespace" remarks did not emerge until sometime later. In the late seventies Isozaki was to dissect the Japanese term *ma*, which can mean "interval" (in time) but also a "space" (or "room"), reinjecting an ethnic dimension into the discourse initiated by van Eyck at Otterlo. Characteristically, however, by that time the whole issue will have lost its high moral or ethical tenor.

. . . AND ITS POLITICS

What in Japanese architecture of the sixties onward may appear, perhaps, to be nothing more than a vernacular shift—or rhetorical foot-shuffling, such as Tange could be relied on to offer—does, nonetheless, possess roots in a recognizable, if generalized, phenomenological schema of more or less arguable validity. Thus, for example, in his famous preface to the *Phenomenology of Perception* (1945), Maurice Merleau-Ponty defines the phenomenological project as providing "an account of space, time and the world as we 'live' them." And it has even been mooted that such a goal might be better expressed in art than by philosophy. Phenomenology's preoccupation with the way in which consciousness perceives objects, as well as its careful attention to the implications of this for the domain of meaning in general, is well expressed in Husserl's celebrated exhortation, "Back to the things themselves!" Accordingly—about the time of Isozaki's postgraduate years and his apprenticeship under Tange—the exacerbation of the conflict between CIAM and its Team X renegades had placed the "meaning" of architectural forms and other components under direct scrutiny. In this light it is not surprising that in van Eyck's Otterlo presentation certain turns of expression bring to mind the phrasing of Martin Heidegger's thought. For example, van Eyck's use of the verb "gather," as in the previously quoted "the time has come to gather the old into the new," recalls Heidegger's etymology of "thing," which he cites as a *gathering*: "Thinging gathers." Likewise, the term "threshold," analyzed by Heidegger in his lecture entitled "Language,"[9] suggests a relationship with van Eyck's "doorstep,"[10] which is so important to the notion of "in between" as already referred to in the Otterlo speech.

Van Eyck's rhetorical question, "What then, I ask, is the greater reality of a door?"[11] is meant to direct attention to "an occasion repeated millions of times in a lifetime between the first entry and the last exit."[12] But in terms of socio-architectural potential the presence of a door also conjures up notions of "part and whole, unity and diversity, individual and collective, inside and outside, closed and open,"[13] at least for an architect such as van Eyck. It is by means of such semantic considerations that he tried to forestall, by defusing it, what he calls "society's genuine love of schizophrenia."[14]

Therefore, Aldo van Eyck viewed his Amsterdam Children's Home—with its 125 child occupants—not merely as a symbolic entity but, more than that, as an operative device he hoped might help "reconcile" polar opposites, like those just enumerated, which he saw as constituting real breaches in society. In the same way that a thinker like Merleau-Ponty used the discoveries of developmental psychology to test and refine his views on human subjectivity, van Eyck exploited the Amsterdam orphanage commission as a kind of controlled experiment. In it he tried to put forward and offer support for notions of how a building might positively reinforce its users' innate perceptual capacities.

Clearly, the Children's Home—one of the most celebrated buildings of the mid-twentieth century—afforded a unique opportunity to erect a therapeutic buffer between its inmates and what van Eyck refers to as the "fatty machinery of society."[15] Here it is not *space* which was "twisted," in keeping with the topological notions already introduced with respect to the architecture of Le Corbusier and Shinohara. Instead, in a shift toward a subjective subject, it is, according to van Eyck, the poor children: "What has happened to them has twisted them in many ways and they need untwisting."[16]

It is not known how far Isozaki was impressed by the socially improving element in van Eyck's theorizing and its occasional unabashedly mystical tenor. The "Space of Darkness" essay may have just been using "topological" considerations in the Dutch architect's discussion of *place* and *occasion* as a springboard for Isozaki's own thoughts on the nature of perception. For better or worse, the impetus afforded by Team X was comparatively short-lived and was not transmitted to the succeeding generation to which Isozaki and other younger architects belonged. While van Eyck's excellent motives are scarcely in question—then as now—still the most important and memorable feature of his Amsterdam building was the practical attempt made in it to treat space directly as an "operative" category. The same treatment that had been aimed at in ideal fashion by the historical avant-garde van Eyck invoked at Otterlo. However, the semantic entities Merleau-Ponty had chosen to refer to as "non-language significations" in his final work[17]—written in the year of the Team X gathering—proved notoriously difficult to grasp and encapsulate from Cézanne onward. A notion of operative signs, as theory, was, hence, unsuited to survival within the unstable and politicized orbiting of Modern Movement aesthetics.

This was precisely the complaint voiced by van Eyck in his contention that, artistically speaking, a postwar, *post*modern society now found itself back in the old "deterministic" or "Euclidean groove."[18] That was to say, a rigidly structured domain between interior and exterior, wherein nonetheless—as phenomenology might have it—a woefully deteriorated, blankly amorphous idiom abrogating the philosophy of consciousness had preempted allegedly non-language territory. Or, as van Eyck did put it, in his presentation at Otterlo: "For 30 years architects have been providing the outside for man even on the inside.... Architecture means providing inside for man even outside—and that goes for urbanism as well."[19]

Here phenomenology, or at least its grass-roots Team X equivalent, was getting more than just symbolically enmeshed in linguistics, as indeed its professional philosophical proponents had been since shortly after World War II. Architecture itself, on the other hand—as opposed to theory and talk—was not quite ready for this engagement with so-called structuralism, and when the moment arrived it afforded fewer results and greater disorder than the polemical revolt of Team X. But this moment was not yet come and—though, in Japanese architecture, Isozaki was to be among those most thoughtfully concerned with such issues—the results showed little cohesiveness and less flair. That may be, of course, owing to the dramatic and intuitive phenomenological bent which seems to mark the unpervertible "non-language" strain of traditional Japanese architecture derived through tea—therefore represented in both the rustic *chashitsu* and its descendant *sukiya*. But this is a thesis to be inferred from Isozaki's own "Space of Darkness" essay, the core of which has not yet been dealt with.

REFLECTIONS AND TRANSPARENCIES

The Children's Home in Amsterdam of 1957–60 contains a number of mirrors, including distorting ones, which may have sparked Isozaki's association with the Magic House at Korakuen. The Dutch building also possesses translucent fenestration reminiscent of *shoji* panels, both in proportions and general manner of insertion into the design. One might wonder whether this feature of van Eyck's design allowed Isozaki to be drawn onto the subject of traditional Japanese spatial modes. But first a brief discussion of baroque architectural spaces is interpolated between Isozaki's comments on the Children's Home and his remarks on Japanese-type space. Ostensibly, in "Space of Darkness," this is to introduce the topic of light. Thus, for example, Isozaki wrote: "I sometimes think that the entire history of European architectural space is the story of techniques developed for the introduction of natural illumination." And, more precisely: "[The distribution of illumination in baroque spaces] simulates perception of the spaces themselves." As a prime example of space illuminated dramatically in late baroque fashion, Isozaki recalls the spectacular highlighting of the Sacrament in its *Transparente*, or retabular tabernacle, in the Gothic cathedral at Toledo. This arrangement (fig. 9.16) was created by Narciso Tomé—working between 1721 and 1732—who removed the Gothic vault, substituting a kind of light chamber in its place. Christian Norberg-Schulz refers to it as "a chapel without walls—that is, so to speak, constructed only of light."[20]

Elsewhere Norberg-Schulz has written—convincingly, I believe—of the transition from Renaissance to baroque spatial handling as "the phenomenization of abstract symbolic space."[21] Space, he says, was at last "conceived as a means of 'direct' expression, and became an object of emotional experience."[22] Accordingly, in the Counter-Reformation: "The general process of phenomenization which took place during the sixteenth century thus suited the purposes of the Church well."[23] After the Council of Trent the purposes of religious art were turned more than ever to persuasion and propaganda. Norberg-Schulz cites "participation" as the ultimate aim and goes on to discuss the role of the Jesuits, who, it should be remembered, also reached the shores of Japan.

As mentioned in the preface to this book, it is tempting to see Jesuit influence in the space of the *chashitsu*, especially as Sen no Rikyu is believed to have entertained Christian sympathies. However, I have no intention of upholding such a proposal and merely refer to Isozaki's aside on baroque spatiality as an overture to his "space of darkness" theme, noting how the eventual argument appears to be corroborated by Norberg-Schulz's remarks on "phenomen[al]ization." It is, surely, sufficient heresy to qualify the rustic *chashitsu* as a baroque space following the terms of this discussion. Yet it is a fact that the space consecrated to the tea ceremony invites and demands our participation—the usual Zen-inspired word being, rather, "concentration." Isozaki is here discussing "Japanese space" in a more extended sense, which includes—but does not limit itself to—*sukiya*-style building derived from tea culture. It is, therefore, with reference to their "participatory," or "operative," quality that van Eyck's orphan's home, baroque spaces in general, and so-called Japanese space merit comparison in Isozaki's essay.

9.16. Tomé: the *Transparente* (toplit altar behind the choir), Toledo Cathedral, 1721–32.

ARCHITECTURE AS METALANGUAGE

Although Husserl and Heidegger[24] were both known in Japanese philosophical circles from the twenties on, the idea of linking phenomenology specifically with architecture scarcely seems to have occurred anywhere before the 1950s.[25] Then, suddenly, for the first time since the Renaissance—or at least the eighteenth century—architecture once more found itself part of a major critique of traditional metaphysics in a way that presupposed juxtaposition of figural with metafigural language. This is, of course, strictly speaking, broad of the mark, since no form of art is conceivable without such a combination. Yet architecture is that public art *par excellence* which must reconcile the internal and formal structures of its own language with certain external or referential effects. By the 1930s the Modern Movement had carried insistence upon identification of its own contemporary but exaggeratedly exclusive figural language with ostensibly public and referential gestures to a level of contradiction begging credibility. This became evident in the crisis which rent CIAM after the war, while reconciliators—like Aldo van Eyck, as discussed here, but also, for instance, Louis Kahn—sought genuinely to redefine figurality in architecture. They, and others, hoped to endow architectural language with a less coldly formalistic and more legitimately intelligible—hence, phenomenological—character that would make it once again truly "public." Van Eyck and Kahn based their approaches, respectively, on an ethos of perception that, I believe, was heavily indebted to De Stijl in the one case, and to the same populist "form follows function" dictum Wright inherited from Sullivan in the other.

Put another way, under the momentous, if unspecifiable, influence of Le Corbusier's late style—discussion of which has been mainly limited here to its repercussions on the Japan Style—a certain bold fluency obtained and the art of quotation was once again practiced. At the beginning of the Modern Movement, all kinds of motifs were necessarily borrowed and appropriated by architects as divergent as Peter Behrens, Hans Poelzig, and, still earlier, Charles Rennie Mackintosh. By none, however, as skillfully—in a way that for long went virtually unrecognized—as by Le Corbusier. However, only in his so-called later style did the play of figural language—developed over the years typically out of vernacular and industrial sources—evolve in so rarefied a manner that it would appear to exclude outside references. Indeed, so distinctive and idiosyncratic did Le Corbusier's idiolect become—founded on rhetorical innovation but including new elements of grammar—that it probably induced relative newcomers, such as van Eyck or Kahn, to follow suit. Moreover, this "late style" at its best was felt, despite its seeming introvertedness, to be advancing into just that domain of shared "non-language significations" envisioned by Merleau-Ponty before his death. Such, then, roughly was the context in the mid-sixties, hence at the moment Isozaki's "Space of Darkness" essay—as well as Shinohara's House of Earth and House in White—were being produced.

One last occurrence with a "phenomenological" bias or lineage—a book—has to be mentioned before we can return with sufficient background to Isozaki's "Space of Darkness." This work was published under the influence of Louis Kahn, who was teaching in the School of Architecture at the University of Pennsylvania, where his own Richards Medical Research Towers was completed in 1961, itself assuming the character of a theorem. These were followed by the Salk Institute for Biological Studies at La Jolla, California, finished in 1965. The next year, 1966, Robert Venturi, a Philadelphia architect, protégé of Kahn's and instructor at Penn, saw his *Complexity and Contradiction in Architecture* issued under the auspices of the Museum of Modern Art in New York. Particularly as Kahn himself committed so few of his ideas to print, Venturi's book—which is, however, a very different text from anything Kahn ever spoke—at once assumed the position of a classic for those concerned specifically with the practice of architecture as a metalanguage. In his contemporary introduction the Yale historian Vincent Scully noted the importance of Aldo van Eyck's presence at the University of Pennsylvania (as a visiting critic), citing van Eyck as one element in a perpetual dialogue which built up around Kahn, the school's mentor and symposiarch. Scully refers to Venturi's treatise as "rigorously pluralistic and phenomenological,"[26] even if—at a distance of twenty years—the former quality seems to have endured over the latter. Thanks in part to the book's ultimately persuasive influence, the semantic urgency of Team X's socially motivated architecture disappeared under the semiotic avalanche of a latter-day "postmodernism"—at its most explicit preoccupied mainly with method as a kind of metafigural self-exposé. Just how some of the responsibility for this can be laid at the door of *Complexity and Contradiction in Architecture* is apparent not so much from the book's textual argument as from its 250 illustrations, as enlarged in the new second edition. By contrast, Venturi's "phenomenological" vocation discernible to Scully a generation ago was genuine but short-lived.

In his impatience to denounce the vogue during the sixties for "Form" as the prevalent—and solipsistic—expression of architectural values, Venturi's treatment of syntactical matters was both attractive and to the point. One of the things *Complexity and Contradiction in Architecture* attempted to do, for example, was promote a reexamination of the language of Western classical architecture: in other words, the distribution and syntax of formal elements derived through the Italian Renaissance from Greece and Rome. Still, it is not too much of an effort to see Isozaki—young as he was—as a kind of Palladian reformer and imagist in contradistinction to Venturi's role as a dour (later camp) Vignola-like figure, although in the early 1960s Venturi was still unquestionably the more mature and significant of the two. In other respects, however, a work like the Oita Prefectural Library (see fig. 9.8), whose realization was exactly contemporary with the publication of Venturi's book, shared something of that overpoweringly form-based approach derided by the Venturian thesis. Shortly,

9.17. Darkness at the heart of the domestic interior.

however, Isozaki made it clear that he would be committed to revival of a moribund tradition—but Japanese rather than Roman, like Palladio. The interiors of the Oita and Daimyo branches (see figs. 9.13-14) of Fukuoka Mutual were to place on offer an alternative kind of postmodern architecture sketched out—as we can at last begin to acknowledge—in latently phenomenological terms. Isozaki's concerns were more rhetorical than syntactical, and the various images they comprised were described by the author as "metaphors." But even the *notion* of metaphor may be seen to have arisen out of Isozaki's meditations on Japanese tradition, as certainly as Palladio's new typologies, such as the temple-front dwelling—and, indeed, his "Romanism"—had emerged from the preprofessional archaeologist's cross-fertilization of antique *rhetorical* modes of building, in a way that Piranesi was to perfect after him.

RETURNING TO A "SPACE OF DARKNESS"

The "Space of Darkness" essay (1964) by Isozaki provides the surest basis for an interpretation of his role and work, although subsequent writings of 1974 ("Rereading 'In Praise of Shadows' ") and 1980 ("Rethinking 'Space of Darkness' ") offer additional clues and pointers. All three make reference to the compelling—even if short—didactic work by the now internationally celebrated novelist and essayist Junichiro Tanizaki entitled "In Praise of Shadows."[27] In spite of a certain desultoriness resulting from adherence to literary conventions, Tanizaki's piece displayed—and still affords today—a remarkable understanding of traditional Japanese aesthetic sensibility. In fewer than fifty English pages, Tanizaki managed, through the use of tightly controlled images embedded in rambling prose, to evoke *in nucleo* a spatial concept, whose "non-language" (i.e., phenomenal) orientation was also, so to speak, "nonspatial."

Tanizaki's ostensible theme was the overemployment of artificial means of lighting in prewar Japan, whether in public places, on the Kabuki stage, or—at night—in towns. More than anything, he was against the tendency to brighten domestic interiors unduly. A high degree of illumination contradicted cultural usage which had evolved over centuries and in accordance with which human life and especially household ritual proceeded in a state of semidarkness (fig. 9.17). This circumstance, Tanizaki urges, produced an aesthetic lifestyle peculiarly suited to the Japanese—even as regards their physiognomy and manners—one that had then persisted throughout the middle ages and well into more recent times.

Numerous and far-reaching complaints are insinuated into a mock diatribe directed mainly against shining, mass-produced materials, like plumbing fixtures and white tile, which for the author induce an unsettling standard of absolute cleanliness. Such conveniences, or so-called improvements, runs Tanizaki's argument, will upset the tranquillity of anyone accustomed to a setting composed wholly of naturally aged, and aging, materials. In the Japanese interior—of unpolished and untreated wood surfaces—illumination levels are conditioned and controlled by the use of papered panels for doors and windows instead of glazing. Originally, buildings had broad roofs of overhanging thatch or dark tiles to provide against a climate of heavy rains as well as glaring summer sun. Whole interior expanses were untouched by sunlight, whose penetration, even in wintertime, was discouraged by the darkness beneath the roof's edge.

Moreover, all ordinary household accouterments—notably utensils and vessels of lacquerware meticulously ornamented with gold, which were used to hold simple nourishment, such as plain white rice and dark miso soup—depended for beauty of effect on the state of perpetual twilight created by the presence of wide eaves. As seemed to befit the Japanese character, limitations imposed by nature were accepted and then cultivated to such an extent that even the canon of female beauty—the genius which presided over these dimly lit interiors—fell under the sway of a preoccupation with darkness. In fact, it was from Japanese womanhood that the abounding darkness—"a pregnancy of tiny particles like fine ashes, each particle luminous as a rainbow"[28]—was observed ultimately to emanate.

The domain of graduated shadow, and what Tanizaki terms "visible darkness"—within the heart of the domestic establishment—was equally well suited to the performance of religious ceremony, as well as its corollary, the traditional Noh drama. Certain architectural features of relatively recent date, such as the *tokonoma* alcove, are literally composed of darkness—or shadow—which, if dispelled, would result in reversion to an undifferentiated void. Yet Isozaki underscores a fact, which even Tanizaki himself was forced to concede, namely, that the "path back to darkness is almost closed." For practical reasons, the modern world of light-filled spaces composed of synthetic materials must be accepted or, at least, endured resignedly.

Nowadays, there is a "net" of intellectual awareness, coextensive with our man-made urban environment, that largely bypasses the role of physical sensation. Our attention is increasingly claimed by sign clusters made up of diverse codes. Our sensibility glides over these new "superficial layers," but we never quite succeed in erasing the consciousness of a "distant, suspended absolute—like darkness."[29] The old darkness itself, then, becomes finally "no more than another metaphor stripped of its absolute status." At best, twilight retains the role of a mediating element permitting signs "to float free instead of being swallowed up in black." Thus, writes Isozaki: "I am now convinced that we must replace darkness with a metaphor of illusoriness. As it gradually becomes a part of this overall illusoriness, darkness floats free and assumes a very different quality from what Tanizaki had in mind." Isozaki's concern, therefore, was the evolution of a working method, or methods, for confronting this new space of illusion.

Isozaki admits that he himself is out of sympathy with Tanizaki's rejection of the bright, shiny implements of daily modern life, but then, even Tanizaki claimed that it would be impossible for a modern Japanese to exist under the conditions sketched in his essay. It is, rather, the speculation that "In Praise of Shadows" provokes which is Isozaki's theme in his "Space of Darkness" essay. In European practice generally—and not only in baroque examples, such as the *Transparente* at Toledo already mentioned—light and shadow are treated as "independent opposing elements." While dramatic effects are obtained under these conditions, light and shadow never mix physically, as they appear to do in Japanese spaces. In traditional Japanese architecture, Isozaki theorizes, "light is something that flickers in the primaeval substance of darkness." Thus, "shadows are not born when light is projected. They are everything left over when light cuts through darkness." "Space," then, such as it exists in Japanese buildings, is conceived of simply as the "degree of intensity of light." Passage of light is an isolated, or ephemeral, occurrence—as, for example, in a candle-lit room; so, when a light source is extinguished, "space reverts to darkness."

Thus, light passes, and space returns to a darkness which is itself absolute in a way that light—in the confines of a Japanese architectural interior—cannot be considered to be. So, for Isozaki as early as 1964, Japanese darkness-space becomes a kind of limiting extreme permitting us to form the notion of "a void without space."

IMPLICATIONS FOR THE CITY

An analogy with the phenomenon of a void which cannot be visualized directly in spatial terms is presented by a pilot flying at night or in bad weather and having to rely upon instruments. Or an urbanite who negotiates the city and is dependent on various codes for reading, or interpreting, the space he or she must confront in virtually blind fashion. Such codes become the operative medium, replacing any sense of the space traversed. They form a "necessary illusion" as over against the "shadows encoded by the technology of modern life." For as Isozaki has it in "Space of Darkness," genuine spatial nuance, or shadow, is restored only when some untoward ordering of events in the life of the city disrupts the programming of these ubiquitous codes that characterize its illusory space.

Observations of this nature led Isozaki to devise a graphlike schema to illustrate the way in which space—such as ordinarily would be experienced in three-dimensional terms—is increasingly forced into polarization. At one pole, according to his visualization of this arrangement in "Space of Darkness," Isozaki places a "spatial order related to the image of darkness" oriented toward psychology, magic, and symbols, hence, the unconscious. At the opposite pole he sets up a "spatial system based on the image of illusion." The latter is an abstract space generated by codes and conducive to a so-called pluralism. On the one hand, this recent type of code-dominated space appears to diversify, and so enliven, the task of the designer; yet, on the other, a major shift in this direction might entail the permanent loss of the other quality of space traditionally vouchsafed by darkness. In Isozaki's view, this could possibly lead to a new nonphenomenological space involving a revived Cartesianism. In order to avoid a cul-de-sac of that kind, architects must seek to infuse the present efflorescence of "cybernetic" spaces with a maximum of metaphorical notions, or "absolutes." Such a thematics of space would possess an analogical relationship to the "space of darkness" that reaches us from an older and more primitive way of life. The space of darkness, according to Isozaki, bypasses the splendor of Western baroque-type spaces (with their unavoidable hallucinatory pitfalls) for the very reason that it sacrifices "total" visualization in favor of more reliable modes of sensory apprehension. Metaphoric space in general would likewise spare us the barren illusoriness of the electronically mediated spaces of our own time by ensuring some link with conventional bodily sensations.

One cannot help but feel the opposition of Isozaki's two orders of space to be more rhetorical than localizable in a real sense. His passage, for example, from the space of darkness to the space of the modern city is ambiguous to say the least. By comparison we shall soon discover how, in the case of Shinohara, his so-called non-Japanese spaces produced during the period of the Second Style become increasingly Japanese, if judged by his own earlier criteria. Almost the same can be said of Isozaki's theoretical transition from traditional "darkness" to contemporary "illusion" spaces. If the space of darkness—because of, yet also in spite of, a certain quotient of "non-visibility"—admirably resists fragmentation by modern communications processes, Japanese cities, owing possibly to their density, still afford a fair similar degree of resistance to comparable wear and tear. For, looked at slightly differently, the virtuality of shadows stresses an innate kinship with that space of the imagination toward which—as Isozaki correctly points out—the city undeniably tends. During the sixties Isozaki's thoughts on urbanism are, for better or worse, bathed in the same emphasis on cybernetics and cybernation that has accompanied all Tange's pronouncements on matters touching the city right down to the present day.

In his "City Invisible" essay of 1966,[30] Isozaki states the theme of the metropolis as a "combination of invisible systems" or a "nest of invisibilities." All the same, cities *are* physical entities, including the "postindustrial" agglomeration understood as the locus of Tange's "information-based society." In order to comprehend this Japanese vision of the city in general as a phenomenon of invisibility, it would be necessary to understand more about the nature and character of Edo, at the height of its prosperity in the eighteenth century, when it was the largest urban conglomerate anywhere on earth. And indeed, one or two important notions can be culled from the popular art and architecture of the Edo era expressing the way in which the imaginative space of Japanese cities was lived and thought.

NEW VALUES IN EVERYDAY THINGS

As contrasted with the high art of earlier periods—where religious expression and the life of the nobility afforded the main motifs and determined its principal forms—an art developed in Edo that comprised all aspects of town life, notably the vagaries of merchant-class culture which to some degree avoided sumptuary restrictions. Apart from language and literature—as well as customs, dress, and even food—this culture of the towns, and Edo in particular, found its expression in two predominant modes. These were the extension of the *sukiya* style in architecture and the invention of the Japanese print, an art destined to revolutionize European aesthetics in the latter half of the nineteenth century. Setting themselves beyond the range of conventions developed by aristocratic and religious art during the preceding centuries, *sukiya* and *ukiyo-e* evolved a certain type of metalinguistic commentary outside the boundaries of officially sanctioned Edo-period art. For its part, the Edo-period print took as its subject eating and drinking, grooming and sex, musical accomplishment, dance, the passage of the seasons, and the life of the professional stage. It merged all aspects of the fashionable "floating world" of the theater and entertainment districts of Edo with the whole subtle procedure of innuendo and also "metaphor." Something has been said about the *sukiya* style of architecture in the previous chapter, but its essence, as an outward growth of the culture of tea, lay principally in the discovery of new values in everyday things.

This process, called *mitate* in Japanese, also found an application in the art of the print, one predating the prints of the "floating world." However, the term refers principally to any transposition of thematic materials, whether grammatical or rhetorical. These were, namely, elements of plot structure or particular scenes, constituting tableaux, drawn from well-known works of literature, mythical narratives, or the classical drama. This borrowing and recasting of artistic materials among different media—one of the hallmarks of Japanese art—is apt to occur as a kind of quotation and with little apparent premeditation—frequently in a much more literal fashion than might be permissible in Western art. In such instances, which may recall the abrupt musical interpolations in modern Indian films, allegory might seem uncomfortably close to parody. Certainly, however, Shakespeare and Milton afford examples of a similar process at work in English literature, as do the Elizabethan or Jacobean periods in architecture vis-à-vis the Italian Renaissance. In ceramic art, on the other hand, where *mitate* figures so prominently in terms of the utensils or vessels for the Japanese tea ceremony, I can think of no parallel Western notion that manages to escape parody or *Kitsch*.

The freedom which metaphor and figural language in general have enjoyed in Japanese art throughout much of its historical development received little expression in architecture, until an open rebellion was undertaken with the elaboration of *sukiya*. If we consider the history of Western architecture, the same is true up until the neoclassical revival now dignified by the term "Renaissance." Or rather, the play of metaphor was surely present, as in the transposition of the Greek orders from wood into stone, but we have no very reliable means of evaluating the process.

By comparison, Buddhist architecture, as imported to Japan from the mainland, was endowed with a system of readings and interpretative schema that were essentially predetermined.

Though in the long run—and particularly as seen from an archaeological point of view—even canonic examples now appear ambiguous and difficult to interpret, early Buddhist buildings were nonetheless highly diagrammatic. It is easy to see, therefore, why architecture was not considered as entering into the system of the arts in either China or Japan, if that be the appropriate terminology. Extremely characteristic, on the other hand, was the closeness between poetry and painting, upon which the transposition of metaphor from one medium to another throve. Moreover, the majority of the tropes employed reveal at least a distant scriptural basis. This served to produce—as in our Metaphysical poets—chains of imagery intimately linked with the panorama of daily sights and other sensory phenomena. The overall effect is a tranquil yet mildly bewildering stream of metaphor from the world of familiar, everyday surroundings in nature and the domestic environment. The rhetorical thrust of this perpetual discourse aims heavenward, but not necessarily in any otherworldly sense—that is, until the time of Edo, which riveted it toward earthly goods and urban sensations.

For Isozaki, the pregnant darkness-space of a Japanese vernacular tradition more ancient than Buddhism operated as a stimulus—through the agency of Tanizaki's essay—toward a gathering-up of notions regarding textual interweavings and polysemy. Later on, certain works by Isozaki were actually based on this conceit of darkness itself. On the whole, however, he sifts the inheritance of the city and its brilliance as categorically as Shinohara had, by contrast, at first confined his interests to folk dwellings and Japanese traditional religious architecture. Above all, it is metaphoricity itself which drew Isozaki beyond "rationalistic" modern architecture to attempt something more. Thus, well before the recent revival of neoclassicism—or at least contemporaneously with the early works of Venturi—he had laid foundations for an architecture to be based on linguistic principle. At the same time, he was Japanese enough to have conceived his vision of "The Future City" in terms of the traditional *mitate-e*, or image based on thematic transposition, or in this case *reversal* (see fig. 9.4). To this elevation of "metaphor" to the status of a principle—which we must now discuss—were added in good measure phenomenological concerns, derived as we have seen from both Modern Movement and Japanese sources. Over all this, Isozaki applied as garnishment his own preference for high-tech and "soft-tech" symbols, a reminder of Tanizaki's shiny implements of modern daily life.

10 | The Present: Between *MAniera* and *Sachlichkeit*

F. L. WRIGHT AND THE UNGRASPABLE TAO

We have touched in the briefest of terms on the distinctive tradition of textual interweavings—consisting, in fact, of metaphoricity itself—which binds the world to the spiritual in Japanese art. It was perhaps this legacy that Frank Lloyd Wright had in mind when he refuted the direct influence of Japanese architecture in his own work and yet openly acknowledged the importance of oriental textiles, painting, ceramics, and folding screens for his architectural vision. Although Wright's buildings are frequently so close to nature as to establish a continuum with it, his work nevertheless adheres with conviction to the hierarchical notion of architecture as encompassing the "lesser" arts and ennobling them in the process. Wright's strategies, then, have little to do with a primal metaphor, such as the darkness plumbed by Junichiro Tanizaki in his famous essay. Nor, I believe, does Wright's architecture ever accede to the "non-spatial" mode of representation (as opposed to containment) practiced by Eastern art. Still and all, like the bulk of Wright's own work, *sukiya*-style building is best within a rural, or make-believe rural, setting. By comparison, the Japanese townsman's dwelling of the feudal period (fig. 10.1)—which had *sukiya* roots—helped define the "invisible" parameters of style in the Tokugawa city but seems a relatively matter-of-fact affair. It does, however, effectively stifle the perception of space *qua* space. On the other hand, a building like Frank Lloyd Wright's Robie House (fig. 10.2) in Chicago (belonging in part to this same town *sukiya* tradition) must be read—in a thoroughly Western context—as a kind of apotheosis. In short, the Robie House, and likewise Unity Temple in Oak Park, are generally retained as milestones of metaphorization along the (boundlessly) open road of the Modern Movement's progress toward a diffuse, self-perpetuating "textuality." The fact can scarcely be overemphasized that this "shift" in principles and corresponding means of expression took place *under the influence of Japanism*. It is understandable, however, that high modernist works of around 1900 in the West differed inevitably and profoundly from a "postmodern" return to Japanese sources —in Japan—more than half a century afterward. At the same time, Japanese tradition could almost certainly never have been taken up again and radically re-formed on its home ground without benefit of the early works of Frank Lloyd Wright and the late style of Le Corbusier.

Spelled out in this way, the identity of Japanese modern architecture takes on the appearance of an upwardly circling spiral: or a series of rising bids in market shares of a spatiality *more open to question than had previously been suspected*. But in more concrete terms, Wright, to my mind, best achieves something relevant to the aims of Japanese architectural space when his building is placed, as was the Robie House, in the midst of an urban, or semiurban, setting but responds by total enclosure at eye level. Such was truer of the Robie House when the garage's enclosing wall still remained (as shown), but the phenomenon may be observed, even today, in the interior of the sanctuary of Unity Temple. Indeed, both designs date to the period when Wright had come under the influence of Okakura's *Book of Tea* (1906).

A later and far grander instance of this type of noncontaining spatial enclosure is the great central administrative space of the Johnson Wax Company at Racine, Wisconsin (fig. 10.3). But in this connection Arata Isozaki has written of "the creation of [*hard* and] *solid space*, textured stone and brick, that could by no means be identified as 'Oriental'"[1] with reference to Wright's astounding work at Racine. The essay in which Isozaki's observation appears is introduced by a quotation from Wright's 1952 American Institute of Architects address,[2] in which Wright himself quotes Lao-tzu as cited by Okakura in the *Book of Tea*. The relevant passage deals with the "metaphor of the Vacuum," and Okakura's paraphrase of the sage philosopher reads as follows: "He claimed that only in vacuum lay the truly essential. The reality of a room, for instance, was to be found in the vacant space enclosed by the roof and walls, not in the roof and walls themselves."[3]

The special interest of Isozaki's commentary lies in his assertion of Wright's misconstrual—indeed reversal—of Lao-tzu's text. Thus: "Wright, however, did not understand this metaphor, but went about making space his object, trying physically to come to grips with it.... [He] seems to have consciously freed empty space from the bonds of metaphor and reinterpreted it, making it a realizable end in itself."[4] Finally, enlarging upon this point of interpretation, Isozaki goes on to say, "As Okakura knew, the space of the tea room, insofar as it manifests vacuity, is part of the revolving universe and is thus in constant motion." He adds that the entire building is transient and "may disappear" (*or* be moved to another place, as frequently happens). Thus, "the tea room is characterized by complete astructurality, which forces [us to recognize in it a sense] of reality and insubstantiality simultaneously."[5] Nevertheless, in his destruction of the box, Wright, according to Isozaki, "did not move toward space that concretely embodied the concept of the vacuum as it ap-

10.1. Japanese town dwelling from Morse's *Japanese Homes and Their Surroundings* (1886).

10.2. Wright: Robie House, Chicago, 1909. Garage wall in original condition.

10.3. Wright: S. C. Johnson Co. Administration Building, Racine, Wisconsin, 1936-39. Main hall.

pears in the tea room, as one might have expected him to do."[6] Instead, his work showed Wright preoccupied with bringing forth modern architecture out of the quagmire of early twentieth-century eclecticism, and his internalization of Lao-tzu's "fundamental principle" constituted an essential "reworking" of it. Proceeding in this manner, Wright achieved "the unprejudiced incorporation of the legacy of every civilization, of Whitman and Lao-tzu, of Aztec and Momoyama Japanese."[7] As such, the quality of the Johnson Wax building, but also that of Wright's architecture in general, became at last an embodiment of "space to which no civilization can lay claim."[8]

SEVEN OPERATIONS OF MANNER (*SIGNED* ISOZAKI)

What Isozaki takes to be "freeing empty space from the bonds of metaphor" on Wright's part can also be seen as a kind of free-floating metaphoricity, as in Isozaki's "space to which no civilization can lay claim" just cited. No matter: it amounted to praise in the highest terms. Yet, by the time his essay went to press in 1970, Isozaki—despite his unbounded admiration for Wright—had become ever more committed to developing *specific* metaphors. Isozaki reminds one of the pre-Socratic philosophers, whom Nietzsche described as having "the courage of their own metaphors," identifying every aspect of reality with one of the four elements: air, earth, water, and fire. Indeed, Isozaki's obsession with metaphor in architecture provides much of the content for his frequently explicated—but still, it seems, widely misread—concept of "manner." This has been interpreted, again and again, in a loose sense as the mere pursuit of a kind of post-Renaissance, "mannerist" individualism. Yet Isozaki has been meticulous in specifying that what he refers to as *maniera* is actually quite *anonymous* in its application. Most importantly, it was a device he invented specifically to deal with that discontinui-

ty between space/architecture and the invisible realms of electronic engineering, as discussed in the previous chapter. For, in a way resembling the Surrealists' proverbial encounter between sewing machine and umbrella on a dissecting table, this confrontation was—for Isozaki—the major event that led up to the present disintegrative crisis in the field of architectural design.

Playing, I imagine, on the same "destruction of the box" metaphor used by Wright to describe his own plight at the start of the century, Isozaki announced the "destruction of architecture" to be his aim. Previously—and until the advent of the seventies—he had pursued two paths to avoid the crushing dilemma which to numerous architects seemed now to be encouraging theories and techniques of fragmentation, thereby threatening the traditional unity of architecture. One of these escape routes had been "megastructural," whereby individual architectural objects were expanded into vast composite structures wistfully believed to connote "urbanistic" scale (see figs. 9.2–4). The other path Isozaki refers to as "vernacularism," a technique in accordance with which "bits of local color or alien vocabulary were introduced in building designs."[9] This afforded, incidentally, an update on Le Corbusier and, indeed, parallels the general evolution of "machine" metaphors in the course of the Modern Movement.

"Manner" was to involve more complex strategies and was conceived of as a means of enabling spaces to generate their own meanings. It was originally envisioned as consisting of seven different operations or methods.[10] And, in confirmation of the phenomenological dimension already alluded to, Isozaki states that "the common point among them is my attempt to locate their physically unreal and phenomenal conclusions."[11] He also mentions that architectural design had recently been "analyzed" from the standpoint of their own "methods" by the likes of Kahn, Venturi, Moore, and Stirling as well as "a number of younger architects."[12] In fact,

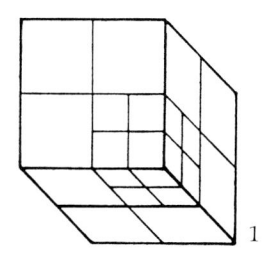

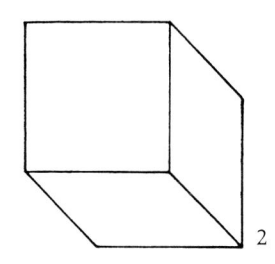

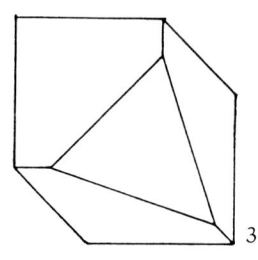

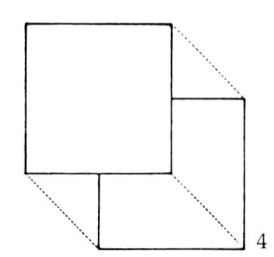

10.4. Isozaki: the Seven Operations of Manner. 1) Amplification, 2) packaging, 3) severing, 4) transferral, 5) projection, 6) *fuseki*, 7) response.

it is Venturi and Moore, with the addition of Cedric Price, Christopher Alexander, Hans Hollein, and members of the Archigram, Archizoom, and Superstudio groups who will provide materials for the critical essays eventually published in Isozaki's monograph *The Destruction of Architecture* (1975).[13] Finally, this manner, or "method," of Isozaki's is, for all its impersonality of execution, "a reflection of personal ideas and not something that will become a universal standard." Moreover—perhaps recalling the early example of Wright, which, I believe, Isozaki always kept in mind— he concludes: "It is something that the individual does not discover; he must invent it."[14]

Briefly, then, what are the operations of Isozaki's manner? Each one is "conceptual" or "phenomenal," but most of them can be represented in terms of a simple procedure of some sort or other. The list (fig. 10.4) comprises amplification; packaging; severing; transferral; projection; *fuseki*, or "chess men"; and response.

Amplification goes back at least as far as Alberti's *Della pittura* (1436), the treatise dedicated to, among others, Brunelleschi. However, Isozaki's version did not imply projection of a finite, Renaissance-type perspective into which all representable objects had to fit, but instead hypothesized an infinite grid in three dimensions, according to the formula 1:1:1. While not necessarily rejecting classical harmony and proportions, its major and characteristic virtue was that of sheer continuity. The grid was thus capable of ensuring production of perfectly "neutral" and lucid spaces, which, according to Isozaki, engendered a sensation of suspension or weightlessness.

Packaging was, by contrast, conceived of as an outright rejection of the Modern Movement's insistence on spatial homogeneity (i.e., the ideal of continuity between a building's interior and exterior). Nevertheless, it may be said that such homogeneity had never been a prime requisite of Japanese buildings even during the thirties when the International Style was in full flower. Through so-called packaging, discontinuity and shadow made an appearance once more in architecture, and spaces became differentiable in terms of texture and meaning. In Isozaki's phrase, a "multifarious spatiality" was aimed for—to replace transparency.

Severing, Isozaki discovered, was a technique that operated in terms of both time and space. Temporal severance somehow forced the architect to confront his own architectural language (past as well as future), though the actual means are never specified. Spatially, severing implied a break in development and extension of any of the various material infrastructures which are a part of modern buildings. Thus, various ducts and beams, which would normally remain hidden, are thrust into visibility, although the process can be either real or symbolic, as in the Oita Prefectural Library (see fig. 9.8).

Transferral relates to the selection process which human beings anywhere in the modern world must exercise with respect to image transmission. Electronically transmitted pictures, for example, are characterized by extreme diffusion of meaning in accordance with the famous phrase "the medium is the message." Through so-called transferral, the image in question can either be made to fit into your hand or blown up to the scale of an entire building. Further "control" can be exercised by manipulating the type of ground against which the image is relayed or projected.

Projection entails the production of virtual images, usually (though not always) in an ordered series. A warping or unbalancing effect takes over, as in an exploded diagram; thus the whole need no longer take precedence over the parts in the controlled, Renaissance fashion. A form of spatial unease or displacement asserts itself (see fig. 9.14). This may be reified by graphics or surface treatment of materials.

The word *fuseki* came from an old text on gardening and involves the concept of "interval" (*ma*). The latter term will shortly become for Isozaki a kind of shorthand notation for an entire constellation of themes related to so-called Japanese space/time. *Fuseki* originally referred to placement of stepping-stones in a Japanese garden, though its present-day use is restricted to deployment of pieces in the game of go. Isozaki emphasizes the practical nature of advice from later gardening manuals, though it often masqueraded in the guise of theory. Formally, intuition rather than rules was stressed. But, in theory, what had started out as careful syntactical placement of objects (such as big slabs of stone or boulders) in a given environment was, in practice, simply and quickly codified. Interestingly, Isozaki points out that what begins in a flash of intuition ends presently in "production of a new rhetoric" replete with ability to generate its own new metaphors. The latter afford a basis for further encodings, and so on, in an endlessly continuing process.

CHESSBOARDS AND MANDALAS

The seventh and final aspect of "manner" Isozaki chose to call *response*, and here he refers once again to information-transmission processes. Architecture, he surmised, must sooner or later merge with these, becoming part of the continuous generation of information of all sorts. Thus architecture is bound, eventually, to acquire a performative aspect. The visual and tactile density of conventional "architectural" materials, as well as the static forms now employed by architects to signify the "modern" machine aesthetic, will be deprived of their meaning by the pulsation of information-relay systems.

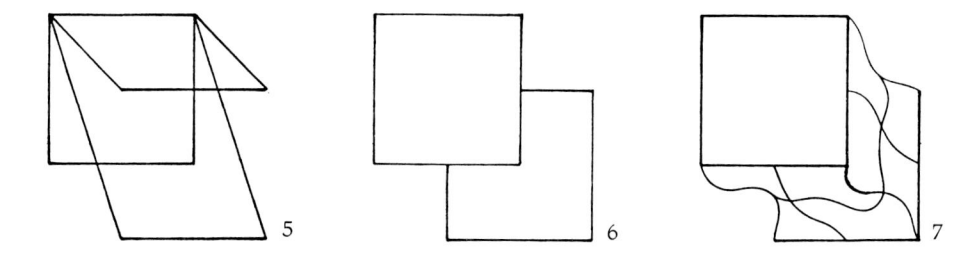

The point Isozaki seems to be making in this seventh category—but also throughout his enumeration of *manner*, that is, method—goes back at least as far as the distinction drawn by Lessing between the *nebeneinander* of spatial representation and the *nacheinander* of speech sounds. During the late eighteenth century, the former category of signs were considered "natural," while the latter, as made use of in poetry, for example, were "arbitrary." For Lessing the realm of the visual arts was reducible to so-called pure Euclidean space or "space as seen." Poetry, on the other hand, was obliged to find a means of elevating its own arbitrary signs to the dignity and force of "natural" ones, the standard being that language of ideal and visible perfection embodied in the media of painting and sculpture. For Isozaki, whose entire theory of architecture has moved toward a metaphor of invisibilty, an inverse difficulty arises.

But just as it was incumbent upon the Enlightenment to attempt a unified conception of the arts, so Isozaki, too, will be driven to pursue a unity of aesthetic representation. The passage of a few more years will see the conflict resolved, at least partially, by a rehabilitation of the traditional concept of "interval," or *ma*. And, in fact, the idea has already been touched upon in the designation of *fuseki* among the operational procedures that constitute *manner*. Using the code name of "chess men"[15] for the *fuseki* operation—his terminology possibly an extrapolation from *go*—allows Isozaki to put forward the interesting example of a spatial model in which grammatical and rhetorical elements interact in a graphic simplification of the profoundly more complex and uninvestigated intermeshing found in the behavior of natural languages. In turn, the example furnished by the chessboard permits the theorist—which by now Isozaki had become to a greater extent than perhaps any contemporary—to recap the argument for "manner" in terms of the mandala. This is defined in the following manner: "In esoteric Buddhism, various ritual articles are placed on an altar in a form prescribed by religious custom and based on mandala representations of the Buddhist cosmos"[16] (fig. 10.5). The relationship with the chessboard is apt and self-evident, although historically the mandala is no more a Japanese attribute than the game of chess is a European one.

The mandala and its mystical-hierarchical world view afford, incidentally, an immediate link for a certain type of Japanese intellectual with the neo-Platonic world of Renaissance high culture, and this association, notably, allows the Isozakian concept of *maniera* to return full circle. Yet, interpreted in this way alone, "manner" appears as little more than an interesting footnote to the style Charles Jencks has had the wit to christen "postmodern classicism." While there is indeed an aspect of this kind of popularizing neoclassicism in Isozaki's works of the eighties, we remain in the present discussion in the early seventies. Thus, Isozaki's treatment of chessboards and mandalas still referred essentially to the enthusiastic turn during those years in favor of semiotics, and his concern for this sort of theory formed part of a vanguard ushering the movement into Japan. But to return to the mandala and Isozaki's use of it, the commentary on *fuseki* says: "The placement of these symbols [in a mandalalike disposition] results in what might be called a high-level syntax."[17] This is true enough, to be sure, and it follows that "from isolated words, one moves to sentences, and then to the larger matter of literary style." Therefore, we find ourselves back once more on the terrain of metaphor, where "the coexistence of differing, even opposed, things produces a distinctive rhetoric." At last, the point is reached at which "the placement of code elements, or of physical things treated as code elements, can result in an allegorical spatial expression." And, in architecture, such code elements, or signs, "must be designed to generate the kind of allegory found in the Buddhist mandala arrangement of esoteric religious implements."[18]

By way of mandalas, a problematic transition from grammatical syntax to rhetoric is achieved and, thence, more easily and naturally to allegory—no mean achievement in a single short paragraph. But exhibit number one constitutes this "high level," or elevated, syntax, which is so much more easily transformable into the rhetorical domain than anything one can hope to pinpoint in linguistic examples. As it happens in Japan, as well as in China, mandalas were never the isolated, ritually constructed objects that they had once been in India. Instead, they were simply drawn or painted, so Isozaki refers to the next best thing—an altar configuration—rather than to the pictorial form, usually mounted on a hanging scroll and without three-dimensional presence. Yet, whatever its form, the mandala is still intended as a world, or cos-

10.5. Altar arrangement based on the mandala: inner precinct, Kanshinji, Osaka, late fourteenth century. Mandala of the Diamond World is visible at left.

mic, image in the broadest sense. As such, it is symbolic of the disintegration of the individual consciousness and its reintegration in an enlightened state of absolute existence. Even *fuseki* in garden art and, decidedly, the rustic *chashitsu* tend toward a like end.

"HARD" AND "SOFT" AND THE FORMALIST LITERARY DEVICE

Like Wright's turn-of-the-century protomodern synthesis—though, as pointed out, arguably different in its spatial character—the *chashitsu*, or room for drinking ceremonial tea, was a new and radical invention of spatial means. There can be no doubt that Isozaki was on a related track, like both Aldo van Eyck in his Amsterdam Children's Home and the European "baroque"—the latter nearly contemporary with the *chashitsu* itself. Isozaki, too, intended his inventions to

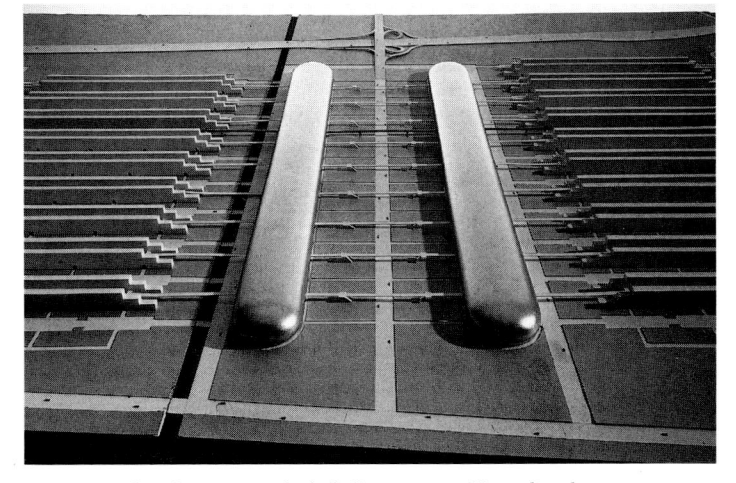

10.6. Isozaki: Computer-Aided City, 1971. Unrealized project.

be "operative" spatial creations and not merely "contemplative" ones. To be sure, the Modern Movement, in general, had made similar assumptions, but these depended, for the most part, on a naive mentalist theory of perception. Nevertheless, some Cubist ideas, the early Purist "experiments" that retained an influence in the later work of Le Corbusier, and aspects of the Bauhaus might be taken as exceptions. The essential difference here was that Isozaki, from the sixties onward, was thinking in terms of new soft technologies. So his ideal—in spite of using "hard" means, such as concrete—was that of a "soft" architecture. This was particularly clear from the essays on the city and on darkness, as well as in the concept of *response*, last among the seven operations of "manner." Indeed, for a number of (at that time) younger architects, the quasifunctional condition of media-responsiveness seemed to promise use of new "soft"-type materials, such as pneumatic or inflatable structures. These were not, to say the least, encouraged by the stringency of Japanese building codes. Whatever the reasons, this "soft architecture" dreamed of by Isozaki and others—illustrated, for instance, by a vast Computer-Aided City project (fig. 10.6) he designed in 1971—failed to materialize. In a slightly different direction, which might be characterized as "hot" rather than "soft and cool"—while remaining "operative"—the "Electric Labyrinth" at the Milan Triennale of 1968 went some way in demonstrating the promise of this ideal.

Overall, Isozaki's grip on his theoretical manipulation of Manner was a firm one, and perhaps owing to the material and spiritual disillusionments of the sixties, the "hard" masterpieces he produced in the seventies are among the most significant and fascinating of all Japanese modern buildings. Following on from the seven categories of manner/method, Isozaki pursued his thoughts on "rhetoric," of which these buildings of the seventies are the fruit. Shortly after the publication of *The Destruction of Architecture* collection of essays in 1975, an article entitled "From Manner, to Rhetoric, to . . ."[19] updated these notions. Isozaki asserts that the concept of architecture needs to be dismantled, destroyed, and/or dissolved, because a consensus as to what is *meant* by "architecture" no longer exists. Nowadays, architecture—as a mere *semantic* vehicle, that is, a form or series of forms capable of transmitting content—demands to be remade, in the image of early twentieth-century Russian "formalist" literary techniques. Henceforth, architecture must become "a machine for the production of meaning."[20]

What should first be remarked here is that Isozaki's easy willingness to assume the possible separation of form from content, or message, has its roots in the history of Japan's first hundred years as a modern nation. The experience of Meiji-period culture, as detailed in the two initial chapters of the present work, explains why this is so. Furthermore, the history of European cultural absorption in Russia suggests why Formalism provided Japan with an attractive and convenient model for demolishing this same notion of separation, once its usefulness had ended and Westernization of Japanese culture attained.

Victor Shklovsky's own belief was that "art does not change little by little. New phenomena accumulate without being perceived, later they are perceived in a revolutionary way."[21] There are parallels between Isozaki's doctrine of Manner and Shklovsky's celebrated essay of 1917 "Art as Technique." In particular, the manner/method discourse places a new emphasis on the notion of a métier, or craft, comprising a range of techniques, or operations, that are specific to it. Whether or not such an idea ought to be considered "new" vis-à-vis, for instance, architecture of the Renaissance or the Modern Movement—as Isozaki somewhat naively implies—is not of great moment. Like Formalism, Manner is not a critique of historical works of art but of contemporary critical attitudes. Architecture is meant to be understood as, above all, *about architecture*, just as, for Shklovsky's circle, literature had to be remade in terms of techniques specific to the "art" of writing, precisely those which involved manipulation of language itself.

The "destruction of architecture" advocated by Isozaki corresponds, at one level, to destabilization of traditional patterns of rhetorical discourse, as aimed at by Formalist theory. At another, each of the operations listed in the mannerist arsenal contributes toward the eventual condition of "defamiliarization" (*ostraneniye*, literally "making strange"). This, according to Shklovsky, allows art to extricate everyday objects from a dangerous "habitualization" or "automatism of perception." Thus, once the International Style had peaked, technology and the machine began to recede as the "subject matter" of architectural discourse, and a confusion of images proliferated. So for Isozaki—as for Shklovsky before him—it no longer behooved the artist to create *new* images but, instead, to manipulate those that already existed in art, as well as all the others that occur in day-to-day life.

SEMIOTICS AND NEO-FORMALISM

Isozaki's injunction against production of "fresh" symbols, or imagery, and his decision to concentrate on such as were already at hand, so to say, could well be interpreted as a critique of Metabolism. For the goal of the Metabolists had been to draw a new code of signs out of the hat by mixing equal parts technology and traditional religious philosophy. Yet, in reality, the bulk of defamiliarizations effected by such Metabolist monuments as eventually got built, like the Shizuoka Press and Broadcasting Center (see fig. 7.22) and, less intentionally, the Tokyo Metropolitan Expressway (see fig. 7.24), were obtained by a single device—deformation of scale. While this type of operation was, to be sure, one possibility of Manner, Isozaki's chief present concern as a neo-Formalist lay in responding to the question "how is an architect to include in a design the image that he holds as a concept?"[22] By 1972, the up-to-date reply was: "If I use semiotics as a hint in explaining my meaning, . . . I [also] use linguistic theories as models. I have been interested in this field personally since the early 1960s. . . . In the seventies, I began attempting to reorganize designs on the basis of a semiotic viewpoint."[23]

Within Manner, the categories of amplification, projection, transferral, and response were felt by Isozaki to exhibit an automatic quality of behavioral performance that related them to grammatical or syntactical procedures. By contrast, the operations embodied in *fuseki*, as well as in packaging and severing, Isozaki saw as various "interventional formulae," more or less subject to the architect's conscious control. They assumed, therefore, for him, the color of rhetorical strategies. In this way, from an earlier theoretical ideal of pure, autonomous "process," Isozaki began to move toward carving out a place for his highly personalized yet seemingly archetypal metaphors. This led to his elaborating a theory of "rhetorical *maniera*," which included abstract images as diverse as catastrophe, ruin, darkness, Marilyn Monroe, mechanical eros, twilight, blue sky, and deep sea. Isozaki's interest in linguistics broadened out from the relatively restricted viewpoint of semiotics in the direction of general semantics, including such popular new-wave notions as the supplementary of textual readings and the deconstructivist idea of full textual autonomy.

Historically, the Formalist movement necessarily had about it an air of expert survivalism, a spirit of improvisation militating at its forefront. Thus one of the principal devices of a writer like Shklovsky was writing in the persona of a bewildered intellectual, the tone of his prose shifting frequently from irony to lyricism and back to irony. This forces a kind of gay and brave despair on the subject of important events of the time made thus to appear beyond the control of any individual. Similarly, the majority of Isozaki's writing also falls into these rhythms, the background he alludes to being—instead of war and revolution—the happenings of 1968 and the crumbling of the Modern Movement's hold over contemporary architecture.

This kind of dramatized autobiographical pessimism about architectural matters is relatively unfamiliar to the American or English reader, although it is more commonly found as an element in European architectural criticism. In Japan, the genre stems from an additional source, which is that tradition of pseudo-autobiographical fiction dating from the Meiji period known as the "I-novel." The cry of the anguished intellectual was thus an accepted rhetorical device. But, more significantly, the position Isozaki assumed is one of the earliest instances anywhere of regarding the Modern Movement more or less consistently as in a state of disorderly retreat.

Yet the whimsy and paradox of Shklovsky's partially fictionalized memoirs comes across, not just in Isozaki's extensive writing, but also in the buildings themselves. We have seen how from the mid-1950s Le Corbusier was already making use of new commissions as an opportunity to generate meanings destined, perhaps even calculated, to subvert the prior logic of his own oeuvre. It was such procedures that, in retrospect, seem to have opened up the vast area of figural praxis that has since assumed the vexed label of "postmodernism." In Japan, meanwhile, the dialectics of exoticism and assimilation were left behind for good by the late sixties, and the highly charged atmosphere of the decade seemed to invite a metafigural climate. While in the Japan Style and Metabolism, too, rhetorical and grammatical elements had demonstrated a degree of mutual interference, the works of Kazuo Shinohara and Arata Isozaki were henceforward to present virtual allegories of incompatibility. In a newly conscious and committed sense, they became metafigural "machines" (the word will be common to both, though it seems originally to have been used by Isozaki), summoning up inherited rhetorical complexities that predate modernism but also extend beyond it.

TWO INCOMPARABLES: POINTS IN COMMON

Till the late 1960s Isozaki had experimented with a theme of "metaphoricality" derived, as he himself explained, from the example of "darkness" initially explored by Tanizaki. In the latter's essay, this quality was taken up empirically as thematic material, toyed with and ironized, then finally developed as a mode of figuration. Subsequently darkness was reproposed by Isozaki as an allegory of seeing (or of its opposite: not seeing).

Shinohara, on the other hand, was preoccupied with his own notion of "abstraction," allowing him, as we have seen, to rediscover the existence of a particular "Japanese" space. Like the "space of darkness" for Isozaki, this commodity may also be interpreted as an allegory of conceptualization, in the sense that a Japanese was still indisposed (i.e., unmotivated) to regard "space" in the Western way familiar to modern architecture. But to state the essential equivalence of Shinohara's and Isozaki's theories of vision (or nonvision) is not necessarily to set their architectural works at an identical level. In fact, among Japanese critics and connoisseurs, such a comparison would have been received as heretical and indecorous. Nevertheless, both architects sought somehow to furnish an answer, or answers, to the difficult question of the identity of Japanese architecture as it had evolved through a filter of Western modernism.

Isozaki, in his bank branches of the late sixties and early seventies (see figs. 9.13–14 and 10.8–11), as well as in his 1972 extension of the Oita Medical Hall, may be thought of as working in tandem with Shinohara, whose "Second Style"—originating in new possibilities of architectural language achieved in the House in White (1966)—was inaugurated with the Incomplete House (see figs. 10.32–33) of 1970. For both architects, these years afforded a breakthrough into a thoroughgoing metafigural or allegorical style that characterizes the mature work of each. At the same time, this change of direction was influential in determining the rhetorical base which underlay the work of a generation of still younger architects, whose point of reference was the year 1968. For, in the period immediately afterward, a number of new offices were set up whose activity has given currency to the notion of a "new wave" of Japanese architecture. On the whole this would not mislead, except that work by Isozaki—as well as the distinguished former Metabolist, Fumihiko Maki—were both included in an exhibition in New York organized under this title.[24] Shinohara, on the other hand, reluctant to be seen as a member of any movement or group, kept aloof. This paid off in a one-man show held a few years later under the auspices of the same institution.[25]

In Japan, where brokerage and patronage are facts of artistic life—as in New York, hub of the world art market—the slogan "new wave" has a generally attractive ring. However, the story of Japanese modern architecture possesses a degree of internal specificity in terms of which "opposites" such as Shinohara and Isozaki can be reconciled only at the risk of a certain loss in referential complexity. Nevertheless, we have seen earlier, in Shinohara's House of Earth of 1966 (see fig. 8.29), a sort of compulsive human physiognomy referring to depths of motivation and, perhaps, endurance. Similarly, the twisted, dispersed, and rising spaces delineated by Isozaki in Fukuoka Mutual's Oita Branch (see fig. 9.14) just one year later might be thought of as recalling certain visions from Piranesi's *Carceri d'Invenzione*. Those great etched plates themselves were an outgrowth of the eighteenth-century Venetian notion of architectural sketches made *al capriccio*—that is, unsubjected to the prevailing rules of art. Equally influential in the formation of Piranesi were the inventions of baroque theater: for example, stage designs, such as those of the Bibiena family, based on the device that came to be known as *scena d'angolo*.[26] When Isozaki speaks of his bank in Oita as an example of "control and violation" (with reference to the way in which its parts relate to the whole), an image of Piranesi's terrifyingly vivid prison scenes registers even more forcefully. In the same connection, it may be appropriate to recall that—during the year in which the bank at Oita was begun—Isozaki had been asked to design sets for a filmed version, by Hiroshi Teshigahara, of Kobo Abe's novel *The Face of Another*. As it happens, these were dissimilar to the approach used at Oita, amounting instead to a potentially surrealistic exaggeration of actual Japanese upper-class bad taste. However, what is more significant is the atmosphere that comes across in the novel itself—a commentary on identity loss and the dehumanizing of social relationships. If only the Oita Branch bank had been completed, it would have provided a superb abstract background for Abe's disturbing work!

Color was deployed in a strongly emotive way in the Oita Branch interiors, just as Shinohara had done in the House of Earth. In 1966, Isozaki introduced these in an exhibition of sculpture, whose title "Space and Color,"[27] supplies a clue to the nature of his special chromatic effects. The tones chosen for the bank were exotic, highly keyed variations of the primary colors favored by Le Corbusier. But it may be added that Isozaki uses these hues "deconstructively," to highlight the already disorienting spatial machinations of this lively transitional building situated in the heart of his hometown.

A DIFFERENT TIME AND PLACE

While James Stirling and Piranesi, an Englishman and an Italian, must have been of equal importance in the genesis of Isozaki's scheme for the branch office of Fukuoka Mutual at Oita, American precedent can also be supposed. As just one example of this, several elements—not only from Oita but also soon to appear in Shinohara's forthcoming Second Style—may be spotted in contemporary designs by Charles Moore in California. Among the best-liked and influential of such works by MLTW was the so-called Sea Ranch Condominium of 1965 on the windswept Pacific Coast north of San Francisco. It is also one of the Moore firm's dourest works, especially if viewed out of context and without its furnished interiors. In fact, it would just be possible to imagine a character from one of Kobo Abe's novels taking refuge there, even though in scarcely any of Moore's other buildings is such a fit conceivable. Other homes by him are, for the most part, gay, airy, and jovial, in spite of the fragmentation of viewpoint and detailing which form an inevitable aspect of his work. Above all, such works were intended to provide Moore's clients with a sense of physical and moral comfort, as the American architect was at pains to emphasize in his forthright and sensitive treatise *The Place of Houses* (1974). Such are precisely those conditions and values from which Abe's existentially oriented heroes flee. Superficially like-minded individuals who inhabit the books of, say, Saul Bellow and Philip Roth may rejoice in starkly comical vernacular attributes of character in a way that Moore, as well as Robert Venturi, permit themselves to do in their architecture. Moreover, to be American in this sense is to approach the vernacularism of an "architecture without architects," while at the same time contriving to show the flag. By a comparable analogy: even though a Japanese lunchbox of the sort consisting of a flat rectangular bed of cold steamed rice with a red pickled plum at its center is referred to as "old glory," Japanese architects and novelists have not—until very recently—been similarly motivated. By contrast, ordinary life in Japan is full of such little ironies, which it is the work of numerous popular cartoonists to expose to public view.

On the whole, then, a Japanese Charles Moore or Robert Venturi would be redundant—even trite—as a few younger architects succeeded in demonstrating by the close of the period under discussion. In the 1960s and throughout most of the seventies, Japanese architecture was either sublime or not at all. Meanwhile product design was seen as an unrelated field, except for a few Italian or Italian-inspired objects. These products alone, along with the earlier postwar wave of Scandinavian enthusiasms, were accepted into a realm of high art. In fact, a principal objection with which the Japan Style can be confronted is that it failed to mediate between this ethereal world and the widespread and burgeoning domain of popular and commercial art.

All in all, from the beginning of Isozaki's career he felt assured in modeling himself after the image of the Renaissance artist as unique, self-formed, and complete. Yet, because of their Japaneseness, even his important public buildings, which we must turn to now, have little to do with that conception of classical unity inherited by the Western architectural tradition. Wright, even in his modernism, had demonstrated faith in this archetypal artist's role as well as the notion of compositional unity. By contrast, the mastery exhibited in Isozaki's works that were inspired by his concept of metaphorical *maniera* is *kaleidoscopic*—as suggested by the great ocular window of stained glass (fig. 10.7) situated in the museum wing of his Municipal Library at Kitakyushu of 1975.

Japanese art up to the modern period is noted for its characteristic ability to fashion astonishing variety out of a restrictive, almost scholastic range of imagery. The window in question actually owes its inspiration to a series of metaphysical diagrams which represent various transformations of matter and spirit devised by the philosopher Baien Miura (1723–89), who lived during the Tokugawa period. Yet, for all the stereotypes and systems—or possibly even because of their self-sufficiency—there is nonetheless a remote possibility that, in the words of a character from an early Abe novel, "maybe there does not exist a Japan at all."[28]

This surmise—despite its overwhelming unlikelihood—contains a threat that is represented on occasion as an option to the modern intellectual. Abe's perennial spokesmen of the Japanese predicament are endowed with an exceptional power to view their own behavior from without, as if torn by force from themselves. That is usually the result of some radical metamorphosis, whether an actual physical change, as in *The Face of Another*, or a total contextual shift, as in *The Woman of the Dunes*, inducing a certain degree of mental duress. In short, in serious modern literary works of this sort—as in architecture—we are confronted with a fable or allegory, although the setting remains palpably real. Char-

BETWEEN *MANIERA* AND *SACHLICHKEIT* 247

10.7. Isozaki, with Baien Miura: diagram of stained-glass window (right) based on Miura's "Gengo" philosophy, for Municipal Library, Kitakyushu, Fukuoka Prefecture, 1973–75.

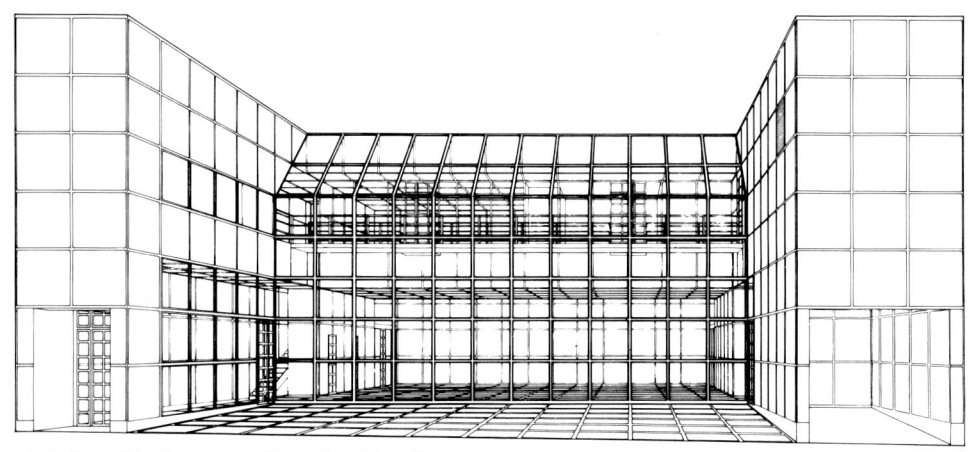

10.8. Isozaki: Nagasumi Branch, Fukuoka Mutual Bank, Fukuoka, Fukuoka Prefecture, 1971. Schematic rendering of main facade.

acters, while pulled this way and that, rarely suffer the disgrace of caricature.

Thus outside, and from the viewpoint of characters other than the protagonist, an illusion of calm-surfaced reality is resourcefully held to at all costs. Japanese "space," whether in literature or in architecture, is a *sine qua non* of everyday reality, be it for the intellectual or the average person. Something analogous happens in American literature—and also in the cinema—but is usually not thought of in connection with building or architecture. Or was not before the theories of Robert Venturi. For there still remains the complication of high art, which is either damned—by the likes of Wright and Sullivan—or looked up to as a metropolitan style by Venturi or Charles Moore in spite of professions to the contrary. It is true that Chinese art once held this position in Japan, but that was a great while ago. Its most important legacy is the Japanese writing system employing Chinese (literally, *Han*) characters. But dialogue with the mainland tradition is today no longer a recognized theme for art, although, as such, it did not die out completely until the present century. Thus, it is probably the disappearance of this cultural dichotomy which has discouraged the establishment in present-day Japan of a pop architecture as advocated by Venturi, Moore, and others in America. As we have seen, difficulties of a comparable sort vexed not only Wright in his attempts to vernacularize the Imperial Hotel, but also the would-be perpetrators of the Imperial Crown style.

The point, in stressing cultural norms and restrictions, is not to emphasize any particular indebtedness on the part of an architect like Isozaki to a novelist like Abe, even if it is known that, as a writer, Isozaki admired and in fact began by imitating Abe's literary style. I should like merely to suggest that over the years Isozaki, as an intellectual, may have reacted along lines that a self-conscious Abe protagonist would have been bound to pursue had he been subjected to comparable stimuli as an artist. Needless to add, Abe himself has never invented such a hero, even in a novel.

MANIERA AND THE CUBE

If Isozaki's earliest works in Kyushu may be called "post-Metabolist" (he being the only architect for whom that potentially descriptive label has any likelihood of validity), the concept of manner/method and the glide toward metaphorical *maniera* show to what extent this relationship was, in reality, little more than circumstantial. It was, as far as can be known, young Isozaki following up Kikutake's initial flight of inspiration who endowed Metabolism with a stable imagery. Meanwhile, the notion of *maniera* he evolved has little to do with the "bad" old art-historical interpretation of so-called Mannerism (as a term for sixteenth-century European art), implying tension and intellectual crisis.[29] On the contrary, Isozaki's adoption of the word is tolerably close to actual Renaissance usage. This, as John Shearman reminds us, "may in all cases be translated into the English word *style.*"[30] Derived from French courtly literature, the term was, in Italy, transferred to the visual arts and retained its meaning of "savoir-faire, effortless accomplishment and sophistication."[31] Metabolism, as is self-evident, was based on quite different premises than a display of "style" for its own sake. Namely, its explicit references to technology and society precluded this sort of performance.

A dual, even three-way, confusion arises, however, due to Isozaki's species of floating metaphor—which ultimately emerges as "metaphorical *maniera*"—and the technological tenor of much of his imagery as well as the social commentary in a work such as the "Electric Labyrinth" of 1968. Thus, too, his notion of the "destruction of architecture" blends all too misleadingly with the latter-day critical endowment of historical "Mannerism" with "virtues peculiar to our time, especially . . . aggression, anxiety and instability."[32] Finally, Isozaki's emulation of Russian Formalist techniques, whose origins are prerevolutionary but whose images are so frequently bound up with revolutionary themes, both before and after 1918, does little to dispel the air of apocalyptic stoicism that informs a proposal like the "Future City" drawing (see fig. 9.4).

Isozaki's work of the seventies, however, thrusts elsewhere, and in it the suspended allegory which haunts Metabolism as well as (at a more pointedly critical level) the fables of Abe became suddenly less apparent. In the buildings of that period, taken as a whole, "effortless accomplishment" and "sophistication" do seem overwhelmingly to prevail. Their mood is *meta*figural, with the emphasis set securely on the prefix, and, among them, the Gumma Prefectural Museum (see fig. 10.14) is probably the most important large modern building in Japan—in the sense that its size precludes any suspicion of its being merely a "folly" or somehow an architectural joke. Stylistically, in terms of manner/method, the immediate predecessors of Isozaki's museum are the Nagasumi and Ropponmatsu branches (see figs. 10.8–11) of the Fukuoka Mutual, both 1971. Although fairly small, each is based on a grid system in facade and/or actual construction, and the

10.9. Isozaki: Nagasumi Branch, Fukuoka Mutual Bank, Fukuoka, Fukuoka Prefecture, 1971. Interior.

"method" used is that of amplification. As has already been mentioned, the conclusive break with Metabolist-type aims and ambiance occurs between these two smaller works and the Fukuoka Mutual Head Office (see fig. 9.11), finished in the same year but begun back in 1968.

In the bank's headquarters, Isozaki was faced with his largest commission to date and one that consisted mainly of potentially undifferentiated office space distributed over eleven stories and two basements of a steel-frame-and-reinforced-concrete structure. Here was a brief which, mentally, he connected with "the task of condensing architecture [into] an oppressive visual simplicity that is always linked with commercial production."[33] It was this "universal space"—which he considered characteristic of Modern Architecture—that he rejected in the design for Hakata (Fukuoka) in favor of what he referred to as an "aggregation of fragments." More specifically, the method he sought was one that "refuses to infer the whole from the parts."[34] The result was a design where "each detail is constantly violating the control system."[35] However, these violations were less a matter of the shape of interior spaces or the pathway denoted by joining a succession of such spaces—as had been the case at Oita—than the imposition of screens and other sculptural forms faced with contrasting materials, such as marble and stainless steel. In fact, in a large building based on a rational structure where connection of spaces was effected on the whole by elevator, Isozaki was in reality deprived of more exciting solutions.

In the miniature branches completed at the end of 1971 in the Nagasumi and Ropponmatsu districts of Fukuoka City, he was dealing, in each instance, with a total of just above 500 square meters distributed over two floors. Each bank consisted of a simple, unencumbered steel-frame structure. At Nagasumi (figs. 10.8–9), vinyl-chloride-covered thermo-

250 BETWEEN *MANIERA* AND *SACHLICHKEIT*

10.10. Isozaki: Ropponmatsu Branch, Fukuoka Mutual Bank, Fukuoka, Fukuoka Prefecture, 1971. Facade detail.

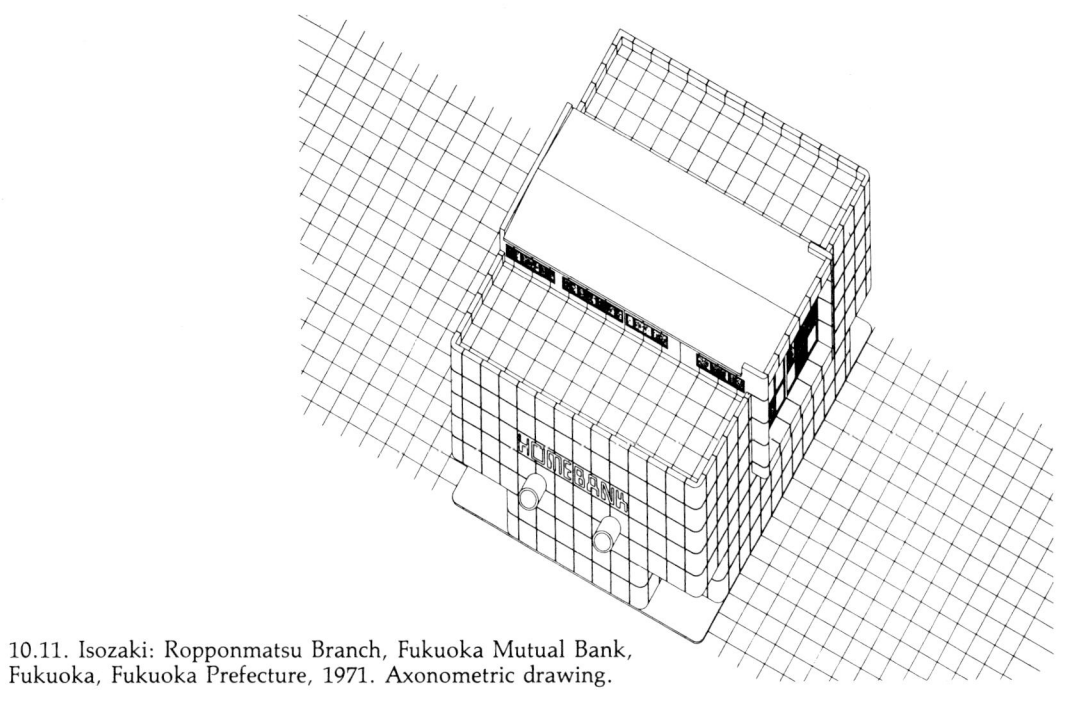

10.11. Isozaki: Ropponmatsu Branch, Fukuoka Mutual Bank, Fukuoka, Fukuoka Prefecture, 1971. Axonometric drawing.

10.12. Wagner: Post Office Savings Bank, Vienna, 1904-6. Main hall.

panels and a good deal of glass were used, while at Ropponmatsu (figs. 10.10–11) there were no windows and the building was wrapped in a shiny aluminum facing. In both buildings a consistent grid was articulated within and without, as well as on the ceiling, and at Nagasumi the grid also extended to floor surfaces. In both buildings, Isozaki's approach was based upon his method of "amplification," yet the effects he achieved were substantially different owing to a varied treatment of details. At Ropponmatsu, the aluminum paneling produced a more ethereal effect than the revetment of asbestos sandwich panels at Nagasumi. On the other hand, the "possibility of infinite expansion" of the equilateral grid was violated at Ropponmatsu by rounding off the corners of the building to create a finite, boxlike enclosure. At Nagasumi, maximum transparency encouraged a feeling of expansiveness and there was refusal of any strong visual focus. This helped generate what Isozaki refers to as the "twilight atmosphere" and sense of weightlessness characteristic of a grid. The building was laid out in accordance with the formula of a *corps de logis* flanked by two forward-projecting wings. To "violate" the strong volumetric effect this would normally have produced and, at the same time, to "control" the sense of independent expansiveness assumed by the grid, the cornice line of the central section was "severed," or sliced off, at an angle of forty-five degrees. Neither of these buildings has weathered particularly well, while the surface-emphasizing qualities of both anticipate a quantity of later structures to such an extent that it is perhaps, now, difficult to appreciate their remarkably novel effect. Moreover, the degree of this illusionism—particularly at Nagasumi—was disproportionate to the relatively restrained methods and cheap materials employed by the architect.

In 1974 the depth of illusion had increased when the Gumma Prefectural Museum of Modern Art (see fig. 10.14) stood finished at Takasaki, the prefectural seat. Begun the year the Nagasumi and Ropponmatsu branch banks were completed, the museum combined, so to speak, the qualities of each, adding as well other properties and devices of the manner/method system. Its scale, however, was sixteen times greater than either of the two small banks. The recent origins of the grid scheme employed by Isozaki at Gumma lay in the post-1968 work of the new Florentine architects' collaborative Superstudio, who had come together in 1966 and whose works formed one chapter in Isozaki's *Destruction of Architecture*. Self-confessedly, elements of irony, provocation, paradox, and mysticism suffused their work,[36] while almost from the beginning there had been an avowed attempt to operate on the scale of the natural and man-made landscape, thus freeing architecture from the production of mere isolated objects or buildings. Cubes were already familiar from the turn of the century in the works of the Viennese architect and theorist Adolf Loos and in the celebrated hall of Otto Wagner's Post Office Savings Bank in Vienna (fig. 10.12; 1904–6). But the "continuous" grid as landscape device appears initially in the first Superstudio "catalogue" of 1966–68, entitled "A Journey through the Regions of Reason."

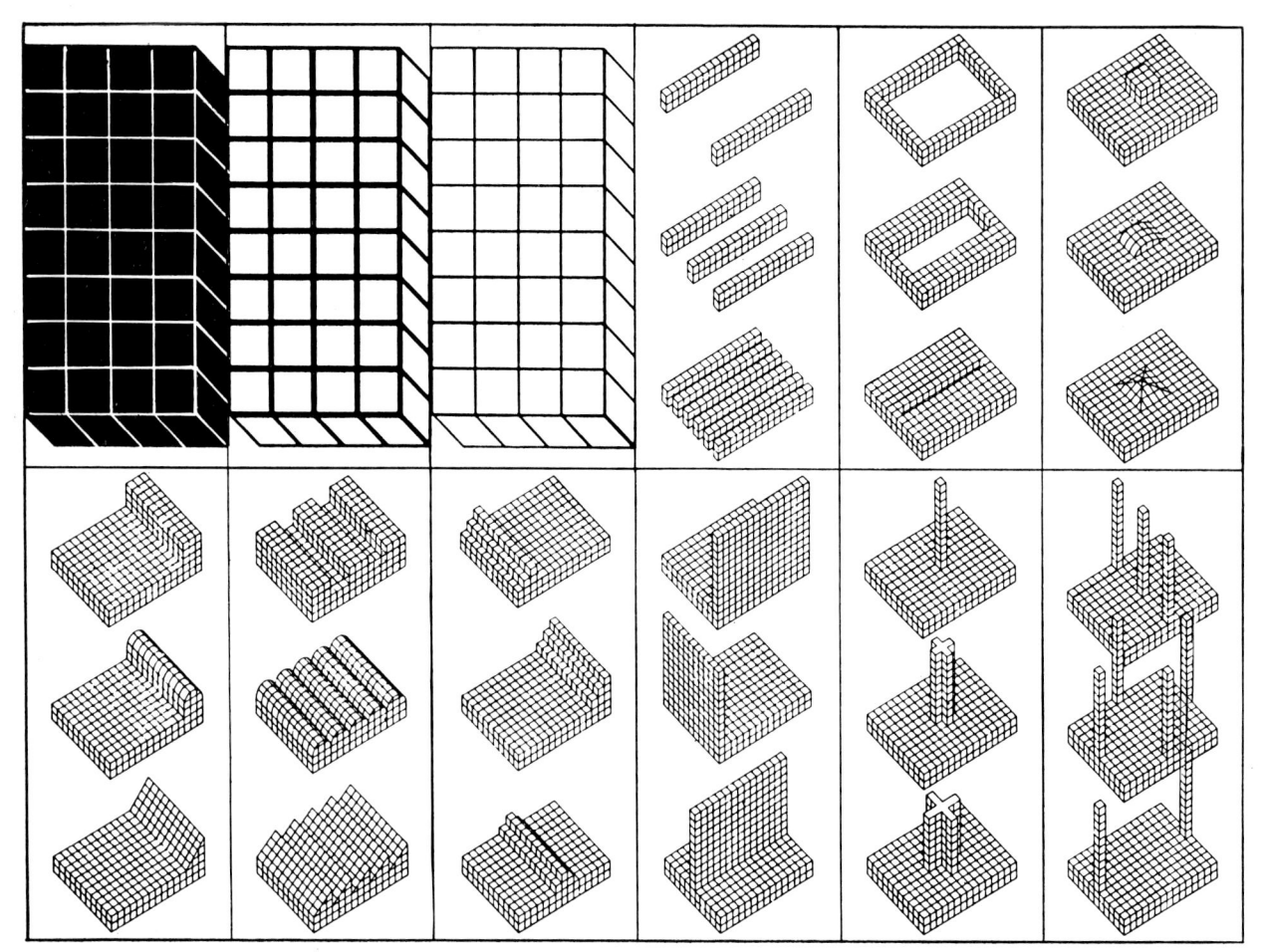

10.13. Superstudio: "Architectural Histograms," 1969.

By publication of the second "catalogue" of plates entitled "Architectural Histograms" (fig. 10.13) in 1969, a more or less pragmatic system of transpositions and metamorphoses had been devised by Superstudio for the cubical grid and its applications. As an ironical tongue-in-cheek search for semantically neutral forms, these schemes were supposed to indicate the futility of continuing to provide furniture and domestic objects that were essentially market-oriented commodities. At the same time, those "histograms" could equally well be referred to casually by their creators, in a Loosian key, as "Tombs for Architects."[37] Yet as early as 1971—the year of Nagasumi and Ropponmatsu—the series of tables and benches known as "Misura" (an embodiment of the 1969 graphics) was in production by Zanotta. Surfaces were elaborated as a three-centimeter grid, giving each individual piece of furniture the illusion of having simply been lifted out of a continuum. In the architectural domain, a "Catalogue of Villas," produced in 1968-70, provides the veritable prototypes for Isozaki's two branch banks at Fukuoka. It must be said, however, that the banks reproduced the intentions of Superstudio far more successfully than the small residence-cum-factory at Pistoia[38] erected by Superstudio itself that same year.

Thus, Superstudio had rendered Japanese architecture the service of developing the axonometric grid as a method of ironical self-inquiry into an increasingly fragmented and commercialized modernism. In his important essay called "The Metaphor of the Cube,"[39] Isozaki also refers to the book by Bruno Munari entitled *The Discovery of the Square* as a font of reference for all sorts of works of art—classical, Renaissance, and modern—that use square or cubical forms. In addition, he calls attention to the works of the American sculptor Sol Lewitt, among which may be mentioned "Untitled Modular," "Three Cube (Straight)," and "Cube by Cube," produced between 1968 and 1969.

The Gumma Prefectural Museum of Modern Art (figs. 10.14-15)—surrounded, untypically for Japan, by an open expanse of lawn—had originated in an arrangement of sculptural elements, similar to Lewitt's, enlarged to the scale of architecture. A principal range of empty cubical frames was laid down and a pair of cubes set at right angles to contain the foyer on the right-hand side. This was balanced by a further pair of matching cubes on the left, which, in the building as built, hovers over a square reflecting pool.

With a building conceived of in this way as a gigantic work of art, it is difficult—if not beside the point—to query its effectiveness as a museum; in any case, there can be no doubt that at present Isozaki's building—as art—outvalues the prefectural art collection housed in it. The museum brief no doubt implied, if it did not actually state, the local government's desire for a monument, especially since the budget issued from funds designated for construction of a regional cultural center. In Japan the "museum" as building type goes back to the Meiji government's decision, evoked at the beginning of this book, consciously to Westernize society. At the prefectural level, where agrobusiness and light industry have come to the economic forefront only since the end of World War II, there is still a good deal of infrastructural upgrading to be accomplished. The museum as a conspicuous monumental commodity remains consequently an even more important architectural category than in the West; and, incidentally, in a country where works of art are subject to an assets tax, considerable stimulus is also given to construction of private museums. A strongly formalist approach, such as the one advocated by Isozaki, enables the architect to hedge his or her bets. It permits the designer to bracket, and, hence,

10.14. Isozaki: Gumma Prefectural Museum of Modern Art, Takasaki, 1971–74. Facade.

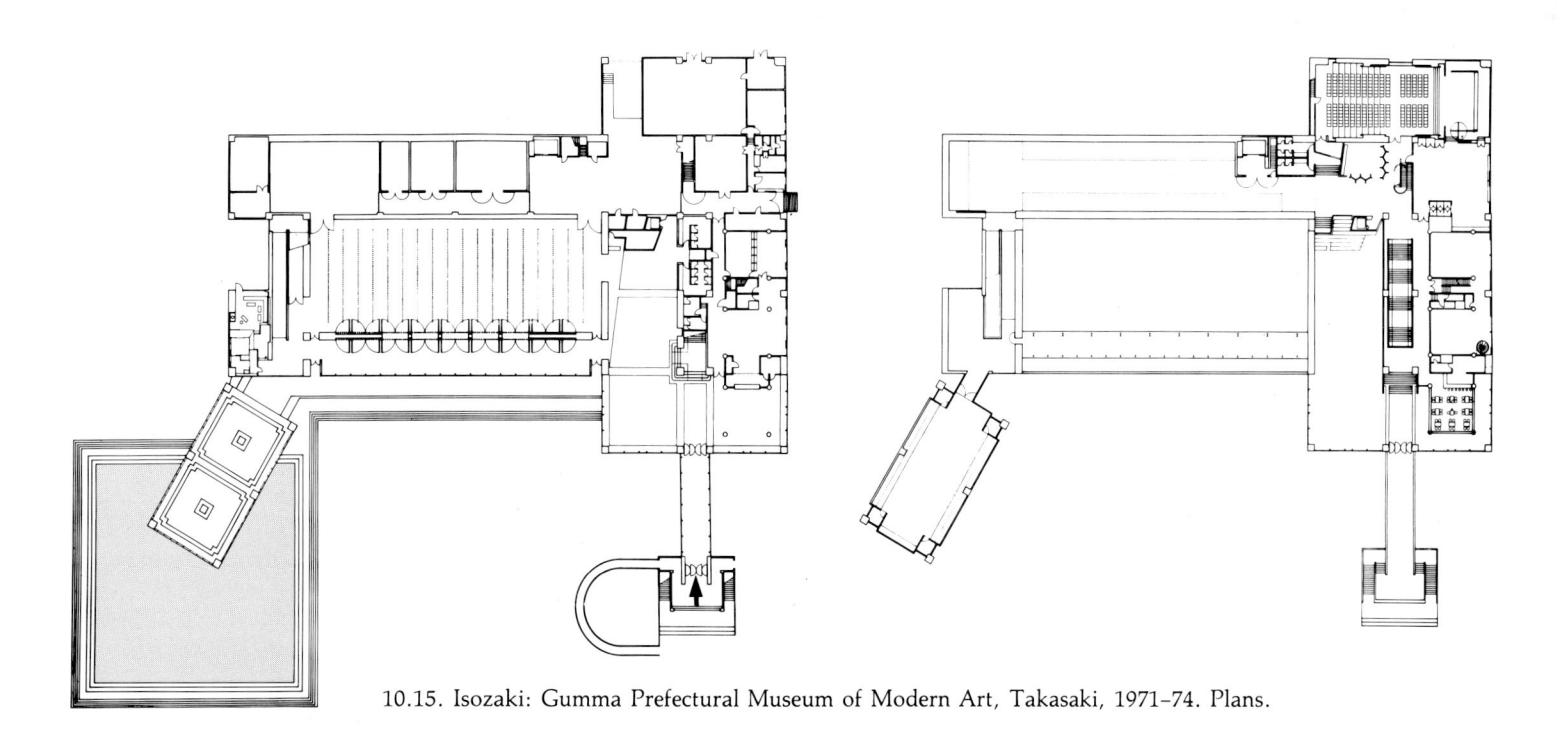

10.15. Isozaki: Gumma Prefectural Museum of Modern Art, Takasaki, 1971–74. Plans.

OKOSHI-EZU (paper model of the Teigyokuken tea-house).

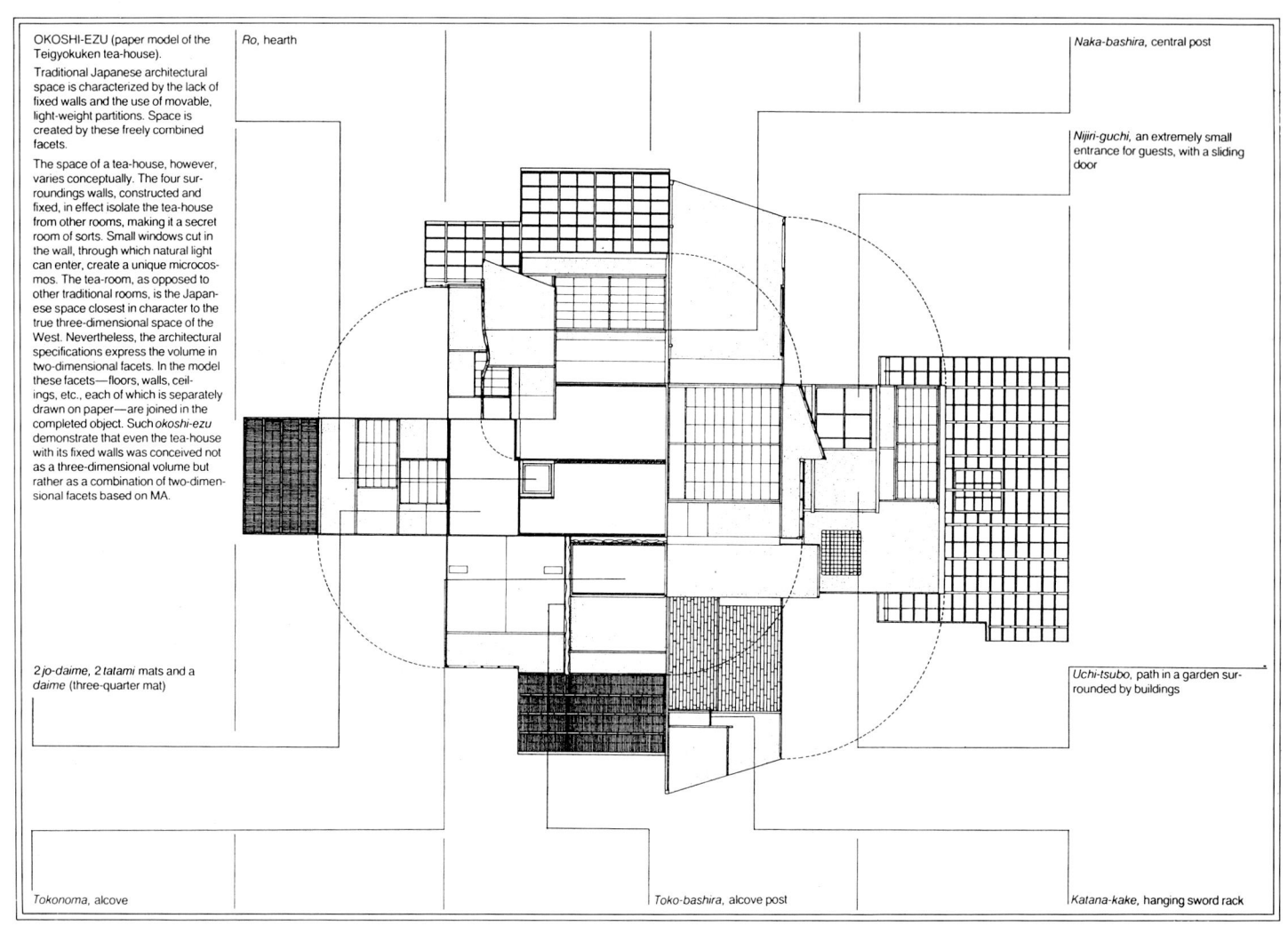

Traditional Japanese architectural space is characterized by the lack of fixed walls and the use of movable, light-weight partitions. Space is created by these freely combined facets.

The space of a tea-house, however, varies conceptually. The four surroundings walls, constructed and fixed, in effect isolate the tea-house from other rooms, making it a secret room of sorts. Small windows cut in the wall, through which natural light can enter, create a unique microcosmos. The tea-room, as opposed to other traditional rooms, is the Japanese space closest in character to the true three-dimensional space of the West. Nevertheless, the architectural specifications express the volume in two-dimensional facets. In the model these facets—floors, walls, ceilings, etc., each of which is separately drawn on paper—are joined in the completed object. Such *okoshi-ezu* demonstrate that even the tea-house with its fixed walls was conceived not as a three-dimensional volume but rather as a combination of two-dimensional facets based on MA.

Ro, hearth

Naka-bashira, central post

Nijiri-guchi, an extremely small entrance for guests, with a sliding door

2 *jo-daime*, 2 *tatami* mats and a *daime* (three-quarter mat)

Uchi-tsubo, path in a garden surrounded by buildings

Tokonoma, alcove

Toko-bashira, alcove post

Katana-kake, hanging sword rack

10.16. Paper model (*okoshi-ezu*) of Teigyokuken teahouse, Shinju-an, Daitokuji, Kyoto (mid-17th century). From *MA: Space-Time in Japan*, catalogue of the exhibition, 1978.

suspend judgment on, questions of referential meaning. Yet the Gumma Prefectural Museum of Modern Art—so far as its design participates in Isozaki's notion of the dissolution (or the destruction) of architecture—also begs to be interpreted as an allegory of issues such as these.

For the rest, Isozaki's infatuation with cubical forms was, he records,[40] a product of the tension he had felt for some time between traditional Japanese and Western techniques of generating architectural containers. In accordance with the *tateokoshi-ezu* (or *okoshi-ezu*) system of model construction, once used by builders in the *sukiya* style, "all of the surfaces of a space are analyzed as if they were floor plans."[41] This technique involves a type of exploded drawing or paper model (fig. 10.16). The floor plan of a given interior afforded a base upon which to construct the wall elevations perpendicularly in a horizontal plane. The walls were then either raised mentally into place or made to stand up, by means of a fold, after cutting away part of the paper. Although the elevational proportions were fully adjusted to meet the requirements of the eye—and post-and-beam construction elements cut to specification prior to assembly—there was "no attempt to deal with the objectification of space, which is a fundamental issue."[42] In fact, the actual space of the room was transformed by this procedure into something merely "left over" in the process of attending to the structural and wall elements of the design.

By contrast, the cube contains and *represents* its own automatically self-determining unit of spatial content, since each of its dimensions is identical and cannot be changed without destroying the proportionally satisfying configuration of the whole. Under the influence of instances ranging from the Renaissance through Le Corbusier to Superstudio, Isozaki determined to accept the objective spatiality guaranteed by the reductive formula of the cube, as embodied in the ratio 1:1:1. But at the same time he would emphasize the form itself as a space-frame by treating it in the *tateokoshi-ezu* manner of post-and-beam construction and repeating this device throughout the museum.

As a formal exercise, Isozaki's entire attention was taken up by the arrangement of his giant cubes, twelve meters on a side, and the adaptation of this configuration to the needs of an earthquake-proof reinforced-concrete frame. This *jeu* entailed the notion of a "gap" between real and ideal structures, and the main theme of the museum became a sort of entasis concentrated on blocking out, or compensating for, perceptions of real structural load and flow throughout the fabric of the building. Thus, conditions of a nonreferential, artificial language were re-created, reminiscent of those that formularized Greek or Roman classicism. In this sense, Isozaki succeeds in "reducing" his building—not to the "metaphor of the cube"—but to that of *language*, through a transposition of ideal cubic structures.

Though visible at certain junctures and, notably, on the interior, for instance in the walls and piers of the vast lobby (fig. 10.17), the greater part of the reinforced-concrete framework of the museum is encased by square aluminum panels. The panel joints constitute a secondary grid, with further complementary rhythms produced in the fenestration as

10.17. Isozaki: Gumma Prefectural Museum of Modern Art, Takasaki, 1971-74. Lobby.

well as by the tiling of the podium that supports the building. Contrastingly, the projecting entrance—which, incidentally, appears to be a quotation and amplification of a similar form devised by Le Corbusier for the Ueno museum—as well as the attic, which is made up of gigantic cubical forms in silhouette, are both of unfaced concrete. The variety and juxtapositions of these surfaces lend a complexity and interest to the grid—breathing life into it—as opposed to the mere exegetic quality of Superstudio's paper architecture. Overall, amplification, packaging, and *fuseki* predominate in the museum, with the last method particularly clear in the adjustment of the two-cube wing on the left, projecting at an angle of 22.5 degrees out of the line of the major axis. Finally, creation of a portico beneath this wing and its reflection in the pool below is a reworking of a neoclassical device that has, according to Isozaki, the effect of making the entire structure "seem to rise" and "saves the building from the inflexibility of total symmetry."[43] If it be true that the Gumma museum strikes, on the whole, an exaggeratedly scenographic note, it should be pointed out that an element of theatricality may be inherent in the very notion of the grid as a controlling device—just as it was in Renaissance perspective.

The square-gridded windows and the extensive veined-marble surfaces of the lobby impart a heightening of awareness that looks back to the architecture of Adolf Loos as well as a metafigural tonality unequaled, perhaps, in Isozaki's other works to date. Another modern master whom the Gumma museum seems to evoke is the Finnish architect Alvar Aalto. His Viipuri Library of 1933-35, which since 1947 has stood in the Soviet Union, possesses two features that invite comparison with Isozaki's building. Notable at once is the window-wall which illuminates stairs leading from the foyer of the library to the administrative offices. In a more general sense, this work by Aalto, which, for some time, has been unavailable for scrutiny, seems to anticipate Isozaki's notion of "packaging." Namely, the interior and exterior of the building exhibit a measure of discontinuity that, according to Isozaki, serves to contradict the spirit of International Style design and promotes the dismantling of a too-insistent functionalism.

Thus, and not leastwise, in the work of one of the greats of modern design, architecture was compelled by an inner logic based on formal considerations to modulate, if not altogether reject, the transparent expression of functional and social demands. Going even further back, the initial project for Viipuri (now Vyborg) had been influenced by Gunnar Asplund's great masterpiece in the neoclassical style, the Stockholm Public Library of 1920-28. In the scheme as built, this earlier library consists of a massive cube surmounted by a vast cylindrical drum in the manner of so-called romantic classicism of the late eighteenth century in France. More than Aalto's work, it almost certainly provides the model for Isozaki's monumental stairway. In addition, Asplund's fenestration, including the massive two-story glass portal surrounded by a veined-marble Egyptian molding, is entirely based on a square grid pattern. Aalto's building, which belongs recognizably to the International Style, retains the notion of monumental stairs and expands the grid into a window-wall. The library at Viipuri, however, also makes good use of acoustics, as well as new heating and ventilation techniques. It may be that the inclusion of such "soft" systems technology served to free Aalto from the compulsion—displayed all too frequently in works by contemporaries—to portray inaccessible technology in terms of an abstract symbolic language.

At Gumma, Isozaki brought the Scandinavian path from neoclassicism to modernism full circle by dialectically reinstating a fresh form of "classical" notation. Yet possibly the most interesting confirmation that Isozaki had been looking at these works by Asplund and Aalto is the existence, in an earlier phase of the Asplund project, of a diminutive piazza, square in form, intended to project out over the rectangular pond fronting the Stockholm library to the right of the entrance. In the event, this charming loggialike feature, which seems more Persian or Mogul than neoclassical, was not built. Whether or not Isozaki could have known of its design at the time of Gumma is less important than the undeniable fact that he felt the need to reinvent a similar device in the wing of the museum to vary the stark insistence of its neo-Platonic forms.

RHETORIC OF THE CYLINDER

The Stockholm library by Asplund posits both of the important formal preoccupations of Isozaki's work of the seventies: one of these, the cube, has already been discussed at length; the other, the cylinder, will now be dealt with. Unlike the square, the circle plays little role in historical Japanese architecture. Thus, it is probable that the half-cylindrical vault reached Isozaki through the tradition of Sullivan and Wright, for instance, in the Auditorium Theater (1890) and the Auditorium Hotel's lobby and main dining room by Sullivan, or in Wright's Susan Dana House (1903; see fig. 10.24), the entrance of the Heurtley House erected the previous year, and the Wright children's own playroom at Oak Park (1895). Moreover, as early as 1971 an intimation of this motif in Isozaki's own work had appeared in the form of the Computer-Aided City project (see fig. 10.6), with its vast caterpillarlike, semisupported, and inflatable semicylindrical components. In this case, just as at Gumma, the tension between later, constructed examples and the ideal, nontectonic hypothesis of the Computer-Aided City units would create a "gap"—as essential to the "rhetoric of the cylinder"[44] as to the "metaphor of the cube."

Actual works completed in this mode of cylindrical rhetoric were the Yano House in suburban Tokyo of 1973–75 (see fig. 10.22), the Fujimi Country Club of 1973–74 at Oita in Kyushu (see figs. 10.18–19), and the Kitakyushu Municipal Library, at Kitakyushu, of 1973–75 (see figs. 10.20–21). Of these, the library at Kitakyushu—remarkable for its sitting and the ingenuity of its plan—is even larger than the Gumma museum, but it is probably the country club that in terms of "rhetorical *maniera*" ought to be considered the opposite number of the museum in terms of the ideal relationship of cylinder to cube.

In the Oita Medical Hall of 1959–60 (see fig. 9.7), Isozaki's earliest realized work, a squashed horizontal cylindrical form, or laterally squared oval-section cylinder, was raised into the air. But the *raison d'être* of this design remained the need to propound an urban significance for such a form, as, indeed, Metabolism would have proceeded to do. In the Computer-Aided City, on the other hand, the semicylindrical form was neutral, unarticulated, and self-referential, for it existed only as an "optimum balance between the weight of the membrane itself and interior pressure."[45] Therefore, technology itself finally expressed its own "form" in the Computer-Aided City rather than just providing the motivation for a vaguely related symbolic shape. Yet this capacity of a pneumatic structure to express outwardly its own force eludes definition, since it depends upon a source of kinetic energy that is quantifiable but invisible. The structural potential of the mile-long pods is realizable via the covering material—without, in a strict physical sense, being embodied in it. Still, apart from this translucent membrane, there need not be, in theory, any other material components specified in the design.

The Fujimi Country Club's field house and club building (figs. 10.18–19) plays on the Computer-Aided City form while transforming it materially and structurally by the imposition of a continuous barrel-vaulting of poured-on-site reinforced concrete. A similar image prevails in the larger and internally more complex Kitakyushu Municipal Library (figs. 10.20–21), but this time the design called for hinged sectional vaulting, whose prefabricated ribbed components were lifted into place like the segments of a bridge. In both cases, the surface of the concrete vaults was protected by copper sheeting, imparting a membranelike quality which recalls the imaginary lightness of the Computer-Aided City. It is thus quite an easy thing to feel the inherent self-modulating perfection of the original shape, "like drops of water resting on flat surfaces."[46] Yet other images are also suggested, such as a

10.18. Isozaki: Fujimi Country Club, Oita, Oita Prefecture, 1973–74. Bird's-eye view.

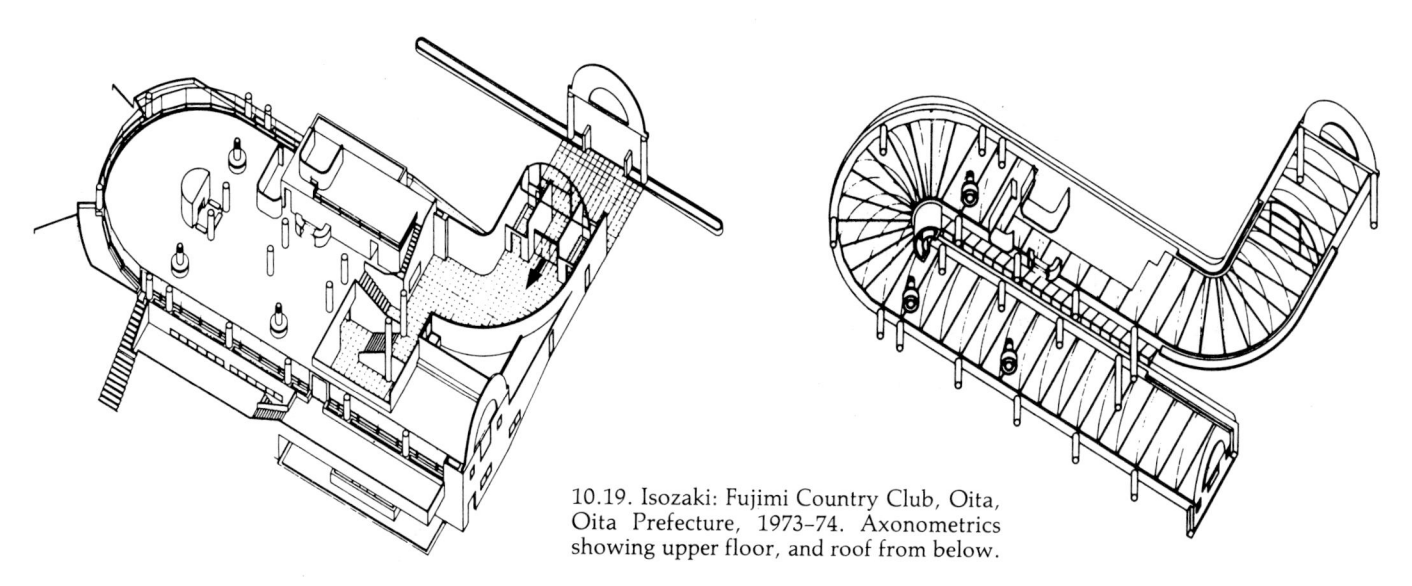

10.19. Isozaki: Fujimi Country Club, Oita, Oita Prefecture, 1973–74. Axonometrics showing upper floor, and roof from below.

giant whale or the observation car of the Twentieth Century Limited for the country club, or a "cave built above ground" in the case of Kitakyushu Library. Thus, no combination or permutation of discrete syntactical operations can be said to account fully for the production of meaning as such. Recourse to the notion of rhetoric enabled Isozaki to recognize the complex and individualistic nature of the chains of signifying elements at work in these buildings. What he could not do, of course, was specify the precise way in which a given space gave voice to a certain phenomenalized experiential content, which, to some extent, was the idealistic goal he had been pursuing in theory.

Another aspect of this complexity was that Fujimi Country Club, especially as regards its frontispiece, had matured

10.20. Isozaki: Municipal Library, Kitakyushu, Fukuoka Prefecture, 1973–75. Bird's-eye view.

BETWEEN *MANIERA* AND *SACHLICHKEIT* 259

10.21. Isozaki: Municipal Library, Kitakyushu, Fukuoka Prefecture, 1973–75. Interior.

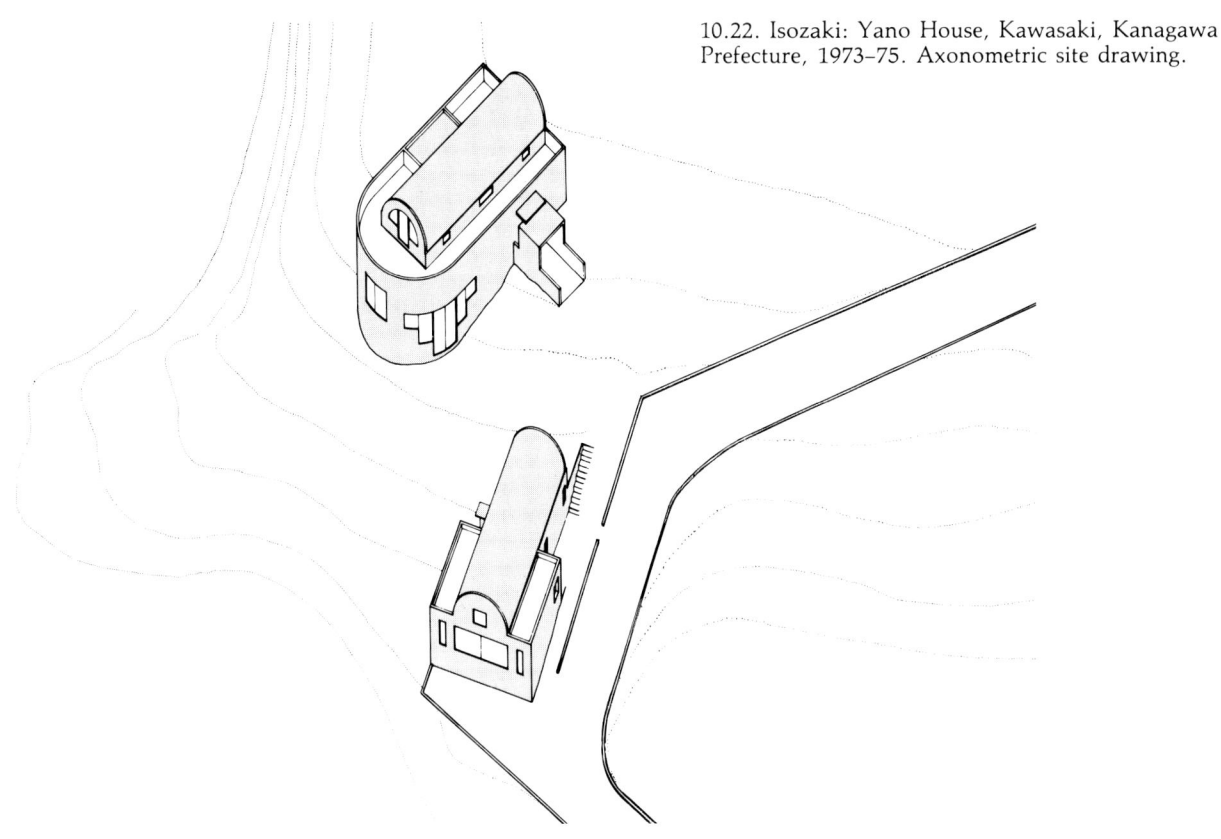

10.22. Isozaki: Yano House, Kawasaki, Kanagawa Prefecture, 1973–75. Axonometric site drawing.

10.23. Ledoux: *Maison des Directeurs de la Loue* from *L'Architecture considérée...* (initial volume, 1804).

under the sign of Palladio and the villa it is believed he designed at Poiana. Thus, similarly—if equally inexplicably—the severed vault section which appears in the lateral wall of the clubhouse recalls the rear facade of Palladio's "Malcontenta." In this way, quotation had leapt back from immediate precedent, such as Aalto and Wright; it had become suddenly daring, particularized, and historicizing, in harmony with the direction taken by Moore and Venturi in the United States. But with Isozaki, and especially in the country club, this seems to have occurred in a thoroughly spontaneous—even semiautonomous—manner, or so he recounts in the "Rhetoric of the Cylinder."[47]

In the Yano House (fig. 10.22), the process of adapting history was more consciously motivated. Employing the same copper-sheathed, semicylindrical vault as the country club, and completed only a little over a year later, this small house for a newspaper journalist was conceived—as is recognizable at once—under the influence of Claude-Nicolas Ledoux. French eighteenth-century "romantic-classicist," or "utopic-rationalist," Ledoux had been one of Isozaki's heroes since his postgraduate days in the 1950s.[48] Like both the library and the clubhouse, the Yano House benefits from very fortunate siting. However, the lentiform profile, originally derived from pneumatic curves, which obtains in the vaulting of the country club, is here abandoned. In its place a horseshoe-shaped wraparound wall of concrete masonry entirely encloses a small rigidly vaulted pavilion on the three sides facing away from the sloped site. Nevertheless, the metaphor—of gas or fluid under pressure—has not been let slip altogether. That is to say, in Ledoux's engraving for a *Maison des Directeurs de la Loue* (fig. 10.23), in the great album which Isozaki possesses, a sluicegate with water streaming from it has been indicated at the very center of the small building to symbolize the existence of the river Loue. This watergate is, of course, not an actual feature of the Yano House, as was, for example, the cascade in Wright's Fallingwater at Bear Run. Still, Isozaki's design and its source do combine to testify in general to the existence of a natural continuity of imagery that may, indeed, be the product of what he calls rhetorical *maniera*.

In his treatise *L'architecture considérée sous le rapport de l'art, des moeurs et de la législations*, Ledoux attempted to

10.24. Wright: Susan L. Dana House, Springfield, Illinois, 1903. Rendering of dining room.

revitalize the academic abstraction into which French classicism had fallen. He succeeded in reinvigorating the rhetoric of architecture, creating what later came to be known as an *architecture parlante*. In purpose, this may be compared with Isozaki's "destruction of architecture," which intended to provoke a like rupture in the language of modernism. Unlike Ledoux's metaphors—which date from the time of the birth of the industrial revolution in France—Isozaki's are emphatically *post*industrial and, in that sense, postmodern— and, for Japan, "postvernacular." Thus, when in the Kitakyushu Municipal Library we are confronted with a space strongly reminiscent of the vaulted gallery or the dining hall in Wright's Dana House (1903) at Springfield, Illinois (fig. 10.24), we may be certain that Isozaki has purposely drawn attention to a particular aspect of the Wrightian canon which could never reasonably be mistaken as neo-Japanese. To this, he attempts to give a new voice, as to the Villa Poiana motif in the *porte-cochère* at Fujimi, which in fact is the selfsame motif with which Wright framed the doorway to the Dana House itself. Instead of Palladian ashlar or Wright's distinctive Roman brick, Isozaki has neatly transposed this (originally Bramantesque) conceit to that bolt-patterned, concrete construction which is practically the hallmark of recent Japanese architecture.

AN AQUEOUS METAPHOR

Some of the wittier buildings Ledoux projected in his treatise, like the house for the Loue River franchise agents, relate directly in terms of their imagery to prevailing local occupations and/or context. There is at least one building by Isozaki which is *parlant*—that is, meaningful or expressive—in virtually this exact sense. It is the so-called West Japan General Exhibition Center (fig. 10.25) in the Kokura district of Kitakyushu City (therefore, not far from the Municipal Library), which was completed in 1977. This extremely large but appealing work (with a total floor space of over 10,000 square meters) cannot receive any detailed attention here, except to note that it originated in several senses as a "metaphor relating with water."[49] This figure is both timeless and highly explicit. The exhibition center, as may be seen, is appropriately situated at the edge of the port in the dockland area of Kyushu's main industrial city.

262 BETWEEN *MANIERA* AND *SACHLICHKEIT*

10.25. Isozaki: West Japan General Exhibition Center, Kokura, Kitakyushu, Fukuoka Prefecture, 1977.

10.26. Isozaki: Kamioka Town Hall, Toyama Prefecture, 1978. Principal (rear) facade viewed from below.

10.27. Isozaki: Kamioka Town Hall, Toyama Prefecture, 1978. First-, second-, and third-floor plans.

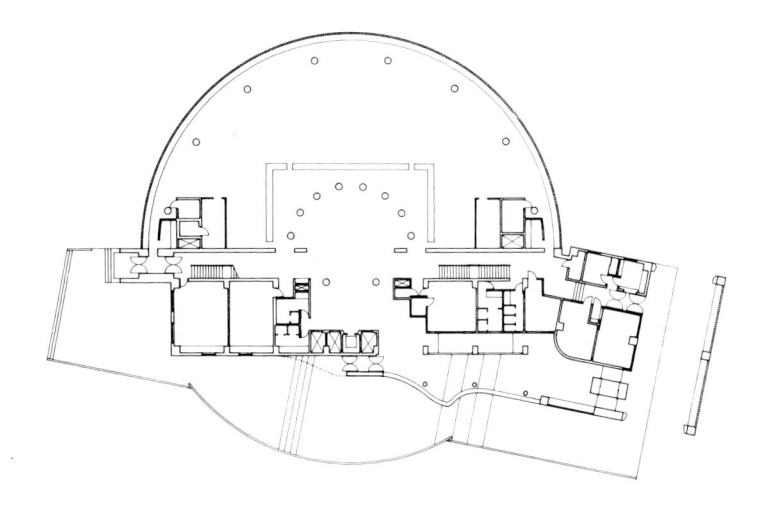

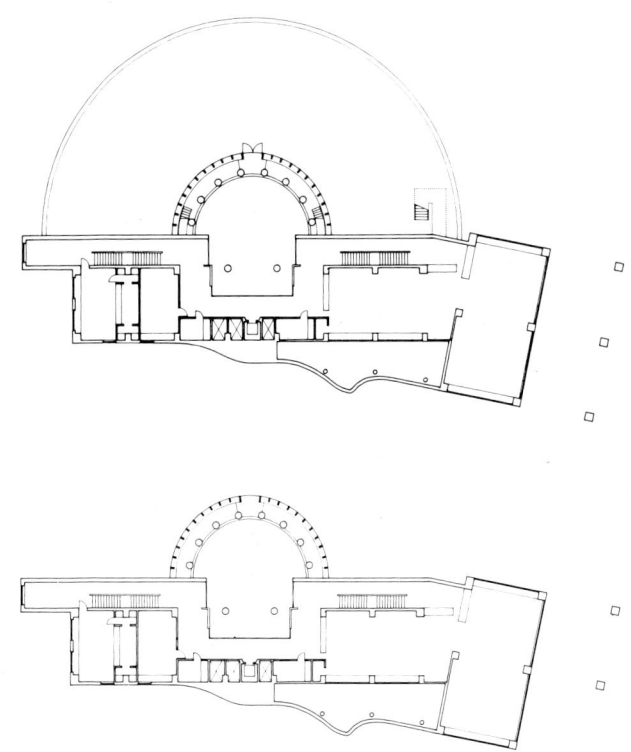

SQUARING THE CIRCLE AT KAMIOKA

We are concerned in this book with the general implications for Japanese architecture of Isozaki's mature style, and the final building by him to be dealt with is the Kamioka Town Hall. It was completed in 1978, although the original competition goes back slightly earlier and the initial project changed completely at least once in the course of design. Kamioka is in one of the most remote parts of Honshu, a mountainous provincial district oriented toward the Japan Sea coast where the main activity is mining. The town itself is built of rough, dark houses and shops in a subvernacular idiom. That it should even possess a town hall worthy of the name, let alone one designed by a major metropolitan architect, may be viewed as a fulfillment of all the political and architectural promises of the Meiji Restoration (fig. 10.26). Yet, in the town hall as built, no single image stands out. Isozaki himself has remarked that the building consists of "forms shaken into place to satisfy function." That, all the same, is a bit of Formalist hyperbole.

What the building (figs. 10.27–28) actually does is to join Isozaki's two paradigmatic metaphorical shapes—the cube and the cylinder—by employment of free-form circulation spaces. In this, the notion of an architectural promenade is somewhat generalized and enlarged upon in a way that, for me, is once again reminiscent of Aalto. What is, of course, different from Aalto is the relative insistence on the Platonic quality of the major forms. In plan, these show as a full circle and a longitudinal axis skewed across it. The building's rear facade—the one that rises above the town—reads as a vast and flat semicylindrical, drumlike terrace surmounted wedding-cake fashion by a narrower, vertical drum with French windows, itself flanked by two cubical forms of comparable height. At left appears an additional freestanding cube, a quarter of which is carved out as a *porte-cochère* to protect against the heavy snowfalls of the region.

In fact, of course, Isozaki's architecture is never quite so far from the Modern Movement as the notion of distance promoted through his "destruction of architecture" slogan may induce us to believe. For example, the office space contained in the lower drum of Kamioka Town Hall could be reworking an idea used by Gropius in 1927–28 for the Municipal Employment Office in Dessau (now East Germany). Likewise, Gropius was familiar with overt demonstrations of the cube, whether in his houses for the Weissenhof Siedlung of 1927 or, in the United States, the Packaged House System of 1943–45, designed with Konrad Wachsmann. On the other hand, Isozaki's main facade, which commands a prospect of Kamioka's descent to the river, has affinities with the Louis Seize style in its unconcealed preference for simplified geometrical forms. For example, one is put in mind of the river facade of the Hôtel de Salm (fig. 10.29; present Palace of the Légion d'Honneur) erected in the early 1780s on the left bank of the Seine in Paris. And, to be sure, it is equally this style and moment to which the works and projects of Ledoux logically belong. The line between formalism and neoclassical formality is here drawn rather fine. Columns and colonnades abound throughout the Kamioka Town Hall, while the delicate and subtle interplay of shapes and claddings—above all the pinkness of granite and the coruscation of aluminum paneling—reinforces this give-and-take exchange between neoclassicism and the heritage of International Modern.

In an article entitled "Formalism"[50] about designing the town hall, Isozaki points out that Kamioka must be evaluated at three different levels. One is the actual environment of the town, another is Isozaki's own "method," and a third he refers to as "interrelations with current architectural trends in general." The first two of these have been dealt with, and I believe the town hall acquits itself rather well in regard to them. As concerns the last, Isozaki goes on to say in the final paragraph of his essay that modern architecture has now

10.28. Isozaki: Kamioka Town Hall, Toyama Prefecture, 1978. Principal (rear) facade seen from across the river.

10.29. Rousseau: Hôtel de Salm, Paris, 1783–86. River facade of one of the largest houses in pre-1789 Paris.

achieved all its goals and that contemporary architects "need do nothing but select the [means and achievements] we want." "But," he continues, "I feel we are in need of a new symbolic-formal structure that will generate a different meaning to help us make the right choice." For example, "the use of pure forms, displacement and articulation of such forms, overscaling, oppositional use of materials, interiors with mazelike qualities, and accumulated quotations from the architecture of the past are all formal methods for the generation of new, independent semantic structures." In the materialization of these eventual symbolic-formal structures, however, "knowing how to mediate the resulting sense of disharmony is difficult."[51]

Whether voiced or unvoiced, such is the most general complaint among so-called postmodernist architects from California to London, Madrid, Berlin, or Sydney. In Japan, the basic stuff of Western architecture has been assimilated long ago, and yet—had we but a souvenir or a recording of it—this might have been the *cri de coeur* of a Meiji architect. No matter, the "disharmony" and "difficulty" cited by Isozaki still persist for all.

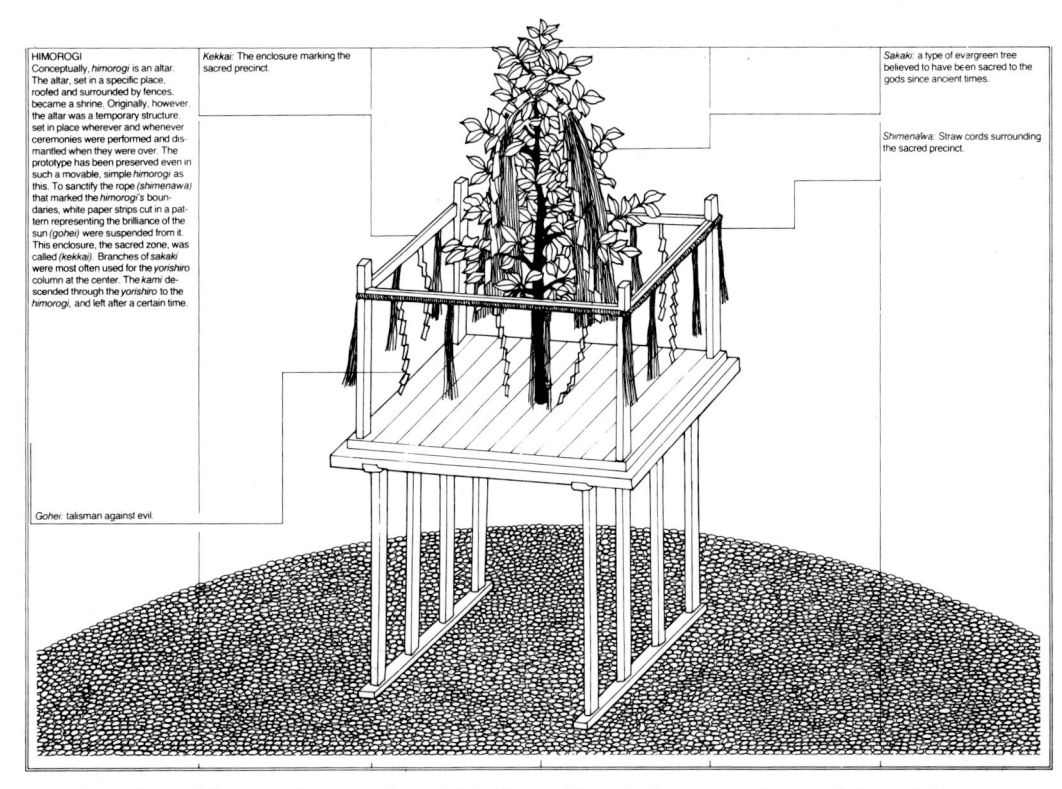

10.30. Isozaki: emblematic drawing from *MA: Space-Time in Japan*, catalogue of the exhibition, 1978.

SPACE-TIME IN JAPAN: PARIS/NEW YORK

As the Kamioka Town Hall weathered its first winter, Isozaki's exhibition "MA: Space-Time in Japan"—inaugurated at the Festival d'Automne in Paris—began a tour which led to Stockholm and various American cities. Ironically, in view of Isozaki's statement of the obstacles which a formalist theory of architecture poses, the "MA" exhibition afforded a brilliant summary of the principles behind (mainly traditional) Japanese cultural production. It consisted of nine thematic tableaux describing the process of Japanese space-making through the ages. These were presented in a thoroughly contemporary manner with examples drawn from various aspects of Japanese life, constituting an anthology of extended meanings and applications (fig. 10.30). The show was, of course, a made-for-export production aimed at Paris and New York. It caused no ripple or repercussion in Japan, where, in any case, it was never shown, an error remedied in the superficially similar 1986 exhibition entitled "Tokyo Form and Spirit" (which was previewed, then shipped abroad).

Ma—itself a Japanese word denoting interval, whether spatial or temporal—was given an imaginative and somewhat specialized interpretation as befitted such an exhibition. The way in which *ma* was explained in the catalogue[52] produced by Isozaki and his staff provides one of the few available introductions to phenomenalized space as the notion relates to Japanese architecture. It also elaborates a number of "devices" similar to *fuseki* in Isozaki's theory of *ma*nner. The purpose of the exhibition was to be selective and representative instead of exhaustive and historically precise in denoting some of the ways Japanese "space-time" either assumes, or induces, full spectator participation. This is the aspect I have called its "operationality" (in a sense similar to the architecture of the Counter-Refor*ma*tion). By the end of the 1960s the influence of Metabolism in bringing neo-Buddhist ideologies out of the closet had spent itself, and it happens that the "MA" exhibition stressed Shinto notions (which contain a good deal of latent Taoist belief, a circumstance insufficiently brought out by the catalogue). But the point of the exhibition was to show how Japanese "space-time" is palpably different from space as generally conceived of in the West, and that in Japan, anyhow, *ma* is everywhere!

Isozaki had realized that the only possible future lay with for*ma*l *ma*nipulation of orthodox International Style themes, an idea also being tried (without italics) in some American schools of architecture. Similar experimentation had taken place earlier in Italy, and the operation Isozaki performed to such effect in severing the flying beams in his Oita Prefectural Library (1962–66) may have originated with Marco Zanuso's Buenos Aires plant for Olivetti of 1960. Likewise, the semicylindrical sections used in construction of the Kitakyushu Municipal Library could relate to the prefabricated, concrete sectional vaulting in Vittorio Gregotti's vast project for Palermo University. Isozaki made no particular bones about such occasional reworkings of current tendencies since the results were couched, inevitably, in a unique and alien spatial tradition—which constituted his own vision and experience, as it always had done for Japanese architects, as early as the first collision between East and West a hundred years before.

10.31. Shinohara: Suzusho House, Miura, Kanagawa Prefecture, 1968. Living-dining area.

SHINOHARA AND THE "SECOND STYLE"

There occurred another, and equally fitting, conclusion to these first 100 years of Japanese building in the Western style, and that was a born-again modernism on the part of Kazuo Shinohara. This trend revealed itself in his works after the House in White of 1966, but—by contrast with Isozaki—Shinohara's buildings remained exclusively within the domain of residential architecture until the 1980s. A reversal of effect was the first sign of change: just as Shinohara's earliest house appeared Japanese in style, though constructed using a steel frame, the Suzusho House of 1968 had a classical Japanese hipped roof but was built of reinforced concrete. Yet, this change was scarcely apparent on the outside except in the unusual breadth of the "traditional" roof span. On the interior, however, the vast living-dining area (fig. 10.31) comprising some 100 square meters was, like that of the House in White two years before, a "neutral," un-Japanese space. Rather, and the point must not be allowed to confuse, it was a quintessentially "Japanese" space without Japanese-type constructional attributes, except for the presence still of paper-glazed *shoji*.

Then, in 1970—the year in which Shinohara was named full professor—came the Incomplete House (figs. 10.32–33), also built of reinforced concrete, but this time on a square plan—like the House in White—yet with a flat roof. In fact, however, the grade line and profile of the house as realized were adjusted in such a way as, for the moment, to minimize the cubical impact of the design. Terms like "neutral" and "cubical" were, as we have discovered, soon to be echoed by Isozaki with reference to the Gumma museum in a few years' time. Conversely, the House with Incomplete Spaces (as Shinohara's work is sometimes referred to) centers around a type of "symbolic" interior space, the product of an intense and contrived axiality, which is reminiscent of the Fukuoka Mutual branches at Oita and Daimyo (see figs. 9.13–14), realized from 1967 to 1969. All in all, one is entitled to suppose that such works derive from a view of the world shared in some way by these two architects. Yet again, too, we meet in the Incomplete House a perfectly credible setting for Kobo Abe's novel plots. Shinohara ascribes the harshness or "neutrality" of his Second Style works to an intensification of his private method of abstraction, evident in the suppression of color and motif from the central space of the house under discussion. This, incidentally, is designed as a living room but could never be one, although it is once in a while used as a surreal setting for convivial dining. Character, in the architectural sense, is harried out of spaces such as these, perhaps in the same way that characterization eventually disappears in the later works of Abe, like *The Box Man* of 1972.

In "Beyond Symbol Spaces," an essay he used to introduce the Incomplete House,[53] Shinohara wrote, "It is no longer necessary to disguise one's belief that the house is a kind of spatial creation based on a criticism of civilization"; that is, it is nothing like a public building or the plan for a city and, thus, not expected to "participate" directly as an aspect or product of society. Additionally, in the Incomplete House and the Shino Residence which followed, two things happened: one was the abandonment of the method of "spatial division" taken over by Shinohara from traditional Japanese planning, and the other was an exchange of the equally traditional theme of "frontality" for a new "multiple" spatiality—emphasis on vertical spaces being just an example. Shinohara also began to insist on restoring a sense of the "irrational" as an accompaniment to the breakup of these traditional methods or certainties in his work. In this—but without actually referring to the heritage of Nietzsche and Freud—he anticipated the architecture of the 1980s. Yet his hold on Japanese tradition remained secure enough to propose "using the certain space [of tradition] to conform to the uncertainties of the world."[54]

The Shino House (fig. 10.34), though substantially smaller than the Incomplete House, presents a similar arrangement:

an enclosed central hall led into by a narrow entrance corridor rising the full two stories of the hall itself. But—whereas this space was white in the Incomplete House, finished in February 1970—in the Shino House, completed in May, it was now papered in gold. Oddly enough, this fissure space, despite its radical appearance, was intended as a device that would serve to reunite or bring closer together the symbolic—or "significant"—space and those other parts of the house designated for more strictly everyday functions, like eating and sleeping. Shinohara at this period had begun to feel that the latter may have suffered from lack of attention in his earlier houses, and his new interest developed as a kind of topology, which came to be defined as "the science of distant and near spaces."[55] For the moment, these retained a sort of analogy with so-called symbolic and functional spaces, but, in fact, a sense of unification was what Shinohara now actively sought.

Although persisting in his belief that such works as the Incomplete House and the Shino House were somehow other than "functional"—or, at best, represented functionality raised to a new level—Shinohara was nevertheless committed to piecing together a notion of continuity. Between the austere symbolic spaces he had achieved earlier using Japanese methods and the simple, practical space of everyday life descended from the Modern Movement, he felt there had to exist some common term. His principal intention was to dephenomenalize the spatial impact of these new constructions, or, in short, to disinvolve the spectator—but only to a certain degree—from the intensity of feeling built up through the praxis evolved in earlier works. Still, this new "multiple"—as opposed to "frontal" (and hierarchical)—approach to space, which Shinohara now expected to derive in geometric terms from his Second Style, would have to come at a price. It would imply an attentiveness to *nonprimary* spaces, investing these with a heightened sense of participation or, in phenomenal terms, "operationality." The new combined emotive quality of the house as "reunified" is, presumably, that aspect endowing it for the time being with a sense of "incompleteness." Therefore, the spectator can neither expect to *exploit* such spaces as the core rooms of the Incomplete House or the Shino House in the usual disregarding, or inattentive, functional way, nor can he or she merely *contemplate* them as before. For, finally, a participatory act is to be exacted even in contemplation, while at the same time function requires in the end a certain obeisance from the architect.

"THIRD STYLE" AND GAP

During the early seventies Shinohara elaborated a series of houses around this new notion of "multiplicity" (the term actually refers to "multiple" geometries, but *plurality* might better illustrate the idea of newfound freedom implicit in the Second Style). As a rule these works were of exposed reinforced concrete and their profiles were rectangular or cubical. The Shino House was an exception since, built of wood, it required a pitched roof in the Japanese climate. From 1970 to 1973, some eight houses were produced in this sequence, with evocative names, such as Repeating Crevice, Cubic Forest, and Sky Rectangle. Naturally, the dimensioning of the concrete reflected prevailing antiseismic standards; this was always kept to the legal minimum and in no sense were the dimensions of posts or beams to be read as an expressive feature of the design. Nevertheless, such features, expressive or not, exact a toll on the awareness of the spectator in a way perhaps unintended by the architect—particularly if one happens not to be familiar with Japan's somewhat spectacular reinforced-concrete standards.

From about 1974, just as Isozaki had sought a counternotion to the cube in the semicylinder, Shinohara—having been trained as a mathematician and a geometer—began to organize his thoughts about prismatic form. They allude to, but never quite coincide with, the shapes of his subsequent houses. The most dramatic and important of these, for the purpose of reconstructing Shinohara's theory of the next years,

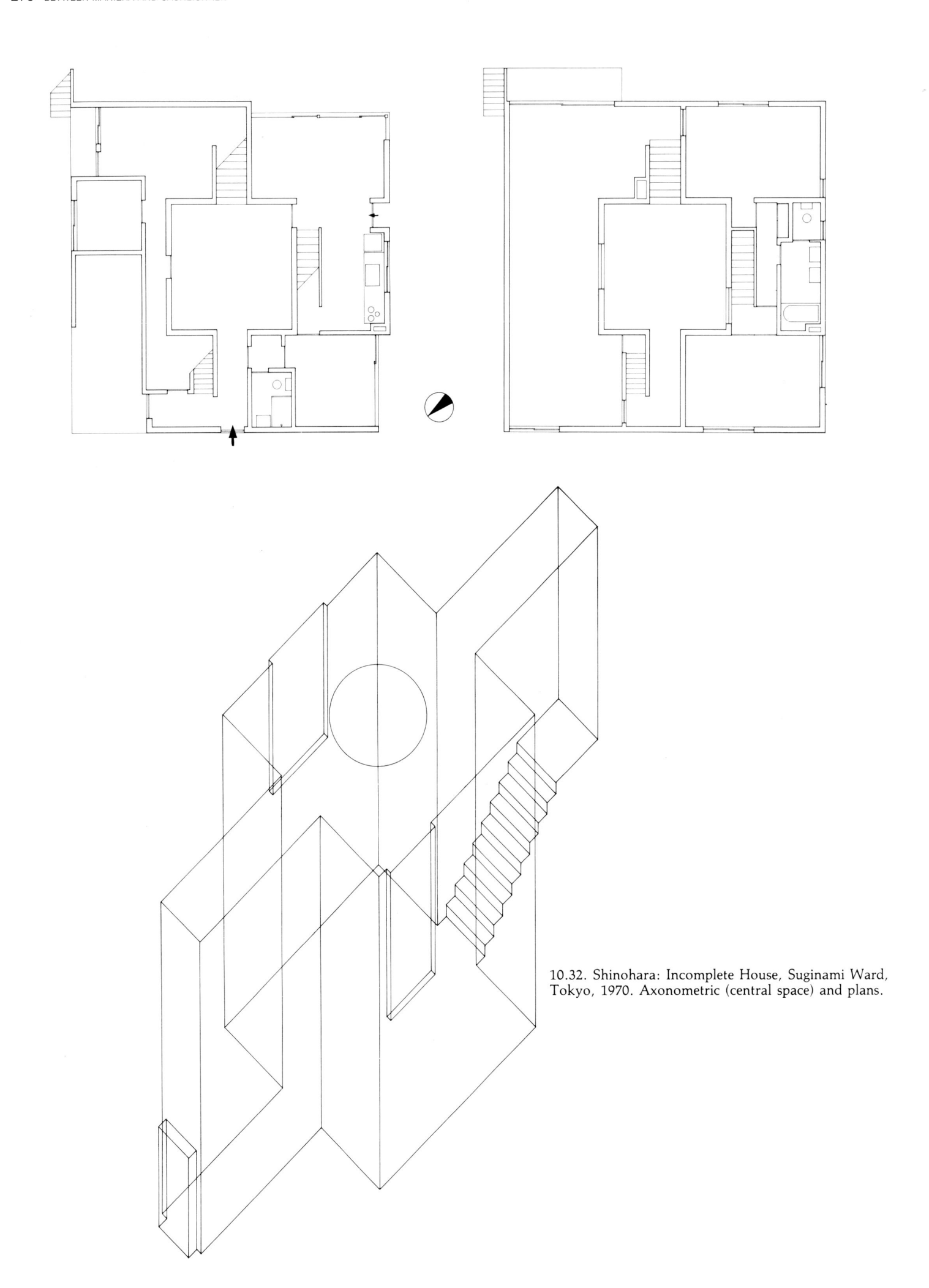

10.32. Shinohara: Incomplete House, Suginami Ward, Tokyo, 1970. Axonometric (central space) and plans.

10.33. Shinohara: Incomplete House, Suginami Ward, Tokyo, 1970. Central space, originally a dining room.

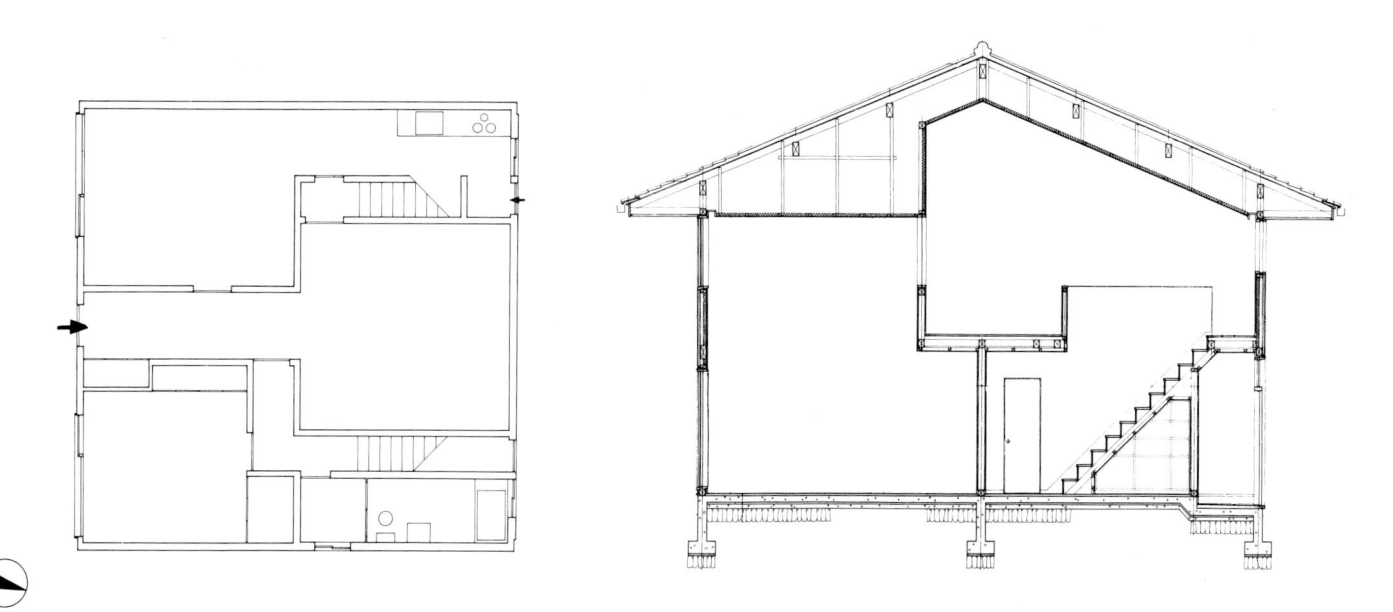

10.34. Shinohara: Shino House, Nerima Ward, 1970. Plan and elevation.

10.35. Shinohara: Tanikawa House, Naganohara, Gumma Prefecture, 1974. Lateral facade.

was a hermitage he designed in Naganohara, near Karuizawa, for the poet Shuntaro Tanikawa, whose Tokyo house Shinohara had built in the First Style back in 1958. This second Tanikawa House (figs. 10.35–37), at the edge of a steep declivity in a mountainous area, marks the beginning of Shinohara's Third Style. The house is of wood surmounted by an ordinary galvanized roof sloping very near to the ground, so that it resembles some unfamiliar form of storage building or barn. The rooms for eating, sleeping, and study are placed to one side; they occupy a fourth portion of the structure, plus a minor projection at the lower end for a bathroom and storage unit. However, access to these living quarters is to be had only through the poetically named "summer space" that takes up the remainder of the building. This consists of no more and no less than the underside of the roof revealed to its full height and supported by the far end wall on one side and two posts—each with a pair of diagonal struts—set in between. The walls and the "ceiling" of this "summer space" are immaculately plastered in white, while the opposed "walls" are of glass. Quotation marks are called for, not only because the roof of the Tanikawa House slopes so low toward the ground, but especially because the house stands on an ungraded slope and the "floor" of this huge vestibule is but bare natural earth. The overall effect

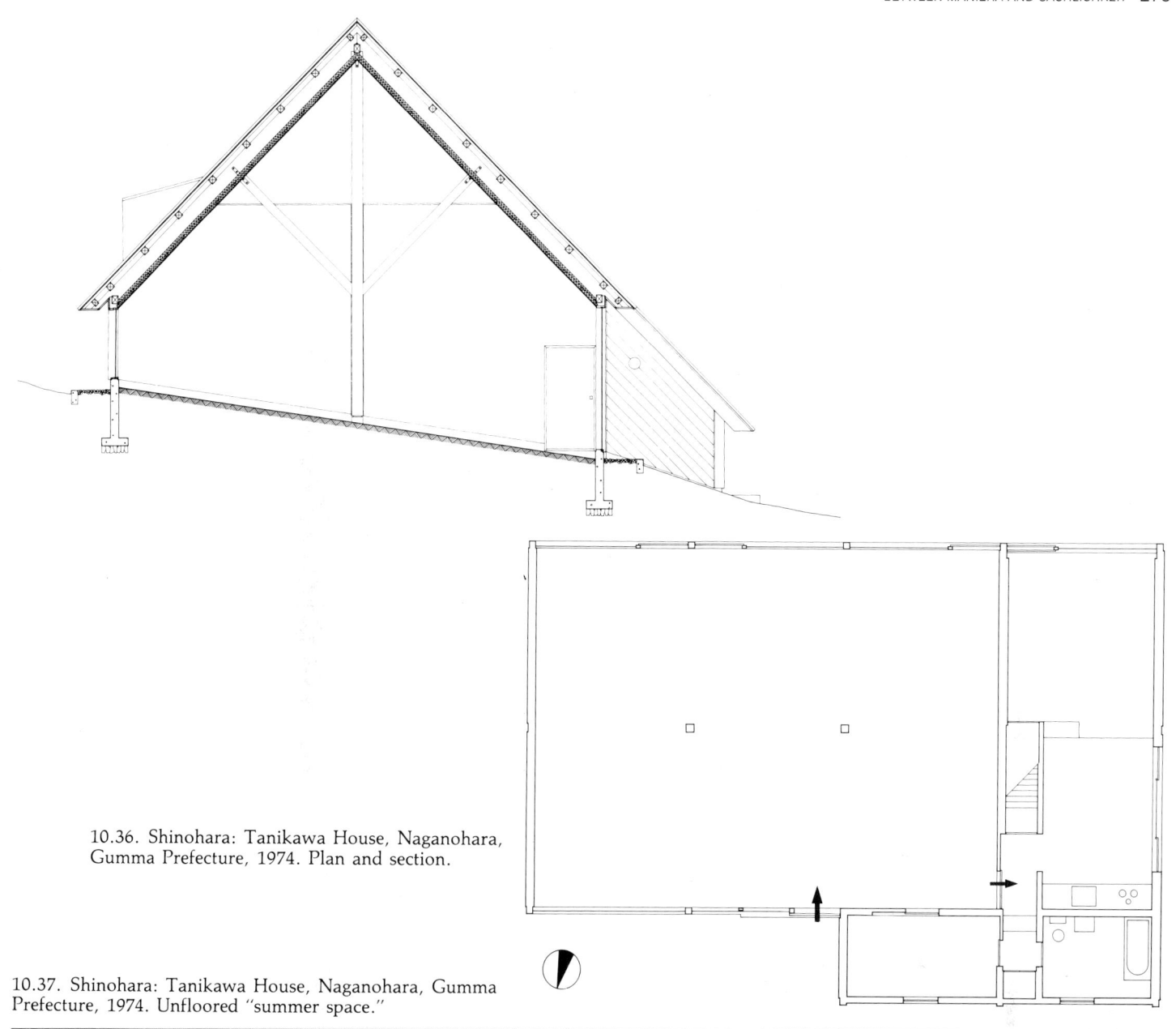

10.36. Shinohara: Tanikawa House, Naganohara, Gumma Prefecture, 1974. Plan and section.

10.37. Shinohara: Tanikawa House, Naganohara, Gumma Prefecture, 1974. Unfloored "summer space."

10.38. Shinohara: Tanikawa House, Naganohara, Gumma Prefecture, 1974. The "summer space" and the notion of "traversal."

is something like that of a Japanese-style garden but devoid of stones or planting of any kind. Inside, the slope dictates a new spatial order which it is the task of the spectator to resolve as best he or she can.

The notion of "gap" already mentioned in connection with Isozaki at Gumma is brought out—here, once more—with its analogy to linguistic formation, that is, to the nature and origin of language itself. According to Shinohara, "Illogical functions emerge from the gap between this slope and the geometric [i.e., summer] space."[56] And also, "I do not think that borrowing the name of the formalists, who were popular a few years earlier, would provide me with a convincing explanation."[57] Indeed, the proffered explanation of the second Tanikawa House—which is among Shinohara's most powerful and intriguing works—is not totally convincing. Shinohara tells us how the design was made after his recovery from a serious illness, the site having been chosen beforehand. It may be that its "summer space" was meant to produce a refractory, or prismatic, effect on the viewer—not so much with respect to one's experience of the space as a "phenomenalized" container, or shell, of "self"-related spatial events, but rather as the imposition of an irrational perceptual grid, or virtual "Space Machine."[58] So far as the explanation can be followed, it was the act of traversing such a field or domain (fig. 10.38) by another person or persons that generated meaning. At another, more concrete level, just as the Second Style was an "antistyle" directed against the specific constitutive elements of the *minka-* and *sukiya-*derived First Style, the Third Style represented pursuit of an "antispace" freed from all secondary or situationally induced meanings. Accordingly: "Posts, walls, and braces express nothing but their own functions. I wondered if I could not realize just this kind of obvious thing," wrote Shinohara. "I would like to eliminate, completely, if possible, various meanings derived from a spatial frame comprised of these elements."[59] Thus, it appears that just as the Gumma museum evokes the notion of "gap," so, too, Shinohara's desire in the Third Style to avoid even that degree of signification deriving from the simplest structure ought to be read as paralleling Isozaki's scheme for the "destruction of architecture."

To digress for a moment from Shinohara's Third Style, how conclusive is this similarity of intentions? Both "traversal" and "destruction of architecture" can be said to reflect—in the dynamics of society as architecture responds to and acknowledges these—something of Merleau-Ponty's concept of intersubjectivity as "a living relationship and tension among individuals."[60] Whereas the category of what may be termed "lived experience" has come increasingly to the fore in our discussion of contemporary Japanese architecture, oddly enough this view of *meaning* as "sociological meaning" has barely called attention to itself since Metabolism. Perhaps the reason ought to have emerged from those parallels we have drawn between outstanding works of the 1960s and 1970s and the novels of Kobo Abe. Yet the tendency for the Western reader is to treat Abe's simple plots—with their brilliant accumulation of heightened detail (the material, in fact, of everyday experience in Japan)—as individualized and introverted searches for the kind of existential self the Westerner is familiar with. Although an "exotic" reading of this kind, whether in books or architecture, cannot definitively be refuted, whoever indulges in such interpretations ignores the fact that the domain of meaning in Japan is overwhelmingly social.

Yet the fact Japanese society is vastly consensual and homogeneous need not imply that it is altogether without seam or crack, and this has proved increasingly true since World War II. Merleau-Ponty's concept of intersubjectivity was a nuanced criticism directed against the danger of trying to use the Durkheimian notion of "collective consciousness" as a practical research tool. If valid, Merleau-Ponty's distinction is, to be sure, universal, but Japan nevertheless offers, it seems to me, a particularly transparent and dramatic instance of how meaning is generated from this kind of socially shared and reciprocal "lived experience." I make no claim that such behavior is unerringly guided along the best channels; neither is it necessary to accept all its goals. Nor, finally, is the majority of Japanese architecture, or the modern city, a socially generated expression of *aesthetic* values. Indeed, this is extremely far from being the case.

Rather, at present, the domain of aesthetics has been preempted by that of "meaning" in general, which is by definition—or by construction—a social one. Owing possibly to the tradition of tea as well as the kind of transparent, even "primitive," vision of society the Japanese possess, architects have been set in a privileged position to exploit these human and cultural data with distinctly powerful results. Again, there is no sense in which Merleau-Ponty could be speaking of a particular race or nation when he insists, "Metaphysics begins from the moment when . . . we apperceive the radical subjectivity of all our experience as inseparable from its truth value. It means two things to say that our experience is our own: both that it is not the measure of all imaginable being in itself and that it is nonetheless co-extensive with all being of which we can form a notion."[61] It is nearly impossible to explain why this "double sense of the *cogito*," to which Merleau-Ponty refers as "the basic fact of metaphysics," should appear to be involved with certain of Isozaki's metaphors or be seen as struggling for recognition in a resort house, like the second Tanikawa residence; or why, indeed, Japanese architecture should, a few years ago, have shifted its direction—and retooled its conceptual apparatus—to become engaged at this level of philosophical generality.

By way of an attempt to respond, we can only reiterate what has already been said of the mandala and its function, namely, that religious devices of this kind aim at symbolizing the "destruction," or dissolution, of individual consciousness; then follows reintegration in a newly enlightened state of absolute existence, which may well be another name for the "intersubjectivity" of Merleau-Ponty's 1947 essay. In any case, a more or less sudden reintroduction of the topic of "religion" cannot be too surprising in any discussion sparked off by a notion of Durkheim's.

From the theoretical construct of "traversal" used in the

10.39. Le Corbusier: terrace of the Beistegui penthouse flat, Paris, 1931, with the Arc de Triomphe de l'Etoile by Chalgrin (1806–36).

explanation of the second Tanikawa House and—borrowed, in fact, somewhat at haphazard from the contemporary French philosopher-critic Gilles Deleuze[62]—Shinohara was to move next to that of savagery (taken over from Lévi-Strauss's *La pensée sauvage*) and, finally, to that of *Sachlichkeit* inherited, as we have seen, from the Modern Movement. In fact, he adopted each of these concepts merely as a starting point—a convenient label—in order to convey an image of the method used in each new work. As opposed to the concatenation of abstract meanings in his "Japanese" works of the First Style, *traversal* was chosen to express the intentional incompleteness and, so to say, open-endedness of the Second Style. In the second Tanikawa House, this was translated, by means of a simple frame construction, into a thinly disguised attack on the notion of "style" itself. From the nascent "spatiality" (in the Western sense, as exemplified, for instance, in Isozaki's critique of the spatial content of Wright's work) of his own Second Style, Shinohara turned to the notion of an anti-space: "From this kind of totality, I hope to find something that will reverse the very totality from which it emerged."[63] And further: "In front of me is the simple question of whether I shall be able to create the style I seek."[64]

The second Tanikawa House can "of course [be] related to the question of Frontality."[65] The traditional sort of Japanese dwelling with its deep eaves results from considerations of climate, and for Shinohara it became a challenge "to design a building that has projecting eaves but that is formally free of limitations of frontality."[66] Thus, compared with the House in White of 1966, Shinohara foresaw here a "different phase of spatial expression" and of "identity." He poses the question: "Is it not possible to remove condensed meaning and to create naked structures, wall surfaces, and spaces?"[67]

For a moment, Shinohara's dialectic with Japanese tradition—which for him was represented, above all, by the notion of frontality and the construction of "symbolic" spaces —may be compared with Le Corbusier's adventures within the Mediterranean tradition. By virtue of the very continuity with which the European Modern Movement has now come to be viewed—as an extension of Western classicism—Le Corbusier's interrogation of the forms and principles of the latter has lost some of its freshness. But in a relatively unfamiliar work known only from contemporary photographs, the Beistegui apartment (fig. 10.39)—or "appartement sur le toit aux Champs-Elysées"—of 1931, Le Corbusier forced the issues of human perceptual awareness rather far in an unusual context eight or nine stories above the most renowned street in Paris. Here, if we mentally demolish the neobaroque furnishings, which were not part of Le Corbusier's program for the Beistegui penthouse, we find ourselves face-to-face with a procedure recalling the *ostraneniye* advocated by Shklovsky or, alternatively, the "gap" which materializes in the Tanikawa House of 1974.

Shinohara uses the term "gap" to qualify the disorienting effect produced by the juxtaposition of the bare slope of the summer space with the angular enclosure it traverses. Likewise, "because of the two-to-one relation of the interior heights of the north and south openings, as one traverses this space [up or down the slope], one's vision alters from perspective to reverse perspective and back to perspective again."[68] In the Beistegui flat, which provides one of the few effective comparisons with the Tanikawa House, just such a "gap" explodes—and with even less subtlety—between the four bare walls of the ninth-floor solarium with its curious antique mantlepiece, the grass and daisies underfoot, and the vault of sky and clouds overhead. Its added furnishings apart, the appointments of the elegantly situated flat were spartan in a way that looked ahead to the simplified restraint of Shinohara's "naked" spaces. For example, despite four kilometers of electrical cables used to activate window-walls of plate glass as well as slidable stands of shrubbery, the flat was illuminated throughout by candles. Similarly, a single opening breached the solarium, and that was hung with a stone slab for a door—a manifestation of frontality which, one might say, puts even the Tanikawa House's "summer space" in the shade.

SACHLICHKEIT ALIVE AND WELL IN UEHARA

Still and all, the Beistegui flat succeeds as an exercise in defamiliarization partly by dint of its interior—and exterior—decoration, which, given a choice, Le Corbusier would most surely have rejected. On the other hand, the second Tanikawa House by Shinohara and the Gumma Prefectural Museum of Modern Art (see figs. 10.14–15) by Isozaki, both works completed in 1974, exhibit a degree of radical formalism—achieved by straightforwardly architectural means—that is without parallel in the development of contemporary architecture. But, as stated, Isozaki had determined, probably from the time of the "Future City" montage of 1961, with its Doric column shafts, that his works—despite their Japaneseness—would be inscribed in the history of world architecture. The museum, therefore, stands in the tradition of Katayama's Hyokeikan (see fig. 2.41) or Yoshida's Tokyo Central Post Office (see fig. 6.8) and, of course, comparable works in other countries, and the assurance that it does so partly accounts for its credibility and success as a design. In contrast, by the time the "MA" exhibition had reached New York, Isozaki admitted that "at the moment [MA] doesn't overlap with my work"[69] in spite of efforts to discover "some point where they come together."

On the other hand, Shinohara does not hide the fact that the issue of cultural identity remains a key factor in his work and that, in this respect, "nakedness" remains intuitively analogous with the spaces of his First and Second styles. In other words, naked space, like the "un-Japanese" type of space which proceeded from the House in White, will ultimately be very Japanese. For the rest, the notion of the work of art as a "machine," used not to *express* meaning but to manipulate or *produce* it, is an old Formalist and Contructivist device, and neither Deleuze's nor Shinohara's rehabilitation of it succeeds very effectively. Invariably, whether we are dealing with Proust or with buildings, everything depends on the particular *method*, to return to Isozaki's term, by which the machine is powered.

One further house, completed in the spring of 1976, may be considered, together with the Tanikawa house at Karuizawa and the Gumma museum, as an apotheosis of nontraditional Japanese building during its first century. This is the House in Uehara (figs. 10.40–41) by Shinohara, which, to my mind, is a more integrated and self-sufficient expression of the notions contained in the Third Style than even the Tanikawa House. In fact, both these houses of the mid seventies are equally dramatic personifications of the devices of "gap" and "nakedness," whereas the House in Uehara embodies wit besides, because of how it deals with a complicated and typical urban dilemma at the root of all Japanese housing: lack of space!

Though situated in a most pleasant upper middle-class neighborhood in Tokyo, the structure with which this book closes was designed for a narrow plot of land having immediate frontage on a narrow street and totally hedged in by existing construction on three sides. A local restriction governed the height of the main structure itself, while a parking space had to be provided, by law, if the client wished to operate an automobile. In the event, it proved possible to form the requisite carport by cantilevering a portion of the upper story, as Shinohara had often done in his Second Style to provide for door and window embrasures. But as the House in Uehara, like works of the prior Second Style, was to be of reinforced concrete and, in order to allow for minimum floor-to-ceiling height requirements, the heavy horizontals which ordinary earthquake-proof concrete framing techniques would have imposed had to be avoided. Toshihiko Kimura—the consultant responsible for all of Shinohara's concrete designs dating from the mid-sixties onward—devised a monolithic concrete envelope or shell, with intermediate wooden flooring inserted to create a sec-

10.40. Shinohara; House in Uehara, Shibuya Ward, Tokyo, 1976. Street facade.

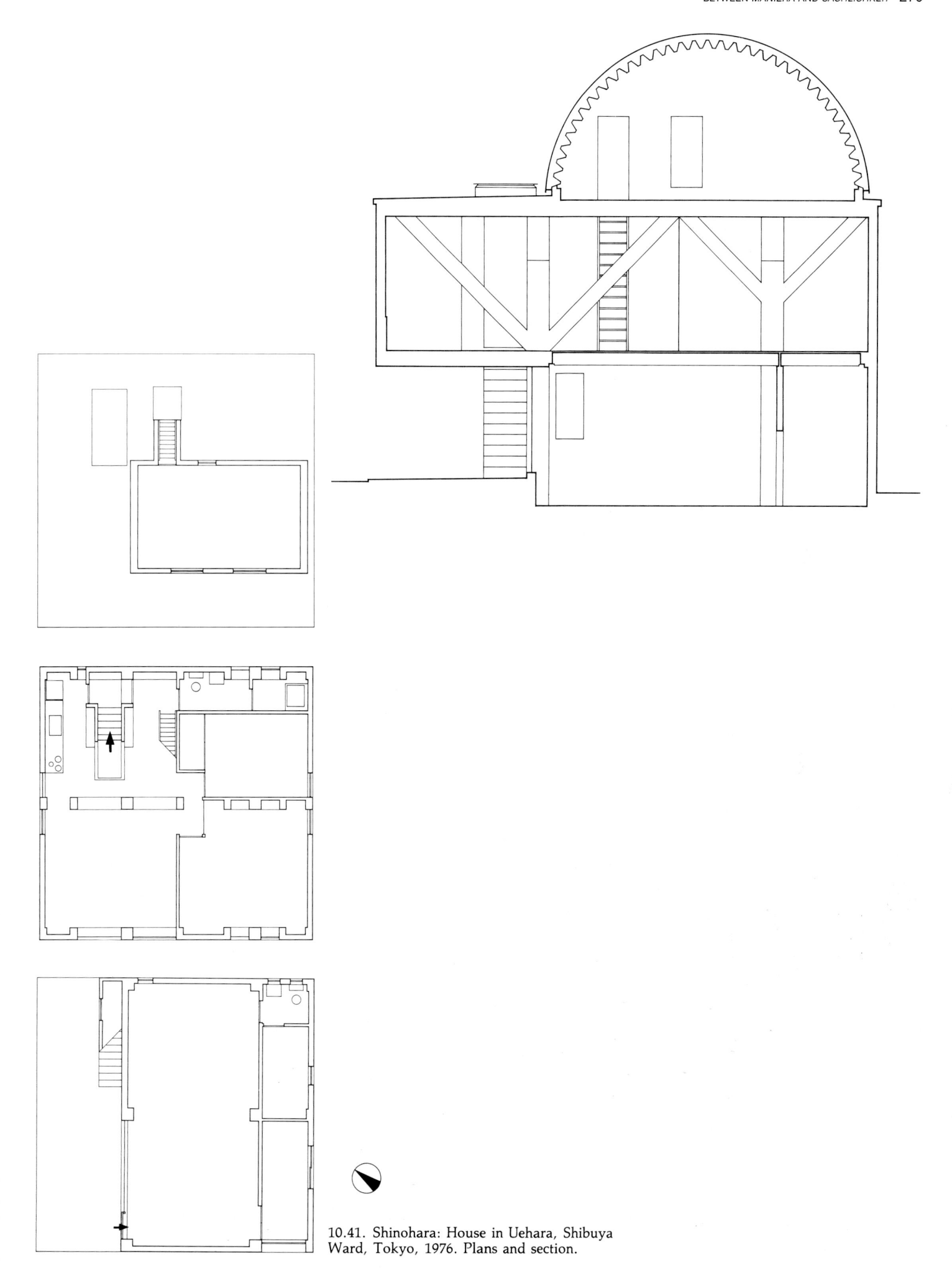

10.41. Shinohara: House in Uehara, Shibuya Ward, Tokyo, 1976. Plans and section.

10.42. Shinohara: House in Uehara, Shibuya Ward, Tokyo, 1976. Living-dining area.

ond level. A system of six supports, with massive angled braces, created a kind of giant forestal order inside the house. These piers were nearly identical in shape to the wooden posts used in the Tanikawa House two years before. Thus, in the end, sufficient headroom is gained at ground-floor level by using an intermediate platform of wood, while in the upper story the same effect is achieved by expressing the transverse beams as diagonals and transposing the structure into a series of vertical planes parallel to the facade.

The client being an architectural photographer, the ground-floor space of the House in Uehara is devoted to his workroom. The upper floor consists of an eighty-one-square-meter space containing principally a kind of family room. This is screened from the kitchen area by one of the six great treelike units (fig. 10.42) holding up the main structure (the rest are embedded in walls), while a bedroom and a simple Japanese-style matted room are also fitted into the plan of this floor. The aedicule at third-story level (fig. 10.43) was requested by the client as a virtual afterthought and is composed of a lightweight vaulted frame of corrugated steel erected autonomously over the main structure and, happily, not liable to height restrictions. It is at present used as a children's sleeping deck and is reached by means of a ladderlike stair mounting through the roof of the main living space below.

The conjunction of a flying visit to several West African capital cities (which Shinohara found eminently civilized and congenial) and his reading of Claude Lévi-Strauss's *Savage Mind* (1962), already mentioned, led to the *a posteriori* baptism of the Uehara house as a "savage machine." There is, indeed, a primitivism—and possibly a feeling of rough man-handling—about the constricted upper floor of the house; but this label supposes a certain tongue-in-check humor, and the house was intended neither as a concrete jungle nor, particularly, as an allegory of Japanese urban lifestyle.[70]

In Shinohara's approach to the work of architecture as a "machine," the aspect of greatest overall significance was the ease with which this machine concept could be made to yield a heightening of awareness while at the same time allowing for the exclusion of any individually "subjective," or personalized, point of view. As suggested by Shinohara's earlier theories, this double provision may be taken as virtually a defining trait of Japanese art, and there is nothing at all "inhumane" about a practice which permits direct and unmediated access to the "operative" mechanism at the core of a work—merely because it is implied that the effect produced would be uniform (even predictable) for every subject. Jokingly, however, Shinohara began to refer to his recent stepped-up impersonalization as a new kind of *Sachlichkeit*, in analogy to European modernism of the 1930s. In this, Japanese architecture may be seen as coming full circle within the tradition of modernism, while, in the interval, building in the once imported "Western" style has become thoroughly Japanese.

10.43. Shinohara: House in Uehara, Shibuya Ward, Tokyo, 1976. View from the third-story room looking toward surrounding houses.

Notes and References

Chapter 1 (pages 13-32)

1. London (Thames and Hudson), 1973, and originally presented as the fifth Walter Neurath Memorial Lecture at Birkbeck College, University of London, the same year.

2. Cited by Basil Hall Chamberlain in *Things Japanese; being Notes on Various Subjects Connected with Japan . . .* , London (Kegan Paul, Trench, Trübner), 1890. Reprint of fifth rev. ed. (1905, Murray) as *Japanese Things*, Rutland, VT, and Tokyo (Charles E. Tuttle), 1971, p. 40.

3. Paul Charles Blum, *Yokohama in 1872; a rambling account of the community in which the Asiatic Society of Japan was founded*, speech delivered at the New Grand Hotel in Yokohama at the ninetieth-anniversary dinner of the society in 1962 and published the following year with line drawings, Tokyo (ASJ). Reprinted by Yumi Press, Tokyo, 1982, p. 65.

4. I would like to thank Peter Spang for pointing out that the standard reference work on views of the China coast remains James Orange, *The Chater Collection: Pictures relating to China, Hongkong, Macao 1655-1860; with historical and descriptive Letterpress*, London (Butterworth), 1924, and Bill Sargent of the Peabody Museum of Salem for showing it to me.

5. *Georgian London*, third rev. ed., Cambridge, MA (MIT Press) and London, 1978, p. 290.

6. The pioneering latter-day account of this subject is Sten Nilsson, *European Architecture in India 1750-1850*, London (Faber and Faber), 1968. The remarks here and those following rely heavily on Margaret Archer, " 'Company' architects and their influence in India," *RIBA Journal*, August 1963, pp. 317-21, and T. H. H. Hancock, "Coleman of Singapore," *Architectural Review*, March 1955, pp. 168-79, both of which are cited by Nilsson. Nor could one refrain from mention of the famous *Original Letters from India* by Eliza Fay (Calcutta, 1817, first printed in Britain by the Hogarth Press, 1925, and reissued in 1986), especially letters 14 and 15 for brief glimpses of Madras and Calcutta.

7. There is, naturally, no equivalent in Japan of the Hong Kong Museum of History's collection of early photographs of the colony, which date from the 1850s onward. I am indebted to Leslie Lu for directing me to this source.

8. In *Through Closed Doors: Western Influence on Japanese Art 1639-1853*, Rochester, MI (Meadow Brook Art Gallery, Oakland University), 1977, p. 32 and following.

Soochow, famous in its own right as a beauty spot and art center, was one of the places visited by Marco Polo. Recalling Venice, it is situated on the Grand Canal and, for a time, was active as an international port. Although Cal French does not specifically say so, the topographical variety of the Soochow print greatly resembles, in its turn, contemporary panoramic views of Venice, such as the one painted by Odoardo Fialetti, a pupil of Tintoretto, and now at Eton College (1611).

9. Ibid., p. 114.

Chapter 2 (pages 33-62)

1. The importance of the relationship between the Meiji government and Glasgow's shipbuilding industry for the foundation in Tokyo of the engineering college is detailed in several articles included in *Charles Rennie Mackintosh* (catalogue of an exhibition held at Isetan Department Store), Tokyo (Japan Art and Culture Association), 1985. The exhibition was mounted by the Glasgow School of Art and the catalogue supervised by Hiroyuki Suzuki.

2. In *The Strange Genius of William Burges: "Art-Architect" 1827-1881*, Cardiff (National Museum of Wales), 1981, p. 10. From the introductory article in the catalogue of this centenary exhibition, written by its editor, J. Mordaunt Crook.

3. From "The Late Dr. Conder" (obituary): Walter Millard, *RIBA Journal*, September 25, 1920, p. 474.

4. Charles Handley-Read, "William Burges," in Peter Ferriday (ed.), *Victorian Architecture*, London (Jonathan Cape), 1963, and Philadelphia and New York (J. B. Lippincott), 1964, pp. 185-220, quotation p. 192.

5. The distinction between the "downtown" section of Tokyo and the more sparsely settled neighborhoods of the aristocratic *yamanote* is played on by the title of Edward Seidensticker's *Low City, High City: Tokyo from Edo to the Earthquake*, New York (Alfred A. Knopf), 1983; paperback, Rutland, VT, and Tokyo (Charles E. Tuttle), 1984. Seidensticker's text is an exhaustive compilation of local and topographical history and anecdotes. It makes the architecture more comprehensible and is developed from a connoisseur's point of view; planning history is dealt with implicitly rather than systematically or in great detail.

6. Cf. *Hermann Muthesius: 1861-1927* (exhibition catalogue: December 1977-January 1978 at Akademie der Künste in Berlin), n.d. (1977), Akademie-Katalog no. 117. The informal photograph appears on p. 54 and also serves as frontispiece in the reduced English-language edition published in London (Architectural Association), 1979.

7. The history of the involvement of Ende und Böckmann, as well as Baurat Hobrecht, with the replanning of the government district is contained in Terunobu Fujimori, *Meiji no Tokyo Keikaku* (Planning in Tokyo during the Meiji Period), Tokyo (Iwanami Shoten), 1982, based on Dr. Fujimori's Ph.D. thesis (Tokyo University, 1979).

8. The significance of Tokyo as a symbol is dealt with by Seidensticker (see note 5, this chap.); it is further discussed and analyzed at length by Henry D. Smith in an article entitled "Tokyo as an Idea: An Exploration of Japanese Urban Thought until 1945" (*Journal of Japanese Studies* 4:1, Winter 1978, pp. 45-80), which includes a bibliography of some eighty items. Smith's study was originally presented at the Workshop on the Japanese City—sponsored by the Social Science Research Council at Mount Kisco, NY, in 1976—and I am indebted to Philip Thiel for calling my attention to it.

9. Cf. *Architecture: Nineteenth and Twentieth Centuries* in The Pelican History of Art, Harmondsworth (Penguin Books), fourth (second integrated) edition, 1977, chaps. 8 and 9, pp. 191-245. The discussion of the German Renaissance mode is given in chap. 9, pp. 219-20 and 222-24.

10. *German Renaissance Architecture*, Princeton (Princeton U. Press), 1981. The Bremen Rathaus, dating from the early fifteenth to the early seventeenth century, is referred to as "the most sumptuous of all German examples of Renaissance civic design" (p. 293). Something of the extent and importance of Hamburg and Bremen in the nineteenth cen-

tury may be gauged by the fact that, in 1886, the steamships of the increasingly powerful North German Lloyd Lines took over the imperial postal service to Australia and the Far East.

11. *Neorenaissance in der deutschen Architektur des 19. Jahrhunderts: Grundlagen, Wesen und Gültigkeit*, Dresden (Verlag der Kunst), 1981. The relevant chapter is entitled "Deutsche Neorenaissance," pp. 278–300; unfortunately, the firm of Ende und Böckmann, mentioned elsewhere by Milde in his work, is not dealt with in connection with this supposedly "Germanizing" version of the neo-Renaissance style.

12. The account which follows is based on Johannes Hirschmeier, SVD, "Shibusawa Eiichi: Industrial Pioneer" in William Lockwood (ed.), *The State and Economic Enterprise in Japan*, Princeton (Princeton U. Press), 1965, pp. 209–47.

13. The new buildings for the Banque Nationale became the object of one of the numerous competitions which were a consequence of the choice of Brussels as the national capital of Belgium. The original winner was Seghers (1859), but the building as built was realized by Henry Beyaert with Wynand Janssens. Its design was studied by the Portuguese and the Prussians, as well as the Dutch, well before Tatsuno's time. See P. Kauch, *Les bâtiments de la Banque Nationale de Belgique à Bruxelles*, Brussels (Imprimerie de la Banque Nationale de Belgique), 1964, especially pp. 22–44.

Although much of the building was replaced in 1957, the original block (rue du Bois Sauvage) survives. It is in an adaptation of Louis XVI, a style more or less faithfully reflected in the Bank of Japan. But, curiously, Tatsuno's domed rotunda appears to derive from a neo-Renaissance stair tower (the so-called tour de Beyaert, now destroyed), placed at the rear of Beyaert's design as a picturesque contextual device. Tatsuno elaborated this tower as the central feature of his own design on a greatly enlarged scale.

14. The fullest contemporary publication of the works of Price was Russell Sturgis, *The Works of Bruce Price*, no. 5 in the Great American Architects Series published by *Architectural Record*, originally June 1899; reprinted, New York (Da Capo Press), 1977. The most detailed modern account is Samuel H. Graybill, Jr., *Bruce Price, American Architect (1845–1903)*, unpublished Ph.D. thesis (Yale University, 1957).

The Canmack Cottage, mentioned below, was identified by Clay Lancaster, *The Japanese Influence in America*, New York, 1963, and republished (Abbeville Press) in 1983, p. 60 and note 6, while the connection between Wright and Tuxedo Park was explored by Vincent J. Scully, Jr., *The Shingle Style and the Stick Style: Architectural Theory and Design from Downing to the Origins of Wright*, New Haven and London (Yale U. Press), 1955 and rev. ed. 1977, p. 159.

15. The orb motif (with rays) is seen atop the Sun Building, an unbuilt project of 1890, which was Price's earliest skyscraper scheme. It reappears, still more in evidence, in the unbuilt Civil War "Peace Monument and Arcade" he designed in 1898 for an unspecified "large northern city." The project for the Sun Building was published in *Architectural Record* in 1891 and that for the Peace Monument in *American Architect and Building News* in 1899.

16. According to Graybill (see note 14, this chap.), Bruce Price exhibited drawings of a palace for the Japanese crown prince in 1901, the year following Katayama's visit to Price, at the Sixteenth Annual Exhibition of the Architectural League of New York. Katayama was listed as architect, Price himself as consulting architect, and Prentice Treadwell, one of Price's regular associates, as "decorator."

Chapter 3 (pages 63–76)

1. The incident is recounted in Frank Lloyd Wright, *An Autobiography* (first published 1932), New York (Horizon Press), 1977, pp. 149–52. It is discussed in H.-R. Hitchcock, "Frank Lloyd Wright and the 'Academic Tradition' of the Early Eighteen-Nineties," *Journal of the Warburg and Courtauld Institutes*, vol. 7, 1944, pp. 46–63.

2. Elizabeth Aslin, *E. W. Godwin: Furniture and Interior Decoration*, London (John Murray), 1986, p. 9.

3. From *The Aesthetic Movement: Prelude to Art Nouveau* (first published 1969), London (Ferndale Editions), 1981, p. 79.

4. In "The Japanese Court in the International Exhibition," *The Gentleman's Magazine and Historical Review*, vol. 213, September 1862, pp. 243–54.

5. Godwin's designs for furniture and wallpaper have been the object of a recent monographic catalogue (see note 2, this chap.).

6. Any appraisal of Godwin's vanished domestic interiors must remain purely speculative, even though in some instances we have extensive notes, such as directions for paint mixing. Whistler's harmonies and happily, above all, his nocturnes survive in reasonable numbers in the collections of the Tate Gallery, London, the Freer Art Gallery (of the Smithsonian Institution), Washington, DC, and the Hunterian Art Gallery, University of Glasgow.

7. *An Autobiography*, op. cit., p. 149.

8. By H. Allen Brooks in his entry on Wright, *Encyclopaedia of World Art*, New York and Maidenhead (McGraw-Hill), 1967 (vol. 13), pp. 858–69, quotation p. 858.

9. Quoted from John Summerson, "Viollet-le-Duc and the Rational Point of View" (first delivered as a lecture in 1947) in *Heavenly Mansions and Other Essays on Architecture*, New York (Norton Library: W. W. Norton), 1963, pp. 135–58, quotation p. 150.

10. Ibid.

11. Cf. "I believed the *Raisonné* was the only really sensible book on architecture." *An Autobiography*, op. cit., p. 97.

12. Published 1854–68.

13. *The Autobiography of an Idea* (first published serially 1922–23, and in book form the following year; variously reprinted), New York (Dover Publications), 1956, p. 233.

In fact, Sullivan had first been introduced to Taine's celebrated *History of English Literature* (1863–64, newly translated into English in 1871, when Sullivan read it). Later, in Paris, he "discovered three small volumes by Hippolyte Taine devoted to the Philosophy of Art in Greece, in Italy and in the Netherlands." These were still recent, dating from 1869, 1866, and 1868, respectively, and represent installments of the lecture course given during the initial five years Taine spent at the Ecole. Together with the first-year series, *Philosophie de l'art* (which appeared in published form in 1865 and was translated into English as *The Philosophy of Art* the same year) and that of the third year, *De l'Ideal dans l'art* (published 1867), all these lectures were eventually collected as *La philosophie de l'art*. Published in 1882, they enjoyed notable success and numerous reprintings well into the twentieth century, even though Taine himself died in 1893.

14. Ibid.

15. "Naturalistic and Humanistic Philosophies of Culture" (as the introduction to *Logic of the Humanities*) and *Logic of the Humanities* (Eng. trans. by Clarence Smith Howe, 1960), New Haven, CT, and London (Yale U. Press), 1971, pp. 13–16, 27–34, and 146–57.

16. In *Contre Sainte-Beuve* (first published in 1954; Eng. trans. by Sylvia Townsend Warner as *By Way of Sainte-Beuve*, 1958), London (Hogarth Press), 1984, pp. 73–74. The introduction to the new edition indicates that Proust conceived this work as an essay "in the manner of Taine" (p. 4).

17. *The Autobiography of an Idea*, op. cit., pp. 235–36.

18. *The Philosophy of Art*, part 2 ("Painting and the Renaissance in Italy"), chap. 4, section 3.

19. D. G. Charlton, *Positivist Thought in France during the Second Empire, 1852–1870*, Oxford (OUP: Clarendon Press), 1959, chap. 7, pp. 127–57, quotation p. 133.

20. Op. cit., p. 330.

21. Ibid., p. 325.

22. Ibid.

23. See Kakuzo Okakura, *The Ho-o-Den (Phoenix Hall): An Illustrated Description of the Buildings Erected by the Japanese Government at the World's Columbian Exposition, Jackson Park, Chicago*, Tokyo (published by K. Ogawa but printed and bound in Chicago), 1893.

The structure was presented to the city of Chicago at the close of the exposition, then served for a number of years as a "tea house" and was finally allowed to deteriorate at about the time of World War II.

24. Ibid., p. 9.

25. Ibid., p. 13.

26. Since the island had originally been designated as a nature preserve, the Japanese petition was initially refused. However, numerous exhibitors, not least among whom was the young Theodore Roosevelt, requested permission to build on the Wooded Island. Roosevelt intended to build a model hunters' camp on it, and the implication, according to Thomas S. Hines, is that the Japanese proposal was accepted as a means of thwarting Roosevelt's ambition. See *Burnham of Chicago: Architect and Planner*, Chicago and London (University of Chicago Press: Phoenix Edition), 1979, p. 109, citing correspondence in the Burnham Papers, Chicago Art Institute Library.

27. Grant Carpenter Manson, *Frank Lloyd Wright to 1910: The First Golden Age*, New York (Van Nostrand Reinhold), 1958, p. 37.

28. Ibid., pp. 38–39. In any case, and more importantly, as we shall see, Wright was extremely anxious that no such assignment be made.

29. Dimitri Tselos, "Exotic Influences in the Architecture of Frank Lloyd Wright," *Magazine of Art*, vol. 46, April 1953, pp. 160–69 and 184, especially pp. 160–62.

30. *An Autobiography*, op. cit., p. 148.

31. *The Autobiography of an Idea*, op. cit., p. 235.

32. Ibid., p. 248.

33. Sullivan records the way "bridges" turned his mind "from the immediate science of engineering toward science in general, and he set forth with a new relish, upon a course of reading covering Spencer, Darwin, Huxley, [John] Tyndall, and the Germans, and found a new, an enormous world whose boundaries seemed destined to be limitless in scope, in content, in diversity." Ibid., p. 249.

34. See Julia Meech-Pekarik, "Frank Lloyd Wright and Japanese Prints" in Edgar Kaufmann, Jr., *Frank Lloyd Wright at the Metropolitan Museum of Art*, pp. 48–56, brochure reprinted (1985) from *The Metropolitan Museum of Art Bulletin* (Fall 1982).

35. Published in "Recollections—United States, 1893–1920," *Architects Journal*, vol. 84, July 1936, pp. 76–78, and quoted by Manson, op. cit., pp. 35–37.

36. "Japan is, or was, a country very much, as regards its arts and handicrafts with the exception of architecture, in the condition of a European country in the Middle Ages, with wonderfully skilled artists and craftsmen in all manner of work of the decorative kind, who were under the influence of a free and informal naturalism." *Of the Decorative Illustration of Books Old and New*, London (George Bell and Sons), 1896, and reprinted 1972, p. 132. The text originated in the Cantor Lectures, at the Society of Arts, for 1889.

37. Ibid., pp. 133–34.

38. Ibid., p. 134.

39. Robert C. Twombly, *Frank Lloyd Wright: His Life and His Architecture*, New York (John Wiley and Sons), 1979, pp. 114–15.

40. *The Japanese Print: An Interpretation by Frank Lloyd Wright*, Chicago (Ralph Fletcher Seymour).

41. On page 3. The text follows an unnumbered title page (cf. fig 3.10) bearing a stylized Japanese crane inscribed within a circle. Over this emblem are superimposed wave motifs in a circle, which lies off center from the first, in the manner that appears in one corner of certain Japanese prints, frequently embossed. There are no illustrations.

42. Idem, p. 3. Among these are Ernest Fenellosa's: *The Masters of the Ukiyoe* (1896) and *An Outline History of Ukiyoe* (1901). I have not been able to determine whether Fenellosa's "Masters of Ukiyoe" exhibition held in New York in January 1896 traveled to Chicago as intended. Wright devotes a short paragraph in *An Autobiography* (p. 548) to the story of Fenellosa's accomplishment in returning Japanese attention to Japanese art and in preserving a number of cultural objects and works of art from destruction at the end of the last century. Fenellosa was a member of the fine-arts jury at the Chicago fair and he spoke there before a meeting of the arts section of the International Congress of Education. From 1902 to 1906, he was a regular lecturer on Chautauqua and women's-club circuits in Chicago and throughout the Midwest, where Wright may have heard him.

43. Idem, pp. 3–4.

44. Idem, p. 4.

45. Idem, p. 5.

46. "And, most important of all, once the comparative study of historic styles is allowed to be legitimate, there is the irresistible analogue of a *new style*. This may be conceived as a personal style, a national style or simply as a rational abstraction from all styles." *The Architecture of the Eighteenth Century*, London (Thames and Hudson: World of Art Library), 1986, p. 76.

   Moreover, Wright regarded his style as the combination of all three possibilities.

47. "In the Cause of Architecture" (earliest of three essays Wright published under the title), *The Architectural Record*, vol. 23, no. 3, March 1908, pp. 155–65, and illustrations, quotation p. 158.

48. Delivered to the Chicago Arts and Crafts Society on March 6, 1901, and reprinted in *Frank Lloyd Wright: Writings and Buildings*, selected by Edgar Kaufmann and Ben Raeburn, New York (New American Library), 1974, pp. 55–73, especially p. 64.

49. The reference is actually to the influence of German architecture in Japan during the nineteenth century, namely the commissioning of Ende und Böckmann by the Japanese government and the style of the first Imperial Hotel (whose architect had trained in Germany, even though this fact was scarcely apparent from the design of the building). Cf. *An Autobiography*, op. cit., pp. 237 and 549, quotation p. 549 (my italics).

50. "In the Cause of Architecture," loc. cit., p. 163.

51. Having once made clear the value of the Machine as a "simplifier," Wright seldom returns to the topic, but in the final paragraph but one of the Hull House lecture (1901) he established "organic law" as the "law to which the great solar universe is but a great obedient machine." "Organic" is the term he will use in the 1908 paper, and throughout his life, to describe his architecture.

52. "In the Cause of Architecture," loc. cit., p. 156.

53. *The Japanese Print*, op. cit., p. 13.

54. Ibid., p. 12.

55. Ibid., p. 13.

56. In the preface to *Ausgeführte Bauten und Entwurfe*, Berlin (Wasmuth), 1910, and reprinted in *Frank Lloyd Wright: Writings and Buildings*, op. cit., pp. 84–106, quotation p. 88.

Chapter 4 (pages 77–89)

1. By Kathryn Smith in "Frank Lloyd Wright and the Imperial Hotel: A Postscript," *The Art Bulletin*, vol. 67, no. 2, June 1985, pp. 296–310.

2. "The Story of the Imperial Hotel," *Japan Architect*, no. 138, January/February 1968, pp. 113–38.

3. Cf. Robert King Reitherman, "The Seismic Legend of the Imperial Hotel: How did it really fare in the Tokyo earthquake of 1923?" *AIA Journal* (American Institute of Architects), vol. 69, June 1980, pp. 42–46 and 70 (adapted by the author from a paper presented at the Seventh World Conference on Earthquake Engineering as "Frank Lloyd Wright's Imperial Hotel: A Seismic Re-evaluation." *Proc. 7th WCEE*, 1980, vol. 4, pp. 145–52).

   I must thank Yoshiaki Yoshimi for locating the latter paper for me, as well as for his own helpful insights with regard to the foundations and subfoundations of the Imperial Hotel, which he examined at the time of the building's demolition.

4. Writing in 1929, Hitchcock characterized the design of the hotel "despite its admirable plan, [as] redundant, overburdened with unskillfully exotic ornament, and except where the quality of the materials is brought out, vastly ineffective. The interiors on which Wright expended apparently a considerable effort are incomparably worse than those however Louis XVI of any coëval Ritz." *Modern Architecture: Romanticism and Reintegration*, New York (Payson and Clarke) and reprint, New York (Hacker Art Books), 1970, p. 115.

5. Smith, op. cit., p. 297.

6. *An Autobiography*, op. cit., p. 247.

7. In *Orientalism*, New York (Random House), 1978 (Vintage Books ed., 1979), pp. 114–15. Said's immediate reference is to Flaubert's satirization of the notion of regeneration in *Bouvard et Pécuchet*.

8. "The Art and Craft of the Machine," loc. cit., p. 56.

9. Ibid., p. 59.

10. Ibid., p. 62.

11. Pp. 218–28 and 228–36, respectively.

12. The section entitled "Reconstruction" deals with Taliesin, also obliquely the Imperial Hotel, and, finally, the reconstruction of Wright's own life after the Taliesin fire. It includes the 1916 visit to Taliesin of Aisaku Hayashi, who helped negotiate the planning of the hotel, pp. 216–17, and is followed by "And Japanese Prints," pp. 217–18. "Building Against Doomsday (Why the Great Earthquake did not Destroy the Imperial Hotel)," pp. 236–48, is about the construction of the hotel. In addition, general information is contained in "Tokio—Japan," pp. 547–50, while "The Print" is the story of Wright's career as a print-dealer, pp. 550–61.

13. Cf. Paul Goldberger, "Design Notebook: The Problems in Preserving a Wright Home," *The New York Times*, July 10, 1980, p. C10.

14. Precise dates for the first and second of Wright's trips to Japan were first given by Robert C. Twombly in his *Frank Lloyd Wright: His Life and Architecture*, New York (John Wiley and Sons), pp. 114 and 152. Subsequently, Smith (loc. cit.) has discovered additional confirmation

in Wright's correspondence regarding the visit of 1913, and she is able to say that "during his stay, Wright drew up preliminary plans, examined the soil conditions, and made suggestions regarding building materials." Pp. 298–99 and note 16.

15. See chap. 3, note 56.

16. Both quotations, *An Autobiography*, pp. 218.

17. Ibid., p. 219.

18. Ibid., p. 220.

19. Ibid., p. 221.

20. Ibid., p. 223.

21. Ibid., p. 224.

22. Ibid.

23. Pater refers to the temptation of Marcus Aurelius in the *Meditations* (incidentally, a favorite work of Taine's) to concretize, thus circumscribing, his own theory of "perpetual" flux. In *Marius the Epicurean: His Sensations and Ideas* (1885), Oxford and New York (OUP: World's Classics), 1986, p. 167.

24. This quotation from Wright is from *An Autobiography*, p. 221. The phrase cited actually refers, not to the inner space of the house, but rather to the "problem" Wright identified as "where [with respect to the house] the garden leaves off and the garden begins."

25. *An Autobiography*, p. 248.

26. Ibid., p. 235.

27. Ibid., pp. 228–29.

28. Ibid., p. 229.

29. Ibid., p. 234.

30. Ibid., p. 235.

31. Ibid., p. 237.

32. Antonin Raymond, *An Autobiography*, Tokyo and Rutland, VT (Charles E. Tuttle), 1973, p. 71.

33. Ibid., pp. 71 and 76.

Chapter 5 (pages 90–106)

1. A city Frank Lloyd Wright compared to Tokyo: "Like Ancient Rome, Ancient Yedo was a capital of seven hills. . . ." *An Autobiography*, op. cit., p. 228. The "hills" refer to the Yamanote. This was a commonplace comparison, and Wright's notion is typical of conflated classical and oriental images in Aestheticism.

2. Continuation of his remarks quoted at the end of chap. 4. (Raymond) *An Autobiography*, op. cit., p. 76.

3. Ibid.

4. (Wright) *An Autobiography*, p. 235.

5. Ibid., pp. 235–36.

6. In "The Imperial Hotel," excerpted from Wright's *Architecture and Modern Life* by Edgar Kaufmann and Ben Raeburn (ed.), *Frank Lloyd Wright: Writings and Buildings*, New York (1960, and New American Library, 1974), pp. 197–208, quotation p. 201.

7. Its organizers were the late Henry-Russell Hitchcock and, ironically, Philip Johnson, godfather of today's neohistoricist architecture. The full title of the exhibition, as well as a book which accompanied it, was *The International Style: Architecture Since 1922*. (The book by Hitchcock and Johnson remains available in a Norton Library edition, 1966, and subsequent printings, under the title *The International Style*.) Buildings that were included in the Museum of Modern Art exhibition have been taken ever since as convenient benchmarks for evaluating the classical or orthodox phase of modern architecture, referred to sometimes as "high modernism."

Three principles guided Hitchcock and Johnson in their selection of material, namely, (1) architectural organization in terms of "space" ("effect . . . of plane surfaces bounding a volume," p. 41) instead of mass; (2) substitution of bilateral symmetry by adjustment of "the irregular and unequal demands of function to regular construction and the use of standardized parts," p. 57; and (3) conscious ("aristocratic rather than puritanical," p. 75) avoidance of applied decoration.

8. (Raymond) *An Autobiography*, op. cit., p. 101.

9. Cf. "Imperial Hotel, Tokyo, Japan," *The Architectural Record*, February 1924, vol. 55, no. 2, pp. 119–23.

10. (Raymond) *An Autobiography*, op. cit., p. 101.

Chapter 6 (pages 107–63)

1. An enticing gloss on the assumption of a possible connection between the Imperial Crown style and Wright can be constructed out of Masami Tanigawa's recent conjecture that the architect Kikutaro Shimoda, in some way through his now lost 1911 design for the Imperial Hotel, influenced the development of the *teikan* style. We know Shimoda worked for a time with the great Chicago architect, Daniel H. Burnham, and later established his own practice in Chicago, which lasted until the time of the Spanish-American War. But Shimoda is also the name of the Japanese draftsman whom Wright engaged and, soon afterward, kicked down the stairs of the Schiller Building. Were these two one and the same—though nothing seems to be known in Japan of the roughing-up episode (recounted by Wright himself in *An Autobiography*, op. cit., p. 148)—then the Imperial Crown style might better be seen as a revenge upon, rather than admiring emulation of, Wright. It is known that Shimoda won a court settlement against the Imperial Household Agency, on account of the commission being finally awarded to Wright.

2. Yoshida left Tokyo Imperial University in 1919 but seems not to have visited Europe until after completing the Tokyo Central Post Office. His trip lasted a year, from the summer of 1931; he is known to have made the acquaintance of the architects Hugo Häring and Ludwig Hilbesheimer in Berlin. On Yoshida, see *Tetsuro Yoshida: Architecture 1919–1956/Yoshida Tetsuro Kenchiku Sakuhinshu*, Tokyo (Tokai U. Press), 1957.

3. For the International Style exhibition held at the Museum of Modern Art in New York (1932) and its explanatory catalogue, cf. chap. 5, note 7.

4. Cited by Mark Girouard in *Sweetness and Light: The "Queen Anne" Movement 1860–1900*, Oxford (OUP) 1977, p. 64.

5. *An Autobiography*, op. cit., p. 135.

6. Ibid.

7. Cf. note 3, this chap. Quotation from Hitchcock and Johnson, op. cit., p. 41.

8. See, for example, the short critical anthology by Toshihiko and Toyo Izutsu, *The Theory of Beauty in the Classical Aesthetics of Japan*, The Hague (Martinus Nijhoff), 1981. The following account of "inconsistency-transiency" (*mujo*), which these authors view as the principal domain of Japanese classical aethetics—". . . things and events of the phenomenal world constitute in a non-temporal space a vast network of accidental coincidences consisting of co-existences, consonances, correlations and contrasts . . ." (p. 56)—might well serve as an ant-eye description of the modern industrial metropolis.

Chapter 7 (pages 164–85)

1. *An Autobiography*, op. cit., p. 211.

2. "Tange came to my attention the year he designed the Hiroshima Memorial. I suspected that he was inspired by the Reader's Digest Building, attracted by the exterior only, not motivated by structural reasons, as the Reader's Digest Building itself was. As the years went by and as Tange came up with increasingly interesting and truly creative buildings, I came to the conclusion that he was an architect of great stature, just as I had predicted that such an architect had to appear in Japan, sooner or later." Ibid., pp. 249–50.

Additionally, ". . . many very prominent architects crudely copied the general form [of the Reader's Digest Building], and even some details, without regard to inner meaning." Ibid., p. 213.

3. Tange: ". . . It seems to me that what you have understood as the tradition of Japanese architecture is different from that conceived by our young architects. . . ."
Raymond: ". . . I expressed my idea of Japanese tradition by mentioning the impression of a Japanese farm building on me upon my arrival in Japan. . . . I want to restate that I find true Japanese tradition in exact agreement with the principles of good design as formulated by the founders of modern architecture early in this century. . . . I fail to understand your use of the English word tradition. I suspect that you mean by it a *new direction*, or perhaps a *reaction* to some aspects of traditional architecture of the Tokugawa and Meiji period. I am forced to criticize the work of some of the young Japanese architects because their work seems to me to be the very opposite of the immortal principles mentioned by me before. Their work is . . . not simple, it is not natural, it is not truly functional, it is too sophisticated and it is criminally *uneconomical*, for a poor country like Japan, in using more materials than necessary." From a radio interview of Antonin Raymond by Kenzo Tange, April 27, 28, and 29, 1960. Partial English version published in *Architectural Design*, February 1961, pp. 56–57.

4. *An Autobiography*, op. cit., pp. 247–49.

5. In *An Architectural Journey in Japan*, London (Architectural Press), 1963, p. 44, and illustrations pp. 47–48.

6. Autobiographical details of Kenzo Tange's life have recently become available in English in the *Japan Architect*, April 1985–June 1986 (fourteen installments). The series is entitled "Recollections: Architect Kenzo Tange" and is an augmented translation of the thirty installments of *Watakushi no Rirekisho* (A History of My Life), originally published in *Nihon Keizai Shimbun*. The "Palace of the Soviets" episode occurs in the earliest installment, *JA* 8504, p. 11, with photographs of Le Corbusier's submission drawing and model reproduced on pp. 10 and 11. Although Tange was, of course, well acquainted with Sakakura as well as Maekawa in the immediate prewar years, it is significant that, even at a young age, Tange had begun to form an idea of Le Corbusier's work which was independent of these men, who were older by half a generation. They had both worked for Le Corbusier, while Tange did not visit Europe until 1951.

7. Ibid., p. 11.

8. *JA* 8505, p. 7, with illustration, otherwise unpublished.

9. Ibid.

10. The article was published in the December, 1939, issue and was apparently some time in preparation.

11. *JA* 8505, p. 7.

12. Ibid., p. 10.

13. Ibid.

14. Ibid., p. 12.

15. *Space Design* 8001, p. 185. (See note 21, this chap.)

16. Ibid.

17. Published anonymously in Paris (Plon), 1941. Republished by Le Corbusier, Paris (Editions de Minuit), 1957, and subsequent reprintings. The Athens-Marseilles meeting aboard the SS *Patris* examined the existing situation of thirty-three towns. The charter comprised 111 points, later reduced to 95, regarding the functions of housing, leisure, work, and pedestrian/vehicular movement, and also included remarks on the subject of historic buildings and town centers.

The historical outline of my discussion is based in part on the useful summary of CIAM and its principles by Reyner Banham in Gerd Hatje (ed.), *Encyclopaedia of Modern Architecture*, London (Thames and Hudson), 1963, pp. 70–73.

18. "La mort atteint les oeuvres aussi bien que les êtres. Qui fera la discrimination entre ce qui doit subsister et ce qui doit disparaître?" *La Charte d'Athenes*, op. cit., 1957 edition, p. 27.

19. "L'esprit de la cité s'est formé au cours des ans; de simples bâtiments ont pris une valeur éternelle dans la mesure où ils symbolisent l'âme collective; ils sont l'armature d'une tradition qui, sans vouloir limiter l'amplitude des progrès futurs, conditionne la formation de l'individu tel que le feront le climat, la contrée, la race, la coutume. Parce qu'elle est une 'petite patrie,' la cité comporte une valeur morale qui compte et qui lui est indissolublement attachée." Ibid., p. 28.

20. Notably, in English, the novelist Kenzaburo Oe's account of the antinuclear movement entitled *Hiroshima Notes* (*Hiroshima Noto*), edited by David L. Swain and translated by Toshi Yonezawa, YMCA Press, Tokyo, 1981 (original edition Iwanami Shoten).

21. In "My Experiences," *SD* 8001, Special Issue: "Kenzo Tange and Urtec," pp. 184–90, quotation p. 185.

22. Ibid.

23. *JA* 8506, p. 10.

24. Loc. cit. (see note 17, this chap.), p. 72.

25. Ibid., p. 73.

26. Ibid.

27. *SD* 8001, p. 189.

28. For Tange's Otterlo presentation, see Oscar Newman (ed.), *CIAM '59 in Otterlo*, Stuttgart (Karl Krämer), 1961, pp. 170–83, including illustrations. A brief discussion between Tange, Ernesto Rogers, Jerzy Soltan, and Peter Smithson appears on p. 182, from which the conclusion cited is drawn.

29. Ibid., pp. 184–85.

30. *JA* 8508, p. 6.

31. Working papers from the World Design Conference were published in English and Japanese as *World Design Conference 1960 in Tokyo*. This bilingual edition was prepared by the World Design Conference Organization and published by Bijutsu Shuppansha (Tokyo), presumably in 1961. It comprises some 300 pages with illustrations.

32. New Haven (Yale U. Press), published jointly with Zokeisha, Tokyo.

33. P. 1.

34. Idem, p. 10.

35. Idem.

36. Idem, p. 4.

Chapter 8 (pages 186–218)

1. *Chuokoron*, January 1965.

2. "Plans are not politics.
Plans are the rational and poetic monument set up in the midst of contingencies.
Contingencies are the environment: places, peoples, cultures, topographies, climates.
They are, furthermore, the resources liberated by modern techniques. The latter are universal.
Contingencies should only be judged as they relate to the entity—'man'—and in connection with man, in relation to us, to ourselves: a biology
a psychology."
From the title page of *La Ville Radieuse*, Paris (Fréal), 1933. English translation: New York and London (Grossman/Faber and Faber), 1967.

3. "Look now at us, at mankind, endowed by heaven with three precise and totally different characteristics that are able to go on producing new effects from their continual interreactions to all eternity: reason, which is an unbroken straight line; the nature of our earthly destiny, which is a long curve rising from our birth then falling to our death; and passion, which is individual, ever varying and irrepressible.

"Any city, and the underlying plan of that city, is also governed by those three powers. Where are the fortunate conjunctions that will decide the future of that city? But those conjunctions may also, alas, be unfortunate ones too!"
Ibid., p. 82.

4. Ibid., p. 83.

5. Cf. ibid.

6. According to a retrospective formulation by Arata Isozaki.

7. In 1964, Tokyo University established a Department of Urban Engineering, in which Kenzo Tange was named to a chair of Urban Design. It was deemed necessary to orient the new division toward civil engineering, hence the name, in order to persuade the Ministry of Education not to withhold support. Predictably, however, emphasis came to rest on issues of city administration rather than design.

8. Poet-philosopher and historian of ideas (1889–1960.) His *Fudo* of 1935 is translated by G. Bownas as *A Climate—A Philosophical Study*, distributed by the Ministry of Education (1961). This essay was intended as a plea against cultural uniqueness written with one eye on the censor. However, it contains numerous arguments which have become general property—often misapplied in casual discourse to furnish evidence for a point of view Watsuji himself would have opposed.

9. *An Autobiography*, op. cit, p. 178.

10. Cf. Alison and Peter Smithson, "The Rebirth of Japanese Architecture" in *Architectural Design*, special Japan issue, February 1961, pp. 66–67.

11. English translation in *Kazuo Shinohara*, catalogue 17 of the Institute for Architecture and Urban Studies, New York (Rizzoli), 1982, p. 20.

12. Arguments of this type are contained in several published writings by Tange, including the introduction to his book on Katsura, op. cit. Cf. also "Creation in Present-day Architecture and the Japanese Architectural Tradition" in *Japan Architect*, June 1956, pp. 25–33, from which the quotations that follow are taken.

13. Le Corbusier, *Oeuvre complete*, op. cit., vol. 6, 1957, p. 152.

14. Cf. ibid., vol. 7, 1965, p. 189.

15. A more comprehensive historical treatment of traditional Japanese buildings in a similar vein is available in Mitsuo Inoue, *Nihon Kenchiku no Kukan*, Tokyo (Kajima Shuppan-kai), 1969. This has now been translated into English by Hiroshi Watanabe as *Space in Japanese Architecture*, Tokyo (Weatherhill), 1985. Inoue graduated from Tokyo Institute of Technology some years before Shinohara, and the above work is based on his Ph.D. thesis, submitted in 1961 to the same university. The distinction between spatial division and connection (or addition) is referred by Inoue to Paul Frankl's *Die Entwicklungsphasen der*

neueren Baukunst of 1914. Cf. note 1 to chap. 4 on p. 194 of Watanabe's translation.

16. Inoue (see previous note) deals with the issue of "frontality" in buildings of the Heian period on p. 49 and at length in a section of chap. 3 called "The Development of Frontality," pp. 60–66. The stroll garden and the characteristic movement it generates are discussed on pp. 165–66, although the topic of movement in general is the theme of chap. 5 entitled "From Geometrical Space to Movement Space," pp. 137–71.

By contrast with Inoue, Shinohara's interpretations are based on analysis of earlier—as well as vernacular—structures, with less emphasis on later changes in Japanese architecture, such as those which occurred during the Edo period.

17. Inoue (see notes 15 and 16, this chap.) ends with a short discussion of the Buddhist notions of *kyomu* (nothingness) and *koku* (emptiness), or at just that point where a number of contemporary Japanese architects seem to derive their design theories. Inoue holds involvement with such themes to have been characteristic of Japanese medieval culture, whereas during the succeeding Edo, or feudal, period "the intention was to create a space full of movement and change, not a boundless abyss." Loc. cit., p. 170.

18. A fairly widespread notion—but one that, on Shinohara's part, is comparatively lightly freighted. By contrast, Inoue is more emphatic "This [notion of 'emptiness'] is the very antithesis of the Western manner of thought, represented by Descartes's *cogito ergo sum*. . . ." Ibid., p. 136. Depending on received interpretations of Cartesian philosophy, the point remains, of course, an arguable one.

19. The quotations in this paragraph, though entirely in the spirit of *Residential Architecture*, are from the first four pages of part 1 of a three-part "Anthology" of Shinohara's writings which appeared in *Space Design* magazine (*SD 7901*, pp. 73–85), a special issue devoted to his work. The anthology was compiled by Akio Kurosaka from seven different published items, *Residential Architecture* being the earliest in date.

20. A natural conclusion for a mathematician, this notion deserves closer analysis. There is a brief discussion of the topological nature of Japanese "movement space" in Inoue, op. cit., pp. 144–45.

21. Now available in the collection *The Mathematics of the Ideal Villa and Other Essays*, Cambridge and London (MIT Press), 1976, pp. 185–203.

22. *Oeuvre complete*, op. cit., vol. 2, 1964, pp. 72–73.

23. Ibid., vols. 4 and 7, pp. 164 ff.

24. Loc. cit., p. 189.

25. Vincent Scully, *The Le Corbusier Archive*, vol. 2: *Le Corbusier 1922–1965*, New York and London (Garland), 1983, p. ix.

26. Loc. cit., p. 191.

27. Ibid., p. 200.

28. At the end of his essay, thus: "the ability to charge depth with surface, to condense spatial concavities into plane, to drag to its most eloquent pitch the *dichotomy* between the rotund and the flat is the absolutely distinguishing mark of Le Corbusier's later style." (My emphasis.)

Chapter 9 (pages 219–36)

1. Special issue of *Space Design*, April 1976, devoted to the work of Arata Isozaki, p. 164 (translation amended).

2. December, 1968.

3. Originally published in *Kenchiku Bunka*, May 1964. Now also available, in Japanese, in the collection *Kukan-e* (Toward Space), Tokyo (Bijutsu Shuppansha), 1971, pp. 146–64.

4. See Oscar Newman (ed.), *CIAM '59 in Otterlo*, Stuttgart (Karl Krämer), 1961, pp. 26–34.

5. Ibid., p. 27.

6. Van Eyck's substitution is typical of the distance Team X ideas had come from the orthodox pronouncements of CIAM. Cf., for example, the title of Siegfried Giedion's famous textbook *Space, Time and Architecture* of 1941. Giedion, together with his friend and compatriot Le Corbusier, were founding members of CIAM but, after Otterlo, became disparagers and chastizers of Team X. Yet van Eyck's building for the Hubertus Association in Amsterdam (completed in 1980) was, it may be noted, dedicated to the memory of Giedion's wife, who died in 1979.

7. In Alison Smithson, (ed.), *Team Ten Primer*, London (Studio Vista), 1965, p. 43 (and quoted in *Architectural Design*, special issue, December 1962). Cf. also MIT Press edition of 1968.

8. Newman (ed.), op. cit., p. 27.

9. First published in 1959, the year of Otterlo, but already presented in 1950 and again in 1951. Titled "Die Sprache," this lecture is based on the example of Georg Trakl's famous poem "A Winter Evening," and is available in English in Martin Heidegger, *Poetry, Language, and Thought*, New York (Harper and Row), 1971 and 1975, pp. 189–210.

10. Attributed, however, by van Eyck to the Smithsons, at the previous CIAM meeting (Aix-en-Provence) in 1954.

11. Newman (ed.), op. cit., p. 28.

12. Ibid.

13. Ibid., p. 33.

14. Ibid., p. 27.

15. Ibid., p. 30.

16. Ibid.

17. *Le visible et l'invisible*, published posthumously: Paris (Gallimard), 1964, and translated as *The Visible and the Invisible*, Evanston (Northwestern U. Press), 1968. Cf. p. 171 of the section "Working Notes of the English Edition."

18. Newman (ed.), op. cit., p. 26.

19. Ibid., p. 28.

20. *Late Baroque and Rococo Architecture*, Milan, 1971, and English translation, New York (Abrams), 1974, p. 311.

21. *Meaning in Western Architecture*, Milan, 1974, and English translation, 1975, rev. ed. New York (Rizzoli), 1980, pp. 145–46.

22. Ibid., p. 145.

23. Ibid., p. 146.

24. On Heidegger, see also Christian Norberg-Schulz, "Heidegger's Thinking on Architecture" in *Perspecta: The Yale Architectural Journal* 20, 1983, pp. 61–68.

25. The earliest attempts must be Heidegger's 1951 lecture entitled *Bauen Wohnen Denken* (Building Dwelling Thinking), published first in 1954 (available in English, loc. cit., pp. 145–61), and Gaston Bachelard's *La poetique de l'espace* (1958), translated as *The Poetics of Space*, 1964, and Boston (Beacon Paperbacks), 1969. Neither bears in particular on the preceding discussion although each affords a (different) phenomenological approach to architectural topics.

26. "Introduction to the First Edition," second edition (1977), p. 9.

27. The essay (in Japanese: *"Inei raisan"*) appeared in two parts in *Keizai Orai*, December 1933 and January 1934. Translated excerpts by E. G. Seidensticker were initially printed in *Atlantic Monthly* (January 1955). A complete edition of this translation was issued at New Haven, CT, (Leete's Island Books), 1977.

28. Ibid., p. 34.

29. Quotations in this paragraph are from "Rereading 'In Praise of Shadows.'" This was Isozaki's directive essay for the 1975 *Shinkenchiku* Residential Competition, published as " 'Inei Raisan' Saidoku" in *Shinkenchiku* (June 1974). It is now also available in *Shuhō ga* (Manner), Tokyo (Bijutsu Shuppansha), 1979, pp. 126–43.

30. Originally published in *Tembo*, November 1967. Now available in Japanese in *Kukan-e*, op. cit., pp. 380–404.

Chapter 10 (pages 237–81)

1. In "Frank Lloyd Wright's View of Space" in Yukio Futagawa (editor and photographer) and Arata Isozaki, *GA 1: Frank Lloyd Wright: Johnson and Son Administration Building and Research Tower, Racine, Wisconsin. 1936–9*, Tokyo (ADA Edita), 1970, pp. 2–7, quotation p. 3 (my interpolation and emphasis).

2. "The Destruction of the Box," addressed to the Junior Chapter of the AIA, New York City. This lecture was published in at least two versions. The quotation given by Isozaki is from Edgar Kaufmann (ed.), *An American Architecture: Frank Lloyd Wright*, New York (Horizon Press), 1955, p. 80. The same talk is reprinted in Kaufmann and Raeburn, op. cit., pp. 284–89, just five years later but without any reference to the venerable Chinese philosopher Lao-tzu. There the effect of destroying the box is ascribed to the "use [of] steel and glass [to provide] a third dimension" (p. 289).

3. Reprint edition, Rutland, VT, and Tokyo (Charles E. Tuttle), 1956, p. 45.

4. In Futagawa and Isozaki, op. cit., p. 3.

5. Ibid.

6. Ibid.

7. Ibid.

8. Ibid., p. 4.

9. This contrast with previous approaches is described in an article entitled *Naze Shuhō ga Nano ka* (proposed English title: Manner to Manipulate Meaning), published in *A + U*, January 1972. It is now also available in *Shuhō ga* (see note 29, chap. 9), pp. 10–33.

10. Systematically catalogued and diagrammed in the article "About My Method" in *Japan Architect*, August 1972, pp. 22–28, as part of a "Special Feature: Recent Works by Arata Isozaki" (pp. 22–76). Works documented in that issue are the Head Office for the Fukuoka Mutual Bank at Hakata, as well as the branches at Nagasumi and Ropponmatsu and the extension of the Medical Hall at Oita.

11. Ibid., p. 22.

12. Ibid.

13. *Kenchiku Kaitai*, Bijutsu Shuppansha; title also translatable as "The Dissolution of Architecture." The component articles appeared in the art magazine *Bijutsu Teicho* from 1969 onward.

14. "About My Method," loc. cit., p. 22.

15. "As each piece on a chessboard carries an individual and symbolic meaning, so physical objects placed within a space—whether interior partitions or a vast wall set in an urban space—become code elements establishing zones of their own." Ibid., p. 24.

16. Ibid.

17. Ibid.

18. Ibid.

19. In *Japan Architect*, April 1976, pp. 64–67

20. Ibid., p. 65.

21. *O Mayakovskom* (Mayakovsky and His Circle), Moscow (Sovetsky Pisatel'), 1940, English translation Lily Feiler, New York (Dodd, Mead) 1972 and London (Pluto Press), 1974, p. 125.

22. Quoted by Isozaki from his own earlier "Space of Darkness" in "From Manner, to Rhetoric, to ...," loc. cit., p. 65.

23. "Han-Kenchiku-teki Noto III" (Semi-architectural Note III) in *Kenchiku Bunka*, December 1972, ibid., p. 66.

24. "A New Wave of Japanese Architecture," at the Institute for Architecture and Urban Studies, New York, September 25 to November 14, 1978. Catalogue 10, IAUS, introduced by Kenneth Frampton.

25. Idem, catalogue 17, *Kazuo Shinohara*, New York (Rizzoli International), 1982.

26. Or *scena per angolo*. This family originated near Bologna and became the leading theatrical designers in early eighteenth-century Italy. Piranesi was born in 1720 in Venice but settled in Rome about 1745. In the stage designs—as in the *Carceri*—the central viewpoint characteristic of Renaissance perspective was dispensed with in favor of a plurality of *foci*, or so it would seem. The perspective system, in reality, is never actually violated or abandoned.

27. At the Minami Gallery, Tokyo. His "sculpture" was a model of the Oita Branch which emitted black light, based on the notion of "making space unreal by means of color." See Yoshiaki Tono, "Architecture for the Miniskirt Age," *Japan Architect*, May 1968, pp. 32–36, quotation p. 33. The actual colors of the first-floor banking hall at Oita were cobalt blue, with red, pink, yellow, and green. Isozaki is quoted as endorsing "the feeling of raw power, of 'incompleteness' they produced" (p. 34). Tono, who organized the "Space and Color" exhibition, adds that the building "promotes in the people within it the feeling that, in moving about, seeing things with their bodies, and touching them with their vision, they are actually creating the space. In other words," he goes on, "the building has something of the incomplete nature of a miniskirt: it invites familiarity and participation ..." (ibid.). Cf. also color illustrations in *SD 7604* (see note 1, chap. 9), pp. 148–49.

28. *Kemonotachi wa Kokyo o Mezasu* (The Beasts Go Homeward), in *Gunzo*, January to April 1957. Quoted from a passage translated by Hisaaki Yamanouchi in his important *Search for Authenticity in Modern Japanese Literature*, Cambridge (CUP), 1978, pp. 155–56.

29. This, to my mind, is the principal difficulty that besets the interpretation of Isozaki's work found in the monograph by Philip Drew entitled *The Architecture of Arata Isozaki*, London (Granada), 1982.

30. In *Mannerism*, Harmondsworth (Penguin Books: Pelican "Style and Civilization" Series), 1967, p. 17.

31. Ibid.

32. Professor Shearman's characterization, ibid., p. 15.

33. Cf. "Control and Violation," *Japan Architect*, August 1972, p. 38.

34. Ibid.

35. Ibid.

36. Cf. Adolfo Natalini, "Presentazione/Descrizione/Dichiarazione" in *Superstudio* (catalogue of the exhibition at Istituto nazionali de architecttura, March 20–23, 1978), Florence (Centro Di, cat. no. 97), 1978, unnumbered (p. 1).

37. Ibid., catalogue entry for item 5.

38. Ibid., photograph item 12. The work of Superstudio was well publicized in Japan by the magazine *Japan Interior Design* as early as 1970 in its special issue no. 138 entitled "Superstudio/Design."

39. Published in English in *Japan Architect*, March 1976, pp. 27–32.

40. Ibid., especially pp. 27–29.

41. Ibid., p. 27.

42. Ibid., p. 28.

43. Ibid., p. 31.

44. "Rhetoric of the Cylinder" was the title of an essay first published in English in *Japan Architect*, April 1976, pp. 61–63. It was preceded by two pages of "Personal Notes on the Cylinder and the Semicylinder," pp. 59–60, just as, one month earlier, "The Metaphor of the Cube" had been introduced by "Personal Notes on the Cube," *Japan Architect*, March 1976, pp. 24–26. Together these notes explain the evolution of Isozaki's two main formal principles of the decade through sixteen of his works and projects.

45. "Personal Notes on the Cylinder and the Semicylinder," loc. cit., p. 59.

46. Ibid.

47. Loc. cit., p. 63.

48. Cf. Arata Isozaki, "The Ledoux Connection," in *Architectural Design* (London), no. 52, January/February 1982, pp. 28–29.

49. See the article of the same name published in English in *Japan Architect*, March 1978, pp. 10–17 plus illustrations.

50. Published in English in *Japan Architect*, January 1979, pp. 9–11 plus illustrations. Following quotation, p. 9.

51. Ibid., p. 11.

52. English-language edition *MA: Space-Time in Japan* published by the Cooper-Hewitt Museum (The Smithsonian Institution's National Museum for Design), New York, no date.

53. Subtitled "An Introduction to Primary Spaces as Functional Spaces." Published in English in *Japan Architect*, April 1971, pp. 81–88. Following quotation, p. 81.

54. Ibid., p. 85.

55. Ibid., p. 88.

56. In "When Naked Space Is Traversed," originally *Shinkenchiku* (October 1975). A barely adequate English version of this almost untranslatable text is available in *Japan Architect*, February 1976, pp. 64–69, quotation p. 65.

57. Ibid., p. 64.

58. Ibid., p. 69.

59. Ibid., p. 66.

60. Cf. "... the social is not *collective consciousness* but intersubjectivity, a living relationship and tension among individuals" in "The Metaphysical in Man" (Le Metaphysique dans l'Homme) in *Revue de métaphysique et de Morale*, nos. 3–4, July 1947. English translation in Maurice Merleau-Ponty, *Sense and Non-Sense*, Evanston (Northwestern U. Press) 1964, p. 90.

61. Ibid., p. 93.

62. In "When Naked Space Is Traversed," loc. cit., Shinohara twice quotes from the Japanese translation of Deleuze's *Proust et les signes*, Paris (PUF), 1970, enlarged edition. The second part of this work is a new essay entitled "La Machine Littéraire"; the construct of *transversales* is introduced on p. 152 as a literary device—posited by Deleuze as having been used by Proust in his *Remembrance of Things Past* to

multiply aspects of character, place, and time in that work. The process is said to be illustrated by the celebrated passage of *Within a Budding Grove* in which the narrator recounts running from one window to another in a train in order to piece together a continuous view of the passing landscape. In fact, the notion is adumbrated by Georges Poulet as follows:

> And behold, all at once, a movement is completed in this emptiness [the Proustian world]. For the first time the mind accompanies an object in its progression. Space is consequently not the endless reiteration of an hiatus, the exclusion of all places by all places, the impossibility of transporting oneself from one locality to another. Space is not negative. It is traversible. The object that crosses it reveals it to the mind.

In *L'espace proustien*, Paris (Gallimard), 1963. English translation, Baltimore and London (Johns Hopkins U. Press), 1977, p. 58. The railroad passage is quoted in full on p. 79. Deleuze's work, then, proposes a modification and extension of Poulet's concept of unity by underwriting it with an augmented notion of *"transversalité."*

63. "When Naked Space Is Traversed," loc. cit., p. 66.
64. Ibid.
65. Ibid.
66. Ibid.
67. Ibid., p. 67.
68. Ibid., p. 68.
69. *Skyline* (New York), May 1979, p. 4.
70. Cf. Shinohara's account in "Now and Function" in *SD* 7901, (see note 19, chap. 8), pp. 6–13.

Additional Sources and Further Reading

With the exception of a few publications to be cited below, virtually all English-language sources have been explained in the notes. In fact, no real bibliography concerning modern Japanese architecture is possible in English, works on this subject in all European languages being meager and, by and large, unsatisfactory. By contrast, in Japanese, resources are numerous but more than usually uneven—extending from chronicle or local history, on the one hand, to an elliptic form of essaylike criticism at the opposite extreme—a spectrum which, overall, provides surprisingly little middle ground in the way of stylistic history. Still and all, for the second half of the one-hundred year span from the late 1860s to the mid-1970s as dealt with here, there is fortunately one alleviating circumstance. Ever since architectural publishing began in earnest in Japan, the principal journals have pursued and maintained their own dogged and relentless chronicle of the nation's building, somewhat in the conscientious manner of our own nineteenth-century publications. In consequence, month by month from the mid-1920s until the present, this account can be followed with a more or less undeviating rhythm. And, still today, the same precedent decrees that a Japanese building be published first in the national press (rather than, say, in an Italian or American magazine) fairly soon upon completion and, frequently, at about the time occupation begins. Criticism, other than the architect's own statement about his work, is usually agreed upon between the architect and the editorial staff of the review in question. A work of real note may appear in rival publications of the same month—with sets of photographs taken on alternate days by staff photographers working exclusively for each magazine, or by independent photographers commissioned by the editors.

Only *Shinkenchiku* (with its postwar English-language edition, *Japan Architect*) has survived the rigors of over half a century, with barely a pause at the height of the Pacific war, when, of course, building as well as publishing were brought temporarily to a halt. Its best (mainly) prewar rival was *Kokusaikenchiku*, and its chief postwar concurrent has been *Kenchikubunka*. Naturally, there are, and have been, other publications in the field. Still, from the point of view of research, it is rather a major inconvenience that no complete run of either *Shinkenchiku* or *Kokusaikenchiku* exists anywhere in Japan, including the National Diet Library (the equivalent of the Library of Congress) or that of the Architectural Institute of Japan. Nor are there archives of any sort for either publication.

All the same, with the help of various university libraries, it has proved possible to get a look at most early issues of these two main periodicals. A parallel resource has been the "complete works," or *sakuhinshu*, and, sometimes, the collected writings, of the architects themselves, although I have not cited any of these by chapter and verse except in the case of direct quotation. Both forms of documentation were realized, in the main, only from the postwar period onward and are easily accessible, by author, for anyone able to make use of a Japanese library catalogue. Nevertheless, there are a few cases of architects either who have left no volume of works, such as Kikuji Ishimoto, or whose self-commemorative book (or books) is so heavily weighted in favor of later work, thus Bunzo Yamaguchi, that very little of historiographical use can be drawn from them, and periodical publications must be resorted to once again. In virtually all instances, prewar documents in autograph form, such as sketches, drawings, plans, and even blueprints have so far proved unavailable. It has, fortunately, nonetheless, been possible to include a few such items among the illustrative material, and it is possible that further pieces still await discovery, especially if they were preserved in safekeeping outside Tokyo during the war period.

* * *

Concerning the Meiji period (1868–1911), where Westernization is the chief issue, the picture is somewhat different. Its architecture stemmed from a new profession—just as did banking or the practice of law—and is part of the panorama of social changes based point for point on an alien order of phenomena. The process of documentation as we know it was a part of that order of things and correspondences are easily plotted, as on a graph. There remains a wealth of information which might be wrought into a visually-oriented social history of this fairly long historical era, whose ethos is still remembered and cultivated by the Japanese. All the same, it would be well to allow as how this has never resulted in any history of a hypothetical Meiji "style." The reason is not far to seek, namely, that any such history—as opposed to, say, one of technique or, alternatively, of sensibility—is foreign to the basic tenets that, even today, underlie Japanese art.

The present book, as may be imagined, has been written from the point of view of Western historiographical notions, in accordance with which the innovator of any particular stylistic feature is entitled, retrospectively, to certain rights or claims. As is generally known, oriental art professes but minor respect for and interest in such ideas. There, instead, the theory is that each return to and reworking of a theme contributes something intrinsic to an unceasing—so to say, basically, immutable—flow of aesthetic sensibility. This understanding should not be confused with our "history of art" or even the broader notion of "history of taste." However, by Western standards, *The Making of a Modern Japanese Architecture, 1868 to the Present* may be found by some to err in an attempt to see the Japanese view in such matters. Even so, from a Japanese perspective, it will doubtless appear bluntly straightforward.

For the very reason that emerges from the sum of these highly condensed, if meditative, considerations on style and on art, there is nothing very like a standard history of modern Japanese architecture in Japanese. I have benefited, all the same, from a few starting points not named in the chapter notes and which I would like now to mention. Most of these works take the notions and practices subsumed under "Meiji architecture" as a beginning, and some even proceed to treat later buildings as part of a continuum of Western architectural ideas reaching forward in time, in a wistfully vague sort of way, toward a present state of affairs with which they have, mildly speaking, remarkably little in common. In fact, although in terms of academic training, the architectural profession does encompass history and affords shelter to historians, there is in practice rather a sharp divide between historical studies and contemporary practice. While some of the works referred to below are clearly limited, as is implied in their titles, to a particular period such as Meiji, in those which are not one should scarcely expect to be carried up to anywhere near the impending final years of the present reign.

Initially, I relied on the two short and classic accounts of Meiji architecture available in English: Teijiro Muramatsu, "Ventures into Western Architecture" in Chisaburoh F. Yamada (ed.), *Dialogue in Art: Japan and the West*, Tokyo and New York (Kodansha International), 1976, pp. 113–48 (illustrations grouped in the text), and Kimimasa Abe, "Meiji Architecture" in Naoteru Uyeno, *Japanese Arts and Crafts in the Meiji Era* (Centenary Culture Council Series: Japanese Culture in the Meiji Era, vol. 8) Tokyo (Pan-Pacific Press), 1958, part 6, pp. 177–98 (and plates 125–62, grouped at the back of the volume). A summary by Professor Abe of his material appeared as "Early Western Architecture in Japan," *Journal of the Society of Architectural Historians* 13:2, pp. 13–18, in 1954.

In addition, *Japan Architect* featured a monthly serialization during the course of 1960 entitled: "A Short History of Modern Japanese Architecture." The articles, of which a total of eight seem to have been published, begin with Meiji and bring the story up to the mid postwar period. The series was edited and written by Shindo Akashi and Yuichiro Kojiro and is partly illustrated. However, as with *Shinkenchiku*, there is no run of *Japan Architect* intact anywhere in Japan; thus, for the English-language edition, the New York Public Library is a good source. With some inevitable repetition, *Japan Architect*, vol. 109, June 1965, is devoted to a topical treatment of historic modern Japanese architecture—in three sections by Teijiro Muramatsu, Hiro Sasaki, and Hiroki Onobayashi—from before the Meiji period to World War II. This issue also contains a useful "Chronological Table of Japanese Architecture: 1840–1945," pp. 85–103, compiled by Masaru Maeno.

The best and most up-to-date general series dealing with the history of modern Japanese architecture is *Nihon no Kenchiku: Meiji–Taisho–Showa (West Meets East: The Japanese Introduction to Western Architecture in [the] 19th and 20th Centuries)*, Tokyo (Sanseido), 1979 onward and subsequent reprintings. It comprises ten volumes dealing, as the series title suggests, with the grafting of Western notions upon the main trunk of Japanese architectural development from the earliest years of Meiji until the hiatus caused by World War II. Regarding the themes I have dealt with in my initial two chapters, three volumes of Sanseido's series are of particular interest: (1) Takeshi Koshino, *Kaika no Katachi* (The Forms of the Opening of Japan), (2) Shigekatsu Onogi, *Yoshiki no Ishizue* (The Foundation of Style) and (3) Terunobu Fujimori, *Kokka no Dezain* (Design for the Nation). The penultimate volume, (9) Masami Tanigawa, *Raito no Isan* (The Legacy of Wright), enlarges upon the topic of the direct influence of Frank Lloyd Wright in Japanese architecture. All volumes are standard in their production and make use of a large number of excellent large-format color photographs of extant buildings.

For the Meiji period itself, several more pioneering volumes may be consulted:

Saburo Horikoshi, *Meiji Shoki no Yofu Kenchiku* (original subtitle: Early Meiji Architecture), Tokyo (Nanyodo Shoten), 1929 and facsimile reprint by Maruzen, Co., Ltd., no date.

Wajiro Kon (ed.), with Hiroichiro Oizumi and Jun Hirasawa, *Kenchiku Hyakunen Shi* (A Hundred-Year History of Architecture), Tokyo (The Hundred-Year History of Architecture Committee), 1957. Somewhat more than half the book deals with Meiji, with the rest covering the period up to 1940.

Katsuhiko Sakamoto, *Meiji no Jinkan: Jinkan, 1858–1912* (original subtitle: Japan's Western Architecture in [the] Meiji Era), Tokyo (Asahi Newspaper Corporation), 1965.

In addition, three more recent works have been produced under direction of Teijiro Muramatsu:

Meiji no Yofu Kenchiku (Meiji Western-style Architecture), special issue of *Kindai no Bijutsu* (Shibundo), January 1974.

Nihon no Yoshiki Kenchiku (Japanese [Classical-]Style Architecture), non-sequential issue of *Shinkenchiku*, June 1976. Mostly, but not wholly, devoted to Meiji architecture.

Nihon Kindai Kenchiku Soran: Kakuchi ni Nokoru Meiji Taisho Showa no Tatemono (A Comprehensive Handlist of Surviving Examples of Buildings from the Meiji, Taisho, and Showa Periods), Tokyo (Gihodo Shuppansha for the Architectural Institute of Japan), 1980. Purports to be exhaustive as regards Meiji building, listing all instances of surviving structures throughout the country.

Concerning the architecture of Josiah Conder, the following are essential:

Yoshiyuki Kawahigashi, *Josaia Kondoru: Kenchiku Zumenshu* (Josiah Conder: Collection of His Architectural Drawings), Tokyo (Chuo Koron Bijutsu Shuppansha), 1981. Three volumes accompanied by a text in Japanese and a brief introduction in English by the compiler.

Hiroyuki Suzuki, "Josaia Kondoru no Kenchikukan to Nihon" in the commemorative volume for Professor H. Ota: *Nihon Kenchiku no Tokushitsu: Ota Hirotaro Hakushi Kanreki Kinnen Ronbunshu*, Tokyo (Chuo Koron Bijutsu Shuppansha), 1976, pp. 457–507. An account of Conder's architectural concepts and Japan, which is paralleled by the same author's *Josaia Kondoru to Eikoku* (Josiah Conder and England) in *Kenchikushi Kenkyu*, 40, September 1976, pp. 1–15.

* * *

On the theme of Japanese urban-planning history, Dr. Shunichi J. Watanabe, who directs the Building Research Institute's Urban Planning Department, is the recognized expert. He was kind enough to provide me with a copy of his paper "Metropolitanism as a Way of Life: The Case of Tokyo, 1868–1930" delivered at the Second International Conference on the History of Urban and Regional Planning, held at Brighton in August 1980. I have pillaged it shamelessly; nevertheless, whoever desires more information on the subject will want to get hold of the same author's "Planning History in Japan: A State of the Art Survey," BRI Research Paper no. 86, August 1980, 25 pages plus notes. The Building Research Institute is a division of the Ministry of Construction, whose various agencies over the years since World War II have issued a number of highly worthwhile papers and pamphlets in English.

By contrast, there is really very little, if anything, in English dealing with the complex issues of Taisho and early Showa architecture. In Japanese, Arata Isozaki has written on stylistic aspects of the 1930s and its architecture, while a more wide-ranging account of that period may be found in the work of the research group Dojidai Kenchiku Kenkyukai entitled: *Hikigeki: 1930 Nendai no Kenchiku to Bunka* (Tragicomedy: Architecture and Culture of the 1930s), Tokyo (Gendai Kikakushitsu), 1981.

In German, there is now an interesting and attractive account of the modern period, which is both more inclusive of diverse types of recent work and more socially oriented than mine (an influence of Waseda University). This compendium is Manfred Speidel, *Japanische Architektur Geschichte und Gegenwart*, Stuttgart (Hatje for the Akademie der Architektenkammer Nordrhein-Westfalen), 1983. It contains writings by a number of living Japanese architects as well as the republication of several essays by Bruno Taut.

* * *

An enduring problem is the challenge of trying to attain a working comprehension of traditional Japanese "design"—including the art and techniques of gardening—as much as possible on its own terms. Of course, there is no single reliable guide in this undertaking, albeit the thirty-volume Weatherhill translation of the Heibonsha Survey of Japanese Art will be available to most English-speaking readers in many libraries and bookshops. A few select books on older Japanese architecture are now appearing in translation, such as Kakichi Suzuki, *Early Buddhist Architecture in Japan*, Tokyo and New York (Kodansha International), 1980. A good overall account may be had in the *Japanese* volume written by Tomoya Masuda in the "Living Architecture" series, London (Macdonald), 1971, or in the edition published a year earlier by Office du Livre, Fribourg. A more recent and simplified general survey, in accessible form with a list of sites and a map, is the English version of Kazuo Nishi and Kazuo Hozumi, *Nihon Kenchiku no Katachi: Seikatsu to Kenchiku-zokei no Rekishi*, entitled *What Is Japanese Architecture?*, Tokyo and New York (Kodansha International), 1983. For classical gardens, Marc Treib and Ron Herman, *A Guide to the Gardens of Kyoto*, Tokyo (Shufunotomo), 1980 and subsequent reprintings, is the handy and indispensable short work on a subject that, otherwise, is ill-adapted to discursive treatment in books.

The best work in English, and likely also one of the best in Japanese, on the delicate and problematic topic of the *sukiya* is Teiji Itoh, *The Elegant Japanese House: Traditional Sukiya Architecture*, New York and Tokyo (Weatherhill/Tankosha), 1969, an adaptation of the author's *Sukiya*, Kyoto (Tankosha), 1967. Incidentally, most older accounts in English of post-medieval Japanese architecture are unreliable (excepting strict chronological matters) in any treatment of the difficult and vexed issues of *shoin* and *sukiya*. In this very connection, it is perhaps insidious to specify one single book dealing with the origins and practice of the Japanese tea ceremony. However, Herbert E. Plutschow, *Historical Chanoyu*, Tokyo (The Japan Times, Ltd.), 1986, written by a foreign tea adept, is both informed and readily understandable without either being dogmatic or pretending to a self-contradictory completeness.

To return, finally, to the matter of "Japanese" space, underlying, as it does, discussion of both traditional, as well as very recent, Japanese architecture, there is a further work of exceptional interest and importance—although it does not deal with buildings at all. This is Noël Burch, *To the Distant Observer: Form and Meaning in the Japanese Cinema*, London (Scholar Press), 1979, a sequel to the same author's earlier *Praxis du cinema* (1967). While the book is written in a style that is occasionally difficult to make out, this is forgivable, since Burch here propounds the first Western analysis of space in the art of the Japanese film. As the explanation of works and, in particular, individual "takes" is fairly technical, the author provides an excellent argument, couched in the terms of another discipline, for anyone remaining unconvinced of the closely related ways in which space is manipulated in old and new Japanese architecture.

* * *

Lastly, although *The Making of a Modern Japanese Architecture, 1868 to the Present* makes no pretense to more than a passing familiarity with the events of nineteenth- and twentieth-century Japanese political history, I believe that one could fare far worse than to be guided (as I have) by the interpretation contained in Richard Storry, *Japan and the Decline of the West in Asia, 1894–1943*, London and Basingstoke (Macmillan), 1979, and more generally by the same author's *A History of Modern Japan*, Harmondsworth (Penguin), 1976.

List of Illustrations

1.1. Tokyo–Yokohama Railway, 1872, showing Yokohama terminal at Sakuragi-cho by Bridgens. Woodblock print by Hiroshige III.
1.2. The Bund, or waterfront, at Yokohama before 1866. Woodblock print by Hiroshige III.
1.3. Nagasaki at the beginning of the Meiji period.
1.4. British and other "factories" at Canton, eighteenth century. Chinese export ware bowl in the Idemitsu Museum of Art, Tokyo.
1.5. Glover Residence at Oura, Nagasaki, 1863. Painting by Soko Ochiai in the Nagasaki Prefectural Museum and early plan with dependencies.
1.6. Waters: the Mint at Osaka, 1868-71. Riverfront alignment of foundry and outbuildings.
1.7. Waters: the Mint at Osaka, 1868-71. Portico of the foundry building.
1.8. Waters: the Mint at Osaka, 1868-71. Sempukan, or reception pavilion, to the rear of the foundry.
1.9. Waters: Takebashi Barracks, 1870-74. Bird's-eye view, from a popular engraving.
1.10. Waters: Takebashi Barracks, 1870-74. Main front.
1.11. Waters: redeveloped Ginza district, or so-called Bricktown, 1872 onward. Woodblock print by Kuniteru II.
1.12. Tateishi: Kaichi Primary School, Matsumoto, Nagano Prefecture, 1876. View from main gate.
1.13. Shimizu: Tsukiji Hotel for foreigners, Tokyo, 1867-68. Woodblock print by Kuniteru II.
1.14. Shimizu: First Mitsui Bank, Kaiunbashi, Tokyo, 1871-72.
1.15. Shimizu: First Mitsui Bank, Kaiunbashi, Tokyo, 1871-72. Woodblock print by Kuniteru II.
1.16. The "Incomparable" British Consulate at Yokohama, completed in 1868. Woodblock print by Kunimasa IV. Smaller view shows three towers superimposed, as in perspective.
1.17. Tateishi: Kaichi Primary School, Matsumoto, Nagano Prefecture, 1876. Porch (detail of figure 1.12).
1.18. Woodblock print depicting the Roman Forum, Toyoharu, before 1814.
1.19. Woodblock print ostensibly of a town in the Netherlands. Toyoharu, before 1814.
1.20. Hayashi: Liberal Arts College, Tokyo, 1873.
1.21. Hayashi: Ministry of Communications (combined with the Nihonbashi Post Office), Nihonbashi, Tokyo, 1874.
1.22. Shimizu: Second Mitsui Bank, Surugacho, Tokyo, 1874. Facade viewed from the right, and lateral elevation.

2.1. De Boinville: auditorium building at the technical college, later Imperial College of Engineering, Tokyo, 1877.
2.2. Tokyo High Court, Tokyo, 1874.
2.3. Burges: Bombay School of Art, 1865. Unrealized project.
2.4. Conder: Ueno Imperial Museum, Tokyo, 1882. Woodblock print and floor plans.
2.5. Conder: Iwasaki Villa, Fukugawa, Tokyo, 1889. Plan shows dependency with conservatory and billiards room.
2.6. Shaw: Alliance Assurance Offices, London, 1881-83.
2.7. Ende und Böckmann: Parliament and Exhibition Grounds near the Imperial Palace, Tokyo, 1887. Existing palace moats with imaginary new construction.
2.8. Ende und Böckmann: Imperial Diet Building, Tokyo. First scheme, 1887 (unrealized).
2.9. Ende und Böckmann: Parliament and Exhibition Grounds near the Imperial Palace, Tokyo, 1887. Proposal for railway extension and location of ministries.
2.10. Ende und Böckmann: Imperial Diet Building, Tokyo. Second scheme, 1887 (unrealized). From *Deutsche Bauzeitung*, 1891.
2.11. Ende: Compromise solution for a public garden (later Hibiya Park) ringed by ministries, 1887 or 1888.
2.12. Tokyo in 1914, showing the Imperial Palace enclosure and location of the fifteen original wards.
2.13. North German Lloyd Lines headquarters, Bremen. Undated bird's-eye view.
2.14. Rathaus, Bremen, late nineteenth-century view.
2.15. Ende und Böckmann: Ministry of Justice, Kasumigaseki, Tokyo, 1895. Lateral view of facade, now altered.
2.16. Ende und Böckmann: Ministry of Justice, Kasumigaseki, Tokyo, 1895. Rear facade, now destroyed.
2.17. Ende und Böckmann: National Supreme Court, Kasumigaseki, Tokyo, 1896, detail of frontispiece. Smaller view shows full facade.
2.18. Conder: Naval Ministry, Kasumigaseki, Tokyo, 1894.
2.19. Conder: Naval Ministry, Kasumigaseki, Tokyo, 1894. Atrium and grand staircase.
2.20. Tsumaki: Tokyo Industrial Club, Babasakimon, 1899.
2.21. Tatsuno: Bankers' Association Assembly Rooms, Sakamoto-cho, Tokyo, 1885.
2.22. Yamaguchi: College of Science Administration Building, Tokyo Imperial University, Hongo, 1888.
2.23. Tatsuno: Shibusawa Mansion, Kabutocho, Tokyo, 1888. Rear facade.
2.24. Serlio: Venetian Palace from *Architettura*, Book IV (1611 English edition).
2.25. Conder: Hokkaido Colonization Agency, Tokyo, 1878.
2.26. Tatsuno: Shibusawa Mansion, Tokyo, 1888. Drawing room (exterior depicted in figure 2.23).
2.27. Kabukiza Theater, Ginza, Tokyo (1889, by Kozo Takahara), depicting the national emblem.
2.28. Tatsuno: College of Engineering, Tokyo Imperial University, Hongo, 1888.
2.29. Conder: Department of Law and Literature, Tokyo Imperial University, Hongo, 1884.
2.30. Tatsuno: Bank of Japan, Otemachi, Tokyo, 1890-96. Plan.
2.31. Tatsuno: Bank of Japan, Otemachi, Tokyo, 1890-96. Detail of courtyard.
2.32. Tatsuno: Bank of Japan, Otemachi, Tokyo, 1890-96. South front.
2.33. Beyaert, with Wynand Janssens: Banque Nationale de Belgique, Brussels, 1860-74. Facade, rue du Bois Sauvage.
2.34. Tatsuno: Tokyo Station, Marunouchi, Tokyo, 1911-14.
2.35. Tatsuno: National Sumo Arena, Kuramae, Tokyo, 1909. Drawing shows roof structure.
2.36. Katayama: Japanese Ministry, Peking, 1886.
2.37. Taki: General Staff Headquarters, Tokyo, 1889.
2.38. Katayama: Nara Imperial Museum, Nara, 1894.
2.39. Katayama: Nara Imperial Museum, Nara, 1894. Detail of main entrance.
2.40. Katayama: Kyoto Imperial Museum, Kyoto, 1895.
2.41. Katayama: Hyokeikan, Ueno, Tokyo, 1901-9. Smaller view shows foundation structure.

2.42. Katayama: Akasaka Detached Palace, Akasaka, Tokyo, 1899–1909. Main front.
2.43. Katayama: Akasaka Detached Palace, Akasaka, Tokyo, 1899–1909. Aerial view of the grounds.
2.44. Katayama: Akasaka Detached Palace, Akasaka, Tokyo, 1899–1909. Grand staircase.

3.1. Godwin: Title-page (pl. 1) and plates 8 and 14 from *Art Furniture...*, 1877. Sales catalogue for Godwin's "Anglo-Japanese" furniture.
3.2. Michelangelo: ceiling frescoes, 1508–12, and altar fresco of the *Last Judgment*, 1534–41, Sistine Chapel, Vatican.
3.3. Kuru: Phoenix Hall, World's Columbian Exposition, Chicago, 1893.
3.4. Hoo-do, Byodo-in, Uji (near Kyoto), 1053, now restored (night view).
3.5. Hoo-do, Byodo-in, Uji (near Kyoto), 1053, plan.
3.6. Kuru: Phoenix Hall, World's Columbian Exposition, Chicago, 1893. Bird's-eye view of Wooded Island, with U.S. and Manufactures pavilions behind it.
3.7. Kuru: Phoenix Hall, World's Columbian Exposition, Chicago, 1893. Plan. From *The Inland Architect and News Record*, 1892.
3.8. Kuru: Phoenix Hall, World's Columbian Exposition, Chicago, 1893. Period interior.
3.9. Nippon Tea House, World's Columbian Exposition, Chicago, 1893 (right half of copyrighted photograph).
3.10. Wright: title page of *The Japanese Print*, Chicago, 1912.

4.1. Wright: Imperial Hotel, Hibiya, Tokyo, 1913–23. Principal Facade.
4.2. Wright: Imperial Hotel, Hibiya, Tokyo, 1913–23. Ornament in dining room and on exterior parapets.
4.3. Driving piles on site of the Imperial Hotel (probably 1920), with National Supreme Court and Ministry of Justice at rear.
4.4. Watanabe: Imperial Hotel, Hibiya, Tokyo, 1888–90.
4.5. Wright: Imperial Hotel, Hibiya, Tokyo, 1913–23. First study. Marginal notation "approved 1913."
4.6. Wright: Imperial Hotel, Hibiya, Tokyo, 1913–23. Looking north along the second-floor promenade.
4.7. Wright: Imperial Hotel, Hibiya, Tokyo, 1913–23. Crossing and north rear entrance.
4.8. Wright: Taliesin, the architect's house and studio, Spring Green, Wisconsin, 1911 onward. Study of about 1916 (after fire of 1914).
4.9. Wright: Midway Gardens, Chicago, 1914. Bird's-eye perspective.
4.10. Japanese workmen erecting one of the eight stone peacocks for the Imperial Hotel's Banquet Hall.
4.11. "Middle-class Japanese Dwelling," drawn for Josiah Conder by R. T. Conder. Elevation and plan. From *Transactions of the RIBA*, 1887.
4.12. Wright: Imperial Hotel, Hibiya, Tokyo, 1913–23. Pair of views detailing circulation.
4.13. Late nineteenth-century view of women awaiting clients in a brothel, Yoshiwara, Tokyo.
4.14. Tea on the Imperial Hotel's terrace, probably late 1930s; and dinner about to be served in the banqueting hall.
4.15. Wright: Imperial Hotel (1913–23). Lobby and *porte cochère* reconstructed at Meijimura, Inuyama, Aichi Prefecture. *Oya*-stone detail has been recarved.

5.1. Nakamura: Tokyo-Taisho Exhibition, Ueno, Tokyo, 1914. View of the grounds, and main gate.
5.2. Olbrich: Hochzeitsturm and exhibition building on the Mathildenhöhe, Darmstadt, 1907–8.
5.3. Nakamura: Josui Kaikan, Kanda, Tokyo, 1918. Rear terrace.
5.4. Sano: Maruzen Book Store, Nihonbashi, Tokyo, 1909.
5.5. Sano: Seitoku Memorial Gallery, Aoyama, Tokyo, 1926.
5.6. Bunri Ha Kenchiku Kai, active 1920–28: four projects.
5.7. Horiguchi: Memorial Tower, Peace Exhibition, Ueno, Tokyo, 1922.
5.8. Ishimoto: Asahi Newspaper Offices, Sukiyabashi, Tokyo, 1927. Main facade.
5.9. Ishimoto: Asahi Newspaper Offices, Sukiyabashi, Tokyo, 1927. Rear facade.
5.10. Ishimoto: Asahi Newspaper Offices, Sukiyabashi, Tokyo, 1927. Plan of the second floor.
5.11. Yamada: Central Telegraph Office, Tokyo, 1925. Inset shows roof terrace.
5.12. Kamahara: Kosuge Prison, Kosuge, Tokyo, 1929–30.
5.13. Horiguchi: Oshima Weather Station, Oshima Island, Shizuoka Prefecture, 1938. Tower.
5.14. Horiguchi: Oshima Weather Station, Oshima Island, Shizuoka Prefecture, 1938. Plan.
5.15. Uchida: Yasuda Hall, Imperial University, Hongo, Tokyo, 1925. Main front.
5.16. Uchida: Yasuda Hall, Imperial University, Hongo, Tokyo, 1925. Auditorium ceiling and plan.
5.17. Raymond: Reinanzaka House, Azabu, Tokyo, 1923–24. Front and rear views.
5.18. Raymond: Reinanzaka House, Azabu, Tokyo, 1923–24. Living room.
5.19. Raymond: Reinanzaka House, Azabu, Tokyo, 1923–24. Plans.
5.20. Raymond: Reinanzaka House, Azabu, Tokyo, 1923–24. Early model.
5.21. Raymond: Reinanzaka House, Azabu, Tokyo, 1923–24. Later model.
5.22. Raymond: Rachel Reid House, Azabu, Tokyo, 1924. Facade.
5.23. Raymond: Rachel Reid House, Azabu, Tokyo, 1924. Plans.

6.1. Goto and Oe: Hobutsu-den, Meiji Shrine, Tokyo, 1921. Elevation.
6.2. Kawamoto: Soldiers' Hall, Kudan, Tokyo, 1934. Front and side elevations.
6.3. Watanabe: Tokyo Imperial Museum, Ueno, Tokyo, 1937. Main front.
6.4. Watanabe: Tokyo Imperial Museum, Ueno, Tokyo, 1937. Composite rendering of ornament, 1931 or after, and architect's view of the proposed building.
6.5. Municipal Office Building, Nagoya, mid-1930s.
6.6. Kanagawa Prefectural Office, Yokohama, mid-1930s.
6.7. Hsinking (Changchun), capital of Manchukuo, late 1930s.
6.8. Yoshida: Tokyo Central Post Office, Tokyo, 1927–31.
6.9. Yoshida: Osaka Higashi Post Office, Osaka, 1931. Entrance.
6.10. Yoshida: Osaka Higashi Post Office, Osaka, 1931. Rear and axonometric rear views.
6.11. Yamada: Ogikubo Telephone Office, Tokyo, 1933.
6.12. Mitsubishi Corporation: Marunouchi Building, Tokyo, 1923.
6.13. Tokyo Municipality: Yotsuya Fifth Primary School, 1934. Glazed stairway, plan, and general view.
6.14. Tokyo Municipality: Takanawadai Primary School, 1935. General view and plan.
6.15. Tokyo Municipality: Nagata-cho Primary School, 1937. Plan and general view.
6.16. Ishimoto: Shirokiya Department Store, Tokyo, 1931. Facade.
6.17. Ishimoto: Shirokiya Department Store, Tokyo, 1931. Lounge.
6.18. Ishimoto: Shirokiya Department Store, Tokyo, 1931. First floor plan and grand staircase.
6.19. Yamaguchi: rendering of Shirokiya, exhibited 1927.
6.20. Ishimoto: Haneda Airport Office, Haneda, Tokyo, 1932. Axonometric proposal.
6.21. Ishimoto: Haneda Airport Office, Haneda, Tokyo, 1932. Terminal building.
6.22. Ishimoto: Togo House, Seijo, Tokyo, 1931. Entrance and plan.
6.23. Ishimoto: Togo House, Seijo, Tokyo, 1931. Atelier.
6.24. Van der Rohe: Tugendhat House, Brno, Czechoslovakia, 1930. Plan of lower level.
6.25. Ishimoto: Aoki House, Seijo, Tokyo, 1931. Garden facade.
6.26. Ishimoto: Aoki House, Seijo, Tokyo, 1931. Plan
6.27. Raymond: Hamao House, Tokyo, 1927–28. South facade.
6.28. Raymond: Hamao House, Tokyo, 1927–28. Plan.
6.29. Fujiyama Mansion, Shiba, Tokyo, ca. 1932–33. Rendering of the garden facade.
6.30. Fujiyama Mansion, Shiba, Tokyo, ca. 1932–33. Plan. Shading indicates enclosed gardens.
6.31. Yamada: House of T, Aoyama, Tokyo, 1931–32. Plans.
6.32. Yamada: House of T, Aoyama, Tokyo, 1931–32. South-facing interior.
6.33. Yamada: House of T, Aoyama, Tokyo, 1931–32. Sunlight diagram.
6.34. Horiguchi: Okada Residence, Omori, Tokyo, 1934. Rear (south) facade showing juncture between Japanese- and Western-style portions.
6.35. Horiguchi: Okada Residence, Omori, Tokyo, 1934. Plan.
6.36. Raymond: Rising Sun Petroleum Executive Residence, Yokohama, 1931.
6.37. Raymond: Rising Sun Petroleum, steel and concrete service station prototypes, 1930.
6.38. Le Corbusier: La Roche/Albert Jeanneret House at Auteuil, Paris, 1922. Initial project.
6.39. Le Corbusier: House for Mr. Errazuris, unrealized project in Chile, 1930.
6.40. Raymond: Raymond House, Karuizawa, Nagano Prefecture, 1933. Rear facade.
6.41. Raymond: Raymond House, Karuizawa, Nagano Prefecture, 1933. Plans.

6.42. Raymond: Raymond House, Karuizawa, Nagano Prefecture, 1933. Living-dining room, view toward rear garden.
6.43. Raymond: Shiro Akaboshi Cottage, Fujisawa, Kanagawa Prefecture, 1931. Elevation.
6.44. Raymond: Shiro Akaboshi Cottage, Fujisawa, Kanagawa Prefecture, 1931. Plan.
6.45. Raymond: Shiro Akaboshi Cottage, Fujisawa, Kanagawa Prefecture, 1931. Interior.
6.46. Raymond: Tokyo Golf Club, Asaka, Saitama Prefecture, 1932. View over roof, and the model.
6.47. Raymond: Tokyo Golf Club, Asaka, Saitama Prefecture, 1932. Rear facade and view of bare concrete work.
6.48. Raymond: Kisuke Akaboshi House, Tokyo, 1932. South facade.
6.49. Raymond: Kisuke Akaboshi House, Tokyo, 1932. Plans.
6.50. Raymond: Kisuke Akaboshi House, Tokyo, 1932. East elevation.
6.51. Le Corbusier: sketch (1927) for the Pavillon des Amis at Ville-d'Avray, near Paris, 1928–29.
6.52. Raymond: Kawasaki House, Azabu, Tokyo, 1934. East facade.
6.53. Raymond: Kawasaki House, Azabu, Tokyo, 1934. Living room with view toward inner garden.
6.54. Raymond: Kawasaki House, Azabu, Tokyo, 1934. Plans.
6.55. Raymond: Tetsuma Akaboshi House, Kichijoji, Tokyo, 1934. North and south facades.
6.56. Raymond: Tetsuma Akaboshi House, Kichijoji, Tokyo, 1934. View from "madam's bedroom" toward dining room.
6.57. Raymond: Tetsuma Akaboshi House, Kichijoji, Tokyo, 1934. Plans.
6.58. Murano: Morigo Shoten office building, Tokyo, 1931.
6.59. Murano: Nakayama House, Ashiya, near Kobe, 1934. Garden facade and plans.
6.60. Murano: Nakayama House, Ashiya, near Kobe, 1934. Vestibule.
6.61. Horiguchi: Kikkawa Residence, Meguro, Tokyo, 1930. Garden front.
6.62. Horiguchi: Kikkawa Residence, Meguro, Tokyo, 1930. Plan.
6.63. Horiguchi: Villa at Warabi, Saitama Prefecture, 1926. Lateral elevation and view of garden.
6.64. Murano: Osaka Pantheon, Osaka, 1933. Entrance, and wall of main block.
6.65. Murano: Osaka Pantheon, Osaka, 1933. Axonometric.
6.66. May: Bruchfeldstrasse Siedlung, Frankfurt/Main-Niederrad, 1925.
6.67. Tsuchiura: Rakuto Apartment, Kyoto, 1933. Perspectives of facade and a representative room interior.
6.68. Yamaguchi: Bancho Siedlung, Bancho, Tokyo, 1933. View from street.
6.69. Yamaguchi: Bancho Siedlung, Bancho, Tokyo. 1933. Site plan.
6.70. Yamaguchi: Bancho Siedlung, Bancho, Tokyo, 1933. Unit facade and plan of rear block.
6.71. Dojunkai: Harajuku Apartments, Aoyama, Tokyo, 1926.
6.72. Dojunkai: Daikanyama Apartments, Shibuya, Tokyo, 1927. Site plan.
6.73. Dojunkai: Daikanyama Apartments, Shibuya, Tokyo, 1927. Representative facade and diverse floor plans.
6.74. Dojunkai: Daikanyama Apartments, Shibuya, Tokyo, 1927. Room interior.
6.75. Dojunkai: Edogawa Apartments, Edogawabashi, Tokyo, 1934. View from the central court.
6.76. Dojunkai: Edogawa Apartments, Edogawabashi, Tokyo, 1934. Model.
6.77. Tsuchiura: Ninomiya Apartments, Kudan, Tokyo, 1937. Rear view.
6.78. Tsuchiura: Ninomiya Apartments, Kudan, Tokyo, 1937. Plans. Shading indicates photographer's ground-floor studio.
6.79. Le Corbusier: League of Nations, Geneva, 1928. Unrealized competition entry.
6.80. Maekawa: Tokyo Imperial Museum, Ueno, Tokyo, 1931. Unrealized competition entry.
6.81. Maekawa: First Mutual Life Insurance Company, Tokyo, 1933. Unrealized competition entry.
6.82. Watanabe: Dai-ichi Seimei Building, Hibiya, Tokyo, 1934–38.
6.83. Le Corbusier: Centrosoyus, Moscow. Submission drawing of 1929.
6.84. Maekawa: Tokyo Municipal Hall, Tokyo, 1934. Unrealized competition entry.
6.85. Maekawa: Dairen Civic Hall, Dairen, 1938. Unrealized winning competition entry, rendering and plan.
6.86. Maekawa: Japan Pavilion, Paris Exposition, 1937. Unrealized project. Axonometric site drawing.
6.87. Maekawa: Japan Pavilion, Paris Exposition, 1937. Unrealized project. Night perspective rendering.
6.88. Sakakura: Japan Pavilion, Paris Exposition, 1937. Facade.
6.89. Sakakura: Japan Pavilion, Paris Exposition, 1937. Plans.

6.90. Tange: Japanese Cultural Center, Bangkok, 1943. Unrealized winning competition entry. Main elevation.
6.91. Maekawa: Japanese Cultural Center, Bangkok, 1943. Unrealized competition entry. Elevations and plan.
6.92. Yamawaki: Migishi House, Saginomiya, Tokyo, before 1935. Main (south) facade and east elevation.
6.93. Yamawaki: Migishi House, Saginomiya, Tokyo, before 1935. Plans.
6.94. Yamawaki: Migishi House, Saginomiya, Tokyo, before 1935. View from atelier into conversation area.
6.95. Yamaguchi: Yamada House, Kita Kamakura, Kanagawa Prefecture, 1934. Facade.
6.96. Yamaguchi: Yamada House, Kita Kamakura, Kanagawa Prefecture, 1934. Plans.
6.97. Neutra: Lovell House, Los Angeles, 1927–29.
6.98. Kurata: White Pillar House, Hakone-Sengoku, Kanagawa Prefecture, before 1937. Facade.
6.99. Kurata: White Pillar House, Hakone-Sengoku, Kanagawa Prefecture, before 1937. Plans.
6.100. Yamaguchi: extension to Nihon Dental College, Tokyo, 1934.
6.101. Yamaguchi: Kurobe Power Station, Kurobe, Toyama Prefecture, 1938.

7.1. Raymond: Reader's Digest Building, Takebashi, Tokyo, 1951. Facade.
7.2. Raymond: Reader's Digest Building, Takebashi, Tokyo, 1951. Plan.
7.3. Raymond: Reader's Digest Building, Takebashi, Tokyo, 1951. Half-section.
7.4. Raymond: Reader's Digest Building, Takebashi, Tokyo, 1951. View from Imperial Palace moat.
7.5. Sakakura: Museum of Modern Art, Kamakura, Kanagawa Prefecture, 1951. View of Japanese-style supports, and axonometric showing plan of upper floor.
7.6. Maekawa: Kanagawa Prefectural Concert Hall and Library, Yokohama, 1954. Elevation sheet.
7.7. Tange: Tokyo City Hall, Tokyo, 1957 (incompletely realized).
7.8. Le Corbusier: Palace of the Soviets, Moscow, 1931. Unrealized competition entry.
7.9. Tange: Greater East Asia Coprosperity Sphere Memorial Building, near Mt. Fuji, 1943. Rendering, and approach map from Tokyo.
7.10. Michelangelo: Capitoline Hill reconstruction, 1538 onward.
7.11. Tange: Peace Park with sports and cultural facilities, Hiroshima, 1949–55.
7.12. Tange: Atomic Memorial Museum, Hiroshima, 1949–55.
7.13. Tange: Peace Park, Hiroshima, 1949–55. Detail of figure 7.11, as realized.
7.14. Kikutake: Skyhouse, Bunkyo Ward, Tokyo, 1958. Rendering, site plan, and main floor plan.
7.15. Kikutake: "Ideas for the Reorganization of Tokyo City," 1959. Visionary scheme from Metabolism (1960).
7.16. Tange: World Health Organization Headquarters, Geneva, 1959. Unrealized competition entry.
7.17. Maekawa: housing at Harumi, Tokyo, 1957–58. Facade of main block.
7.18. Maekawa: housing at Harumi, Tokyo, 1957–58. Side elevation and structural section.
7.19. Maekawa: housing at Harumi, Tokyo, 1957–58. Unit layout plan and sectional locator for three-floor grouping.
7.20. Tange: "Tokyo Plan: 1960." View of model.
7.21. Tange: "Tokyo Plan: 1960." Detail of figure 7.20.
7.22. Tange: Shizuoka Press and Broadcasting Center, Shimbashi, Tokyo, 1966–67.
7.23. Kurokawa: Nakagin Capsule Building, Shimbashi, Tokyo, 1972.
7.24. Tokyo Municipality: Metropolitan Expressway, from 1959 onward.

8.1. View of Shinohara's Umbrella House under construction in Nerima Ward, Tokyo, 1961. See also figures 8.23–24.
8.2. Tange: seaboard megalopolis, Tokyo to Osaka, 1965.
8.3. Demonstration against United States–Japan Security Treaty, 1960.
8.4. Maekawa: Kasama House, Komaba, Tokyo, 1938. Facade.
8.5. Maekawa: Kasama House, Komaba, Tokyo, 1938. Plans.
8.6. Maekawa: the architect's house, Meguro, Tokyo, 1940–41. Facade.
8.7. Maekawa: the architect's house, Meguro, Tokyo, 1940–41. Plan and section.
8.8. Raymond: the architect's house, Shibuya, Tokyo, 1953. Facade.
8.9. Raymond: the architect's house, Shibuya, Tokyo, 1953. Section.
8.10. Raymond: the architect's house, Shibuya, Tokyo, 1953. Interior.
8.11. Seike: Mori House, Bunkyo Ward, Tokyo, 1951. Facade.

8.12. Seike: Mori House, Bunkyo Ward, Tokyo, 1951. Plan.
8.13. Seike: Saito House, Ota Ward, Tokyo, 1952. Facade.
8.14. Seike: Saito House, Ota Ward, Tokyo, 1952. Plan.
8.15. Seike: Miyagi House, Ota Ward, Tokyo, 1953. Facade.
8.16. Seike: Miyagi House, Ota Ward, Tokyo, 1953. Plan.
8.17. Breuer: the architect's first house at New Canaan, Connecticut, 1947. Plan.
8.18. Breuer: the architect's first house at New Canaan, Connecticut, 1947. Right elevation.
8.19. Shinohara: House at Kugayama, Suginami Ward, Tokyo, 1954. Facade.
8.20. Shinohara: House at Kugayama, Suginami Ward, Tokyo, 1954. Plans and section.
8.21. Shinohara: Tanikawa House, Suginami Ward, Tokyo, 1958. Elevation.
8.22. Shinohara: Tanikawa House, Suginami Ward, Tokyo, 1958. Plan.
8.23. Shinohara: Umbrella House, Nerima Ward, Tokyo, 1961. Plan and mid-section.
8.24. Shinohara: Umbrella House, Nerima Ward, Tokyo, 1961. Interior.
8.25. Shinohara: House with an Earthen Floor, Kita Saku, Nagano Prefecture, 1963. Section and plan.
8.26. Shinohara: House with an Earthen Floor, Kita Saku, Nagano Prefecture, 1963. Interior.
8.27. Shinohara: House of Earth, Nerima Ward, Tokyo, 1966. Night view and living room interior.
8.28. Shinohara: House of Earth, Nerima Ward, Tokyo, 1966. Plan and section.
8.29. Teshigahara: still from *Woman of the Dunes* (1964).
8.30. Imamura: still from *Insect Woman* (1963).
8.31. Shinohara: House in White, Suginami Ward, Tokyo, 1966. Facade.
8.32. Shinohara: House in White, Suginami Ward, Tokyo, 1966. Plan and section.
8.33. Shinohara: House in White, Suginami Ward, Tokyo, 1966. Living room.
8.34. Pure Land Hall, Jodoji, Ono, Hyogo Prefecture, 1192.
8.35. Shinohara: North House in Hanayama, Kobe, 1965. View through bedroom from living-dining area.
8.36. Shinohara: North House in Hanayama, Kobe, 1965. Plan and section.
8.37. Katsura Villa, Kyoto, mid-seventeenth century. Bird's-eye view with gardens.
8.38. Tange: Kagawa Prefectural Office, Takamatsu, 1955–58.
8.39. Great South Gate (Nandaimon) at Todaiji, Nara, 1199. Half-elevation and partial section.
8.40. Le Corbusier: National Museum of Western Art, Ueno, Tokyo, 1957–59. Facade.
8.41. Le Corbusier: National Museum of Western Art, Ueno, Tokyo, 1957–59. Plans.
8.42. Le Corbusier: National Museum of Western Art, Ueno, Tokyo, 1957–59. Nineteenth Century Hall interior.
8.43. Le Corbusier: National Museum of Western Art, Ueno, Tokyo, 1957–59. Sketch for Nineteenth Century Hall.
8.44. Maekawa: Tokyo Metropolitan Festival Hall, Ueno, Tokyo, 1961. Elevation drawing of the east facade.
8.45. *Chashitsu*, Ryokakutei, Ninna-ji, Kyoto, ca. 1688.
8.46. Audience hall at Nishi Honganji, Kyoto, 1618, in the *shoin* style.
8.47. Le Corbusier: four views of La Tourette monastery, near Lyons, 1957–60, and axonometric.
8.48. Le Corbusier: preliminary sketch for National Museum of Western Art, Ueno, Tokyo (March 1956), showing Boîte à Miracles.
8.49. Le Corbusier: Musée du XXe Siècle, or Musée d'Art Contemporain, 1930 onward. Unrealized project.
8.50. Le Corbusier: Notre-Dame-du-Haut, Ronchamp, 1950–55. Diagram showing double-shell roof construction.
8.51. Maekawa: Tokyo Metropolitan Festival Hall, Ueno, Tokyo, 1961. Overhead view (see also figure 8.44).
8.52. Tange: Totsuka Country Clubhouse, Totsuka, Kanagawa Prefecture, 1960–61.
8.53. Tange: Nichinan Cultural Center, Nichinan, Miyazaki Prefecture, 1960–62. Lateral facade.
8.54. Tange: Nichinan Cultural Center, Nichinan, Miyazaki Prefecture, 1960–62. Plan and section.
8.55. Kikutake: Miyakonojo City Hall, Miyakonojo, Miyazaki Prefecture, 1966.
8.56. Le Corbusier, with Iannis Xenakis: Philips Pavilion, Brussels World's Fair, 1958. Schematic drawing.
8.57. Tange: National Olympic Stadiums, Yoyogi, Tokyo 1961–64.

9.1. Tange: Tsukiji Plan, Tokyo, 1960–64. Unrealized project.
9.2. Isozaki: "City in the Air," 1961 (or 1962).
9.3. Isozaki: "Joint Core System," possibly 1960.
9.4. Isozaki: "Future City," photomontage, 1962.
9.5. Isozaki: "Destruction of the Future City," 1968.
9.6. Isozaki: "Electric Labyrinth," 1968. Exhibit for the Milan Triennale, included figure 9.5 as mural background. Axonometric and plan.
9.7. Isozaki: Oita Medical Hall, Oita, Oita Prefecture, 1959–60. Axonometric.
9.8. Isozaki: Oita Prefectural Library, Oita, 1966.
9.9. Isozaki: Oita Branch, Fukuoka Mutual Bank, Oita, Oita Prefecture, 1966–67. Axonometric drawing.
9.10. Stirling and Gowan: Leicester University Engineering Building, 1959–63. Axonometric drawing.
9.11. Isozaki: Head Office, Fukuoka Mutual Bank, Hakata, Fukuoka, Fukuoka Prefecture, 1968–71.
9.12. Stirling: Cambridge University History Faculty, 1964–67. Partial axonometric of interior.
9.13. Isozaki: Oita Branch, Fukuoka Mutual Bank, Oita, Oita Prefecture, 1966–67. "Image drawing." (See also figure 9.9.)
9.14. Isozaki: Oita Branch, Fukuoka Mutual Bank, Oita, Oita Prefecture, 1966–67. Main banking hall.
9.15. Distorting mirror: "Perhaps it is all truly 'funny'."
9.16. Tomé: the *Transparente* (toplit altar behind the choir), Toledo Cathedral, 1721–32.
9.17. Darkness at the heart of the domestic interior.

10.1. Japanese town dwelling from Morse's *Japanese Homes and Their Surroundings* (1886).
10.2. Wright: Robie House, Chicago, 1909. Garage wall in original condition.
10.3. Wright: S. C. Johnson Co. Administration Building, Racine, Wisconsin, 1936–39. Main hall.
10.4. Isozaki: the Seven Operations of Manner.
10.5. Altar arrangement based on the mandala: inner precinct, Kanshinji, Osaka, late fourteenth century.
10.6. Isozaki: Computer-Aided City, 1971. Unrealized project.
10.7. Isozaki, with Baien Miura: diagram of stained-glass window based on Miura's "Gengo" philosophy, for Municipal Library, Kitakyushu, Fukuoka Prefecture, 1973–75.
10.8. Isozaki: Nagasumi Branch, Fukuoka Mutual Bank, Fukuoka, Fukuoka Prefecture, 1971. Schematic rendering of main facade.
10.9. Isozaki: Nagasumi Branch, Fukuoka Mutual Bank, Fukuoka, Fukuoka Prefecture, 1971. Interior.
10.10. Isozaki: Ropponmatsu Branch, Fukuoka Mutual Bank, Fukuoka, Fukuoka Prefecture, 1971. Facade detail.
10.11. Isozaki: Ropponmatsu Branch, Fukuoka Mutual Bank, Fukuoka, Fukuoka Prefecture, 1971. Axonometric drawing.
10.12. Wagner: Post Office Savings Bank, Vienna, 1904–6. Main hall.
10.13. Superstudio: "Architectural Histograms," 1969.
10.14. Isozaki: Gumma Prefectural Museum of Modern Art, Takasaki, 1971–74. Facade.
10.15. Isozaki: Gumma Prefectural Museum of Modern Art, Takasaki, 1971–74. Plans.
10.16. Paper model (*okoshi-ezu*) of Teigyokuken teahouse, Shinju-an, Daitokuji, Kyoto (mid-17th century). From *MA: Space-Time in Japan*, catalogue of the exhibition, 1978.
10.17. Isozaki: Gumma Prefectural Museum of Modern Art, Takasaki, 1971–74. Lobby.
10.18. Isozaki: Fujimi Country Club, Oita, Oita Prefecture, 1973–74. Bird's-eye view.
10.19. Isozaki: Fujimi Country Club, Oita, Oita Prefecture, 1973–74. Pair of axonometrics showing upper floor, and roof from below.
10.20. Isozaki: Municipal Library, Kitakyushu, Fukuoka Prefecture, 1973–75. Bird's-eye view.
10.21. Isozaki: Municipal Library, Kitakyushu, Fukuoka Prefecture, 1973–75. Interior.
10.22. Isozaki: Yano House, Kawasaki, Kanagawa Prefecture, 1973–75. Axonometric site drawing.
10.23. Ledoux: *Maison des Directeurs de la Loue* from *L'Architecture considérée...* (initial volume, 1804).
10.24. Wright: Susan L. Dana House, Springfield, Illinois, 1903. Rendering of dining room.
10.25. Isozaki: West Japan General Exhibition Center, Kokura, Kitakyushu, Fukuoka Prefecture, 1977.
10.26. Isozaki: Kamioka Town Hall, Toyama Prefecture, 1978. Principal (rear) facade viewed from below.
10.27. Isozaki: Kamioka Town Hall, Toyama Prefecture, 1978. Plans.
10.28. Isozaki: Kamioka Town Hall, Toyama Prefecture, 1978. Principal (rear) facade seen from across the river.
10.29. Rousseau: Hôtel de Salm, Paris, 1783–86. River facade of one of the largest houses in pre-1789 Paris.

10.30. Isozaki: emblematic drawing from *MA: Space-Time in Japan*, catalogue of the exhibition, 1978.
10.31. Shinohara: Suzusho House, Miura, Kanagawa Prefecture, 1968. Living-dining area.
10.32. Shinohara: Incomplete House, Suginami Ward, Tokyo, 1970. Axonometric (central space) and plans.
10.33. Shinohara: Incomplete House, Suginami Ward, Tokyo, 1970. Central space, originally a dining room.
10.34. Shinohara: Shino House, Nerima Ward, 1970. Plan and elevation.
10.35. Shinohara: Tanikawa House, Naganohara, Gumma Prefecture, 1974. Lateral facade.
10.36. Shinohara: Tanikawa House, Naganohara, Gumma Prefecture, 1974. Plan and section.
10.37. Shinohara: Tanikawa House, Naganohara, Gumma Prefecture, 1974. Unfloored "summer space."
10.38. Shinohara: Tanikawa House, Naganohara, Gumma Prefecture, 1974. The "summer space" and the notion of "traversal."
10.39. Le Corbusier: terrace of the Beistegui penthouse flat, Paris, 1931, with the Arc de Triomphe de l'Etoile by Chalgrin (1806–36).
10.40. Shinohara: House in Uehara, Shibuya Ward, Tokyo, 1976. Street facade.
10.41. Shinohara: House in Uehara, Shibuya Ward, Tokyo, 1976. Plans and section.
10.42. Shinohara: House in Uehara, Shibuya Ward, Tokyo, 1976. Living-dining area.
10.43. Shinohara: House in Uehara, Shibuya Ward, Tokyo, 1976. View from the third-story room looking toward surrounding houses.

Photographic Credits

The author and publishers wish to acknowledge use of graphic and photographic materials courtesy of the following government agencies, foundations, institutions, business firms, and individuals:

Ambassade de Belgique (Tokyo): 2.33.
Masao Arai: © Shinkenchikusha 8.1, 9.11, 10.14, 10.17, 10.18, 10.25, 10.35, 10.38.
Avery Architectural and Fine Arts Library (Columbia University, New York): 3.6 (C. D. Arnold).
British Architectural Library (RIBA, London): 2.3, 2.6, 4.11.
Centro Di (Florence): 10.13.
Chicago Historical Society: 3.3 (ICHI-17539), 3.9 (C. D. Arnold).
Cooper-Hewitt Museum (New York): 10.16, 10.30.
Dai-ichi Seimei (Tokyo): 6.82.
ENIT (Tokyo): 3.2, 7.10.
The Far East: 1.6.
Fondation Le Corbusier: © SPADEM 6.39, 6.51, 6.83, 7.8, 8.43, 8.47 (axonometric), 8.48, 8.50, 8.56.
Geihinkan: 2.42, 2.43, 2.44.
Chuji Hirayama: 7.17, 8.11, 8.13, 8.34, 8.40, 8.42.
Terutaka Hoashi: 10.43.
Sutemi Horiguchi: 5.13, 6.61, 6.62, 6.63.
Saburo Horikoshi: 1.22 (elevation).
Kazuo Hozumi: 8.39.
Idemitsu Bijutsukan: 1.4.
Imperial Hotel: 4.1, 4.2, 4.3, 4.6, 4.7, 4.10, 4.12, 4.14, 4.15.
Taikichi Irie: 10.5.
Ishimoto Kenchiku Jimusho: 5.8, 5.9, 6.19, 6.20, 6.21, 6.22, 6.23.
Yasuhiro Ishimoto: 9.8.
Arata Isozaki Atelier: 9.3, 9.4, 9.5, 9.6, 9.7, 9.9, 9.13, 10.4, 10.7, 10.8, 10.11, 10.15, 10.19, 10.22, 10.27.
Iwanami Shoten: 2.11 (Terunobu Fujimori).
Kanagawa Kenritsu Hakubutsukan: 1.16 (full view).
Kikutake Kiyonori Kenchiku Sekkei Jimusho: 7.14, 7.15, 8.55.
Kobe Shiritsu Hakubutsukan: 1.18, 1.19.
Kodansha Ltd.: 2.42, 2.43, 3.4, 8.3.
Kokkai Toshokan: 3.8.
Kokusaikenchiku: 5.14, 6.9, 6.10, 6.68, 6.69, 6.70, 6.78, 6.86, 6.87, 6.93 (plan), 6.98, 6.99, 6.100.
Kyoto Kokuritsu Hakubutsukan: 2.40.
Kyu-Kaichi Gakko Kanri Jimusho (Matsumoto): 1.12.
Lucien Hervé (Paris): © SPADEM 10.39.
Maekawa Kunio Kenchiku Sekkei Jimusho: 7.6, 7.18, 7.19, 8.44.
Maruzen: 5.4.
Akihisa Masuda: 1.17, 2.31, 2.39, 2.44.
Meiji Jingu (Tokyo): 6.1.
Mitsubishi Jisho: 6.12.
Osamu Murai: 7.22, 8.6, 8.26, 8.27, 8.31, 8.33, 8.35, 8.38, 8.53, 8.57, 9.1, 9.2.
Murano Mori Kenchiku Jimusho: 6.58, 6.59, 6.60, 6.64, 6.65.
Musée National de la Légion d'Honneur et des Ordres de Chevalerie (Paris): © SPADEM 10.29.
Nagasaki Shiritsu Chuo Toshokan: 1.3, 1.5.
Nagatacho Shogakko (Tokyo): 6.15.
Nara Kokuritsu Hakubutsukan: 2.38.
Nihon Doro Kodan: 7.24.
Nihon Kenchiku Gakkai: 1.7, 1.8, 1.10, 1.14, 1.20, 1.21, 1.22, 2.1, 2.2, 2.5, 2.7, 2.8, 2.9, 2.15, 2.16, 2.17, 2.18, 2.19, 2.20, 2.22, 2.25, 2.27, 2.28, 2.30, 2.32, 2.34, 2.35, 2.36, 4.4, 5.1, 5.7, 6.90, 6.91, 7.9.
Nikkatsu Shuppan: 8.30.
Takeshi Nishikawa: 8.45.
Taisuke Ogawa: 10.21.
Tomio Ohashi: 7.23, 10.26, 10.28.
Takashi Oyama: 8.55.
Point and Line: 9.15 (Shinobu Oda).
Rhetoria (Tokyo): Shunji Kitajima, 9.17; Yukio Futagawa, 8.37, 8.51, 9.14, 10.3, 10.12; M. Otsuka: 8.24.
Yoshikatsu Saeki: 8.19.
Sakakura Kenchiku Kenkyujo: 6.88, 6.89, 7.5.
Kiyosi Seike: 8.12, 8.14, 8.15, 8.16.
Shibusawa Shiryokan: 2.21, 2.23, 2.26.
Shinkenchiku: 6.4, 6.25, 6.26, 6.29, 6.30, 6.34, 6.65, 6.67, 6.77, 6.80, 6.81, 6.84, 6.85, 6.92, 6.93, 6.94, 6.95.
Kazuo Shinohara: 8.20, 8.21, 8.22, 8.23, 8.25, 8.28, 8.32, 8.36, 10.32, 10.34, 10.36, 10.41.
Shokokusha: 10.6 (Shigeo Okamoto), 10.10.
Showa Jutaku-shi (Shinkenchikusha): 6.22, 6.35, 6.41, 6.54, 6.59, 6.63, 6.96, 8.4, 8.5, 8.7.
James Stirling Michael Wilford and Associates: 9.10, 9.12.
Takanawadai Shogakko (Tokyo): 6.14.
Koji Taki: 10.31, 10.33, 10.37, 10.40, 10.42.
Hiroaki Tanaka: 10.9.
Tange Kenzo Toshi Kenchiku Sekkei Jimusho: 7.7, 7.11, 7.12, 7.13, 7.16, 7.20, 7.21, 8.2, 8.54.
Teishin Hakubutsukan (Tokyo): 5.11, 6.8.
Teshigahara Productions: 8.29.
Tokyo Daigaku: 2.29, 5.6, 5.15, 5.16.
Tokyo Kokuritsu Hakubutsukan: 2.4, 2.41, 6.3.
Tokyo Toritsu Chuo Toshokan: 1.11, 1.13, 1.15.
Yuzuru Tominaga: 8.47 (photographs).
Frank Lloyd Wright Memorial Foundation: 4.5, 4.8, 4.9, 10.2, 10.24.
Yokohama Kaiko Shiryokan: 1.1, 1.2, 1.16 (detail).
Yotsuya Daigo Shogakko (Tokyo): 6.13.

While every effort has been made to trace copyrights and secure permission for the use of copyrighted materials, individuals or entities holding rights to documents or photographs here reproduced inadvertently without permission or misattributed are invited to inform Kodansha International of any omissions or errors of attribution, so that the necessary rectification can be made.

Index

Aalto, Alvar, 255, 260, 265
Abe, Kobo, 248, 275
—novels: *Box Man, The,* 268; *Face of Another, The,* filmed by Teshigahara, 245, 246; *Woman of the Dunes,* filmed by Teshigahara, 200, 246, *fig. 8.29*
Adler and Sullivan, Chicago, 66. See also Sullivan, Louis
aestheticism, 76, 79, 85. See also Aesthetic Movement
Aesthetic Movement, 64-65, 69, 74, 75
Akasaka Detached Palace (Togu Gosho), Tokyo (1909), 58-59, 62, 63, 64, 81, 93, *figs. 2.42-44*
allegory (allegorical spatial expression), 241, 245, 246, 248, 254
Amsterdam: Children's Home (1960), 228-30
Amsterdam School (of protoexpressionism), 96, 112, 113
Anderson, William, 35
Ansei Treaties (1858), 16
apato (low-cost apartment housing), 147
Architectural Institute of Japan, 36
architecture
—periodicals (Japanese): *Gendai Kenchiku,* 171; *Kenchiku-zasshi,* 92, 94; *Kokusaikenchiku,* 154; *Shinkenchiku,* 114, 125-26, 129, 148, 154, 179, 193
—profession of (in Japan): compromised by engineering in Taisho era, 92; control of public building by, in Meiji era, 33; in Manchuria and northern China, 111; effect of 1960's protest movement on, 140; influence of *teikan yoshiki* on, 111, 145
—Wright's notion of "truth" in, 66-69, 73, 74, 75, 76, 79, 81, 85, 90
Art Deco style, 79
Art Nouveau style, 65, 79, 93
Asahi Newspaper Offices, Tokyo (1927), 96, 118, *figs. 5.8-10*
Asaka, Saitama Prefecture: Tokyo Golf Club (1932), 135, 165, *figs. 6.46-47*
Ashiya, Hyogo Prefecture: Nakayama House (1934), 143-44, *figs. 6.59-60*; Yamamura Villa (1924), 143
Aslin, Elizabeth, on Japanese art, 64, 64n2, 65, 65n3
Asplund, Erik Gunnar, 154, 255, 256
Athens Charter. See CIAM: fourth meeting

Bakema, Jacob, 179
Banham, (Peter) Reyner, on CIAM and Team X, 173n17, 176
Bankers' Association Assembly Rooms, Tokyo (1885), 48
Bank of Japan, 50; building, Tokyo (1896), 52, 54, 56, 58, 81, *figs. 2.30-32*
baroque
—neo-, idiom of, introduced by Akasaka Detached Palace, 59
—planning (axial): contrasted with Japanese urban forms, 41, 188; contrasted with Japanese building forms, 148; "Tokyo Plan: 1960," *ville radieuse,* and, 182; Tange and, 164. See also Tange: and Michelangelo
—roots of *giyofu* style in, 29
—space, 9-10, 230, 231, 242; *chashitsu* as, 231; "total" visualization of, 234-35. See also Norberg-Schulz
Barry, Charles, and A. W. Pugin, 34
Baton Rouge, LA: Old State Capitol (1849), 35
Bauhaus, 105, 115, 183

beauty, notion of, 10, 146. See also taste (Japanese)
Beaux-Arts (style). See Ecole des Beaux-Arts
Behrens, Peter, 94, 232
Bell, Henry, 29
Berlin, 38, 39, 44; Altes Museum (1830), 175; Bauakademie (1835), 55; Palais Reichenheim (1881), 45, 47
Berlin-Charlottenburg: Haus des Rundfunks (1931), 99
Berlin-Köpenick: Dorotheen-Schule (1929), 114
Berlin-Steglitz: electricity-gauge factory (1928), 114
Beyaert, Henry. See Brussels: Banque Nationale de Belgique
Bibiena family, 245
Bloc, André, 181
Böckmann, Wilhelm. See Ende und Böckmann
Böhm, Dominikus, 100
Bombay: School of Art project (1865), 35-36, *fig. 2.3*
Bonatz, Paul, 100
Booth, General William, 43
Boston, 32, 33. See also Tange, Kenzo: and urban planning (MIT student project for Boston Bay)
Boyd, Robin, 182
Bremen: North German Lloyd headquarters planned for, 44, *fig. 2.13*; Rathaus, 39, *fig. 2.14*
Breuer, Marcel, residence, New Canaan, CT (1947), 195, *figs. 8.17-18*
brick construction
—"bricktown" (Tokyo's Ginza), 22
—curtain walling in, 95
—in Queen Anne revival, 38, 95
—shift to, in Meiji era, 33: in Akasaka Detached Palace and Hyokeikan (both 1909), 59; in Bank of Japan (1896), 52; in Maruzen Book Company (1909), 95; in Sempukan (1871), 20
Bridgens, R. P., 27, 31
British Consulate, Yokohama (1868), 27, *fig. 1.16*
British Legation, Tokyo (1872), 20; and in Yokohama (1867), 27
Brno, Czechoslovakia: Tugendhat House (1930), 119, 138, *fig. 6.24*
Brussels, 105
—Banque Nationale de Belgique (1874), 54, *fig. 2.33*
—World's Fair (1958): Philips Pavilion, 218, 222, *fig. 8.56*
Buber, Martin, 229
Buddhism, 145, 154, 156, 171, 182, 183, 205, 206, 231; architecture of, 71, 236; "Daibutsu" style, 206, *fig. 8.39*; concept of enlightenment in, 10; mandala as spatial model, 241, *fig. 10.5*; Metabolism and, 133, 267; Zen sect of, 31, 183, 205
building codes (Japanese), 46, 243
Bund (Yokohama waterfront), 17, *fig. 1.2*
Bunri Ha Kenchiku Kai (Japanese Secession, or Secessionist Architectural Society), 95-96, 98-99, 112, 113-14, 115, 146, *fig. 5.6*
bureaus. See under Japan: Government of
Burges, William, 33, 35, 36, 37, 38, 47, 52, 65, 74; Brisbane Cathedral (1859), 30; Bombay School of Art (project, 1865), 35, *fig. 2.3*; Trinity College, Hartford, CT (project, 1873), 52
Bute, (Lord John P. Crichton-Stuart), 35

Calcutta, 18, 18n6, 20
Cambridge, University of, 110; History Faculty building (1967), 226, *fig. 9.12*
Canmack, Addison, 59

carpentry (Japanese), 15, 22-23, 27, 33, 96, 197
Cassirer, Ernst, 67
castle towns (*jokamachi*), 41, 173-74
Central Post Office, Tokyo. See Tokyo Central Post Office
Central Telegraph Office, Tokyo (1925), 96, 100, 113, *fig. 5.11*
Chamber of Commerce, Tokyo, 142. See also Tokyo Industrial Club
chashitsu. See tearoom
Cheney, Mamah Borthwick, 85
chessboard, 241. See also *fuseki*; mandala
Chicago
—Midway Gardens (1914), 79, 83, *fig. 4.9*
—(Frank) Robie House (1909), 105, *fig. 10.2*
—World's Columbian Exposition (1893), 59, 69, 73; Nippon Tea House, 71, 73, *fig. 3.9*; Phoenix Hall (Ho-o-Den), 69, 71, 73, 74, 112, 126, *figs. 3.3, 6-8*
China (Chinese), 10, 236, 248
—artistic influence of, 18, 24, 27, 29, 30, 55, 65
—cities of, and urban form, 41, 43, 182
—Dairen (Ta-lien): Civic Hall competition (1938), 154, *fig. 6.85*
—Hong Kong, 16, 18-19, 20, 22, 29
—Manchuria (Manchukuo), 107, 110-11, 154, 171; Hsinking (Changchun) capital, *fig. 6.7*
—in Nagasaki, 29
—model for Japanese open ports, 16, 17, *fig. 1.4*
—Peking: Japanese Ministry (1886), 55, *fig. 2.36*
—Shanghai, 107, 154, 164
—Soochow souvenir prints, 29
—Japan at war with, 14, 59, 107, 110-11, 154
CIAM (Congrès Internationaux d'Architecture Moderne), 172, 174. See also under Tange, Kenzo: and urban planning
—first meeting (La Sarraz), 152
—second meeting (Frankfurt) 114
—fourth meeting (Athens-Marseilles), 173: Athens Charter (1933), 173, 175, 176, 182, 190
—fifth meeting (Bridgewater) and sixth meeting (Bergamo), 173
—CIAM VIII (Hoddesdon), 173, 175, 176, 182, 186
—CIAM X (Dubrovnik) and Team X, 173, 176, 179, 181
—CIAM '59 (Otterlo), 176, 177, 178
cinema (Japanese), 92. See also Imamura, Shohei; Teshigahara, Hiroshi
city planning, 41, 42, 46, 90-91, 182, 184-85, 188, 190-91, 243. See also China: cities of; CIAM: fourth meeting (Athens Charter); Le Corbusier: writings (*La Ville Radieuse*); Tange, Kenzo: and city planning; Tokyo: city planning
Coleman, George, 18
College of Engineering, Tokyo. See under Tokyo (Imperial) University
Commemorative Peace Exhibition, Tokyo (1922), 93, 96, 152, *fig. 5.7*
Commercial Museum, Tokyo (1871), 20
concrete, 203, 280. See also earthquakes: and earthquake-proof construction
Conder, Josiah, 33, 35-37, 38, 47, 48, 55, 56; Hokkaido Colonization Agency, Tokyo (1878), 50, *fig. 2.25*; Iwasaki Villa, Tokyo (Fukagawa, 1889), 38, *fig. 2.5*; Kummo-in, Tokyo (1879), 36; Naval Ministry, Tokyo (1894), 47, *figs. 2.18-19*; Rokumeikan, Tokyo (1883), 79-80; Tokyo Imperial University, Dept. of Law and Literature (1884), 52, *fig. 2.29*; Ueno Imperial

298

Museum, Tokyo (1882), 36, *fig. 2.4*
Constructivism, 105, 129, 144, 146, 159, 277; neo-, 164, 170; Russian, 119, 226
Copenhagen: Ny Carlsberg Glyptothek (1895), 58
Crane, Walter, 74, 75
cybernetics, 228; and electronics, 183; and "manner," 239–41; metaphor and, 234–35

Dahlerup, J. V., 58
"Daibutsu" style, 206, *fig. 8.39*
Dai-ichi Seimei (First Mutual Life Insurance) Building, Tokyo (1934–38), 153–54, *fig. 6.82*
Dairen (Ta-lien), China. *See under* China
danchi (low-income housing), 147
darkness. *See* space; Isozaki, Arata; Tanizaki, Junichiro
Darmstadt (Mathildenhöhe): Hochzeitsturm (1908), 93, *fig. 5.2*
de Boinville, A. C. (Chastel de Boinville, Alfred), 33; auditorium at the technical college, Tokyo (1877), *fig. 2.1*
Deleuze, Gilles, 276, 277
demographical statistics (Japanese), 107, 111
—population growth: Meiji era, 14, 188; Taisho and early Showa eras, 146
—urban expansion: Meiji era, 41; post-World War II, 186
Descartes, René, 189–90, 235
Deshima, Nagasaki, 29
De Stijl, 112, 113, 232
Deutscher Werkbund, 145, 149
Dojunkai (housing association), 147, 150–52; Daikanyama Apartments, Tokyo (1927), 150, *figs. 6.72–74*; Edogawa Apartments, Tokyo (1934), 150, 152, *figs. 6.75–76*; Harajuku Apartments, Tokyo (1926), 150, *fig. 6.71*
doma (earth-paved domestic workspace), 200
Doshi, B. V., 179
dozo-zukuri. *See under* fires
Dudok, W. M., 119
Dyer, Henry, 33

Eames, Charles, 195
earthquakes: and earthquake-proof construction, 45, 77–79, 83, 94, 95, 100, 129, 150, 163, 165, 188, 191, 254, 277; Great Kanto (1923), 36, 77, 90, 91, 96, 100, 116, 147, 188; Nobi (1891), 47
Ecole des Beaux-Arts, 34, 68, 94; architectural planning, 54, 81, 82, 94; classicism of, 58, 64, 69; instruction at, 67
Edo (Yedo: pre-Meiji-era Tokyo), 13, 41, 90n1, 92, 182, 235, 236. *See also* Tokugawa era
—building style carried over, 24, 27
—Castle, 35, 41; suite of rooms of, copied in Phoenix Hall (Ho-o-Den), 71
—fires, 43; *dozo-zukuri* fireproofing, 26
—living conditions, 41, 43
—Wright on (and Yoshiwara), 86–87, 90
Ekuan, Kenji, 179
Emerson, William, 29
Ende, Hermann. *See* Ende und Böckmann
Ende und Böckmann, Berlin, 39, 43, 45–47; Ministry of Justice, Tokyo (1895), 43, 45, 46, *figs. 2.15–16*; National Supreme Court, Tokyo (1896), 43, 46–47, *fig. 2.17*; Imperial Diet and surroundings (projects), 1887), 39, *figs. 2.7–11*
Endo, Arata, 81, 143
engawa verandah, 152
engravings, European, 29
expressionism, 92–96, 99–100; and Modern Movement in Japan, 191; of Gropius, 96; and early Bauhaus, 119; in painting, 100, 105. *See also* Bunri Ha Kenchiku Kai

fascism: German and Italian, and architecture, 143, 145, 153; Japanese, 107, 145; and Greater East Asia Coprosperity Sphere Memorial (1943), 172, *fig. 7.9*
Fenellosa, Ernest, 75n42, 111–12
Feurstein, Bedrich, 129
Fiesole, Tuscany, 76
Fillmore, Millard, 14
film. *See* cinema
fires (in Tokyo and Yokohama): destruction by, 22, 23, 27, 43, 87; and fireproof construction (*dozo-zukuri*, *namako-kabe*), 26–27, 46, 129
Fischer, Oskar, 119
Floto, Julius, 105
formalism, 83, 197, 252, 277; denounced by Venturi, 232; disapproved of by Smithsons, 197; disclaimed by Shinohara, 274; Japanese neo-, 244–45, 265; and phenomenological approach, 231–32; Russian, 243, 248, 277. *See also* Shklovsky, Victor
Fowler, Charles, 22
France (French): architectural influence (including International Second Empire style), 43, 47, 50, 55, 56, 58; Art Nouveau influenced by Japanese art, 65; Art Nouveau influence on Secessionism, 93; military technology of, 14. *See also* Paris; Vaux-le-Vicomte
Frankfurt/Main: Bruchfeldstrasse Siedlung (Niederrad, 1925), 148, *fig. 6.66*. *See also* CIAM: second meeting
French, Cal, 29, 30
Fujii, Koji, 192
Fujisawa, Kanagawa Prefecture: S. Akaboshi Cottage (1922), 134, *figs. 6.43–45*
Fukuoka, Fukuoka Prefecture
—Fukuoka Mutual Bank: Head Office, Hakata (1971), 224–25, 249, *fig. 9.11*; Nagasumi Branch (1971), 249, 251, *figs. 10.8–9*; Ropponmatsu Branch (1971), 249, 251, *figs. 10.10–11*
furniture: Ishimoto and, 119; the Raymonds and, 100, 119, 134–35, *fig. 5.18*
fuseki, 240, 241, 255
fusuma doors, 211

Galveston, TX, Customs House, 20
"gap" (architectural and/or semantic), 254, 269, 272, 274–77
Garnier, J.-L.-C., 43
gas street lighting, 50
General Grant style, 50, 56
General Staff Headquarters, Tokyo (1899), 56, *fig. 2.37*
Geneva: League of Nations competition (1928), 152–53, *fig. 6.79*
genkan entryway, 159
German neo-Renaissance style, 43–48, 55, 56
Germany (German), 14, 39; architectural influence cited, 75n49, 159; Hamburg, 44; Katayama influenced by, 55–56; Prussia, 14, 38, 39; Schwerin, 44; Stuttgart, 105, 149. *See also* Bauhaus; Berlin; Bremen; expressionism; Frankfurt/Main; German neo-Renaissance style; Secession style
GHQ, American Occupation Forces, Tokyo. *See* Dai-ichi Seimei Building
Giedion, Siegfried, 175, 177
giyofu (pseudo-Western) style, 22–25, 27, 29–31, 33, 34
Glasgow, University of, 33, 35
Glover, Thomas Blake, 18–19; residence of, Nagasaki (1863), 17, *fig. 1.5*
godown (storeroom), 26
Godwin, E. W., 65, 74; furniture by, *fig. 3.1*
Gookin, Frederick W., 81
Gothic Revival style, 34–36, 47, 65, 68. *See also* Tokyo (Imperial) University: Yasuda Hall
Goto, Keiji, and Shintaro Oe: Hobutsu-den at Meiji Shrine, Tokyo (1922), 107, *fig. 6.1*
Gowan, James. *See* Leicester, University of, Engineering Building
Grant, Ulysses S., 50, 56
Great Britain, 17, 18, 43, 50, 91; architectural influence of, 15–62 passim. *See also* Cambridge, University of; Glasgow, University of; Leicester, University of; Liverpool; London; Oxford, University of
Greene and Greene, Pasadena, 63
grid (architectural), 240, 251–52, 254–55, 274–75. *See also* Superstudio
Gropius, Walter, 96, 118, 150, 152, 159, 162, 191, 195. *See also* Bauhaus
—buildings: Municipal Employment Office, Dessau (1928), Packaged House System (1945), and Weissenhof Siedlung houses (1927), 265
—and Tange, 175, 177, 183, 195
—writings: "Architecture in Japan," in Ishimoto and Tange, *Katsura* (1960), 183–84; *Internationale Archtektur* (1925), 105

Hakodate, Hokkaido, 16, 17
Hakone-Sengoku, Kanagawa Prefecture: White Pillar House (c. 1936), 162–63, *figs. 6.98–99*
Hamao, Arata (Baron), 111; house for, 125, *figs. 6.27–28*
Hamburg, 44
Hanayama, Hyogo Prefecture: North House (1965), 205, *figs. 8.35–36*
Hasenauer, Karl von, 59
Hayashi, Tadahiro, 31
Hegel, G. W. F., 67, 68
Heian-era architecture. *See shinden-zukuri* style
Heidegger, Martin, 229, 231
Hennebique, François, 95
highway construction, 22, 91. *See also* municipal improvement
Hindu-Saracenic style, 47, 55, 56
Hiroshige, 63, 74
Hiroshima, Hiroshima Prefecture, 183

—Isozaki's "Destruction of the Future City" (1968), 221–22, *fig. 9.5*
—*Hiroshima Notes* (Oe), 174n20
—Peace Center competition (1949), 168, 172, 173, 174–75; Atomic Memorial Museum (1949–55), 175, 197, *fig. 7.12*; Peace Park (1949–55), 175, *figs. 7.11, 13*; master plan (1949–55), 175
historicism, 22, 33, 45, 63, 64–65, 75, 83
Hitchcock, Henry-Russell, 43, 44, 64n1, 79, 96n7, 113, 129
Hobrecht, James, 39, 39n7
Hobutsu-den, Meiji Shrine, Tokyo (1921), 107, *fig. 6.1*
Hokkaido: Colonization Agency building, Tokyo (1878), 50, *fig. 2.25*; Hakodate, 16, 17; Office for Development building, Sapporo (1873), 31
Hokusai, 65, 76
Holland (Dutch), 14, 15; Amsterdam Children's Home (1960), 228–30; Amsterdam School of protoexpressionism, 96, 112, 113; architectural influence, 23, 25, 29–30, 145, *fig. 1.19*; factory, Deshima, Nagasaki, 29; Rotterdam, 119; Utrecht, 105
Hollar, Wenzel, 29
Hong Kong, 16, 18–19, 20, 22, 29
Hoo-do, Byodo-in, Uji (1053), 69, 71, *figs. 3.4–5*
Horiguchi, Sutemi, 96, 112–13, 126, 129, 146
—buildings: Kikkawa Residence, Tokyo (1930), 144, *figs. 6.61–62*; Memorial Tower (1922) at Commemorative Peace Exhibition, Tokyo, 96, 152, *fig. 5.7*; Okada House, Tokyo (1934), 125, 129, 138, 144–45, *figs. 6.34–35*; villa at Warabi, Saitama Pref. (1926), 145, *fig. 6.63*; Weather Station, Oshima Island, Shizuoka Pref. (1938), 99, *figs. 5.13–14*
—writings: "Japanese Taste as Expressed in Modern Architecture" (1932), 145; *Modern Dutch Architecture* (1924), 112
houses and housing (Japanese): early modern example of, 100, 105, 106, *figs. 5.17–21*; 1950's case-studies of, 193–95; family investment in, 188–89; special features of, 124–25; group, 146–50, 152, 190–92; housing association (Dojunkai), 147, 150, 152; *minka* and vernacular theme in, 10, 134, 143, 170; north-south orientation of, 144, 162; typology (pre-World War II), 124–26; Wright's perception of, 85, 105, 237. *Note*: All post-Meiji-era residences are indexed by location
Husserl, Edmund, 9, 226, 231
Hyokeikan. *See* Ueno (Imperial) Museum

illusion. *See* semiotics; space
Imamura, Shohei, 200, *figs. 8.30*
Imperial Crown style. *See teikan yoshiki*
Imperial Diet, 13; building and surroundings (projects, 1887), 39, *figs. 2.7–11*; competition for (1917–18), 107; constructed (1936), 107, 153
Imperial Hotel, Tokyo: first (1890), 56, 75n49, 79, *fig. 4.4*; second (1923), 9, 43, 54, 76, 77, 79–83, 86, 89, 90, 100, 110, 110n1, *figs. 4.1–3, 5–7, 10, 12, 14–15*
Imperial Household Ministry, 55, 56, 62
Imperial Museum, Kyoto. *See under* Kyoto
Imperial Museum, Nara. *See under* Nara
Imperial Museum, Tokyo. *See* Ueno (Imperial) Museum
Imperial Palace, Tokyo, 41, 55–56, 173–74, *fig. 2.12*
Imperial University, Kyoto, 94. *See also* Kyoto: Rakuto Apartment
Imperial University, Tokyo. *See* Tokyo (Imperial) University
India: neoclassical colonial architecture, 15–16; Presidency towns of, 17–18. *See also* Bombay: School of Art project; Hindu-Saracenic style; Le Corbusier: buildings (Chandigarh)
Inoue, Mitsuo, 211n15–18
"I-novel" (Japanese literary genre), 244
International Second Empire style, 43, 47, 50, 56
International Style, 9, 92, 99–100, 135, 138, 142, 146, 159, 191; "The International Style: Architecture Since 1922," exhibition at Museum of Modern Art, New York (1932), 96n7, 113, 129; Tokyo primary schools as example of, 116, 118, *figs. 6.13–15*; Wright, Tsuchiura, and, 148–49. *See also* modernism (Modern movement)
Inumaru family, 77
invisibility, 235, 235n30, 241. *See also* space; Isozaki, Arata
Ishimoto, Kikuji, 96; Aoki House, Tokyo (1931), 124, *figs. 6.25–26*; Asahi Newspaper Offices, Tokyo (1927), 96, 118, *figs. 5.8–10*; Shirokiya Department Store, Tokyo (1931), 118–19, *figs. 6.16–18*; Togo House, Tokyo (1931), 119, 124, 138, *figs. 6.22–23*; Tokyo Airport Office (1932),

119, figs. 6.20-21
Ishimoto, Yasuhiro, 183
Isozaki, Arata, 218ff
—buildings: Fujimi Country Club, Oita, Oita Pref. (1974), 256, figs. 10.18-19; Fukuoka Mutual Bank, Daimyo Branch, Fukuoka, Fukuoka Pref. (1969), 226, 233; Fukuoka Mutual Bank, Head Office, Hakata, Fukuoka, Fukuoka Pref. (1971), 224, 249, fig. 9.11; Fukuoka Mutual Bank, Nagasumi Branch, Fukuoka, Fukuoka Pref. (1971), 249, 251, figs. 10.8-9; Fukuoka Mutual Bank, Oita Branch, Oita, Oita Pref. (1967), 223, 226, 228, 233, 245, 246, 249, 268, figs. 9.9, 13-14; Fukuoka Mutual Bank, Ropponmatsu Branch, Fukuoka, Fukuoka Pref. (1971), 249, 251, figs. 10.10-11; Gumma Prefectural Museum of Modern Art, Takasaki (1974), 248, 251, 252, 268, 277, figs. 10.14-15; Kamioka Town Hall, Toyama Pref. (1978), 265-66, figs. 10.26-28; Medical Hall, Oita, Oita Pref. (1960), 223, 245, 256, fig. 9.7; Municipal Library, Kitakyushu, Fukuoka Pref. (1975), 246, 256, 261, 267, figs. 10.7, 20-21; Oita Prefectural Library, Oita (1966), 223, 226, 232, 240, 267, fig. 9.8; West Japan General Exhibition Center, Kitakyushu, Fukuoka Pref. (1977), 261, fig. 10.25; Yano House, Tokyo (1975), 256, 260, fig. 10.22
—and darkness, 226, 234-36, 244-45. See also "Space of Darkness" under "Writings"
—and the destruction of architecture, 219, 239, 243, 248, 254, 261, 265, 275
—exhibitions: "Electric Labyrinth" at the Milan Triennale (1968), 222, 226, 243, 248, fig. 9.6; "MA: Space-Time in Japan," Paris (1978), 267, 277, figs. 10.16, 30; participated in "Space and Color," Tokyo (1966), 245, 245n27
—on Magic House, Korakuen Amusement Park, Tokyo, 228, 230, fig. 9.15
—and idea of the future city, 219-22, 236
—on mandala, 240-41, fig. 10.5
—on manner, maniera, 246, 248, fig. 10.7; seven operations of, 236, 239-40, fig. 10.4
—and Metabolism, 219, 221-22, 223, 244, 248
—projects: "City in the Air" (c. 1961), 219, fig. 9.2; "Computer-Aided City" (1971), 243, 256, fig. 10.6; "Destruction of the Future City" (1968), 222, fig. 9.5; "Future City" (1962), 219, 221, 222, 223, 248, 277, fig. 9.4; "Joint Core System" (c. 1960), 219, fig. 9.3
—and "soft" systems, 226, 236, 242-43
—on vacuum, 237
—writings: "City Invisible" (1966), 235; The Destruction of Architecture (1975), 240, 251; "Formalism" (1979), 265; "From Manner, to Rhetoric, to ..." (1976), 243; "The Metaphor of the Cube" (1976), 243; "Rereading 'In Praise of Shadows'" ("'Inei Raisan' Saidoku," 1974), 233-34, 234n29; "Rethinking 'Space of Darkness'" (1980), 233; "Rhetoric of the Cylinder" (1976), 260 "Space of Darkness" ("Yami no Kukan," 1964), 9, 228, 230-31, 232, 234
Italianate style (nineteenth century), 22, 23, 32
Ito, Chuta, 110, 192
Ito, Hirobumi, 62
Iwakura Mission, 33, 50

Janes, L. L., 24
Janet, Pierre (-M.-F.), 68
Janssens, Wynand. See Brussels: Banque Nationale de Belgique
Japan: Government of. For other government buildings, see variously under Imperial, National bureaus: Department of Works, 38-39; Hokkaido Colonization Agency, building, Tokyo (1878), 50, fig. 2.25; Printing Office, building (1876), 33; Railways Bureau, 31; Agency for Reconstruction, 172
—ministries: Communications Architectural Dept. of, 113-16; Communications Ministry, building, Tokyo (1874), 31, fig. 1.21; Education, 48; Finance (Treasury), 48, 49; Finance, Public Works Bureau of, 19, 20, 31; Foreign, 41-42, 43, 90-91, 154; Home Affairs, 14, 37, 42, 43, 56; Home Affairs, city planning section of, 90, 91; Home Affairs, and Dept. of Local Affairs, 147; Home Affairs, Public Works Bureau of, 31; Justice, 43, 99; Justice Ministry building, Tokyo (1895), 45, figs. 2.15-16; Naval Ministry, building, Tokyo (1894), 47, figs. 2.18-19; Technology, 14, 23, 31, 33, 34, 37, 38, 55
Japanese Empire, pan-Asian ideology of: and Murano, 142-43; and Tange, 157; and Tange's entry for Greater East Asia Coprosperity Sphere memorial competition, 172, fig. 7.9. See also China: Manchuria
Japanese Print, The (1912), by Wright, 64, 74, 76, 79, fig. 3.10
Japanism, 64, 237. See also Aesthetic Movement; historicism
Japan Style, 186, 190-92, 200, 206, 210, 218, 223, 224, 244, 246
Jesuits, 10, 231
Jodoji Pure Land Hall, Ono, Hyogo Pref. (1192), 202, fig. 8.34
Johnson, Philip, 96n7, 113, 129
Jones, Inigo, 49
Josui Kaikan, Tokyo (1918), 93, fig. 5.3

Kabukiza, Tokyo (1889), 50, fig. 2.27
Kagoshima, Kagoshima Prefecture, 18, 20
Kahn, Louis, 179, 184, 219, 232
Kaichi Primary School. See Matsumoto, Nagano Prefecture
kaikashiki (Restoration style), 22, 23. See also giyofu style
Kaisei Gakko (Liberal Arts College), Tokyo (1873), 23, 31, fig. 1.20
Kamahara, Shigeo: Kosuge Prison, Tokyo (1930), 99, fig. 5.12
Kamakura, Kanagawa Prefecture: Museum of Modern Art (1951), 169, 210, fig. 7.5. See also Kita Kamakura
kamban (signboard) architecture, 30
Kamioka, Toyama Prefecture: Town Hall (1978), 265-66, figs. 10.26-28
Kanagawa, Kanagawa Prefecture, 16, 27. See also Yokohama
kara-hafu ("Chinese-style") gable, 27, 31
Karuizawa, Nagano Prefecture: Raymond House (1933), 133-34, figs. 6.40-42
Kasumigaseki Building, Tokyo (1968), 188
Katayama, Tokuma, 55-56, 58-59; Akasaka Detached Palace (Togu Gosho), Tokyo (1909), 58-59, 62, 63, 64, 81, 93, figs. 2.42-44; Hyokeikan, Tokyo (1909), 58-59, 62, 277, fig. 2.41; Imperial Palace interiors (1888), 55-56; Japanese Ministry, Peking (1886), 55, fig. 2.36; Japanese Resident-General's Palace, Seoul (1909), 62; Kyoto Imperial Museum (1895), 56, 58, fig. 2.40; Nara Imperial Museum (1894), 56, 58, figs. 2.38-39; Red Cross Society Hospital, Tokyo (1890), 56; Tokyo Central Post Office (1891), 56
kato mado ("flame-headed" window), 31
Katsura Villa. See Kyoto: Katsura Detached Imperial Villa
Kawamoto, Ryoichi: Soldiers' Hall (Gunjin Kaikan), Tokyo (1934), 107, 110, fig. 6.2
Kawazoe, Noboru, 179
Kayser und Grossheim, Berlin, 45
Kent, William, 33, 34
Kikutake, Kiyonori, 178, 248; "Ideas for the Reorganization of Tokyo City" (project, 1959), 177, 181, 184, 219; Miyakonojo City Hall, Miyazaki Pref. (1966), 216, fig. 8.55; Skyhouse (Kikutake House), Tokyo (1958), 177, 197, 214, fig. 7.14
Kimura, Toshihiko, 277
Kirishiki, Shinjiro, 79
Kishida, Hideto, 152, 170, 171, 191, 192, 197; (with S. Uchida) Yasuda Hall, Tokyo Imperial University (1925), 100, 170, figs. 5.15-16
Kita Kamakura, Kanagawa Prefecture: Yamada House (1934), 159, 164, figs. 6.95-96
Kitakyushu, Fukuoka Prefecture: Kitakyushu Municipal Library (1975), 246, 256, 267, figs. 10.7, 20-21; West Japan General Exhibition Center (1977), 261, fig. 10.25
Kita Saku, Nagano Prefecture: House with an Earthen Floor (1963), 200, figs. 8.25-26
kiwari system of structural proportions, 207
Kobe, Hyogo Prefecture, 16, 17, 31, 91
Koening, Pierre, 177
Kofu, Yamanashi Pref.: Yamanashi Press and Radio Center (1966), 184, 219
Korakuen Amusement Park, Tokyo, Magic House at, 228, 230, cf. fig. 9.15
Korea, 59, 62, 65, 107, 184
Korin (Ogata), 76
Kosuge Prison, Tokyo (1930), 99, fig. 5.12
Kumamoto, Kumamoto Prefecture, 24
Kummo-in, Tokyo (1879), 36
kura (storehouse), 26, 138
Kurata, Chikatada: White Pillar House, Hakone-Sengoku (c. 1936), 162-63 figs. 6.98-99
Kurobe, Toyama Prefecture: Kurobe Power Station (1938), 163, fig. 6.101
Kurokawa, Kisho (Noriaki), 179; Nakagin Capsule building, Tokyo (1972), 184, fig. 7.23
Kuru, Masamichi: Phoenix Hall (Ho-o-Den), World's Columbian Exposition, Chicago (1893), 69, 71, 73, 74, 112, 126, figs. 3.3, 6-8
Kyoto, 13, 43, 79, 85, 91, 129, 182; Imperial Museum (1895), 56, 58, fig. 2.40; Imperial Palace, 110, 171, 197; Institute of German Civilization (1935), 145; Katsura Detached Imperial Villa (mid-17th c.), 129, 183, 197, 205, 211, fig. 8.37; Rakuto Apartment (student hostel, 1933), 147, 148-49, fig. 6.67
Kyoto (Imperial) University, 94. See also Kyoto: Rakuto Apartment

Lao-tzu, 237, 239
Le Corbusier (Charles-Edouard Jeanneret), 9, 39, 44, 83, 106, 165, 168-71, 175-76, 183, 207, 210, 212, 214, 232, 243, 245
—buildings: Municipal Museum (1957), Ahmedabad, India, 207, 216; Centrosoyuz, Moscow (1929), 154, 170, fig. 6.83; Chandigarh (various and master plan), India (1951-65), 164-65, 169, 175, 206, 207, 210, 216, 225; Cook House, Boulogne-sur-Seine (1926), 135; Errazuris House, Chile (1930), 133-34, fig. 6.39; La Roche/Albert Jeanneret House, Anteuil (initial project, 1922), 129, fig. 6.38; National Museum of Western Art, Tokyo (1959), 206, 207, 210, 214, 215, figs. 8.40-43, 48; Notre Dame-du-Haut (Ronchamp, 1954), 168-69, 190, 213, 215-16, fig. 8.50; Ozenfant atelier, Paris (1922), 105; Philips Pavilion, Brussels World's Fair (1958), 218, 222, fig. 8.56; Sainte-Marie-de-la-Tourette, nr. Lyons (1960), 213, 225, fig. 8.47; Villa Savoye, Poissy (1930), 134, 195; Swiss Students' Hostel, Paris (1931), 207; Unité d'Habitation, Marseilles (1953), 165, 175; Villa at Vaucresson (1923), 105, 119, 152; Villa at Ville-d'Avray (1929), 138, fig. 6.51; Wanner flats, Geneva (1929), 152
—Cartesian aspects of, 189-90
—and CIAM, 172-73. See also CIAM: esp. fourth meeting (Athens Charter)
—and Citrohan prototype, 135
—post-International Style influence of, in Japan, 190-91, 206-7, 232
—and Maekawa, 152-54
—and crisis in modernism, 190-91, 212, 232, 244
—projects: Bôite à Miracles, Tokyo (1959), 214, fig. 8.48; League of Nations (1928), 152-53, fig. 6.79; Musée d'Art Contemporain (from 1930), 214, fig. 8.49; Palace of the Soviets, Moscow (1931), 170, 190, fig. 7.8
—and Purism, 243
—and Sakakura, 156-57
—and Tange, 164, 170, 171
—writings: L'Art decoratif d'aujourd'hui (1924), 152; Le Modulor (1948), 210; La Ville Radieuse (1935) and implementations of the ville radieuse scheme, 165, 172, 173, 182, 190
Ledoux, Claude-Nicolas, 260-61; Maison des Directeurs de la Loue engraving (1804), 260, fig. 10.23
Leicester, University of, Engineering Building (1963), 223, 226, fig. 9.10
Lessing, Gotthold E., 241
Le Vau, Louis, 62
Lévi-Strauss, Claude, 276, 280
Lewitt, Sol, 252
Liberal Arts College (Kaisei Gakko), Tokyo (1873), 23, 31, fig. 1.20
Liberal Democratic Party (Jiyu Minshu-to), 186
Liverpool, 43
London, 15, 22, 33, 34, 38, 44, 59, 118, 164; Exhibition of 1862, Japanese Court at, 65; Greater London Plan (1944), 184; Metropolitan Board of Works, 42; and Tokyo, comparisons with, 13, 41, 91
Loos, Adolf, 143, 145, 255
Los Angeles, 185; Lovell House (1929), 159, 177, fig. 6.97
Louis Seize style, 265
Lutyens, Edwin (Sir), 110-11

ma (interval), 229, 240, 241; "MA: Space-Time in Japan" exhibition, Paris (1978), 267, 267n52, 277, fig. 10.30
MacArthur, General Douglas, 154, 165
machine (analogy in architecture), the, 75, 76, 239, 243, 244, 277, 280
Macintosh, Charles Rennie, 232
Madras, 18, 18n6
Maekawa, Kunio, 152-57, 179, 181, 182, 189, 191, 210
—buildings: Harumi housing, Tokyo (1958), 178, figs. 7.17-19; Kanagawa Prefectural Concert Hall and Library, Yokohama (1954), 169, fig. 7.6; Kasama House, Tokyo (1938), 192-93, figs. 8.4-5; Kishi Memorial Gymnasium, Tokyo (1940), 154; Maekawa House, Tokyo (1941), 154,

192–93, figs. 8.6–7; Morinaga candy store, Tokyo (1936), 152; Shanghai Commercial Bank (1939), 154; Toho Films office, Tokyo (1940), 154; Tokyo Metropolitan Festival Hall, Ueno (1961), 210, 215–16, figs. 8.44, 51
—at CIAM VIII (1951), 175
—competition entries: Dairen Civic Hall, China (1938), 154, fig. 6.85; Japanese Cultural Center, Bangkok (1943), 157, fig. 6.91; Japan Pavilion, Paris Exposition (1937), 154; figs. 6.86–87; Showa Steel administration building (1937), 154; Tokyo Hinomoto Kaikan (1935), 154; Tokyo Municipal Hall (1934), 154, fig. 6.84; Ueno Imperial Museum (1931), 153, 157, fig. 6.80
—and Le Corbusier, 152, 154
—and Raymond, 152–53, 193
—and Tange, 154, 164, 171, 192–93
Mainichi newspaper, 29
Maki, Fumihiko, 179, 245
Manchuria (Manchukuo). See under China
mandala, 240–42, 275, fig. 10.5
maniera. See Isozaki, Arata: on manner; also Shearman, John
"mansion" (high-priced apartment housing), 147
Manson, Grant C., 71
Marunouchi Building (Marubiru), Tokyo (1923), 114, 153, fig. 6.12
Maruzen Book Company, Tokyo (1909), 54, 95, fig. 5.4
masonry, 110. See also brick construction; fires: and fireproof construction
Matsumoto, Nagano Prefecture: Kaichi Primary School (1876), 23, 27, 29, figs. 1.12, 17
Matsuzaki, Bancho, 38, 39
May, Ernst, 114; Bruchfeldstrasse Siedlung, Frankfurt/Main (Niederrad, 1925), 148, fig. 6.66
Medical College, Tokyo (1876), 23, 31
Meiji era (1868–1912), 13, 91, 164; architecture of, 15–62
Meiji Insurance Building, Tokyo (1934), 114
Memorial Tower, at the Commemorative Peace Exhibition (Tokyo, 1922), 93, 96, 152, fig. 5.7
Mendelsohn, Erich, 96, 118
Merleau-Ponty, Maurice, 229, 230, 232, 275
Metabolism (Metabolist movement), 184, 189, 256, 267. See also Kikutake, Kiyonori; Kurokawa, Kisho; Maki, Fumihiko
—evolution of, 179, 181, 182
—fading away of, 210
—fulfillment of, 184–85
—and Isozaki, 219, 221–22, 223, 244, 248
—and Shinohara, 200, 211
—and Tange, 177–78, 182, 219, fig. 9.1
—foremost examples: Miyakonojo City Hall, Miyazaki Pref. (1966), 216, fig. 8.55; Nakagin Capsule Building, Tokyo (1972), 184, fig. 7.23; Shizuoka Press and Broadcasting Center, Tokyo (1967), 184, fig. 7.22
metaphor, 228, 232–37, 245; of the cube, 252, 254–56; future urban ruin as, 219, 221–22, figs. 9.4–5; in Greek architecture, 236, 254; language as, 254; of "the machine," 239; and manner, *maniera*, 244, 248; of the vacuum, 237, 239; relating with water, 261; Wright and (according to Isozaki), 237, 239
Mewes and Davis, London, 59
Michelangelo: reconstruction of the Capitoline Hill, 172, 175, fig. 7.10; Sistine Chapel frescoes, discussed, 67, 68, 73, 74, 75, fig. 3.2; Tange's study of, 164, 171
Milan Triennale (1968): "Electric Labyrinth" exhibition at, 222, 223, 226, 243, 248, fig. 9.6
Milde, Kurt, 44, 45
ministries. See under Japan: Government of
minka (farm- or vernacular-style house), 10, 134, 143, 170
mitate and *mitate-e*, 236
Mitsui Bank Headquarters, Tokyo: first (1872), 23, 24–26, 27, 32, 39, figs. 1.14–15; second (1874), 32, fig. 1.22
Mitsukoshi Department Store, Tokyo (1934), 114, 153
Miura, Baien, 246, fig. 10.7
Miura, Kanagawa Prefecture: Suzusho House (1968), 268, fig. 10.31
Miyakonojo, Miyazaki Prefecture: City Hall (1966), 216, fig. 8.55
modernism (Modern Movement), 67, 69, 76, 92, 100, 105–6, 115, 172, 191–92, 212, 229, 230, 231, 237, 240. See also International Style
—beginnings of, 63–64, 66–69
—demise of, 244. See also Isozaki, Arata: and the destruction of architecture; Le Corbusier: and crisis in modernism; postmodernism
—Metabolism and, 221
—and *modanizumu*, 91, 92, 114, 146, 163

—and Murano, 142
—and Shinohara, 206, 269
—and Western "space," 9, 212
—and Tange, 176
—utopianism of, 75
Moore, Charles, 239, 246, 248, 260
Morigo Shoten, Tokyo (1931), 142, fig. 6.58
Morris, William, 75
Moscow: Centrosoyuz (project, 1929), 154, 170, fig. 6.83; Palace of the Soviets (unrealized project, 1931), 170, 190, fig. 7.8
Mullet, Alfred B., 50, 56
Munari, Bruno, 252
municipal improvement, 41, 42, 91. See also city planning
Murano, Togo, 142, 146, 147
—buildings: Institute of German Civilization, Kyoto (1935), 145; Morigo Shoten, Tokyo (1931), 142, fig. 6.58; Nakayama House, Ashiya (1934), 143–44, figs. 6.59–60; Osaka Pantheon (1933), 147–48, 149, figs. 6.64–65
—writings: "Be above style!" ("*Yoshiki no ue ni are*," 1919), 142, 145; "The Economic Environment of Architecture" (1926), 142; "Looking While Moving" ("*Ugokitsutsu Miru*," 1931), 142
Muthesius, Hermann, 39

Naganohara, Gumma Prefecture: (second) Tanikawa House (1974), 272, 274–77, figs. 10.35–38
Nagasaki, Nagasaki Prefecture, 16, 17, 19, 20, 29, 34; Glover House (1863), 18–19, fig. 1.5
Nagato-cho Primary School, Tokyo (1937), 116, fig. 6.15
nagaya (tenement housing), 146
Nagoya, Aichi Prefecture, 91, 110, 111
Nakagin Capsule Building, Tokyo (1972), 184, fig. 7.23
Nakamura, Jumpei, 93–94
namako walling, 26, 27
Nara, Nara Prefecture, 43; Imperial Museum (1894), 56, 58, figs. 2.38–39; Todaiji (1199), 83, 205, 206, fig. 8.39
Nash, John, 22
National Diet Building, Tokyo. See Imperial Diet
National (Diet) Library, Tokyo, 59
National Mint. See under Osaka
National Museum of Western Art, Tokyo (1959), including Nineteenth Century Hall of, 206, 207, 210, 214, 215, figs. 8.40–43, 48
National Olympic Stadiums, Tokyo (1964), 164, 171, 179, 190, 218, fig. 8.57
National Sumo Arena, Tokyo (1909), 54, fig. 2.35
National Supreme Court, Tokyo (1896), 43, 46, fig. 2.17
Naval Ministry, Tokyo (1894), 47, figs. 2.18–19
Naval Reception Hall, Tokyo, 24
Needham, Joseph, 10
neoclassicism, 15–16, 17, 22, 219, 221–22, 232–33, 236, 241, 246
Neutra, Richard, 159; Lovell House, Los Angeles (1929), 159, 163, 177, fig. 6.97
New Canaan, CT: Breuer House (1947), 195, figs. 8.17–18
New Objectivity. See *Sachlichkeit*, *Neue Sachlichkeit*
New Orleans, 20
New York City, 142, 164, 186
Nichinan, Miyazaki Prefecture: Cultural Center (1962), 216, figs. 8.53–54
Nietzsche, Friedrich, 205, 239, 268
Nihon Dental College Hospital, Tokyo (extension, 1934), 163, fig. 6.100
Nihon Kosaku Bunka Remmei (so-called Japanese Werkbund), 145
Niigata, Niigata Prefecture, 16
Nikko, Tochigi Prefecture: Toshogu (shrine, 1636), 27
nishiki-e prints, 27, 29
Noda, Toshihiko, 94, 96
Noel, Miriam, 85, 89
Noguchi, Isamu, 165
Noh drama, 234
Norberg-Schulz, Christian, 231, 131n24

Oita, Oita Prefecture: Fukuoka Mutual Bank (1967), 223, 226, 228, 233, 245, 246, 249, 268, figs. 9.9, 13–14; Fujimi Country Club (1974), 256, figs. 10.18–19; Medical Hall (1960), 223, 245, 256, fig. 9.7; Prefectural Library (1966), 223, 226, 232, 240, 267, fig. 9.8
Okada, Shinichiro, 114
Okakura, Kakuzo, 71n23, 111, 112, 237
Okura, Kihachiro (Baron), 80
Olbrich, Joseph Maria, 93, 96
Ono, Hyogo Prefecture: Jodoji Pure Land Hall

(1192), 202, fig. 8.34
Ordnance (G.B.), 20, 22
Osaka, 16, 91; Higashi Post Office (1931), 114, figs. 6.9–10; Kanshinji (late 14th c.), altar arrangement based on mandala, fig. 10.5; National Mint (1871), 19, 20, 24, 31, figs. 1.6–7; Pantheon (1933), 147–48, figs. 6.64–65; Sempukan (belonging to the National Mint, 1871), 20, 24, fig. 1.8; Town Hall (1874), 23
Oshima Island, Shizuoka Prefecture: Weather Station (1938), 99, figs. 5.13–14
Ostberg, Ragnar, 142
Otaka, Masato, 179
Oxford, University of, 25
Ozenfant, Amédée, 105

Palladio, Andrea, and Palladian style, 22, 24, 25, 31, 232, 233, 260, 261
paquebot style, 149
Paris, 49, 186; Beistegui apartment (1931), 276, 277, fig. 10.39; Hôtel de Salm (1786), 265, fig. 10.29; Japanese Pavilion (student hostel), Cité Universitaire, 154; Japan Pavilion, Paris Exposition (1937), Maekawa entry for, 154, figs. 6.86–87; Japan Pavilion, Paris Exposition (1937), Sakakura entry for, 156–57, figs. 6.88–89 (as realized); Louvre, extension (1852–57), 43, and Square Court (begun 1546), 58; Luxembourg Palace (early 17th c.), 54; "MA: Space-Time in Japan" exhibition, Festival d'Automne (1978), 267, 267n52, fig. 10.16, 30; "Paris Parallèle" scheme (1959), 181
parliament (Japanese). See Imperial Diet
Pater, Walter, 85
Peking: Japanese Ministry (1886), 55, fig. 2.36
Perret, Auguste, 129, 183
Perry, Matthew C., 13, 14
perspective, 63–64, 240, 245; -viewing machines, 29
phenomenology, 229, 231, 236, 267; contrasted with Cartesianism, 235; contrasted with formalism, 232; Isozaki and, 229, 233, 239; and linguistics, 230; and Tanizaki's *In Praise of Shadows*, 233; Venturi and, 232. See also Heidegger, Martin; Husserl, Edmund; Merleau-Ponty, Martin
Phoenix Hall (Ho-o-Den), at the World's Columbian Exposition, Chicago (1893), 69, 71, 73, 74, 112, 126, figs. 3.3, 6–8. See also Uji: Hoo-do
Pierce, Franklin, 14
Piranesi, Giovanni Battista, 219, 233, 245, 245n26, 246
Plesum, Guntis, 222
Poelzig, Hans, 99, 105, 232
polychromy, 29, 159, 245
Post, Emily, 59
postmodernism, 221, 230, 232, 233, 237, 239, 244, 246, 249, 252, 260. Cf. 236, 241
Prairie House style, 73, 82, 85, 105, 110, 205
Presidency towns (India), 17–18
Price, Bruce, 59, 59n14, 62, 62n15, 62n16, 64
prints (Japanese). See *nishiki-e* prints; *ukiyo-e* prints; also China: Soochow souvenir prints; engravings, European
Proust, Marcel, 67, 68, 276n62, 277
Prouvé, Jean, 179
Prussia. See under Germany
Punitzer, Martin, 114
putti, 27, 29

Queen Anne revival style, 37–38, 43, 73, 95, 118

rabbit hutch dwellings, 91
Racine, WI: S. C. Johnson Co. administration building (1939), 237, 239, fig. 10.3
Raffles, Sir Stamford, 18
railways, 22, 27, 31, 91, 111, 119, fig. 1.1
ramma (openwork transom), 195
rationalism, 113–163, 236. See also Viollet-le-Duc; modernism (Modern Movement)
Raymond, Antonin, 89ff. See also Raymond, Noémi
—buildings: K. Akaboshi House, Tokyo (1932), 135, figs. 6.48–50; S. Akaboshi Cottage, Fujisawa, Kanagawa Pref. (1931), 134, figs. 6.43–45; T. Akaboshi House, Tokyo (1934), 136, 138, 152, 162, 165, figs. 6.55–57; American Embassy, Tokyo (1928), 129; P. Claudel residence, Tokyo (1923), 106; French Embassy, Tokyo (1930), 129, 138, 152; K. Fukui Villa, Atami, Shizuoka (1934), 136; Hamao House, Tokyo (1928), 125, figs. 6.27–28; Kawasaki House, Tokyo (1934), 136, 138, 142, 152, 165, figs. 6.52–54; house at Montauk Point, NY, 193; Raymond House, Karuizawa, Nagano Pref. (1933), 133–34, 192, 193, figs. 6.40–42; Raymond House, New Hope, PA (remodeled in 1939), 193; Raymond

House, Tokyo (1953; see also Reinanzaka House, this entry), 193, figs. 8.8-10; Reader's Digest Building, Tokyo (1951), 165-68, figs. 7.1-4; R. Reid House (1924), 106, figs. 5.22-23; Reinanzaka House (1924), 100, 105, 106, figs. 5.17-21; Rising Sun Petroleum Co., Yokohama, employee housing (1928), 129; Rising Sun Petroleum General Office Building (1929), 129; Rising Sun Petroleum Manager's Residence (1931), 129, fig. 6.36; Rising Sun Petroleum service station prototypes (1930), 129, fig. 6.37; St. Alban's Church, Tokyo (1955), 193; Saloman House, Tokyo (1952), 193; Soviet Embassy, Tokyo (1929), 129; Tokyo Golf Club, Asaka, Saitama Pref. (1932), 135, 165, figs. 6.46-47; Tokyo Women's Christian College (1922), 106
—An Autobiography (1973), 89n32
—on the Japanese upper-middle-class house, 124-25
—influence of, on younger architects, 168, 168n2, 168n3
—disapproval of Le Corbusier's postwar style, 165, 168-69
—and Maekawa, 152, 193
—and Modern Movement, 106
—contrasted with Murano, 142-44
—criticism of Tange by, 182, 189
—and architectural "truth," 90
—and Wright, 89-90
Raymond, Noémi, 89, 119, 129, 135, 136. See also Raymond, Antonin
Reader's Digest Building, Tokyo (1951), 165-68, figs. 7.1-4
Reamer, Robert C., 82-83
Red Cross Society Hospital, Tokyo (1890), 56
Regency period, 15, 22
Ribot, T.-A., 68
Richards, J. M. (Sir James), 169, 169n5
Richardson, H. H., 65
Rietveld, G. T., 105
Rohe, Mies van der, 165, 195, 212; Tugendhat House, Brno, Czechoslovakia (1930), 119, 138, fig. 6.24
Rokumeikan, Tokyo (1883), 79-80
Rome, 90, 172, 182. See also Michelangelo
Ronchamp: Notre-Dame-du-Haut (1954), 168-69, 190, 213, 215-16, fig. 8.50
Rotterdam, 119
Rowe, Colin, 213, 214, 215
Royal Institute of British Architects (RIBA), 34, 36, 37
Rudolph, Paul, 179, 223
Ruhlmann, Emile-Jacques, 138
Ruskin, John, 32, 48, 49, 50, 66, 68, 83, 152
Russia (Soviet Union), 14, 16, 43, 59, 85, 146, 243. See also Moscow

Saarinen, Eero, 170, 218
Sachlichkeit, Neue Sachlichkeit (New Objectivity), 105, 114, 126, 146, 159, 276, 277, 280
Said, Edward, 83
Sakakura, Junzo, 164, 179; Japan Pavilion for the Paris Exposition (1937), 156, 210, figs. 6.88-89; Kamakura Museum of Modern Art, Kanagawa Pref. (1951), 169, 210, fig. 7.5
Salem, MA, 32
Sano, Riki (also Toshikata), 94-95; Maruzen Book Company, Tokyo (1909), 54, 95, fig. 5.4; Seitoku Memorial Gallery, Tokyo (1926), 95, fig. 5.5
Sapporo, Hokkaido, 31
Sartre, Jean-Paul, 190
Scandinavian modern style, 195, 246
Schinkel, Karl Friedrich, 55, 175
Schwerin, Mecklenburg, 44
Scott, George Gilbert (Sir), 35
Scott, Sir Giles Gilbert, 110
Scully, Vincent, 232
Secession style: Viennese 93, 145; Japanese (see Bunri Ha Kenchiku Kai)
Seidensticker, Edward, 38n5
Seike, Kiyosi, 195, 197, 198; Miyagi House, Tokyo (1953), 195, figs. 8.15-16; Mori House, Tokyo (1951), 193, 195, figs. 8.11-12; Saito House, Tokyo (1952), 195, figs. 8.13-14
semiotics (architectural), 224-26, 228, 230, 233, 234-35, 236, 241-42, 244
Semper, Gottfried, 36, 44, 55, 59
Sempukan. See under Osaka
Sen no Rikyu, 10, 85, 231. See also tea
Seoul, 62
Serlio, Sebastiano, and Serlian style, 33-34, 45, 48, 49, 50, fig. 2.24
Sert, José-Luis, 156, 175
Severud, Fred, 218
Shanghai, 107, 154, 164
Shankland, Edward, 59

Shaw, (Richard) Norman, 38, 44
Shearman, John, 248
shell structures, 179, 210, 215-16, 218
Shibusawa, Eiichi, 42, 47, 49-50, 80
Shibusawa Mansion, Tokyo (1888), 49-50, figs. 2.23, 26
Shimbashi Station, Tokyo (1872), 22
Shimizu, Kisuke, II, 23, 34; Mitsui Bank Headquarters, Tokyo, first (1872), 23, 24-26, 27, 32, 39, figs. 1.14-15, and second (1874), 32, fig. 1.22; Shimizu Gumi, 23; Tsukiji Hotel, Tokyo (1868), 23, 27, 31, 79, 80, fig. 1.13
Shimoda (Kikutaro), 73, 110n1
shinden-zukuri style, 110, 157, 171, 212
Shinohara, Kazuo, 9, 197ff. See also under space (Japanese)
—and abstraction, 198, 202, 245
—buildings: House at Kugayama, Tokyo (1953), 197-98, figs. 8.19-20; House in Uehara, Tokyo (1976), 277, 280, figs. 10.40-43; House in White, Tokyo (1966), 202, 205, 210, 211, 215, 223, 228, 232, 245, 268, 277, figs. 8.31-33; House of Earth, Tokyo (1966), 200-202, 210, 212, 216, 232, figs. 8.27-28; House with an Earthen Floor, Kita Saku, Nagano Pref. (1963), 200, figs. 8.25-26; Incomplete House, Tokyo (1970), 245, 268-69, figs. 10.32-33; Shino House, Tokyo (1970), 268-69, fig. 10.34; Suzusho House, Miura, Kanagawa Pref. (1968), 268, fig. 10.31; Tanikawa House (first), Tokyo (1958), 198, figs. 8.21-22; Tanikawa House (second), Naganohara, Gumma Pref. (1974), 272, 274-77, figs. 10.35-37; Umbrella House, Tokyo (1961), 198, 205, figs. 8.1, 23-24
—Isozaki and, 236, 244-45
—and Metabolism, 200, 211
—Seike and, 197
—and space: "black" (psychopathological) space, 200, 212; a "fourth" space, 211; "Japanese" space, 9, 206, 210-12, 218, 228, 245; "non-Japanese" space, 205, 235, 268, fig. 10.31; multiple spatiality, 268, 269, 276; "naked" spaces, 274n56, 277; "Space Machine," 275
—styles: First, 197, 198, 200, 202, 205, 210, 218, 235, 275; Second, 205, 206, 210, 235, 245, 246, 267, 268-69, 275; Third, 275, 277
—and traversal, 275, 276, fig. 10.38
—writings: "Beyond Symbol Spaces" (1971), 268; Residential Architecture (1964), 211; "When Naked Space Is Traversed" (1975), 274n56
Shintoism, 85, 110, 171, 182, 184, 205 267
Shizuoka Press and Broadcasting Center, Tokyo (1967), 184, fig. 7.22
Shklovsky, Victor, 243, 244, 276
shoin, shoin style, 10, 129, 155. See also kiwari
Showa era, 92, 107, 170, 186; architecture of, 113ff
Silsbee, J. L., 65
Singapore, 18, 20
Sino-Japanese War, 59
Sistine Chapel frescoes. See under Michelangelo
Smith, T. Roger, 37
Smithmeyer, John I. and Paul V. Pelz, 58
Smithson, Alison and Peter, 179, 197, 223
soan chashitsu. See tearoom
Soldiers' Hall (Gunjin Kaikan), Tokyo (1934), 107, 110, fig. 6.2
Sone-Chujo, Tokyo, 92-93
Soochow souvenir prints, 29
Soriano, Raphael, 179
space (Japanese), 9, 63-64, 148, 191, 211-12, 234, 235, 237; antispatiality, 76; and the city, 234-35; frontality and, 211, 214-15, 268, 276, 277; and identity of modern Japanese architecture, 228-29, 245; "Japanese" space of Shinohara, 9, 206, 210-12, 218, 228, 245; and "MA: Space-Time in Japan" exhibition, Paris (1978), 267, 267n52, 277, figs. 10.16, 30; nonexistence of, in Japanese architecture, 211; spatial division as technique of composition, 184, 211, 212, 214, 268; related to sukiya, 231; related to tateokoshi-ezu, 254; topological nature of, 212, 226, 230, 241, 268. See also allegory; perspective; taste (Japanese); tearoom
Spain, architectural influence of, 16, 20
Speer, Albert, 145
Springfield, IL: Susan Dana House (1903), 256, 261, fig. 10.24
steel, use of, 56, 110; in Bank of Japan, Tokyo (1896), 52, figs. 2.30-32; (steel combined with concrete) in City Hall, Miyakonojo, Miyazaki Pref. (1966), 216, fig. 8.55; in House at Kugayama, Tokyo (1953), 197, figs. 8.19-20; in Maruzen Book Company, Tokyo (1909), 54, 95, fig. 5.4; (steel trussing) in Miyagi House, Tokyo (1953), 195, figs. 8.15-16; in Reader's Digest Building, Tokyo (1951), 165, 168, figs. 7.1-3; in

Rising Sun Petroleum Co. service station prototype, Yokohama (1930), 129, fig. 6.37; (steel combined with wood) in Yamada House, Kita Kamakura, Kanagawa Pref. (1934), 159, figs. 6.95-96
Stirling, James, 246; Cambridge University, History Faculty building (1967), 226, fig. 9.12; (with James Gowan) Leicester University, Engineering Building (1963), 223, 225, 226, fig. 9.10
Stockholm 142, 154, 255, 256
Stone, Edward Durell, 138
Stuttgart, 135, 149
sudare (reed blinds), 134, 211
sukiya, sukiya style, 10, 71, 73, 129, 195, 212, 236, 237; and confrontation/recognition, 145; and Edo, 235; in relation to "Japanese space," 231, 254; and Japan Style, 191; non-language aspects of, 230, 233; and mitate, 236; structural notions of, 207; -shoin style, 129; Tange's Kulturkritik and, 205; and tateokoshi-ezu, 254. See also tearoom
Sullivan, Louis, 64, 75, 79, 232, 248
—author of The Autobiography of an Idea (1922-23), 67, 68, 69
—buildings: Auditorium Theater, Chicago (1890), 256; Transportation Building, at the World's Columbian Exposition, Chicago (1893), 69
—on the Sistine Chapel, 68, 73
—and Taine 66, 67, 67n13
Summerson, Sir John, 15, 16, 17, 27, 67n9, 75
Superstudio, 240, 251-52
Surrealism, 105, 164, 190
surveying, surveyors, 17-18, 19, 22, 30, 39, 172, 174
Suzuki, Hiroyuki, 59

Taine, Hippolyte, 67-68, 67n13, 69, 75, 85n23, 173
Taisho era, 41, 58, 90, 91-92, 107, 113, 114
Takamatsu, Kagawa Prefecture: Kagawa Prefectural Office (1958), 176, 177, 206, fig. 8.38
Takasaki, Gumma Prefecture: Gumma Prefectural Museum of Art (1974), 248, 251, 252, 268, 277, figs. 10.14-15
Takebashi Barracks, Tokyo (1870-74), 20, 23, figs. 1.9-10
Taki, Daikichi, 56
Tange, Kenzo, 143, 168, 170-79, 181-85, 191, 228
—buildings: Ehime Sports Center (now Kemminkan), Matsuyama, Ehime Pref. (1953), 179; Hiroshima Peace Center, Hiroshima Pref. (park and Atomic Memorial Museum, 1949-55), 168, 169, 172, 173, 175, 197; figs. 7.11-13; Japanese Embassy, Mexico City (1974), 171; Kagawa Prefectural Gymnasium, Takamatsu (1965), 218; Kagawa Prefectural Office, Takamatsu (1958), 176, 177, 206, fig. 8.38; Kurashiki City Hall, Okayama Pref. (1960), 190, 218; National Olympic Stadiums, Tokyo (1961-64), 164, 171, 179, 190, 218, fig. 8.57; Nichinan Cultural Center, Nichinan, Miyazaki Pref. (1962), 216, 222, figs. 8.53-54; St. Mary's Cathedral, Tokyo (1964), 218; Shizuoka Meeting Hall, Shizuoka, Shizuoka Pref. (1957), 215; Shizuoka Press and Broadcasting Center, Tokyo (1967), 184, 219, fig. 7.22; Sogetsu Kaikan, Tokyo (1958), 178-79; Tange House, Tokyo (1953), 195, 197; Tokyo City Hall (1957, unfinished), 169, 176, 177, fig. 7.7; Tosho Printing Works, Numazu (Haramachi), Shizuoka Pref. (1955), 179; Totsuka Country Club, Kanagawa Pref. (1961), 216, fig. 8.52; Yamanashi Press and Radio Center, Kofu, Yamanashi Pref. (1966), 184, 219
—and Isozaki, 218, 219, 224
—Kulturkritik and a national style, 205-6, 210
—influence of Le Corbusier on, 169-71, 190, fig. 7.8
—Maekawa and, 154, 164, 171, 192
—and Michelangelo, 164, 171, 172, 175, fig. 7.10
—Raymond and, 168, 175n22, 175n23, 182
—and urban planning: Boston Bay student project at MIT, 177-78; attendance at CIAM VIII (Hoddesdon, 1958), 173-74, 175-76; at CIAM '59 (Otterlo), 176-77, 197; Hiroshima (and Master Plan, 1946), 175 (see also Hiroshima Peace Center, in this entry, under "buildings"); contrasted with Kikutake, 177-78, 179, 181; seaboard megalopolis proposal (1965), 189, fig. 8.2; "Tokyo Plan: 1960," 181-82, 189, 219, figs. 7.20-21; at Tokyo University, Department of Urban Engineering, 223; Tsukiji Plan (unrealized, 1960-64), 219, fig. 9.1; WHO project (unrealized, 1959), 178, 182, fig. 7.16
—wartime competitions won (unrealized): Greater East Asia Coprosperity Sphere (1942), 157, 172, 175, fig. 7.9; Japanese Cultural Center, Bangkok (1943), 157, 172, fig. 6.90

—writings: "Eulogy for Michelangelo as an Introduction to a Study of Le Corbusier" (1939), 171; (with Gropius and Y. Ishimoto) *Katsura: Tradition and Creation in Japanese Architecture* (1960), 183, 205; "Technology and Man" (1960), 179, 183–84
Tanizaki, Junichiro, 233–34, 236, 245, *fig. 9.17*
taste (Japanese), aesthetic and architectural, 107, 110, 111–12, 142–46, 146n8, 183. *See also* space (Japanese)
Tateishi, Seiju, 23, 31
tateokoshi-ezu (okoshi-ezu), 254
Tatsuno, Kingo, 37, 38, 48–50, 52, 54–55, 56, 94; Bankers' Association Assembly Rooms, Tokyo (1885), 48, *fig. 2.21*; Bank of Japan, Tokyo (1890–96), 52, 54, 56, 58, 81, *figs. 2.30–32*; National Sumo Arena, Tokyo (1909), 54, *fig. 2.35*; Shibusawa Mansion, Tokyo (1888), 49–50, *figs. 2.23, 26*; Tokyo Imperial University, College of Engineering (1888), 50, 52, *fig. 2.28*; Tokyo Station (1911–14), 41, 54, 96, *fig. 2.34*
Taut, Bruno, 105, 115, 154, 191
Taut, Max, 114
tea, art of, 10, 71, 143, 146, 275. *See also* tearoom
tearoom *(chashitsu)*, 10, 198, 212, 215, 230, 231, 237, 242–43; Ryokakutei, Ninna-ji, Kyoto (ca. 1688), *fig. 8.45*; Shogetsu-an, abbot's residence of Sampo-in, Kyoto (uncertain date), 129; Teigyokuken, Shinjuan, Daitokuji, Kyoto (mid-17th c.), *fig. 10.16*. *See also* tea, art of
Technical College, Tokyo, 33, 34, 36, 38, 111. For post-1885 entries, *see* Tokyo (Imperial) University: College of Engineering
teikan yoshiki (Imperial Crown Style), 107, 110, 110n1, 111–12, 145, 154, 156, 171, 248
Teshigahara, Hiroshi, 200. 245, *fig. 8.29*
Tessenow, Heinrich, 145
Togo, Seiji, 119
Togu Gosho. *See* Akasaka Detached Palace
tokonoma alcove, 234
Tokugawa era, 13, 14, 15, 41, 43, 86–89, 90, 211–12
Tokyo, 38–39, 90–91, 184–86, 188–89. *See also* Edo; *also see under individual buildings* except "houses and housing" (indexed below)
—city planning, 41–42; City Planning Act (1919), 91
—exhibitions. *See* Ueno Park, Tokyo
—expansion (post-World War II), 164
—fire, 22, 27, 87
—Ginza district, 22, 38, 50
—government district (and Hibiya Park), 38–39, 41–42, 79, 171
—Great Kanto Earthquake (1923), 36, 77, 90, 91, 100, 116, 147
—houses and housing: K. Akaboshi House (1932), 135, *figs. 6.48–50*; T. Akaboshi House (1934), 136, 138, 152, 162, 165, *figs. 6.55–57*; Aoki House (1931), 124, *figs. 6.25–26*; Bancho Siedlung (1933), 149–50, *figs. 6.68–70*; P. Claudel residence (1923), 106; Daikanyama Apartments (1927), 150, *figs. 6.72–74*; Edogawa Apartments (1934), 150, 152, *figs. 6.75–76*; Fujiyama Mansion (ca. 1932–33), 126, 138, *figs. 6.29–30*; Hamao House (1928), 125, *figs. 6.27–28*; Harajuku Apartments (1926), 150, *fig. 6.71*; Harumi housing (1958), 178, *figs. 7.17–19*; House at Kugayama (1953), 197–98, *figs. 8.19–20*; House of Earth (1966), 200–202, 210, 212, 216, 232, *figs. 8.27–32*; House of T (1932), 126, 129, *figs. 6.31–33*; House in Uehara (1976), 277, 280, *figs. 10.40–43*; House in White (1966), 202, 205, 210, 211, 215, 223, 228, 232, 245, 268, 277, *figs. 8.31–33*; Incomplete House (1970), 245, 268–69, *figs. 10.32–33*; Kasama House (1938), 192–93, *figs. 8.4–5*; Kawasaki House (1934), 136, 138, 142, 152, 165, *figs. 6.52–54*; Kikutake House (*see below under* Skyhouse); Maekawa House (1941), 154, 192–93, *figs. 8.6–7*; Migishi House (pre-1935), 159, *figs. 6.92–94*; Miyagi House (1953), 195, *figs. 8.15–16*; Mori House (1951), 193, 195, *figs. 8.11–12*; Ninomiya Apartments (1937), 152, *figs. 6.77–78*; Okada House (1934), 125, 129, 138, 144–45, *figs. 6.34–35*; Raymond House (1953), 193, *figs. 8.8–10*; Raymond House at Reinanzaka (*see below under* Reinanzaka House); R. Reid House (1924), 106, *figs. 5.22–23*; Reinanzaka House (1924), 100, 105, 106, *figs. 5, 17–21*; Saito House (1952), 195, *figs. 8.13–14*; Shino House (1970), 268–69, *fig. 10.34*; Skyhouse (1958), 177, 197, 214, *fig. 7.14*; Tange House (1953), 195, 197; Tanikawa House (1958), 198, *figs. 8.21–23*; Togo House (1931), 119, 124, 138, *figs. 6.22–23*; Umbrella House (1961), 198, 205, *figs. 8.1, 23–24*; Yano House (1975), 256, 260, *fig. 10.22*
—industrialization of, 42
—as Metabolist "model," 184
—Metropolitan Expressway System (from 1959), 185, 244, *fig. 7.24*
—National Capital Region Development Law (1956), 184
—Olympics: 1940 Olympics (proposed), 145; 1964 Olympics, 164, 185; National Olympic Stadiums (1961–64); *see under* Tokyo Olympic Games
—population and comparative densities, 42–43, 90, 186
—railway and streetcar systems, 91
—school construction (early Showa era), 116, 118
—slums, 43
—suburbanization, 41, 90–91, 195
—Tokyo City Improvement Ordinance (1888), 42
—"Tokyo Plan: 1960." *See under* Tange, Kenzo: and urban planning
—Tsukiji Plan (project, 1960–64). *See under* Tange, Kenzo: and urban planning
—waterways, 96
—Yoshiwara, 87–89, 90
Tokyo Bunka Kaikan. *See* Tokyo Metropolitan Festival Hall
Tokyo Central Post Office: 1891 building, 56; 1927–31 building, 113, 114, *fig. 6.8*
Tokyo Chamber of Commerce. *See* Tokyo Industrial Club
Tokyo City Hall: 1867 building, 27; 1957 building (unfinished), 169, 176, 177, *fig. 7.7*
Tokyo Fine Arts Academy, 69, 111, 112
Tokyo High Court (1874), 34–35, *fig. 2.2*
Tokyo Imperial Museum. *See* Ueno (Imperial) Museum
Tokyo (Imperial) University, 31, 37, 94, 95. *See also* Kaisei Gakko
—College of Engineering (1888), 52, 56, *fig. 2.28*. For pre-1886 entries, *see* Technical College, Tokyo
—Department of Law and Literature (1884), 52, *fig. 2.29*
—College of Science, Administration Building (1888), 48, *fig. 2.22*
—Yasuda Hall (1925), 100, 170, *figs. 5.15–16*
Tokyo Industrial Club (Tokyo Chamber of Commerce), 42, 49; building (1899), 47, *fig. 2.20*
Tokyo Metropolitan Expressway (from 1959), 185, 244, *fig. 7.24*
Tokyo Metropolitan Festival Hall (Tokyo Bunka Kaikan, 1961), 210, 215, *figs. 8.44, 51*
"Tokyo Plan: 1960." *See under* Tange, Kenzo: and urban planning
Tokyo Olympic Games: stadium complex (1961–64), 164, 171, 179, 190, 218, *fig. 8.57*. *See also* Tokyo: Olympics
Tokyo Station (1911–14), 41, 54, 96, 113, *fig. 2.34*
Tokyo-Taisho Exhibition (1914), 92–93, *fig. 5.1*
Tokyo World Design Conference (1960), 178–79, 182, 183, 189, 219
Toledo (Spain): Cathedral, the *Transparente* (1721–32), 231, 234, *fig. 9.16*
Tomé, Narciso. *See* Toledo (Spain)
Totsuka, Kanagawa Prefecture: Country Club (1961), 216, *fig. 8.52*
transportation, 91, 188. *See also* railways; Tokyo Metropolitan Expressway
Treaty of Nanking (1842), 16
Treaty of Versailles (1919), 107
Treaty Port Settlements, 16. *See also* Hakodate; Kobe; Nagasaki; Yokohama
"trepang." *See namako* walling
Triple Intervention (1895), 38
Tselos, Dmitri, 71, 73
tsubo (courtyard garden), 25, 126, 129, 138, 144, 148, 162
Tsuboi, Yoshikatsu, 218
Tsuchiura, Kameki: Ninomiya Apartments, Tokyo (1937), 152, *figs. 6.77–78*; Rakuto Apartment, Kyoto (1933), 147, 148–49, *fig. 6.67*
Tsukiji Hotel, Tokyo (1868), 23, 26, 27, 31, 79, 80, *fig. 1.13*
Tsumaki, Yorinaka, 46, 47, 48
Tuscan architectural order, 19, 22, 45
Twombly, Robert, 74, 85n14

Uchida, Shozo, 171; Yasuda Hall, Tokyo (Imperial) University (1925), 100, 170, *figs. 5.15–16*
Ueno (Imperial) Museum, Tokyo, 36, 56, 58, 69, 71, 111; early building (1882), 36, 49, 56, *fig. 2.4*; Hyokeikan (1901–9), 58, 62, *fig. 2.41*; Main Building (1937), 107, 110, 153, *figs. 6.3–4*; Main Building, Maekawa design for (1931), 153, 157, *fig. 6.80*
Ueno Park, Tokyo: Commemorative Peace Exhibition (1922) at, 93, 96, 152, *fig. 5.7*; Tokyo-Taisho Exhibition (1914) at, 92–93, *fig. 5.1*. *See also* National Museum of Western Art; Tokyo Metropolitan Festival Hall; Ueno (Imperial) Museum
Uji (nr. Kyoto): Hoo-do, Byodo-in (1053), 69, 71, *figs. 3.4–5*. *See also* Chicago: World's Columbian Exposition (Phoenix Hall)
ukiyo-e prints, 10, 81, 92; Edo, *sukiya,* and, 235–36; Hiroshige, 63, 74; Hokusai, 65, 76; Wright and, 63, 65, 74–76, 74n34, 85, 87, 90. *See also nishiki-e* prints
United States, 13, 14, 15, 16, 18, 20, 31, 65, 75, 81; architectural influence of, 50, 56, 165; Corps of Engineers and Engineering, 20; Treasury, Construction Branch, 20; US-Japan Security Pact, protest against (1960), 189, *fig. 8.3*; Works Progress Administration (WPA), 115, 154. *See also under individual cities and towns*
Utagawa, Toyoharu: 30, *figs. 1.18–19*
Utrecht: Schroeder House (1924), 105

vacuum, 237, 239
van der Rohe, Mies, 165, 195, 212; Tugendhat House, Brno, Czechoslovakia (1930), 119, 138, *fig. 6.24*
van Eyck, Aldo, 228–30, 232, 242
Vardy, John, 33
Varese, Edgar, 222
Vaux-le-Vicomte, château at, 62
Venturi, Robert, 232, 236, 239–40, 248, 260
vernacular materials and themes, 236. *See also minka;* wood and wood construction
—in Horiguchi's villa at Warabi, Saitama Pref. (1926), 145, *fig. 6.63*
—of Isozaki, 239
—and neotraditional themes. *See* Maekawa, Kunio: buildings (Kasama House, Maekawa House); Raymond, Antonin: buildings (Raymond House, Tokyo)
—post-, 261
—Raymond's prewar employment of, 133–34; contrasted with Murano, 143
—in Shinohara's First and Second styles, 205, 268
—compared to Seike's work, 198, 200
—discussed in Tanizaki's *In Praise of Shadows,* 233–34
Vienna, 38, 49, 111; Post Office Savings Bank (1906), 251, *fig. 10.12*. *See also* Loos, Adolf; Secession style, Viennese
Viollet-le-Duc, Eugène Emmanuel, 10, 66, 67, 68, 69, 74, 75, 76, 83
Visconti, L.-T.-J., and L.-M. Lefeul, 43
Vladivostok, 16
void. *See* space (Japanese); vacuum

wafu-jutaku (Japanese-style house), 124
Wagner, Otto: Post Office Savings bank, Vienna (1906), 251, *fig. 10.12*
Wallace, Lila Acheson (Mrs. DeWitt), 165
Warabi, Saitama Prefecture: Horiguchi's villa at (1926), 145, *fig. 6.63*
Washington, DC, 50, 56, 58
Watanabe, Jin: Dai-ichi Seimei Building, Tokyo (1934–38), 153–54, *fig. 6.82*; Ueno (Imperial) Museum, Main Building, Tokyo (1937), 107, 110, 153, *figs. 6.3–4*
Watanabe, Setsu, 142
Watanabe, Yuzuru: first Imperial Hotel, Tokyo (1890), 56, 79, *fig. 4.4*
Waters, Thomas James, 18, 19, 20, 22, 23, 24, 26, 30, 31, 34
—and redevelopment of Ginza district of Tokyo, 22, 31, 38
—Government Printing Office design, Tokyo, 33
—National Mint, Osaka (1871), 19, 20, 24, 31, *figs. 1.6–7*; Sempukan, 20, 24, 29, 31, *fig. 1.8*
—Takebashi Barracks, Tokyo (1874), 20, 23, *figs. 1.9–10*
Watsuji, Tetsuro, 192
wayo-kongo jutaku (combined Western/Japanese-style dwelling), 124–26, 129, 136, 193
Whistler, James A. McNeill, 64, 65, 65n6
Wilde, Oscar, 65
Willets, Ward W., 73, 85
wood and wood construction, 111, 147, 159, 171, 191, 193, 195. *See also* carpentry; *kiwari;* vernacular materials and themes
World Design Conference, Tokyo (1960). *See* Tokyo World Design Conference
World's Columbian Exposition, Chicago (1893). *See under* Chicago
World War I, 14, 39, 90, 146, 147
World War II, 14, 75–76, 154, 173; atomic bombing of Hiroshima and postwar architectural significance, 174, 183; material stockpiling and its effect on Japanese architecture, 111; reconstruction of Tokyo, 164, 165, 171; and Metabolism, 184

Wren, Christopher, 25, 49
Wright, Frank Lloyd, 63ff
—and the Aesthetic Movement, 74–75
—buildings: S. Dana House, Springfield, IL (1903), 256, 261, *fig. 10.24*; Fallingwater, Bear Run, PA (1936), 163, 260; Heurtley House, Oak Park, IL (1902), 256; Imperial Hotel, Tokyo (1923), 9, 43, 54, 76, 77, 79–83, 86, 89, 90, 100, 110, 110n1, *figs. 4.1–3, 5–7, 10, 12, 14–15*; S. C. Johnson Administration Building, Racine, WI (1939), 237, 239, *fig. 10.3*; Larkin Administration Building, Buffalo, NY (1905), 59, 62; D. Martin House, Buffalo, NY (1904), 83, 202; Midway Gardens, Chicago (1914), 79, 83, 86, 87, *fig. 4.9*; F. Robie House, Chicago (1909), 105, 237, *fig. 10.2*; Taliesin, Spring Green, WI (from 1911), 83, 85, 86, 89, *fig. 4.8*; Unity Temple, Oak Park, IL (1906), 112, 237; W. Willets House, Highland Park, IL (1902), 73, 85; Wright House, Oak Park, IL (remodeled 1895), 73, 256; Yamamura Villa, Ashiya, Hyogo Pref. (1924), 143
—on the "destruction of the box," 237, 239
—and the Machine, 75–76
—and the Modern Movement, 63
—notion of style, 75–76, 91–92
—Oak Park period (1890s–1909), 65, 73, 74, 112
—influence of Okakura's *Book of Tea* on, 237
—"organic" architecture of, 68, 76n51
—and the Phoenix Hall (Ho-o-Den) at the World's Columbian Exposition, Chicago (1893), 69, 71, 74
—influence of Bruce Price on, 59, 64
—and Japanese prints, 63, 65, 74–76, 74n34, 85, 87, 90
—and Raymond, 89, 90
—spaces in work of, 82, 212
—and "truth" in architecture, 66–69, 73, 74, 75, 79, 81, 85, 90
—and Tsuchiura, 148–49
—and Viollet-le-Duc's *Raisonné*, 67, 74
—writings: "Art and Craft of the Machine, The" (1901), 75; *Autobiography, An* (1932), 65, 68, 74, 79, 83, 85, 86–87, 90, 106; *Japanese Print, The* (1912), 63, 74, 76, 79, *fig. 3.10*

Xenakis, Iannis, 218, *fig. 8.56*

Yamada, Mamoru, 96, 114; Central Telegraph Office, Tokyo (1922–25), 96, 100, 113, *fig. 5.11*; Electrical Laboratory (1930), 113–14; House of T (*Ein Wohnhaus*), Tokyo (1932), 125, 126, *figs. 6.31–33*; Ogikubo Telephone Office, Tokyo (1933), 114, *fig. 6.11*
Yamaguchi, Bunzo, 96, 118, 119, 182; Bancho Siedlung, Tokyo (1933), 149–50, *figs. 6.68–70*; Kurobe Power Station, Toyama Pref. (1938), 163, *fig. 6.101*; Nihon Dental College Hospital, Tokyo (extension, 1934), 163, *fig. 6.100*; Shirokiya Dept. Store, Tokyo: 1927 drawing of facade, 119, *fig. 6.19*; Yamada House, Kita Kamakura, Kanagawa Pref. (1934), 159–63, *figs. 6.95–96*
Yamaguchi, Hanroku: College of Science Administration Building, Tokyo Imperial University (1888), 48, *fig. 2.22*
Yamawaki, Iwao: Migishi House, Tokyo (pre-1935), 159, *figs. 6.92–94*
Yamazaki, Minoru, 179
Yasuda, Yojuro, 171
yofu-jutaku (Western-style dwelling), 124
Yokohama, Kanagawa Prefecture, 14, 15, 16, 17, 24, 27, 31, 42, 91, *fig. 1.2*
—British Consulate (1868), 27, *fig. 1.16*
—British Legation (provisional, 1867), 27
—City Hall (1867), 27
—Kanagawa Prefectural Building (1871), 23
—Kanagawa Prefectural Concert Hall and Library (1954), 169, *fig. 7.6*
—Kanagawa Prefectural Office (mid-1930s), 110, *fig. 6.6*
—Rising Sun Petroleum Co. (1928–31) employee housing and General Office Building, 129; Manager's Residence, 129, *fig. 6.36*; service station prototypes (*see under* Raymond: buildings)
—Sakuragicho Station (1872), 22, 27, *fig. 1.1*
—U.S. Minister's Residence (1867), 27
—Yokohama Cathedral (1962), 19
Yoshida, Tetsuro, 114, 115; Osaka Higashi Post Office (1931), 114, *figs. 6.9–10*; Tokyo Central Post Office (1927–31), 113, 114–15, 277, *fig. 6.8*
Yoshimura, Junzo, 134, 135, 138, 142, 193
Yoshiwara. *See* Edo: Wright on
Yoshizaka, Takamasa, 210
Yotsuya Fifth Primary School, Tokyo (1934), 116, *fig. 6.13*
Young, Ammi B., 20

Zen, 31, 183, 205. *See also* Buddhism

定価9,500円
in Japan